The Fourth Ghost

SOUTHERN LITERARY STUDIES
Fred Hobson, Series Editor

THE FOURTH GHOST

WHITE SOUTHERN WRITERS AND EUROPEAN FASCISM, 1930–1950

ROBERT H. BRINKMEYER JR.

Louisiana State University Press
Baton Rouge

PUBLISHED BY LOUISIANA STATE UNIVERSITY PRESS
www.lsupress.org

Copyright © 2009 by Louisiana State University Press
All rights reserved. Except in the case of brief quotations used in articles
or reviews, no part of this publication may be reproduced or transmitted
in any format or by any means without written permission
of Louisiana State University Press.

Louisiana Paperback Edition, 2021

DESIGNER: Michelle A. Neustrom
TYPEFACES: Warnock Pro, Bureau Agency, Century Gothic
TYPESETTER: J. Jarrett Engineering, Inc.

LIBRARY OF CONGRESS CATALOGING-IN-PUBLICATION DATA

Brinkmeyer, Robert H.
The fourth ghost : white Southern writers and European fascism,
1930-1950 / Robert H. Brinkmeyer, Jr.
p. cm. — (Southern literary studies)
Includes bibliographical references and index.
ISBN 978-0-8071-3383-5 (cloth : alk. paper) 1. American literature—
Southern States—History and criticism. 2. American literature—White
authors—History and criticism. 3. Fascism and literature—Southern
States—History—20th century. 4. Authors, American—Southern States—
Political and social views. 5. Southern States—In literature. 6. Fascism in
literature. 7. Racism in literature. I. Title.
PS261.B744 2009
810.9′975—dc22

2008019088

ISBN 978-0-8071-7623-8 (paperback) | ISBN 978-0-8071-3480-1 (pdf) |
ISBN 978-0-8071-4841-9 (epub)

Portions of this book have been published previously in different form, as
"Carson McCullers, European Totalitarianism, and the Southern Literary
Imagination," in *Roots and Renewal: Writings by Bicentennial Fulbright
Professors*, ed. Mark Shackleton and Maarika Toivonen (Helsinki: Renvall
Institute, 2001), and as "Slavery Old and New: Styron's Sophie's Choice,"
in *Transatlantic Exchanges: The American South in Europe—Europe in
the American South*, ed. Richard J Gray and Waldemar Zacharasiewicz
(Vienna: Verlag der Österreichischen Akademie der Wissenschaften,
2007), and are reprinted here with permission.

To my Mother and in memory of my Father

CONTENTS

ACKNOWLEDGMENTS ix

ABBREVIATIONS xiii

INTRODUCTION
The Fourth Ghost 1

1 DANGEROUS LIAISONS
The Nashville Agrarians 24

2 SAVAGERY ON THE FRONTIER
W. J. Cash 71

3 PASTORALISM AND EXTINCTION
William Alexander Percy 96

4 GEORGIA ON MY MIND
Lillian Smith 119

5 YOU CAN'T GO TO GERMANY, AGAIN
Thomas Wolfe 146

CONTENTS

6 DEMOCRACY'S TALL MEN
  William Faulkner..............................176

7 SOMETHING DEATHLY IN THE AIR
  Katherine Anne Porter........................203

8 DISPATCHES FROM THE HOME FRONT
  Carson McCullers..............................229

9 PRAGMATISM, IDEALISM, RESPONSIBILITY
  Robert Penn Warren...........................251

10 RAVAGERS OF THE EARTH
   Lillian Hellman...............................280

   CODA
   The Long Shadow 309

   NOTES 327

   BIBLIOGRAPHY...............................373

   INDEX...401

ACKNOWLEDGMENTS

The origins of this book stretch back twenty years or so, to when I was first struck by the fact that in 1941 both W. J. Cash and William Alexander Percy, two writers of very different political stripes, used references to Nazi Germany to describe the cultural landscape of the South. Like one of Walker Percy's searchers, I felt that I was onto something. Over time, the project grew dramatically in scope as I discovered more and more southern writers who were grappling with Fascism and its relevance—or what they claimed to be its irrelevance—to southern culture. At some point I realized that this was a long-term project that would require a great deal of reading and a great deal of digesting. As my research widened, there were times when I wondered whether the project was becoming unmanageable. Working steadily became more difficult after I got involved in administrative work. I never abandoned my Fascism project completely, but for a while I was unsure whether I would ever complete it.

Receiving a Guggenheim Fellowship in 2003 was just what I needed to bring the project into order. The year off that the fellowship afforded me allowed me to complete the first draft of the book. My first thanks, then, go to the John Simon Guggenheim Memorial Foundation and to Dean Don Bobbitt, of the Fulbright College of Arts and Sciences at the University of Arkansas, whose support allowed me to accept the Guggenheim Fellowship and work for a year without financial worry.

Many people helped me along the way. I'll start with my colleagues at the University of Mississippi, where I began work on the project, particularly Charles Eagles, Don Kartiganer, Jay Watson, Barry Hannah, Charles Wilson, Ted Ownby, Annette Trefzer, Robbie Ethridge, Ann Fisher-Wirth, Peter Wirth, Karen Raber, Katie McKee, Bill Ferris, Bob Haws, and Tom Rankin. While at the University of Mississippi, I received a National Endowment for the Humanities Summer Stipend for early work on the project. That award was important, coming at a time when I needed some validation that my ideas were worth pursuing.

Also while at the University of Mississippi, I received a Distinguished Fulbright appointment, serving as the Bicentennial Chair in American Studies at the University of Helsinki for the academic year 1994–95. That was a marvelous experience, and during the year many Finns got to hear about my project and give me feedback. Deeply felt thanks go particularly to Seppo Tamminen, Markku Henriksson, Mikko Saikku, Mikko Toivonen, Roy Goldblatt, Michael Coleman, Maarika Toivonen, Tuula Pentillä, and Renvall Institute Director Eino Lyytinen.

I have already mentioned the support of Dean Don Bobbitt, but there were others at the University of Arkansas who encouraged me in my work, including Susan Marren, Bob Cochran, Davis McCombs, Pat Slattery, Dave Chappell, Lyna Lee Montgomery (for taking over as interim chair of the department during my Guggenheim year), and all of the sympathetic members of the chair's faculty advisory committee. And special, special thanks go to Miller and Jordan Williams.

Those who have heard the most about this project are my colleagues in the Southern Studies Forum and others in southern studies. Perhaps appropriately for a project on southern literature that looks outward across the seas, I presented versions of this material at conferences in numerous countries, including England, Spain, Poland, Finland, Norway, Russia, Greece, Ukraine, Germany, Denmark, Holland, and Austria. All of the following people played a part in shaping this book: Richard Gray, Richard Godden, Jack Mathews, Suzanne Jones, Constante González, Waldemar Zacharasiewicz, Noel Polk, John Burt, William Bedford Clark, Jan Nordby Gretlund, Walter Edgar, Leon Jackson, Jim Cobb, Don Doyle, Lothar Hönnighausen, Anneke Leenhouts, Marcel Arbeit, John Lowe, Leigh Anne Duck, Youli Theoldisiadou, Anne Firor Scott, Michael Cass, Tom McHaney, Pearl McHaney, Tom Inge, Francois Pitavy, Charles Joyner, Peter Lurie, Hans Skei, Anne Goodwyn Jones, Peter Nicholaisen, Susan Donaldson, Dan Carter, Mark Newman, Danielle Pitavy-Souques, Dieter Meindl, Joe Urgo, Sharon Monteith, Nahem Yousaf, Dawn Trouard, Arno Heller, Owen Robinson, Helen Taylor, Jacques Pothier, Barbara Ladd, Karl Zender, Valeria Gennaro Lerda,

ACKNOWLEDGMENTS

Martin Crawford, Sarah Robertson, A. Robert Lee, Tjebbe Westendorf, and the late Stuart Kidd (you are missed dearly, pal).

I wish I could list all of my students at the Universities of Mississippi, Helsinki, and Arkansas, but that would be impossible. But I thank them as a group for all the worthwhile discussions in and out of class.

The editors at LSU Press have all been great, particularly John Easterly, whose support is appreciated more than he knows. Lee Sioles and George Roupe have guided me with assurance through the process. The series editor, Fred Hobson, has been supportive all along, and I thank him for both his friendship and his guidance. Thanks, too, to my copyeditor, Joanne Allen, for her fine work; to William Duke for helping me chase down quotes; and to Bob Ellis for doing the index.

Closer to home, Debra gets top billing. Throughout our time together she has heard me talk endlessly about this project, and she has read every word of every version of the manuscript. As always, she has done a great job advising and editing. She alone knows how much I owe to her. My children, Mary, Eliza, and Emma, have all lent their support to their quirky father, and it has been much appreciated.

My father passed away a few days after my Guggenheim Fellowship began, just when I was gearing up for full-time work on the project. Those were dark days for the family, most particularly of course for my mother. This book is dedicated to her, in recognition of her great strength in persevering, and to the memory of my father, who did not always understand why I wanted to study southern literature but never questioned my decision and never failed to support it.

ABBREVIATIONS

AKM Warren, Robert Penn. *All the King's Men.* 1946. New York: Harcourt Brace Jovanovich, 1982.

BSC McCullers, Carson. *"The Ballad of the Sad Café" and Collected Short Stories.* Boston: Houghton Mifflin, 1955.

CP Tate, Allen. *Collected Poems, 1919–1976.* New York: Farrar, Straus & Giroux, 1977.

CPW Warren, Robert Penn. *The Collected Poems of Robert Penn Warren.* Ed. John Burt. Baton Rouge: Louisiana State University Press, 1998.

CSF Faulkner, William. *The Collected Stories of William Faulkner.* New York: Random House, 1950.

CSP Porter, Katherine Anne. *The Collected Stories of Katherine Anne Porter.* New York: Harcourt, Brace and World, 1965.

GDM Faulkner, William. *Go Down, Moses.* 1942. New York: Vintage International, 1990.

HLH McCullers, Carson. *The Heart Is a Lonely Hunter.* Boston: Houghton Mifflin, 1940.

ITMS Twelve Southerners. *I'll Take My Stand: The South and the Agrarian Tradition.* 1930. Baton Rouge: Louisiana State University Press, 1977.

KD Smith, Lillian. *Killers of the Dream.* New York: W. W. Norton, 1949.

KPD Mead, Margaret. *And Keep Your Powder Dry: An Anthropologist Looks at America.* New York: William Morrow, 1942.

L Percy, Walker. *Lancelot.* New York: Farrar, Straus and Giroux, 1977.

ABBREVIATIONS

LCDT Davidson, Donald, and Allen Tate. *The Literary Correspondence of Donald Davidson and Allen Tate.* Ed. John Tyree Fain and Thomas Daniel Young. Athens: University of Georgia Press, 1974.

LL Percy, William Alexander. *Lanterns on the Levee: Recollections of a Planter's Son.* 1941. Baton Rouge: Louisiana State University Press, 1973.

LLS Smith, Lillian. *How Am I to Be Heard? Letters of Lillian Smith.* Ed. Margaret Rose Gladney. Chapel Hill: University of North Carolina Press, 1993.

LP Porter, Katherine Anne. *The Letters of Katherine Anne Porter.* Ed. Isabel Bayley. New York: Atlantic Monthly Press, 1990.

LTL Lytle, Andrew, and Allen Tate. *The Lytle-Tate Letters: The Correspondence of Andrew Lytle and Allen Tate.* Ed. Thomas Daniel Young and Elizabeth Sarcone. Jackson: University Press of Mississippi, 1987.

LTW Wolfe, Thomas. *The Letters of Thomas Wolfe.* Ed. Elizabeth Nowell. New York: Charles Scribner's Sons, 1956.

MH McCullers, Carson. *The Mortgaged Heart: Selected Writings.* Ed. Margarita G. Smith. Boston: Houghton Mifflin, 1971.

MOL Wolfe, Thomas, and Aline Bernstein. *My Other Loneliness: The Letters of Thomas Wolfe and Aline Bernstein.* Ed. Suzanne Stutman. Chapel Hill: University of North Carolina Press, 1983.

MS Cash, W. J. *The Mind of the South.* 1941. New York: Vintage, 1991.

MW McCullers, Carson. *The Member of the Wedding.* Boston: Houghton Mifflin, 1946.

NTW Wolfe, Thomas. *The Notebooks of Thomas Wolfe.* Ed. Richard S. Kennedy and Paschal Reeves. 2 vols. Chapel Hill: University of North Carolina Press, 1970.

P Hellman, Lillian. *Pentimento: A Book of Portraits.* Boston: Little, Brown, 1973.

SC Styron, William. *Sophie's Choice.* New York: Random House, 1979.

SLF Faulkner, William. *Selected Letters of William Faulkner.* Ed. Joseph Blotner. New York: Random House, 1977.

SLW Warren, Robert Penn. *Selected Letters of Robert Penn Warren.* Vol. 2,

ABBREVIATIONS

The "Southern Review" Years, 1935–1942. Ed. William Bedford Clark. Baton Rouge: Louisiana State University Press, 2001.

SP   Hellman, Lillian. *Six Plays.* New York: Modern Library, 1960.

ST   Hellman, Lillian. *Scoundrel Time.* New York: Little, Brown, 1976.

SW   Hellman, Lillian. *"The Searching Wind": A Play in Two Acts.* New York: Viking, 1944.

TWA   Reeves, Paschal. *Thomas Wolfe's Albatross: Race and Nationality in America.* Athens: University of Georgia Press, 1968.

UW   Hellman, Lillian. *An Unfinished Woman: A Memoir.* Boston: Little, Brown, 1969.

WET   Warren, Robert Penn. *World Enough and Time: A Romantic Novel.* New York: Random House, 1950.

The Fourth Ghost

Introduction

THE FOURTH GHOST

In her memoir and commentary on southern culture, *Killers of the Dream* (1949), Lillian Smith identifies three "ghosts" of segregation haunting the consciousness of white southerners: the black woman with whom the white man oftentimes had sex; the rejected child resulting from mixed-race coupling; and the black mammy whom the southern child first loves and then must later reject as unworthy of love. All three of these ghosts, Smith argues, threatened to demystify the South's tightly structured and rigidly controlled social system, since they were manifestations of the transgressive desires and acts that whites pursued despite all social conditioning. Smith opens *Killers of the Dream* by describing a southern people outwardly serene but inwardly deeply troubled, beset by a terrifying awareness, often not rationally acknowledged, that everything they have been taught to believe is somehow wrong. "Even its children know that the South is in trouble," Smith writes in the text's startling opening sentence, and she goes on:

> No one has to tell them; no words said aloud. To them, it is a vague thing weaving in and out of their play, like a ghost haunting an old graveyard or whispers after the household sleeps—fleeting mystery, vague menace, to which each responds in his own way. Some learn to screen out all except the soft and the soothing; others deny even as they see plainly, and hear. But all know that under quiet words and warmth and laughter, under the slow ease and tender concern about small matters, there is a heavy burden on all of us and as heavy a refusal to confess it. The children know this "trouble" is bigger than

they, bigger than their family, bigger than their church, so big that people turn away from its size. They have seen it flash out like lightning and shatter a town's peace, have felt it tear up all they believe in. They have measured its giant strength and they feel weak when they remember. (*KD* 15)

Segregation, Smith argues, not only divides the races but divides the white southern mind, a fracture that Smith reports one of the girls attending her summer camp as characterizing this way: "I'm all confused. My mind is full of barbed wire. It isn't right for any one [*sic*] to feel the way I feel—inside" (*KD* 46).

The camper's reference to barbed wire in a book appearing in 1949 no doubt would have called to mind the Nazi concentration camps, a reference that Smith makes explicit shortly thereafter.[1] To her camper's declaration that she will teach her children to accept unthinkingly the strict southern codes so that they will not suffer the type of inner turmoil she does, Smith responds: "In other words, you would make little Nazis of them" (*KD* 47). Smith's maneuver here, setting the South's segregated system alongside Nazi Germany's totalitarianism, points to the central question that this book explores: with the ghostly presence of European Fascism lurking on the cultural horizon, how did white southern writers during the 1930s and 1940s understand their homeland and represent it in their work?[2]

Merely asking this question challenges the traditional interpretation of white southern writing from the period, a view that holds that most writers were xenophobic in their regional concerns and allegiances, their backs turned, their eyes closed, and their ears plugged to the cultural dialogue then being anxiously voiced in America and Europe concerning the future of democracy and the threat of totalitarianism. In exploring what many critics are now calling the "global South," this book argues something quite different: that rather than being turned incestuously inward, white southern writers during these two decades were actually turned fearfully outward, haunted by the ghostly presence of Fascist Italy and Nazi Germany (and, to a lesser extent, as another manifestation of totalitarianism, the Soviet Union).[3] While these writers continued to set their work almost exclusively in the rural South, they nonetheless portrayed the cultural forces shaping the South in the context of the world situation, particularly as the nation, responding to the threat of world war, embraced a nationalism and internationalism that downplayed the significance of local customs and regional allegiances. White southern writers were themselves aware of and responsive to this cultural crisis. Their literature shows them repeatedly engaging issues central to the democracy-totalitarianism debate and reconfiguring, in response to this engagement, their understandings not only of their region (and particularly of the South's system of segregation) but also of themselves as southerners and of the nature and significance of their art.

Because of the ubiquity of its threatening presence in white southern writing of the 1930s and 1940s, I have designated European Fascism as "the fourth ghost," looming alongside the other three "ghosts" that Lillian Smith sees fracturing the consciousness of white southerners. While white southern writers, like other Americans, associated totalitarianism with both Fascism and Communism, Fascism wielded the greater power for demystifying southern ideology, whether that was to the writers grave threat or welcome liberation. There are several clear reasons for this. To begin with, in the 1930s a number of commentators from both the North and the South began noting similarities between the political and social orders of the South and those of Fascist countries, particularly Nazi Germany. The South's system of racial segregation, together with its one-party political system, including its enforcement of widespread voting restrictions, came under intense scrutiny, the benighted South looking a good deal more benighted in the context of Fascist Italy and Nazi Germany.

Were these comparisons being made only by radical leftists from, say, New York and Chicago, their impact upon white southern writers might have been slight unless a particular southern writer happened already to be decidedly leftist. But that was not the case. Indeed, to view southern society alongside Nazi Germany was a widespread practice, coming from respectable commentators, southerners and northerners alike, including President Roosevelt. In a 1938 speech delivered in Gainesville, Georgia, the president noted that the South's essentially feudal social system was causing the region to suffer terrible economic privation. "Things will not come to us in the South if we oppose progress—if we believe in our hearts that the feudal system is still the best system," Roosevelt said, adding darkly: "When you come down to it, there is little difference between the feudal system and the Fascist system. If you believe in one, you lean to the other."[4] The title of Roosevelt's speech, "The United States Is Rising and Is Rebuilding on Sounder Lines," underscored an important point that other commentators on the South were frequently making: that there was a fundamental difference between the South and the rest of America and that specifically in the 1930s the South seemed to be going one way, while the rest of America seemed to be going another.

Of course identifying the South as different was nothing new in terms of regional and American identity. The South had long been used by the rest of the nation as a foil against which to define itself, with aspects of national culture that cut against democratic ideals displaced comfortably onto the South. As Jennifer Rae Greeson has shown, such displacement began as early as the nation's founding, establishing what Greeson calls a nationalization "built in part upon an intra-national, regionally-inflected symbolic geography, in which the terms 'South' and 'U.S.' formed an ideological opposition."[5] The symbolic geography became real with the Civil War, and from then on the South embraced its own history and culture; both southerners and non-southerners alike came to see the region as standing both within and without the nation. In perhaps the most famous discussion of the South's oppositional stance, C. Vann Woodward observed that the South's foundational myths—derived from a history of defeat, shame, and poverty—stood fundamentally opposed to the American myths of progress and opportunity.[6] For Woodward, writing in 1968, the South's oppositional stance was not such a bad thing; he saw it as serving as a check, or a ballast, to America's progressive vision that, ignoring past folly, gazed continually forward to an always better future. In other words, while the South suffered under the burden of history, the rest of the nation benefited.

Few Americans, though, would have made that observation in the 1930s, when the South was typically characterized not only as the nation's number one economic problem, as Roosevelt put it in another speech in 1937, but also as the nation's number one social and political problem as well. Except for the years immediately leading up to the Civil War, the South had probably never seemed to the rest of America quite so alien, threatening, and dangerous. During this period, aspects of southern culture—lynching, sharecropping, rural poverty, poor education, demagoguery, brutal prison conditions, restricted voting rights, and, of course, the entire segregated social system that all of these things supported—were repeatedly investigated and denounced. If America proclaimed itself as having been founded on Enlightenment ideals, derived from the universal applicability of rights and rationality, the South seemed to have missed all that. Rather than rational, the South appeared irrational, sunk in a miasma of local customs, beliefs, and superstitions that were never going to change, no matter what anybody said about evolution or anything else.[7]

INTRODUCTION

Not surprisingly, black writers in particular, many of whom viewed literature as a weapon for social change, zeroed in on the white South's irrationality, particularly its to-the-death defense of its restrictive racial codes and its explosive acts of racial violence, including lynchings. The South of Jean Toomer's *Cane* (1923), for instance, is soaked in emotion and mystery, beauty and violence swirling together in ways that confound the narrator, a visitor from the North. The most stunning conflation of violence and beauty comes in the poem "Portrait in Georgia," in which the poet describes a woman's beauty in a series of images from a lynching, its final lines portraying her "slim body, white as the ash / of black flesh after flame."[8] Richard Wright's South is less mysterious but more violent, an intricately mapped world of regulations and boundaries that cannot be violated without brutal retribution. Wright's autobiographical essay "The Ethics of Living Jim Crow" reveals that surviving under the South's rigid racial order demands, not ethical choices, but ingenuity and dissembling, what he identifies as the skills necessary for playing "that dual role which every Negro must play if he wants to eat and live."[9]

White writers, too, often portrayed an irrational South, or at least a South that appeared irrational to non-southern readers, as in much of Faulkner's and Erskine Caldwell's writing from the 1930s. Perhaps the most explicit depiction of a threatening, irrational South, however, appeared in a memoir/travelogue by a northerner living in the South, Carl Carmer's *Stars Fell on Alabama* (1934), which recounts his experiences in the state during the late twenties and early thirties, when he was teaching at the University of Alabama. A New Yorker living in the South for the first time, Carmer found Alabama alien and dangerous, a world, as he describes it in his foreword, enveloped by some sort of dark spell:

> Alabama felt a magic descending, spreading, long ago. Since then it has been a land with a spell on it—not a good spell, always. Moons, red with the dust of barren hills, thin pine trunks barring horizons, festering swamps, restless yellow rivers, are all part of a feeling—a strange certainty that above and around them hovers enchantment—an emanation of malevolence that threatens to destroy men through dark ways of its own. It is difficult to translate this feeling into words, yet almost every visitor to this land has known it and felt in some degree what I felt with increasing wonder during the six years I lived there. Hill-billies and niggers, poor whites, and planters, Cajans and

Lintheads are sometimes aware of the intangible net that encompasses them. But the stranger is more apt to realize that sorcery is at work on these people and know that the land on which they live is its apprentice.[10]

Carmer, who was deeply interested in folklore, cites several Native American legends as possible explanations for the spell but then suggests that "those who really know, the black conjure women in their weathered cabins along the Tombigbee," say that Alabama's destiny took its dark turn one night during the days of slavery when a blazing star shower streaked the skies, a time now marked as "the year the stars fell." "What had been written in eternal symbols," Carmer writes, "was thus erased—and the region has existed ever since, unreal and fated, bound by a horoscope such as controls no other country" (xiv). Lest the reader think that he is kidding in all this, Carmer concludes the foreword with this warning:

Let those who scorn such irrationalities explain this state-that-is-another-land in ways they prefer. They may find causes economic and sociological quite as incredible as these fables and much less interesting. But few of those who know this ground and those who live on it will deny that the curious traveler will find his journeying amply repaid here. The Congo is not more different from Massachusetts or Kansas or California. So I have chosen to write of Alabama not as a state which is part of a nation, but as a strange country in which I once lived and from which I have now returned. (xiv)

Underscoring the difference between Alabama (and more generally the Deep South) and the rest of the nation, the page immediately following the foreword, a full-page illustration opening the book's first section, "Tuscaloosa Nights," portrays a full-scale Ku Klux Klan rally.

Even more chilling are Carmer's comments in his afterword. After saying that he finds it hard to believe that he ever lived in Alabama, his memories appearing "as an unreality stumbled upon long ago" (270), he observes that he knows two things for sure: that the spell over Alabama has not been lifted and that dark days lie ahead. He closes with an ominous commentary:

And in my old home, the river-bordered town of Tuscaloosa, dreaming most of its days away beneath the shade of elms and live oaks and magnolias, the fateful compulsion is at work again. As I write this, news comes that a mob of a thousand men has surrounded the dingy yellow courthouse. A machine gun mounted on the steps looks bleakly down on them. I can picture them milling about on the lawn of the Snow place next door, talking in excited groups near the Baptist church across the street. There will be dark doings soon. The men in khaki uniforms who serve the machine gun and stand guard with their rifles at the doors look nervous and uncomfortable. The mob is made up of their friends. But the guardsmen have seen the glint in the eyes out there. They know that the old irresistible urge is upon the shifting crowd. No ties will hold them when that madness lowers. The spell cast in the "years the stars fell" is not yet broken. (271)

Soldiers in the streets, machine guns, mob violence—these were images that in the coming years would be icons of Fascist dictatorship, particularly that of Nazi Germany.[11]

If Carmer did not explicitly connect the Deep South with Fascism, others soon would, often focusing on what was perceived as the shared irrationality of southern and Fascist cultures. By the late 1930s a growing number of commentators were interpreting Fascism as fundamentally an expression of irrational barbarism, what Hermann Rauschning, in his influential book of the same name, identifies as "the revolution of nihilism," a manifestation of powerful barbaric forces threatening to plunge Western civilization into chaos.[12] Rauschning argues that rabid antirationalism was propelling the Nazi revolution and that the revolution's "subversive course involves the utter destruction of all traditional spiritual standards, utter nihilism. These values are the product of the intellectual and historical unity of Western civilization, of historic intellectual and moral forces."[13] Reflecting this analysis, Rauschning entitles his study of Nazi Party members *Men of Chaos* (1942) and his analysis of the crisis facing Western civilization at the end of World War II *Time of Delirium* (1946). Other commentators, deeply influenced by theories of psychoanalysis, focused on psychological reasons for Fascism's compelling attraction for the masses. Jung, for instance, believed that Fascism was best understood as the eruption of the collective unconscious, while Wilhelm Reich, influenced by Freud, interpreted Fascism as a return of the repressed, "the expression of the irrational structure of mass man," which had been long suppressed through social conditioning.[14]

One of the earliest and most explicit commentaries yoking together the irrationalism of Fascism and that of southern politics comes in Virginius Dabney's essay of alternative history, "If the South Had Won the War." Published in the *American Mercury* in 1936, the year that Dabney assumed the editorship of the *Richmond Times-Dispatch,* the essay posits that whatever social and economic gains the Confederacy might have achieved by winning the war and thus not suffering "the ten-year saturnalia of thievery and corruption euphemistically termed Reconstruction," the Southern nation would in all likelihood be suffering under the thumb of a Fascist dictator.[15] Dabney locates the origins of this dictatorship in the political ascendancy of the poor whites in the 1880s and 1890s, observing that once the poor whites had gained power, the Confederate Congress would have been controlled "by a group of unmannerly zanies," demagogues such as "Ben Tillman, Tom Watson, Jeff Davis of Arkansas, Tom Heflin, Cole Blease, and Huey Long" (202). From there, Huey Long would have easily stepped into the presidency, transforming the government into a dictatorship, ultimately taking "control of everything from the local fire brigades to the Supreme Court, as he did in Louisiana" (202). Imagining life in Long's South, Dabney writes that "we denizens of Dixie might have found ourselves slapped in the face by his storm-troopers for failing to salute the piscatorial insignia on ceremonial occasions, and belabored with *Gummiknüppel,* à la Nazi, for failure to leap at the piscatorial command" (202). "Under the leadership of *Führer* Long," Dabney adds, the Confederacy would have had a huge standing army and a populace continuously preparing for war, "holding gas drill and teaching its six-year-olds how to toss hand-grenades, against the day when the embattled Union launched its long-awaited program of vengeance" (204). Dabney concludes that it is far better that the South lost the Civil War rather than being "lashed to the chariot wheel of Huey Long and wearing such stigmata as must inevitably have accompanied subjection to the hero of the Sands Point washroom" (205).[16]

Dabney's essay makes vivid what a number of Americans were at that time beginning to fear: that while not avowedly Fascist, the South nonetheless was potentially a seedbed of Fascist irrationalism, and that without the tough-minded guidance of the rational North, the nation's nether region might erupt as a dangerous threat to American democracy (this mapping of the "body" of the nation has long been a part of the interplay between the two regions). No doubt this fear only intensified as the world ground its way toward war and Americans, in response, began rallying behind what is now called "the democratic revival." Besides its ringing endorsement of democratic principles, this upsurge in patriotic fervor ushered in a redefinition of American identity, one grounded less in ethnicity than in belief, specifically belief in the ideals of freedom and democracy.[17] The South, with all its social and political problems, only looked more alien, more un-American, in light of this version of Americanism.

Typical of the works engendered by the democratic revival is Margaret Mead's *And Keep Your Powder Dry* (1942), a study of the strengths and weaknesses of America's national character, what she identifies as "the psychological equipment with which we can win the war" (*KPD* 24). As a cultural anthropologist, Mead argues that a nation's fundamental characteristics derive, not from the ethnicity of its people, but from the "character structure" of its culture, that is, a universally accepted value that shapes a nation's patterns of behavior and its belief system. For Mead, the character structure of America is democracy, and she argues that democratic thought is the fundamental ingredient of American identity, shaping everything Americans do and are, as well as everything America is and does:

> Democratic procedures are not something people have, like automobiles or hot-dog stands or a way of building roads. Democracy is not something which can be added or subtracted; it is not one of an array of items found on closet shelves, in stores or text-books, not just one more detail in a hodgepodge of furniture models, written laws, and grammar books. The way in which people behave is all of a piece, their virtues and their sins, the way they slap the baby, handle their court cases, and bury their dead. It would be impossible suddenly to introduce "democracy," which is a word for a type of behavior and an attitude of mind which runs through our whole culture, through our selection of candidates for office, our behavior in street cars, our schools and our newspapers, into an undemocratic society—as it would suddenly to introduce feudalism into a modern American city. (*KPD* 20)

Mead's reference to feudalism may or may not be a deliberate echo of President Roosevelt's comment that the South's feudalism was something alien to America (an expression of Fascism rather than of democracy); but even if it is not, elsewhere in *And Keep Your Powder Dry* Mead suggests that the South's character structure is not the same as America's, pointing to the conclusion that the South is not really "American" at all. In her initial discussion of American character, Mead attaches a footnote to clarify that her comments are not meant to apply to the South:

> Statements about the culture of the United States have to be qualified in many cases, if they are to apply both to the North and the South. The introduction in the South of the bi-racial classification of humanity means that caste is sometimes a directly formative element in developing standards of behavior. The generalizations in this book should be regarded as based primarily on the North, Middle West, and West, and should not be called into question because certain elements of Southern culture differ from them, as this is inevitable. A discussion which overrode the very considerable differences between North and South would often be too abstract to be fruitful. (*KPD* 24)

Without elaborating further, Mead in effect writes the South out of the nation.

Given that *And Keep Your Powder Dry* looks continually toward restructuring the postwar world, designating the South as un-American places the region among the nondemocratic cultures that need to be remade through American guidance and ingenuity in order to create a better, more peaceful world. Mead models her postwar project on the battle against contagion, saying that the sick must immediately be segregated and remain quarantined until a cure is developed. "We must devise a phrasing of the postwar reconstruction, in which we handle those institutions which breed men committed to warfare and dominance and ruthless cruelty as if they were dangerous viruses and treat those individuals who are deeply infected with them as carriers of fatal social diseases," Mead writes. "We must analyze the social organization of Prussia and Japan, especially, and attempt scientifically to strike out those elements which produce the convinced fascist" (*KPD* 245–46).

While Mead never specifically mentions the South in her social engineering plans, she does drop a number of hints that Dixie's remaking is in order, including her call for democracies to enforce their own brand of segregation.[18] In her discussion of the dangers involved in misconstruing social problems as racial problems, moreover, she writes:

> We can say: "This element is linked with the race of those who practice it: the practice of superordination is inextricably bound up with

the German race; an inability to see either themselves or Negroes as simply human beings is an instinct of the American Southern white race; a tendency to cringe and invite sadism is an instinct of the Hindu race." If we say this we become fascists quickly, even though we started out with the best intentions. This phrasing of the problem is unsuitable to the end we have in view. (*KPD* 243)

Besides listing southern racial practices here, equating them both with Nazi racial practices and more generally with the worldwide problems facing America in its reconstruction work, Mead repeatedly comments that in eradicating the world's disorders America must at the same time clean up its own. "We cannot demand anything from those whom we have conquered which we are not willing to demand from ourselves," she writes. "This does not mean that we should disarm because we must disarm our enemies, as many might lightly interpret it to mean. But we must set out to remove—inside our own culture—all those tendencies which would lead us to misuse the arms which we keep, and with equal vigor we must set about developing within the culture of our enemies those tendencies which will enable them to use well the freedom which they have never had" (*KPD* 247). While Mead leaves unsaid the specific internal "tendencies" that must be rooted out and rechanneled, it seems altogether likely, given her rhetoric elsewhere in *And Keep Your Powder Dry*, that she had the South in mind and, furthermore, that she expected the reader to have it in mind as well.

Besides highlighting southern culture's undemocratic character, identifying it as an internal threat to the idea of the nation, the democratic revival delivered a crushing blow to regionalism and regional identity as concepts significant to America and its future and contributed heavily to the demise of the political and cultural movements that had formed around those concepts. As Robert Dorman explains so well in his history of the movement, regionalism emerged as a significant cultural and political force in the 1920s and early 1930s.[19] While the various regionalist groups were quite different in specific goals and attitudes—these groups included, among others, the Nashville Agrarians (discussed in chapter 1 of this study); the Chapel Hill sociologists; the "Texas Triumvirate" of J. Frank Dobie, Walter Prescott Webb, and Roy Bedichek; Lewis Mumford and his circle in the Northeast; Maria Sandoz and the artists John Steuart Curry, Grant Wood, and Thomas Hart Benton in the Midwest; and the artists' colonies of Santa Fe and Taos—they all shared a similar perspective on culture and nation grounded in localism and particularism. According to regionalist thinking, America was less a single, unified culture than a wide assortment of diverse cultures, each shaped by its particular environment, customs, and beliefs (usually understood as those of the folk). These cultures needed to be nurtured rather than flattened by modernity; in contrast to a melting pot, with all the ingredients blended together into one big, all-in-one stew, regionalists characteristically viewed America, in Waldo Frank's wonderful term, as a "symphonic nation," a country of unique regional cultures harmoniously working together, a pluralist nation respecting, protecting, and thriving upon regional uniqueness.

Regionalism's powerful critique of the modern industrial state initially cloaked its failure to offer effective alternatives, but by the early 1930s that failure was seriously undermining the movement, with the lingering economic chaos of the Great Depression further sapping popular support. While the economic collapse in 1929 initially spurred interest in regionalism as an alternative to finance capitalism (and also an alternative to the Socialism others were touting), after a few years of continued economic downturn that interest waned, regionalism's decentralized economic model appearing inadequate to deal with the large-scale economic forces that were pulverizing the nation. In this new light, regionalism appeared backward and naive, an unrealistic attempt to return to an idyllic past, a pipe-dream of nostalgic pastoralism. Economically discredited by the mid-1930s, regionalism was politically discredited by the early 1940s, falling victim to the democratic revival that swept over the nation as political conditions in Europe deteriorated.

The them-or-us ideological battle then raging between proponents of democracy and Fascism (typified by the title of Melvin Rader's 1939 analysis of Fascism's threat to Western civilization, *No Compromise: The Conflict between Two Worlds*)[20] doomed regionalism politically by aligning the movement with Fascism. Democracy, in these binary terms, was associated with universal rights and principles, freed from the irrational prejudices of race and nation; Fascism, on the other hand, manifested those prejudices, spurning the universal for the particular. From this perspective, despite its fervent appeals for decentralized government and authority, regionalism appeared to draw from the same irrational thinking and loyalties as Fascist ideology; regionalist valorization of folk and place, for instance, took on a very dark cast when read alongside the Nazis' celebration of "blood and soil." Melvin Rader's comment on Fascism's fundamental antiuniversalism characterizes the type of critique that regionalism was also facing: "If we should try to condense in a single formula the essence of Fascism, we should maintain that it is *the denial of universality*. The universality of truth, of value, of law, of human rights—in other words, the solidarity of mankind—is rejected in favor of the partnership of race, nation, and class."[21] It is one of the terrible ironies in American history that regionalism, a movement begun largely in resistance to modern industrial society's grinding forces of homogeneity and centralization, in the end was widely perceived as being not merely undemocratic but Fascist and traitorous.

Of all the attacks on regionalists, those leveled against Grant Wood, Thomas Hart Benton, and John Steuart Curry were probably the most vocal and intense.[22] Wood, Benton, and Curry were frequently lumped together as a regionalist group, primarily because much of their work centered on rural American life, often derived from folk traditions and narratives; moreover, all three largely rejected the techniques of artistic modernism, which they associated with Europe, in order to promote an indigenous American art. Leftist critics early on attacked the three for their avoidance of social realism (contrasting them with such painters as Edward Hopper), and one of these critics, Stuart Davis, himself a painter, in 1935 savaged Benton for what he saw as his jingoism and racial chauvinism. Benton "should have no trouble in selling his wares to any Fascist or semi-Fascist type of government," Davis wrote,[23] adding that Hitler and Huey Long would love aspects of Benton's mural in the library of New York's Whitney Museum of American Art:

> [Benton's] opinion of radical thought is clearly symbolized [in the Whitney mural]. It shows a Jew in vicious caricature holding the New Masses and saying "the hour is at hand." Hitler would love that. For Huey Long he can point to his Puck and Judge caricatures of crap shooting and barefoot shuffling negroes. No danger of these negroes demanding a right to vote even if the pole [sic] tax has been taken off. If art forms have meaning and purpose and are inseparable from human ways of perceiving and doing, then in the examples given it is quite clear what Benton has perceived and what the purposes of his forms are. (13)

Other leftist critics about this time began comparing the subject matter and style of the regionalists with those of the artists officially sanctioned by the Nazis in their campaigns to promote German nationalism and to stamp out the "degenerate art" of the modernists.

The regionalist slide into insignificance continued during World War II, as localism seemed terribly irrelevant in light of the global war. Reviewing the opening of Grant Wood's exhibit at the Art Institute of Chicago in 1942, Peyton Boswell observed that with the nation at war, Wood's once popular paintings seemed completely out of touch with the internationalism marking America's political and cultural life. "Today, the United States is perhaps more international-minded then ever before," Boswell writes. "Grant Wood and all those associated with him in the long crusade for a genuine native expression in the arts are in eclipse."[24] If, as Boswell suggests, the regionalists were in eclipse in 1942, by the end of World War II they were completely out of the picture, their coffin nailed shut by H. W. Janson's influential essay "Benton and Wood, Champions of Regionalism" (1946). Janson here argues that the regionalists hoped to use their art to lead America into political authoritarianism. He observes that despite the movement's waning appeal, regionalism remains "sufficiently dangerous to invite the closest scrutiny of its sources, aims, and methods, as well as the underlying reasons for its popular success. Since the movement has been nourished by some of the fundamental ills of our society—the same ills that, in more virulent form, produced National Socialism in Germany—it would be vain to expect its complete disappearance in the immediate future; nevertheless, a clear understanding of its nature will at least enable us to recognize its implications and reduce its influence."[25] Later in the essay, Janson explicitly declares that regionalist aesthetics are those of the Nazis, claiming that "almost every one of the ideas constituting the regionalist credo could be matched more or less verbatim from the writings of Nazi experts on art" and that "many of the paintings officially approved by the Nazis recall the works of the regionalists in this country" (186). Besides burying the regionalists, "Benton and Wood, Champions of Regionalism" looks forward to the emergence of the conception that abstract expressionism was the art of democracy, its universalist nonrepresentationalism liberated from both the social and political repression of the authoritarian state and the chauvinism and jingoism of regionalism.

The demise of the regionalist painters is merely one story of many related to the more general collapse of regionalism as a cultural and political movement in the late 1930s and 1940s. White southern writers were deeply affected by regionalism's demise, particularly the confirmed regionalists, such as the Nashville Agrarians, who faced similar attacks to those leveled at Benton, Curry, and Wood. But many other white Southern writers also felt the impact, as the rising tide of the democratic revival not only undermined many of the foundational supports of white southern identity but also sullied the whole notion of "southernness." In the 1930s and 1940s many southern writers were easily dismissed as "regional writers"; some, including Faulkner, were tagged as Fascists, not because they were supporters of Hitler and Mussolini, but because they became associated with the South they were depicting in their fiction, a South awash with the same sort of irrational violence that commentators were finding at the heart of Fascism.

The weakened foundations of white southern identity, cracked by the democratic revival, crumbled further during World War II, as blacks grew increasingly vocal in their protests against segregation. As had the democratic revival, black protest swelled in part because of events overseas: many blacks openly questioned the war effort, wondering why they should fight to protect freedom in other nations when they themselves lacked equality at home, even in the armed services, which remained persistently segregated throughout the war, as did the blood supply. Doxey A. Wilkerson, in his essay for the wartime collection *What the Negro Wants*, summarizes the thinking embraced by many blacks, particularly early in the war: "Why fight fascism in Germany when we have fascism right here in America?"[26] Rallying to aid Great Britain, with its long history of imperialism, did not inspire a great deal of enthusiasm in the black community, nor did the war with the Japanese, who were seen by some as people of color fighting the white man. Not forgetting their situation in the United States, many blacks endorsed a "Double V" campaign—victory abroad and at home. Near the end of the war, looking forward to its aftermath, Walter White, president of the NAACP, warned that America and the other Allied nations "must choose without delay one of two courses—to revolutionize their racial concepts and practices, to abolish imperialism and grant full equality to all of its people, or else prepare for World War III."[27] White noted that World War II had taught American blacks, particularly black soldiers, that in their struggles for freedom they stood alongside oppressed people from all over the world:

> World War II has given to the Negro a sense of kinship with other colored—and also oppressed—peoples of the world. Where he has not thought through or informed himself on the racial angles of colonial policy and master-race theories, he senses that the struggle of the Negro in the United States is part and parcel of the struggle against imperialism and exploitation in India, China, Burma, Africa,

> the Philippines, Malaya, the West Indies, and South America. The Negro soldier is convinced that as time proceeds that identification of interests will spread even among some brown and yellow peoples who today refuse to see the connection between their exploitation by white nations and discrimination against the Negro in the United States. (144)

White delivered some of his most caustic attacks on those southern Democrats who were doing everything they could in Congress to retard social change.

Four years before White's warning, and before the United States entered the war, Zora Neale Hurston also cast the plight of American blacks in a global context, castigating white nations for their hypocrisy in professing ideals of liberty and freedom while practicing imperialism. "All around me, bitter tears are being shed over the fate of Holland, Belgium, France, and England," Hurston wrote. "I must confess to being a little dry around the eyes. I hear people shaking with shudders at the thought of Germany collecting taxes in Holland. I have not heard a word against Holland collecting one twelfth of poor people's wages in Asia."[28] President Roosevelt, Hurston added, was calling loudly for action to protect freedom overseas, "but he evidently has not the courage to speak even softly at home. Take away the ocean and he simmers right down. I wish I could say differently, but I cannot. I will fight for my country, but I will not lie for her" (251).

Hurston's comments, written in 1941, appeared in "Seeing the World as It Is," a chapter with which she intended to close her autobiography, *Dust Tracks on a Road* (1942). That chapter, however, along with another, was cut from the final manuscript at her editor's insistence, judged to be too critical of the United States during a time of war. Hurston's comments point to a significant difference in the responses of black southern writers and white southern writers to the rise of Fascism and World War II, a difference that is one reason for my decision to limit my study to white southern writers. While white southern writers for the most part focused on what Fascism and totalitarianism did or did not reveal about traditional southern culture, black southern writers, not needing the example of Nazi Germany to understand the terrors of southern segregation, for the most part brought Fascism to bear on America as a whole, focusing on the contradiction between the nation's professed ideals of equality and its widespread practice of discrimination against blacks.[29] Fascism, in other words, highlighted racial discrimination as an American rather than merely a southern problem, even if conditions were more severe in the South.[30]

Richard Wright's *Native Son* and his essay about the novel's creation, "How 'Bigger' Was Born," both published in 1940, probably best illustrate how black southern writers used their understanding of Fascism more to make the racism of their nation than to make that of their region visible. In his essay, Wright reveals that his voracious reading about Nazi Germany throughout the 1930s—"I read every account of the Fascist movement in Germany I could lay my hands on," he writes,[31] his interest no doubt shaped largely by his Communist politics—profoundly shaped his belief that virulent racism was a widespread American problem. Wright comments that the political developments rocking the world led him to see that "the Southern scheme of oppression was but an appendage of a far vaster and in many respects more ruthless and impersonal commodity-profit machine" (861). In fact, so insignificant was Fascism in terms of helping him understand southern racism that Wright observes, in an extraordinary statement, that his early reading about Nazi Germany reminded him not of the South's segregated system but of the sermons of black preachers that he had heard as a child, those telling "of a life beyond this world, a life in which the color of men's skins would not matter, a life in which each man would know what was deep down in the hearts of his fellow man" (864). "What struck me with particular force was the Nazi preoccupation with the construction of a society in which there would exist among all people (*German* people, of course!) *one* solidarity of ideals, *one* continuous circulation of fundamental beliefs, notions, and assumptions," Wright explains. "I am not now speaking of the popular idea of regimenting people's thought; I'm speaking of the implicit, almost unconscious, or pre-conscious, assumptions and ideals upon which whole nations and races act and live" (864).

Wright of course eventually came to see the vicious racism and stifling regimentation structuring Nazi Germany, and he used that knowledge in *Native Son* to portray American racism as darkly mirroring that of the South, in large part by depicting the racial landscape of Chicago as distinctly and recognizably southern. The parallels are striking: blacks are shunted to Chicago's South Side; Bigger is threatened with lynching (with many echoes of the violence directed at southern blacks that Wright had previously portrayed in *Uncle Tom's Children*); the Ku Klux Klan burns a cross atop a building; and the whites, in dehumanizing Bigger and other blacks, speak with the same bestial-racial rhetoric characteristically used by racist southerners, complete with the fearful image of the black beast violating the southern-turned-northern belle. "It is a sad day for American civilization," the prosecutor says in his closing argument at Bigger's trial, "when a white man [Bigger's lawyer] will try to stay the hand of justice from a bestial monstrosity who has ravished and struck down one of the finest and most delicate flowers of our womanhood." He goes on: "Every decent white man in America ought to swoon with joy for the opportunity to crush this black lizard, to keep him from scuttling on his belly farther and farther over the earth and spitting forth his venom of death."[32] The manhunt for Bigger, with street-by-street house searches and countless shakedowns of innocent blacks, characterized by Bigger's lawyer as "something unheard of in democratic lands" (806), suggests the workings of both the racist South and the police state.

Wright gives the novel its international context largely through Bigger's repeated comments voicing his emotional admiration of Fascist dictators. In discussing Bigger's origins in "How 'Bigger' Was Born," Wright comments that while obsessively reading about Nazi Germany he was startled to discover "either from the side of the Fascists or from the side of the oppressed, reactions, moods, phrases, attitudes that reminded me of Bigger, that helped to bring out more clearly the shadowy outlines of the negative that lay in the back of my mind" (864). "From page to page," Wright adds, "I encountered and recognized familiar emotional patterns" (864). Those patterns, as Wright explains and as he himself had felt in the early 1930s, had to do mostly with blacks' admiration for Hitler and Mussolini, not because "of any intellectual comprehension of the forces at work in world, but because they felt that these men 'did things,' a phrase which is charged with more meaning than the mere words imply" (860).

The Fascist enterprise, Wright observes, brought out in blacks "a wild and intense longing (wild and intense because it was suppressed!) to belong, to be identified, to feel that they were as alive as other people were, to be caught up forgetfully and exultingly in the swing of events, to feel the clean, deep, organic satisfaction of doing a job in common with others" (860). This is precisely why in the novel Bigger looks to the dictators abroad to give him hope at home:

> He liked to hear of how Japan was conquering China; of how Hitler was running the Jews to the ground; of how Mussolini was invading Spain. He was not concerned with whether these acts were right or wrong; they simply appealed to him as possible avenues of escape. He

felt that some day there would be a black man who would whip the black people into a tight band and together they would act and end fear and shame. He never thought of this in precise mental images; he felt it; he would feel it for a while and then forget. But hope was always waiting somewhere deep down in him. (551)

In jail Bigger feels no remorse for his murderous acts because in killing Mary Dalton and Bessie he felt himself a man of action and thus, at least momentarily, free; his violent acts, in other words, were a version writ small of the acts of Fascist dictators he admired for their manhandling of nations. "But I ain't worried none about them women I killed," he says. "For a little while I was free. I was doing something" (776).

It is immensely significant to the novel's national and international perspectives that Bigger's defense lawyer is Jewish, less because Jews themselves were often victimized in America and were generally supportive of blacks' demands for civil rights than because the Jewish lawyer's scathing denunciation of America's oppression of blacks resonated in 1940 as a scathing denunciation of Nazi oppression, with American racism seen through a palimpsest of Nazi racism. There is no need to work through the lawyer's long closing argument, in which he delivers his attack, but one haunting comment takes the logic of black oppression to its logical extremes and looks eerily forward both to the forced emigration of Jews out of Germany (which began in the fall of 1940, roughly six months after the publication of *Native Son*) and then to the creation of extermination camps: "You cannot kill this man, Your Honor, for we have made it plain that we do not recognize that he lives! . . . But if we say that we must kill him, then let us have the courage and honesty to say: 'Let us kill them all. They are not human. There's no room for them.' Then let us do it" (825).

Given the ferocity of its depiction of American racism, Wright must have been surprised when the Book-of-the-Month Club chose *Native Son* for one of its monthly dual selections (among other things, the club's editors requested that Wright cut the masturbation in the movie theater and shorten the courtroom summation of Bigger's lawyer). Four years later, the Book-of-the-Month Club was not so welcoming when Wright's editor submitted the manuscript of *American Hunger*, his two-part autobiography of childhood in the South and young adulthood in Chicago, which continued his assault on American racism. With America now at war and the invasion of Europe under way, the depiction of American racism apparently was no longer deemed acceptable for the American reading audience, a reality that Hurston had faced in the excision of the chapters from *Dust Tracks on the Road*. While expressing interest in selecting *American Hunger*, the novelist Dorothy Canfield Fisher (writing under the name Dorothy Canfield), one of the Book-of-the-Month Club's chief editors, who had strongly advocated the club's selection of *Native Son*, demanded that Wright cut the Chicago section and rewrite the ending of the southern section to make it more upbeat and patriotic. Canfield Fisher wanted Wright to locate his dream of freedom and dignity solidly in America's democratic creeds; doing so, Canfield Fisher wrote to Wright (1 July 1944), "would hearten all those who believe in American ideals." Characterizing the South as a "prison of injustice" and "that Bastille of racial oppression," she posited that perhaps Wright's dream had been inspired by the sight of the American flag.[33]

For whatever reason, Wright agreed to the changes. If cutting the second section was easy, rewriting the first section's ending to Canfield Fisher's specifications was not; she kept insisting that Wright include more fulsome praise of America and American writers. As finally published with its new title, *Black Boy* (1945), Wright's autobiography completely redirected the thrust of the original manuscript. *American Hunger*, as its title indicates, portrays racism as an American problem, embedded deeply in the social structures of both the North and the South. In the Chicago section, Wright repeatedly attacks America's flawed democracy and its refusal to right itself. At one point Wright goes so far as to declare that given the systematic exclusion of blacks from American life, he would prefer to live under totalitarianism if that system, unlike American democracy, recognized the humanity of black people. "In order to escape the racial attack that went to the roots of my life, I would have gladly accepted any way of life but the one in which I found myself," Wright comments, adding: "I would have consented to live under the most rigid type of dictatorship, for I felt that dictatorships, too, defined the use of men, however degrading that use might be."[34]

Black Boy, however, has none of this criticism of America and instead reads like a modern-day slave narrative, with Wright at the end boarding a train in Memphis that will carry him to Chicago, to the promised land. *Black Boy*'s final paragraph looks hopefully forward to Wright's envisioned new life in the land of liberty and justice:

> With ever watchful eyes and bearing scars, visible and invisible, I headed North, full of a hazy notion that life could be lived with dig-

nity, that the personalities of others should not be violated, that men should be able to confront men without fear and shame, that if men were lucky in their living on earth they might win some redeeming meaning for their having struggled and suffered here beneath the stars.[35]

The message is not just clear but trumpeted: the South is a terrifying world of irrational racism, and the North is America, home of liberty and justice for all.

To make sure that no one missed any of this, Canfield Fisher characterized *Black Boy* in the *Book-of-the-Month Club News* as a heartstopping thriller, a story of an American living in a world as dark and dangerous as the occupied nations of Europe (in other words, the slave narrative transformed into the modern-day tale of escape from a Nazi-occupied country). "No story of desperate, hopeless, but doggedly persistent European resistance to Nazi oppressors, set upon killing the soul of man," Canfield Fisher writes, "is more breathtaking than this true story of a greatly gifted human being's stubborn resistance to the pressure on him to deny and renounce the best in his nature, than this factual account of a fellow-citizen of ours who tells us that he knew 'the safety of my life in the South depended on how well I concealed from all whites what I felt.'"[36] Indeed, Canfield Fisher immediately corrects the comment she had quoted, saying that "from our wider viewpoint, we know that he was quite inaccurate in saying 'all whites,'" that throughout the nation "conscientious and intelligent white Americans, many of them, are trying to open the door of decent opportunity to colored people" (2). While acknowledging that there were even some southern whites who were acting civilly, she makes it clear that these sane voices are anomalies in a region rigidly controlled by a Gestapo-like white populace:

> That this door of opportunity is not nearly open enough is shown by the perfect unconsciousness of the Black Boy that there was in the white population around him any save members of a sort of informal, unofficial, but—as far as he could see—all-pervasive Gestapo, spying upon his every action and gesture, determined to leave him no instant of time in which he could act freely, in accordance with his finest impulses. The terrified anxiety of these white people, the only ones with whom he came in contact, is always felt by those who try to hold others in subjection, since they know that their own safety depends on the suppression not only of action but of the thought. Like

the Gestapo in later phases of the German occupation of formerly free countries, they were nervously on the alert for any sign of inner independence. At the mere scent of it, they pressed close on him in alarm, trying to divine from the expression of his face (or from its lack of expression) what he felt. For he must be prevented at all costs from feeling what he felt. (2–3)

Only by implication does Canfield Fisher suggest that the South needs to be liberated from its occupiers, but the commentary on the inside front dust jacket, clearly looking forward to the postwar era, poses a question that makes it clear that America can no longer tolerate southern culture's threatening irrationality: "What kind of America, the reader may well ask, are we building for ourselves when such things as are set forth in this book can be?"[37]

This question, together with Canfield Fisher's commentary, brings us back to the primary questions that the present book explores: amidst a cultural crisis rocking the foundations of southern identity and culture, when commentators inside and outside the South routinely equated southern culture with European Fascism, how did white southern writers of the 1930s and 1940s understand themselves and their culture? How did they represent the South, and particularly its system of racial segregation, in their work? How did the European crisis become integrated into their writing? And how did World War II and its aftermath affect their writing? All of these questions are central to this study, and merely asking them points toward the possible reconfiguration of white southern literature from this period. Traditionally, this literature has been seen to be turned decidedly, if not incestuously, inward, focusing almost exclusively upon southern matters entirely isolated from the larger world.[38] While modernity, of course, occasionally is seen as penetrating the southern literary landscape, that penetration is usually identified only in manifestations of finance and business, with the traditional South trying to hold off the Yankee invasion of dollars and capital investment. Rarely are the issues central to European Fascism and totalitarianism seen as significant to the white southern literary imagination; Europe's influence upon that imagination is generally understood to be confined to matters of literary form and technique, that is, to the influences of and resistance to literary modernism.

While to date a few studies have explored white southern writers in the context of Fascism and totalitarianism, these have all been articles or chapters looking specifically at one writer and often merely at one or two works.[39] As good as these studies are, none of them argues what this book does, that for at least two decades a large number of white southern writers were haunted by Fascism's long shadow over the South and that this haunting fundamentally shaped their imaginations, work, and careers. As we shall see, Fascism influenced different writers in different ways, largely determined by the writers' fundamental political outlook and, in some cases, by their travels in Europe. For some, such as W. J. Cash and Lillian Smith, viewing the South in the context of Fascism was liberating, defamiliarizing southern ideology and providing a powerful perspective from which to critique the traditional South. For others, such as the Nashville Agrarians and William Alexander Percy, the Fascist-southern connection was ridiculous and dangerous, and they felt compelled to defend the traditional South and refute the alleged ties to Fascism; frequently they also had to defend themselves from similar allegations of Fascist thinking. To their eyes, the traditional South was actually the last line of defense against what seemed like a worldwide trend toward corporate capitalism and its final manifestation, the Fascist state. For the imaginative writers—those writing fiction, poetry, and drama rather than cultural criticism—the impact of Fascism was more complex and often less visible, usually surfacing in their fiction and drama in manifestations of the crushing power of the authoritarian state and its threat to individual liberties. White southern writers who struggled with these issues include William Faulkner, Carson McCullers, Katherine Anne Porter, Robert Penn Warren, Thomas Wolfe, and Lillian Hellman.[40] All but Faulkner and McCullers, it is worth noting, traveled to Nazi Germany or Fascist Italy during the 1930s, returning home transformed, their fiction and drama turning decidedly darker and more focused on authoritarian politics and control. European Fascism, in other words, haunts these writers' work even when it is not mentioned outright, serving as a backdrop to their narratives, at times clearly visible, at times not. It is against this backdrop that their literature is perhaps best read, with the menace of Fascism not only shaping the crucial issues of their work but also bringing their work into the cultural dialogue that was then determining America's future.

I

DANGEROUS LIAISONS

THE NASHVILLE AGRARIANS

In "Reconstructed but Unregenerate," his essay from *I'll Take My Stand: The South and the Agrarian Tradition* (1930), John Crowe Ransom looked to Europe in order to conceptualize southern culture. "The South is unique on this continent for having founded and defended a culture which was according to the European principles of culture," Ransom writes; "and the European principles had better look to the South if they are to be perpetuated in this country" (*ITMS* 3). As Ransom goes on to make clear, the Europe about which he spoke was not contemporary Europe but premodern, traditional Europe, that is, Europe before various forces of modernity, including industrialism and equalitarianism, had destroyed the central belief system that had structured its culture, what Ransom characterized as "the core of unadulterated Europeanism, with its self-sufficient, backward-looking, intensely provincial communities" (*ITMS* 5). Equating the South with traditional Europe was a popular trope for many of the Agrarians, one that Allen Tate, in his contribution to *I'll Take My Stand*, "Remarks on the Southern Religion," takes to its limit when he flatly declares that the Old South "*was* Europe; that is to say, the South had taken root in a native soil" (*ITMS* 171). Indeed, the characteristic Agrarian view had it that southerners were the world's last Europeans, since by their definition Europe no longer existed, societies there having long since forsaken traditional culture for the corporatism of the modern industrial state. The Agrarians were taking their stand to make sure that that did not happen in the American South.

As we have already seen, by the mid-1930s the antimodernism of the regionalist impulse in America was becoming deeply suspect in the popular imagination, regarded as a potentially dangerous tribal irrationalism standing opposed to the universally held ideals of freedom and democracy upon which America had been founded. Some critics of the Agrarians, from both the North and the South, for instance, followed their lead in contextualizing the southern culture within the recent history of Europe but reached a startlingly different conclusion: the defenders of the traditional South certainly looked very European, but the Europeans they resembled were not backward-looking traditionalists but the Fascists and the Nazis. As we shall see, the association with Fascism became the Agrarians' albatross; never able fully to refute the charge, by the late 1930s the Agrarians were in disarray. While not the only reason for their demise, the long shadow of the Fascist allegations, together with the nation's mounting fervor of patriotic nationalism against the Fascist enemy, played a large part in the Agrarians' undoing and particularly affected the literary careers of three of its leaders, John Crowe Ransom, Donald Davidson, and Allen Tate.[1]

Although the Agrarians fiercely embraced localism, most of them from the beginning of the movement conceptualized southern culture and constructed their defense of it according to what they saw happening in faraway Europe. Tate's *Jefferson Davis: His Rise and Fall* (1929) works from this global perspective, configuring the Civil War as a battle between large cultural forces that were remaking both America and Europe.[2] "The War between the States," he writes,

> has a remote origin, and it cannot be understood apart from the chief movements of European history since the Reformation. It was another war between America and Europe, and "America," in the second great attempt, won. The South was the last stronghold of European civilization in the western hemisphere, a conservative check upon the restless expansiveness of the industrial North, and the South had to go. The South was permanently old-fashioned, backward-looking, slow, contented to live upon a modest conquest of nature, unwilling to conquer the earth's resources for the fun of the conquest; contented, in short, to take only what man needs; unwilling to juggle the needs of man in the illusory pursuit of abstract wealth. It is a mistake to suppose that the surrender of Lord Cornwallis at Yorktown in 1781 freed "America" from the bonds of the European tradition: that some-

what mottled blessing required for its success one more surrender—that of Lee at Appomattox in 1865. The War between the States was the second and decisive struggle of the Western spirit against the European—the spirit of restless aggression against a stable spirit of ordered economy—and the Western won.

In a sense, all European history since the Reformation was concentrated in the war between the North and the South. For in the South the most conservative of the European orders had, with great power, come back to life, while in the North, opposing the Southern feudalism, had grown to be a powerful industrial state which epitomized in spirit all those middle-class, urban impulses directed against the agrarian aristocracies of Europe after the Reformation. The transformation of Europe, its Americanization, within Europe, has been gradual, but the transformation of Europe in America was, because its two spiritual poles clashed here, sudden and dramatic.[3]

In this remarkable passage, Tate rotates the North-South cultural axis characteristically used by southerners to conceptualize their culture (with the North embodying everything that the South was not—urbanism, industrialism, progressivism, etc.) so that the axis points West-East, with the North now as the West, the South now as the East. While the basic values associated with each pole remain the same, the dramatically revised orientation contextualizes southern history as a reconfiguration of world history, with the South corresponding to the cultural stability of premodern Europe and the North to the rapacious expansionism that had torn asunder traditional Europe and then later, in this new reading, the Old South. Several lines from Tate's "The Mediterranean" (1933) capture the destructive power of this westering force of his expansionism:

> What country shall we conquer, what fair land
> Unman our conquest and locate our blood?
> We've cracked the hemispheres with careless hand!
> Now, from the Gates of Hercules we flood
>
> Westward, westward . . .
> (*CP* 67)

By the time of *I'll Take My Stand*, almost all of the Agrarians were using the East-West axis to celebrate southern culture's grounded origins and to attack the westering impulse they saw defining the rest of America. In "Reconstructed but Unregenerate" John Crowe Ransom describes the values the typical southerner embraces in his commitment to place, history, and tradition: "He identifies himself with a spot of ground, and this ground carries a good deal of meaning; it defines itself for him as nature. He would till it not too hurriedly and not too mechanically to observe in it the contingency and the infinitude of nature; and so his life acquires its philosophical and even its cosmic consciousness" (*ITMS* 19–20). The forces of progress threatening the South, which the Agrarians labeled with the catchall term *industrialism*, represent the aggressive expansionism associated with westward exploration and pioneering. "It is only too easy to define the malignant meaning of industrialism," Ransom writes. "It is the contemporary form of pioneering; yet since it never consents to define its goal, it is a pioneering on principle, and with an accelerating speed" (*ITMS* 15).

In its ruthless pragmatism and endless pursuit of wealth and new markets for its goods, industrialism, the Agrarians believed, destroyed the values holding together traditional societies, particularly the bond with the soil. Industrialism valued time over place, movement over stasis, individualism over community, fostering a psychology of transience that Ransom summarizes in this directive: "Do not allow yourself to feel homesick; form no such powerful attachments that you will feel a pain in cutting them loose; prepare your spirit to be always on the move" (*ITMS* 6). "Time is money now, not property," Andrew Lytle observes in his essay "The Hind Tit," adding that southerners "should dread industrialism like a pizen snake. For the South long since finished its pioneering. It can only do violence to its provincial life when it allows itself to be forced into the aggressive state of mind of an earlier period" (*ITMS* 236, 234). Lytle underscores the connection between industrialism and westward movement when he flatly declares that the modern view holds that "industrialism is *manifest destiny*" (*ITMS* 207). Lytle's words point to a simple image from American history, one that I have suggested elsewhere, for contrasting the Agrarians' characterization of industrialism and traditionalism: industrialism is a wagon train pushing forever west; traditionalism is the fort from which the wagon train has departed.[4]

Certainly in part because the Agrarians attacked industrialism from this East-West perspective, several of them objected loudly to the decision to entitle their collection of essays *I'll Take My Stand*, a phrase from the song "Dixie," which suggested not only that the symposium was primarily a "southern" book, with its arguments merely sectional in significance, but that its defense of southern culture was conceived along neo-Confederate lines, with the Agrarians simply following in the steps of their ancestors. Even though all of the Agrarians were committed to defending southern traditionalism (that was what brought them together), they often disagreed about the group's practical goals.

The disagreement over the symposium's title reveals the fault lines that would only grow more visible over time. The strongest defenders of the title were Davidson and Clarence Nixon (who at one point had suggested the title "The Promise of a Southern Life: A Collection of Essays by a Group of Rebels of the Third Generation"),[5] together with Ransom; those most opposed were Robert Penn Warren, Lytle, and Tate. Warren and Tate were particularly concerned that the title would cast the group as sentimental Old South escapists. "I think that the title, 'I'll Take My Stand,'" Warren wrote to Tate and his wife, Caroline Gordon (19 May 1930), "is the god-damnedest thing I have ever heard of; for the love of God block it if you can."[6] Not long after, Warren wrote Davidson (25 June 1930) that he hoped "to the Lord . . . that the title is not to be *I'll Take My Stand.* Compliments to its contriver, but I don't think that a worse could be picked; it seems to me to inject an entirely false note into our performance."[7] Tate himself was even uncomfortable with the designation *Agrarian,* fearing that people would perceive the group merely as back-to-the-farm crusaders. Upon hearing that T. H. Alexander, an editor at the *Nashville Tennessean,* had made just that connection, Tate wrote Davidson (7 September 1930) that such thinking "reduces our real aims to nonsense" and that "by not making our appeal through the title to ideas, we are at the mercy of all the Alexanders—for they need only to draw portraits of us plowing or cleaning a spring to make hash of us before we get a hearing. My melancholy is profound" (*LCDT* 255). Tate's fears were to be proved well founded.

Tracts Against Communism was the title preferred by Tate, Warren, and Lytle. At first glance, their choice appears wildly inappropriate, for Communism is barely mentioned in the symposium. But actually, in relation to the East-West axis structuring Agrarian thinking, *Tracts Against Communism* was perfectly appropriate, because the Agrarians at this point believed that the ultimate end of industrialism, once its power was centralized through finance capitalism, was Communism.[8] Thus in the long run it was finally Communism, rather than Yankee industrialism, against which the Agrarians were taking their stand. At least this was how Tate, Warren, and Lytle saw it. Lytle was particularly enthusiastic about the proposed new title, writing to Tate (June 1930) that he liked "the tactical import of *Tracts Against Communism*; the selling value; and the added surprise which the contents would give the reader, expecting a discussion of the Reds and the activities of New York's idle who form the bulk of the supposed Communistic party in this country" (*LTL* 38–39). In another letter to Tate (spring 1930), Lytle wrote that to Ransom's objections that using the new title would mean that an essay on Communism would have to be added to the symposium, he had responded "that no paper was needed, because the defense of agrarianism was, itself, an attack on Communism" (*LTL* 42).

Tate, Warren, and Lytle lost their battle, in part because they raised the issue when the book was already speeding toward production, in part because Ransom and Davidson stood firm in defending the original choice. After enduring several months of Tate's carping, Davidson finally exploded, writing his friend an angry and dismissive letter (5 September 1930) in which he characterized Tate's efforts to change the title as "like stopping to polish your shoes in the midst of a headlong charge, just before you reach the enemy's breastworks; or like pausing to argue about the wording of the motto on the flag—'Are we right sure, Soldiers and Comrades, that it should be "Sic semper tyrannis?" Would not "Lux et veritas" better describe our dignified array?'" (*LCDT* 253). While Ransom remained steadfast in his support of the original title, in his late revisions of *I'll Take My Stand*'s opening manifesto he did include a statement equating industrialism with Communism. After commenting that "the true Sovietists or Communists ... are the Industrialists themselves," he added, "They would have the government set up an economic super-organization, which in turn would become the government. We therefore look upon the Communist menace as a menace indeed, but not as a Red one; because it is simply according to the blind drift of our industrial development to expect in America at last much the same economic system as that imposed by violence upon Russia in 1917" (*ITMS* xli–xlii).[9] In a final concession to Tate, who was threatening to pull his essay from the book, Davidson and Ransom allowed him to include a footnote stating his disagreement with the symposium's title.

The Agrarians' attacks on industrialism in *I'll Take My Stand* are long on idealism and short on pragmatics, with few of the contributors going much further, in terms of offering practical solutions, than Ransom's declaration that "the theory of agrarianism is that the culture of the soil is the best and most sensitive of vocations, and that therefore it should have the economic preference and enlist the maximum number of workers" (*ITMS* xlvii). Tate, however, the Agrarian who had his eyes most on Europe, went further than most, at least in offering a broadly conceived vision of an agrarian society, suggesting that the South needed to model itself after medieval Europe, anchoring itself with a central and authoritative (and by suggestion, authoritarian) religious faith (obviously Roman Catholicism) structuring all areas of life. Tate believed that in conceiving a blueprint for a new agrarian South, the Agrarians needed to learn from the failures of the Old South, particularly its failure to organize itself around religious faith. In "Remarks on the Southern Religion" he argues that the Old South "was a feudal society without a feudal religion" (*ITMS* 166) in that it had focused on matters social and political, being bolstered by an individualistic Protestantism—which he characterizes as "in origin, a non-agrarian and trading religion; hardly a religion at all, but a result of secular ambition" (*ITMS* 168)—that had sundered, rather than knitted together, community ties. With the defeat of the Civil War and the onslaught of Reconstruction, southern culture had collapsed because of its fundamental spiritual poverty. Tate thus concludes that "the South would not have been defeated had it possessed a sufficient faith in its own kind of God. It would not have been defeated, in other words, had it been able to bring out a body of doctrine setting forth its true conviction that the ends of man require more for their realization than politics. The setback of the war was of itself a very trivial one" (*ITMS* 174).

"Remarks on the Southern Religion" points to the concept of culture that underlies Tate's agrarianism: to be stable and civilized, society must be structured around a central faith demanding discipline and allegiance. From the beginning of his interest in agrarianism, Tate focused his efforts on preparing the way for such a society, which can be seen clearly in his letters from the late 1920s. To Andrew Lytle (31 July 1929) Tate declared forthrightly that Agrarianism should establish "a whole, religious, philosophical, literary, and social program, anti-industrial on the negative side, and all that implies, and, on the positive, authoritarian, agrarian, classical, aristocratic" (*LTL* 34). A few days later, in a remarkable letter written to Davidson (10 August 1929), Tate outlined tactical plans for remaking the South along these programmatic lines, calling specifically for

1. The formation of a society, or an academy of Southern *positive* reactionaries made up at first of people of our own group.
2. The expansion in a year or two of this academy to this size: fifteen active members—poets, critics, historians, economists—and ten

inactive members—lawyers, politicians, private citizens—who might be active enough without being committed at first to direct agitation.

3. The drawing up of a philosophical constitution, to be issued and signed by the academy, as the groundwork of the movement. It should be ambitious to the last degree; it should set forth, under our leading idea, a complete social, philosophical, literary, economic, and religious system. This will inevitably draw upon our heritage, but this heritage should be valued, not in what it actually performed, but in its possible perfection. Philosophically we must go the whole hog of reaction, and base our movement less upon the actual old South than upon its prototype—the historical social and religious scheme of Europe. We must be the last Europeans—there being no Europeans in Europe at present.

4. The academy will not be a secret order: all the cards will be on the table. We should be *secretive*, however, in our tactics, and plan the campaign for the maximum of effect. All our writings should be signed "John Doe, of the —— ——," or whatever we call it.

5. Organized publication should be looked to. A newspaper, perhaps, to argue our principles on the lower plane; then a weekly, to press philosophy upon the passing show; and, third, a quarterly devoted wholly to principles. This is a large scheme, but it must be held up constantly. We must do our best with what we can get. (*LCDT* 229–30)

Tate noted that extreme times demanded extreme positions that would both draw out the enemy and rally the supporters. He wrote Davidson that he wanted to compel southerners to take a stand one way or the other, "crystalliz[ing] into opposition or complete allegiance the vaguely pro-Southern opinions of the time." "We must crush minor differences of doctrine under a single idea," Tate added, stressing the need for unrelenting discipline, an idea he returned to later in the letter when he declared, "*Organization and discipline are indispensable*" (*LCDT* 230–31).

Tate admitted to Davidson that his proposal for action appeared to contradict one of the Agrarians' key principles—that Agrarianism stood fundamentally opposed to centralization and its crushing power of standardization. This was particularly important to Davidson, who as an artist and scholar celebrated folk culture and expression and believed that America was headed, through progressive economic and political consolidation, toward what he would later call "a Leviathan state."[10] Davidson must have been surprised, then, at Tate's proposal for a southern academy and his declaration that "we cannot merely fight centralization; we must envisage a centralization of a different and better kind" (*LCDT* 230–31). Whatever Davidson's feelings about the academy—in his reply to Tate (20 August 1929) he did not comment on its creation (*LCDT* 233–34)—Tate believed that it was crucial for the Agrarians' success and should be modeled, as he wrote to Andrew Lytle (31 July 1929), on L'Action Française (*LTL* 34).[11] The primary goal of the academy, he wrote Davidson (10 August 1929), was to "*create an intellectual situation interior to the South*" (*LCDT* 230); that is, they would control the ideas that defined southern culture. "I underscore it," Tate added, "because, to me, it contains the heart of the matter" (*LCDT* 230). In his letter outlining his program to Lytle (29 July 1929), Tate wrote that the group should suppress all reservations and work together in a united front. "There's no use taking half measures," he wrote. "We must go the whole hog, or we shall end by merely brooding over the past. Instead, we must *use* the past for daring and *positive* ends" (*LTL* 34).

While Tate's plans for a southern academy never materialized, the "intellectual situation interior to the South" that he called for became an important goal for the Agrarians in their resistance to industrialism. Read in this light, *I'll Take My Stand* was the group's attempt not only to identify the crisis of industrialism but also, more importantly, to define the terms and establish the categories for interpreting that crisis. Following Tate's notion that extreme positions would generate extreme responses, the Agrarians hoped the symposium would crystallize southern opinion. To that end, in the immediate aftermath of *I'll Take My Stand*'s publication they participated in five public debates focused on issues raised by the book, with Ransom most often representing the group. The debates were well publicized and well attended; three thousand people attended the first debate, in Richmond, Virginia, with Ransom paired off against Stringfellow Barr, editor of the *Virginia Quarterly Review*.

The Agrarians' initial enthusiasm soon faded, however, as *I'll Take My Stand* appeared to flush out decidedly more enemies than partisans; the stack of negative reviews grew increasingly tall, with many of the harshest appearing in southern newspapers.[12] As Tate had feared, many reviewers dismissed the Agrarians as ivory-tower intellectuals, romantic idealists nostalgically celebrating the virtues of farm life, even as the South's real farmers were locked in a bare-bones struggle to survive. "Of such a philosophy," Gerald Johnson, the influential southern liberal columnist, wrote of *I'll Take My Stand*'s agrarianism, "one can only say that it smells horribly of the lamp, that it was library-born and library-bred, and will perish miserably if it is ever exposed for ten minutes to the direct rays of the sun out in the daylight of reality."[13] Johnson hit even harder in another review of the symposium, writing that the Agrarians' ideas "would seem to indicate that their sole knowledge of the South has been gleaned from the pages of Joel Chandler Harris and Thomas Nelson Page." He wrote that the Agrarians appeared oblivious to both the hardscrabble conditions in the southern countryside—the poverty, pellagra, and hookworm—and the region's dangerous demagogues, whom he characterized as "the delight of Southern agrarianism."[14] Johnson underscored that however silly the Agrarians' ideas appeared, those ideas in the end were less frivolous than dangerous, because they threatened to increase southern misery and oppression. Characterizing the Agrarian' project as "sniveling and excuse-hunting on the part of intelligent Southerners," Johnson added that their work was "a worse betrayal of their ancestors than are Gastonia, lynching, demagoguery, and religious fanaticism combined."[15] The danger posed by the Agrarians, particularly in light of political developments in Europe, would soon be the focus of many of their critics, particularly after 1933, the year they joined forces with Seward Collins, publisher and editor of the *American Review*.

Before linking up with Collins, the Agrarians endured two disappointing and frustrating years. The group met at times to kick around a number of promising projects, including starting an agrarian political party, buying a county newspaper, organizing a second symposium, and hosting public lectures and discussions, but little came of these discussions. Other than an occasional essay or two by someone in the group, agrarianism threatened to become merely the stuff of parlor talk. Enthusiasm waxed and waned, with personal needs and problems pressuring individual commitments. Ransom was perhaps the most consistent in his activism, immersing himself, while in England on a Guggenheim Fellowship, in the study of economics in order to devise practical means for self-sufficient farming. Tate and Davidson, however, by 1932 seemed mired in miasmic gloom, though neither had entirely abandoned his agrarian faith. In a letter to Tate in October of that year Davidson suggested that the Agrarians were floundering because "we have never quite made up our minds whether we are crusaders or not" and that, in the end, none of them were "really crusaders who will risk all in the fight" (*LCDT* 276, 275). Davidson argued for tactical retrenchment:

> We like to think of ourselves as crusaders; in our mind's eye, we can see ourselves doing a kind of Pickett's charge against industrial breastworks, only a *successful* charge this time. But we don't actually do the crusading. We merely trifle with the idea a little. And while we trifle with it, we neglect the other role in which we really can accomplish something, though results will be very slow. We are, after all, writers before everything else—and only secondarily, if at all, cavalry commanders, orators, lobbyists, and ward-heelers. We ought to write, then, and keep writing. And we should organize our effort around our writing, as we have done in the past, with the sure conviction that if our ideas are right, we shall in the end reach the people who can do the other needful things; and if our ideas are not right, then they deserve to fail. (*LCDT* 276)

Believing that the Agrarians lacked, as had the Old South, an authoritative and authoritarian spiritual center, Tate responded to Davidson (10 December 1932) that "the trouble with our agrarianism is not that we don't believe in it enough to make sacrifices; it is rather that we don't believe in it in the way that demands sacrifice. In other words not one of us has a religion that any of the others can understand. That sort of understanding is necessary to fire the enthusiasm of a group; it is reciprocal in its action. *Vide* my Remarks on the Southern Religion." Tate concluded that by all appearances "the Agrarian Movement has degenerated into pleasant poker games on Saturday night" (*LCDT* 280); he added that while the group might, like the Phoenix, renew itself, he felt that the buzzard more likely heralded the group's future.

Renewal of enthusiasm came in 1933, when Seward Collins offered the Agrarians a significant role in his new conservative political journal, the *American Review*. Collins envisioned the journal as the primary publishing organ for four traditionalist groups: the British Distributists (including G. K. Chesterton and Hillaire Belloc); the Neo-Scholastics (Christopher Dawson and Father D'Arcy); the New Humanists (Irving Babbitt and Paul Elmore More); and the Agrarians.[16] He did not expect complete uniformity of opinion among the four groups, nor did he demand that one group endorse the ideas of another; instead he wanted to bring together four broadly compatible groups to launch a powerful assault on what he saw as America's moribund economic and political systems.

The Agrarians invited Collins to Lytle's Alabama farm, where over two days, 31 March–1 April 1933, he and eight Agrarians discussed the proposed alliance and hammered out an agreement. Neither side, apparently, was totally honest with the other: the Agrarians did not talk about their plan to manipulate Collins and eventually turn the *American Review* into an Agrarian journal, and Collins did not discuss his pro-Fascist views.[17] It is not clear exactly what the Agrarians knew about Collins's Fascist beliefs, though they probably knew more than they later let on, since Tate had been a contributor to Collins's earlier journal, the *Bookman*, and had had a vicious dispute with him, in part political, after Collins rejected his essay "The Fallacy of Humanism."[18] Knowing of Collins's interest in European affairs, Tate wrote him (26 March 1933) that the Agrarians were more internationally minded than they might appear from *I'll Take My Stand* and that they were willing to support other antimodernist groups, including those in Europe. "I think we are and were a little more aware of the world movement towards reaction than *I'll Take My Stand* indicated," Tate declared, recalling his earlier hope to model the Agrarian enterprise along the lines of L'Action Française. "We suppressed for reasons of strategy, most of the references to a similar movement in England and France. Our reason was this: We felt that if we could present the whole case for reactionary agrarianism in southern terms, we should make a strong appeal to those very foreign allies whom we ignored. We were not only talking about an idea; we had the concrete basis for its realization."[19]

If the Agrarians were unaware of Collins's Fascist sympathies before the alliance, they could have later remained so only if they were not reading the *American Review*, which seems unlikely.[20] The journal's first issue, which appeared in April 1933, contained an article by Harold Goad that praised Italy's Fascist system, declaring it a "new form of 'disciplined' or 'harmonized' democracy" that possessed a "clarity and continuity of policy [that] avoids the grave dangers of uncertainty, vacillation, or even oscillation between extremes, which is the consequence of an alternation of parties in power. It abolishes press or popular agitation and speculation on the chances of a change in government."[21] While not precisely endorsing Goad's views, Collins wrote in his initial editorial statement that Goad's essay was the first of several that would examine the Italian government. "The Fascist economics, in particular, which have received scant treatment by our universally liberal and radical press, are badly in need of sympathetic exposition," Collins comments. "The rise of Hitler to power in Germany brings us still further aspects of the Fascist question which will be discussed." Collins added that with the increasing number of European countries that were abandoning parliamentary politics, together with the expanding power of the American president, "the whole question of the relative worth of monarchy and republicanism" needed to be explored.[22]

Collins made his political views, including his unusual interpretation of *monarchy*, explicitly clear in the second issue. In "Editorial Notes: The Revival of Monarchy," Collins argues that America had become a "plutocratic state called Capitalism" and that "the only way to abolish a plutocracy is by establishing a monarchy."[23] Collins explains that by *monarchy* he does not mean hereditary dynasties and royalty, but rather what he calls the "monarchical principle," that is, rule by an all-powerful sovereign. "A monarch," Collins writes, "is a man (or woman, or, formally, child) in whom all governmental responsibility of a State is vested; he governs in the interest of the whole State, and in secular matters stands above all individuals and groups in the State. The ultimate sovereignty of the people is symbolized in him and is by him realized in action" (246). In Collins's eyes, Europe was currently in the throes of reviving its ancestral model of government, since both the Fascist and the Communist revolution aimed at overthrowing capitalism and establishing "the New Monarchies which are altering the course of history" (253). Although both revolutions embodied the same monarchical principle, Fascism was more constructive and effective, because it preserved the assets of the plutocratic state while ridding it of its evils; Communism, on the other hand, answered "the Capitalist abuse of the rights of property with [its] silly but sinister over-simplification, *abolishing* private ownership of productive property" (254). Collins praised Fascism's fundamental opposition to Communism and attacked the American press for maligning Nazi Germany by focusing on its treatment of the Jews. "Even if the absurd atrocity stories were all true," Collins writes, "the fact would be almost negligible beside an event that shouts aloud in spite of the journalistic silence: the victory of Hitler signifies the end of the Communist threat, *forever*" (248). Near the end of his essay, Collins announces that at another time he hopes to discuss the possibility of a monarchical revival in America, and he closes, with a nod to the Agrarians, by imagining a transformed America "in which liberty and the family are safeguarded by widespread opportunity for ownership, in which the working of the land is raised to its rightful place as the first and best of industries, in which the fruits of nature and of man's inventiveness can be equitably shared, in which the spiritual and creative sides of life are richly nourished and given full freedom" (256).[24]

If Collins at times nodded to the Agrarians in his essays, they rarely acknowledged him in theirs, even though the *American Review* almost overnight became the journal where they published most of their political essays. Unlike in their essays from *I'll Take My Stand*, which largely kept to general principles, the Agrarians now directed their attention at practical economic and political matters. Ransom, for instance, often focused on the competing economics of industrialism and independent farming, buttressing his analysis with specific suggestions for federal legislation and tax reform that would encourage small-scale rather than commercial farming.[25] He also proposed, for economic and political reasons, that the nation's capital be moved to a new location somewhere along the Mississippi River.[26] Davidson, meanwhile, focused primarily on political and cultural issues, particularly regionalism, sectionalism, and federalism. Following the lead of William Yandell Elliott and Frank Owsley, both of whom had proposed constitutional reform to reshape the nation's governing structure, Davidson called for dividing the states into regional confederations.[27] He believed that with the power to tax and legislate, the confederations could better defend regional interests and cultures against competing claims from other regions and from the federal government.

Tate, as always, stood as the Agrarians' point man, fervently championing the movement and aggressively defending it from attacks. In one of the most savage pieces he ever wrote, "The Problem of the Unemployed: A Modest Proposal," Tate (obviously drawing inspiration from Jonathan Swift) suggests, in the name of American progress and efficiency, that the economic potential of male desire could be tapped through a large-scale program of prostitution and that the problem of massive employment could be solved through mass executions, completed "quietly, and in the ordinary routine of industrial technology."[28] "I need not suggest that the method be painless," Tate writes. "We are too humane for the axe, guillotine, rope, or firing-squad. I should personally prefer some kind of lethal gas, but not being a chemist, I leave that proposal to the specialists" (148). In addition to the social benefits of reducing the number of unemployed, the corpses would be refined for their useful materials. "For example," Tate explains, "that 'deep inward satisfaction' the public gets out of a fine, animal-skin glove would deepen further could men and women wear the whole skin of a hand meticulously removed and tanned into a soft, seamless glove. The 'fine art of cookery' would get a richer base for oleomargarine and the shortening oils. The potash and sodium chloride would revise the slogan, '25¢ is enough to pay for toothpaste,' to: 'This toothpaste is cheap at any price: Human dentifrice for humanity'" (149). "The Problem of the Unemployed" looks hauntingly forward to the Nazi extermination camps and illustrates the rhetorical extremes to which Tate was willing to take his assaults on industrialism. In fact, he was willing to take these extremes even further, since the essay was apparently heavily revised by Collins in order to make it, as Tate put in a letter to Lytle (2 June 1933), "innocuous to club ladies" (*LTL* 83).

The Agrarians' relationship with Collins and the *American Review* reached a crisis in 1936, not long before publication of their second symposium, *Who Owns America?* To their dismay, they found themselves publicly smeared as homegrown Fascists, a charge that not only splintered their relationship with the British Distributists (who under the leadership of Hillaire Belloc, after the death of G. K. Chesterton, had turned more clearly toward Fascist thinking)[29] but also hastened their own breakup. The crisis began with the publication, in the February 1936 issue of *Fight against War and Fascism*, of Grace Lumpkin's interview with Collins, "I Want a King." Lumpkin's goal in talking with Collins, as quickly becomes evident, was twofold: to tease out Collins's Fascist beliefs and to link the Agrarians with those beliefs. "Because I am a Southern writer," Lumpkin begins in addressing Collins, "I have been asked to make a talk on the Southern agrarian movement, and hearing that you are connected with it I came up to see you."[30] She proceeds to lead Collins through a discussion in which he asserts that he and the Agrarians share the same broad aims, calling for the destruction of factories and the establishment of guilds, together with the institution of an educational system for instructing a select few while keeping the masses ignorant. The interview then takes a devastating turn:

> Q. Some of the things you have said make me think that you are a fascist. Are you?
>
> MR. COLLINS: Yes, I am a fascist. I admire Hitler and Mussolini very much. They have done great things for their countries. I do not agree with everything they do, but . . .

Q. Do you agree with Hitler's persecution of the Jews?

MR. COLLINS: It is not persecution. The Jews make trouble. It is necessary to segregate them.

Q. It seems to me it is Hitler who has made the trouble.

MR. COLLINS: Oh, no. It's the Jews. They make dissension and trouble wherever they are. (3, 14)

Seeming utterly oblivious to Lumpkin's goadings and to the way the interview is developing, Collins goes on to say that besides wanting a king and a royal court in America, he wants to do away with modern conveniences and to segregate Jews and blacks and bar them from schooling. Lumpkin closes "I Want a King" with a statement linking together Collins, the Agrarians, and Hitler:

> This short interview can give only the superficial aspects of the movement which Mr. Collins and the Southern Agrarians represent. I felt after the interview like a person who watches a magician pulling white rabbits out of a top hat. One knows the magic is all bluff, but the rabbits are real. People laughed at Hitler's magic until the rabbits got out of the hat and multiplied and devoured a country and a people.
>
> I think it is not necessary to say that I do not believe Fascism is already upon us. I do believe after reading a number of books like "God Without Thunder," "I [sic] Take My Stand," and copies of the *Southern Review* and *The American Review,* that in those who write for them (some of them very sensitive and fine writers) there is the beginning of a group that is preparing the philosophical and moral shirt-front for Fascism with its top hat from which the rabbits come. (85)

The cover of *Fight against War and Fascism* suggests a similar conclusion. In the foreground stands a troubled Abraham Lincoln, perhaps contemplating the situations discussed in the two articles listed on the cover—the Italian invasion of Ethiopia and Collins's dream of a Fascist monarchy. In the background a soldier is bayoneting a black man. While the obvious reference is the Italian invasion of Ethiopia, the image also suggests, in light of the Lumpkin interview, the end result of Collins's dreams—the suppression of blacks in the South and an Italian-like Fascism in America. No wonder Lincoln looks so glum.

Although by this time the Agrarians no doubt were fully aware of Collins's beliefs—Tate, for instance, had written Collins two years earlier (9 September 1933) that "your discussion of monarchy is in line with this program, though we all thought that the terms you employed needed some popularization, if we are to make the idea palatable"[31]—they were stunned by his performance with Lumpkin. This was not the sort of popularization the Agrarians were hoping for, and they scrambled to limit the damage, looking for an effective way to repudiate the accusation that Collins's Fascism was also theirs. Immediately after the interview's publication, Herbert Agar, the editor of the *Louisville Courier-Journal*—who had joined the Agrarians and was coediting with Tate *Who Owns America?*—wrote to Tate that the group had to confront Collins. Tate agreed and forwarded Agar's letter to Davidson (23 February 1936), asking him to share it with the Agrarians in Nashville. "However valiant [Collins] has been in the cause," Tate wrote, "we can't let him make us Fascists when the big plank in our platform is that we are offering the sole alternative to Fascism." He stressed the urgency of an Agrarian response, writing that "we've got to seize this occasion to clear up all the nonsense that has been said about us," and suggested that the Agrarians draw up a statement of principles pointing out "our opposition to Fascism and our indifference to the restoration of the Middle Ages, monarchy, etc." for publication in the *American Review*. "If he published it," Tate wrote, speaking of Collins, "we could refer to the statement and prove that he doesn't represent us; if he refuses to publish it, that would signify a definite break, and we could print the statement elsewhere as a matter of record" (*LCDT* 296). Tate knew that such action risked causing a total break with Collins, but he also knew that the Agrarians were doomed if they continued "to have everything we write discredited with charges of mediaevalism and Fascism" (*LCDT* 297).

After the Agrarians apparently decided not to follow through on his suggestions, Tate voiced his own strong response to Lumpkin's article in an open letter that was published, along with Lumpkin's response, in the *New Republic* in May 1936.[32] Tate here defends himself and those he identified as "the distributists-agrarians" against charges of Fascism. "First, I do not believe in fascism," he writes. "I hold the political views that I do hold because they alone seem to me to stand between us and the Fascist state."[33] Tate adds that should he have to choose between the two slave states of Fascism and Communism, he would choose Communism, since "the aim of fascism must be realized by force, while the aim of communism, ideally at least, looks toward order and consent" (75). In his defense of the Distributists and Agrarians, Tate first denies Lumpkin's charge that they, like Collins, want to restore the Middle Ages, observing that the group does "not want to restore anything whatsoever. It is our task to create something" (75). That something is an alternative to the dehumanized world wrought by finance capitalism. To the charge that the Distributists and Agrarians are the "stuffed shirts of fascism," Tate responds that actually the Communists deserve that designation. "Are we not justified in deploring the waste of political energy represented by the Communist Party?" Tate writes. "Its zeal is lost to a political movement that might have some real chance of success in America. Communism is a hopeless, visionary cause, and if its energy represents, as it well may, the balance between fascism and the Property State, then when fascism comes the Communist, in our view, will be chiefly responsible" (75).

Lumpkin responded to Tate by pointing out that it was not she but Collins who had said that the Agrarians shared his Fascist views, and she went on to say that Tate should not be amazed, given what the Agrarians had written, that other people would reach the same conclusion. After citing a few lines from *I'll Take My Stand*'s introductory chapter, she zeroes in on Tate's famous lines from "Remarks on the Southern Religion": "How may a Southerner take hold of his tradition? The answer is by violence.... Reaction is the most radical of programs. It aims at cutting away the overgrowth and getting back to the roots."[34] Taking Tate's calls for violence literally, Lumpkin discusses the implications of his words in the context of recent developments in Fascist Italy and Nazi Germany: "Retake Southern traditions by violence? Does Mussolini want more than to recapture Roman slave-owning traditions by violence? Reaction is most radical? Hitler in his fraudulent radicalism calls for a return to the pre-trust era."[35] After citing several more lines from Tate's essay, together with several from John Gould Fletcher's essay "Education, Past and Present," which called for the creation of an intellectual elite,[36] Lumpkin notes that while the Agrarians might not feel "'spiritually close' to Mr. Collins" (76), they often wrote statements that were similar to his. "The above statements in themselves do not make you fascists," Lumpkin concludes, referring to her quotations from the Agrarians. "But they are the theoretical foundation of a reactionary movement. Any kind of honest examination of the theoretical basis of fascism by you and your group should make you uncomfortable at the similarity. If you are serious in saying you are against fascism, I am sure you will be responsible enough to reconsider your beliefs to find out whether they are leading you to a real search for the truth, or into a morass of intellectual confusion" (76).

No doubt Tate hoped that his exchange with Lumpkin would put the issue of Fascism to rest and that the whole matter would be quickly forgotten. He was wrong. Two weeks later the *New Republic* published a letter by Collins, a response by Lumpkin, and an editorial commentary, grouping all three statements together under the title "The Sunny Side of Fascism," a thinly veiled reference to the popular phrase *the sunny South*.[37] Collins begins his letter by asserting that Lumpkin had distorted his comments to make it seem as if the Agrarians agreed with everything he had said. "I said nothing to indicate that I was speaking for Mr. Tate, the Southern Agrarians, or anyone but myself," Collins declares. "On the contrary, I specifically stated, and repeated it whenever the questions seemed to involve others, that I was voicing my own ideas, and that many of the contributors to The American Review, including the Southern Agrarians, differed with me."[38] Collins then addresses Lumpkin's charge that the Agrarians are Fascists. Whatever distance Collins was trying to put between himself and the Agrarians, he had all but eliminated it by the end of the following paragraph:

> As to whether the Southern Agrarians are "fascists," Mr. Tate has abundantly shown that he despises both the word and the thing, and prefers communism. On this he and I stand in sharp disagreement. I believe his opinion rises from a misunderstanding of the nature of fascism, which he identifies with its plutocratic aspect, whereas I see it as essentially and ultimately a "petit bourgeois" movement tending toward an agrarian and distributist society. It is for this reason that I do not mind being called a fascist, but rather enjoy it: though I naturally regret that this should afford occasion for contributors to my magazine being labeled with the abhorrent word. But as I have pointed out to them, and as Miss Lumpkin's letter illustrates, there is too much similarity between their avowed ideas and those prevalent in fascist movements to escape being called fascists, were I not alive. (132)

Looking forward to the possibility of a Fascist government in the United States, Collins underscores what he sees as the Fascism of the Agrarians' thinking, observing that "we will be lucky if the fascist regime we will get is half so good—half so sympathetic to agrarian-distributist ideals—as the regime of Mussolini or Hitler" (132).

In her response to Collins, Lumpkin acknowledges that she now recognizes that the Agrarians' loyalty to southern traditions differs from Collins's outright Fascism. Lumpkin depicts Tate as a misguided innocent rather than a misguided Fascist, and she closes her letter by saying that she feels "genuine regret and sadness as he goes about with his butterfly net busily recapturing Southern traditions."[39] While Lumpkin backed off from the issue of the Agrarians and Fascism, the editorial commentary that followed the two letters did not, returning to the philosophical similarities between the Agrarians and European Fascists.[40] Asserting that they are glad Tate prefers Communism to Fascism, the editors add, "We wish that he would reflect on a point emphasized by Mr. Collins as well as Miss Lumpkin, namely, that some theories of the Southern Agrarians are quite close to part of Hitler's and Mussolini's programs—the demagogic part of them naturally. The danger is that the American fascists, now completely lacking in intellectual respectability, will seize hold of Mr. Tate's ideas and some of his associates also."[41] In other words, despite their stated opposition to Fascism, the Agrarians seemed to be laying the intellectual groundwork for Fascism in the United States.

As suggested by Lumpkin, particularly in her letter in "Fascism and the Southern Agrarians," and then echoed by both Collins and the *New Republic*'s editors in "The Sunny Side of Fascism," the Agrarians were perceived as being hand in hand with European Fascists largely because of their shared antimodernism. As we have already seen in the case of the regionalist painters Grant Wood, John Steuart Curry, and Thomas Hart Benton, by the mid-1930s regionalist movements in America—and the very concept of regionalism—were being tagged as dangerously close in philosophical origins to Fascism, most notably in the celebration of the folk and of local tradition. Regionalist localism, according to this line of thinking, was the same as provincial jingoism, similar to that which underlay Nazi and Italian nationalism and which stood opposed to universal ideals of freedom and democracy. Moreover, the antiurbanism of most regionalist movements, which contrasted the unstructured decadence of city life to the virtuous stability of rural life, with like-minded folks living intimately in touch with the land, seemed to echo, however distantly, the Nazis' celebration of blood and soil.

Being die-hard supporters of segregation opened the Agrarians to further criticism that they endorsed a native Fascism. As seen in the editorial commentary in "The Sunny Side of Fascism," the Agrarians were at times indiscriminately lumped together with southern demagogues, who with the rise of Hitler and Mussolini now seemed all the more dangerous. Moreover, the Agrarians' unapologetic hostility toward blacks connected them in the public's eye with the worst form of southern race-hating and, at times, with the Nazis' racial ideology and violent treatment of Jews. Most of the time, this hostility was largely unspoken; that is, the Agrarians said little about the place of blacks in their envisioned social order because racial segregation was an unquestioned cornerstone of that order. No discussion was necessary. At times, however, particularly when events brought southern racial practices under close national scrutiny, members of the group openly voiced their racial views.

Such was the case during the controversial Scottsboro trials (the case was originally tried in 1931, and it was retried in 1933), in which nine African American youths in Alabama were charged with and tried for raping two white women.[42] While several of the Agrarians commented on the case, arguing that outside agitators, representing forces of industrialism and Communism, were using the trial to undermine southern traditionalism, John Gould Fletcher's comments stand out for his extreme views.[43] In a letter to the editors of the *Nation* Fletcher excoriates what he saw as that magazine's irresponsible commentary on the trial, accusing the editors of trying to incite a civil war between whites and blacks. He predicts the conviction and execution of those charged, and he adds that what might seem like injustice to northern leftists would be justice for southerners, since "justice is in itself an abstract matter, and as every great lawyer knows, has always to yield to the morals, the usages, the customs and conveniences of a living and functioning community."[44] Fletcher goes on to argue, in an extraordinary statement, that the recent lynching of four blacks, all probably innocent, proves that southern traditionalism is alive and well:

> That the South is such a community was proved this very summer. With the Scottsboro case still in doubt, the people of Tuscaloosa County turned out and lynched four other Negroes. Three of them were probably innocent, and in the case of the fourth there is considerable doubt. But the fact of the matter is that [the northern attorney for the defendants] Mr. Leibowitz's conduct, as well as the taunts of the metropolitan press, have unstrung that section of the South which adjourns Scottsboro. We will not suffer further dictation from the North as to what we are to do about the Negro. All that we built up again out of the ruins of Civil War and of Reconstruction is again

at stake. Rather than permit our own peculiar conceptions of justice to be questioned, we will take the law into our own hands, by a resort to violence. (735)

Statements such as Fletcher's, suggesting the extreme ends to which localism (and more generally, regionalism) could be taken, including advocating vigilante violence as the expression of community (as opposed to universal) justice, were precisely what made critics of the Agrarians worry that their line of thought might ultimately lead to an American Fascism.

With the publication of the joint Agrarian-Distributist symposium, *Who Owns America? A New Declaration of Independence* (1936), the Agrarians hoped to distance themselves from Collins and quiet the critics who were linking them with Fascism. Except for Douglas Jerrold's "Whither Europe?" which concludes that democratic governments had a good deal to learn from the Fascists and the Nazis (since Italy and Germany protected the rights of property holders more effectively than democracies, which were falling under the control of corporate power), most of the essays wholeheartedly attacked the Fascist enterprise. While often quite different in approach and subject, the essays share a basic political outlook, calling for the widespread distribution of property in order to preserve civil liberties and democracy. Above all, the contributors stood opposed to monopoly capitalism, believing that its concentration of wealth in large corporations was leading democracies toward economic collectivism and political plutocracy, a process that, unless stopped, would ultimately lead to Communism or Fascism. Only a propertied revolution could avert this nightmarish prospect, a belief cogently voiced by Frank Owsley: "The right to life, the right to liberty, to the pursuit of happiness, the right to govern oneself, the right to own property, all natural rights must give way to the fascist or communist totalitarian State which guarantees security and denies freedom—unless private property is put back into the hands of the disinherited American people."[45]

The Agrarian contributors were particularly vocal in savaging what they saw as the tyranny of Fascism and Communism. Corporations, observes Lyle Lanier, "have become the instruments of an economic fascism which threatens the essential democratic institutions of America."[46] "If monopoly goes its way," Agar notes, "it will drift into fascism—the political tyranny that must implement an economic tyranny. And if we once get fascism, we shall probably get communism in the end, for the reason that fascism is too bad to be endured."[47] Unless Americans "return to real politics, resume our political character, and reassert the rights of effective ownership," comments Tate, "we shall drift with the corporate structure of emasculated ownership until all trace of widespread control vanishes: that would be the tyrant State where corporations would be bigger than now and the two thousand men reduced, say, to twenty."[48] Americans must reassert the fundamental Jeffersonian principles upon which the nation was founded, Owsley writes, so that these principles "guide our political action and our conduct of government. Otherwise we cannot escape the communist or fascist totalitarian State."[49] Davidson, arguing for a restructured federal government that would grant the regions more autonomy, likewise feared a totalitarian future in which, through centralized planning, the nation's regions would be brought "to heel with the lash of a dictatorial whip." "Such a regionalism is not American," Davidson adds. "It belongs to Russia and other home-lands of the totalitarian State."[50]

Only Robert Penn Warren specifically addressed the accusation that the Agrarians' localism smacked of Fascism. He came to this charge by way of literature, contrasting what he designated as regionalist writing (literature grounded in a specific place and drawing upon the specific traditions of that place, attempting to forge a vital tradition between the past and the present) with proletarian writing (dogmatic, left-wing literature that embraces an international rather than a local perspective, rejecting the past in an effort to create a new, revolutionary future). While noting that proletarian writers find the regionalist literature's grounding in the life and customs of a specific place "smack[ing] of antiquated religion, patriotism, or even fascism,"[51] Warren argues that actually it is the thoroughly politicized proletarian fiction that most resembles the Fascist enterprise. "This type of politicized literature," Warren writes, "just like organized Nazi or Fascist literature, is usually based on a conception of literature as instrument; both types, communist or fascist, are attempts to reason the writer into an appropriate relation to politics" (356–57).

In contrast, regionalist literature, says Warren, expresses a fundamental opposition to the modern industrial state, from which Fascism and Communism spring. Drawing upon the Distributist ideas running throughout *Who Owns America?* Warren writes that "the regional writer connects the idea of property, that is, real property as opposed to abstract property, with his idea of the relation of man to place, for ownership gives a man a stake in a place and helps to define his, for the regional writer, organic relation to society" (354–55). The regional artist for Warren is the model citizen within a democracy, a person who rather than merely blindly following the dictates of political dogma uses his critical intelligence for "inspecting the aims of society from which he stemmed and in which he moved, and of pondering the inevitable puzzles proposed to him by the spectacle of human existence" (347). Such effort, representing the responsibility demanded of citizens living within a democracy, is the fundamental means for resisting plutocracy and totalitarianism.

Critics made little of the Agrarians' efforts to disassociate themselves from Fascism in *Who Owns America?* In his review of the collection, Dwight McDonald acknowledged that while the Agrarians were not out-and-out Fascists, their economic and political plans, if enacted, might eventually lead to Fascism. "Provincialism befogs the social and economic thinking of the Southern Agrarians, and provincialism is also the force that makes their doctrines potentially dangerous," McDonald writes. "They aren't Fascists, and Mr. Agar goes out of his way to state that if it is a choice between Communism and Fascism, he would choose Communism. But the Agrarian's [sic] point of view, being reactionary, confused and sentimental, could easily be used as a cloak for a movement which would outrage no one more than the idealistic authors of the present volume."[52] V. F. Calverton, in his 1936 essay "The Bankruptcy of Southern Culture," discussed the Agrarians under the subheading "Fascism Rears Its Head." Dwelling on the Agrarians' connection with Collins, Calverton notes that Collins had declared that the Agrarian movement was part of "the international fascist appeal to the farmers to fight the industrialists and financiers in an attempt to replace the power of Wall Street by that of Main Street." Calverton declares the goals of Collins and the Agrarians "not only most reprehensibly naïve and fantastic but most dangerously reactionary."[53]

In a less virulent attack, John Chamberlain, in the *Saturday Review of Literature*, wrote that while emotionally he could not help but be attracted to the Agrarians' vision, he found their plans so unrealistic and unworkable that he feared that their crusade might, ironically, lead the nation to the Fascist state they deplored. Chamberlain looked to the experience of Germany for his economic analysis, complete with a prediction of coming concentration camps if the Agrarians' ideas were carried out: "Like the 'little man' who turned to Hitler in Germany in the hopes that the bankers, the large chain stores, and the big industrialists would be curbed, and the economic world made 'free' for the small producer, Mr. Agar's friends are all for using the State to enforce differential taxation, to grant subsidies, and to evolve legal tricks to keep the farmer on the land and to prevent the mortgaging and subsequent alienation of property," Chamberlain writes. "The net result would be to freeze the capitalistic system on a certain level, and the one remaining variable—the human unit of labor power—would be forced beyond certain numbers into the concentration camps simply because the static equation of the existing system would not be able to contain it and remain an equation."[54] A few years later, Corliss Lamont, characterizing Agar and the Agrarians as "that school of Utopian retrogressives," also envisioned a dictatorship emerging from Agrarian policy, though Lamont posited that dictatorship would emerge because implementing the Agrarians' impracticable plans would require "central planning and a government dictatorship," complete with "a huge bureaucracy to keep small business small and to enforce that 100 per cent system of competition so dear to the hearts of our backward-lookers."[55]

When Lamont wrote those words, in 1939, the Agrarians had already disbanded, with the principal literary figures, except for Davidson, having abandoned explicitly political work for literature and criticism. While there had been some effort in 1936 to follow through with the collaboration between the Agrarians and the Distributists, including a conference in Nashville to establish a formal alliance, little in the end came of the efforts, with the charges of Fascism hanging over both groups. By late 1936 not only were the alliances with others (including Collins and Agar) either broken or soon to be, but the Agrarians themselves were falling apart as a political group.

Ransom was one of the first to resign. After reviewing Tate's new collection of poetry, *The Mediterranean and Other Poems,* Ransom wrote to Tate (17 September 1936) about his joy in doing literary criticism again and his recognition of the dangers to art, both to his own and to Tate's, of deliberately mixing politics with aesthetics. "It has started me on an exciting excursion of thought which I want to bring before you," he wrote, speaking of his review. "I say there is one place that *patriotism* is eating at lyricism. What is true in part for you (though a part that is ominously increasing) is true nearly in full for me: *Patriotism* has nearly eaten me up and I've got to get out of it."[56] By *patriotism* Ransom of course meant his and Tate's agrarianism, and his break with the movement was highlighted in 1937, when he left Vanderbilt for Kenyon College and the editorship of the *Kenyon Review.* That same year Tate declared his break, writing to Davidson (30 March 1937) that in leaving he was not repudiating the group's principles, but merely following his desire to be "a creative writer once more, a mere man of letters."[57]

Despite watching the Agrarian movement come undone, Davidson continued in the coming years to work for the cause. His 1938 collection of essays, *Attack on Leviathan: Regionalism and Nationalism in the United States,* summarized his regionalist views, including his belief that the defeat of the South in the Civil War had paved the way for the creation of what he called the Leviathan state, a powerful federal government that, he feared, would soon be enforcing uniformity in all areas of life. Drawing from the observations of Frederick Jackson Turner, particularly those in his essay "The Significance of the Section in American History," Davidson argues that only through the preservation of vital sectional cultures and the establishment of strong sectional governments can America survive as a democratic nation. He paints a grim picture of America's future if the sovereignty of the sections is not recognized and protected, suggesting that the nation will either split apart or be held together by a dictatorship. "And if Fascism or Communism ever arrives in America," Davidson adds, Americans have Lincoln to thank, since "by letting himself be used by the idealistic front for the material designs of the North, Lincoln not only ruined the South but quite conceivably ruined the North as well."[58]

Davidson continued defending southern traditionalism during the wartime 1940s, taking an unyielding stance against attacks on southern culture and segregation. Two essays stand out from this period: his review of W. J. Cash's *The Mind of the South,* "Mr. Cash and the Proto-Dorian South"; and his essay on "the Negro problem," "Preface to Decision."[59] In "Mr. Cash and the Proto-Dorian South" Davidson finds many things wrong with Cash's interpretation of southern history, but what most angers him is Cash's assertion that the South had established a tightly bound system of repression and taboo (what Cash calls "the savage ideal") to enforce a rigid conformity resembling that of the totalitarian state.[60] After quoting Cash's statement that the South had put in place the savage ideal "almost as truly as it is established in Fascist Italy, Nazi Germany, in Soviet Russia—and so paralyzed Southern culture at the root," Davidson comments:

> These are terrible words—terrible, as suggesting the contempt of Mr. Cash's heart for the role of religion in the South; terrible, for what they imply as to the future he would desire. But it is not the first time I have heard this pronouncement. Clifton Fadiman, that bright fellow of "Information, Please," and self-styled propagandist for democracy, has announced over the radio that he, too, would put the

South of former days in the same class with Nazi Germany. If Fadiman will say it, then I know it is a fashionable sentiment in New York. And does Mr. Cash, who holds that even the modern South has not changed its mind, mean to imply that the modern South is also in essence Fascist? What a sentiment to offer a South which, as I write, is being celebrated in the newspapers as exceeding all other sections in its enthusiasm for aid to England if not for war! (9)

Later in the essay Davidson argues that it is not the South but the American nation that enforces binding conformity, loudly proclaiming liberty and freedom while quietly crushing those very ideals. "We keep the fiction of democracy, but behind the fiction, what do we see?" Davidson asks, and then gives his answer: "The strongest central government we have ever known; the most elaborately restrictive and regulative laws; a continually increasing tendency of the government to call for and indeed to exact unanimity of opinion, to brook no criticism, to demand almost servile obedience.... And now, too, with war shaking the whole world, what prospect is there that this savage ideal will quickly relax its hold upon us?" (18–19). Those wanting to witness true democracy, as outlined in the nation's founding principles, Davidson continues, must turn their eyes to the South, a region that he says is so fundamentally democratic that "not only could the South never have imagined or understood Hitler's Germany or Stalin's Russia; it could not have understood even the England of Chamberlain and Churchill; and, I strongly suspect, does not now understand the America of Roosevelt" (19).

Perhaps letting his anger get the best of him, Davidson ends the essay by imagining himself and a group of southerners standing in judgment of Cash at a lynching party, complete with burning cross. "And now fellow Southerners, Proto-Dorians, the moon is setting, and the Fiery Cross is burning low," Davidson writes. "You all know what we came out here for tonight, and let's get through with it. You all have heard what Mr. Cash has had to say, and I have tried, the best I could, to make plain to you what it means. Now what do you say? Shall we use the gun or the rope? Or ride him on a rail? Or just turn him loose?" (19). In the end, Davidson and the others decide to let Cash go unharmed because he is a southerner, and they even invite him back for a meal, an invitation Davidson clearly means as a final retort to Cash, indicating that the South lives less by the savage ideal than by graciousness and hospitality. Ironically, however, the entire episode highlights the smothering conformity demanded by southern traditionalists—a conformity enforced by the lynch mob. Adding to the passage's disturbing undercurrents is the fact that Cash, hounded by psychological demons not unlike those manifested in Davidson's threats, had committed suicide by the time of the article's publication.

In "Preface to Decision" Davidson rails against blacks who called for an end to segregation, largely in hostile response to Charles S. Johnson's *Patterns of Negro Segregation* (1943) and to Rayford W. Logan's *What the Negro Wants* (1944), a collection of essays by fourteen black leaders and activists. Davidson opens his essay by attacking sociological investigations that foreground universal ideals rather than custom and history, seeing these investigations as primary tools of authoritarian governments for establishing centralization and uniformity. He argues that America is evolving into a totalitarian state, seen clearly in the federal government's treatment of the South since the Civil War, which Davidson characterizes as a long history of "iron despotism" (410) and a Nazi-like occupation. Concerning Reconstruction, Davidson writes that "the so-called state governments set up in the South . . . were as truly 'puppet governments' as anything established in Europe by the Nazi armies. The white Southern renegades who participated in them, once called scalawags, were the precise equivalent of the Quislings and Vichyites now held in deserved contempt" (405). Since Reconstruction, Davidson goes on, the South has suffered ongoing scapegoating and appropriation of its resources, all in the name of democracy. "We now have the Leviathan state of the New Deal model," Davidson writes, "which talks democratic slogans with its mouth but abridges both corporate and individual freedom with every effective step it takes. It moves toward a totalitarian form of government" (409). Looking forward to his antidesegregationist activism in the 1950s, Davidson calls for a southern leadership to resist federal intervention into any area of southern life.

Davidson's two-volume history of the Tennessee River, *The Tennessee*, published after the war but written during it, continued his attacks on what he saw as the authoritarian practices of the federal government and its efforts to destroy the traditional South. Those attacks come mainly in his discussions of the Tennessee Valley Authority's reshaping of the once untamable Tennessee into a commercial waterway for the production of electricity. His early description of the TVA's work suggests that the river's diminishment mirrors that of traditional cultures—and individuals—before the manipulations of the Leviathan state:

> Now, at long last, the old wild river is submerged, is lost in its great progeny, the river of the TVA. Destiny, or whim, or some man's bold wish, or some Platonic dream, has decided that this untamed river creature should become, of all the rivers in the world, the one most deftly chained, the one most thoroughly subdued to man's designing will. The Tennessee is now a civil and obliging stream. One flick of a switch by the tenderest human finger, and the Tennessee is any man's obedient slave, though he be a thousand miles away. Tourists stare at it in immaculate safety from observation booths placed on points where long ago, it was as much as a man's life was worth to be seen. The Indians are gone, and the Indian river wears the manacles and dress of civilization. How all this came about is a long story and a strange one. It begins with legend. It ends with statistics.[61]

For Davidson, the TVA represents the nightmare of an all-powerful central government destroying local landscapes and cultures in the name of progress and efficiency, one more step in the nation's evolution toward totalitarianism. To politicians in Washington who were praising the TVA as proof "that a democratic government could be even more efficient than a totalitarian regime, and yet be kind and good and not in any way oppressive,"[62] Davidson answers that the TVA is instead proof that America's so-called democratic government mirrors that of totalitarian regimes, employing authoritarian methods in the name democracy.

Davidson's outspoken agrarianism during the years following the demise of the Nashville group in 1937 contrasts sharply with the turn from activist politics to aesthetics taken by Ransom, Tate, and Warren (whose story is told in detail in a later chapter). In making this turn, these writers reformulated the fundamental principles of their agrarianism, particularly its critique of the modern industrial state; rather than seeing regionalism as a means to resist the modern state's oppressive uniformity, they now saw that resistance in the intellectual freedom manifested in art and aesthetics. With what is now known as the "New Criticism," Ransom and Tate confronted head-on the increasingly strident demands for openly patriotic art that colored cultural debate in the late 1930s and then into World War II. Both believed that such demands smacked of the totalitarianism to which democracy stood opposed. Rather than through simplistic patriotic subject matter, they argued, art best manifested—and thus defended—democratic principles through its complicated interior dynamics.

In a series of lectures delivered at Princeton University during the winter of 1940–41, later published as "Criticism as Pure Speculation," Ransom presented a striking analysis of the role of art in a democratic society, characterizing the opposition between poetry and prose as that between democracy and totalitarianism:

> A poem is, so to speak, a democratic state, whereas a prose discourse—mathematical, scientific, ethical, or practical and vernacular—is a totalitarian state. The intention of a democratic state is to perform the work of state as effectively as it can perform it, subject to one reservation of conscience: that it will not despoil its members, the citizens, of the free exercise of their own private and independent characters. But the totalitarian state is interested solely in being effective, and regards the citizens as no citizens at all; that is, regards them as functional members whose existence is totally defined by their allotted contributions to its ends; it has no use for their private characters, and therefore no provision for them. I indicate of course the extreme or polar opposition between two polities, without denying that a polity may come to us rather mixed up.
>
> In this trope the operation of the state as a whole represents of course the logical paraphrase or argument of the poem. The private character of the citizens represents the particularity asserted by the parts in the poem.[63]

As Ransom goes on to explain, the poem, like the democratic state, has both consistency and diversity; that is, within the poem's overarching structure, what he calls its "central frame of logic," numerous independent elements variously support and oppose one another. "A poem is a *logical structure* having a *local texture*," Ransom writes, echoing the Agrarian vision of a nation consisting of diverse cultures, and he concludes that "the poem was like a democratic state, in action, and observed both macroscopically and microscopically" (110).

As founding editor of the *Kenyon Review*, which began publication in 1939, Ransom attempted to put these views into practice, seeing the journal as a bulwark of freedom and democracy against the growing wartime demands for literary and political conformity. With the spring 1941 issue, Ransom began using brief editorial commentaries, which continued through the war, to defend what he saw as the democratic politics of his editorial policy. In the first of these editorials, "Muses and Amazons," Ransom expresses disappointment that a new journal, *Decision,* had apparently recruited a number of artists for patriotic commentaries on the European war. Declaring these commentaries a "waste of talent," Ransom adds "that it is just as much a patriotic duty in our present short-of-war economy to keep the arts going—or for that matter the sciences going, and the colleges and the homes—as to attend to the military effort or the state of public opinion."[64] The mission of the *Kenyon Review,* he declares, is to keep the arts free from political conformity and didacticism; and in responding to recent criticisms of this policy by Margaret Marshall in the *Nation* and Malcolm Cowley in the *New Republic,* he notes that despite their magazines' excellent literary departments, the significance of the arts has recently diminished in both publications. For the past several years, Ransom notes, the literary pieces in these magazines have been written "largely by persons who have conceived themselves as fighting in the front lines for some aspect of freedom. It has brought about a certain mitigation from their otherwise unwavering fidelity to the arts" (241–42). No such mitigation, Ransom makes clear, will take place in his journal.

In an editorial from 1942, "War and Publication," Ransom suggests that his editorial position resembles that of the four Londoners in Dryden's "Annus Mirabulus," who intently discuss the nature of dramatic art within earshot of battling Dutch and English fleets. Ransom indicates that as editor he has followed the lead of Dryden's Londoners, remaining devoted to aesthetics (and the democratic politics manifested in those aesthetics) while the war rages. He goes on to admit, however, that his position has grown increasingly difficult to maintain, particularly with funding for the arts having been drastically reduced, highlighted by the recent demise of the *Southern Review* and the money problems then facing the *Kenyon Review* itself. Those problems, it turned out, soon forced Ransom to suspend publication for one issue while he campaigned for financial backing. When the journal resumed publication that fall, Ransom noted in his editorial "We Resume" that his previous editorial policy would continue. "The *Kenyon Review* by its nature plays no direct part in the war effort," Ransom declared.[65] Nonetheless, at the end of his editorial, no doubt responding to the public pressure to support the war, he wrote that his commitment to art did not undercut his support of the Allied cause and that he trusted that the journal's readers shared in his patriotism. "The Editors personally await any call that may come to them to play some direct part in the war," Ransom comments, adding that "while we wait we can only attend to the job in hand, which is that of teaching and editing. Finally, we feel reasonably assured that our readers are similarly in order and are not neglecting the war effort in order to receive and read the *Review*" (406).

Two years later, in his 1944 commentary "Artists, Soldiers, Positivists," Ransom responded to the frequent complaint that his was the position of the overly refined aesthete, that the literature he supported and published had no relevance in the larger and more significant social and political realms, particularly during wartime. Sounding exasperated, Ransom early on poses a number of questions regarding the artist's social responsibility and utility:

> The time scarcely comes when there is enough of dedicated public service to fight the evil in the world, and improve the lot of citizens; when is there time for art? How can we ever do less than ask to see the artist's service stripes, and certificate of honorable discharge from duty? In war time, the indulgence which the public extends to the artist, if he would have his person deferred in the draft, is that he may enlist his art. But at any time: what is the public service which art renders, that it should hope for reputation and favor?[66]

While not specifically echoing his argument from "Criticism as Pure Speculation," that the interior dynamics of the poem mirror those of the democratic state, Ransom argues that the aesthetic experience expresses civilization's highest ideals, so that whatever apparent public utility a poem does or does not have (as put forth in its literal argument), its very nature as an artifact speaks vitally to and about the public sphere. Mirroring each other, the dynamics of poetry and the dynamics of society transform instinctual experience into aesthetic experience, both structured by the principles by which civilization orders itself. "Let the basic satisfactions be secured by total war if necessary, or by total Positive technology," Ransom concludes his essay. "We will assume that they are already assured to the citizens at the stage where the arts begin" (281).

Ransom's affirmation of aesthetic experience as a concrete manifestation of civilization's principles and ideals signals how far he had moved from the practical politics of his agrarian period. In his 1945 essay "Art and the Human Economy" Ransom characterizes his former belief in agrarianism as a nostalgic fantasy, a misguided rejection of civilization in the hopes of recovering pastoral innocence. He argues that a pastoral culture by its very nature means the death of civilization, for in that world there would be "not only no effective science, invention, and scholarship, but nothing to speak of in art, e.g., Reviews and contributions to Reviews, fine poems and their exegesis."[67] Ransom thus concludes that the Declaration of Potsdam, asserting that Germany should return to an agrarian economy, is a heavy if not inhumane punishment, since "people in the natural course of things have left the garden far behind" (687). Most of the Agrarians themselves, Ransom notes, had left the garden far behind, repudiating pastoralism and affirming aesthetics in order to protect civilized values and order. "Whatever may be the politics of the agrarians," he writes, "I believe it may be observed that they are defending the freedom of the arts, whose function they understand" (687).

If Ransom's observations here do not speak for all the Agrarians—Davidson, for instance, had previously written to Tate that he wanted nothing to do with Ransom's aesthetics, and he was infuriated with Ransom's comments on the Agrarians in "Art and the Human Economy" (*LCDT* 331–32, 344–45)—they certainly come close to speaking for Tate, who after leaving the Agrarians strongly defended the freedom of the arts and of critical thought in the face of what he saw as an increasingly authoritarian society. Tate addressed this issue most directly in his 1940 essay "The Present Function of Criticism," asserting that the dominance of what he designates as positivist thinking—by Tate's definition, the belief that all experience can be ordered scientifically and that realms of experience outside of science, such as religion and literature, are insignificant—is leading America toward becoming a servile state. Seeing positivism spreading throughout all areas of American life, spearheaded by social scientists, Tate argues that America is becoming increasingly bereft of moral and religious authority, its once sound democratic order reduced to a "democracy of appetites, drives, and stimulus-and-response."[68] "What we thought was to be a conditioning process in favor of a state planned by the Teachers College of Columbia University will be a conditioning equally useful for Plato's tyrant state," Tate writes. "The actuality of tyranny we shall enthusiastically greet as the development of democracy, for the ringing of the democratic bell will make our political glands flow as freely for dictatorship, as, hitherto, for monopoly capitalism" (238). Tate sees America's future in Europe's totalitarian states, writing that "under the actuality of history our sociological knowledge is a ready-made weapon that is now being used in Europe for the control of the people, and it will doubtless soon be used here for the same purpose" (239). He paints a grim picture of the coming repression in arts and letters, suggesting that it will be even more absolute than that in Nazi Germany:

> What will happen to literature under the totalitarian society that is coming in the next few years—it may be, so far as critical opinion is concerned, in the next few months? The question has got to be faced by literary critics, who as men of explicit ideas are responsible to imaginative literature for the *milieu* in which it works. The first ominous signs of this change are before us. The tradition of free ideas is as dead in the United States as it is in Germany. For at least a generation it has suffered a slow extinction and it may receive the *coup de grâce* from the present war. The suppression of the critical spirit in this country will have sinister features that the official Nazi censorship, with all its ruthlessness, has not yet achieved, for the Nazis are, towards opinion, crude, objective, and responsible. Although it has only a harsh military responsibility, this censorship is definite, and it leaves the profession of letters in no doubt of its standing. Under this régime it has no standing at all. Increasingly since 1933 the critical intelligence under National Socialism has enjoyed the dilemma of extinction or frustration in exile. (237)

That Tate focused so emphatically on the demise of the critical spirit in his post-Agrarian essays underscores the crucial role that he believed the profession of letters plays in civilized societies. Tate saw literature (and its study, the practice of criticism) opposing the cultural conditioning that, in the case of America, was preparing citizens "for the realization of a *bourgeois* paradise of gadgets and of the consumption, not of the fruits of the earth, but of commodities" (237). Literature affirmed what he characterized as the humane imagination, that is, the free and unchecked mind striving to grasp the completeness of human experience. "The greater poets give us knowledge, not of the new programs, but of ourselves," Tate writes in the preface to *Reactionary Essays on Poetry and Ideas* (1936),[69] a self-knowledge whose significance extends ultimately to the social, fostering the independent-minded, responsible citizens necessary for a humane, civilized society. For Tate, then, poetry—its creation and its interpretation—becomes a model of responsible citizenship. "Poetry is one test of ideas; it is ideas tested by experience, by the act of direct apprehension," Tate comments further in the preface (xi), and it is precisely this interrogation of ideas in the social realm—as, for instance, the testing of the utopian prophecies of totalitarian regimes, measured against a full knowledge of the human experience—that keeps a society from falling prey to the irrational and ensures that its overarching ideals are grounded in and restrained by fully apprehended human experience.

Positivist attacks on the profession of letters, Tate believed, only intensified as Europe and then America slid toward and then into war, with writers being pressured to become citizen soldiers. Tate found this patriotic pressure, voiced most vociferously by Archibald MacLeish and Van Wyck Brooks, a dangerous manifestation of the very totalitarian menace against which MacLeish and Brooks railed. "Could the outlook be worse for the future of criticism?" Tate writes in "The Present Function of Criticism." "In the United States we face the censorship of the pressure-group. We have a tradition of irresponsible interpretation of patriotic necessity" (237). Tate's designation of patriotic necessity as "irresponsible interpretation" is clearly his comeback to MacLeish, who in his well-known essay "The Irresponsibles" slapped that label upon writers who were not using their art openly to boost democracy.[70] In his preface to *Reason in Madness* (1941) Tate described the dangers facing America when, as he claimed was then happening, everyone was compelled to limit "the whole human problem to the narrow scope of the political problem."[71] "We are justified in saving democracy if democracy can save something else which will support it," Tate writes. "That 'something else,' which we name with peril, so great is our distress, hovers round the periphery of these essays. Unless we consider it, everything we write will look, after a generation, when the historical irony becomes visible, like another tale of the tub" (x). While Tate never specifically names the "something else" he sees necessary for democracy's preservation, the collection's title, *Reason in Madness*, suggests that that something else is freethinking, rational inquiry—inquiry that stands opposed to unthinking, and thus irrational, patriotism. Tate concludes by declaring that all the essays in his collection attack the type of unquestioned and unchallenged "knowledge" that he sees misshaping mind, art, and world: "It asks of people who profess knowledge: What do you know? But that is only another way of asking oneself the same question. I don't hear it asked very frequently these days" (x).

No doubt Tate's fears of the authoritarian power of those calling for patriotic literature increased with President Roosevelt's creation, in July 1941, of the Office of the Coordinator of Information, the forerunner of the Central Intelligence Agency, which besides being charged with collecting information through espionage also had as its mission the dissemination of information to the public. Under the leadership of Colonel William "Wild Bill" Donovan, the information office quickly grew, with more than eight hundred writers, journalists, and broadcasters working within the propaganda department.[72] One of these was Archibald MacLeish, who became a chief recruiter for the Research and Analysis Branch. A week after the attack on Pearl Harbor, Tate wrote to Cleanth Brooks (15 December 1941), then co-editor with Robert Penn Warren of the *Southern Review*, proposing that the journal organize a symposium attacking what he saw as the government-authorized movement to suppress literature and criticism. Dangerous forces were organizing that needed to be resisted, Tate stressed to Brooks:

> I happen to get every week some inside information on the doings of MacLeish; when I add it to what I hear about Van Wyck Brooks' influence and the workings of the Donovan committee, I am convinced that something like a conspiracy is under way to suppress critical thought in the United States. Brooks' doctrine is the official program of the movement. Mark the repudiation of rational intelligence in criticism, the dishonest use of the idea of "primary literature" which comes out of the "life-drive" and "biological patterns"; the spurious regionalism, which is only a dodge which allows him to use a good slogan for a base purpose. It all adds up to Dr. Goebbels. Behind this movement are frustrated men like Van Wyck Brooks and MacLeish, who have an account to settle with modern literature. The Donovan committee is undertaking a high-powered campaign to discredit all the good writing of the past twenty years.[73]

"Please consider [the symposium] seriously," Tate added. "It ought to be done without delay. I don't want to sound ominous, but you must consider even the probability that the S.R. may be suppressed. It sounds fantastic. . . . There is no time to lose" (84).[74]

As the war progressed, Tate came to see publishing houses joining in the conspiracy to suppress critical thought. In response to an invitation to contribute to a forthcoming anti-Axis anthology, *War Poems of the United Nations*, edited by Joy Davidman, Tate voiced his dismay in a letter to the editor in the *New Republic*. Tate zeroed in on Davidman's statement of acceptable subject matter: "The only limitation in subject is that all the poems must make their contribution to defeating the Axis—whether by attacking fascism and its horrors, celebrating individual deeds of heroism, building morale and the spirit of resistance, crying for action, fighting racial discrimination, or by any of the hundred other methods of aiding the war effort." Appalled at the project, Tate wrote that while some decent war poetry had been written, he could not allow himself "to see the poets grimly manufacturing morale. The spectacle would break my own." He included a copy of the letter he had returned to Davidman, saying that it offered one of the hundred other ways of contributing to the war effort, and clearly the way that Tate endorsed:

> I do not as a rule reply to circular letters, yet I find yours of October 28 so interesting that I cannot forbear. In spite of your very kind suggestion, I cannot contribute to your anthology of anti-Axis poetry, which I nevertheless hope will have a great success. All poetry, if it is poetry, is anti-Axis; and all poetry which is a mere call to action, however desperately necessary the action may be, is pro-Axis, particularly if it fails to invite us to look at reality. And the full reality might compel us to consider a reflection such as the following: if we are going to justify the great cause for which we are presumably fighting, we shall have to confess that some verse which even seems to favor the immediate cause of the Axis, is poetry, and anti-Axis in the deepest sense. We shall have no difficulty with this idea if, as we are contending, our side represents civilization; the other, barbarism. We do not elevate our cause and its prestige by going over, in the arts, to the other side, in the belief that we are strengthening the immediate power of our own. I am sure you will not think that I am saying here that your anthology will not contain some genuine poetry.[75]

Tate here defined his notion of patriotic poetry: it was poetry grounded in a full knowledge of reality; by its very nature and regardless of subject, such poetry endorsed civilization against barbarism.[76]

Tate gave his fullest account of fears of authoritarian censorship in "The State of Letters," an essay published in 1944, the year he assumed the editorship of the *Sewanee Review*. After first lashing out at writers and critics who judge art by its social usefulness, Tate defends his editorial position to judge submissions solely on artistic merit. His attack singles out Van Wyck Brooks and Bernard De Voto, who were all but demanding that American writers choose between art and patriotism. Tate characterizes what he sees as

Brooks's and DeVoto's dangerously simplistic logic: "If you believe in 'standards,' who is going to uphold them but 'authority'? And what other authority is there than the authority of force?"[77] Tate responds icily: "It is my impression that in the late fascist countries a 'choice' was made, and that upholders of intellectual authority had to be liquidated to make way for 'authority' of another kind; and I suspect that many American anti-fascists give their case away to fascism in their loss of insight into the meaning of authority other than that of force" (610). Predicting that the union of democracy and nationalism, as proposed by Brooks and De Voto, will soon "become the religion of the next age" (611), Tate asserts that he and the *Sewanee Review* will have nothing to do with this new form of "democracy":

> I say this largely to reassure those of my readers who a few years ago liked to think that I was not only un-democratic but anti-democratic; I should not wish, on this of all occasions, to disappoint them. I am not a democrat if Mr. Bernard De Voto is a democrat; but then I do not think that Mr. De Voto is a democrat; I think he is a literary obscurantist. Critics of this kidney are likely to be for any successful political movement, if it can be called "liberal" and if they are "in on it." As Mr. Auden points out in this issue of THE SEWANEE REVIEW, fascism in Europe came out of a liberalized society. THE SEWANEE REVIEW will oppose, when it is necessary for a literary review to consider politics, the democratic or any other state, if like the fascist state it shall make an all-engrossing demand for our loyalty and shall thus become the national religion. Then, regardless of what the state may call itself, it will be totalitarian. (611–12)

Toward the end of "The State of Letters" Tate writes that he fears that the American literary establishment is moving toward endorsing what he calls "an official literature . . . not officially censored but spontaneously conforming to official beliefs, morally dead and quite sinister" (613). Tate finds the growing spread of such conformity a situation so dire that "we must contemplate the possibility in the next generation of a society here as well as in Europe so precarious in its footing that men may come, for a time, to believe what they are told to believe: imaginative literature as we still know it may go underground or temporarily disappear" (613). Rather than give in to the gathering forces of darkness, Tate vows to use the *Sewanee Review* to foster "the insights that have kept man alive" in previous ages of oppression. "That—to keep alive the imagination and what it has meant historically—is perhaps a good enough cause," Tate writes, "for a quarterly like THE SEWANEE REVIEW to do what little it can to support" (614).

Beginning in the late 1930s and then throughout the war years, Tate wrote fiction and poetry that interrogated many of the issues that the European crisis was bringing into cultural debate. While rarely openly political in subject (that is, in terms of arguing for specific political action), this work nonetheless is deeply political in its underlying positions regarding the failures of modernity, drawing from Tate's agrarian thinking and its critique of authoritarianism. Tate's novel, *The Fathers* (1938), though set during the days immediately before and after the outbreak of the Civil War, explores crises of politics and identity that Tate clearly believed relevant to what he saw as the increasing authoritarianism of 1930s America. Early on, the elderly narrator, Lacy Buchan, poses questions that were haunting Tate during this period:

> Is it not something to tell, when a score of people whom I knew and loved, people beyond whose lives I could imagine no other life, either out of violence in themselves or the times, or out of some misery or shame, scattered into the new life of the modern age where they cannot even find themselves? Why cannot life change without tangling the lives of innocent persons? Why do innocent persons cease their innocence and become violent and evil in themselves that such great changes may take place?[78]

Dominating Lacy's narrative is George Posey, who represents the emerging modernity that, by the 1930s in its later, fuller forms, Tate saw pushing the world toward barbarism. Tate's depiction of George is straight out of *I'll Take My Stand*'s representation of the modern industrialist: George is an updated version of the mythic American frontiersman, an aggressive businessman whose endless pursuit of money is disrupting traditional order and relations. As Tate himself suggested in a letter to John Peale Bishop (28 September 1938), George represents "the American dream, which you've often called the American nightmare."[79] At one point in the novel, Lacy comments on George's aggressiveness, observing that George "had to keep moving; but where? I always come back to the horseman riding over the precipice" (179). And it is to the precipice of barbarism—and the nightmare of authoritarianism—that Tate in the late 1930s saw modern industrialists, George's progeny, pushing Western civilization toward and into.

Tate explored this global nightmare, together with his own sense of personal crisis in a world coming undone, in his wartime poetry, typically either in harshly satiric attacks on American idealism or in deeply confessional interrogations of the spirit and the self.[80] The war looms large in both groups of poems, in terms not only of subject matter but also of poetic inspiration, the forbidding times prompting Tate to search for understanding and purpose. "I write better when I am in trouble," Tate wrote to John Peale Bishop (4 December 1942), adding that "the trouble of the world answers the purpose."[81] The opening lines of "Winter Mask" (1942) typify the tone and character of Tate's confessional poems:

> Towards nightfall when the wind
> Tries the eaves and casements
> (A winter wind of the mind
> Long gathering its will)
> I lay the mind's contents
> Bare, as upon a table,
> And ask, in a time of war,
> Whether there is still
> To a mind frivolously dull
> Anything worth living for.
> (*CP* 111)

Originally entitled "Dejected Stanzas," "Winter Mask" portrays the poet pondering a grim and forbidding world in which people are bound together in treachery rather than love. Primarily through allusions to Dante's *Inferno*, the poet suggests that while Christian salvation is a thing worth living for, the world takes no notice and proceeds along in its murderous ways.

In "More Sonnets at Christmas" (1942) the poet equates his personal failures with those of the world at war, portraying his divided sensibilities in the cruel ironies that mark the celebration of Christ's birth in a world, as he writes, "unstalked by Christ" (*CP* 105). In the first of the four sonnets, the poet describes Christ as a mummy, drained of power and presence; and he goes on to imagine himself piloting a bomber, with satanic voices whispering in his ear to continue his mission without guilt. As the poet makes clear, to be at war is to lose one's moral judgment, metaphorically to lose one's head and to lose one's way, one's "capital yoke" (the yoke controlled the aircraft's altitude):

> Yes, the capital yoke—
> Remove it and there's not a ghost to fear
> This crucial day, whose decapitate joke
> Languidly winds into the inner ear.
> (*CP* 104)

Tate's world at war is indeed a "decapitate joke," a world without morality, a world without reason, a world in which Christ too appears headless, crouching "head crammed between his knees" (*CP* 104), in the same position as those waiting out the bombing raid.

In the second and third sonnets, the poet portrays Christmas during the current war as a grim day absent of faith and cheer, with people merely going through the motions of traditional festivities, all the while selfishly focusing on their own well-being. Prayers are lifted up not to Christ but to American empire:

> Give me this day a faith not personal
> As follows: The American people fully armed
> With assurances policies, righteous and harmed,
> Battle the world of which they're not at all.
> (*CP* 105)

In the final sonnet, the poet suggests that life in America has become a totalitarian nightmare, with the individual having become not only "Albino man bleached from the mortal clay, / Mild-mannered, gifted in your master's ease" but also "Plato's kept philosopher"(*CP* 106), that is, as Radcliffe Squires points out, the silent conniver in the tyrant state.[82]

America as a nation gone awry, headed possibly toward the tyrant state, is voiced even more forcefully in two of Tate's most openly political poems, "Jubilo" (1943) and "Ode to Our Young Pro-consuls of the Air" (1943). That Tate wrote such explicitly political satires, given his belief that the internal dynamics of art—rather than its subject matter—best worked to defend democracy, suggests how grave his feelings were at this time concerning the war and America's future. "Jubilo" draws upon the Civil War song of the same title, which was popular with slaves as they looked forward to a world made right by emancipation and the defeat of the Confederacy. Tate equates what he sees as the naiveté of the blacks' vision of the "Kingdom comin'" in the post–Civil War South with the naiveté of those now looking forward to a new world of democracy and freedom on "the Day of Jubilo" (*CP* 101), the end of World War II. "Who will count the gains and the losses / On the Day of Jubilo?" (101), the poet asks, and he continues with startling lines suggesting the great cost of the war, in terms of both wartime casualties and social devastation:

> Public accountant with double entry
> Enter in red war's final cast
> In the black column the pacing sentry,
> Old women picking the hogs' mast
>   For the Day of Jubilo.
>   (*CP* 101)

The images of the pacing sentry and the foraging women suggest the militarization and hardship coming in the postwar world. Despite the vast devastation of the war, however, people continue to look hopefully forward to a utopian society freed from the burdens of history, believing that they will "never be / Trapped in a fox-hole of decay / Nor snip nor glide of history / After the day of Jubilo" (*CP* 102). Tate goes on to suggest the futility of such thinking, suggesting the emptiness of both the dreamers and the dream, and concludes with the image of modern man as a patient being drained of blood, Tate's frightening vision of the coming totalitarian state's power to suck the life out of its citizens, condemning them to lives of empty anonymity.

"Ode to Our Young Pro-consuls of the Air" presents Tate's response to the jingoism being voiced during the war, suggesting that America is fighting less to defend democracy than to extend its power and influence throughout the world. As he does in "Jubilo," Tate here invokes an earlier poem, Michael Drayton's "To the Virginian Voyage" (1606), in order to comment on contemporary matters. For a poem written during wartime, Tate's satirical ode approaches the scandalous, envisioning America's war effort as one more in a long line of imperial adventures, beginning with its very founding.[83] Tate signals his skeptical stance immediately, the poem's opening stanzas describing, in drastically diminished terms, the American war effort and the Japanese enemy:

> Once more the country calls
> From sleep, as from his doom,
>   Each citizen to take

>   His modest stake
>   Where the sky falls
>   With a Pacific boom.
>
>   Warm winds in even climes
>   Push southward angry bees
>   As we, with tank and plane,
>   Wrest land and main
>   From yellow mimes,
>   The puny Japanese.
>   (*CP* 107)

After continuing this diminishment by surveying, in debunking verse, America's wars from the Revolutionary War up to the opening of World War II ("Sad day at Oahu / When the Jap beetle hit!" [*CP* 109]), Tate describes the efforts of "Brave Brooks and lithe MacLeish" to rally modern poets "grown Eliotic" (*CP* 109) into becoming patriotic. "We follow / *The Irresponsibles*," Tate writes (*CP* 109), a double-edged comment savaging both the modern poets who blindly toe the patriotic line and also Brooks and MacLeish themselves, who, along with their followers, are the true irresponsibles.

At this point the poet begins his address to American pilots about to begin a combat mission, echoing Drayton's call to the Virginia voyagers to extend the English empire into the Americas. In harking back to Drayton, Tate suggests that the American enterprise in World War II is just that—an enterprise, and specifically an enterprise to increase America's dominance throughout the world. Go forward, the poet invokes the pilots in withering irony, "And like a man / Swear you to keep / Faith with imperial eye" (*CP* 110). Moreover, Tate's lines echo, as filtered through his ironic vision, Henry R. Luce's famous editorial "The American Century" (1941), in which Luce vigorously called for America's entry into the war in order to extend American influence throughout the world. It was time for Americans, Luce wrote, "to accept wholeheartedly our duty and our opportunity as the most powerful and vital nation in the world and in consequence to exert upon the world the full impact of our influence, for such purposes as we see fit and by such means as we see fit."[84] While Luce noted that it was not America's purpose "to impose democratic institutions on all mankind including the Dalai Lama and the good shepherds of Tibet" (63), he nonetheless argued that America, as the inheritor of "all the great principles of Western civilization," had a duty "to be the powerhouse from which the ideals spread throughout the world and do their mysterious work of lifting the life of mankind from the level of the beasts to what the Psalmist called a little lower than the angels" (65).

Tate draws specifically from Luce's comments, envisioning in the poem's final two stanzas the end results of the cultural imperialism for which Luce was calling—a cultural imperialism that, in Tate's eyes, would indeed have an impact on "the Dalai Lama and the good shepherds of Tibet":

> Take off, O gentle youth,
> And coasting India
> > Scale crusty Everest
> > Whose mythic crest
> Resists your truth;
> And spying far away
>
> Upon the Tibetan plain
> A limping caravan,
> > Dive, and exterminate
> > The Lama, late
> Survival of old pain.
> Go kill the dying swan.
> > (*CP* 110)

As M. E. Bradford notes, Tate's poem anticipates James Branch Cabell's later comment on opening the world to American ideals and interests with "airplanes of altruism" and "battleships of brotherhood."[85]

Images of the world war also haunt Tate's most spiritual poem from the period, "Seasons of the Soul" (1944). As in Tate's other wartime poems, the destructive madness of war is represented as humanity's spurning of rationality and morality, the ripping away, returning to words from "More Sonnets at Christmas," of humanity's "capital yoke," the war a manifestation of a terrible, terrible "decapitate joke." Tate makes several specific references in "Seasons of the Soul" to the war's disruption of sanity and vision:

> No head knows where its rest is
> Or may lie down with reason
> When war's usurping claws
> Shall take the heart escheat—
> > (*CP* 115)

And later:

> In time of bloody war
> Who will know the time?
> Is it a new spring star
> Within the timing chill,
> Talking, or just a mime,
> That rises in the blood—
> Thin Jack-and-Jilling seas
> Without the human will?
> (*CP* 121)

Judging from "Seasons of the Soul," the spiritual certainty for which Tate was searching eluded him during the war, as the poem ends inconclusively, with the poet's invocation to Saint Monica for guidance remaining unanswered.

Tate's perilous spiritual seeking would not end until after the war, when in 1947 he joined the Roman Catholic Church. Although he had severed his Agrarian connections a decade earlier, joining the Catholic Church might best be understood as both Tate's return to and his repudiation of his Agrarian past. That is, his conversion to Catholicism both repudiates the significance of locating traditional order in secular history and practical politics (the Agrarian enterprise as the group generally defined it) and affirms the centrality of religious faith for structuring civilized life (Tate's interpretation that Agrarianism was primarily a religious movement, together with his belief that the Old South lacked the proper religion—Catholicism—for its essentially feudal order).[86]

Despite Tate's break with the practical politics of Agrarianism and his turn to an aesthetics that he believed was fundamentally democratic and antiauthoritarian, his days of being tagged as a Fascist were not entirely behind him. That charge surfaced most vociferously in 1949, when the Fellows in American Letters of the Library of Congress—a group that included Tate, Robert Penn Warren, T. S. Eliot, W. H. Auden, Conrad Aiken, Louise Bogan, Paul Green, Robert Lowell, Katherine Anne Porter, Willard Thorp, Leonie Adams, and Katherine Garrison Chapin—awarded Ezra Pound, then under indictment for treason, the Bollingen Award for *Pisan Cantos*. The ensuing controversy focused on what was perceived as the antidemocratic ideology underlying the aesthetics of the New Criticism endorsed by Tate, Warren, and other of the fellows, recalling previous charges leveled at Tate and Ransom during the war. Norman Cousins and Harrison Smith, in their editorial "Ezra Pound and the Bollingen Award," for instance, characterized the New

Critical praise for Pound's verse as "the incredible and dangerous intellectual snobbery that is the dominant strain of the 'new criticism.'"[87] "We beg to differ," Cousins and Smith added, attacking what they saw as the New Critics' dangerous separation of political and artistic judgments. "Art cannot be separated from life and attain true greatness; an artist's work cannot be entirely divorced from the man himself; evil and madness and inhuman conceptions are not a part of the composite structure of a work of genius" (21).

In two *Saturday Review* essays, Robert Hillyer went even further than Cousins and Smith, suggesting that the New Critics were preparing the way for a new American authoritarianism. Mainly attacking T. S. Eliot and his widespread influence, particularly with the New Critics, Hillyer concluded that the actions of the Bollingen committee reveal that "the clouds of an intellectual neo-Fascism and the new estheticism have perceptively met and on a horizon too near for comfort."[88] Hillyer argued, moreover, that the committee's decision smacked of dictatorial strong-arming, with Eliot and his disciples smothering dissent and cowing their few opponents into accepting the party line. "The performance of the Bollingen committee," Hillyer wrote, "is disagreeably reminiscent of what happens when a dictatorial will moves through a group wherein right and wrong are no longer clearly distinguishable from each other. History shows us that a civilization is always destroyed on the cultural level before the politicians and military take over" (38). Hillyer was not done. He ended the essay with a vigorous call to arms against the growing menace to freedom:

> An uncompromising assault on this new estheticism is long overdue. The award to Pound made it inevitable. In a spiritual morass where language, ethics, literature, and personal courage melt into something obscure and formless, a guided impulse has stirred the amorphous haze into something approaching form, something shaped out of stagnant art by groping Fascism. When I began the research for these articles I was quite unaware how deviously the trails would lead me toward one concept: totalitarianism. It is not genteel authoritarianism or the desire for order in a disordered world, as polite critics have called it. It is the mystical and cultural preparation for a new authoritarianism. (38)

Not long after Hillyer's articles appeared, Robert Gorham Davis, in an essay in the *American Scholar*, argued that the New Critics were part of a powerful neotraditionalist network that had launched a "general intellectual assault on the assumptions of democratic liberalism at a time when the United States is contending with Russia for world leadership in the name of democratic liberalism."[89] Davis echoed Hillyer in arguing that the New Critics were paving the way for an authoritarian state, their approach to literature based on "a complex of ideas which made poetic sensibility, purity of language, and the integrity of art inextricably involved with ideas of authority, aristocracy and reaction, and at odds with the ethos of a liberal democracy" (12). In their classrooms, journals, and textbooks, Davis continued, the New Critics were quietly brainwashing Americans with authoritarian ideology. "Over the last two decades, in the journals of the New Criticism," he wrote, "*authority, hierarchy, catholicism, aristocracy, tradition, absolutes, dogma, truth* became related terms of honor, and *liberalism, naturalism, scientism, individualism, equalitarianism, progress, protestantism, pragmatism,* and *personality* became related terms of rejection and contempt" (10). Davis concluded that the New Critics, along with other neotraditionalists, were working to replace America's democratic traditionalism with an alien authoritarianism.

Attacks similar to Davis's upon Tate, Ransom, and other New Critics would continue in the coming years, waxing and waning in intensity as the critical and political climate shifted back and forth with the cold war, the civil rights movement, and the turbulent 1960s. With their critical positions evolving largely from the earlier agrarianism, Tate and Ransom ultimately fell victim to those very origins, their traditionalism (including their racism, though this did ameliorate with time) becoming associated with their aesthetics—an association that doomed them to be finally swept aside by the powerful waves of intellectual and social change that washed over America in the late twentieth century.

2

SAVAGERY ON THE FRONTIER

W. J. CASH

In a 1938 editorial in the *Charlotte News*, "Problem in Definition: Now, What Is a Liberal?" W. J. Cash presents perhaps his most succinct analysis of his own political stance as a cultural critic in the 1930s. Drawing on a recent comment from President Roosevelt, who had observed that a liberal was someone who looked to solve old problems with new methods, Cash notes that the president's definition could include any number of crackpots and demagogues who were anything but politically liberal. He amends the president's definition, writing that the liberal "insists that these new ways of solving the problems shall be such as are compatible with the preservation of civil liberty and with sincerity and intelligence."[1] "The true liberal," Cash adds, "will certainly be the man who remembers that skepticism is, after all, the very essence of the spirit of the liberal tradition." Turning then to the status of the liberal in the modern world, Cash observes that as important as the liberal was in the nineteenth century, when the world was a good bit simpler, he now stands as a small fry in an age given to centralized and authoritarian political systems, created in part to deal with increasingly complex and disruptive economic and political problems. "Perhaps the liberal is only a quixotic soul who is doomed in the modern world," Cash writes. "Maybe there is no way out which really faces and attempts to solve modern problems and which at the same time can be reconciled with the liberties whose names at least we have so long revered. But it's what we have to hope and strive for—or make up our minds to surrender to totalitarianism."

Cash's definition of a liberal in effect reflected his own political position, and his words on the liberal's quixotic status in the twentieth century expressed his own deep-seated concerns about the ominous social and political developments that threatened civil liberties and critical thinking. Those developments, which Cash interpreted as the undoing of civilization and the return to barbarism, took their most dangerous form in the totalitarian state of Nazi Germany. So concerned was Cash about what seemed like the world's headlong rush toward authoritarian politics that he defined himself against everything totalitarianism stood for (part of the reason he saw himself as quixotic—the lone man standing against the power of the modern state). Liberal skepticism, for Cash, questioned totalitarian utopianism; the defense of civil liberties challenged totalitarianism's suppression of those liberties; critical thinking stood opposed to totalitarianism's mind-numbing tribalism and uniformity.

In his fear of authoritarian politics and totalitarianism, Cash shared a great deal with the Nashville Agrarians, but his perspective on the threat and its diagnosis was totally different from theirs.[2] Unlike the Agrarians, Cash found the totalitarian menace embedded deep within southern (not American) society, and while he did not see the Agrarians as consciously Fascist, he did believe that their defense of southern traditionalism masked disturbing ideological doctrines that southern traditionalism shared with Nazism. Cash's obsession with European Fascism (his fury also extended to Japan) profoundly shaped his understanding of southern society, as can be seen both in his newspaper writing and, more significantly, in his monumental reading of southern history and culture, *The Mind of the South* (1941). While Cash did not see the American South as identically mirroring Fascist Italy or Nazi Germany, he did see important connections that suggested that the South had for generations nurtured its own version of totalitarian control, a control that Cash hoped to expose. For Cash, one either took a stand against totalitarianism or surrendered to it; and Cash vowed never to surrender, either to the enemies abroad or to those within southern culture.

—✗ ✗ ✗ ✗—

Cash's difficulties with writing *The Mind of the South*—it would take more than ten years to complete—resulted in large part from his increasing concern over European totalitarianism, which not only distracted him but caused him to revise his thoughts on southern culture and his original plans for the book. Cash began work on the project in late 1929, not long after publication of his essay "The Mind of the South," which had appeared earlier that year in H. L. Mencken's *American Mercury*. Encouraged by Blanche Knopf's invitation to send the publisher a sample chapter and an outline for the book, Cash began organizing his materials and seeking advice from Howard Odum, at the University of North Carolina. In March 1930 Cash wrote Knopf that the book's thesis "is that the Southern Mind represents a very definite culture, or attitude towards life, a heritage, primarily, from the Old South, but greatly modified and extended by conscious and unconscious efforts over the last hundred years to protect itself from the encroachments of three hostile factors: the Yankee Mind, the Modern Mind, and the Negro."[3]

As his letter to Knopf suggests, Cash at this point was working with the basic idea from his 1929 essay: that despite great social and economic change in the South, the essential consciousness of southerners had never developed beyond its frontier origins. Cash observes in the essay that even though the New South landscape looks like "a chicken-pox of factories on the Watch-Us-Grow maps," the mind of the New South populace is "basically and essentially the mind of the Old South. It is a mind, that is to say, of the soil rather than of the mills—a mind, indeed, which, as yet, is almost wholly unadjusted to the new industry."[4] He describes the "ancient mind of the South" (187) as intensely individualistic, intensely passionate and violent, intensely religious, and intensely resistant to critical thinking.

What would be central in the book—an analysis of the authoritarian forces under which southerners lived—is almost entirely absent in the essay. About as far as Cash goes in this regard is his statement, upon which he does not elaborate, that the contributions to higher education made by the South's newly rich, including that by James Buchanan Duke in creating Duke University, are "motivated by a desire to perpetuate the old order, not to create an enlightened new one" (191). Cash suggests that rather than prisoners of authoritarian forces, southerners are prisoners of their own thoughtlessness and their determination *not* to analyze. "All problems are settled categorically," Cash writes. "Maxim and rule are enough. Precedent is inviolable. And nice distinctions are, of course, impossible" (190). Lacking a critical consciousness, the southern mind has remained "almost impervious to change" and has "successfully resisted the steadily increasing pressure of industrialism, blithely adopting the Kiwanis moonshine—all those frothy things it found compatible—but continuing, in the main, to move through the old rhythms" (190).

Not surprisingly, given his emphasis on personal responsibility for southern recalcitrance, Cash ends his essay by saying that with time the ancient southern mind will inevitably evolve into something new, with southerners slowly leaving the old ways behind as they work themselves fully into the new order. "Perhaps, indeed, the beginning of [the change] is already at hand," Cash writes. "For, undeniably, there is a stir, a rustling upon the land, a vague, formless, intangible thing which may or may not be the adumbration of coming upheaval. Tomorrow—the day after—eventually—the cotton-mill peon will acquire the labor outlook and explosion will follow" (192). Eventually, Cash predicts, not without some chagrin, the South will be indistinguishable from the North, the iconic Confederate General apotheosized into George Babbitt.

Cash worked on expanding "The Mind of the South" and its thesis for the next several years. Although battling chronic ill health, he had apparently written about sixty thousand words by late 1932 and was looking to finish the project in the next year.[5] At some point around this time, however, he set the manuscript aside; when he returned to it, probably in 1935, he destroyed everything he had written and started over again. "I discovered that I knew a great deal less about the South than I thought I knew, and above all I grew to dislike the attitude with which I had begun," Cash recalled later. "When it was complete, I looked at it and found that, while it seemed to me to contain some excellent ideas and some passages of good writing, it was neither reasonably fair nor organized into a continuous piece. And so I deliberately destroyed it, without sending it to the publisher at all."[6] Cash never explained the attitude that he had grown to dislike, but it seems clear, judging both from the essays he wrote for the *American Mercury* during the time when he had set the manuscript aside and from the final shape of *The Mind of the South*, that he had reached an entirely different conclusion concerning the continuity of the southern mind: rather than seeing it as remaining unchanged because of southerners' thoughtlessness and close-mindedness, he now saw it as crippled and controlled by the authoritarianism of southern culture.

The six essays that followed "The Mind of the South" in the *American Mercury* provide telling evidence of Cash's shift in perspective, with the essays from 1930 and 1931 differing significantly from those written from 1933 to 1935.[7] The early essays for the most part continue in the same vein as "The Mind of the South," exposing southern wrongheadedness and ignorance and looking forward hopefully to the passing of ancient ways and the emergence of the new. In "The War in the South" (1930), an examination of labor troubles in the textile industry, Cash predicts that the violent labor wars will end with "not only the victory of the labor union and the beginning of striking changes in the South generally, but also the passing of the cotton-mill baron as a type."⁸ "Paladin of the Drys" (1931), a fierce attack on North Carolina senator Cameron Morrison, likewise looks hopefully forward, ending with the suggestion that Morrison's revolting politics (Morrison at one point had been a leader of the white supremacist group the Red Shirts) might in the long run actually help heal rifts in the Democratic Party and lead to the purging of Morrison and other like-minded politicians.

Cash's later essays from the *American Mercury* present a darker, more forbidding vision of a locked-down, authoritarian South, with Cash much less confident about the inevitability of better days ahead. "Close View of a Calvinist Lhasa" (1933), an examination of the social and cultural life of Charlotte, North Carolina, portrays southern traditionalism and economic self-interest joining hands to create a tightly controlled, closed society. It is not merely that life there is "one continuous blue law,"⁹ but that those laws—and everything else having to do with the social and economic system—must be accepted without question. "To question Babbittry is to question God," Cash writes, "and to question God is to question Babbittry, and to question either . . . And so, plainly enough, liberalism, the university, whatever questions and challenges in North Carolina, must be destroyed" (449, Cash's ellipses). Cash goes on to make it clear that Charlotte's citizens live imprisoned not in ignorance but in fear; or as Cash puts it, they submit to authority "not because everybody is inherently so stupid as to be unable to rise above it, but because nobody or nearly nobody (the town has two or three somewhat querulous and rabbitty 'liberals') ever *dares* rise above it. These people are not without the elements of mind. Take them out of here and they often distinguish themselves" (450). Only behind locked doors can Charlotte's citizens be individuals; in public they become indistinguishable members of the compliant masses. "Let the word come down and they become simply a herd," Cash writes, in effect describing an authoritarian dystopia upheld by enforced conformity and allegiance; "their idiosyncrasies and their private convictions slough away and they click into line like so many marionettes, slide through the grooves of their *Kultur*-pattern with all the inevitability of Hardy's dynasts in the coils of the Immanent Will. If any man hesitates, he is lost" (450).

"Holy Men Muff a Chance" (1934), another of Cash's *American Mercury* essays, presents a frightening view of the fear and despair gripping people in the midst of the Great Depression. Coloring Cash's essay, as he makes clear early on, is the pessimism of Oswald Spengler's *Decline of the West* (Spengler argued that Western civilization was headed for inevitable ruin, following the organic pattern of life and death through which he saw all civilizations passing) and his own despair over the dehumanization ushered in by the modern industrial state. "The nation is frightened half out of its wits," Cash observes, adding that "sometimes it seems to me that everybody in America must have read that book of Oswald Spengler's."[10] People, he goes on, "look at you with scared eyes and ask you what *you* think is going to happen, and before you can frame a reply, race on to answer it themselves with 'Chaos!' or what serves in their vocabularies for the term. It isn't revolution they mean, either. What they talk—what everybody in the nation is talking, I gather—is essentially the thing Spengler talks: that the world has got too complex for one man's mind to get around, that civilization is cracking down—ruin—the New Middle Ages" (113). While Cash later says that he doubts that Western culture faces the destruction Spengler predicts, he adds that "it does seem likely that we may be working toward a Big Change all around—in culture as in economic structure. Yes, even in religion" (115). That change, he says, is "the machine view of things" (115), which regards all existence, from the human body to the universe itself, as operating by verifiable mechanical laws. People may still desperately yearn for what Cash calls "the old, deep, dark, mysterious humanity" (116), but they will not find it in the modern age.

In "Genesis of the Southern Cracker" (1935), his final essay in the *American Mercury,* Cash portrays poor whites as victims of a crushing social and economic system, thoroughly revising his earlier argument from "The Mind of the South" that poor whites had only their own ignorance to blame for their wretched condition. Working with an idea that would be important in *The Mind of the South,* Cash argues that the plantation system began the oppression of poor whites by forcing them deep into the back country, far from southern culture's social and economic centers. "Nor were they only driven back," Cash adds. "Because of the peculiar static quality of the Southern order, they were locked up and closed in—completely barred from any economic and social advance as a body."[11] There in the back country the spiraling slide into degeneracy started, greased by malnutrition and poor living conditions. That slide continued later when New South industrialism entrapped poor whites in an exploitative system, ruled over by "an army of new masters" (108)—the factory owner, the banker, and the absentee landlord, to name three. Ground into poverty by this new system and suffering "the ennui, the bitterness, the viciousness, bred in him by the always-narrowing conditions of his life," the poor white devolved further, becoming ever more dangerous and violent, "at his worst a dangerous neurotic, a hair-trigger killer, a man-burner, a pig quite capable of incest—in brief, everything that William Faulkner and Erskine Caldwell have made him out to be, and perhaps something more" (108). With this reinterpretation of poor whites, Cash laid the foundation for his analysis of southern authoritarianism in *The Mind of the South*; and it was apparently about the time that Cash wrote "Genesis of the Southern Cracker" that he destroyed his initial book manuscript and began anew.

Political developments in Europe certainly played a significant role in shaping Cash's new perspective on the South. Cash's analysis of southern authoritarianism began in 1933 (with "Close View of a Calvinist Lhasa"), the year that Hitler came to power and that the world began taking serious notice of the Nazis. Precisely when Cash began paying close attention to Hitler is not known, but it is clear that by 1935, when he started writing editorials for the *Charlotte News*, his interest in Fascism and Nazism had become an obsession. That obsession intensified as the world situation worsened, so that by the late 1930s Cash was known to explode into paroxysms when the subject of the Nazis came up in conversation. His authoritative biographer Bruce Clayton memorably describes Cash's flareups in the newsroom:

> By late 1939, with his fears fixated on Hitler, the merest mention of the dictator's name caused Cash's anger to flare. He would begin by rubbing his forehead vigorously and squinting his eyes. Then he would start pacing, muttering about Hitler's villainy. Then his voice would rise as he flailed his arms in denunciation. When reading something disturbing about the international scene, he would at first sit staring at the newspaper or magazine. Then he would jump up, fling the paper on the floor, and grind it under his heel. Hitler was a demon, a filthy monster. Cash would stand staring at the giant wall map at the *News*, carefully and silently tracing Hitler's movements. Then he would begin to scream epithets: Hitler was a madman, a maniac, a Ku Kluxer, white trash. Cash's screams could be heard throughout the newsroom and beyond.[12]

In his editorials, Cash's dismay over international politics surfaced almost immediately. In one of his earliest pieces for the *Charlotte News*, "What Price Mussolini" (11 November 1935), Cash characterizes Mussolini's invasion of Ethiopia as a reckless effort to preserve power that threatened to unleash general warfare in Europe. "Fiercely, like the cry of a wounded wolf, Mussolini bares his fangs and snarls his defiance of the nations," Cash writes. "He is convincingly poised to spring, and it may be that Ethiopia will soon be forgotten as the desperate imitator of the Caesars deliberately creates a European ocean of blood for his own suicide." Later that year Cash drew attention in his editorials to Japan's incursions into China, and by 1936 he was agonizing over Nazi Germany's growing militarism, particularly after the German reoccupation of the Rhineland. Two months after that reoccupation, Cash predicted world war, writing in "War and Peace: Note on Pacifism" (10 May 1936) that an insatiable demand for new markets and raw materials would drive Italy, Germany, and Japan into conflict with France, England, and Russia—and finally, perhaps, the United States. "And so today," Cash writes, speaking of Germany, Italy, and Japan, "they roll inexorably forward, mad, fanatical, and immeasurably hungry," adding that soon the Fascist countries "will strike fully home—never doubt it. And undoubtedly, and though they may not necessarily strike as allies, they will all strike at one and the same time. Tomorrow, Britain, France, Russia must surrender tamely to endless demands—or go into a battle for which the only end will be their own complete ruin or the complete breaking of the power of their challengers."

In this same editorial, Cash argues that Fascism and Nazism represent not a step into the future but a step backward into the past, a devolution into barbarism. Cash writes that the Fascist countries "have fallen back into an essentially barbaric pattern—into the permanent organization of society as a military unit. And as the heart and center of that, they have fallen back, too, into the essentially barbaric idea of themselves as a chosen and superior people, coming down from gods or demi-gods, and destined by ineluctable fate to rule over mankind—as the heirs to the Caesars, to Woden and the Gothic hosts, or to the conquering Children of the Sun." As the decade wore on, Cash returned repeatedly to this idea, in ever fiercer terms. In "Spengler Comes True: Dawn for Dictators, Evening in the West" (27 February 1938), Cash argues that the barbarism of Germany and Italy points to the fulfilment of Oswald Spengler's dire prophecies of civilization's decay. Cash characterizes barbarism as the "complete suppression of the individual by the group" and the group's "complete subordination to the military end of conquest," and he continues: "The organization of Germany and Italy now is ominously like the organization, and the watchwords of Blood and Soil are ominously like the watchwords, with which the Visigoths and the

Ostrogoths, the Alani and the Huns, the Suevi and the Vandals, the Saxon and the Dane, poured over Europe between the Second and Ninth Centuries." On the day that Germany invaded Poland, beginning World War II, Cash wrote in his editorial "A Fanatic Menaces Civilization" (1 September 1939) that Nazism was "a system invented by a gang of criminals for the deliberate purpose of taking a whole nation back into barbarism, and using it as an instrument to carry barbarism over the whole earth. . . . Its purpose is naked and ruthless conquest by the sword—conquest which spares neither woman nor child. And, for brutality, the man who heads it makes Genghis, Tamerlane, Attila, Genseric, Theodoric—any of the old barbarian conquerors—look pale by comparison."

While delivering scathing attacks on Nazi aggression, Cash was devoting himself to studying the Nazi philosophy and psychology. He pored over Hitler's *Mein Kampf*, filling his copy with marginal comments, and he sought out translations of the full, unexpurgated text, not the shortened one approved by the Nazi government that was commercially distributed in the United States.[13] He also studied writers whom he believed had inspired Nazism, particularly Nietzsche, and he read all the contemporary commentary on the Nazis he could find.[14] To doubters of the Nazi menace, he recommended Hermann Rauschning's book *The Revolution of Nihilism: Warning to the West* (1939), which argued that Nazism was a revolutionary barbarism with no goals other than power for its own sake. Intriguingly, he also looked to one of his favorite authors, Joseph Conrad, for help in understanding Nazism, writing in "A Note on Joseph Conrad: Death by Honor" (3 April 1938) that Kurtz's descent into barbarism and despair in *Heart of Darkness* is mirrored in the philosophy of the Fascist and Nazi state, specifically the tenet "that man is under no bond whatever to his fellows—that he is simply a beast subject to no law save that of force." In a later book-page editorial, "Time Shows Conrad Knew Real Germany" (5 November 1939), Cash wrote that he had changed his mind about Conrad's categorical hatred of Germans and that he now agreed with him. Again citing *Heart of Darkness*, Cash observes that "the German mind is a rigid, uncompromising mind, and in conflict with the native mind it will not give an inch but demands instead that the native shall conform to German ideas. And when that happens, the native, a curiously fragile creature, simply succumbs, dies out, disappears."

Cash's grapplings to understand Nazism and the Nazi mind—he went so far as to apply for a Guggenheim Fellowship in 1936 to spend a year in

Germany—paralleled his grapplings to understand the southern mind, and it is clear that his obsessive focus on Nazism was influencing his thinking on the South, particularly concerning its racial ideology and practice. By the mid-1930s Cash was attacking the racial underpinnings of Nazi ideology and the Nazi campaign against the Jews. In "Hitler's Germany" (2 January 1936) Cash quotes heavily from the resignation letter of James G. McDonald (McDonald had stepped down from his League of Nations post overseeing German refugees, in part to publicize the terrors of Nazi persecution), in which McDonald describes in detail the plight of Germany's Jews, who, he says, are "condemned to segregation within the four corners of the legal and social ghetto which has now closed upon them." After presenting McDonald's explicit descriptions of Nazi oppression, Cash concludes: "This, incomprehensible as it may seem, is taking place in Germany under Hitler in the Twentieth Century."

In later editorials and reviews Cash savaged Nazi racial ideology and its claims of Aryan superiority. In "Papa Franz Boas: He's a Testy and Aged Teuton, Who Proves that Racial Blood Streams are as Fickle as the Waters, and as Lively" (12 July 1936), Cash praises Boas's argument that not only are there no pure races but there are no races at all, since every "race" is in fact a racial hodgepodge, or in Cash's words, a "mongrel crew," descended from diverse, not common, ancestors. The next year, in "Scoffs at Hitler's Talk of 'Race' in *Study of Man*" (4 July 1937), Cash wrote that Ralph Linton's *Study of Man: An Introduction* made it absolutely clear that "such notions as 'race' as Hitler and his barbarians are propagating are romantic myths with not a whit of fact to back them up." In a stunning statement for a white southerner in the 1930s, Cash notes that current anthropological research points "to the belief that there is little or no real difference in the native intelligence of the various great races—that certainly there is none as between the Nordic and 'The Latin'—and that even our boasting superiority to the 'inferior' groups of Asia and Africa rest [sic] finally and simply upon the fact that, 'Whatever happens, we have got The Maxim gun and they have not.'" Cash concludes that Linton's work establishes that there is "no ground to believe in any evolutionary superiority of the white race," since that position of superiority was a relatively recent development. "If the white man's superiority arises from innate qualities," Cash writes, turning to Linton's observations, "he says that we must suppose a mutation which took place not earlier than the Fifteenth century, for down to that time the white man was always on the defensive as against the hordes swinging out of Asia. And, of course, as he says, everyone knows that what we call civilization was invented and worked out not by Europeans but by Asiatics."

Cash began explicitly connecting Nazi racial ideology and practice with the South in 1936, first by noting similarities between the Nazis and the Ku Klux Klan. At the end of his 1936 editorial on Franz Boas, Cash states that he looks forward to Boas's planned anthropological study aimed for the general reader, adding that "it won't do any good in his native Germany, for it will not be read there under the Terror. But perhaps it will get some sense into the heads of some of our American Ku Kluxers who seem so hotly bent on taking us into Fascism, willy-nilly." In other editorials, Cash reversed the terms of the German-southern connection, characterizing the Nazi leadership as Klansmen. In a piece discussing Nazi misreadings of Nietzsche, "The Synthetic Supermen: Europe's Ku Kluckers, They Invoke Nietzsche" (5 September 1937), Cash calls Hitler "a somewhat inferior Grand Dragon Clarke" who, like Mussolini, masked his Klan identity behind the mantle of the Nietzschean superman. Such cloaking, Cash observes, is "a savage irony," since "what Nietzsche really worshipped was the natural aristocrat, the strong bold intelligence which dared to look at the shape of reality, and which ruled through its inherent force—not Ku Kluckers appealing to fools with lying clap-trap, and ruling through stupidity in the fear of a beating—or death."

Besides the specifics of Nazi racial policy, the more general issue of political authoritarianism as highlighted by Nazi Germany was also shaping Cash's stance as cultural critic of the South.[15] Several of Cash's editorials defending southerners who dared to criticize the South look forward to the position he himself adopted in *The Mind of the South*. His appreciation of novelist Evelyn Scott, "The Lovely Evelyn Scott: Iconoclast of Charm" (24 October 1937), defends Scott's burlesque of southern legends and argues that Scott's stinging critiques of Dixie earned her the title, not of southern traitor (as she was frequently deemed), but of southern patriot.[16] Scott, Cash explains, embraces "the highest form of patriotic devotion"—the courage to criticize and challenge her homeland and to stand up to those who blindly worshiped "a brummagem legend compounded out of hurt feelings and tinsel romancing." The previous year, Cash had defended himself against a similar charge of southern betrayal, writing in "Criticism of Criticism; or, Rather, Some Remembered Winces by a Young Man who Wrote as He Pleased" (5 July 1936) that it was a person's patriotic duty to challenge society when it no longer manifested ideals of truth and dignity:

> For truth is the first value of humanity, and loyalty to truth is the highest loyalty to humanity. And loyalty to humanity is the first loyalty—a loyalty that transcends and embraces all other loyalties such as loyalty to America and the South. And whatever in this America or this South that does not fit with truth and humanity is no proper object of loyalty. On the contrary, to support it becomes the very greatest disloyalty. Yes, even if it should be so—as I am perfectly convinced it isn't—that the things we commonly call American or Southern are knit together in a single inseparable fabric—that to attack the evil is necessarily to attack the good. For then the whole would be incompatible with the actual interest of the American people or the Southern people and would deserve to be destroyed.

As his comments here suggest, Cash saw forces of authoritarianism, both on the regional and the national level, pressing to shut down cultural dialogue, to dictate truth rather than to discover it. He believed that discovering truth through dialogue and dissent lay at the heart of the democratic process and that while democracy was not the most efficient way of governing, its inefficiency was actually in some ways its greatest strength, keeping it responsive to the voices of the people.

Perhaps conceiving it as his patriotic duty to complete *The Mind of the South,* Cash returned to the manuscript in 1938, delivering a big chunk of the manuscript to Knopf in October. The growing troubles in Europe were pulling him in two directions with regard to the book: on the one hand, they were distracting him (he would not finish the manuscript for another two years); and on the other hand, they were compelling him to complete it, since by this time he had come to see his critical examination of southern culture as an effective means to defend it from authoritarian forces, both from within and from without.

Cash explicitly detailed this critical position in his commencement address at the University of Texas at Austin, "The South in a Changing World," which he delivered a few months after publication of *The Mind of the South*.[17] Cash begins by telling his audience that he is turning a critical eye on his—and their—homeland because the turbulent times in the world demand that people be clear-eyed about their cultures and their traditions. He quickly identifies totalitarianism as the major threat to Western civilization, including, he emphasizes, to Texas and the South. "Totalitarianism is apparently sweeping over the world," Cash says. "It certainly swept over Europe and is at the present threatening the United States." He adds that "since tradition is everywhere under attack—since the whole tradition of the Western world is under attack, and our tradition in the South of course is ultimately just a part of that tradition of the Western world—I think it is very necessary that we should try not only to approach the problems of the times that are coming with good will, but also with as intelligent as possible understanding of what our tradition is." Cash explains that because he does not have time to discuss the entire tradition of the Western world, he will focus specifically on the traditions of Texas and the South.

Cash then zeroes in on what he calls southern tradition's retreat into unreality, and he urges his audience to step forward *into* reality—the reality of the worldwide threat of totalitarianism. Making that step means abandoning regional isolation and joining forces with the nation and with other nations to fight the enemy. Cash chastises those Americans who believe that totalitarianism is an "irresistible wave . . . [and] who say that the only rational thing for us to do is to give up quietly, that we are seeing the decay and death of an order of civilization."[18] He underscores that Fascism is not, as Anne Morrow Lindbergh puts it, "the wave of the future" but instead is, as R. H. Markham's designates it, "the wave of the past," that is, the return to barbarism and brutality.[19] He exhorts his audience to stand tall as Texans, southerners, Americans, and members of Western civilization against that barbarism.

Nowhere else would Cash make such an explicit statement asserting the power of tradition, informed by critical appraisal, to counter the forces of totalitarianism, not even in *The Mind of the South* itself. While it shares the general thrust of "The South in a Changing World," the book is far less hopeful about a rejuvenated southern tradition standing powerfully against the world's disorder. In its darker analysis, *The Mind of the South* develops an idea that Cash did not share with his audience at the University of Texas: that the American South continues to be gripped by an authoritarianism that dates back to the Old South and shares a number of disturbing traits with European Fascism. Cash's primary goal in *The Mind of the South* was to expose the dangers of southern authoritarianism and to provide the means, through open inquiry and critical thinking, for southerners to free themselves from their psychological bondage.

Cash argues in *The Mind of the South* that southern authoritarianism originated in the culture's folk mind, which was established in the region's early settling. By *mind* Cash means something close to collective consciousness, in his words "a fairly definite mental pattern, associated with a fairly definite social pattern—a complex of established relationships and habits of thought, sentiments, prejudices, standards and values, and association of ideas" (*MS* xlviii). Two major attributes of this primitive, uncritical mind stand out: radical individualism and enthusiastic romanticism, both developing from the harsh conditions of the early frontier. In perhaps his most striking interpretive move, Cash argues that the repeated onset of frontier conditions in the South (*frontier* interpreted loosely, suggesting conditions of social upheaval that impede social development), brought about by the Civil War, Reconstruction, and World War I, has kept the southern mind from progressing beyond its primitive state, leaving it open to control by authoritarian forces. From the beginning of its settlement, Cash argues, the South has been "a world in which horses, dogs, guns, not books, and ideas and art, were [southerners'] normal and absorbing interests" (*MS* 96); thus southerners have never developed "the complexity of mind, the knowledge, and, above all, the habit of skepticism essential to any generally realistic attitude" (*MS* 45). With no capacity for making level-headed, informed appraisals of the real world, the characteristic southerner is a "child-man . . . [in] that the primitive stuff of humanity lies very close to the surface in him, that he likes naïvely to play, to expand his ego, his senses, his emotions, that he will accept what pleases him and reject what does not, and that in general he will prefer the extravagant, the flashing, and the brightly colored—in a word, that he displays the whole catalogue of qualities we mean by romanticism and hedonism" (*MS* 45).

Cash sees the individualism and romanticism of the frontier South as crucial in the emergence of the southern authoritarianism that began with the creation of the Old South's plantation society. He argues that the plantation society established frontier conditions for the large majority of white southerners—the poor whites and the yeoman farmers—who were banished to the margins of society, far from the centers of wealth, prestige, and power. There, viewing the world with "essentially naive, direct, and personal eyes" (*MS* 35), they remained unaware not only of the social and economic forces controlling them and their world but also of their very marginalization. It was an ideological triumph for the planter elite. Believing themselves free and embracing a radical individualism, common whites lived happily imprisoned "within the enclosing walls thrown up by the plantation . . . [and] not one in a thousand of the enclosed ever even remotely apprehended the existence of such walls. And so it happened, finally, that the old basic feeling of democracy was preserved practically intact" (*MS* 39).

Other forces cemented the planter elite's system for maintaining order and control, including, most importantly, the South's rigid racial ideology. What Cash calls the "Proto-Dorian bond" joined whites of all ranks in superiority over blacks, fostering the comforting illusion for common whites that they were legitimate members of the ruling class. In its "vastly ego-warming and ego-expanding distinction between the white man and the black" (*MS* 38) the Proto-Dorian bond elevated the common white "to a position comparable to that of, say, the Doric knight of ancient Sparta. Not only was he not exploited directly, he was himself made by extension a member of the dominant class—was lodged solidly on a tremendous superiority, which, however much the blacks in the 'big house' might sneer at him, and however much their masters might privately agree with them, he could never publicly lose. Come what might, he would always be a white man. And before that vast and capacious distinction, all others were foreshortened, dwarfed, and all but obliterated" (*MS* 39). Identifying themselves with the master class, common whites threw their support wholeheartedly behind the very system that oppressed them.

The perceived threat of the Yankee, and particularly the abolitionist, further solidified the bond between ruling elites and common whites, joined in their defense of the southern way of life. "Yeoman and cracker turned to the planter," Cash writes, "waited eagerly upon his signal as to what to think and do . . . because he was their obviously indicated captain in the great common cause" (*MS* 67). In discussing common whites' lack of class awareness and their unquestioned allegiance to the planter, Cash quotes the baffled Hinton Helper, who had unsuccessfully tried to communicate to poor whites their wretched subservience: "The stupid and sequacious masses, the white victims of slavery . . . believe whatever the slaveholders tell them; and they are cajoled into the notion that they are the freest, happiest, and most intelligent people in the world" (*MS* 67). Loyalty to the South against the threatening Yankee is for Cash "the final development of the paternalistic pattern" (*MS* 67) established by the planter elite.

In all this, Cash describes the Old South as bearing a striking resemblance to the modern totalitarian state, with its elaborate cultural system tightly controlling all areas of southern life. No dissent was tolerated, as Cash emphasizes. "From the taboo on criticism of slavery, it was but an easy step to interpreting every criticism of the South on whatever score as disloyalty—to making such criticism so dangerous that none but a madman would risk it," Cash writes. "And from that it was but another and just as easy—an almost inevitable—step to a state of affairs in which criticism of any sort at all was not impossible, surely, but an enterprise for bold and excitement-loving spirits alone" (*MS* 90). Behind the rhetoric of the Old South's cultured society was actually the anticivilizational barbarism that Cash found in twentieth-century totalitarianism. And behind the rhetoric of rugged individualism was a society in which all people were cut "to a single pattern" and restrained by "strait-jacket conformity" (*MS* 88). Cash's description of the mind of the Old South was in effect a description of the mind of those living under the modern authoritarian state: unthinking, uncritical, and, most frighteningly, loyal to an enslaving system.

Cash argues that despite the collapse of the Old South and the plantation system, southern authoritarianism not only maintained but actually increased its stranglehold on the southern mind after the Civil War, particularly during the chaotic times of Reconstruction. Cash argues that immediately after the Civil War the South collapsed back into a newly configured frontier, a "jungle growth of poverty and ruin" (*MS* 146) in which southerners "were once more without mastery of their environment and must begin again from the beginning to build up social and economic order out of social and economic chaos" (*MS* 103). With that rebuilding came the continuation of the region's authoritarian ideology, now centered on unquestioned allegiance to the Lost Cause and undying worship of a legendary southern civilization made even glorious through romantic nostalgia. "With the antebellum world removed to the realm of retrospect, the shackles of reality, as so often happens in such cases, fell away from it altogether," Cash observes. "Perpetually suspended in the great haze of memory, it hung, as it were, poised, somewhere between earth and sky, colossal, shining, and incomparably lovely—a Cloud-Cuckoo-Land wherein at last everybody who had ever laid claim to the title of planter would be metamorphosed with swift precision, beyond any lingering shade of doubt, into the breathing image of Marse Chan and Squire Effingham, and wherein life would move always in stately and noble measure through scenery out of Watteau" (*MS* 124). Not unlike the cult worship of a romanticized Aryan past encouraged by the Nazis to solidify German nationalism, the southern worship of the Lost Cause bound white southerners tightly together ideologically and blinded them to the authoritarian system imprisoning them.

As the Old South had been, postbellum southern society was organized essentially as a military state. The system demanded loyalty and discipline, and common whites for the most part loyally followed the orders of their leaders, the planter elite. Cash describes the postwar South:

> During these thirty years the South was like nothing so much as a veteran army. The people—crackers and farmers—stood to their captains in very much the same way that, say, the troopers of Austerlitz and Marengo stood to Bonaparte and his marshals; gave them much the same idolatry, the same high faith, the same quick and sure response to suggestion; waited upon their word with the same respectful attention; were cast down by their frowns, elevated by their smiles, and, in a word, were scarcely less dependent upon the favor of their commanders for a good opinion of themselves than the most zealous trooper. (*MS* 112)

The ideological mastery of southern authoritarianism continued, with the common whites once again identifying themselves uncritically with the oppressive system. In Cash's words, the common white "so absolutely identified his ego with the thing called the South as to become, so to say, a perambulating South in little, and hence found in the prescriptions of his captains great expansion for his ego—associated the authority yielded the master class, not with any diminution of his individuality, but with its fullest development and expression" (*MS* 113).

Besides its broadly based militarism and authoritarianism, Cash's Reconstruction South shares a number of startling similarities with his reading of Nazi Germany. In contrast to the Nashville Agrarians, who argued that the South's antimodernism represented the preservation of Western civilization (modernity, to them, being barbaric), Cash presents the South's resistance to modernity as the death of civilization and its traditions. As he finds underlying Nazi ideology, Cash sees southern antimodernism as tribal and insular, standing opposed to the openness of the Western intellectual tradition and the ongoing evolution of Western civilization. In snuffing out critical inquiry, what Cash sees as the basis of the modern mind, the South enforces its authoritarian system, with southerners indoctrinated to associate the hated Yankee with destructive forces of modernity threatening southern traditionalism. In this campaign to shut down free inquiry, Cash writes, the Yankee easily morphed into a horrific amalgamation of "Darwin, Huxley, Ben Butler, Sherman, Satan" (*MS* 139).

Echoing the Nazis' campaigns to cleanse themselves and their society of the Jews and other "pollutants," Cash describes the postwar South's "consuming monomania" (*MS* 168) to protect the purity of its blood and culture against the threat of blacks, establishing a rigid system of racial segregation buttressed by ritual violence. During Reconstruction, as Cash describes it, lynching became a community ritual, "an act of racial and patriotic expression, an act of chivalry" (*MS* 118). All white people were supposed to participate and, according to Cash, almost all of them did.

Cash argues that when forces of industrial capitalism poured into the South near the end of the nineteenth century, southern culture was pushed back to yet another frontier of social chaos. From all appearances, Cash notes, this era of rapid and momentous social change signaled the demise of the old order, as large numbers of people moved into towns and cities, factories and mills went up all over the South, and speculative capitalists manipulated the economy. In Cash's eyes, however, the transformations of the cultural landscape were merely cosmetic; the forces of southern authoritarianism still reigned. The new factory system, Cash argues, was merely a reconfiguration of the plantation system. Referring to the factory as merely "a plantation, essentially indistinguishable in organization from the familiar plantation of the cotton fields," Cash concludes that in the industrialization of the South "the *plantation* remained the single great basic social and economic pattern of the South—as much in industry as on the land" (*MS* 200). Like the plantation masters before them, the factory owners completely controlled their workers' lives; Old South paternalism, without the stigma of chattel slavery, was "fortified by force and turned into true prescriptive right" (*MS* 201). The old pattern of self-policing held firm, with common whites continuing to embrace the Proto-Dorian ideal and to see their interests as coinciding with those of the bosses. Cash thus concludes that, above all, New South industrialism illustrates how seamlessly forces of southern authoritarianism adapted to changing times while keeping the underlying authoritarianism intact. "There was no revolution in basic ideology and no intention of relinquishing the central Southern positions and surrendering bodily to Yankee civilization involved in the genesis of dream and program," Cash writes, adding that "far from representing a deliberate break with the past, the turn to Progress clearly flowed straight out of that past and constituted in a real sense an emanation from the will to maintain the South in its essential integrity" (*MS* 179). For Cash, then, the New South was new only in "that it would be so rich and powerful that it might rest serene in its ancient positions, forever impregnable" (*MS* 184).

Those "ancient positions" were even more solidly reinforced after World War I plunged the South into yet another frontier era; like much of the Western world, the South was beset by an ideological crisis that Cash characterizes as a "vast mass neurosis" (*MS* 292). "Strange new ideas and faiths and systems were sweeping through the Western lands, and all the old ideas and faiths and systems were under attack, in danger, crumbling or even vanishing in places," Cash writes. "Everywhere were doubt and change and chaos and flux and violence" (*MS* 293). Already resistant to change and new ideas, the South responded to the cultural crisis with a passionate revival of regional loyalty. "The stream of fears and hates generated by the war and conditions in the Western world poured back within the frame of the South itself, fixed upon Southern themes and translated itself into Southern terms, met and merged with certain rising fears and hates native to the old Southern pattern, and so contributed to the renewal of a concern like that which had reigned in the years before 1900—a concern which fixed itself precisely on the line of the old Southern patriotism and the will to the preservation of the ancient pattern" (*MS* 296).

In no area of southern life did that fanatic loyalty rage as it did in race relations, seen visibly in the rebirth of the Ku Klux Klan. So powerful did the Klan emerge at this time that Cash goes so far as to suggest that in the 1920s the Klansman embodies the essentials of the southern mind. Cash describes the Klan's organization in terms of a body made up of the entire population of white southerners:

> Its body was made up of the common whites, industrial and rural. But its blood, if I may continue the figure, came from the upper orders. And its bony framework and nervous system, the people who held it together and co-ordinated and directed it, were very near to being coextensive with the established leadership of the South. People of great prominence in industry and business, indeed, were often though not always, chary about actually belonging to it, but they usually maintained liaison with it through their underlings and the politicians. And its ranks swarmed with little business men. Except in North Carolina and Virginia, the rural clergy belonged to it or had traffic with it almost *en masse,* and even in those two states the same

thing was true in many districts. It was true, too, in many towns throughout the South, and everywhere the great body of the ministers either smiled benignly on it or carefully kept their mouths shut about it. Planters joined it by the wholesale, and more often than not worked with it when they did not join it. So did the landowning farmers generally; indeed, in proportion to their numbers, these perhaps went into it or sympathized with it more generally than even the unpropertied commons. (*MS* 335–36)

Incorporating the entire white South, the Klan manifests characteristic southern hates and fears within "the ancient Southern pattern of high romantic histrionics, violence, and mass coercion of the scapegoat and the heretic" (*MS* 337). Cash identifies the Ku Klux Klan as a folk movement "at least as fully as such as the Nazi movement in Germany, to which it was not without kinship" (*MS* 335).

In equating the Klan—and by extension the entire white South—with the Nazis, Cash points to what he has been arguing all along in *The Mind of the South:* that the South and Nazi Germany share similar ideological underpinnings and authoritarian structures; and further, that the modern South might be devolving into a dangerous version of Nazi barbarism. Rather than seeing the traditional South as a bulwark against the frightening extremes of modernity, as the Agrarians did, Cash sees the traditional South as not traditional at all but actually a frightening version of modern authoritarianism. Cash's rebuke to the Agrarians might best be understood as his reconfiguration of the Agrarians' geocultural axis. Agrarian thinking, as we have seen, links the South with premodern Europe (East) and the North with unchecked modernity (West), while Cash, using the same East-West axis, also links the South with Europe, but with a very different Europe—the Europe of Nazi Germany.

Cash's suggestion that the South might devolve further, approaching the extremes of Nazi Germany, largely derives from what he sees as southern culture's stranglehold on thought and expression, seen most visibly in its ongoing demands for conformity and allegiance to the southern way of life—what Cash calls the "savage ideal." That ideal, he argues, reached terrifying proportions during Reconstruction, when tolerance "was pretty well extinguished all along the line, and conformity made a nearly universal law. Criticism, analysis, detachment, all those activities and attitudes so necessary to the healthy development of any civilization, every one of them took on the aspect of high and aggravated treason" (*MS* 135). No area of life escaped regulation:

> Here, under pressure of what was felt to be a matter of life and death, was that old line between what was Southern and what was not, etched, as it were, in fire and carried through every department of life. Here were the ideas and loyalties of the apotheosized past fused into the tightest coherence and endowed with all the binding emotional and intellectual power of any tribal complex of the Belgian Congo. Here was that mighty frame the Democratic Party, as potent an instrument of regimentation as any totemic society that ever existed. In a word, here, explicitly defined in every great essential, defined in feeling down to the last detail, was what one must think and say and do. (*MS* 134)

Cash here describes his totalitarian nightmare, a South in which everyone became "in all their attitudes, professions, and actions, virtual replicas of each other" (*MS* 91). In perhaps his most damning indictment of traditional southern culture, Cash writes that the savage ideal was established in the South "as it had not been established in any Western people since the decay of medieval feudalism, and almost as truly as it is established today in Fascist Italy, in Nazi Germany, in Soviet Russia—and so paralyzed Southern culture at the root" (*MS* 134).

In his analysis of southern authoritarianism, Cash exposes what he sees as perhaps the greatest irony of southern history: that southern culture's rhetoric of fervent traditionalism, which opposes the traditional South to the modern state, masks the South's own authoritarian system, mirroring that of the modern totalitarian state. This masking of the South's underlying authoritarian structures explains why southerners could rage against Nazi racism while being racist themselves, blind to the similarities they shared with the Nazis. It also explains why Cash, who stood fundamentally opposed to the Nashville Agrarians, defends them against the charge that they are "consciously inclined to Fascism" (*MS* 382). In Cash's eyes, the Agrarians are like most other southerners, mystified by the southern mind and blind to the faults of the southern system; while not out-and-out Fascists, they nonetheless promote a way of life sharing ideological underpinnings with Fascist authoritarianism, all the while remaining unaware of those underpinnings.

Near the end of *The Mind of the South*, Cash surveys the contemporary South, finding reason for both hope and regret. On the one hand, he notices signs of new habits of analysis and perception that are starting to undermine the authority of the southern mind. As evidence, he points to a surge of sophisticated southern literature, improvements in education, a rise in unionization and mill organizing, a growing trend of sociological analysis of southern society (particularly by the Chapel Hill sociologists), a decline in Klan membership, and a weakening of southern fundamentalism. In one of his more hopeful moments, Cash suggests that it is possible that the modern mind has furtively "plant[ed] the tiny germ of inward doubt" (*MS* 341) into the minds of southerners, an initial step toward clear-sighted awareness of self and region. In another moment of uncharacteristic hopefulness, Cash goes so far as to say that perhaps even the wave of enthusiasm for the Klan and religious fundamentalism in the 1920s might be evidence of the southern mind's undoing, since perhaps these proponents "proceeded from that distrust of themselves which I have before noted in Southerners, and represented an ultimately unsuccessful attempt to draw themselves back upon the ancient pattern to escape the feeling that, against their wills, the seeping in of change might claim them also" (*MS* 341).

Despite these visible signs of hope in the contemporary South, Cash finally concludes that the ancient pattern is holding, that the cracks he has found in its walls are not gaping fissures that could bring down the structure. Moreover, he sees compelling signs that the southern mind is forcefully reasserting itself. He notes gloomily that the contemporary South seems to be living less by the longstanding southern virtues of honor, courtesy, and bravery and more by its traditional vices, which he enumerates as "violence, intolerance, aversion and suspicion toward new ideas, an incapacity for analysis, an inclination to act from feeling rather than from thought, an exaggerated individualism and a too narrow concept of social responsibility, attachment to fictions and false values, above all too great attachment to racial values and a tendency to justify cruelty and injustice in the name of those values, sentimentality and a lack of realism" (*MS* 428–29). Particularly disheartening to Cash was the South's turn against Roosevelt and the New Deal, an about-face he sees as the South's return to the "old complete individualism of economic outlook" and "the ancient incapacity of the great body of Southerners to examine and analyze a case realistically even when their own fate hinged upon it, the tendency to take the easiest answer as explaining all their ills" (*MS* 398). Even more disturbing was the failure of the region's intellectual leaders (the Chapel Hill sociologists among others) to reach the general public with their message and to effect meaningful change. This situation, he writes, "was the final great tragedy of the South as it stood in 1940," and he elaborates: "The tragedy was that this leadership was almost wholly unarticulated with the body of the South. If the people of the region were not entirely unaffected by what the men who represented the new analytical and inquiring spirit were doing, they were still affected by it only remotely and sporadically" (*MS* 418–19).

Looming behind Cash's commentary and adding to Cash's urgency to break the stranglehold of southern authoritarianism with *The Mind of the South* was the European war then under way. In his final paragraph, Cash looks forward, with much trepidation, to the fast-approaching time when the South will face an inescapable challenge:

> In the coming days, and probably soon, [the South] is likely to have to prove its capacity for adjustment far beyond what has been true in the past. And in that time I shall hope, as its loyal son, that its virtues will tower over and conquer its faults and have the making of the Southern world to come. But of the future I shall venture no definite prophecies. It would be a brave man who would venture them in any case. It would be a madman who would venture them in face of the forces sweeping over the world in the fateful year of 1940. (*MS* 429)

Cash's final words carry forward the vision of *The Mind of the South*, expressing his fear that the world war, and the crushing power of the Third Reich, would someday soon usher the South into a new "frontier" experience. Cash was not envisioning an invasion of Nazi soldiers, but an invasion of Nazi ideology that would only strengthen the power of southern authoritarianism; that invasion, he feared, would sink the South back into frontier barbarism and steel the southern mind against developing an enlightened, critical sensibility. The virtues of the South would then certainly not "tower over and conquer its faults" but would fall before them, the ancient pattern once more exerting its powerful control.[20]

Cash clearly hoped that *The Mind of the South* would help undo that ancient pattern and free the southern mind from the bonds of authoritarianism. Cash hoped to do that not only through his narrative of southern history but also through his skeptical analysis, encapsulating precisely the type of mind that Cash hoped the southern mind would become. At the same time, however, he concealed that analysis with the mask of the down-home storyteller spinning out yarns with rhetorical flourish, hoping his history would engage everyday people and not merely academics. Indeed, with *The Mind of the South* he hoped to provide the leadership that he believed academics, by and large, were failing to provide the South. As Anne Goodwyn Jones argues, Cash strove to be something of a Gramscian "organic intellectual," one who drew from his or her humble origins in order to speak to the people and whose work was deeply involved not merely with scholarship but with material conditions. Jones insightfully suggests that the story of the Trojan Horse is one way to understand how Cash hoped his modern dismantling of the southern mind would itself work its way into the readers' minds: "Disguised—by means of its rhetorical strategies—as a gift, *The Mind of the South* could, once 'opened' and read, give birth to a new and alien way of thinking, accomplishing the political end of restructuring not only the mind, or hegemony, of the South but its political economy as well."[21] The German word *Gift*, one might add to Jones's analysis, means "poison," another way to understand Cash's subversive goal: he wanted to poison the body of southern authoritarianism.

Given this goal, it is not surprising that *The Mind of the South* is not a full and complete history of the region, nor a traditional intellectual history along the lines of, say, Perry Miller's *New England Mind*, which was published two years before Cash's book. With the threat of world war looming, and with Cash unearthing what he saw as frightening ideological connections between the South and Nazi Germany, Cash keeps his focus tightly on the South's authoritarian system and those who, blinded by its ideological mystification, came most to support it: the common whites. Cash does not focus on the plight of blacks and women, because for the most part they remained outside of the power structure. In this, Cash shares much with the contemporary commentators on the Third Reich, most of whom closely and urgently examined the authoritarian apparatus erected by the Nazis, paying more attention to how that apparatus worked to blind its citizens to its terrors than to how that apparatus excluded and marginalized its enemies. And, finally, Cash shares much with the many social psychologists and psychoanalysts of his day who were exploring Fascist and Nazi "minds." Indeed, it is alongside these other deeply ideological and profoundly polemical interpretations of authoritarianism that *The Mind of the South* is best read.

Several months after the publication of *The Mind of the South*, Cash committed suicide in Mexico City, apparently convinced that he was being pursued by Nazi agents. Whatever dark obsessions drove him into madness, it does not seem far-fetched to think that Cash feared the Nazis had targeted him because they had read and understood well the danger of *The Mind of the South,* a book working to unmask the savagery of the authoritarian state, both in Germany and in the American South.

3

PASTORALISM AND EXTINCTION

WILLIAM ALEXANDER PERCY

The same year that Cash's *Mind of the South* was published, so too was another deeply personal and profoundly polemical work analyzing southern traditionalism, William Alexander Percy's *Lanterns on the Levee: Recollections of a Planter's Son* (1941). Working from a perspective similar to that of the Nashville Agrarians, positing traditional southern society against the horrors of modernity as seen most frighteningly in European Fascism, Percy reached an entirely different conclusion from Cash's: to his eyes, not only was southern traditionalism fundamentally opposed to the modern industrial state but it was entirely free from its taints. Unlike the Agrarians, however, Percy found that in a time when modernity had already completed its sweeping destruction of the Mississippi Delta (and, more generally, of the South), the virtues of the southern way of life were entirely irrelevant, as was, in this context, his autobiography itself, which he designated in his foreword as merely "a pilgrim's script—one man's field-notes of a land not far but quite unknown—valueless except as that man loved the country he passed through and its folk, and except as he willed to tell the truth" (*LL* n.p.). Rather than seeking to reconstruct the fallen culture and its values, as the Agrarians tried to do, Percy sought to memorialize southern traditionalism in an elegiac work focused on his own life and that of his family. With the war to defend southern traditionalism already lost, Percy presented himself as the weary soldier looking back at the hard-fought struggle and its heroes, assured that "it is better to remember, to be sure of the good that was, rather than of the evil that is, to watch the spread and pattern of the game that is past rather than engage feebly in the present play. It was a stout world thus far, peopled with all manner of gracious and kindly and noble personages—these seem rather a pygmy tribe" (*LL* n.p). Before the final passing, Percy looked inward to the comforting world of memory, his only refuge. "So while the world I know is crashing to bits, and what with the noise and the cryings-out no man could hear a trumpet blast, much less an idle evening reverie," Percy writes, "I will indulge a heart beginning to be fretful by repeating to it the stories it knows and loves of my own country and my own people" (*LL* n.p.).

Lanterns on the Levee is thus Percy's elegy for his Lost Cause, not the Lost Cause of the South following the Civil War, but the Lost Cause of southern traditionalism in the twentieth century, an era dominated by war and the rise of the modern industrial state. But as we shall see, Percy's most crucial elegiac strategy—constructing the strict opposition between the rural innocence of traditional culture and the urban evil of the modernity—ultimately collapses in upon itself, so that *Lanterns on the Levee*, for all its praise of southern traditionalism, in the end ironically suggests conclusions not unlike those reached by W. J. Cash in *The Mind of the South*. The traditional South, both of these texts end up illustrating, has less to do with pre-industrial Europe than it does with the modern state; and even more disturbingly, the South's racial ideology and codes come close to mirroring those of Nazi Germany. From Cash's perspective, Percy would stand right alongside the Agrarians, as both he and they, in their common blindness to the dangers of the southern system, unwittingly promoted a traditional way of life that was structured by ideology mirroring that of the modern state they railed against.

—✷ ✷ ✷ ✷—

Given Percy's numerous trips to Europe and his abiding interest in classicism, it is not surprising that Europe infuses Percy's imaginative vision.[1] Percy first went to Europe in 1904, after graduating from the University of the South, spending a year visiting France, Italy, Egypt, Germany, and Switzerland. He returned to Europe often throughout his life, finding respite in his travels from the rigid confines of Greenville, Mississippi, society and his pressing responsibilities as a lawyer and planter. Mediterranean culture he found particularly appealing. Capri and Taormina were two of his favorite destinations; there, far from the prying eyes of his hometown, Will communed with other writers and artists and enjoyed the social ease and openness of the large homosexual communities.² There Percy found the pastoral innocence for which he always yearned.

Of course, very little of Europe in the twentieth century was a pastoral paradise, as Percy knew, and his participation in World War I, first in Belgium as a relief worker and then later in France as a combatant, underscored modernity's threat to traditional order. Significant in terms of his later conceptualization of modernity's barbarism, Percy's war experiences intensified his dislike for Germany and Teutonic culture, which came to represent for him the worst of the modern menace. Jay Tolson observes that unlike many Americans of the period, Percy felt that America's entry into World War I was justified; he saw Germany as the aggressor threatening Western civilization, and France and England as the Western world's defenders.³ Percy's relief work in Belgium confirmed his feelings about German culpability; he was deeply affected by the harsh rule of the German occupiers, particularly the forced transportation of men to labor camps and the widespread hunger resulting from the tight food restrictions. His later combat service added to his ill will toward German aggression and the devastating destruction it had wrought upon the continent. When Percy heard that the armistice had been signed, he wrote to his mother, signaling the depth of his feelings about the war, that he was having a hard time realizing that he was "playing in the last act of the world's greatest tragedy" (*LL* 213). Percy felt the impact of that tragedy, particularly in his antipathy for Germany, for the rest of his life.

That antipathy evolved into something close to rage after Hitler came to power in 1933. As later became evident in *Lanterns on the Levee*, Percy saw Nazism as an extreme manifestation of the modern state, terrifying and barbaric in its power and social control. He was deeply troubled when, in 1934, his adopted son, the future novelist Walker Percy (Walker and his two brothers had moved in with Percy after the death of their parents), sought his permission for a summer trip to Germany sponsored by one of his professors at the University of North Carolina.⁴ Percy urged Walker to go to France instead but eventually gave in and allowed him to make the trip. He probably regretted his decision. Walker returned from Germany deeply impressed by Nazi culture, for reasons not unlike those that had attracted many Europeans to Fascism: Nazism gave a dispirited people identity, purpose, discipline, and pride.⁵ In Bonn, Walker befriended a member of the Hitler Jugend and was bowled over by the young man's enthusiasm and commitment. "He was *not* like an American Boy Scout," Walker said years later in an interview. "He was dead serious, with this impressive uniform, and he was graduating from the Hitler Jugend and going into the Schutzstaffel. I remember he talked about the Teutonic knights, and taking the oath at Marienberg, the ancient castle. There was a tremendous mystique there."[6] If Walker ever shared his feelings with his adoptive father (Walker later saw the error of his ways but remained haunted by the fact that he had been enticed by Nazi authoritarianism), certainly Percy would have pointed out the threat to traditional society posed by Nazism and other mass movements supported by the modern industrial state.

Percy's sympathy for and allegiances with what he later came to see as the opposite of Nazism—the traditional cultures of "old Europe," untouched by the transformations wrought by modern politics and economics—can be seen in his poetry written before *Lanterns on the Levee*. His verse harkens back to classical times, peopled with shepherds and satyrs and the like; typically the poems involve tensions between carnal and spiritual love, youth and age, individual and community duty.[7] Not surprisingly, critics sympathetic to modernist experimentation dismissed Percy's verse, zeroing in often on its archaic diction and manner. To Faulkner, Percy as poet seemed like "a little boy closing his eyes against the dark of modernity which threatens the bright simplicity and the colorful romantic pageantry of the middle ages with which his eyes are full."[8] Percy, of course, chafed against such criticism, and in a letter to Donald Davidson (18 May 1928) he bemoaned his standing with the critics: "I get so damned tired of people assuming that because I use medieval and Greek themes, I am interested only in archaeology or history or literature. As far as I can recall neither Shakespeare nor Milton nor Dante nor any of the great Greeks used contemporary themes to any considerable extent, and yet their emotion and thought did not lag behind the emotion and thought of their own time."[9]

Percy could make such a statement because he knew, even if the critics did not, that his verse frequently derived from and explored contemporary issues, even when cloaked in faraway times and archaic language. Such was the case with "Enzio's Kingdom," Percy's most ambitious poem. A long dramatic monologue spoken by Frederick II's son Enzio, recalling both his father's heroic efforts to unite thirteenth-century Europe and his own despairing sense of uselessness, "Enzio's Kingdom" owed its inspiration, as Percy himself admitted, in part to Woodrow Wilson's futile efforts to unite the world with the League of Nations.[10] The poem was also inspired by Percy's father, LeRoy, who in Percy's view had against all odds struggled to maintain traditional order and community in Greenville by holding in check the rebellious poor whites who were disrupting the town's social and political structures. Just as Frederick was ultimately defeated, so too was LeRoy Percy, both victims of an increasingly powerful mass culture that refused to recognize the authority and vision of the traditional order and its leaders.

While Percy clearly intended to praise his father, together with the traditional order for which he stood, his retelling of the story of Frederick II unearths a dark undercurrent suggesting the dangerous extremes to which traditionalism might be taken by zealous proponents. As Lewis Lawson observes, the reign of Frederick II can be read less as the defense of traditionalism than as its death, with Frederick's millennial vision ultimately reconfiguring the structures of the traditional order into those of the modern authoritarian state.[11] Compelling Frederick's aims at conquest was his belief that he was fulfilling divine prophecy and that ultimately he would purge the world of the Antichrist (the pope). "Frederick, in short," Lawson writes, "sets in the European imagination the legend of the secular leader who comes in the fullness of a known scheme; who commands absolute obedience; who in order to fulfill his destiny must purge his people of their traditional institutions (so that his personality, the only institution, will expand to its possibility and) so that they can respond to the truths of their blood; who will lead them to victory if they are worthy or to destruction (the very fact of which would be proof that they had not risen to his visionary demands)" (400–401). As Lawson admits, it is not clear whether Percy meant to invoke this reading of Frederick II in writing about his father through him; even if he did not, however, linking LeRoy Percy with Frederick II at the very least suggests the possibility that embedded in southern traditionalism might be the driving force of modernity—a suggestion that also haunts *Lanterns on the Levee*.

Percy was deeply shaken when the European war broke out in 1939, and the war profoundly affected his work on his autobiography.[12] On the one hand, the war spurred Percy to write, as he saw *Lanterns on the Levee* as another means to draw attention to the Nazi threat. Lewis Baker notes that in early drafts of his chapter "1914–1916" Percy made specific comparisons between American isolationism during World War I and in 1939 and argued, in Baker's words, that "the Germans were still barbarians, and excoriat[ed] Americans who refused to face the current menace" (166). On the other hand, the war also distracted him, drawing him away from his writing; as the European situation worsened, Percy fell into depression, with everything seeming insignificant in the face of the crisis. In June 1940, in the midst of a productive period of writing and revising, Percy set aside the unfinished manuscript and apparently contacted the federal government about volunteering to help in the preparations for war. With the war dominating his thoughts, Percy realized that he might never finish the manuscript, and he fluctuated between burning it and submitting it unfinished. On the day Paris fell, 14 June 1940, Percy wrote to his friend Huger Jervey that he hoped to get the manuscript off to the publisher and that "it will be rotten and I don't care—nothing seems worthwhile but the war."[13] Percy ended up not submitting the unfinished manuscript and instead hid it in a sofa, where it was later found by David Cohn, who persuaded Percy to complete it. Percy soon after departed for the Grand Canyon, where he hoped to write without distraction. It was not his first choice, as he wrote his cousin Janet (28 August 1940): "I wish there was the old Europe to go to for six months. . . . But our world is definitely gone, and I feel superfluous, if not posthumous."[14] Once the manuscript was complete, Percy made another attempt to join the war effort (nothing had come of his earlier offer to the federal government), this time contacting the Canadian government. Nothing came of that request either.

Not only did wartime developments haunt Percy during the writing of *Lanterns on the Levee* but wartime issues, particularly those significant to the question of American intervention, affected the manuscript's final shape. Following the advice of his editor at Knopf, Harold Straus, Percy agreed to make two significant cuts from the final manuscript: several World War I letters from the chapter "At the Front" and a chapter entitled "The White Plague," a discussion of the deleterious effects of civilization upon native life, written after Percy visited Samoa in 1936. Straus suggested cutting the letters from "At the Front" because he feared that their graphic descriptions of battlefield suffering might encourage American isolationism, something neither Straus nor Percy supported. No doubt Straus insisted that "The White Plague" be cut because, as Lewis Baker observes (168), he did not want Western civilization taken to task in wartime for exploits overseas that smacked of imperialism.

In its final shape, *Lanterns on the Levee* focuses on the conflict between southern traditionalism and modernity, often expressed in a pastoral opposition between rural innocence and urban evil. From Percy's perspective, there was no healthy middle ground between the two cultures, no possibility that traditional society could successfully absorb fundamental axioms of modernity and still remain traditional. And he knew that all was lost, that forces of modernity had already swept through and polluted the traditional South, including his beloved Mississippi Delta, its once gracious, amiable, and mannered life now a grotesque combination of the traditional and the modern.[15] There is no Bakhtinian laughter in Percy's grotesque, only horror at a world become monstrous:

> The old Southern way of life in which I had been reared existed no more and its values were ignored or derided. Negroes used to be servants, now they were problems; manners used to be a branch of morals, now they were merely bad; poverty used to be worn with style and dignity, now it was a stigma of failure; politics used to be the study of men proud and jealous of America's honor, now it was a game played by self-seekers which no man need bother his head about; where there had been an accepted pattern of living, there was no pattern whatsoever. (*LL* 312)

Without a pattern of conduct and morality, what Percy sees as traditional values and morality have collapsed, leaving the culture careening madly into the future. "Behind us a culture lies dying," Percy writes, "before us the forces of the unknown industrial world gather for catastrophe" (*LL* 24). In this world, "the good die when they should live, the evil live when they should die; heroes perish and cowards escape; noble efforts do not succeed because they are noble, and wickedness is not consumed in its own nature" (*LL* 154).

The only refuges for the honorable person in this blasted world, Percy argues throughout *Lanterns*, are the small world of the self and the almost as small immediate world that the self inhabits. The individual needs to keep both pure and undefiled by holding fast to personal ideals of honor and integrity and by performing small, everyday acts of goodness, what Percy deems "minute heroic efforts" (*LL* n.p.), rather than by engaging in grand social and political schemes. In this, Percy casts his lot with the emperor Marcus Aurelius, whose *Meditations* Percy read throughout his life; and it was his father LeRoy whom Percy found the living example of Aurelius's stoicism. Percy heartily endorses the observations made by his father in a letter to a supporter after his humbling 1912 electoral loss to James K. Vardaman:

> If I can keep this small corner of the United States in which I reside, comparatively clean and decent in politics and fit for a man to live in, and in such condition that he may not be ashamed to pass it on to his children, I will have accomplished all that I hope to do.
>   A good deal has been written about "shooting at the stars." I have never thought much of that kind of marksmanship. It may be characterized by imagination, it is lacking in common sense. I rather think it is best to draw a bead on something that you have a chance to hit. To keep any part of Mississippi clean and decent in these days, is a job that no man may deem too small. (*LL* 152)

"No matter how far defeat pierces," Percy writes, echoing his father, the interior life of the honorable person remains unassailable and thus untouched: "when all is lost, it stands fast" (*LL* 313).

With cultural and individual purity as his defining virtues, Percy attempts in *Lanterns* to portray the Delta's traditional culture and its aristocracy (and most significantly his father) as pure in motive and deed.[16] Percy employs a number of narrative strategies to cleanse the messiness of history, one of the most important being to position himself above the fray of his narrative. Throughout *Lanterns* Percy observes and comments upon traditionalism and modernity while standing in various elevated places—on levees, atop buildings, on mountaintops. From this virtuous "high ground," Percy delivers stern judgment on the sordid world of modernity. "Like gods we looked down," Percy writes, describing his visit to the Empire State Building, and like a god he passes withering judgment on those below him: "We peered into the chasms they had made and saw long files of metal beetles trekking a bare yard when the chains of rubies turned to emeralds. And then we spied the lesser insects on the bottom. We watched their tiny scurryings, their nervous sorties and returns, their feverish small haste, and their bewildered pauses" (*LL* 342, 343).

Percy's comments from atop the Empire State Building point to the distortions that frequently come when he passes judgments from on high, reducing the individuals walking the streets of New York to an indistinguishable mass—and a mass not of people but of insects. From the distanced stance he repeatedly assumes, Percy intends his pronouncements, such as his dismissal of New York as "the city of Babel on Manhattan" (*LL* 342), to stand as unquestionable and unchallengeable; from there, he confidently disparages American culture, poor whites, the *Chicago Defender*, and everything else he finds offensive. Jonathan Daniels probably had Percy's elevated, authoritative stance in mind when he wrote that Percy was "more nearly a citizen of the solar system" than of Mississippi.[17]

Besides attacking modernity, Percy praises southern traditionalism from the same elevated perspective, leading him to simplify human and cultural complexity into static images. To Percy's eyes, southern traditionalism stands as an exemplar of pastoral harmony, illustrated most clearly in his discussion of sharecropping and tenant farming. Literally and imaginatively far from the fields in which tenants toiled, Percy concludes quite simply that "profit-sharing is the most moral system under which human beings can work together" and that "if it were accepted in principle by capital and labor, our industrial troubles would largely cease" (*LL* 278). "Our plantation system," he adds, "seems to me to offer as humane, just, self-respecting, and cheerful a method of earning a living as human beings are likely to devise. I watch the limber-jointed, oily-black, well-fed, decently clothed peasants on Trail Lake and feel sorry for the telephone girls, the clerks in chain stores, the office help, the unskilled laborers everywhere—not only for their poor and fixed wage but for their slave routine, their joyless habits of work, and their insecurity" (*LL* 280). Since he owned a plantation but lived in town, it was of course easy for Percy to reach these conclusions; away from its everyday operations, Percy could readily represent his plantation as a pastoral paradise, peopled with happy, fit, well-fed, and nicely clothed peasants. And it was just as easy from afar to rail against the antipastoral hell of modern industrialism, where in Percy's eyes suffered a mass of exploited urban wage earners.

Percy directs some of his most withering ire at those who criticized sharecropping and tenant farming as economic exploitation, particularly those from outside the Delta, whom he views as invading marauders of modernity. Percy angrily dismisses the report of a sociologist from Chapel Hill who completed a socioeconomic analysis of Percy's Trail Lake plantation, finding it ludicrous that the author reduced the workings of the plantation to simple numbers and statistics. Such analysis, Percy believes, communicates nothing of what he sees as the humane principles structuring the system and the valuable benefits provided to the workers—job security, long periods of inactivity, the noblesse of generous planters. Ironically, Percy here reads his own elevated position onto the sociologist, suggesting that his abstracted, distorted view of the plantation derives largely from his standing too far above it.

For Percy, the Chapel Hill sociologist and other critics of sharecropping and tenant farming represent the social planning of the modern state, which he believed was leading the nation toward the most complete manifestation of social control—totalitarianism. "I woke to the discovery that in pseudo-intellectual circles from Moscow to Santa Monica the Improvers-of-the-world had found something new in the South to shudder over," Percy writes. "Twenty years ago it had been peonage. In the dark days when the collapse of the slave-trade had almost bankrupted good old New England, it had been slavery. Now it was the poor share-croppers—share-croppers over the whole South, but especially in the Delta. That very partnership of Fafar's [Percy's grandfather, William Alexander Percy] which had seemed to me so just and practical now was being denounced as avaricious and slick—it was Mr. Roosevelt's 'infamous system'" (*LL* 281).

While holding fast to the image of pastoral harmony, Percy at the same time admits that abuses sometimes occur in the sharecropping and tenant-farming system, not because the system is flawed but because its operators sometimes are. Those owners who abuse the system, Percy makes clear, are not from the true planter class but are modern interlopers masquerading as the aristocracy, speculators who have bought up land for profit and care nothing about the trust and obligations that property ownership entails:

> Property is a form of power. Some people regard it as an opportunity for profit, some as a trust; in the former it breeds hubris, in the latter, noblesse oblige. The landed gentry of Fafar's time were of an ancient lineage and in a sober God-fearing tradition. Today many have thought to acquire membership in that older caste by acquiring land, naked land, without those ancestral hereditaments of virtue which change dirt into a way of life. On the plantation where there is stealing from the Negro you will generally find the owner to be a little fellow operating, as the saying goes, "on a shoe-string," or a nouveau riche, or a landlord on the make, tempted to take more than his share because of the mortgage that makes his title and his morals insecure. These, in their pathetic ambition to imitate what they do not understand, acquire power and use it for profit; for them the share-cropper system affords a golden opportunity rarely passed up. (*LL* 283)

Here is another frightening version of the southern grotesque into which Percy sees the modern South evolving, with outsiders, disguised as true-blooded nobility, infiltrating and corrupting traditional culture.

By defending the system of sharecropping and tenant farming while attacking its interloping abusers, Percy upholds his pastoral image of the plantation and Delta life. He uses a similar strategy to explain away abuses arising from southern traditionalism: he attributes flaws in the system to outsiders, forces of modernity, who are disrupting the traditional South and its stability. In terms of the Delta, Percy singles out the large number of poor whites who have migrated into the area from the hill country. Their presence has altered the Delta's social and political landscape, undermining its once stable foundations and pushing it toward chaos. Before poor whites began drifting into the Delta, Percy argues, life was orderly and tranquil, whites and blacks living together without rancor, everyone knowing his or her place and everyone staying there, everyone living gracefully by a commonly accepted social code manifested in southern manners. Two races set off by an easily recognized color line made the social structure simple: "White folks and colored folks—that's what we were—and some of us were nice and some weren't" (*LL* 231). Problems that occurred, as Percy's final observation suggests, derived merely from the vagaries of human nature that were present in all social systems.

The coming of the poor whites, however, drastically disrupted this social stability, including upsetting the racial order by introducing a new breed of white people into the mix. To Percy's eyes, poor whites are not an economic class but a distinct race whose bloodlines consist mainly of degenerate Anglo-Saxon stock. Poor whites are "a nice study in heredity and environment," Percy comments (*LL* 19), sounding a good bit like a eugenicist, their devolution over generations illustrating the destructive effects of inferior genes and horrible living conditions. "If it was ever good," Percy writes of poor whites' blood, "the virus of poverty, malnutrition, and inter-breeding has done its degenerative work: the present breed is probably the most unprepossessing on the broad face of the ill-populated earth" (*LL* 19–20).

The arrival of the poor whites skewed the Delta's biracial order; now there were three significant races, and skin color was no longer the universal marker of racial identity. "The newcomers weren't foreigners or Jews, they were an alien breed of Anglo-Saxon" (*LL* 230), Percy writes, locating the destructive power of poor whites in their whiteness. Previous newcomers—foreigners and Jews—were easily visible and could be easily "placed"; poor whites, however, were invisible in their whiteness. This invisibility allowed the poor whites to go unnoticed as they moved into the Delta and wreaked their destructive work on the region's social and political structures. Percy describes the infiltration:

> Unbeknownst, strangers had drifted in since the war—from the hills, from the North, from all sorts of odd places where they hadn't succeeded or hadn't been wanted. We had changed our country attractively for them. Malaria had been about stamped out; electric fans and ice had lessened the terror of our intolerable summer heat; we had good roads and drainage and schools, and our lands were the most fertile in the world. We had made the Delta a good place in which to live by our determination and our ability to endure hardships, and now other folks were attracted by the result of our efforts. The town was changing, but so insidiously that the old-timers could feel but could not analyze the change. (*LL* 230)

The changes being wrought by the poor whites became readily apparent once they started organizing politically and voting, a flexing of muscle that eventually threatened to undo the ruling elite's traditional control.

As he characteristically does with other threats to southern traditionalism, Percy contextualizes the poor whites' disruption of Delta society within the contemporary global disorder, and particularly the war in Europe. He equates the rise of the poor whites with the emergence of radical democracy and equalitarianism, which he identifies as two of modernity's fundamental ideologies that are dismantling the hierarchal order of traditional societies. His discussion of his father's unsuccessful Senate campaign records his horror at democracy's corrosive power. At one point, Percy describes his feelings as he looks out at the crowd gathered at a political rally, writing that he feels as if he is staggering in a nightmare, knowing that this "gang of poor degenerates" has a voice in determining the election. "They were the sort of people that lynch Negroes, that mistake hoodlumism for wit, and cunning for intelligence, that attend revivals and fight and fornicate in the bushes afterwards," Percy writes. "They were undiluted Anglo-Saxons. They were the sovereign voter. It was so horrible it seemed unreal" (*LL* 149).

Percy's disdain for democracy centers on what he sees as its pernicious philosophy of equalitarianism. "In time we are all good democrats; in the manger we look the same and in the grave," Percy writes, taking his stand against the philosophical basis of democratic government. "I rejoice to be of a caste which, though shaken and scattered, refuses to call itself Demos"

(*LL* 60). Demos, Percy makes clear, is wreaking havoc not merely in Mississippi but throughout the world:

> True, it was not the South alone that had been killed, but its ideals and its kind of people the world over. The bottom rail was on top, not only in Mississippi, but from Los Angeles to New York, from London to Moscow. In different quarters the effects were dissimilar, but the cause was always the same. In Russia, Germany, and Italy Demos, having slain its aristocrats and intellectuals and realizing its own incompetence to guide or protect itself, had submitted to tyrants who laughed at the security virtues and practiced the most vile of the survival virtues with gangster cynicism. In the democracies Demos had been so busy providing itself with leisure and luxury it had forgotten that hardihood and discipline are not ornaments but weapons. Everywhere the security virtues appeared as weaknesses and the survival virtues as strength and foresight. (*LL* 312)

In his suggestion here that totalitarianism evolves from the social chaos wrought by radical democracy, Percy both echoes the political thinking of the Agrarians and carries their thinking to new extremes. These extremes become clearly visible when, discussing the enfranchisement of poor whites (the secret ballot another manifestation of their invisibility), he equates their electoral power with the authoritarianism of Nazi Germany and Soviet Russia: "It was my first sight of the rise of the masses, but not my last. Now we have Russia and Germany, we have the insolence of organized labor and the insolence of capital, examples both of the insolence of the parvenu; we have the rise of the masses from Mississippi east, and back again west to Mississippi. The herd is on the march, and when it stampedes, there's blood galore and beauty is china under its hoofs" (*LL* 153).

Besides by voting, poor whites, according to Percy, destroy traditionalist society by organizing themselves into the Ku Klux Klan, another force of modernity. In discussing its disruptive power, Percy underscores that the new Klan, begun in 1915 by Colonel William Joseph Simmons, has nothing to do with the Klan that held sway during Reconstruction. The original KKK, Percy argues, was an admirable force of law and traditional order and kept the South from sliding into complete chaos after the Civil War. Whatever its tactics in enforcing order, the old Klan for Percy had remained steadfastly honorable in its defense of traditional society. The new Klan, in contrast, is for Percy another force of modern misrule, "a money-making scheme without ideals or ideas" and "not even a bastard of the old organization" (*LL* 232). As poor whites had earlier drifted unnoticed into the Delta, the new Klan too had begun its work unseen; rather than donning robes (which, while keeping Klansmen's faces hidden, would have made their group's presence visible), the new Klansmen schemed behind closed doors, quietly working to place their members in key positions in the city government. Only after one of the Klan's members invited a national organizer to speak at a rally did the group's presence in Greenville become known to the general population. Percy sees the Klan's secret organizing in Greenville as another manifestation of the worldwide destruction of traditional order by authoritarian forces, the Klan's strategy for seizing power "a fifth-column tactic before there was a Hitler" and its rhetoric "an example of Nazi propaganda before there were Nazis" (*LL* 232, 233).

By equating the Klan with the Nazis, Percy signals that the battle for Greenville's political future in 1922 is best understood in terms of the current world war: forces of barbarism were at work that must be stopped.[18] "It's hard to conceive of the mumbo-jumbo ritual of the Klan and its half-wit principles—only less absurd than the Nazi principles of Aryan superiority and lebensraum—as worthy of an adult mind's attention," Percy writes. "But when your living, your self-respect, and your life are threatened, you don't laugh at that which threatens. If you have either sense or courage you fight it. We fought, and it was high time someone did" (*LL* 235). But fighting the Klan proves difficult, as Percy makes clear, because the organization is indeed the Invisible Empire: unless Klansmen are wearing their robes, it is impossible for Percy and his allies to see them. Klansmen are like spies, Percy declares, Nazi spies: "Like German parachute jumpers, they appeared disguised as friends.... Everyone was under suspicion: from Klansmen you could expect neither frankness nor truth nor honor, and you couldn't tell who was a Klansman. If they were elected judges and law-enforcement officers, we would be cornered into servility or assassination" (*LL* 237).

By linking the Ku Klux Klan (and more generally, poor whites) with Nazism, Percy both attacks the barbarism of modernity and defends the purity of southern traditionalism, answering liberal critics such as W. J. Cash, who were linking the ideology and racial practices of the traditional South with Nazism. Percy asserts that racial violence in the South arises, not from the southern system, but from those moderns bent on destroying the system—the poor whites, who to Percy's eyes are not southern at all, no matter where they come from (because they are not loyal traditionalists).

According to Percy's line of thinking, then, traditional southern society not only is not violently racist but stands opposed to the violent racists in their midst, the Nazi-like Ku Klux Klan. The champions of racial conciliation are thus southern traditionalists.

Percy has to do a good bit of historical cleansing to reach this conclusion. In presenting the Klan as a Nazi-like organization, peopled almost entirely by poor white outsiders at odds with traditional southern society (as opposed to Cash's interpretation of the Klan, which held that the Klan manifested the authoritarian ideology of southern traditionalism), Percy downplays the fact that the new Klan characteristically drew heavily from the middle class and largely championed middle-class virtues.[19] Not only were the motives of the Klansmen opposed to Percy more complicated than he makes them but so were those of the traditionalists who stood against them. Percy presents these traditionalists as acting entirely selflessly, motivated by noblesse oblige and committed to serving the community regardless of personal cost. While noblesse oblige was no doubt important to some of the Delta's planters, the issues involved in their battles with the Klan also involved a good deal of self-interest.

Even Percy's father, in his famous 1922 speech against the Klan (subsequently published in the *Atlantic Monthly*), suggested the complexity of the planter elites' motives. In that speech LeRoy Percy acknowledged that the one of the gravest threats posed by the Klan involved labor—when the Klan moved in, he warned, black laborers moved out, emptying areas so quickly of workers "as to afford no opportunity for readjustment to changed conditions, resulting in industrial paralysis and ruin. This is one of the terrifying potentialities of the Klan's work in these sections."[20] Retaining sufficient labor, it should be noted, had been an ongoing problem for the Percys and other Delta planters, and LeRoy Percy had previously been actively involved in various schemes to recruit domestic and foreign workers into the region.[21] One would never know any of this from *Lanterns on the Levee*. In his discussion of his father's speech in *Lanterns*, Percy focuses only on his own and the crowd's reactions, saying nothing of the speech's content. Nor does he discuss the serious threat that the Klan posed to the godfatherlike control that LeRoy Percy, together with a few associates, wielded over Greenville and Washington County.[22] Standing up to the Klan, in Percy's rendition, was entirely a matter of honesty and decency.

Honesty and decency, for Percy, define the southern aristocracy, no matter what their behavior. Percy can make such an outrageously simplistic claim because throughout *Lanterns* he presents the aristocracy less as a class than as a distinct race with essentialist racial characteristics. Oddly enough, however, Percy suggests that the gentry's racial identity is not a matter of blood but one of possessing a mysterious spiritual blessing that makes a person, in Percy's word, "nice." Exactly what this spiritual blessing is, or how a person gets it, Percy never makes entirely clear, but he says that people know if they have it and can recognize it in others. Thus, when Percy discusses his ancestry, he is less concerned with displaying bloodlines than he is with establishing that family members possessed an inner grace, making them racial brethren to "good people" throughout the world.

> The Percys were nice people; the Bourges were nice people—voilà tout! But I cannot help wondering what were the qualifications that admitted to the post-Civil-War aristocracy. Apparently not pedigree, certainly not wealth. A way of life for several generations? A tradition of living? A style and pattern of thinking and feeling not acquired but inherited? No matter how it came about, the Bourges and Percys were nice people—that is what I breathed in as a child, the certainty I was as good as anyone else, which, because of the depth of the conviction, was unconscious, never talked of, never thought of. Besides Southerners, the only people I have ever met graced with the same informal assurance were Russian aristocrats. (*LL* 40–41)

Perhaps the most specific Percy gets in defining this inner grace is his description of students at Sewanee, who, he says, possess an innate style of manners, "the kind not learned or instilled but happening, the core being sweet" (*LL* 101). This inner grace binds the students (whom he deems "Arcadians") in a common identity, the lineage of which, Percy indicates, includes "Socrates and Jesus and St. Francis and Sir Philip Sidney and Lovelace and Stevenson" (*LL* 101). "It is to be marveled that they never change," Percy observes about their essential core—and thus racial—identity. "They may not be quite the same faces or the precise bodies you met a few years back, but the alterations are irrelevant—a brown eye instead of a blue one, a nose set a little more to the left. The lining is the same" (*LL* 100).

His judging people entirely by what he perceives as their inner lining—their racial identity—means that Percy everywhere downplays the significance of performative acts. To Percy, people are what they are, as established by their inner core, no matter how they behave, and all races have their essential and unchanging characteristics. Blacks, for instance, may at times be able to imitate whites, but they can never "be" white. Percy heaps his harshest scorn on those who believe that "there is no relation between what you see of [a black person] and what there is of him" and that a black person, as a human being, is the same as a white person, or, as Percy puts it, "a white man inside" (*LL* 84). Percy believes instead that the inner life of black people is so different from that of whites that fundamental communication between the two races is impossible, as is, of course, living together on equal terms. Blacks remain to Percy "deeply alien and unknowable" (*LL* 298). Poor whites, likewise, are always poor whites, racially distinct from other white people, no matter where they end up socially and economically. Thus, when a former Klansman asks Percy, nearly twenty years after the Klan's campaign to control Greenville, why he has never forgiven him, Percy responds: "Forgiveness is easy. I really like you. The trouble is I've got your number and people's numbers don't change" (*LL* 241).

Nor do the aristocracy's numbers ever change. Indeed, so secure is Percy in his racial taxonomy that in discussing Greenville's history he presents a ruling elite who can do no wrong even when they *are* doing wrong; that is, even when they are breaking the law or otherwise acting dishonorably, the ruling elite remain upstanding and honorable, their racial identity unbesmirched. Perhaps the most obvious example of Percy's essentializing comes in his commentary on General Ferguson, a city leader and "a man of unimpeachable rectitude, of untarnished honor" (*LL* 70), who embezzles money from the levee board and, when discovered, flees to South America.[23] General Ferguson's actions mean nothing to Percy in terms of judging his honor: since he carries the trait of honor, he will always be honorable. Even in describing General Ferguson's return to Mississippi many years later, by which time the general is a madman obsessed with his crime, Percy uses his story to illustrate, of all things, the tribulations facing honorable men who must live in a dishonorable—that is, modern—world. "People steal public funds now, but the public is cynical, no one is horrified, and the accused, guilty or innocent, seldom goes mad," Percy explains. "Going mad for honor's sake presupposes honor. In our brave new world a man of honor is rather like the Negro—there's no place for him to go" (*LL* 72). Percy seems oblivious to the absurd extremes that his racial thinking here carries him. While going mad for honor's sake does indeed presuppose honor, stealing public funds does not; and for those "honorable" men like General Ferguson, there *was* a place to go—South America, where General Ferguson (along with, later, scores of Nazis) fled. There he avoids just—and honorable—punishment and restitution.

Presenting southern elites, the nobility of southern traditionalism, as paragons of virtue is of course crucial in Percy's portrayal of southern culture's stand against modernity. But the more Percy allows history into the text, as in the case of General Ferguson, the more the reader sees the aristocracy's purity as impure, masking motives of self-interest and greed, if not downright lust for power. This is particularly true in Percy's presentation of his grandfather and father. Percy's narrative of his grandfather's efforts during Reconstruction to restore white supremacy—a task that "required vote-buying, the stuffing of ballot-boxes, chicanery, intimidation" (*LL* 274)—ends up ironically suggesting that his grandfather used methods every bit as lawless as those of the forces he was fighting against, if not more so. Although Percy certainly does not mean it this way, his description of Reconstruction as "one glorious orgy of graft, lawlessness, and terrorism" (*LL* 274) aptly describes his grandfather's behavior; but while Percy acknowledges that the actions required of his grandfather were "heart-breaking and degrading," he goes on to make it clear that his grandfather emerged neither brokenhearted nor degraded. Immediately following his discussion of Reconstruction, Percy praises his grandfather, seconding his own father's judgment that he was "superior to any human being he had ever known" and that "he had a finer mind, a greater gusto, a warmer love of people, and a more rigid standard of justice than any of his sons" (*LL* 274).

Percy also unwittingly undercuts both his own and his father's nobility in his discussion of the 1927 flood that devastated Greenville and many other towns along the Mississippi River. Percy blames all of the unrest and problems plaguing the relief efforts on outside agitators and Greenville's gullible blacks. His angry criticism of the local black population centers on their discontent at being forcefully resettled in a huge refugee camp along the levee (at one point the camp stretched for more than eight miles and contained more than thirteen thousand people) rather than being evacuated (as the white population had been).[24] Despite the camp's notorious conditions, which eventually prompted the federal government to launch an investigation into charges of abuse and peonage, Percy (who as chairman of the Flood Relief Committee was in charge of the camp) goes so far as to suggest that Greenville's blacks only got the idea that they were suffering because that was what black newspapers, such as the *Chicago Defender*, were saying. Before the black newspapers began sowing their discord, Percy writes, Greenville's blacks were content with their life of ease in the camp. "The camp life on the levee suited their temperaments," Percy observes. "There was nothing for them to do except unload their rations when the boats docked. The weather was hot and pleasant. Conditions favored conversation. They worked a little, talked a great deal, ate heartily of food which somebody else had paid for, and sang at night" (*LL* 264). All that contentedness changed, according to Percy, once "the Negroes at home read their Northern newspapers trustingly and believed them far more piously than the evidence before their own eyes" (*LL* 264). The evidence before their eyes, Percy fails to mention, included these conditions: no one without a pass could enter or leave the camp, which was patrolled by the National Guard; all men were required to work in order to receive food; no compensation, other than food, was given for work.[25] Although Percy never makes this connection, the conditions in Greenville's refugee camp resemble, if they were not much worse than, those he describes Germany enforcing in occupied Belgium during World War I.[26] Percy summarizes those conditions as "the wholesale enslavement of the able-bodied males of a helpless little country," and in his angry denunciation he adds that they are "an example of wicked stupidity that Germans alone could have been capable of" (*LL* 162). Not the Germans alone, apparently.

Percy's anger over what he calls "the embittering influence of the *Chicago Defender*" (*LL* 265) recalls his bitter attack of outside critics of sharecropping, who, he declares, are blind to the humane workings of the system. In both cases, Percy draws more on the image he wants to preserve than on the reality before him (in effect, mirroring the blindness he attributes to the blacks reading the *Chicago Defender*), presenting the planter elite as long-suffering practitioners of noblesse oblige. Before a black gathering called in response to a black man's shooting by a policeman, Percy lashes out at those he see as his ungrateful charges:

> For four months I have struggled and worried and done without sleep in order to help you Negroes. Every white man in this town has done the same thing. We served you with our money and our brains and our strength and, for all that we did, no one of us received one penny. We white people could have left you to shift for yourselves. Instead we stayed with you and worked for you, day and night. During all

this time you Negroes did nothing, nothing for yourselves or for us. (*LL* 267)

Percy's words here echo his general commentary on blacks throughout *Lanterns*: they are "without moral stamina, without discipline, without standards" (*LL* 306), condemned genetically to inferiority, laziness, irresponsibility, and criminality. They are, quite simply, the white man's burden, childlike people who run amok if not looked after. Before outside agitators began their disruptive work, according to Percy's history of Greenville, blacks recognized the goodness of the planter elite and happily accepted their position in the southern system, which Percy identifies as "the tiller of our soil, the hewer of our wood, our servants, troubadours, and criminals" (*LL* 21).

The challenges Percy faced during the flood of 1927 point to the problem that threatens in *Lanterns* to expose the impurity of his southern traditionalism: that noblesse oblige masks the gentry's own self-interest. Strikingly, as we have already seen, Percy repeatedly presents evidence that allows readers to view this impurity, even as his rhetoric asserts the virtues of southern traditionalism, with Percy suggesting that impure actions have nothing do with a person's (and by extension, a culture's) innate and unchanging purity. Percy even presents two deeply personal incidents that momentarily unmask his own stance as paternal planter, both involving Percy's black helper, Ford, or as he is better known, "Fode." In one, Fode pierces the image of the powerful planter when, after seeing Percy standing naked in the shower, without his habiliments of authority, he pronounces, "You ain't nothing but a little old fat man" (*LL* 287). In the other, Fode explains to Percy his misinterpretation of one of his tenants designating Percy's car as "*us* car." "How sweet it was to have the relation between landlord and tenant so close and affectionate that to them my car was their car," Percy comfortably muses. Fode lets him know better: "He meant that's the car *you* has bought with *us* money. They all knew what he meant, but you didn't and they knew you didn't. They wuz laughing to theyselves" (*LL* 291). Both incidents scald Percy so painfully as to suggest that he knows full well that Fode's observations have uncovered his and his culture's pretensions.[27] But Percy makes no acknowledgment of that recognition and instead quickly returns to a continued defense of southern paternalism.

The two incidents with Fode point to the crucial issue that Percy sees signaling the doom of the southern aristocracy: that neither blacks nor poor whites acknowledge the inner grace of the aristocracy, the "niceness" that establishes their pedigree. In other words, the distinguishing racial characteristic that in earlier times had guaranteed the gentry their leadership position in society is now worthless in the public sphere; "niceness" is now merely a private virtue, a devaluation that underlies Percy's comment that he feels "superfluous, if not posthumous."[28] Having fallen from the heights of public leadership, the gentry are left with only a gritty private stoicism, their final defense against the modernity that is about to overwhelm them. Unrecognized and unappreciated, the aristocracy is passing away, with Percy portraying himself, as the text winds down, as its last gentleman. His memoir ends appropriately with Percy in Greenville's cemetery, resting with the only people left of his race—his dead ancestors.

Percy portrays the struggle for survival between the aristocracy and the poor whites, the Delta's two white races, as the gentry's fading from visibility to invisibility and the poor whites' emergence from invisibility to visibility.[29] Beneath these mirrored motions lies perhaps the deepest irony of the text: that the gentry and the poor whites are not as utterly distinct as Percy presents them, a fact that Percy himself at one point comes close to acknowledging. In one of his discussions of the demise of the aristocrats, Percy suggests that over time a new aristocracy might be reborn from among the descendants of those poor whites who were then rising to power. As the gentry move toward extinction, Percy notes, "the vulgar are increasing and multiplying and prospering and will continue to do so until their children or their children's children, having attained security, will begin all over to admire and cherish the forgotten virtues we were not strong enough to maintain. Perhaps in every age an aristocracy is dying and one is being born" (*LL* 62). This is Percy at his most hopeful, but it is not his characteristic position and, indeed, cuts against the racial logic Percy everywhere else employs.

More characteristic of Percy's racial thinking, as we have seen, is his essentializing of purity, a view that he also uses metaphorically in defending southern traditionalism against modernity's taint. It is also a view that shares disturbing similarities with the Nazis' belief in racial superiority, a connection that Percy never acknowledges but nonetheless unwittingly suggests in his vilification of both poor whites and blacks as threats to the planters' superior blood.[30] Percy's frightening warnings to blacks regarding assimilation in his chapter "A Note on Race Relations" make this connection most visible. Believing that social equality between the races will eventually break down the sexual barrier, particularly the taboo prohibiting relations between black men and white women, Percy declares that that barrier is inviolable and that merely for blacks to question it will provoke a devastating response by whites:

> The Negro, not having assimilated the white man's ethics, giving only lip service to the white man's morality, must for his own peace and security accept whole-heartedly the white man's mores and taboos. In the South the one sacred taboo, assumed to be Southern, but actually and universally Anglo-Saxon, is the untouchability of white women by Negro men. It is academic to argue the wisdom or justice of this taboo. Wise or unwise, just or unjust, it is the cornerstone of friendly relations, of interracial peace. In the past it has been not the eleventh but the first commandment. Even to question it means the shattering of race relations into hideous and bloody ruin. (*LL* 307–8)

Percy's great fear and loathing is hybridization—of races and cultures—and he notes that he has learned a great deal about crossbreeding from gardening. "If you happen to flush me, trowel in hand, over a patch of coco grass," he writes, "be not deceived: my mind is not on gardening, but on people" (*LL* 333). And here is one thing he thinks about:

> It took years of battle with root-rot to teach me that it does not ravage with equal devastation every variety of iris. The older purer strains seem immune to it, its greatest toll is from the ranks of the hybrids, in which we have learned to fear Mesopotamican blood. But when we cross human beings we give no thought to the racial compatibility of the bloods fused and neglect to observe whether the human hybrids we produce are unhappily subject to rot of one kind or another. In gardening we have learned that death is the best cure for many diseases. (*LL* 333)

Not long after Percy made this observation, the Nazis began enforcing a similar cure in the death camps.[31]

Percy's racial taxonomizing and his idealizing of racial purity do not, of course, make him a Nazi. But Percy's need to deny the dangerous extremes to which his thinking was taking him led this very unsentimental man to construct a very distorted and sentimental history of himself, his family, and the Mississippi Delta aristocracy. In writing that history, Percy avoided seeing the deep ironies that everywhere pervade his text, including the two that undo everything he is arguing: that the traditional South, at least since Reconstruction, was already quite modern and that the planter class, including the Percys, had been and were probably the most modern southerners of all, active participants in the new economy and the driving force behind the Delta's modernization.[32] Those planters who prospered after the Civil War, as C. Vann Woodward observes, were not those who only farmed but those who "moved to town, opened stores, ran gins, compresses, and banks, invested in railroads and mills, and played the speculative markets."[33] LeRoy Percy, presented in *Lanterns* almost exclusively as a planter, was in actuality the type of successful man described by Woodward; among other things, he was a prominent lawyer (who represented the Illinois Central Railroad), a partner in a cotton factorage firm, a large holder in stocks and bonds (and a man who typically borrowed money from Wall Street banks rather than local ones), a leader in the efforts for federal support of levee construction, a director of a Federal Reserve bank, a director of the Rockefeller Foundation, a trustee of the Carnegie Foundation, a founder of a small railroad, and a chief promoter of railroad expansion in the Delta. Particularly noteworthy in LeRoy's résumé is his deep involvement with railroads, for the construction of an efficient rail system more than anything else made possible the coming of modernity to the Delta; and imaginatively, too, the arrival of railroads has long suggested the destruction of American pastoral, Leo Marx's "machine in the garden."[34]

Ironically, then, as James Cobb puts it, "the Delta's dramatic emergence of the New South's Old South was largely attributable to the rapid modernization of its economy and transportation network,"[35] and this modernization was spearheaded by the Delta planters themselves. In other words, the Delta society that Percy idealizes as traditional is already the terrifying hybrid he fears that it is destined to become, modernity masking itself as traditional. Percy's representation of Delta culture and gentry as purely traditional is ultimately troubled to the point of desperation and might best be understood as another manifestation of what Faulkner saw in Percy's poetry, Percy's attempt to close his "eyes against the dark of modernity," at least in terms of seeing it in the life he loved. Or put another way, Percy's narrative strategies, as the title of his memoir suggests, are a manifestation of his attempt to shore up a levee to keep out the flood of modernity,[36] a levee that ironically had long ago been blown apart, not by a flood but by his very ancestors.

4

GEORGIA ON MY MIND

LILLIAN SMITH

A vocal critic of southern traditionalism, Lillian Smith was shocked when she read William Alexander Percy's *Lanterns on the Levee*. In her review of Percy's memoir, Smith dubs it "an anachronism with a highly rubbed patina," declaring that "a book like this is more disturbing . . . than a Georgia demagogue's cheap tricks. It is easy for intelligent people to reject violent and vulgar expressions of race chauvinism; it is more difficult for them to resist the seductive chanting of those same words if modulated and muted to a well-bred softness."[1] Beneath a text that appears to express little more than a "lyrical longing to be a gentleman" (6), Smith finds psychological dynamics that she believes also underlie the cultural crisis that had carried the world into war. "Driven by our insecurities, aching with unconscious and conscious fears and dreads and frustrations," Smith writes, reading the world's chaos through Percy, "we feverishly continue to blow ourselves up from miniature dimensions to the magnificent proportions of a super race and a super class" (6). How ominous for the nation's future, Smith adds, that Percy's memoir has become immensely popular both in the North and the South, Americans reading with pleasure "words which burn candles at the shrine of racial and class superiority at the very moment they are sending their sons to die for democracy and the brotherhood of man" (6). "It is a grotesque and comic thing," Smith concludes about *Lanterns*. "One could forget it in a great gust of sane and healthy laughter were it no so malevolent in its effects upon mankind" (6).

Smith felt quite differently about W. J. Cash's *Mind of the South*, as she and Cash shared a fundamental perspective that southern culture was less traditional than authoritarian. Both believed that powerful cultural forces, masked by sentimental myths, held southerners in a totalitarianlike grip, keeping them from developing the critical intelligence needed for the full development of self and culture. Not surprisingly, Cash and Smith, together with Paula Snelling, Smith's companion, had for several years been lending each other support. Smith and Snelling had published an excerpt, "The Reign of the Commonplace," from *The Mind of the South* in their journal *Pseudopodia* (later titled *North Georgia Review* and finally *South Today*), and Snelling had later favorably reviewed *The Mind of the South* in the journal. Cash, meanwhile, had written a favorable column on *Pseudopodia* for the *Charlotte News* book page (19 July 1936), had contributed a review of Francis Griswold's *Sea Island Lady* to the journal (Spring 1940), and had mentioned Smith and Snelling favorably in an excerpt from *The Mind of the South*, "Literature in the South," published in the *Saturday Review of Literature* (28 December 1940).

A few weeks after the publication of *The Mind of the South*, in March 1941, Cash and his wife visited Smith and Snelling at their home atop Old Screamer Mountain, near Clayton, Georgia. In hindsight, this weekend gathering seems fateful, for four months later Cash committed suicide in Mexico City, leaving Smith the most important leftist white cultural critic in the South, determined to demystify the region's authoritarian system.[2] Even more so than Cash, Smith focused her analysis on the crippling effects of segregation, exploring the damaging neuroses besetting southern children and the destructive manifestations these neuroses later took in adulthood. Her "mind of the South" was thus even more frightening than Cash's folk mind; it was a mind that, as Smith writes in *Killers of the Dream* (1949), was from birth brought under relentless social conditioning, which destroyed the human spirit and transformed southern children into "little crooked wedges that fit into the intricately twisting serrated design of life which THEY WHO MAKE THE RULES had prepared for us in Dixie" (*KD* 87).

※ ※ ※ ※

While it is impossible to locate precisely the origins of Smith's deep-seated radicalism, clearly her three years in China as a young adult had a profound impact on her political perspective and her views of the South. Before that time, Smith, who grew up in a small town in northern Florida, had spent most of her life as a privileged southerner, though she had left the South for several years to study music in Baltimore and had taught school in rugged conditions in northern Georgia. Her years in China, however, brought her face to face with Western, and particularly British, imperialism of the worst sort. Smith later recalled her shock at witnessing senseless beatings of coolies and at experiencing her "first big confrontation with naked, hideous, obscenely exposed poverty."[3] Even more significant was her recognition that even well-meaning colonials, including Christian missionaries, lived hypocritically, their professed goodness masking what she called "white arrogance." She wrote that she found "white colonialism in all its manifestations smoothed over by Christian talk—and poisoned by unChristian acts. Always, always, we British and Americans segregated the Chinese—even the Christian Chinese from our 'fun' etc. We prayed with them but we didn't play tennis or swim with them."[4] Segregation in China turned her thoughts, now with something of an outsider's view, to segregation at home. She did not like what she saw. "Seeing it happen in China made me know how ugly the same thing is in Dixie," she wrote later. "For the first time in my life I was ashamed of my white skin. I began almost to believe that 'whiteness' cast an evil spell over all that it came in contact with."[5]

Smith returned to Georgia in 1925 to help her parents run their summer girls' camp. In 1929 she bought the camp from her parents, and with Paula Snelling, who became her companion, she directed it until its closing in 1949. Sometime after her father's death in 1930 she began writing fiction, by the mid-1930s completing two novels, one set in China and the other in the South, and three novellas.[6] All of this work remained unpublished, most of it destroyed much later in a house fire. In 1936 Smith and Snelling agreed to start a literary journal, envisioning it as an outlet for southern writers who were struggling with new material. Its title, *Pseudopodia,* as they explained in their first issue, embodied their goal: "For the artist no less than the amoeba inhabits an adamant world in which cherished efforts at locomotion fail not always through inner capacity. A pseudopod differs from an ordinary foot in that it is not a specialized and differentiated organ fully equipped with toenails and calloused but a temporary and tender projection of the nucleus or inner-self, upon the success of whose gropings the nucleus is entirely dependent for its progress and sustenance."[7]

Smith and Snelling also noted in their opening editorial that they were looking for new, striking work that avoided the "petrification [that] follows inevitably from looking too exclusively at the past; at past glories no less than past orgies." The editors, they wrote, "are not interested in perpetuating that sterile fetishism of the Old South which has so long gripped our section."[8] Nor were they interested in perpetuating tired southern stereotypes, declaring in the journal's announcement letter (1936) that "we have so often been outraged by the axiom: 'Different, therefore wrong' that we are almost tempted to set up as a working postulate: 'Different, therefore right'" (*LLS* 24). As Louise Blackwell and Frances Clay point out, Smith and Snelling from the beginning staked out a cultural position opposed to the Nashville Agrarians and their conservative defense of traditional southern society.[9] Noting in an editorial that the second issue would contain a review of the Agrarians' second symposium, *Who Owns America?*, Smith commented that "perhaps most of us remember Mr. Tate best for his contribution to *I'll Take My Stand* which some of us thought brilliantly untenable."[10]

John D. Allen's review of *Who Owns America?* "Southern Agrarianism: Revised Version," led off the second issue and sharply attacked the Agrarians' social and economic philosophies, voicing a position close to Smith's.[11] "It is a pity that a program so futile, a social philosophy so warped and partial," Allen writes, "can be urged with a charm and vigor so dangerously seductive."[12] The danger with the Agrarians, Allen makes clear, is not that their ideas will carry the South back into the past but rather that they might lead the region into the future—into Fascism. Allen writes that the Agrarians believe that "socialism (particularly the Russian variety) and fascism are identical twins, sired by liberalism out of industrialism. And yet, if choice must be made, the world would do well to choose fascism. For it does discipline the masses, protect property, and recognize the role in society of the privileged classes" (2). On the reforms that the Agrarians declared would make real "the American dream," Allen comments that "the petty bourgeoisie of Italy and Germany once were lulled by similar visions" (3).

Signaling their own expanding interests and political commitment, Smith and Snelling in the spring of 1937 announced a change of title and direction for the journal: the newly titled *North Georgia Review: A Magazine of Southern Regions* would explore matters of southern culture in general, not merely literary expression. The subtitle, echoing Howard Odum's *Southern Regions of the United States* (1936), sent another clear signal of opposition to the Agrarians and allegiance with the liberal Chapel Hill sociologists. Smith had already praised Odum's work in the fall 1936 issue, writing that *Southern Regions* should be "in the office of every county administrator throughout the Southeastern region, in every library, in every newspaper office (it could be the source of a text for at least one editorial a week), in every banker's office, in every high school library. For we Southerners need above all else knowledge of the historical origins of our present difficulties and an understanding, as Mr. Odum says so frequently throughout the book, 'of the immensity and time quality of cultural reconstruction and the exceedingly complex nature of the regional culture involved' in order to 'focus upon a relatively small number of elemental factors toward which practical study and planning may be directed.'"[13]

Throughout the ten-year run of the journal Smith wrote a regular column entitled "Dope with Lime" (a reference to Coca-Cola, or "dope," as it was then frequently called), in which she commented on matters mostly southern in a down-home, folksy style (the Coca-Cola) that frequently zeroed in on issues with deadly seriousness (the lime). Those from 1936 contained little of controversy and no political commentary; typically, Smith told a few vignettes about life on the mountain, announced new southern books, and identified contributors with brief biographical statements. That pattern continued throughout most of 1937, but at the end of the year Smith began openly addressing world affairs, and particularly political developments in Asia and Europe and their relevance to domestic issues, most pointedly those in the South. Her column from the winter 1937–38 issue, composed as a catechism, works through her and Snelling's various political positions, asserting that being anti-Fascist does not necessarily mean being interventionist, that confronting antidemocratic forces at home is more important than confronting such forces abroad, that reductive political oppositions gloss over complex political issues, and that profound social and psychological disorders underlie the world's crisis. "Is there any evil on earth greater than fascism?" Smith asks, and then answers, "Yes. Its progenitors."[14] These, she goes on to identify, include war, poverty, hate, and stupidity. In this column Smith looks forward to the issues that would dominate her commentaries during the late 1930s and the wartime 1940s: the danger of unquestioned nationalism, the uselessness of war for settling disputes, the need for the nation to confront its own social problems before addressing the world's, and the psychological disorders underlying the world's growing conflicts.

Smith's emphatic turn to strident political commentary in late 1937 was likely triggered by the outbreak of war between Japan and China that summer. Since returning from China in 1925, Smith had kept a close eye on that nation's political struggles, and she was deeply troubled by the Japanese occupation. In her essay "He That Is without Sin . . . ," which also appeared in the winter 1937–38 issue, Smith comments on the absurdity that recently published pictures of the Panay incident (Japanese warplanes had sunk the USS *Panay* near Nanjing on 12 December 1937) were provoking American calls for war against Japan—calls from a nation long involved in imperialist enterprises and long blind to oppression and suffering within its own borders:

> "The Japanese have no right in China; we can't sit by and see them steal her wealth and kill her people!" You hear it everyday. But we Western imperialists have been stealing her wealth and killing her people for 100 years. "We can't sit by . . . there's our national honor . . ." No? We sit by and let our neighbors' children starve and do nothing about it. We sit by and see Negroes lynched and make no effort to punish the mob. We are not outraged when textile workers are killed, when miners starve. Here where we could defend our national honor with no bloodshed, with no risk of a collapse of civilization, we do nothing. We've closed our eyes to the depredations Great Britain has made upon India; Gandhi has been for most of us only a stooge for our wisecracks. We forget Africa; we forget Mexico; the Philippines.[15]

Smith closes her essay by saying that the nation seems headed toward war, signaled by President Roosevelt's massive armament program and the rising jingoistic chorus condemning "the 'menace' of fascism; the 'menace' of communism" and affirming "the new cry, and its old death-echo, 'Make the world safe for democracy'" (32).[16]

Smith's concern about America's entry into another world war intensified as the political situation deteriorated; steadfastly refusing to acknowledge Nazi Germany's threat to Europe and, more generally, to democratic societies throughout the world, she kept her eyes focused on domestic issues, fearing that the nation's internal problems would be overlooked in the rush toward armament.[17] To her dismay, Smith found Americans growing more bellicose and intolerant, and she noted in a letter to Glenn Rainey (19 September 1940) that even the girls at her summer camp were showing ill effects from the European war. During that summer, she told Rainey, she had watched with great discouragement "war creep into our midst and twist feeling and thought," adding that the girls "were less tolerant of the Negro this summer (some holding bravely to their decency but others wavering) more inclined to defend the South . . . America . . . to hate Hitler and the Germans" (*LLS* 46, Smith's ellipses). "It is not the physical part of war that sickens me," she added, "as it is what is happening to our minds and feelings" (*LLS* 47).

In her spring 1940 column Smith attacked both the president and the press for their efforts to whip up the nation's martial spirit. "As this is being written," Smith writes, "we as well as our President are once more on a stampede of the mental texture, the emotional quality of the 1938 Martian panic; of the brute power and carelessness of a horde of crazed cattle. There is something chilling and fantastic about the talk on the streets; the copy in newspapers."[18] Smith argues that both Roosevelt and the mainstream American press, in their zealousness to rally support for war, are neglecting the nation's domestic ills. Roosevelt, she writes, is "a President whose eyes are so fixed upon Europe's high speed carnage that he cannot spare a glance at our own slow death" (4); and most American journalists, she adds, are "whipping the masses of people into a mood of fear and lust for blood—they are singing a battle hymn of hate" (6). She just as angrily criticizes Americans for their gullibility, or as she put it, for "gulping down and smacking our lips over the same mess of propaganda (be it out of London skillet or Washington pan) that gave us colic before and which we'd swore we'd spue out of our mouths if it was ever offered us again" (6). Those already fighting and dying in Europe, she says, are victims "of the stupidity and dull hate, the greed and egotism of old men and middle-aged men" (6).

No doubt in large part because of what she had seen of British colonialism in China, Smith had very little patience with those arguing that America needed to enter the war in order to save Britain. To go to war for Britain, she repeatedly commented, would not be to save democracy but to keep white England free to oppress its colored colonies. In her winter 1940–41 column Smith says it is shameful that America is becoming England's toady rather than the leader in establishing international democracy, "a framework which is surely the only rational alternative the world has now to endless nationalistic wars."[19] "We bluster and sling our arms around and step all over our feet like a foolish loud-mouthed country boy," Smith writes, "and when time to act comes we sneak dumbly behind England, urging that cosmopolite to lead the way even to the ruin of the earth" (5).

Smith's attacks on British imperialism parallel those she was aiming at what she saw as America's flawed democracy, and particularly its most visibly flawed manifestation, southern segregation. Noting similarities with British colonialism, Smith found America guilty of ballyhooing democratic freedoms while denying those freedoms to its black population. She saw the possibility, as America inched toward war in the late 1930s, that African Americans might soon face the same troubling and ironic fate that British colonials did, that of being enlisted to defend the very nation that denied them their freedom. In an angry editorial, "Mr. Lafayette, Heah We Is—," published in the journal's spring 1939 issue, Smith attacked with Swiftian venom "the proselytizers of the Democratic Religion,"[20] who ignored the blighting of democracy at home while calling for the defense of democracy in Europe. Smith proposed that America send to war all those people who "are a blotch on our fair democracy, all the human beings who persist in casting their shadows on our gleaming purity: the sharecroppers, the unemployed, the slum-dwellers, the undernourished, and the Negroes" (15). After saying that it would be easy to persuade these folk to "sacrifice themselves in order to make democracy safe for the rest of us" (15), Smith delivers one of the bitterest attacks she would ever write:

> We'd send the Negroes as our shock troops, since they have the longest and most persistent record of being splotches. They could go, calling out in their deep mellow voices: "Mister Lafayette, heah we come! Leastways, all of us cept the 5,000 or so who was lynched a while back. Mr. Lafayette, heah we is. They don't call us mister back home and they don't let us ride in their railroad cars or eat at their tables or sleep in their hotels or let us vote;—and they gives us what scraps are lef as to jobs and we knows to say 'thankee Boss.' And we take what's lef over in the way of schools and hospitals and houses and sewer systems and sech liddle things like that, and tips our hats. But we live in Gawd's country en that's a fact, en it's a fine place to live in ef yo knows yo place, and we knows our place, yeah Lawd! Now we'se come to lay down our lives for those Jews Mister Hitler's been pickin on. We hear tell he takes their property and their money and kicks them about and spits on 'em and burns their books. An' all that makes our democratic blood about boil over. Yas suh! For hit sho must be terrible to live in a country whar yo has yo money tuk (our ways a lot better cause we has no money to be tuk—jus a little furnish which is et up and gone fo yo can say scat) and it sho must be awful sight to have to have yo books burned—hit's a lot better never to learn how to read and write like us, we'se telling you. And to be spit at in the face! That just shows the awful wickedness of that fascism business. Now in our country things are worked out mighty well, a sight

better'n that. Theah's plenty of back streets to walk on in every town and back doors what you can go in and out of. And theah's always the Quarters. Yo don need to scrouge up close to folks, close enough for 'em to spit at yo! You kin always step off the sidewalk. And if worse comes to worst you kin run yo tail off and make it to the Swamp. Yeah Lawd . . . there ain't nothin so plumb democratic as a good cypress swamp. . . . Ef them Jews hada jes had a coupla cypress swamps it'd sho help them get rid of fascism. Yeah man. . . ." (15)

Not surprisingly, Smith was deeply saddened by the Japanese attack on Pearl Harbor and the United States' declaration of war. The journal's winter 1941 issue was already in proof when war was declared, but Smith and Snelling quickly attached an editorial, "As We Go to War," expressing their profound misgivings about the coming conflict. "We share with other Americans a profound sorrow that our nation and other nations have once more failed to settle their economic conflicts by rational means," they write. "We dread, as does every thoughtful American with us, the hard years ahead of our people, the bloodshed, the grief, the psychic disintegration, the moral regression that war inevitably brings, the democratic losses which may not be inevitable yet have always in the past come in its wake."[21] As their final words here suggest, Smith and Snelling deeply feared that wartime jingoism would stifle efforts to make American democracy more equitable and just. In contrast to the standard calls for patriotic support, Smith and Snelling call for a patriotic citizenry who will thoughtfully discuss the war and its aims. "It is urgently needful for emotionally mature and intelligent men and women of good will to stem the tide of chauvinism," they write, "to enunciate civil rights, to define moral and creative values and acts at a time when regressive violence makes such values and acts seem to lose authenticity" (25).

Thoughtful discussion of the war became Smith and Snelling's primary goal for the journal during the war years, and to that end they initiated a series of writing contests, reading lists, quotations, editorials, and symposia designed to provoke discourse on the war's impact on American democracy. In their first issue after America's entry into the war, spring 1942, they announced their new focus, writing that "it is fitting that a southern magazine devote many of its pages to consideration of the aims and strategies which press with such conflicting urgency upon America today. For in a very special sense, America's failures are the South's failures, American sins are southern sins. The obligation rests heavily upon southerners during this war to see that the wages of our sins against democracy is not the death of democracy."[22] Highlighting this issue is an eighteen-page symposium, "Winning the World with Democracy: A Symposium of Questions and Answers concerning Aims and Strategies, Ends and Means," in which a number of distinguished citizens, including journalists, social scientists, churchmen, and political activists, responded to four questions on the war: "Do we know what we are fighting for?" "If we are fighting for democracy, whose democracy are we fighting for?" "Can this war be won for ourselves alone? by ourselves alone?" and "Do we want to win the people of the world to a belief in democracy?" (8–9). For each of the four questions there were a number of subquestions, clearly intended to guide the responses (and provoke the reader) and just as clearly intended to signal the line of Smith and Snelling's thinking. Here, for instance, are the questions below "Do we know what we are fighting for?":

> are we fighting for world markets? for rubber and tin?
> for colonies—economic or political?
> to help England retain her imperialistic holdings?
> are we fighting for national sovereignty even while we say that a world-order is inevitable?
> are we fighting so that the race and nations which have dominated other peoples may continue dominating them?
> are we fighting to preserve "our way of life" because it is ours without regard to its worth or the price others pay that we may live it?
> by our way of life do we mean the way open to members of our more fortunate economic groups, or the way open to our 13,000,000 Negroes, our 10,000,000 sharecroppers? (8)

Among the many questions below "Do we want to win the people of the world to a belief in democracy?" are these two: "is not Jim Crow a greater menace to democracy than Hitler? will he not have to be conquered in our hearts before Hitler can be conquered in Germany?" (9). While the respondents gave different answers, most worked from positions close to Smith and Snelling's, so that the symposium ended up for the most part elaborating their own positions on the war—as no doubt they intended it to.[23]

In this same issue, Smith used her bitter Swiftian voice again in "Portrait of the Deep South Speaking to Negroes on Morale," a dramatic monologue of a white southerner cajoling blacks to support the war while at the same time attempting to silence their demands for equality.[24] The speaker works through a number of arguments and speaks in a number of voices. Here, as indicated in Smith's directions, he speaks in a roaring voice:

> THIS IS WAR! COLORED FOLKS!
> WHERE'S YOUR UNITY!
> This fool equality
>   you keep whining about
>   equal votes
>   equal education
>   equal chance for jobs and pay
>   equal chance for children to play—
> these little things you call America's foundations
> don't you know they're interior *decorations?*[25]

The monologue ends with a fierce indictment of the fact that in a war declared to be for democracy blacks faced a very undemocratic segregation, both on the battlefield and on the home front:

> Come on darkies, time to start a song
> time to open your mouths now and bellow out strong
> and show the world you as good
> an American
> as we are
> and you'll fight to the last drop
> of your blood
> for us
>   (but stop that fool complaining
>   about Red Cross separating it
>   you know they can't mix white and nigger blood!)
>
> Yeah, we'll fight, you'll fight
> and we'll fight
> to the last Jim Crow drop
> to rid the world of Hitlerism
> and Nazism
> and all them OTHER ISMS
> and save the American Way

>   so that things can go on forever
>   and ever
>   and
>   ever
>   and
>   ever
>   just as they are
>   down
>   here
>   today.
>   (37)

Although Smith later admitted that the monologue's satire was perhaps too raw to be effective, "Portrait" nonetheless accurately voiced Smith's predominant feelings about the war effort.[26]

Those feelings received a fuller and more reasoned expression in Smith and Snelling's essay "Buying a New World with Old Confederate Bills," which appeared in the journal's autumn–winter 1942–43 issue. Early in the essay, Smith and Snelling suggest that recent world developments directly challenge the logic of southern racism. "It is just possible," they write, "that old answers which seemed 'true' in the tight, rigid frame of the Southern past are based on assumptions that are no longer valid. It is just possible that the white man is no longer the center of the universe. It is just possible that even German nazis, British imperialists, and white southerners will have to accept a fact that has been old news to the rest of the world for a long, long time."[27] In this larger international context, Smith and Snelling continue, southern segregation's apparent naturalness is revealed as perversely unnatural:

> We now have a bigger frame in which to hang the old race problem. And it is a good thing to know, a good thing to remember that a line of reasoning that seemed "realistic" in one frame of reference becomes absurd when the frame is altered. Racial and minority needs in the South, in India, in Java, in Germany and everywhere else in the world are hung now within an international frame, and can no longer be viewed save in a context of global human needs. Against the backdrop of total war, of a double-headed race-economic world revolution, of a great earth-hunger for freedom, we of the South now watch the South, the white man, the Negro and their common problems,

begin to shrink from gigantic dimensions over which human emotions have so long grown frenzied to a reasonable size which human intelligence can deal with. (11–12)

Smith and Snelling go on to argue that only by keeping the international situation in view could southerners move forward. It is, they write, a matter of reading maps: "Unless we keep the world map open before us we shall slip back into the old, bad habit of looking down at our own feet, and if we do we shall find ourselves at the same place where we first began. We must learn to read our maps simultaneously: regional map, national map, world map" (12).

Without specifically calling it totalitarian, Smith and Snelling nonetheless describe the South as totalitarianlike in its enforced conformity. They note that "when people who are different, who possess different minds, different feelings, different jobs, different values, different interests, act the same way, talk the same way, do the same way," then clearly "something bigger than they is pushing them all in the same direction" (17). That something, they conclude, much as Cash does in *The Mind of the South*, is an interlocked group of planters, industrialists, bankers, and politicians who control southern society and its cultural system. That system, Smith and Snelling continue, "pumps race prejudice and hopelessness through the arteries, veins, and capillaries of the whole South" (17), creating a populace of psychological cripples who have "incorporated the habits, the 'customs' of sickness into their personalities and enhaloed them with that over-esteem with which one tends to regard all aspects of himself" (19). Their imaginations, Smith and Snelling add, have "shrunk to the dimensions of the sickroom" (19).

Smith and Snelling proceed to level their fiercest attack on southern liberals, who they believed lacked the courage to live their convictions. The liberals' capitulation to the southern system, Smith and Snelling write, "is a chilling sight," made all the more so in light of the world's contemporary chaos:

> At a time when the South needs, as it has never needed, leaders of wisdom and courage and bold vision; on a globe where millions of boys think they are dying for world freedom; in a year when men in profound thought are creating great charters for the people of the earth to live by;—the southern liberal is busily concocting little recipes for sweetening the old segregation, refining the old color codes,

rubbing out and drawing in little lines which no one walking on southern soil may step across; and explaining all the while to a tired, puzzled world why this is not the right time for the freedom millions are now dying for. (24)

In their short coda, "Wanted: A New World," Smith and Snelling argue that now is the time for building a new world order based on "the democracy of the human spirit." They envision a world in which people live "with intelligence, with creative understanding, with love, with life itself," spurning the lucre of the past, the "old Confederate bills of race slavery and prejudice and frustration" and "the imperialistic British pound of arrogant exploitation" (30).

"Buying a New World with Old Confederate Bills" signals the beginning of Smith's angry campaign against southern liberals for their failure to call for an end to segregation. As Morton Sosna observes, the full-fledged assault on segregation by blacks during the war brought southern liberals to a crisis of conscience.[28] Up until this time, southern liberals generally avoided the issue of segregation, working to improve the conditions of black people (by, say, upgrading education or stopping lynching) without confronting the injustices of the system itself. During the war, however, as Sosna writes, "segregation and all it represented had finally become *the* race issue in the South."[29] Walter White, executive director of the NAACP, laid down the challenge in 1942: "Prove to us that you are not hypocrites when you say this is a war for freedom. Prove it to us."[30]

Most prominent southern liberals ended up arguing that segregation needed to be maintained for social order and racial peace. Many voiced the argument that "the time is not right," often pointing to the need for social stability during wartime. Others put it more harshly. While chairing the President's Committee on Fair Employment Practices, Mark Ethridge, editor of the *Louisville Courier-Journal*, declared in 1942 that "there is no power in the world—not even in all the mechanized armies of the earth—which could now force the Southern white people to the abandonment of the principle of social segregation."[31] The prominent liberal David Cohn, a close friend of William Alexander Percy's and Hodding Carter's, warned in a 1944 essay in the *Atlantic Monthly* that should the federal government enact laws prohibiting segregation, "every southern white man would spring to arms and the country would be swept by civil war."[32] A year earlier, Virginius Dabney, also in the *Atlantic Monthly*, had also warned of war in the streets, opening his essay, "Nearer and Nearer the Precipice," with a dire scenario of disaster for the nation (and the world):

> A small group of Negro agitators and another small group of white rabble rousers are pushing this country closer and closer to an interracial explosion which may make the race riots of the First World War and its aftermath seem mild by comparison. Unless saner counsels prevail, we may have the worst internal clashes since Reconstruction, with hundreds, if not thousands, killed and amicable race relations set back for a decade. There may also be far-reaching and heavily adverse effects upon the colored peoples of China, India, and the Middle East—peoples whose attitude can be of crucial importance to the allies during the war.[33]

At about the time that Dabney's essay appeared, Julian Harris, an outspoken critic of lynching and the Ku Klux Klan and editor of the *Columbus (GA) Enquirer-Sun*, criticized Smith for her calls to end segregation, saying that she was "dropping bombs on Georgia's peace."[34] Harris's criticism was merely one of the many attacks leveled at Smith by white liberal journalists (most notably Ralph McGill), who saw her activism during the war as dangerous both to the South and to the war effort.[35]

That criticism only increased with the publication in 1944 of her controversial novel *Strange Fruit*, which portrays the psychologically crippling stranglehold in which a small southern town (Maxwell, Georgia) held its citizens.[36] Most controversial, however, was the interracial love affair at the novel's center between white Tracy Deen and black Nonnie Anderson. Much of the novel follows Tracy's agonizing conflict between his love for Nonnie and the demands of family and culture. His transgressive attraction to Nonnie represents his dream of a new world in which people live free from the constraining nets of culture.[37] Ultimately, however, Tracy forgoes his dream and bows to the commands of southern tradition, segregating (or at least trying to) his love for Nonnie from his "proper" life as a white southerner, choosing to live within the safety—and confinement—of the community. Tracy's final choice indicates both his own weakness and southern tradition's power; indeed, they are inseparably linked, as Tracy's failure to live his dream results from the psychological crippling inflicted upon him during his upbringing. All of the white characters in the novel are likewise psychologically broken; they differ only in their level of awareness of their fractured condition. Near the end of the novel, two of Tracy's friends admit their alienation. One says that only by fleeing the South can he and others escape their conditioning. "Right now I have some ideas," he says, speaking of thoughts that do not mesh with those of the community. "If I stay here twenty years, I won't have them. Now I see things without color getting in the way—I won't be able to, then. It'll get me. It gets us all. Like quicksand. The more you struggle, the deeper you sink in it—I'm damned scared to stay—." Tracy's other friend, however, knows that the psychological wounding inflicted upon southerners runs so deep that merely fleeing the region solves little. "You can't run away from a thing like this," she says. "It'll follow you all over the world."[38]

This last observation points to Smith's own deepening, psychologically based understanding of southern segregation. By the mid-1940s Smith was focusing on both the immediate end of the South's specific racial codes and the long-term healing of the schizophrenia engendered by its segregated system. In a letter to Guy B. Johnson (12 June 1944) Smith discussed the psychological disorder that she saw manifested in the South's system of segregation:

> Segregation is not merely a southern tradition, a result of poverty, of certain economic patterns, etc., etc. Segregation is an ancient, psychological mechanism used by men the world over, whenever they want to shut themselves away from problems which they fear and do not feel they have the strength to solve. When men get into trouble they tend to put barriers between themselves and their difficulties. We white people got into deep trouble long ago when we attempted to enslave other human beings. A trouble we have never faced fully and never tried with all our strength to solve. Instead, we have tried to push it away from us; and in trying, we have used a mechanism so destructive that it, in itself, has become a menace to the health of our culture and our individual souls. Segregation is a way of life that is actually a form of cultural schizophrenia, bearing a curious resemblance to the schizophrenia of individual personality. It is a little chilling to note the paranoid symptoms of those among us who defend segregation: their violence, their stereotyped replies to critics, their desire to withdraw from everything hard to face. (*LLS* 86)

In foregrounding segregation as a psychological disorder, Smith reconfigured her understanding of southern authoritarianism and the means to combat it. If segregation was a deep-seated schizophrenia rather than merely a set of legal codes, then psychological and cultural health could only come with profound changes in personality development and child-rearing (and not merely by changing legal codes, though of course that was an important first step). In the same letter to Johnson, Smith wrote that "racial segregation, political and economic isolationism cannot be considered apart from man's whole personality, his culture, his needs. Neither can man's needs be considered apart from the destroying effects of segregation. Nor can the South's major problems be solved by trying to put a loaf of bread, a book, and a ballot in every one's [sic] hand. For man is not an economic or political unit. To believe that he is, by ignoring personality, we oversimplify a complex, subtle, tragically profound problem" (*LLS* 86). To attack the problem, Smith advocated that white southerners begin by engaging in small acts of behavior modification, such as using titles when speaking to black people, subscribing to a black magazine or newspaper, and spending a little time every day thinking about how it must feel to be a black person in the South. In the essay in which she makes these and many other suggestions, "Addressed to Intelligent White Southerners," Smith writes that while these small deeds might seem insignificant and undramatic, when "done by tens of thousands of southern individuals they would change the South. And the change would begin to take place where it must take place first: in a man's own heart and mind."[39]

Smith also emphasizes in "Addressed to Intelligent White Southerners" that for the creation of a new democratic order, children need to be raised in nurturing, nonfearful environments in which values of tolerance, creativity, and justice are taught. Smith speaks broadly of her goals:

> We can train them in good racial manners; to respect all people regardless of race or economic status; to oppose injustice, whether economic, racial, sexual, political or psychological. We can avoid those frustrations of spirit in childhood that prepare the emotional soil for aggression. We can train them to do long-range planning, to think of ends and means as one continuous process of indistinguishable quality. We can give them a sensitive appreciation of human personality. We can make them fearless of new ideas. We can give them awareness of their identification with all children of the whole earth. (39)

In other work from this period, Smith placed child-rearing at the center of her social and political criticism. The spring–summer 1944 issue of

South Today, for instance, includes a photo essay on children in China and America at play (those in America are African American), together with a collection of quotations from notable people on establishing psychological and cultural health, most of which affirm that the future of democracy rests with wholesome child-rearing. Some of the quotations were especially timely, diagnosing the psychological disorders facing children during wartime and arguing for extensive care for the young during periods of conflict. Several years later, Smith called for the establishment of an international center for the welfare of children; she proposed that mothers from throughout the world gather there to discuss methods of raising and nurturing the young.[40]

Smith's growing concern during World War II for children, together with her interest in the means by which cultures acculturated their young, added to her growing fears regarding authoritarian societies. Not insignificantly, one of her earliest references linking southern traditionalism with Nazism, which appeared in "Addressed to Intelligent White Southerners," comes in her call for southerners to raise their children not as "little Nazis" but as "democratic world citizens" (39). While Smith does not elaborate on the southern-Nazi connection, "Addressed to Intelligent White Southerners" reads in many ways like a wartime call to arms against southern traditionalism, an internal enemy of true democracy. Smith ends the essay's first section with this stirring statement: "Whatever our reasons for wanting to act: whether we are stirred by our love for the South or love for democracy; by our shame at being a party to injustice, our desire to win the war, or our belief in the teachings of Jesus Christ; whether by vision of a new world in which men of all races will have an equal chance for food and freedom, or fear of a race riot in our home town;—whatever our reasons for wanting to ease race tension, there are things we can do NOW" (35).

Smith made another call to arms against southern authoritarianism in her 1944 essay "Humans in Bondage." While Smith here makes clear that she sees all southerners, white and black, as "humans in bondage," she focuses her comments (as she usually does) on the destructive psychosis that southern traditionalism inflicts upon white people. "Whether they wear frock coats or overalls, the toga of leadership or the stripes of the chain gang," Smith writes of white southerners, "they are the casualties of a culture which promotes hate more assiduously than love, which makes it so hard for men to live in dignity with each other that, in despair, they tear to pieces the good along with the bad, hardly knowing one from the other as they search in great hunger for something they lost in their childhood, and which nothing in their culture gave back to them."[41] Malformed by "the steel frame of segregation" (35), most white southerners, despite supporting the war against Nazi Germany, remain ignorant of their fractured condition and of the virulent racism that shapes their thinking. "We are willing," Smith writes, "for black children to be humiliated, bruised, hurt daily, subjected to a psychic brutality that would arouse us to fury if our white children were subjected to it—that *has* aroused our fury when it has happened to Jewish children in Germany" (34). The few white southerners who are aware of their broken conditions and the crushing power of southern culture, Smith adds, cower in fear rather than calling for change, as do citizens living in totalitarian societies. "We have no Gestapo in America to invade the privacy of our homes and punish us for civilized and Christian tastes," Smith writes, making it clear that she sees southern authoritarianism as another form of Nazism. "Yet we make a Gestapo of our fears and become cowards at the sound of our own heart-beat, mistaking it for the heavy clump of disaster" (45).

In the aftermath to World War II, Smith continued to use European parallels in her attacks on southern authoritarianism, but for the most part she now drew comparisons with the Soviet Union rather than with Nazi Germany. Like many other Americans, she apparently saw the Soviet Union sharing much with Nazi Germany, the two systems' differing political ideologies overshadowed by their shared totalitarianism (Communism configured as "Red Fascism").[42] In a letter to the editors of the *New York Times* (written 22 March 1948, published 4 April) Smith wrote that southern liberals' failure to fight for human rights in the South mirrored the free world's failure to stand up against Communism. "Caution, vacillation, no real program, no strong affirmations of human freedom—these are poor weapons to use against real enemies," she writes (*LLS* 120). Observing that southern liberals are maintaining their "old grim silence" in the face of racist demagogues, Smith declares outright that the South is a totalitarian society:

> It is hard to understand such timidity at a time like this, unless we remember that Georgia, U.S.A., still has a lot in common with Georgia, U.S.S.R. Totalitarianism is an old thing to us down home. We know what it feels like. The unquestioned authority of White Supremacy, the tight political set-up of one party, nourished on poverty and ignorance, solidified the South into a totalitarian regime under which we

were living when communism was still Russian cellar talk and Hitler had not even been born.

To keep us that way, our political demagogues used and still use the same tricks Stalin uses today: an external enemy to hate (the damnyankee), an internal enemy to fear (the Negro), an iron curtain which was first forged out of the reluctance of the democratic few to take an open stand against such powerful forces. During those bitter decades liberalism was driven completely underground. Caution was a necessity, temporizing was virtue. This was the only way men could work for human rights under a system that exacted such heavy penalties from its "deviationists" as did Southern tradition. (*LLS* 120)

Adjusting her attacks on liberals to the cold war, Smith adds that the regional isolationism embraced by southern liberals (following the old argument, "Whatever is done has to be done by us alone and has to be done under the segregation system" [*LLS* 122]) mirrors the "Russian denial of freedom of speech, book-banning, national isolationism" and represents a dangerous "withdrawal from the realities of the world we live in" (*LLS* 121). Near the end of the letter, Smith suggests, astoundingly, that southerners might in the end embrace Communism, acclimated as they are to living under totalitarianism. Saying that the current situation in the South must change, she adds that "it is a tragic fact, but true, that people long used to one authority find it easy to accept another. The Solid South founded on the authority of White Supremacy, held firm by one party and a hatred of 'those enemies outside,' might not find it too hard to accept the authority and one-party system of the Solid Soviets" (*LLS* 122).

Smith's far-fetched fears of a Communist South suggest how consuming her fear of southern authoritarianism had become in the late 1940s. In the following year, she expanded her analysis of southern authoritarianism in *Killers of the Dream* (1949), a work that carries forward Smith's writings and interests from the 1930s and 1940s, weaving together autobiography, social analysis, narrative, psychology, and polemic, creating a text that speaks in all manner of discourses and moves in all sorts of directions. That multiplicity extends to the text's primary subject—segregation. Initially focusing on the ways that southern segregation destroys the dream of racial democracy, the text evolves, while remaining grounded in the southern experience, to explore the damaging psychological segregation enforced by totalitarian states, and specifically the Soviet Union, which Smith presents as the potential killer of her dream of world democracy. The first line of the foreword signals the text's international context: "This book is addressed to men and women who are concerned with the continued existence of an earth trembling between past and future" (*KD* 9).

As in her letter to the *New York Times*, Smith presents southern culture in *Killers* as a rigidly totalitarian society that controls its citizens through ruthlessly efficient socialization. Using her own upbringing as an example, and then moving to experiences she shared with girls at her summer camp, Smith explores how southern culture warps the psychological development of its children and how that warping later (mis)shapes its adults. Early in the book, focusing primarily on her life narrative, Smith characterizes southern culture as "dissonant," demanding that southerners simultaneously embrace contradictory ideas without seeing them as contradictory. Describing her own education in southern thinking—or not-thinking—Smith writes:

> I learned that it is possible to be a Christian and a white southerner simultaneously; to be a gentlewoman and an arrogant callous creature in the same moment; to pray at night and ride a Jim Crow car the next morning and to feel comfortable in doing both. I learned to believe in freedom, to glow when the word *democracy* is used, and to practice slavery from morning to night. I learned it the way all of my southern people learn it: by closing door after door until one's mind and heart and conscience are blocked off from each other and from reality. (*KD* 20)

As Smith repeatedly underscores, the South's segregated social system mirrors the segregated, fractured southern mind: "Minds broken in two. Hearts broken. Conscience torn from acts. A culture split in a thousand pieces. That is segregation" (*KD* 31).

The segregated mind is also, Smith argues, a version of the mind under totalitarianism. She describes southerners as automatons, mindlessly following not a dictator but a dictating idea—white supremacy. That idea controls all aspects of southern life, its reach extending everywhere, from Main Street to the bedroom. "We did not use the word *dictator*," Smith writes, "for we thought of ourselves as free Americans, but we obeyed this invisible power as meekly as if Hitler or Stalin had given the orders. It seemed to us that we had no other choice" (*KD* 66). Elsewhere she comments that "southern tradition may be only a ghost stalking our land, while the Politburo is a police authority with real live guns, but both have the power, by the use of fear, to take from men their freedom to do right" (*KD* 202). Smith sees that fear and terror clearly manifested in lynching, which she argues is a primary tool for enforcing segregation; in her enthusiasm to cement the southern-Nazi connection, Smith even goes so far as to assert, astoundingly, that lynching is the South's version of the death camp. She writes that even though the institutionalizing of white supremacy involves "no massive sadistic orgies as in Germany, no gas chambers, concentration camps, no Buchenwald and Dachau," nonetheless southern tradition has murdered and continues to murder countless numbers of black people, in mind if not always in body. Continuing the parallel between lynching and the death camps, Smith writes that the number of people lynched since the end of the Civil War (about five thousand) "is different in quantity and quality from the six million Jews killed so quickly in Germany. Different and in a way more evil. For we used those lynchings as a kind of symbolic rite to keep alive in men's minds the idea of white supremacy and we set up a system of avoidance rites that destroyed not bodies but the spirit of men" (*KD* 62).

After establishing what she sees as the totalitarian dimensions of southern culture, Smith looks closely at what she sees as its thoroughgoing indoctrination of children. She characterizes this indoctrination as a continuous dance lesson, with youths practicing the intricate steps of southern segregation over and over until they move across the floor naturally and mindlessly. Once mastered, the dance becomes the master:

> So we learned the dance that cripples the human spirit, step by step by step, we who were white and we who were colored, day by day, hour by hour, year by year until the movements were reflexes and made for the rest of our life without thinking. Alas, for many white children, they were movements made for the rest of their lives without feeling. What white southerner of my generation ever stops to think consciously where to go or asks himself if it is right for him to go there! His muscles know where he can go and take him to the front of the streetcar, to the front of the bus, to the big school, to the hospital, to the library, to hotel and restaurant and picture show, into the best that his town has to offer its citizens. These ceremonials in honor of white supremacy, performed from babyhood, slip from the conscious mind down deep into muscles and glands and on into that region where mature ideals rarely find entrance, and become as difficult

to tear out as are a child's beliefs about God and his secret dreams about himself. (*KD* 91)

As Jay Watson, drawing on Althusser, discusses, performing "the collective lockstep" of Smith's dance is in the end less the expression of ideological belief than the production of that belief in the individual[43]—who, of course, loses his or her individuality once the body acts instinctively as trained. Or as Smith describes the process, "we learned our way of life by doing" (*KD* 91). Watching over all are invisible, Orwellian forces of authority, "THEY WHO MAKE THE RULES" (*KD* 86).[44] "You never considered arguing with teacher," Smith writes, "because you could not see her. You only felt the iron grip of her hand and knew you must go where all the other children were going. And you learned never, never, to get out of step, for this was a precision dance which you must do with deadly accuracy" (*KD* 91). Smith ends her chapter on the training of southern youth with an image both suggesting Hitler's SS and recalling Smith's comment on the South's production of "little Nazis": "So Southern Tradition taught her bleak routines with flashes of lightning to quicken our steps" (*KD* 92).[45]

Structuring the ideology of segregation, Smith argues, are the interlocked ideologies of sin, sex, and segregation (what might be called Smith's "SSS"), which tie together the South's teachings on religion, the body, and race. To question anything, Smith emphasizes, is to question everything, so that to commit the smallest transgression is to risk standing in error before the Almighty God, who oversees all. Smith describes the fear and guilt suffered by children whose lives are triangulated by the ideology of the SSS:

> By the time we were five years old we had learned, without hearing the words, that masturbation is wrong and segregation is right, and each had become a dread taboo that must never be broken, for we believed God, whom we feared and tried desperately to love, had made the rules concerning not only Him and our parents, but our bodies and Negroes. Therefore when we as small children crept over the race line and ate and played with Negroes or broke other segregation customs that were known to us, we felt the same dread fear of consequences, the same overwhelming guilt that was ours when we crept over the sex line and played with our body, or thought thoughts about God or our parents that we knew we must not think. Each was a "sin," each "deserved punishment," each would receive it in this

world or the next. Each was tied up with the other and all were tied close to God. (*KD* 78)

Having learned that their bodies are mapped into restricted and non-restricted areas—"parts of your body are segregated areas which you must stay away from and keep others away from" (*KD* 81)—white southern children have little trouble accepting the similar mapping of segregated society. "The lesson on segregation was only a logical extension of the lessons on sex and white superiority and God," Smith writes. "Not only Negroes but everything dark, dangerous, evil must be pushed to the rim of one's life. Signs put over doors in the world outside and over our minds seemed natural enough to children like us, for signs had already been put over forbidden areas of our body" (*KD* 84–85). Lacking self-consciousness and critical-thinking skills, southern children grow into unquestioning pawns of the system, accepting what THEY WHO MAKE THE RULES dictate "as uncritically as the Communists accept their Stalin-stamped lives" (*KD* 149).

In the final section of *Killers*, "The Dream and Its Killers," Smith contextualizes the South primarily in terms of the worldwide threat of Communism, recalling totalitarian fears she had expressed in her letter to the *New York Times*. Smith sees the non-Communist world in chaos following World War II, adrift without a vital faith and poised to fall before the forces of totalitarianism. "Today, confusion encircles the world," she writes, adding that "men believing the same things [are] fighting each other to death for different reasons; men believing in different things [are] becoming allies against those who share their own beliefs" (*KD* 238). Amidst the carnage, Smith adds, lie scattered "the symbols of man's broken faith with himself," and her list of these symbols, juxtaposing images from Europe with those from the South, underscores that the coming struggle for true democracy necessarily involves defeating totalitarianism at home and abroad: "concentration camps and Jim Crow, firing squads and the KKK, Dachau and burning crosses, NKVD, mental hospitals, starving children, and in the foreground the most gruesome trials that the world has known since the Inquisition" (*KD* 238).

Adding to Smith's urgency is the threat of nuclear war. Smith writes that the world changed dramatically on the day Hiroshima was bombed; time, she says, is now our mortal enemy, because the time for finding solutions to the world's chaos is no longer on our side: nuclear warfare threatens to destroy everything before humanity establishes a just and lasting peace. Moreover, Smith sees the nuclear age pushing people into a frightening schizophrenia. On the one hand, the atomic bomb brought the world's people together by demolishing barriers that once separated them: "Walls fell. Barriers crumbled. Distances snapped together like a piece of elastic. Color, race, religion, nationality no longer had relevance. We were just people, two and one-third billion frightened people, clinging to one small earth which could give us no protection against the hate in men's heart and this dread power in their hand" (KD 236–37). On the other hand, the bomb closed people off from one another: panic-struck by the void of the nuclear future, people were regressing to childhood fears and hates, closing ranks and closing minds, searching for security in rigid ideologies.

Amidst this confusion and panic, Smith argues, humanity has forgotten its most cherished dreams of dignity and freedom, of democracy, of a hopeful future. To make these dreams real—and to secure the survival of the world—America faces a daunting challenge: "We must see to it that every man on earth is given his civil rights and we must do it quickly if man the human being is to win his fight against totalitarianism" (KD 242). That fight must be won, Smith underscores, because totalitarianism is the killer of dreams, demanding that people give up their dignity and sovereignty:

> Communism tells us that in order to have the shoes and roof and loaf of bread we must give up the freedom of mind and spirit and act; that we must do work that the state tells us to do, not that which fits into our talents and inner needs; that we can esteem only the state and must give up the luxury of esteem for each other and ourselves; that not only must we relinquish our need to change things around but above all else we must be full of anxiety, despairingly fearful, so that we shall watch each other and betray each other in order to cajole the powers that are above us. Communism tells us that there is no time and place for the dreamer, that only by giving up the dream can man have the things he wants for his body. And fascism, whose whispers are soft but powerful these days, echoes these things. And Dixiecrats say them also in part, in southern accents, and Republicans have been known to say them, and the church at its worst and certain Socialists and even liberals say words that sound curiously as if they too believe—at least in part—that these conditions are valid on which man is asked to surrender his sovereignty in order to live or to let the power that controls him live. (KD 246–47)

Here, then, are Smith's "killers of the dream"—systems of political authoritarianism that in the name of the state destroy human potential and growth.

In looking forward to the South's future, Smith at the end of *Killers* presents a quite different scenario from that in her letter to the *New York Times*. In that letter, as we have seen, Smith suggests that southerners, long attuned to living under a totalitarian system, might one day embrace Communism, the Solid South becoming the Solid Soviet. In *Killers*, however, Smith presents southerners remaining fiercely anti-Communist because Communism challenges their own brand of authoritarianism. Smith writes that southerners "hated communism because it was a new way of sinning when the old ways of sinning were good enough for us; it was a new way of making money and using money; it was a new concern with people" (*KD* 229). Communism represents drastic and intolerable change that challenges all aspects of southern authoritarianism: "It seemed to mean that workers were no longer just 'hands,' and in their minds southerners tied communism up with labor unions and high wages for both were new in the South; and their politicians tied it fast to every manifestation of concern for people's welfare and every movement that might limit their own power, and to everything that might make it more difficult for them to win an election; while the churchmen tied it up with psychoanalysis and 'free love' and hostility to the church. Communism to our people was confusion and confusion is a powerful weapon with which to lacerate the mind and to fill it with terror" (*KD* 229).

It is finally the South's anti-Communism that provides Smith with a ray of hope for the future. She believes that if southerners could ever break free from the binding chains of their own totalitarianism, a liberation that she hoped *Killers of the Dream* might help bring about, they would not be seduced again by other forms of authoritarianism. Speaking about those few southerners who she believed had broken free, as she had, of the traditional mind-set, Smith observes that it was to freedom and dignity, rather than to authority, that they turned:

> We had struggled too hard to free ourselves from southern Tradition to creep now under the coat of Russian Tradition. We feared being dictated to, having been dictated to so long by a force in the South that is as vague, as invisible, and almost as successful in making southerners conform as is the party line for the Communists; we had fallen in love with freedom for all men regardless of race, in a land of

white supremacy, and could not give it up to any party or group anywhere in the world. How could we forgive Russia its iron curtain, its putting of state rights above human rights when we opposed with all our heart and mind and skill the states' righters of our own South! Segregation was too much our mortal enemy—and to make it so we had been compelled to break too many childhood chains and sometimes the hearts of those we loved—for us to tolerate segregation in any of its communist disguises. We had learned the hard way to be loyal to belief in the dignity of man and the honor of the individual. It was not easy to bribe us with a few quick "social goals." Having learned to look at the faults of this South where we were born, we could not blind ourselves to the sins of Russia to which we had no deep ties at all. (*KD* 230)

It is these southerners, once crippled by segregation but now standing tall in their democratic faith, their dreams once shattered but now revived, who stand as Smith's hope for creating a new world democracy. And it is these southerners whom Smith hoped her work would help create, liberating those imprisoned by southern authoritarianism and leading them into a world of freedom and justice.

5

YOU CAN'T GO TO GERMANY, AGAIN

THOMAS WOLFE

Perhaps no southern writer was influenced as deeply as Thomas Wolfe by the rise of Nazi Germany. From his youth Wolfe felt a special connection with Germany, drawn to what he saw as its magnificent culture, particularly its intellectual and literary traditions. This connection, however, eventually went far deeper, with Wolfe coming to feel more at home in Germany, at least before the Nazis came to power, than in any other place. Wolfe found the Nazis' transformation of Germany hard to understand and accept; and it was not until after two fateful trips there, in 1935 and 1936, that he finally came to see that the Nazis were destroying what he found wonderful about the country. He was left stunned and troubled, and not long thereafter he began to reexamine many of his fundamental beliefs, including those on race, politics, nation, and art. Wolfe returned to the United States in 1936, transformed and in some ways chastened, an artist with an entirely new mission and understanding of himself and the world.

✶ ✶ ✶ ✶

Before Wolfe visited Nazi Germany in 1935 and 1936, he had already made four trips to the country—in 1926, 1927, 1928, and 1930—and was fascinated by Europe in general and Germany in particular.[1] His first trip across the Atlantic, in 1924, began a pattern of extended European stays, during which Wolfe usually buried himself in work.[2] He repeatedly characterized his time in Europe as productive and purposeful, and he rarely missed an opportunity to contrast himself with the expatriate American writers, including Ernest Hemingway and F. Scott Fitzgerald, who had come to be dubbed "the lost generation." Wolfe saw these writers largely as lazy escapists, looking for a way to avoid the hard work of writing, what Wolfe described in "The Story of a Novel" as "the necessity of grappling squarely with ourselves and the stern and bitter necessity of finding in ourselves, somehow, the stuff to live by, to get from our own lives and our own experience the substance and material of our art which every man who ever lived and wrote a living thing has had to get out of himself and without which he is lost."[3] In one of his unkinder moments, Wolfe characterized those of the lost generation as "cheap literary fakes sicklied o'er with a pale coat of steer-shit" (*LTW* 273).[4]

Wolfe felt profoundly connected to Germany even before he went there. Not long before his first visit, Wolfe wrote to his lover Aline Bernstein (9 November 1926) that Germany "is a land where this life shall find a home[.] I am going to Germany because there—I will tell you—below old dreaming towers a river runs; upon the rocks Lorelei comb their hair; the winds about the castle crags at night are full of demon voices; and the gabled houses of the toyland towns are full of rich and gluttonous warmth" (*MOL* 118). Describing his feelings when his train crossed the border into Germany, Wolfe wrote to Aline (10 December 1926) that he was "nearly crazy with excitement and exultancy, rushing from one side of the compartment to the other to look down upon the river" (*MOL* 134). His initial impressions of the country confirmed all his dreams: he felt right at home amidst a landscape he found magical and a people he found kind, simple, and honest. "I am alone in the kind of adventure that excites me, discovering, voyaging, renewing myself, soaking in it" (*MOL* 135), he wrote in the same letter, adding that "yesterday I met the hills, the woods, the crazy villages for the first time—they *sounded* in me, I gave them life that had never existed before" (*MOL* 136).

Not surprisingly, Wolfe's rose-colored views of the Germans began to darken as he moved about the country, coming face to face with some of the uglier aspects of Weimar society. Among the rowdy crowds in German beer halls Wolfe discovered a brutish streak in what he had hitherto believed was the noble German spirit. Writing to Aline (13 December 1926), he characterized one of these drinking establishments as "one enormous sea-slop of beer, power, Teutonic masculine energy and vitality," adding that the crowd seemed like "some tremendous yeast unfolding from its own bowels—it was the core, heart, entrails of that strength—the thing unfolding and unpremeditated that cannot be stopped or stoppered" (*MOL* 137). On his second trip to the country, Wolfe concluded, as he wrote to Aline (1928), that the beer-hall crowd "is the real Germany—it is impressive and powerful and yet, after a time I dislike it. Nevertheless, I think this country interests me more than any in Europe—can you explain this enigma?—here is this brutal, beer swilling people, and yet I doubt if there is as much that is spiritually grand in any other people in Europe as this one" (*MOL* 212).

Wolfe continued to affirm his love for Germany through his fourth trip, in 1930, clearly seeing himself in the German character as he perceived it, with its striking conflation of nobility and brutishness: at the same time that he embraced a Joycean aesthetic confirming himself as a priest to his art, Wolfe hungered for worldly experience, driven by a gargantuan appetite. Quite simply, he wanted it all: to read every book, to see every museum, to visit every major city, to meet every person, to sleep with every woman, and so on. He kept long lists documenting his progress in meeting these goals. As ascetic as he was in his devotion to his writing, he thrived, when not writing, on Teutonic excess; it was not merely as a detached observer that Wolfe sought out the German beer halls.

During his 1928 and 1930 visits to Germany, Wolfe began to take closer note of the nation's economic and political turmoil, expressing sympathy for the struggles facing everyday Germans amidst the disastrous economic conditions. His comments now focused less on brutishness in the beer halls than on brutishness in the government; he described German politicians as arrogant, corrupt, and imperialistic. Regarding the 1930 national elections, Wolfe wrote in his notes that nationalist fervor was being whipped up by "fat corrupt faces all over Germany," an apparent reference to the leaders of the nineteen political parties vying for power (*NTW* 2:514). It was during this trip that Wolfe first took note of the Nazis; despite the tremendous gains they had made in the elections (their Reichstag representation rose to 107 from 12), Wolfe dismissed them as worthless hotheads who posed no threat to German stability. To his brother Fred, Wolfe wrote (26 September 1930) that "the German fascisti" were merely "young fellows... hot under the collar about the international situation"; and he added that he shared the Nazis' anger over the French occupation of the Rhineland.[5]

Even after the Nazis came to power and began transforming Germany into a repressive state, Wolfe found little to criticize them for and little to fear from them. On his 1935 trip he noticed little amiss, perhaps being distracted by his own status as a literary sensation, with his German hosts wining, dining, and bedding him in a promiscuous whirlwind of activity. Rarely at a loss for words, Wolfe wrote to Maxwell Perkins (23 May 1935) that he had "not space or power enough here to tell you how beautiful and fine and magical this trip has been" (*LTW* 460). H. M. Ledig-Rowohlt, a partner in the German publishing house that published Wolfe and who spent time with him in 1935, later recalled that their talks had "remained predominantly unpolitical" and "that only occasionally did our conversation touch on the murky political situation and on the 'Dark Messiah,' as Wolfe would later call Hitler. His political skepticism was still glossed over by joy at his literary success; and besides, he loved Berlin more than any other European capital."[6]

Wolfe's resistance to acknowledging the dangers of the Nazis, however, extended beyond his literary stardom and his love for Berlin. Feeling fundamentally connected with the Germans, he found it hard to believe that they would embrace Nazism if it were as terrible as the Western press was describing it. Wolfe was convinced that most of what the foreign press wrote about the Nazis was ill-informed and biased, and for the most part he ignored what he read, vowing to form his own judgments based on his own observations. Those observations, of course, were not as unbiased as Wolfe acknowledged (to himself or anyone else), and indeed David Herbert Donald is clearly right in his suggestion that Wolfe's refusal to believe in Nazi oppression in 1935 stemmed in part from how he construed the Nazi enterprise. As Donald observes, at this point Wolfe "believed that Hitler was accomplishing much that was positive," particularly when seen against the social and economic disorders that had plagued Germany in the late 1920s and early 1930s. On his previous visits, Donald writes, Wolfe "had witnessed the poverty, the unemployment, and the fierce political battles that had racked Germany," and in 1935 "he could not help being impressed by the new sense of order."[7] Seeing himself as somewhat of a homeless nomad, torn between the desire for wandering and new experience and the desire for fixity and repose, Wolfe admired the German people for giving themselves over to a cause larger than themselves, establishing identity and purpose within a community of believers.

This is not to say that Wolfe was entirely naive about the Nazi enterprise and its attendant repression. Fears and warnings voiced by his German friends forced him to acknowledge the widespread unease among Germans. In the same letter to Perkins in which gushed about his wonderful visit, Wolfe admitted his growing concerns. After saying that he did not see how anyone who traveled to Germany "could possibly fail to love the country, its noble Gothic beauty and its lyrical loveliness, or to like the German people who are, I think, the cleanest, the kindest, the warmest-hearted, and most honorable people I have met in Europe," he added: "I tell you this because I think a full and generous recognition must be made of all these facts and because I have been told and felt things here which you and I can never live or stand for and which, if they are true, as by every reason of intuition and faith and belief in the people with whom I have talked I must believe, are damnable" (*LTW* 460). Perplexed and torn between his love for Germany and his fears about what it was becoming, Wolfe wrote to Perkins that he wished he could sit down with him so he could fully explain "all that has been wonderful and beautiful and exciting, and about those things that are so hard to explain because one feels they are so evil and yet cannot say so justly in so many words as a hostile press and propaganda would, because this evil is so curiously and inextricably woven into a kind of wonderful hope which flourishes and inspires millions of people who are themselves, as I have told you, certainly not evil, but one of the most child-like, kindly and susceptible people in the world" (*LTW* 460). In a striking passage, Wolfe attempted to sort through his confusion, acknowledging the difficulty of accusing Nazi Germany of evil without acknowledging that evil in himself and indeed in all humanity:

> Someday I should like to write something about it, but if I now wrote even what I have heard and felt in two weeks, it might bring the greatest unhappiness and suffering upon people I have known here and who have shown me the most affectionate hospitality. But more and more I feel that we are all of us bound up and tainted by whatever guilt and evil there may be in this whole world, and that we cannot accuse and condemn others without in the end coming back to an accusal of ourselves. We are all damned together, we are all tarred by the same stick, and for what has happened here we are all in some degree responsible. This nation to-day is beyond the shadow of a vestige of a doubt full of uniforms and a stamp of marching men—I saw it with my own eyes yesterday in one hundred towns and villages across two hundred miles of the most peaceful, lovely and friendly-looking country I have ever seen. A thousand groups, uncountable divisions of the people from children eight years old to men of fifty, all filled beyond a doubt with hope, enthusiasm and inspired by a belief in a fatal and destructive thing—and the sun was shining all day long and the fields are greenest, the woods the loveliest, the little towns the clean-

est, and the faces and the voices of the people the most friendly of any I have ever seen or heard, so what is there to say? (*LTW* 460–61)

As his words suggest, confronting the dark side of Nazism involved for Wolfe confronting his own dark side. So, indeed, what was there to say about Nazism? About himself?

In struggling to understand Nazism and its transformation of Germany, together with what Nazism had to do with his own feelings and beliefs, Wolfe was facing up to the challenge that he believed necessary for intellectual and imaginative growth. As he said repeatedly throughout his career, the primary reason he traveled to Europe was to enlarge his vision and deepen his self-understanding by immersing himself in different cultures, with the imaginative interplay between old and new forcing him to rethink his accepted beliefs and to reconfigure his characteristic lines of sight. In this process of reformulation, Wolfe wrote, "all of my powers of memory and experience were constantly brought to bear as I compared the life of which I was a part, the country from which I came, with this new and alien life in which I lived and wandered as a stranger."[8] The interplay most at work during his travels to Nazi Germany centered on Wolfe's deeply ingrained thoughts and feelings about race, including his bitter anti-Semitism. Dovetailing as they did, at least broadly, with Nazi ideology, Wolfe's racial beliefs were made manifest in the Nazi system, and this manifestation pressured him to reevaluate his thinking, including his political and artistic commitments.

Wolfe's ideas on race, which were bound up with his troubled attitudes toward women and sexuality, combined characteristic white southern prejudice against blacks with hardcore American nativism, as popularized in the work of the historians Madison Grant and Lothrop Stoddard. While it is not known whether Wolfe read Grant and Stoddard, he clearly knew their general arguments, which were circulating freely in 1920s and 1930s America, and his ideas on race, including his basic racial taxonomy, closely parallel theirs.[9] Put simply, and in the words of one of their admirers, Grant and Stoddard advocated a "hereditary interpretation of history."[10] Mixing history, anthropology, and eugenics, both argue that history is first and foremost the story of races struggling to survive and prosper and that in this ongoing struggle, maintaining the purity of the superior races' blood—and all the genetic materials it carried—is history's fundamental value. All manifestations of society and culture are secondary to blood and genetics, because all these manifestations are, finally, themselves expressions of blood. Of the achievements of the white race up into the nineteenth century Stoddard writes that "all these marvellous achievements were due solely to superior heredity, and the mere maintenance of what had been won depended absolutely upon the prior maintenance of race-values. Civilization of itself means nothing. It is merely an effect, whose cause is the creative urge of superior germ-plasm. Civilization is the body; the race is the soul. Let the soul vanish, and the body moulders into the inanimate dust from which it came."[11]

Grant's and Stoddard's work, like Wolfe's own racial thinking, focuses on the problems facing the white race—the superior race whose blood purity needs to be protected in order for civilization to advance. In looking at the world following World War I (which, as Stoddard puts it, "was nothing short of a headlong plunge into white race-suicide. It was essentially a civil war between closely related white stocks" [179]), Grant and Stoddard find the white race threatened not only by the rising power and numbers of other races but also by the competition between the white race's three different stocks—Nordic, Mediterranean, and Alpine, of which the Nordic was the highest. "All three are good stocks, ranking in genetic worth well above the various colored races," Stoddard writes, but he adds that "there seems to be no question that the Nordic is far and away the most valuable type; standing, indeed, at the head of the whole human genus" (162). The Nordic is "the white man par excellence,"[12] Grant comments, concluding that "the backbone of western civilization is racially Nordic, the Alpines and Mediterraneans being effective precisely to the extent in which they have been Nordicized and vitalized."[13] The great race of Grant's title, *The Passing of the Great Race*, is not, as one might expect, the white race, but the Nordic.

Perhaps Wolfe's clearest statement confirming his awareness of Grant and Stoddard's racial taxonomy comes in a short essay that he wrote in 1925 about the Tower of London. In poking fun at the superior methods of torture developed by the civilized British, Wolfe writes that "it will no doubt be pleasing to all of us who are quite sure of the Nordic supremacy in all matters requiring character and courage and honesty, and who believe that only by the continued domination of the Nordic may civilization be saved, to know that in the matter of devising abominable and revolting cruelties for the torture of the unconvinced we Nordics have shown the same superiority" (*TWA* 115–16).[14] More significant here than the gentle satire of Nordic civility (which does not undercut unquestioned Nordic racial superiority) is

Wolfe's self-identification not only as a Nordic but also as being "quite sure of Nordic supremacy." As Pascal Reeves notes in his close study of Wolfe's racial attitudes, Wolfe's "Nordic self-identification" remained unwavering throughout his career (*TWA* 115).

Expressions of Wolfe's nativist thinking appear throughout his letters and notebooks. In a letter to his mother (31 August 1923) Wolfe discussed the decline of American civilization, comparing its vulgarization to that of ancient Rome's final days (a comparison frequently made by Grant and Stoddard), when "there was the same vulgar display of wealth, the same vulgar waste, the same worship of cheap, low, trivial things" and when the great rulers and poets had been replaced by "freaks and degenerates."[15] Wolfe continued, in a passage that bears citation in its entirety:

> I do not know if you can observe it at home—possibly not—for the South is still conservative, and, for the most part, of undiluted stock, but the signs of unrest up here are appalling. For one thing our constitution has perpetrated the most damnable political theory ever conceived—namely that men are created equal. Now, I appeal to your judgment,—to your, good, hard sense—did you ever see two people who were equal in any respect? in intelligence, in physical strength, in imagination, in courage, in judgment, in any of the things that help us through this tempestuous world. Furthermore—we Southerners, more than anyone else, recognize the falsity of the doctrine in practice at any rate, while defending it, hypocritically, in practice. Do we admit the equality of the Negro? Do we give him the vote? Yet no one is better at whooping up equality than one of our quack Congressmen on the stump. It sickens you. Yet, yearly we are bringing hundreds of thousands of inferior people—the Latin races, undeveloped physically, dwarfed mentally, into this country. From them will grow the America of to-morrow—"the hope of the world[.]" It is impossible to regard them without a sinking of the heart. How can anything good come from it? I am no pessimist, but why try to side-step the facts? (49–50)

Wolfe's tirade here could almost be read as a gloss on Grant and Stoddard, complete with a racialist perspective of culture valorizing "undiluted stock," an appreciation of the South's unbending racial consciousness that protects its bloodlines, a call to end unchecked immigration because the nation is being inundated with inferior genetic stock, and an attack on equalitarianism, if not democracy itself. In another letter to his mother (3 June 1927) Wolfe bemoaned America's democratic masses, what he satirically labeled "the great intelligent self-governing public of this noble land—the amalgamated Boosters, Kiwanians, Lions, and, in general, the Federated Half Breeds of the world" (118).

Paschal Reeves, noting similarities between Grant and Wolfe, argues that Wolfe's nativism derived from "the combination of his rural, pioneer point of view and his having grown up in a homogenous region" and mirrored nineteenth-century American "notions of racial superiority, exclusiveness, veneration for established tradition, distrust of unassimilated cultural patterns, and suspicion of urban values" (*TWA* 5, 6). While perhaps oversimplifying American cultural thought, Reeves is no doubt correct that Wolfe's nativism looked backward to simpler and more heroic times. And it is also clear that Wolfe most identified with heroes of the past. In a letter to his mother (26 April 1930) Wolfe wrote about his allegiance to the "old" rather than the "new" America:

> I am proud of my people, proud of my pioneer and mountaineer and Pennsylvania Dutch ancestry, and proud of the place I came from, although I have been told they do not want me back there, and that I am no longer welcome. As I walk through the crowded and noisy streets of this immense city, and look at the dark swarthy faces of Jews, Italians, Greeks, and all the people of the New America that is roaring up around us here, I realize more keenly than ever that I come from the Old Americans—the people who settled the country, who fought in its wars, who pushed westward. (162)

Like a number of southern writers from the period, including William Alexander Percy and William Faulkner, Wolfe repeatedly contrasted what he found as the puny stature of modern humanity (typically characterized as urban hordes) with the rugged tall men of the past (typically characterized as wilderness frontiersmen). Eugene Gant, for instance, one of Wolfe's autobiographical heroes, ruminates in *Of Time and the River* (1935) on what Wolfe liked to call "lost America" and the great men who "knew the wilderness, but who had never lived in cities: three hundred of his blood and bone, who sowed their blood and sperm across the continent, walked beneath its broad and lonely lights, were frozen by its bitter cold, burned by the heat of its fierce suns, withered, gnarled, and broken by its savage weathers, and who fought like lions with its gigantic strength, its wildness, its limitless savagery and beauty, until with one stroke of its paw it broke their backs and killed them."[16] Those of the "new America" Eugene characterizes as "the million-footed crowd" flooding the nation out from New York City, which he describes as "the last and largest colony of the great mongrel and anonymous compost that makes up America" (593).

Eugene Gant's observations illustrate Wolfe's own nativist interpretation of American history: that America had drastically declined since the great men of the past "sowed their blood and sperm across the continent," that the nation was being overrun by immigrants, "mongrel and anonymous compost," whose inferior racial stock was destroying American (Nordic) bloodlines. Wolfe's harsh characterization of the immigrant population is typical of his sweeping dismissal of immigrants from countries of southern and eastern Europe, those who, in Grant and Stoddard's racial taxonomy, were Mediterraneans and Alpines. Writing on shipboard on his return trip from Europe in 1929, Wolfe commented on the immigrant passengers: "This boat too is America—this swarthy stew of Italians, Greeks, and God knows what other combinations. This morning they are 'spikking Eenglis' (How are yew, Mister? etc.) and going about in their cheap new American clothes" (*NTW* 1:299). Wolfe clearly saw no hope of these people ever becoming "true" Americans; speaking English and wearing American clothes (cheap or otherwise) were inconsequential next to their swarthy—that is, racial—identity.

As Paschal Reeves argues, "Wolfe's standard for evaluating the foreigner is the nativistic touchstone of Americanization—the degree to which the foreigner is capable of complete acculturation" (*TWA* 115). For Wolfe, only whites from northern Europe—the Nordics—were capable of that acculturation. All others were interlopers, American wannabees. In this, Wolfe closely followed Grant and Stoddard, whose discussions of the United States focused on the decline of Nordic presence and influence, and particularly on the threat to Nordic blood posed by racially inferior immigrants. To their eyes, the American colonies had been settled and the nation later established largely by Nordics, whom they designated as "native Americans." Although the United States remained primarily a Nordic nation up through the late nineteenth century, historic events were undermining its Nordic solidarity and purity. These events included the heated debates on slavery that divided the nation (a split, says Grant, "inimical to the Nordic race, because it thrust aside all national opposition to the intrusion of hordes of immigrants of inferior racial value and prevented the fixing of a definite American type" [86]), the Civil War ("fought almost entirely by unalloyed native Americans" [86]), and the flood of immigration after the War ("the European governments took the opportunity to unload upon careless, wealthy, and hospitable America the sweepings of their jails and asylums" [89]). Concerning immigration's effect on the Nordic nation, Grant comments: "The result was that the new immigration, while it still included many strong elements from the north of Europe, contained a large and increasing number of the weak, the broken and the mentally crippled of all races drawn from the lowest stratum of the Mediterranean basin and the Balkans, together with hordes of the wretched, submerged populations of the Polish Ghettos. Our jails, insane asylums and almshouses are filled with this human flotsam and the whole tone of American life, social, moral and political has been lowered and vulgarized by them" (89–90).

In seeing American history much as Grant and Stoddard did, Wolfe found easy justification for his belief, grounded in his southern upbringing, that blacks were genetically incapable of progressing far up the ladder of civilization. Blacks could imitate the civilized, Wolfe believed, but they could never *be* civilized, a point Stoddard also emphasized: "The negro is a facile, even eager, imitator; but there he stops. He adopts; but he does not adapt, assimilate, and give forth creatively again" (100–101). "When left to himself, as in Haiti and Liberia," Stoddard added, "[the black person] rapidly reverts to his ancestral [that is, savage] ways" (100). At about the same time that Stoddard wrote these words, Wolfe wrote, in a preface intended for his play "Niggertown" (later changed to *Welcome to Our City*), that "the negro race has no moral or cultural background to give it spine. Let the optimistic call it lack of education, opportunity or what they will, but the fact remains that the race is incapable of making the simplest ethical decisions." He went on to say that social change would not fundamentally affect the black character, since "the background from which a well-developed race must come is the product of centuries of slow and painful upbuilding" (qtd. in *TWA* 10). And in a fragment for an essay from the early 1920s, Wolfe commented that if blacks were magically transported back to the jungle ("a dream in which most Southerners at one time or another indulge"), one "would see completed in twenty years the cycle from savagery to savagery" (qtd. in *TWA* 9). While Wolfe later grew more conscious of and sympathetic about the suffering of blacks in America, particularly during and after the Depression, apparently he still clung to his fundamental belief that blacks were never far from jungle primitivism.[17]

Wolfe's nativism also lies at the heart of his anti-Semitism. Indeed, much of Wolfe's discussion of Jews, particularly in the early 1920s (before Wolfe's intense and explosive relationship with Aline Bernstein, who often became the flashpoint for his anti-Semitism), focused on their tribalism, which he said problematized their acculturation as Americans. In notes written on his first trip to Europe in 1924, Wolfe discussed at length "the relation of the Jew to American life":

> The Jew has everywhere insisted in maintaining a religious and social isolation, and where he has discarded the religious isolation, he has held to the social. This is his right, but every nation is an island and one may live upon an island, but one may not, without complication, create an island upon an island. He demands a walled city for himself, in which he may live, without ingression, and from which he may go to share in Every suffrage of the nation. Wherever he has been, wherever he goes, he has been confronted with the problem of God and the law. He entreats the right to other people's law, but he insists on his own right to furnish his own God; and two Gods and one Caesar is a difficult, an almost insoluble combination. (qtd. in *TWA* 48)

Wolfe added that Jewish resistance to national identity and nation building, while often breeding resentment and persecution from non-Jews, actually best explained Jewish survival:

> It has been held by many that the remarkable evidence of the Jew's persistence is that he has maintained his race while losing his nation; but it is doubtless because of this rather than in spite of it that he exists. For it is quite often not the absence of empire which kills a people, but the possession of it. The Jew unharmed by civil strife, political dissension, and the ambitions for Empire of rapacious and uncompassionate rulers, save when these evils have been imposed on him by alien hands, has had, it seems to me, unequalled opportunity for survival. (qtd. in *TWA* 48–49)

Wolfe saw the Jew in America not merely surviving but thriving, since Americans—that is, non-Jews—"have created a commercial life whose conditions fit him like a glove" (qtd. in *TWA* 48). Non-Jews, he wrote, "are hopelessly outmatched at the beginning in any such rivalry with people to whom our greatest subtleties of trade seem banal; who have inherited all the shrewdness of five thousand years of trading; and who, at the age of two, begin to finger their father's coat sleeve deftly in order to judge the quality of the cloth" (qtd. in *TWA* 48). In notes from 1928 Wolfe commented that "there was growing up in America a new race of millionaires with strange and forbidding names—Schultes, and Gimbels, and Fleischmans, and Kahns, a race whose thousand millions made the hundreds of the Pierces and the Goulds and the Astors look paltry" (*NTW* 1:193). And that wealth and power, he added, was taking control of American culture, including the arts, a view he had held at least since the early 1920s, when he was a struggling playwright. In notes from that time, Wolfe blamed Jews for his failures as a dramatist:

> Artistically, at any rate, the Jew is a menace. He controls the theatre in New York. If this were all, he might be compelled, by properly enlightened audiences, to advance his standards and improve in the quality of his dramatic selections. But the character of New York audiences is itself determined, in large measure, by the members of his race. They dominate the occasion and their demand is ever for the sensual, the thinly veiled, or the materialistic. The explanation for our country's noble and unique contribution to drama—the "success play"—that is, the play where the brisk and breezy young "American" shows his employer how to double the sale of dill pickles, and thereby wins the old man's daughter, may be found in the strong zest the Semitic audience has for this type of play. (*NTW* 1:21)

Once Aline entered into his life, Wolfe's anti-Semitism grew more virulent, now intertwined with his passionately conflicted feelings toward women and sexuality. Wolfe's gargantuan sexual appetite was laced with bitter misogyny, particularly directed at independent and sexually active women, to whom he was drawn and by whom he ultimately felt threatened. "Women have no morals: they only have the sense of fashion," Wolfe commented in some notes from 1930. "If the fashion is for adultery: they will adulterate openly; if the fashion says niggers are better than white men, they will have niggers, if the fashion says niggers are loathesome, they will loathe niggers" (*NTW* 2:483). Typically he nestled into relationships with women, only to have them founder on his paranoia concerning women's sexual desire and betrayal of men. "And where dies faith? Where does the heart go rotten?" Wolfe asked in a letter to Aline (25 October 1926) and then gave his answer: "Why, when a woman lifts her skirt, behind the door; with sow grunts and belly burlesque" (*MOL* 104). No one triggered these conflicting feelings toward women more intensely than Aline, the Jewish woman who, as he wrote to her in another letter the same day, was run into his heart like a thorn (*MOL* 102). Wolfe's consuming love for Aline—"I love you with a single and absolute love that rises above and dominates everything in my life," he wrote to her (11–12 August 1928)—was matched by his equally consuming disgust (*MOL* 190). Aline, he announced on another occasion, was merely "a titillative New York Jew with a constantly dilating and palpitative vagina."[18] In his fictional portrayal of his relationship with Aline in *The Web and the Rock* Wolfe describes his autobiographical hero, George Webber, pondering the face of Esther (the Aline figure), seeing it as "flamed like a strange and opulent jewel; in his feverish imagination it smouldered drowsily with all the slumberous and insatiate passions of the East, it spoke of a desire illimitable as the ocean, a body to be taken by all men, and never to be possessed by any."[19]

This powerful combination of misogyny and virulent anti-Semitism, a combination that Wolfe was far from alone among modernist writers in demonstrating,[20] lies behind George Webber's outbursts in *The Web and the Rock* that Esther is participating in a Jewish plot to entrap Gentiles: "Why is it that every damned one of you is out to get a Christian if you can? . . . You know it's true! Why, every God-damned one of you, man or woman, will crawl upon your hands and knees—yes!—creep and crawl and contrive until you have a Gentile in your clutches!" (591). George imagines "a dark regiment of Jewish women in their lavish beauty, their faces melting into honey, their eyes glowing, their breasts like melons. . . . They were the living rack on which the trembling backs of all their Christian lovers had been broken, the living cross on which the flesh and marrow of Christian men had been crucified" (547–48). Jewish temptresses, following the logic of Wolfe's racialist history, threatened the genetic health of America itself, with engulfing Jewish women drawing Nordic American men away from their proper mates. The nativist underpinnings of Wolfe's anti-Semitism surface most clearly in the draft of a letter to Aline:

> You put up a poor whining mouth in your letters about being "broke" and having lost your money—Well, being broke in the understanding of most of us does not mean apartments at the Gotham Hotel and buying homes in Westchester County and trips to California—My own people fought in the wars of this country and helped settle

it and have endured all its poverty and danger and suffering. You and your kind who belong to an alien and disloyal race have fought in none of our wars and done none of the building or working or pioneer work that made the country. I have often heard you and your kind sneer at this country and at its people—my own people—and talk of our ignorance and crudity and babbittry—Well, if it had not been for us there would have been no such rich pickings for smooth soft-handed German Jews who were able to exploit simple ignorant people through the dishonest speculations and by doing so keep their wives and daughters in Park Avenue apartments and able to entertain select gatherings of Lesbians, pederasts, and other vicious people that are spawned out of the theatre. (*NTW* 2:663)

Wolfe wrote these words in 1934, one year after Hitler's ascension to power and nine years after Hitler had forthrightly declared in *Mein Kampf* that "the Jew was no German" and that, among many other things, Jews were sapping the strength of German nationalism and were responsible for "nine tenths of all literary filth, artistic trash, and theatrical idiocy" that was flooding German society.[21]

Bringing up Hitler at this point is not to equate Wolfe with the Nazi dictator but to point to the intriguing question of what happened to Wolfe's nativism, founded so solidly on racial thinking and anti-Semitism, when he visited Nazi Germany and came face to face with a dictatorial regime that made real, by law and fiat, many of Wolfe's racialist thoughts. Answered simply, Wolfe's experiences in Nazi Germany challenged his nativism but in the end left it fundamentally unchanged. While certainly Wolfe emerged more socially and politically aware after his trips to Nazi Germany in 1935 and 1936, he was never able to free himself entirely from his emotionally charged nativism. Lillian Smith's description of the deep-seated psychological hold segregation had on southerners also characterize the grip nativism had on Wolfe: the rituals of southern supremacy, Smith writes, "slip from the conscious mind down deep into the muscles and glands and on into that region where mature ideals rarely find entrance, and become as difficult to tear out as are a child's beliefs about God and his secret dreams of himself" (*KD* 91).

The main challenge to Wolfe's nativism came during his 1936 trip. At the beginning of the trip Wolfe seemed utterly oblivious to the fact that the Nazis were turning Germany into an oppressive and militaristic state. Upon his arrival, Wolfe gushed as he always had about the wonders of Germany, writing that "if there was no Germany, it would be necessary to invent one. It's a magical country. I know Hildesheim, Nuremberg, Munich, the architecture, the soul of the place, the glory of its history and its art. Two hundred years ago my forefathers emigrated from southern Germany to America."[22] But before long that joy began to give way to dismay, with Wolfe commenting less on Germany's glorious past than on its troubled present, particularly its grim political situation. Whereas H. M. Ledig-Rowohlt remembered his apolitical discussions with Wolfe during his 1935 visit, he noted that in 1936 "the 'Dark Messiah' was the recurring subject of our conversations.... [Wolfe] feared still greater mischief to come [from the Nazis], and he realized bitterly that everywhere men of good will were being oppressed by the men of power, and that Hitler was unleashing nothing but evil in the world."[23] Once dismissing critics of Nazi Germany as ignorant and biased, Wolfe now saw that these critics had been largely right—that the Nazis were establishing a tightly regulated militarized state. Wolfe now took seriously the stories he heard, both from German friends and from officials at the American embassy, concerning the Nazi suppression of civil liberties and the resulting fear and paranoia infecting everyday German life.

Nevertheless, Wolfe refused to reject the Nazis outright, still believing that the foreign press was misrepresenting their programs and that in some ways the Nazis' political positions were more forthright than those of compromised democracies. Wolfe struggled to work through his thoughts on the Nazis in order to gain what he hoped would be a balanced perspective, not only on the German situation but also on his own political beliefs and biases, many of which, as we have seen, broadly echoed Nazi ideology. Wolfe's notebook entries in 1936 frequently focused on issues highlighted by the contrast between the Nazi and American political systems, as in the following fragment entitled "On Freedom of Speech and Thought":

> We say in America that we are free to speak and write and think as we please, but this is not true. We also say that in Germany people can not speak and write and think as they please. This also is not true. People are free to speak, and write and think some things in Germany that they are not free to speak and write in America. For example, in Germany you are free to speak and write that you do not like Jews and that you think Jews are bad, corrupt, and unpleasant people. In America you are not free to say this. (*NTW* 2:829)

In another fragment Wolfe diagramed his conflicting feelings toward the Fascist enterprise:

FASCISM

For	Against
Physical Clean-ness	Repression of Free Speech
Healthy People	A Cult of Insular Superiority
Effective Relief	With This A Need For Insular Domination
A Concentration of National Energy	

(*NTW* 2:831)

Wolfe no doubt saw his own efforts to understand Nazi Germany standing in contrast to the behavior of those critics who merely denounced, without any critical appraisal, everything Nazi or Fascist. Indeed, Wolfe felt that the Nazi haters in America had become so powerful that no reasoned discussion of the German political system was possible, a dangerous development that threatened to counter one form of totalitarianism with another. In some notes made immediately after Wolfe returned from Germany in 1936, and after he had become decidedly anti-Nazi, he commented on the need for intellectual and political honesty in confronting the Nazi menace:

> There have been too many false stories—too many distortions of fact, twisting of evidence, and just plain lies. Surely, if the conscience of the men of good will throughout the world is so deeply and earnestly convinced that what has happened in Germany is against the true current of the nation's spirit, and the true current of the spirit of the world—and I, for one, am so convinced—is it not a matter of the deepest urgency that we keep, so far as possible, scrupulously exact our account of what has happened there? Are we to fight fire with fire—subdue contagion by the spreading of a plague?—or meet a lie with another lie of our own formulation? It will not do. (*NTW* 2:840)

Wolfe designated unthinking anti-Fascists "slot-machines," because he felt that no matter what the discussion, they repeatedly spat out the same ideologically acceptable comments, stifling open dialogue. In another notebook entry from 1936 he zeroed in on what he saw as the anti-Fascist suppression of free inquiry, noting that the anti-Fascists' tactics ironically mirrored those used in Fascist dictatorships:

The Slot Machine
1. We can make any criticism we like, however violent, about the inhabitants of the state of Kansas. But it is very dangerous to make any criticism, even a mild one, about Jews.
2. Nothing good can be said about the Italian or German Dictatorships. If one suggests that benefits from these dictatorships have been considerable, the slot-machine answer, with a slight sneer, is, "Oh, yes, we know—the streets are clean and the trains run on time, but do you think these blessings compensate for the loss of human liberties, freedom of speech, etc., etc."

It is useless to tell the Slot-Machines that the benefits of the Fascist Dictatorships have resulted in far more considerable benefits than "clean streets and trains on time," and that if we are really going to combat the evil of Fascism, we must first begin by understanding its good. (*NTW* 2:829–30)

Particularly sensitive to issues of freedom of speech and of the press (Wolfe frequently complained of being savaged by the press), Wolfe seemed torn between what he saw as the excesses of both political systems. In another fragment, he imagined a Fascist dictatorship coming to power in the United States, noting that "freedom of speech and freedom of the press would be suppressed, but so would freedom of Press-Filth, Press-Lies, etc., be suppressed" (*NTW* 2:832). Although it is not precisely clear, Wolfe seemed happy to give up the former for the latter.

By the time Wolfe left Germany in September 1936 he had come to see that whatever the immediate benefits ushered in by Fascist dictatorships—such as transforming chaotic social orders into powerful modern states by focusing national pride and energy—these were outweighed by the dangerous aims and methods ushering in these changes, particularly (as Wolfe designated in his Fascism chart, above) Fascism's xenophobic ideology calling for "A Cult of Insular Superiority" with "A Need For Insular Domination." Although Wolfe continued to condemn "slot-machine" criticism of the Nazis, he was now aware of the Nazi threat to both Germans and the world. Wolfe's description of the 1936 Olympics (which he attended and where he saw Hitler), eventually published in *You Can't Go Home Again*, reveals the ominous danger underlying the otherwise magnificent discipline and order of the games:

> One sensed a stupendous concentration of effort, a tremendous drawing together and ordering in the vast collective power of the whole land. And the thing that made it seem ominous was that it so evidently went beyond what the games themselves demanded. The games were overshadowed, and were no longer merely sporting competitions to which other nations had sent their chosen teams. They became, day after day, an orderly and overwhelming demonstration in which the whole of Germany had been schooled and disciplined. It was as if the games had been chosen as a symbol of the new collective might, a means of showing to the world in concrete terms what this new power had come to be.[24]

Outside the stadium, lines of soldiers stretched for miles down the main thoroughfare, waiting not merely for Hitler's entourage but also, as Wolfe's comments make clear, for the coming conflagration: "They stood at ease, young men, laughing and talking with each other—the Leader's bodyguards, the Schutz Staffel units, the Storm Troopers, all the ranks and divisions in their different uniforms—and they stretched in two unbroken lines from the Wilhelm-strasse up to the arches of the Brandenburger Tor. Then, suddenly, the sharp command, and instantly there would be the solid smack of ten thousand leather boots as they came together with the sound of war" (627).

Beyond the threat of Nazi militarism, Wolfe now understood the fear and paranoia infecting the everyday lives of Germans under the grip of Nazi totalitarianism. In a passage eventually published in *You Can't Go Home Again*, Wolfe interpreted Germans' interest in American writers as an effort to maintain their intellectual lives amidst Nazi censorship and repression. "Under these conditions," Wolfe writes, "the last remnants of the German spirit managed to survive only as drowning men survive—by clutching desperately at any spar that floated free from the wreckage of their ship" (633). Wolfe goes on to describe George Webber's growing awareness of "this shipwreck of a great spirit. The poisonous emanations of suppression, persecution, and fear permeated the air like miasmic and pestilential vapors, tainting, sickening, and blighting the lives of everyone he met. It was a plague of the spirit—invisible, but as unmistakable as death. Little by little it sank in on him through all the golden singing of that summer, until at last he felt it, breathed it, lived it, and knew it for the thing it was" (633).

A few years after his return from Germany, in a 1938 lecture at Purdue University, Wolfe discussed his final visit to Germany and his witnessing of the nation's quiet suffering under the Nazis. "Sometimes it came to me with the desperate pleading of an eye, and the naked terror of a sudden look, the swift concealment of a sudden fear," Wolfe comments. "Sometimes it just came and went as the light comes, just soaked in, just soaked in—words, speech and action, and finally in the mid-watches of the night, behind thick walls and bolted doors and shuttered windows, the confession of unutterable despair, the corruption of man's living faith, the inferno of his buried anguish—the spiritual disease and death and strangulation of a noble and a mighty people." He adds that once he began noticing the spiritual disease, he found it everywhere: "And day by day the thing soaked in, soaked in until everywhere, in every life I met, and in every life I touched, I met and saw and knew the ruin of its unutterable pollutions; and it still came in, it kept coming in, so known now and understood at last beyond all depths of intellectual understanding, since the cancer and the root both came out of the body I had loved."[25]

On the train taking him out of Germany in 1936 Wolfe witnessed Nazi terror firsthand, an experience he described later in his story "I Have a Thing to Tell You."[26] When the train reached the German border, Nazi guards arrested a man who was riding in the same compartment as Wolfe and several other travelers; the Germans in the compartment later explained that the arrested man was a Jew apparently attempting to leave the country with more money than the strict currency restrictions allowed (ten marks). Wolfe and the others watched silently as the man was taken away; and Wolfe held in his pocket the ten marks that he had volunteered to take out of the country for him. It was a stunning moment for Wolfe, lashing together Nazi repression with his silent complicity. The hugely famous writer, a man large in bulk and stature, was reduced to another of the meek and helpless bystanders, gripped by the same fear and enchained by the same servility as the Germans living under the Nazis.

Back in Paris, Wolfe began almost immediately to work on a story describing his experience on the train. Wolfe originally entitled the story "I Have Them Yet," referring to the coins the arrested man had given him, which he kept on his writing table.[27] Haunted by the experience, Wolfe saw the Jew's arrest as emblematic both of the dangers of Nazi anti-Semitism (with which, as we have seen, Wolfe was not unsympathetic) and more generally of the authoritarian state, particularly its power to crush the humanity of its citizens. At one point in the story (as later worked into *You Can't Go Home Again*), after the Jew has been pulled from the train and is looking back at his fellow travelers, the narrator comments that "in that gaze there was all the unmeasured weight of man's mortal anguish. George and the others felt somehow naked and ashamed, and somehow guilty. They all felt like they were saying farewell, not to a man, but to humanity; not to some pathetic stranger, some chance acquaintance of the voyage, but to mankind; not to some nameless cipher out of life, but to the fading image of a brother's face" (699). In the Jew's gaze back Wolfe acknowledged his own failure to recognize fully the evils of Nazism; humbled and shamed, he also acknowledged, as Richard Kennedy observes, "the claims of brotherhood with a strength that his self-centered individualism had not allowed to emerge before."[28]

Wolfe was fully aware that publishing "I Have a Thing to Tell You" would mean severing his ties with Germany, a painful step he nonetheless knew he had to make. Not long after completing the story, Wolfe wrote to Elizabeth Nowell from Paris (16 September 1936): "I've written a good piece over here—I'm afraid it may mean that I can't come back to the place where I am liked best and have the most friends, but I've decided to publish it" (*LTW* 541). And later, shortly before the story's first installment appeared in the *New Republic*, Wolfe wrote Dixon Wecter (5 March 1937): "I've crossed the Rubicon as far as my relations with the Reich are concerned. It cost me a good deal of time and worry to make up my mind whether I should allow the publication of the story because I am well known in Germany, my books have had a tremendous press there, I have many friends there, and I like the country and the people enormously. But the story wrote itself. It was the truth as I could see it, and I decided that a man's own self-respect and integrity is worth more than his comfort or material advantage" (*LTW* 614).

Besides a break with Germany and the Nazis, "I Have a Thing to Tell You" signaled a reconfiguration in Wolfe's thinking and art, away from the fierce Romantic individualism that had shaped *Look Homeward Angel* and *Of Time and the River* and toward, in the words of an early critic, "Wolfe's new democratic 'social consciousness.'"[29] Bella Kussy observes that in reorienting his artistic vision Wolfe in effect remade himself, working through renunciations not only "of opinions, which are comparatively easy to change, but of instincts, of temperamental attitudes and reactions, virtually of his entire personality" (321). Whether he underwent changes as fundamental as Kussy claims, clearly Wolfe returned from Germany a very different artist, his vision now closely focused on social and political issues, particularly those concerning democracy and totalitarianism. "I think you'd be surprised if you saw how politically-minded I've become," he wrote to Jonathan Daniels (23 October 1936) not long after his return to America. "I've become enormously interested in politics for the first time in my life, not only in Europe, but even more here at home" (*LTW* 552).

Like so many of his views and attitudes, Wolfe's politics were deeply impressionistic and mercurial. That said, his political feelings at this point were decidedly leftist, an extension of his sympathies for the working class, in large part resulting from his witnessing of widespread suffering during the early years of the Great Depression.[30] In a letter to one of his childhood teachers in Asheville, Margaret Roberts (20 May 1936), Wolfe affirmed his sympathies with the workers, saying "that by instinct, by inheritance, by every natural sympathy and affection of my life, my whole spirit and feeling is irresistibly on the side of the working class, against the cruelty, the injustice, the corrupt and infamous privilege of great wealth, against the shocking excess and wrong of the present system, the evidences of which are horribly apparent I think, to anybody who lives here in New York and keeps his eyes open" (*LTW* 519–20). During this time, Wolfe became increasingly vocal in his criticism of monopoly capitalism and particularly of the power wielded by corporations to shape economic and social policy.

While calling for a change in the political system, Wolfe never made precisely clear what change he was advocating, typically affirming a vague variety of democratic socialism. "If I had to state my politics I'd call myself a social democrat," Wolfe observed in some undated notes (probably in 1938). "And by social democrat I would understand a man who believes in socialism but not in communized socialism, and in democracy but not individualized democracy" (*NTW* 2:915). In some other notes from this same period Wolfe declared that he believed "in the preservation of the idea of democracy at any cost, as the most valuable idea of government and life that has been produced," but that he did "not believe in the preservation of the capitalist system as it now exists." He added: "I believe that it must either change voluntarily by directive force within; or that it will be changed forcibly by pressure from without. I do not hold that the idea of democracy, and the idea of free capitalist enterprise are synonymous" (*NTW* 2:915). Wolfe's vigorous defense of democracy here points to his growing patriotic fervor as the Nazi threat grew and the world situation deteriorated and stands in sharp contrast to his earlier bewailing, during the 1920s, of the dangers of democracy, with the democratic voter as mindless and corruptible and the nation's foreign policy directed toward, as he says in *Look Homeward, Angel*, "making the world safe for hypocrisy."[31]

As we have already seen, the late 1930s was a time when America itself was awash with patriotic fervor, what is now frequently called the "Democratic Revival," and clearly Wolfe was caught up in its spirit. A new hopefulness for America penetrated his thinking and work. Whereas Wolfe had in *Of Time and the River* portrayed a nation overwhelmed by economic and social upheaval and a people whose spirit was beset by a "foul, corrosive poison," by the late 1930s he was looking more hopefully toward a rejuvenated and reinvigorated America.[32] Not that he no longer saw problems in America—he most certainly did—but now amidst his analysis of what he called the betrayal of America, Wolfe frequently foregrounded the unquenchable American spirit and the possibility of renewal. "The people! Yes, the people!" Wolfe gushed in his talk "Writing and Living." "The people that cannot be defeated or betrayed—the betrayed and defeated people, the corrupted and misguided people, the duped and superstitious people, the inert and the submissive people—but in the end, always the people!—just the people—the rock bottom of the invincible and the everlasting people!"[33]

Clearly Wolfe's thinking in all this was vastly influenced by what he saw as the Nazi betrayal of the Germans. Wolfe found a similar betrayal of Americans by corrupt and exploitive political manipulators. If not as organized and bellicose as the Nazis, those who preyed on America nonetheless inflicted deep injuries to the country's spirit and health, as Wolfe made clear in George Webber's comments in *You Can't Go Home Again*:

> But it was not only in the South that America was hurt. There was another deeper, darker, and more nameless wound throughout the land. What was it? Was it in the record of corrupt officials and polluted governments, administrations twisted to the core, the huge excess of privilege and graft, protected criminals and gangster rule, the democratic forms all rotten and putrescent with disease? Was it in "puritanism"—that great, vague name: whatever it may be? Was it in the bloated surfeits of monopoly, and the crimes of wealth against the worker's life? Yes, it was in all of these, and in the daily tolling of

the murdered men, the lurid renderings of promiscuous and casual slaughter everywhere throughout the land, and in the pious hypocrisy of the press with its swift-forgotten prayers for our improvement, the editorial moaning while the front page gloats.

But it is not only at these outward forms that we must look to find the evidence of a nation's hurt. We must look as well at the heart of guilt that beats in each of us, for there the cause lies. We must look, and with our own eyes see, the central core of defeat and shame and failure which we have wrought in the lives of even the least of these, our brothers. And why must we look? Because we must probe to the bottom of our collective wound. As men, as Americans, we can no longer cringe away and lie. Are we not all warmed by the same sun, frozen by the same cold, shone on by the same lights of time and terror here in America? Yes, and if we do not look and see it, we shall be all damned together. (328–29)

Here and elsewhere, Wolfe underscored that America suffered not from the evils of democracy but from the evils of democracy's corrupters, most notably big business, the media, and the legal system. "I do not think political democracy has failed," he commented in notes from 1938, "but I think its processes have been so corrupted and weakened everywhere that its failure is possible, and its survival dubious. As a method of individual life and general government the democratic ideal still seems to me to be the best one that men have conceived" (*NTW* 2:916).

Like many Americans at the time, Wolfe feared that a weakened, corrupt democratic system was vulnerable to Fascism, both from without and, more ominously, from within. Although Wolfe believed, as he wrote in 1938, that Franklin Roosevelt enjoyed "a restricted dictatorship granted freely to him through the free mandate of the people," he trusted that Roosevelt would not "manipulate that trust and that mandate to his own purposes in such a way as to secure for himself, or for more dangerous successors, an arbitrary and dictatorial command of power" (*NTW* 2:901). At the same time, however, Wolfe feared that rootless Americans might be attracted to the order and purposefulness of Fascism, which prompted him to write in 1938 that "there is a grave Fascist danger, and it is with Fascism that I am concerned" (*NTW* 2:916). His dread of an American Fascism called forth nativist rhetoric; in notes from 1938 he characterized America as "just a mongrel and disordered mob—a jargon of a thousand tongues, the mouthpiece of a million vicious and sensational rumours—but with no *faith*, no *freedom*, no *belief*—a slave-like swarm without the dignities of slavery—a duped, doped horde who seek or want no remedy for the diseases that prey upon them—and themselves so vicious, infamous, and base, that one does not know which is more hateful or more odious—the fools who take it, or the knaves who dupe?" (*NTW* 2:918). Wolfe feared that Fascism would in all likelihood come to America, not through violent upheaval, but by quiet political manipulation. In notes probably written in 1937 he identified "Potential Fascist Literary Groups and Individuals," including, among others, the *Saturday Review of Literature*, the *New York Times Sunday Book Review*, the National Academy of Arts and Letters, the *New York Sun*, the *Virginia Quarterly*, Bernard DeVoto, and the Southern Agrarians (*NTW* 2:887). Elsewhere he described the possibility of Fascism's insinuation into the American system:

> It will just speak to you the same old words—"Fellow Americans"—"freedom"—"our great people"—
> And there will be no drums beat, and no grim compulsive beat—
> It will just come in quietly into the yards of a silent plant—
> And say "let the wheels turn"—
> When it happens, if it happens, as it happens.[34]

For all his concerns about America's self-betrayal and perilous future, Wolfe did not see a Fascist takeover as inevitable, and he took it upon himself as an artist to help prevent that from happening. While maintaining his belief, as he put it in a letter to Margaret Roberts (20 May 1936), that "the artist who makes his art the vehicle for political dogma and intolerant propaganda is a lost man" (*LTW* 520), after his turn against Nazism Wolfe affirmed that the artist should be responsible to both art and society. He now believed that the artist should participate in his era's important cultural dialogues, while maintaining artistic excellence. The American writer of the late 1930s, Wolfe believed, should work to reawaken America's democratic spirit by forging, as he wrote in "The Story of a Novel," "a new tradition for himself, derived from his own life and from the enormous space and energy of American life." "Out of the billion forms, the huge and single substance of America," Wolfe added, "out of the web, the flash, the thrust, the savage violence and dense complexity of all its swarming, million-footed life; out of the million little things that we have known all our lives but for which we never found a word; out of every flick and dart of evanescent memory; from all the things remembered and forgotten; from the last and deepest adyt of the ancient and swarm-haunted mind of man; from the unique and single substance of this land and life of ours, must we draw the power and energy of our own life, the articulation of our speech, the substance of our art."[35]

Echoing his earlier calls for clear-sighted understanding of Nazism—recognizing its virtues in order to understand its faults, rather than relying on one-sided "slot-machine" thinking—Wolfe argued that only by presenting America in all its fullness—its strengths and weaknesses, its successes and failures, its beauty and its ugliness—could the artist inspire a vigorous nationalism powerful enough to counter the forces betraying America. While continuing to berate Americans for letting themselves be duped by the ruling powers, Wolfe remained stubbornly hopeful about America's ability to cleanse itself. In *You Can't Go Home Again* Wolfe identifies "a curious paradox about America," that amidst the despair and suffering of the Depression there remained in the unemployed workers "an almost quenchless hope, an almost boundless optimism, an almost indestructible belief that something is bound to turn up, something is sure to happen." "This is a peculiar quality of the American soul," he continues, "and it contributes largely to the strange enigma of our life, which is so incredibly mixed of harshness and of tenderness, of innocence and of crime, of loneliness and of good fellowship, of desolation and of exultant hope, of terror and of courage, of nameless fear and of soaring conviction, of brutal, empty, naked, bleak, corrosive ugliness, and of beauty so lovely and so overwhelming that the tongue is stopped by it, and the language for it has not yet been uttered" (429). Near the end of the novel George Webber envisions America's glorious future: "I think the true discovery of America is before us. I think the true fulfillment of our spirit, of our people, of our mighty and immortal land, is yet to come. I think the true discovery of our own democracy is still before us. And I think that all these things are certain as the morning, as inevitable as noon" (741).

To speak to and for Americans, galvanizing them to fight against the Fascist threat, became Wolfe's dream in these late years. He now saw his art as a call to arms for the war he saw forthcoming. In a letter to the *Nation* (2 April 1938) Wolfe observed that "the wheels of a great war machine, such as that which Germany has today, are not going to be stopped, once they have begun to roll, by a handful of reproving phrases, or by a batch of diplomatic protests" (*LTW* 735). Fascist aggression, he added, was proceeding almost unchecked because the world's democracies had not taken a united stand against it. "Sooner or later, it seems to me, they will have to," Wolfe went on.

"They will have to when they decide that democracy is valuable enough to be saved, and is worth fighting for, if need be, by those who believe in it. In the end, I think we may all have to make that decision. For Fascism is a creature that thrives but is not appeased by compromise" (*LTW* 736).

This was Wolfe's final dream: to be the American bard, to write the American epic, to cleanse America of its betrayers, to inspire Americans to embrace democracy and fight Fascism. Fulfilling his dream, however, demanded that Wolfe accept America in all its diversity, an acceptance that, as Paschal Reeves observes, Wolfe could never finally make because of his deep-seated racism and nativism (*TWA* 136–38). Evidence of his intransigent racism surfaced throughout Wolfe's late career, most often in his comments on Jews. At a dinner party in 1937, for instance, Wolfe erupted in anger and disbelief when Sherwood Anderson's wife said that she had heard Wolfe was half-Jewish.[36] What Wolfe took as a damning insult festered for weeks, and he finally wrote to Anderson (20 December 1937) about his wife's comment:

> I do have to tell you this, however, and then I hope I am done with it: I just can't agree that it is something that should not be taken seriously, because it seems to me the implications not only to myself, but to a lot of obscure decent people are pretty serious, and whether you will agree with my point of view or not, you must have understanding enough to see that such a thing would affect them pretty tragically in so many of the fundamental relations of life and their marital relations, their social and business relations, and so on. And I think also it would affect me pretty seriously too. I have been mighty fortunate as a writer, people have said some mighty fine things about me. I don't know whether they were right or not, or whether it means anything, but apparently a lot of people have thought I was a pretty American sort of writer, and what I did was indigenous to this country. I hope this is true. At any rate, I am mighty proud of it, and I would like to live up to it, and I say this honestly without a word or thought of prejudice toward any people, any race, or any creed. (*LTW* 689)[37]

The logic in these final sentences of this letter harks back to Wolfe's earlier racial conceptualization of America and American identity: America was originally a Nordic nation and thus only Nordics were "native Americans"; all other races, including Jews, could never be true Americans, whatever their efforts at assimilation. His concluding remark, asserting that his commentary is without prejudice, underscores the deep-seated nature of Wolfe's nativism. So, too, does his outburst after the publication of Aline Bernstein's novel *The Journey Down* (1938), which was based on her relationship with Wolfe: late one night, Wolfe arrived in a fit at the Bernsteins' apartment and, according to Bernstein, raged that Jews should be wiped off the face of the earth and then called out three cheers for Hitler.[38]

Indeed, Wolfe's nativist prejudices were always threatening to explode forth, even during a time when he was declaring himself America's democratic bard and calling for a democracy open to all races. Wolfe's 1937 story "The Child by Tiger" illustrates such an explosion. While the story suggests Wolfe's developing social consciousness and his growing sympathies for the suffering of southern blacks, at the same time it ironically portrays the return of his repressed racism. The story depicts the seemingly inexplicable shooting spree undertaken by a deeply religious African American, Dick Prosser, and his later lynching by a vicious mob. While the story at first glance suggests humanity's primal savagery (the lynch mob's violent outburst mirroring Prosser's), the story's racial taxonomy actually foregrounds the savagery of only two groups—blacks and poor whites—and suggests that that savagery derives from their racial heritage and genetics.[39] Prosser's outburst clearly points to the savagery and degeneracy of blacks, while the lynch mob's viciousness points to that of the poor whites, one of whose leaders is described as a genetic misfit, "a little ferret-faced man with a furtive and uneasy eye, a mongrel mouth, and wiry jaw muscles."[40]

This description of the poor white leader brings us back to George Webber's—and Wolfe's—repulsion at poor white degeneracy expressed in *The Web and the Rock*. Webber's comments on poor whites cover several long pages, and a large portion bears citation, beginning here after a brief discussion of "the rotten sneering names" of poor white boys:

> Boys who had these names were never any good—a thin-lipped, sneer-mouthed, freckled, blear-eyed set of hair-faced louts, who had unpleasant knuckly hands, and a dry, evil, juiceless kind of skin. There was always something jeering, ugly, unwholesome, smug, complacent, and triumphant about these people. Without knowing why, he always wanted to smash them in the face, and not only hated everything about them, but he hated the "very ground they walked on," the

houses they lived in, the streets on which they lived, the part of town they came from, together with their fathers, mothers, sisters, brothers, cousins, aunts, and close companions.

    He felt they were not only foully different from the people that he liked in all the qualities that make for warmth, joy, happiness, affection, friendship, and the green-gold magic of enchanted weather—he felt there was also in them a physical difference, so foul and hateful that they might be creatures of another species. In blood, bone, brains, white-haired, juiceless-looking flesh, in sinew, joint, and tissue, in the very spittle of their mouths—which would be a vilely ropy, glutinously murky stuff of the very quality of their blear eyes and their sneering lips—as well as in all the delicate combining nerves, veins, jellies, cements, and fibrous webs that go to knit that marvelous tenement, that whole integument of life that is a human body, these people whose very names he hated would be found to be made of a vile, base, incalculably evil stuff. It was a substance that was as different from the glorious stuff of which the people that he liked were made as a foul excrement of fecal matter from the health and relish of the sound, wholesome, life-begetting food. It was a substance not only of the mind and spirit but of the very texture of the body, so that it seemed they had been begot from acid and envenomed loins, and nurtured all their lives on nameless and abominable rations. He could not have eaten of the food their mothers cooked for them without choking and retching at each mouthful, feeling that he was swallowing some filth or foulness with every bite he took.

    And yet, they seemed to score an evil and unfathomable triumph everywhere he met them. It was a triumph of death over life; of sneering mockery and ridicule over gaiety, warmth, and friendly ease; of wretchedness, pain, and misery over all the powerful music of joy; of the bad, sterile, and envenomed life over the good life of hope, happiness, and the glorious belief and certitude of love. (44–45)

Later in the novel, Webber directs his ire at the wretchedness of poor white women and what he sees as the "unbroken progressions of their loathsome fertility": "The idiot proliferations of blind nature which these wretched rakes and hags and harridans of women so nakedly and brutally revealed as they stood there stupidly proposing their foul, swollen bellies in the merciless and shameful light of the hot sun filled Monk with such a feeling of choking and wordless fury, loathing, and disgust that every natural emotion of pity and sorrow was drowned out below the powerful flood tide of revulsion, and his antagonism to the women and their wretched children was scarcely to be distinguished from blind hatred" (58).

Webber's comments on poor whites mirror the racial taxonomy of "The Child by Tiger," a story that in the end suggests the dangerous threat posed to the superior white race and its civilization by the degenerate races of whites and blacks. As William Alexander Percy did in his defense of the southern aristocracy, Wolfe here displaces racial violence and degeneracy entirely onto poor whites and blacks, keeping the South's better bred, such as the mayor (who tries to stop the mob), entirely free of taint. In all this, the story of Dick Prosser finally expresses less Wolfe's move away from racial prejudice and nativism than his inability to do so, Prosser's violent, uncontrollable outburst ironically depicting the similarly uncontrollable and explosive outbursts of Wolfe's virulent racism, in both his life and his art.

And so despite the evil and oppression Wolfe saw in Germany; despite the suffering and economic exploitation he witnessed during the Great Depression; despite the betrayal of American democracy he now recognized, together with the need for national unity in the face of the Fascist threat; despite the social responsibility of the American artist for which he now called—despite all this, Wolfe's racialist thinking continued to befoul, and to betray, his larger, more hopeful vision. Dreaming of stepping forward as the bard of America and its incorruptible human spirit, Wolfe to the end remained mired in a morass of a filthy racism that, slightly altering Lillian Smith's phrase, was the killer of his dream. In a letter to Aline Bernstein (7 June 1928) Wolfe apologized for his recent bad treatment of her, explaining that "the snake headed furies that drive us on to despair and madness are inside us: how to unroot them from the structure of our soul is a problem that gets me sick with horror" (*MOL* 147). Wolfe never found a way to unroot these furies, either in his feelings for Aline or in his imaginative vision and his art, despite knowing full well that similar furies underlay, not the beloved America of his bardic dreams, but the nation—Nazi Germany—that stood fundamentally opposed to it.

6

DEMOCRACY'S TALL MEN

WILLIAM FAULKNER

In 1956 a neighborhood boy asked Faulkner what made him so different from other people in Oxford, Mississippi. Faulkner told the boy to ask around town. When he saw the boy again, Faulkner asked him what he had found out. "I asked two people," the boy said, "and all I could find out was that you're a nigger-lover." Taken aback, Faulkner replied, "Well, I guess that's better than being a fascist."[1] Faulkner's reply carries a good bit more freight than first appears, for indeed Faulkner had been tagged "nigger-lover" and Fascist at different points in his career. In the 1950s his public declarations against segregation had angered many of his fellow Mississippians, provoking them to challenge Faulkner's allegiances to the white race and to the southern way of life. But earlier, in the 1930s and 1940s, Faulkner had sometimes been tagged a Fascist, not because of any expressed political views, but because his fiction, particularly to the eyes of a number of leftist critics, seemed rooted in a destructive and irrational violence similar to that which they saw as the foundations of Fascist ideology.

Faulkner, of course, was not a Fascist or a Fascist sympathizer. Indeed, beginning in the late 1930s Faulkner began voicing strong anti-Fascist positions that eventually not only worked their way thematically into his fiction but also guided the aesthetic choices he made in constructing that fiction. More than anything else, and more than is generally acknowledged, it was Faulkner's anti-Fascism, particularly as manifested in his strident defense of democracy during World War II, that led him, in a profound reconfiguration of his understanding of art and the artist, to affirm the artist's responsibility to society and democracy. That affirmation, in turn, led him to reconfigure the Yoknatapawpha saga in his postwar fiction, in effect rewriting his earlier novels by the lights of his new, socially responsible vision.

—✕ ✕ ✕ ✕—

Attacks suggesting the possible links of Faulkner's fiction with Fascist ideology began in the early 1930s, with Alan Reynolds Thompson's influential essay "The Cult of Cruelty" (1932). While he did not explicitly call Faulkner a Fascist, Thompson argued that Faulkner's work, along with Robinson Jeffers's, represented a disturbing trend in modern writing that he termed "the cult of cruelty." These writers, Thompson wrote, exploited obscenity and horror merely to arouse humanity's gross animal instincts, and more disturbingly, they embraced a "pessimistic skepticism, to which morals and aspirations are merely customs and dreams, and the world is an inhuman mechanism."[2] Two years later, in *The Foreground of American Fiction* (1934), Harry Hartwick entitled his chapter on Faulkner "The Cult of Cruelty," with the section heads "Reductio Ad Aburdsum," "Savagery Among the Honeysuckles," and "Dead End." Hartwick characterized Faulkner's work as "reptilian," writing that art "should be a 'mansion of philosophy,' invigorating as well as vigorous, and a source of inspiration for all those who draw their values from Nature rather than Man, not [as with Faulkner] a haunted house, dark and cold, inhabited only by spiders and morons."[3]

Hard-line leftist critics were also attacking Faulkner's heavy use of the grotesque and horror, seeing it as gratuitous rather than useful for understanding economic injustice and for initiating revolutionary social change. In *The Great Tradition* (1933) Granville Hicks declared that Faulkner's focus on the sensational precluded any rational analysis of the social ills of the South. Hicks wrote that Faulkner "will not write simply and realistically of southern life. . . . Nothing but crime and insanity will satisfy him. If he tried to see why life is horrible, he might be willing to give a more representative description of life, might be willing to occupy himself with the kind of suffering that he can see on every hand, the kind of crime that is committed every day, and the kind of corruption that gnaws at every human being in this rotten society. As it is, he can only pile violence upon violence in order to convey a mood that he will not or cannot analyze."[4] Philip Rahv, in his review of *Absalom, Absalom!* (1936), found Faulkner locked within his brooding and suffering consciousness, blind to the workings of history.[5] Summing up Faulkner's critical reception from the early 1930s through the mid-1940s, Robert Penn Warren commented that until the publication of Malcolm

Cowley's *Portable Faulkner* (1946), Faulkner, with a few notable exceptions, had been characterized by literary critics as "a combination of Thomas Nelson Page, a fascist and a psychopath, gnawing his nails. Of course, this picture is usually accompanied by a grudging remark about genius."[6]

In his characterization of Faulkner's critical reception Warren probably had foremost in mind Maxwell Geismar's comments in *Writers in Crisis* (1942). Geismar characterized Faulkner essentially as an unreconstructed southerner, venting his hatred for the demise of the traditional South, brought about by the forces of northern industrialism, upon two scapegoats—blacks and women, figures he deemed "the twin furies of Faulkner's deep southern Waste Land."[7] After observing that emancipated blacks are for Faulkner "the cause of the destruction of all he held dear," Geismar writes that in "showing this negro as Joe Christmas, as Jim Bond, as the inhuman criminal, the degenerate who will dominate the civilization which freed him, Faulkner proclaims at once his anger and his revenge upon those who have destroyed his home" (179). Faulkner's rage toward women, Geismar adds, likewise illustrates "the universal debasement of modern times," with "the pure Lady [transformed] into the contemporary Female, now wanton, graceless, and degraded" (180). Geismar concludes that Faulkner's scapegoating of blacks and women mirrors the Fascist scapegoating of Jews and that his rage against modernity (which, Geismar observes, "threatens the entire western hemisphere" [179]) mirrors that of the Fascist enterprise. "I have used the title of Maurice Samuel's penetrating study of the Fascist superstitions, 'The Great Hatred,'" Geismar writes, "to best describe Faulkner's work as a whole. For it is in the larger tradition of reversionary, neo-pagan, and neurotic discontent (from which Fascism stems) that much of Faulkner's writing must be placed—the anti-civilizational revolt which has caught so many modern mystics, the revolt rising out of modern social evils, nourished by ignorance of their true nature, and which succumbs to malice as their solution" (182). Geismar claims at the end of his chapter that Faulkner repudiates not merely the modern South but "our society from 1860 to 1929," an act, he says, of "total cultural rejection" (183).

It is not clear whether Faulkner ever read *Writers in Crisis*, although Malcolm Cowley did mention the book to him in a letter (22 July 1944), commenting that while Geismar was "not so dumb for a professor" (actually, Geismar was not a professor) and that while he did a good job analyzing Hemingway, "when he comes to Faulkner, you might as well have written your novels in Minoan or Hittite for all the sense he makes of them."[8]

(Cowley did not mention to Faulkner that in his own 1939 review of *The Wild Palms* he had written that the tall convict was a man who "will perform deeds of physical courage, even heroism, to escape from the need of moral effort" and was thus "the ideal soldier for a fascist army.")[9] If Faulkner did read *Writers in Crisis*, no doubt he was stung by Geismar's accusations of his proto-Fascism, as he certainly was when other leftist critics made similar observations. Joseph Blotner points out that years later Faulkner still rankled at being called "a Gothic fascist" during the 1930s and 1940s.[10]

Such accusations were no doubt particularly galling to a man who by the mid- to late 1930s was publicly taking a stand against Fascism. In 1938 Faulkner responded to an appeal from the League of American Writers with the following statement: "I most sincerely wish to go on record as being unalterably opposed to Franco and fascism, to all violations of the legal government and outrages against the people of Republican Spain."[11] That same year, he contributed his manuscript copy of *Absalom, Absalom!* to a relief fund for the Spanish Loyalists and offered to send other manuscripts. By 1940 Faulkner's gloomy assessment of the European political situation was deepening his already serious depression, which stemmed primarily from ongoing financial problems, and affecting his desire to write. Faulkner wrote to Robert Haas (27 May 1940) that "maybe the watching of all this [the situation in Europe] coming to a head for the last year is why I cant write, dont seem to want to write, that is" (*SLF* 125).[12] While saying that he knew he still had things to say with his fiction, he expressed concern that given the world situation whatever he did write would be worthless. He feared, too, that the war threatened his literary legacy, writing that "surely it is still possible to scratch the face of the supreme Obliteration and leave a decipherable scar of some sort. Surely all these machines that can destroy a thousand lives or stamp out an entire car gassed and oiled and ready to run in two seconds, can preserve, even by blind mischance and a minute fault in gears or timing, some scrap here and there, provided it ever was worth preserving" (*SLF* 125). In this same letter, Faulkner admitted getting out his old RAF uniform and contemplating whether he should try to join the war effort. "Of course I could do no good, would last about two minutes in combat," he wrote. "But my feeling now is better so; that what will be left after this one will certainly not be worth living for" (*SLF* 125).

Faulkner was not always this gloomy during 1940. He did complete some writing, including several of the stories that would later appear, significantly revised, in *Go Down, Moses* (1942) and *Knight's Gambit* (1948). He also explored ways to get involved locally in the war effort, including preparing to teach navigation and radio at a flight school and trying to organize a National Guard unit with a commission for himself. On 5 October he wrote to Robert Haas that he had "become better adjusted mentally to the condition of this destruction-bent world," though in the next sentence he described a helter-skelter world torn by dispute in a way that probably failed to reassure Haas (*SLF* 137). Retreating into the woods, as always, gave him solace. In his Christmas letter to his editors and friends at Random House (15 December 1940) Faulkner spoke about all the hunting he had been doing, adding that that was "one nice thing about the woods: off there hunting, I don't fret and stew so much about Europe" (*SLF* 138).

Faulkner's attempts to join the war effort continued through 1941 and into 1942. Long before the attack on Pearl Harbor, Faulkner worked at organizing a committee of aircraft spotters, eventually setting up an office on the Oxford Square and enlisting enough volunteers to have all the county's beats covered (an effort not everybody in Oxford took very seriously). With the United States' entry into the war Faulkner's war fever increased, as did his efforts at participation. "This world is bitched proper this time, isn't it?" he wrote to Robert Haas (21 January 1942). "I'd like to be dictator now. I'd take all these congressmen who refused to make military appropriations and I'd send them to the Philippines. This day a year and I dont believe there will be one present second lt. alive" (*SLF* 148). In this same letter, Faulkner wrote that his local work on air defense was not enough for him now and that he was looking into teaching air navigation for the navy. That spring he went to Washington, DC to appear before a naval board in hopes of getting a commission with the Bureau of Aeronautics. "I dont like this desk job particularly," Faulkner wrote to Haas in a letter received on 27 March 1942, "but I think better to get the commission first and then try to get a little nearer the gunfire, which I intend to try to do" (*SLF* 149). Faulkner apparently hoped that once commissioned, he could eventually get a pilot's rating. None of these efforts panned out, however, and Faulkner remained a civilian throughout the war.

In the early 1940s Faulkner began making specific references in his fiction to the war in Europe, voicing scorn for the Fascist enemy. The unpublished story "Snow," which Faulkner wrote in 1942, opens with a child's question, "Father, what was Europe like before all the people in it began to hate and fear Germans?" and ends with his father's answer: "It was just the same. The people in Europe have hated and feared Germans for so long that nobody remembers how it was."[13] Another story, "Knight's Gambit," the first version of which Faulkner completed in 1942, ends with a decidedly patriotic ring: the would-be murderer, given a choice between going to jail and joining the army, chooses the army; Captain Gualdes decides to enlist; and Charles (Gavin's nephew) departs to rejoin his military unit, having been called back from leave after the attack on Pearl Harbor. *"Sending Jap scalp for wedding present,"* Charles wires to his uncle on his trip west. "Don't send it bring it," Gavin wires back to close the story.[14]

Issues of the war more seriously impact "Delta Autumn," which Faulkner completed in 1940 and then later revised for inclusion in *Go Down, Moses*. On a hunting trip, Ike McCaslin and several others discuss the possibility of war. One of the men, Boyd, voices deep cynicism about America's ability to defend itself, both internally and externally, while Ike argues that America is poised for a renewal of patriotic spirit and heroism. To Boyd's mocking commentary, Ike responds:

> "So that's what's worrying you," McCaslin said. "I ain't noticed this country being short of defenders yet when it needed them. You did some of it yourself twenty years ago and did it well, if those medals you brought back home mean anything. This country is a little mite stronger and bigger than any one man or even a group of men outside or inside of it either. I reckon it can cope with one Austrian paper hanger, no matter what he calls himself. My pappy and some other better men than any of them you named tried once to tear it in two with a war, and they failed."[15]

With this exchange between Ike and Boyd, Faulkner voiced both sides of the question that in the early 1940s deeply concerned him about the war against Fascism: with American individualism diminished by corporatism and big government, had the nation become vulnerable to takeover and dictatorship? In his fiction at least, Faulkner fluctuated widely in his feelings about this issue, sometimes voicing cynical views similar to Boyd's, at other times sounding more hopeful, like Ike affirming a renewal of American spirit.

In three stories of the home front, "The Tall Men" (1941), "Two Soldiers" (1942), and "Shall Not Perish" (1942), all written for the popular press, Faulkner was at his most hopeful, locating the source of American rejuvenation in the common folk of the southern countryside. All three stories suggest that the American Dream still lives within southern farmers, whose unquestioned loyalty and patriotism embody that dream. The fiercely independent small farmers know that their independence depends on the independence of the nation. Southern plain folk, Faulkner suggests in these stories, are the tall men of America, and it is to them that America must look for its deliverance in wartime.

As Faulkner makes clear in "The Tall Men," tallness relates not to physical height but to uncompromising individualism.[16] The tall men of the story are the McCallums, independent farmers who have resisted government incursions into their way of life. Rather than participate in what they see as illogical government planning, with a distant and unknowing government dictating how farms should be run, the McCallums keep farming their own way. Buddy McCallum thus does not register his land with the government; he will have no one tell him what, when, and how much to plant. Nor do his two sons register for military service (as the law requires them to do), seeing no reason to since the nation is not at war; when there is a war to fight, they will enlist, knowing full well that it is their duty to defend the country. Thus, when a government investigator arrives to arrest his sons, Buddy misunderstands, thinking he is there to call his sons off to war. Himself a World War I hero and the son of a man who walked from Mississippi to Virginia to join up with Stonewall Jackson's army, he tells his sons to get packing: "The Government done right by me in my day, and it will do right by you. You just enlist wherever they want to send you, need you, and obey your sergeants and officers until you find out how to be soldiers. Obey them, but remember your name and don't take nothing from no man" (*CSF* 53).

Buddy's words here embody Faulkner's vision of the American Dream alive and well in the southern plain folk, who instinctively believe in individual liberty and are ready to fight to preserve it. While the investigator does not recognize that New Deal programs, by restricting individual freedom, are sapping American vitality, the sheriff, who undoubtedly speaks for Faulkner, does. "The trouble is, we done got into the habit of confusing the situations with the folks," he explains to the investigator, adding that while the investigator means well, "you just went and got yourself all fogged up with rules and regulations. That's our trouble. We done invented ourselves so many alphabets and rules and recipes that we can't see anything else; if what we see can't be fitted to an alphabet or a rule, we are lost" (*CSF* 59). They are lost, the sheriff goes on, because in a world increasingly defined by and controlled by rules and regulations, the individual no longer exercises choice and responsibility. People are not tall anymore. They have lost their backbones:

We have come to be like critters doctor folks might have created in laboratories, that have learned how to slip off their bones and guts and still live, still be kept alive indefinite and forever maybe without even knowing the bones and guts are gone. We have slipped our backbone; we have about decided a man don't need a backbone any more; to have one is old-fashioned. But the groove where the backbone used to be is still there, and the backbone has been kept alive, too, and someday we're going to slip back onto it. I don't know just when nor just how much of a wrench it will take to teach us, but someday. (*CSF* 59)

As the sheriff continues, he conjectures that it might take "trouble, bad trouble," to make people realize that "honor and pride and discipline . . . make a man worth preserving" (*CSF* 60). The bad trouble here is of course the war in Europe: perhaps America's entry into the war, the sheriff suggests, will knock people to their senses and regenerate their backbones, making them tall again, like the McCallums.

Significant in the sheriff's discussion is his suggestion that with the McCallums the line of southern heroism dating back to the Civil War and before remains undiminished. The McCallums, that is, are as tall as those who came before them, their heroism matching that of their forefathers. Old Anse, Buddy's father, learned those virtues in the Civil War and passed them along to his sons; now Buddy is doing the same. "Did you notice how all Buddy had to do was to tell them boys of his it was time to go, because the Government had sent them word?" the sheriff asks the investigator. "And how they told him good-by? Grown men kissing one another without hiding and without shame. Maybe that's what I am trying to say" (*CSF* 60). What the sheriff is also trying to say is that the McCallums' heroic virtues support not only their family but the nation: they have a fighting faith, instinctive and vital, that America at large sorely needs, particularly in a time of world disorder.

An even more explicit message that the simple folk possess the source of power to revitalize the American character comes in the slightly later story "Two Soldiers." Here Pete Grier, a young man in a farm family similar to the McCallums, insists upon enlisting after hearing radio broadcasts about the Pearl Harbor attack. "I got to go," he says. "I jest ain't going to put up with no folks treating the Unity States that way" (*CSF* 83). When his concerned parents prod him about his motives, Pete can only keep repeating, "I got to go." (The second soldier of the title is Pete's eight-year-old brother, who sneaks off by himself to Memphis hoping to join the army so he can accompany Pete.) Embodying the virtues of the southern plain folk, Pete acts not from mindless jingoism but from deeply felt loyalty and responsibility to his family, community, and nation. Like the McCallums in "The Tall Men," he stands with the heroic stature of his forefathers. Pete's mother recognizes this stature, grudgingly accepting her son's plans to enlist after she comes to see that Pete's desires mirror those of her brother Marsh, who joined up to fight in World War I. "He had to go to that one when he wasn't but nineteen," she says of Marsh, "and our mother couldn't understand it then any more than I can now. But she told Marsh if he had to go, he had to go. And so, if Pete's got to go to this one, he's got to go to it" (*CSF* 84–85). There is no loss of stature here between generations, nor is there any in Pete's brother's lighting out to accompany him, a childhood quest, complete with adversity and tests of skill and bravery, that mirrors Pete's journey off to war. The story suggests that whatever happens to Pete, there will be others every bit as heroic following after him.

In "Shall Not Perish" Pete does indeed perish, going down with a ship sunk in the Pacific. But like "Two Soldiers," this story makes clear that the national spirit that drove Pete continues to live in those coming after him, a point underscored by the story's title and its echoing of Lincoln's Gettysburg Address ("that government of the people, by the people, for the people, shall not perish from the earth").[17] In "Shall Not Perish" this national spirit emerges forcefully in Mrs. Grier, who after Pete's death enlists in the homefront effort, consoling those in her community who have lost men in the war. Mrs. Grier's first task takes her to the home of Major de Spain, where his son, a pilot recently killed in combat, lies in state. When Mrs. Grier announces herself, de Spain angrily denounces what he sees as her simple-minded ideas about courage, duty, and honor. De Spain finds nothing heroic in his son's death—or any other American soldier's death, for that matter. For him, the war and his son's death are meaningless acts in a meaningless world. Speaking with a cynicism similar to Boyd's in "Delta Autumn," de Spain says that rather than virtue and honor the war is about being duped by the machinations of the rich and powerful. American ideals are merely illusions, de Spain claims, telling Mrs. Grier that his son did not fight and die for his country, because in truth he had no country. "His country and mine both was ravaged and polluted and destroyed eighty years ago, before even I was born," de Spain says. "His forefathers fought and died for it then, even though what they fought and lost for was a dream. He didn't even have a dream. He died for an illusion. In the interests of usury, by the folly and rapacity of politicians, for the glory and aggrandisement of organized labor!" (*CSF* 108).

De Spain's tirade ironically speaks most tellingly about his own diminishment rather than the South's or the nation's. For de Spain himself, described as "a banker powerful in money and politics both . . . [who] had made governors and senators too in Mississippi" (*CSF* 107), is actively involved in the very financial and political machinations about which he complains. Rather than carrying forward the heroic life of his ancestors, de Spain disavows that life, claiming that there is no connection between the heroic past and the present. That is certainly true in his case, underscored by the fact that de Spain was "not a real major but just called that because his father had been a real one in the old Confederate war" (*CSF* 107). And so when Mrs. Grier and de Spain wrestle for his son's pistol—a manifestation of the martial virtues by which de Spain's son has lived—she rightfully bests him. It is Mrs. Grier, and not Major de Spain, who has inherited and lives by the traditional virtues.

After chastising de Spain for his defeatism, Mrs. Grier confidently announces the unbroken connection between the heroes of the Civil War and those of World War II, celebrating the ongoing line of southern heroes. She admits that she cannot quite grasp why men are driven to take up arms, but she says that whatever compels them must be noble, since southern men continue to do it:

> But my son knew why [he had to go fight]. And my brother went to the war when I was a girl, and our mother didn't know why either, but he did. And my grandfather was in that old one there too, and I reckon his mother didn't know why either, but I reckon he did. And my son knew why he had to go to this one, and he knew I knew he did even though I didn't, just as he knew that this child here and I both knew he would not come back. But he knew why, even if I didn't, couldn't, never can. So it must be all right, even if I couldn't understand it. Because there is nothing in him that I or his father didn't put there. . . . I know it came a long way. So it must have been strong to have lasted through all of us. It must have been all right for him to be willing to die for it after that long time and coming that far. (*CSF* 109–10)

In her showdown with de Spain, Mrs. Grier humbles him and silences his cynicism. She achieves a victory similar to the one she had achieved when she humbled her sons and her husband for making fun of her grandfather in a movie theater. Awakening and seeing horses on the screen, her grandfather had believed that he was back in the Civil War and had called out for people to make way for Bedford Forrest's troops. "Fools yourselves," Mrs. Grier had told her sons and husband after they called her grandfather an old fool. "He wasn't running from anybody! He was running in front of them, hollering at all clods to look out because better men than they were coming, even seventy-five years afterwards, still powerful, still dangerous, still coming!" (*CSF* 114). Her message here is the same one she delivers to Major de Spain: the heroes of the present stand every bit as tall as their forefathers, their actions mirroring those of previous generations. The heroic line remains intact; men may perish, but the heroic force that drives them shall not.

"Shall Not Perish" closes with a bold vision of the South as the source of American character and its fighting faith in freedom and democracy. The vision comes to Pete's brother after he remembers his mother's chastising words at the movie theater. He visualizes the heroes who have come before him, configuring their exploits as spokes on a wheel, extending out from the center point of Frenchman's Bend. The spokes reach out into the lands opened up and defended by these brave men, heroes "who lasted and endured and fought the battles and lost them and fought again because they didn't know they had been whipped, and tamed the wilderness and overpassed the mountains and deserts and died and still went on as the shape of the United States grew and went on" (*CSF* 114). "I knew them too," he says, going on to echo his mother, as he thinks of the heroes who have gone before him and who will come after: "the men and women still powerful seventy-five years and twice that and twice that again afterward, still powerful and still dangerous and still coming, North and South and East and West, until the name of what they did and what they died for became just one single word, louder than any thunder. It was America, and it covered all the western earth" (*CSF* 114–15). The vision closing "Shall Not Perish" stands as Faulkner's most hopeful statement of the heroism embodied in the spirit of the southern folk, an instinctive faith affirming individual freedom and American democracy.[18]

Faulkner's attitudes toward the war, the South, and the American democracy in the early 1940s were not always as hopeful as those expressed in "The Tall Men," "Two Soldiers," and "Shall Not Perish," all of which targeted a popular audience through simple, patriotic expression. A more gloomy view, particularly in terms of his attitudes toward American democracy, structures *Go Down, Moses*, which he was revising for publication at about the same time he was writing these three stories. With Ike McCaslin's failed quest to expiate both his family's curse, set in motion by his grandfather's act of incest, and the South's curse for its enslavement of black people, *Go Down, Moses* points to a breakdown in the line of southern heroism that the three stories affirm. This breakdown can be seen not only in Ike's failure to halt the endlessly repeating line of misdeeds arising from both curses—"Delta Autumn" ties Roth's affair with and abandonment of his black kinswoman to the overall miserable state of southern society itself, the result of long and grinding decline—but also in the fact that Ike breaks the line of his patrimonial heritage by renouncing his inheritance and his place as head of the family.[19]

Further underscoring the broken line of southern heroism is the contrast between the "tall men" of Ike's generation and those southerners coming after, characterized at one point as the indistinguishable masses, "men myriad and nameless even to one another" (*GDM* 185). Roth, one of these small men, knows well the diminishment of modern southerners, and he zeroes in on that depletion in his conversation with Ike in "Delta Autumn" concerning dictatorship and America's future. What will happen to America, Roth asks (in the novel Roth replaces Boyd as the challenger to Ike), "after Hitler gets through with it? Or Smith or Jones or Roosevelt or Willkie or whatever he will call himself in this country?" (*GDM* 322). As he had in the earlier version of "Delta Autumn," Ike dismisses his challenger with rousing bravado, but now, within the novel's overarching context of depletion and decline, with southern society falling to pieces, it is clearly the challenger, and not Ike, who speaks authoritatively. Replaying and reversing the outcome of Mrs. Grier and Major de Spain's showdown in "Shall Not Perish," the conversation portrays Ike's affirmation of ongoing southern heroism as fanciful and naive in the face of Roth's evocation of Depression-era America drifting toward social chaos and political dictatorship:

> Half the people without jobs and half the factories closed by strikes. Half the people on public dole that wont work and half that couldn't work even if they would. Too much cotton and corn and hogs, and not enough for people to eat and wear. The country full of people to tell a man how he cant raise his own cotton whether he will or wont,

and Sally Rand with a sergeant's stripes and not even the fan couldn't fill the army rolls. Too much not-butter and not even the guns— (*GDM* 323)

Roth's words to Ike point to a diminished American democracy facing forces of dictatorship from both within and without, a far cry from Faulkner's unabashedly patriotic and propagandistic stories "The Tall Men," "Two Soldiers," and "Shall Not Perish."[20] *Go Down, Moses* shows old-fashioned southern heroism entirely absent in the 1940s South, with little suggestion that any renewal is possible except in Ike's clouded mind. By the end of the novel Faulkner's tall men have devolved into the little people of modernity, faithless and feckless, the shooters of does, not Germans.

If in the early 1940s Faulkner's vision of America and American democracy alternated between the unabashed call to arms and hopefulness of his three home-front war stories and the despairing gloom of *Go Down, Moses*, that alternation for the most part ended when Faulkner returned to Hollywood in 1942 for another stint as a screenwriter for Warner Brothers. Deeply supportive of the war, Faulkner worked on several propaganda-film screenplays, including "The De Gaulle Story" and "Battle Cry" (neither of which ended up being produced), embracing his role as defender of democracy. While Faulkner could not serve on active duty (none of his many efforts to join in the war panned out), he could use his art to aid in the war between democracy and Fascism, helping to forge the "fighting faith" that he felt democracy desperately needed.[21]

Not long after his arrival in Hollywood, in a letter to his nephew Malcolm (5 December 1942) Faulkner signaled that he was reassessing his role as artist and the purpose of his art, suggesting that he wanted his fiction to be more accessible and socially responsible. He wrote that he was looking forward to the time when the war would be over, commenting that after the young men had preserved liberty in the battlefield, older men like himself would be needed to preserve it at home. "Then perhaps the time of the older men will come," Faulkner wrote, "the ones like me who are articulate in the national voice, who are too old to be soldiers, but are old enough and have been vocal long enough to be listened to, yet are not so old that we too have become another batch of decrepit old men looking stubbornly backward at a point 25 or 50 years in the past" (*SLF* 166). Faulkner's comments here, particularly his desire to be "articulate in the national voice," suggest that he was considering a more straightforward and politically conscious art, particularly concerning issues of political freedom and democracy—an art, that is, that had more to do with "The Tall Men," "Two Soldiers," and "Shall Not Perish" than with *Go Down, Moses.*

Faulkner began testing out his more activist artistic stance in his screenplays, particularly "The De Gaulle Story" and "Battle Cry." In "The De Gaulle Story," his first assignment at Warner Brothers, Faulkner manifests his new vision in a chorus of voices expressing faith in the enduring force of democracy and the human spirit.[22] Not only does de Gaulle make pronouncements—"Freedom is not just an idea," he says at one point. "Freedom is bread. Without freedom, you don't live"[23]—but so do the many everyday French people, supporters of de Gaulle, who are the screenplay's primary focus (which was one reason the film was not made, as the producers thought there was not enough material on de Gaulle himself). The village priest, for instance, in the original story treatment of the script delivers a powerful affirmation of the human spirit, which he says will survive the Nazis: "Oppression and suffering come upon mankind and even destroy him as individuals. But they cannot destroy his immortal spirit. That endures. It is more than the simple will to freedom and contentment. It is his immortality, his hope and belief that out of his suffering his children and all the children of man to follow him will be free. In his suffering and his resistance to tyranny and evil and oppression he finds himself" (31–32). Equally powerful are Emilie's words on "the little people," the everyday people, who, while not necessarily strong and heroic as individuals, stand as a powerful force—they become, in Faulkner's terms, "tall"—when unified. "It's like those little ants in the jungle that nothing can stand against—not the biggest and fiercest and the most powerful—nothing," Emilie says. "You can kill them by the millions just by stepping on them, but they keep on coming because they are so little" (190–91). Emilie goes on to characterize the connection between the little people and the great leaders, saying that "there is something of the little people in the very great: as if all the little people who had been trodden and crushed had condensed into one great one who knew and remembered all their suffering. And the little ones themselves are never afraid as long as they believe that the other little ants coming behind them will finally eat the elephant" (191).

Emilie's words point to the script's specific patriotic message: because the human spirit survives in the face of all oppression, the Nazi occupation of France (and, by implication, of other European countries) is ultimately doomed to failure. That spirit lives on not only in the people oppressed by the Nazis but also, as Faulkner notes in his original script (there are several versions), in the Nazis themselves, though the force is repressed deep within their consciousness. Whatever the Nazis' military might, their enterprise carried within it the seeds of their own destruction; ultimately they would be undone by their humanity, in a powerful return of the repressed. Or as Faulkner put it: "Naziism is inherent with its own ultimate downfall to the extent that Nazis are at bottom human beings, too, when this quality can be reached" (48). When that day comes and the collective human spirit reemerges in the Nazis, they will recognize their crimes against humanity and see that Hitler, as one of the characters observes, "is nothing: a little clod of rotten dirt before God. He will pass" (32).

Faulkner's celebration of humanity's enduring spirit continues in "Battle Cry." As originally conceived by Howard Hawks and his agent, Charles Feldman, "Battle Cry" was to portray, in separate story lines, the exploits of various heroic resistance fighters (including American, British, French, Russian, Chinese, and Greek), their stories unified by the theme of undying desire for freedom.[24] By framing these story lines within the film's overarching celebration of the American dream of democracy—the script begins and ends with scenes celebrating American patriotism—Faulkner suggests that this desire for freedom, while universal, is most recognizably American. What finally links the stories of the Allied freedom fighters, in other words, is their belief in America.

In a move emphasizing his national, not southern, vision and voice, Faulkner invokes Abraham Lincoln—and not Robert E. Lee or some other southern hero—in presenting the Civil War as the antecedent to World War II. As we have already seen, Faulkner had made reference to Lincoln's Gettysburg Address in "Shall Not Perish," but here Lincoln himself takes center stage. Not only do characters repeatedly talk about Lincoln but verses from the "Lincoln Cantata," which was based on an African American folk legend that Lincoln had not died but had lived on to fight for freedom, are interspersed with backdrops of his funeral train throughout the script.[25] Lines from the cantata state the film's fundamental message:

> Freedom's a thing that has no ending,
> It needs to be cared for, it needs defending;
> A great long job for many hands,
> Carrying freedom across all the lands.[26]

As both the screenplay and the cantata itself underscore, and as Daniel Brodsky and Robert Hamblin point out regarding the script, "Lincoln's dream of freedom must be extended to all nations."[27]

By invoking Lincoln and the Civil War, Faulkner presents World War II as another necessary war against slavery. While affirming the undiminished line of American heroism (as he had done in "The Tall Men," "Shall Not Perish," and "Two Soldiers"), Faulkner now locates the source of that heroism, not in the southern yeoman, but in those who defended the nation against the southern rebellion. Early in the script a garrulous old man sounding a good bit like Mr. McCallum and Mrs. Grier from the earlier stories tells his grandson just why he is going off to war: "You're going to fight for the folks that ain't free, that have been enslaved. And this ain't the first time boys from this town [Springfield, Illinois] left this very station to go and fight against slavery. Hell fire, there was a man from this very town . . . that said, there ain't room in all North America for a nation to exist half slave and half free. And now we got the same fight on our hands that old Abe had, only worse, because we know now there ain't room even on this whole earth for people to exist half slave and half free" (192). When his grandson responds that all that was in 1865, a time when one did not have "to go to the end of the world to fight slavery," his grandfather answers: "That's jest where we want slavery; at the end of the earth! Then we can shove it the rest of the way off!" (194). In this construction, World War II pits individual freedom against the modern-day equivalent of the Old South slave system: Fascist totalitarianism.

In a scene in which one of the American soldiers visits an English pub, Faulkner acknowledges that while the American democratic system might be flawed, democratic ideals are not. Faulkner's directions for filming this scene showing the soldier listening to the patrons criticize the government underscore that flawed democratic governments are not to be abandoned, but improved: "He hears them criticize the government and the running of the war, talk atheism, anything they want to in freedom, and he realizes that this is democracy and that there is something in democracy, for all its waste and clumsiness in government, that can't be destroyed" (86). Other soldiers later reach agreement on precisely this point. When an American soldier says that "we are fighting for the right to keep on living in the way we want to live" and adds that "maybe that way is wrong, unjust to some, and will change later—," a British soldier interrupts him to continue the sentence: "—but you want to change it yourselves, without help. It was like a man of America's people, Joe Louis, who said it about as well as I know, good enough, anyway: 'There's a heap wrong with this world, but Hitler can't fix it'" (94). Joe Louis's comment both acknowledges American democracy's gravest flaw—longtime inequities based on race—and suggests, in the context of the conversation, that those inequities will eventually be made right. Furthermore, Louis's comment on Hitler contextualizes that flaw within the war against Fascism, suggesting that internal problems of American democracy pale before the external threat posed by Nazi Germany.

The idea that World War II extends straight back to the Civil War, both being wars against slavery and oppression, surfaces repeatedly in the screenplay, particularly in the discussions and banter of the American soldiers. In one exchange, a soldier's story of enlisting in the current war merges directly with the narrative of the "Lincoln Cantata." In the cantata, Lincoln, reportedly dead but actually alive, sits quietly at the back of a small black church in Alabama, listening to a sermon declaring that the time of slavery is over. In Faulkner's screenplay, a country boy named Akers tells of coming upon a small black church in the Alabama backwoods and listening to the preacher's sermon, hearing precisely what Lincoln does in the cantata:

> We got a new land!
> Ain't no riding boss with a whip,
> Don't have no backbiters,
> Liars can't go, cheaters can't go,
> Ain't no deputy to chain us,
> No high sheriff to bring us back!
> (299)

Upon hearing the preacher, Akers immediately knew he was going to enlist, although he could not then (and still cannot) articulate what exactly compelled him. He just knew. Akers's sudden decision looks back to "Two Soldiers," where Pete Grier immediately decides to enlist upon hearing news of the attack on Pearl Harbor, his only explanation being, "I got to go" (*CSF* 83). But whereas Faulkner had characterized Grier's heroism as extending in an unbroken line from his southern forebears, Akers's heroism originates in his direct connection with the spirit of Lincoln. Indeed, in placing Akers at the same church where Lincoln sits in the cantata, Faulkner makes Akers a manifestation of Lincoln, ready to fight in this new war against slavery.

The symbolic resonance here points to Faulkner's quest to articulate a national voice, as does the name of the black soldier in the screenplay—America. Besides his name, America has tremendous symbolic significance: his severe wound suggests the terrible burden blacks have suffered in the United States; and his complete acceptance into the unit, once he has proved himself to be every bit as good a soldier as his white companions, points to a future nation in which whites and blacks (who are fully capable of assuming the responsibilities of citizenship) live and work together on equal terms. That vision comes up in the soldiers' conversations, which frequently circle around race and racial politics. These conversations underscore further that World War II continues the Civil War's fight against slavery and that blacks are ready for (and deserving of) full citizenship. America himself makes it clear that however violently and irresponsibly blacks have acted in the past, they have put all that behind them and are now fighting the true enemy—Fascism. Or as he puts it: "That's done over now. All folks got better fighting than that to do now" (290).

Some of the most charged discussions of racial politics in America come in the conversations between the American soldiers and their two prisoners, one Italian, the other German. The Italian, surprisingly enough, is a strong admirer of the United States (he says that he lived there for a number of years) and speaks confidently of gradually improving racial conditions. Indeed, the Italian voices the gradualist approach to southern race relations that Faulkner himself would soon be endorsing in public comments and in his fiction, often through the comments of Gavin Stevens. When one of the American soldiers attacks southern segregationists for denying blacks the vote, the Italian predicts that all that will change once Americans stop pressuring the South and start paying more attention to the plight of blacks in their own regions. "I think it will be changed just as soon as the people outside that part of the country, whose concern it is not, stop trying to force them to give America's people a vote," the Italian says. "When the people outside that part of the country have cleaned their own house a little, as they had promised to do on the first day of January, 1863" (102).

The German prisoner, on the other hand, speaks contemptuously of the United States. An orphan who has found meaning and purpose in the Nazis, the German soldier represents both the appeal of Fascism and its ultimate danger: he has gained a meaningful place in the Nazi community, but he has had to give up his individuality in his submission to it. In talking with an American soldier named Reagan (it is not clear whether Faulkner wanted Ronald Reagan for the part), the German describes how Nazism has galvanized Germans, presenting them with "the pattern which could take the homeless and parentless like me, and in exchange for simple absolute fidelity and obedience, offer them in return a concept of power, of will, of force, whose reward would be the world" (252). He sees Americans as entirely vacuous and driven by a desire for money, pursuing material goods "which you neither deserve nor need, with which you try to drug yourselves into believing that ease is the same thing as security" (253). The German argues that rather than a means for purchasing comforts, wealth should be the means for creating power, "the sinews of strength, the reins to control the force which only the strong dare handle—not for the moiling worthless mass of mankind, but for the power and glory of that race which has the strength to declare its own godhead, and so becomes godhead." "America," he concludes. "An empty continent waiting for its master as a woman waits for hers" (254).

So frightening is the German's vision that one American soldier, Franklin, must be restrained from shooting him, calling out as he is held back, "Kill him! Kill him, somebody! They're mad! They're monsters! There ain't any hope for them! We got to kill them all! There ain't room in the world for them and us, too! We got to kill them all to save ourselves!" (254). While Franklin may be raving, he nonetheless clearly understands the threat posed by Nazis like the German prisoner: in giving themselves over entirely to the state, Nazis lose their humanity and become unthinking automatons, slaves to the system. The American soldiers, in contrast, are united in purpose but maintain their individual dignity and identity. The dynamics of their military unit represent those of the democratic system; they argue and debate, but they stand as one when the votes are counted (at one point the soldiers take a vote on whether to retreat or hold their ground). And so it is appropriate that the response to the German comes in the very dynamics of the unit, a point driven home by a British soldier, Loughton. After first standing aghast that the Americans soldiers at times make military decisions based on votes rather than simply following orders, Loughton sees his mistake and concludes, "Maybe you Americans don't know yet what you're fighting for, and maybe you haven't quite learned yet how to do the fighting, but . . . No. That's wrong. I think you not only know what you're fighting for, whether you can say it or not, but you know the best way to do the fighting, too. Go on. Vote" (341).

"Battle Cry" ends with a full-blown celebration of American democracy, with the freedom train of 1865 dissolving into the opening scene's troop train, now roaring off with its banner "BERLIN TOKYO OR BUST" (407). Significantly, the screenplay reaches this patriotic affirmation only after it has examined a number of the faults in the implementation of America's democratic system, including ongoing racial inequities and the nation's (not just the South's) failure to fulfil Lincoln's promise to grant equal citizenship to blacks—precisely the concerns that Faulkner was himself examining in his newfound patriotism, weighing the system's workings in the context of Fascism and a world at war.

In a letter to his nephew Malcolm (4 July 1943), written when he was feverishly revising his first script of "Battle Cry," Faulkner expressed ideas similar to those in the screenplay, affirming the values of democracy while pointing to the flaws in America's system and specifically calling for full democracy for blacks. He points to a startling and deeply troubling juxtaposition between bravery abroad and murder at home: on the same day that black fighter pilots performed heroically over Africa, white mobs killed twenty blacks in the streets of Detroit. Faulkner asks his nephew to imagine the following scenario of living in Africa as a minority:

> Suppose you and me and a few others of us lived in the Congo, freed seventy-seven years ago by ukase; of course we cant live in the same apartment hut with the black folks, nor always ride in the same car nor eat in the same restaurant, but we are free because the Great Black Father says so. Then the Congo is engaged in War with the Cameroon. At last we persuade the Great Black Father to let us fight too. You and Jim say are flyers. You have just spent the day trying to live long enough to learn how to do your part in saving the Congo. Then you come back down and are told that 20 of your people have just been killed by a mixed mob of civilians and cops at Little Poo Poo. What would you think? (*SLF* 175–76)

Faulkner then makes his thoughts clear with regard to America: "A change will come out of this war. If it doesn't, if the politicians and the people who run this country are not forced to make good the shibboleth they glibly talk about freedom, liberty, human rights, then you young men who live through it will have wasted your precious time, and those who dont live through it will have died in vain" (*SLF* 176).

By the fall of 1943, not long after this letter, Faulkner had begun to experiment in his fiction with what he considered his new national, rather than specifically southern, literary voice. In order to express his more openly political vision, Faulkner adopted a new style of writing that foregrounded ideas and social issues, a move that David Minter characterizes as one "from short stories and novels toward exempla and fables, from indirectness toward directness, from modes of fiction that made 'nothing happen' toward modes that were at least arguments for change."[28] Faulkner, in short, wanted his fiction to bring about large-scale changes in American attitudes—and with time large-scale changes in American democratic practice. He started work at this time on a story that much later evolved into *A Fable*, the postwar novel that best exemplifies his new authorial positioning. Writing to Harold Ober (30 October 1943), Faulkner characterized his story as "a fable, an indictment of war, perhaps" (*SLF* 178), and several months later, in a letter to Robert Haas (15 January 1944), he described its basic plot and argument, clearly articulating his new artistic stance:

> The argument is (in the fable) in the middle of that war, Christ (some movement in mankind which wished to stop war forever) reappeared and was crucified again. We are repeating, we are in the midst of war again. Suppose Christ gives us one more chance, we will crucify him again, perhaps for the last time.
>
> That's crudely put; I am not trying to preach at all. But that is the argument: We did this in 1918; in 1944 it not only MUST NOT happen again, it SHALL NOT HAPPEN again. i.e. ARE WE GOING TO LET IT HAPPEN AGAIN? now that we are in another war, where the third and final chance might be offered us to save him. (*SLF* 180)

Despite his disclaimer, Faulkner was indeed trying to preach (as his admonitions and writing in all capitals suggest), and preachiness would soon be a large element in almost all of his postwar fiction.

Although it would be several years before he completed any new fiction, Faulkner buzzed excitedly in his letters about the new direction in his writing. In a letter to Bennett Cerf and Robert Haas (10 January 1945) he characterized the turn in his work as a coming of age, a maturing from the passionate strivings of youth:

> Unless I am wrong about it, have reached the time of an artist's increasing years when he no longer can judge what he is doing, I have grown up at last. All my writing life I have been a poet without education, who possessed only instinct and a fierce conviction and belief in the worth and truth of what he was doing, and an illimitable cour-

age for rhetoric (personal pleasure in it too: I admit it) and who knew and cared for little else.

Well, I'm doing something different now, so different that I am writing and rewriting, weighing every word, which I never did before; I used to bang it on like an apprentice paper hanger and never look back. (*SLF* 188)

Faulkner's emphasis on rewriting signaled his priority of clearly and effectively communicating his political message, and this priority lay behind his comments to Richard Wright (probably 11 September 1945) faulting *Black Boy* for what Faulkner believed would be its limited political usefulness. Faulkner wrote that although he found *Black Boy* well written, "it will accomplish little of what it should accomplish, since only they will be moved and grieved by it who already know and grieve over this situation." "I think you will agree," Faulkner commented later in the letter, "that the good lasting stuff comes out of one individual's imagination and sensitivity to and comprehension of the suffering of Everyman, Anyman, not out of the memory of his own grief" (*SLF* 201).

Committed to using his art to help strengthen democratic America, Faulkner by the mid-1940s was imaginatively rereading his earlier fiction in the context of its political effectiveness in the battle between totalitarianism and democracy. As indicated in his letter to Bennett Cerf and Robert Haas, Faulkner saw his earlier fiction as not reasoned out or carefully written, in contrast to his new, democracy-inspired writing, suggesting that on some level he may have feared that the sources of his fiction lay in an irrationalism perhaps akin to that from which Fascism sprang—an opinion, as we have already seen, that leftist critics had long been voicing about Faulkner's work.[29] In this context, his characterization of himself as "an apprentice paper-hanger" is anything but innocuous, echoing, as it does, Ike McCaslin's characterization, in *Go Down, Moses,* of Hitler, himself a failed artist and, in Ike's words, "one Austrian paper-hanger" (*GDM* 323). This is not to say that Faulkner saw himself as a Fascist (he did not). Rather, it is to say that he saw his earlier work as springing from different sources than did his current work and that he was determined, in his future writing, to reconfigure Yoknapatawpha according to his new vision, underscoring its—and the South's—need for a more just democracy.[30]

That reconfiguration began when, at the request of Malcolm Cowley, Faulkner added an appendix to *The Sound and the Fury* for inclusion in *The*

Portable Faulkner. The appendix, written in 1945, in effect recontextualized the novel in light of World War II and Faulkner's new democratic vision. If the four-part structure of *The Sound and the Fury* represented, as Faulkner once said, his four attempts to portray Caddy,[31] the appendix represented his fifth attempt, and its inclusion drastically redirected the thrust of the novel. Faulkner here carried Caddy's life forward all the way to Nazi-occupied France, describing a county librarian in 1943 noticing a magazine picture of Caddy riding alongside a German staff general. The picture, aglow "with luxury and money and sunlight—a Cannebiere backdrop of mountains and palms and cypresses and the sea," shows the two riding in "an open powerful expensive chromiumtrimmed sports car," Caddy's face "hatless between a rich scarf and a seal coat, ageless and beautiful, cold serene and damned."[32] The year is 1940, and this is the last we see of her.

It is tempting to read, as many have done, Caddy's sitting alongside a Nazi general as Faulkner's misogynist indictment of a strong-willed and sexually active woman, cold and calculating in her pursuit of power and influence, a version writ small (and female) of the Nazi quest for dominance. If she is not necessarily a Nazi, Caddy appears happy to be with one (though it is not precisely clear why Caddy is riding in the car; for all we know, she may be working for the resistance).[33] That reading, however, cuts against the thrust not only of the novel as originally written but also of the appendix itself. In this fifth effort at understanding Caddy, Faulkner focuses, as he does in the novel proper, less on Caddy herself than on those observing her, in this case the librarian and those to whom she shows the photograph, Jason and Dilsey. All three judge Caddy as she has been judged all along in the novel proper, damning her without question. While the librarian, in an initial rush of feeling, tells Jason that they must try and save Caddy—though clearly she has no idea how that could be done—she later concludes that she has merely refused to see the truth about her: "*Yes* she thought, crying quietly *that was it she didn't want to see it know whether it was Caddy or not because she knows Caddy doesn't want to be saved hasn't anything anymore worth being saved for nothing worth being lost that she can lose*" (342). Even Dilsey turns her back on Caddy, refusing to acknowledge that it is she in the photograph.

By directing attention away from Caddy to her fiercely judgmental observers, the appendix underscores the smothering authoritarianism of southern culture, turning the reader both back to the novel proper (where Caddy has been similarly judged, scorned, and banished by the dysfunctional Compson family, representing the voice of southern culture) and forward to the rise of Nazi Germany. In this dual look, yoking together southern and Nazi authoritarianism, Faulkner points to the punishing power wielded by both cultures and, even more damningly, suggests that the two share fundamental structures of control. That crushing power, demanding submission and conformity, is seen in the victimization suffered by both Caddy and the librarian for not embracing the prescribed roles of wife and mother. The vital and sexually active Caddy is driven out of the South, while the mousy spinster librarian is imprisoned by it, pathetically identifying with the very system that has locked her away, spending most of her time keeping sexually suggestive fiction out of youthful hands. By portraying in the appendix the victimization of two southern women under the shadow of Nazi Germany, Faulkner comes close to portraying a view of southern culture similar to that of W. J. Cash and Lillian Smith, both of whom saw southern traditionalism masking a punishing authoritarianism, if not an outright totalitarianism. Underscoring the appendix's significance, Faulkner wrote to Robert Linscott, at Random House (13 March 1946), that he wanted it published as the novel's first section, since it "was the key to the whole book." After reading the appendix, Faulkner added, "any reader will understand the other sections" (*SLF* 228).

The reconfigured *Sound and the Fury* presents the South in desperate need of transformation, particularly with regard to issues of race and citizenship, political issues now central to Faulkner. Besides portraying the crushing authoritarianism of the South, the appendix in its very structure, which divides the white and black characters, re-creates the system of racial segregation. Dividing the discussions of the white and black characters is this stark line of type: "And that was all. These were not Compsons. They were black" (348). Moreover, the summaries of the black characters, appropriate to their second-class status in southern culture, are so brief as almost to be nonexistent; and just as appropriately, they come at the back of the appendix. "They endured" is all that marks Dilsey's future in the appendix: it is a fitting description for the situation Faulkner saw facing blacks in 1945 America, who had little other than endurance for weathering their oppression.

Issues of race and citizenship are also central to *Intruder in the Dust*, with the terrors of European totalitarianism shadowing the novel's call for a just democracy for both blacks and whites. That call comes primarily through the voice of Gavin Stevens, who, though not without fault (he is much better at talking about problems than he is about fixing them), nonetheless expresses political positions Faulkner would himself echo repeatedly in public statements throughout the 1950s. Stevens calls for the gradual dismantling of the barriers of racial segregation, a view similar to that voiced by the Italian prisoner in "Battle Cry." Stevens's position is fairly simple: democracy demands that blacks be given full citizenship, but change should come slowly and judiciously, since the process involves not merely changing laws but changing customs and attitudes. In the slow dismantling of the system of segregation, the rights of both whites and blacks must be protected. Stevens believes that if the South does not take the responsibility for ending segregation, it runs the risk of federal intervention, which he sees as a potentially dangerous expansion of the federal government into local and regional affairs. That expansion, which Stevens configures as a step toward the totalitarianism of Nazi Germany and the Soviet Union, would undermine the bedrock of American democracy, individual rights.[34] In a remarkable outburst (as filtered through Chick's memory), Stevens compares the position of southerners facing northern interference to that of citizens of Germany and Russia facing totalitarian rule:

> *We are in the position of the German after 1933 who had no other alternative between being either a Nazi or a Jew or the present Russian (European too for that matter) who hasn't even that but must be either a Communist or dead, only we must do it and we alone without help or interference or even (thank you) advice since only we can if Lucas' equality is to be anything more than its own prisoner inside an impregnable barricade of the direct heirs of the victory of 1861–1865 which probably did more than even John Brown to stalemate Lucas' freedom which still seems to be in check going on a hundred years after Lee surrendered.*[35]

Here Stevens expresses Faulkner's dual-edged concern regarding the shoring up of American democracy: the flaws of the democratic system, particularly racial inequities, need to be corrected, but in a way that protects individual rights, particularly in the face of a powerful federal government. It makes no sense, in other words, to grant blacks political equality by a process that enslaves all Americans, including the blacks themselves, under a totalitarian slavemaster.[36]

Set against Stevens's nightmare of federal intervention is the gradualism manifested in the relationship between Lucas and Chick. In his quiet and bold dignity Lucas resembles the black soldier America in "Battle Cry": not only are both worthy of citizenship but both possess the tall-man individualism that Faulkner believes must not be destroyed by big government. Moreover, just as America gains the respect of his fellow soldiers, Lucas gains the respect of Chick, who through helping Lucas will certainly grow up to be more sensitive to the plight of blacks. In this regard Chick represents the coming change in racial attitudes in the South. Indeed, it is in the interplay between Lucas and Chick, particularly their ongoing trading of indebtedness, that Faulkner suggests the gradual process that will undo southern racism: acts of kindness to whites by blacks will set in motion a sort of "pay it forward" process whereby whites will eventually return all the kindnesses given to them, along the way reaching an understanding of their shared humanity with black people.[37] Faulkner thus puts the agency of social change in the hands of blacks—not hands raised defiantly in fists but hands making offerings to whites that will in time be returned in mutual respect. The naiveté of this plan for social change needs no comment.

The political vision of *Intruder in the Dust* suggests the extent to which issues involved with European totalitarianism permeated and shaped Faulkner's thinking in the late 1940s. As he does in the novel, Faulkner typically configured domestic politics in light of the Soviet Union, conflating Nazism and Communism (as did many Americans at the time), seeing them as essentially the same in their shared totalitarianism.[38] Several years later, in one of his interviews in Nagano, Japan, Faulkner went even further, equating capitalist magnates' ferocious pursuit of wealth with totalitarian thinking. He began by saying that he did not like any form of totalitarian government and that what had once seemed so hopeful and good about Communism had vanished, current-day Communism having become a frightening manifestation of a monolithic state "in which men use the mass of peoples just like the rich men in my country established their power and their aggrandizement on beaver pelts. It seems to me that the totalitarian people use people just like they use beaver pelts, just for their own power."[39]

Faulkner's concerns about totalitarianism only intensified during the 1950s, profoundly shaping his fiction and his thinking on democracy, individual rights, and integration in the South. By the time he finally finished *A Fable*, in 1954, it had evolved into a large and complicated tale of authoritarianism and militarism, the two working together to keep the forces of rebellion silenced. As Joseph R. Urgo rightfully comments, the novel "is Faulkner's most blatantly anti-authoritarian and anti-establishmentarian novel," depicting in all its horror "the ideology of bureaucratic professionalism, of hierarchy, of authority, and of corporate control over human behavior."[40] Standing against the crushing power of the state in the novel is the corporal, a manifestation of Christ, who inspires a short-lived rebellion that threatens to undo the vast bureaucracy whose reach stretches into all areas of life. That bureaucracy, as Faulkner underscores, braids together, not merely one nation, but all nations:

> the Prime Ministers and Premiers and Secretaries, the cabinet members and senators and chancellors; and those who outnumbered even them: the board chairmen of the vast establishments which produced the munitions and shoes and tinned foods, and the modest unsung omnipotent ones who were the priests of simple money; and the others still who outnumbered even these: the politicians, the lobbyists, the owners and publishers of newspapers and the ordained ministers of churches, and all the other accredited travelling representatives of the vast solvent organizations and fraternities and movements which control by coercion or cajolery man's morals and actions and all his mass-value for affirmation or negation—all that vast powerful terror-inspiring representation which, running all democracy's affairs in peace, comes indeed into its own in war, finding its true apotheosis then.[41]

In the following years, Faulkner in numerous interviews, talks, and speeches continued his assault on authoritarianism, typically by attacking the Soviet Union. In his calls for ending segregation in the South, he frequently spoke about the ways integration would aid America in its cold war against Communism. "We must have as many people as possible on the side of us who believe in individual freedom," he wrote to David Kirk (8 March 1956). "There are seventeen million Negroes. Let us have them on our side, rather than on that of Russia" (*SLF* 395). His statement here is neither surprising nor unusual. As we have seen, ever since the late 1930s, when the world was sliding into war, Faulkner had kept one eye on Europe; if he had earlier in his career seen everything primarily from the long view of southern history, he was by the early 1940s seeing things shaded and illuminated by European Fascism and totalitarianism. Reorienting his vision meant reorienting his art—his postage stamp of Mississippi soil was by the 1940s imprinted with a foreign postmark.

7

SOMETHING DEATHLY IN THE AIR

KATHERINE ANNE PORTER

At a 1956 conference sponsored by the Institute of International Education, Katherine Anne Porter responded to the question whether living in another culture necessarily cut writers off from their roots: "A human being carries his 'roots' in his blood, his nervous system[,] the brain cells. Even his attempts to disguise them will betray his origins and true nature. I think foreign travel and experience are good for everybody—not just writers, but for writers they are an invaluable, irreplaceable education in life." Porter added, in responding to another question, that she was particularly thankful to the Guggenheim Foundation, whose fellowship had allowed her to travel to Germany in 1931 and to stay in France for several years after that. "Without that grant," Porter commented, "I might have just stayed in Mexico, or here at home; I should certainly not have gone to Europe when I did; and so in the most absolute sense, that Guggenheim Foundation Fellowship has helped me nourish my life as a writer to this day; I am today unable to imagine even faintly what I should have done without my wonderful years in Europe."[1]

At twenty years distance and through the reworkings of memory, it was easy for Porter to configure her time in Europe as "wonderful years," but that characterization glosses over the tension and turmoil that she also experienced, particularly during the five and a half months she spent in Berlin, from early September 1931 to mid-February 1932. Even during her more comfortable and easygoing time in Paris, where she lived after leaving Germany until 1936, she was dogged by the growing power of European Fascism and the looming threat of war. These were crucial years in Porter's artistic development, providing her with subject matter for her fiction and insight into the era's troubling social and political issues. Even more importantly, her time in Europe, particularly that in Germany, profoundly affected her imaginative vision, turning its focus upon issues of political authoritarianism, typically as it was manifested in the everyday dynamics of both the family and southern culture.

―××××―

Porter and her lover Eugene Pressly departed for Europe on 22 August 1931, sailing from Veracruz, Mexico, to Bremerhaven. Her two primary goals for her fellowship year were to write fiction (she was already an established, if somewhat struggling, writer) and to develop her political thinking. While her political sympathies at this time were decidedly leftist, Porter's overall political views were muddled and inconsistent, often fluctuating wildly between revolutionary idealism and southern conservatism.[2] Her itinerary in Europe was aimed largely at gaining some coherence of thought by observing firsthand the striking political transformations taking place on the Continent. Long before her departure, and even before she knew she would be going, Porter wrote Josephine Herbst (11 February 1931), who had just returned from three years in Europe and a trip to Soviet Russia, about the political education she hoped to receive: "I mean to spend most of my time in Russia, and Germany maybe, but I want to hear from you how Germany is now. I'd like a look at several other countries for the sake of getting the whole idea" (*LP* 32–33).

Porter never made it to Russia, but she had many experiences that sharpened her political thinking, beginning with her mingling with the Germans on board the ship to Bremerhaven. In a long letter to Caroline Gordon (begun 28 August 1931, last dated 24 September 1931) Porter described the many Germans on board and her growing affection for them. She wrote that all the Germans she had met "have soft voices and good manners. Their words of greeting and goodbye and thanks are very musical: it is all a great relief after the harshness, the nasty public manners, the shrillness and meanness of Mexico, where only the Indian gives any charm of being" (*LP* 60). Once in Germany, Porter was immediately impressed by what she saw as the order and purpose of German society, and she happily looked forward to immersing herself in the culture of Berlin.

Porter's enthusiasm was short-lived. Not long after her arrival, she began suffering from a suffocating depression that took its toll on her physical health. That the winter was particularly brutal did not help matters. Nor did the fact that she was suffering alone, as Pressly soon after their arrival had departed for Madrid to seek work. While Porter initially welcomed his departure, their cramped living quarters having strained their relationship, she soon found herself painfully isolated. Sick, lonely, and unable to speak German, Porter wrote to Gordon (14 December 1931) that despite there being a great deal to do in Berlin, "only, only, I am here so alone that all other alonenesses of my whole life seem crowded by comparison" (*LP* 68).

With time Porter came to see how misguided her initial impressions of Germany were. Rather than enjoying boon times, Germany was suffering from economic and political chaos; and even though, as Thomas Austenfeld observes, Porter was poorly equipped to understand the complexities of Germany's problems, the large-scale turmoil and suffering were hard to miss.[3] From the beginning, Porter brought her leftist sympathies to bear in her efforts to understand Germany's situation. Not long after her arrival in Berlin, she visited the offices of TASS, the Soviet news agency, to set up a meeting with the leader of the German Communist Party, and she expressed interest in writing for several Communist-backed publications.[4] In December 1931 she attended a large rally celebrating the thirtieth anniversary of the German Communist Party, and in a letter to Herbst (16 January 1932) she noted the haunting contrast between the gaunt, despairing workers and the heavily armed, fierce-looking police who patrolled the rally.[5] At the same time that she was mingling with Communists, she was also attending parties with well-heeled and powerful Nazis, including Hermann Göring, whom she apparently met on several occasions.[6] Porter later reported to Herbst (16 October 1933) that Göring had boasted that the Jews would be expunged from all positions of power once Hitler came to power.[7] In later years Porter claimed that she had immediately recognized the evil of Hitler and the Nazis, though there is little evidence from the time to support that claim.

Clearly, Porter was deeply affected by all that she was witnessing and experiencing. Her work with the Communists, rather than strengthening ties, instead enhanced the frustration with Communist politics she had begun to experience in the aftermath of the Mexican Revolution. She was increasingly resistant to what she saw as the Communists' demands for the sacrifice of individuality; and as an artist, she was particularly alarmed at what she saw as their stifling proscriptions on art. "Russia seems to have this effect on most people who are convinced by what they find there," Porter wrote to Herbst (11 February 1931); "they begin to despise artists." In demanding unquestioned allegiance and in silencing all voices but their own, Communist leaders, she added, reduced the complexity of life and art into simplistic "slogans and the latest Ultimate Truth" (*LP* 34). Porter knew that for the artist such restraints were fatal, and she told Herbst that art must instead revel in the multiplicity of life's voices and perspectives:

> Life comes first, an art not rooted in human experience is not worth a damn, but different kinds of minds have different kinds of experience, and all I ask of any man is validity; and there should be a place for every type and kind of mind. I don't want to lose any testimony; it may be necessary for one man to sit wound up in his own vitals in order to find out what he needs to know, and his discoveries will be valuable if he is capable of telling the truth. Another must be wound up in the world around him . . . some must be active, and some contemplative. (34)

Porter's frustration with the Communists brought to the surface her deeply felt but often repressed antiauthoritarianism. A few years before, in her unfinished biography of Cotton Mather, Porter had expressed these feelings in her depiction of Mather as a dictatorial mastermind consumed with a monomaniacal belief in his godlike authority. The recent executions of Sacco and Vanzetti, in 1927, had also stoked her antiauthoritarianism, as Porter had come to the conclusion that the pair of immigrant anarchists were victims of not only of a modern-day witch hunt by the government but also a conspiracy led by the very people who were organizing protests on their behalf, the Communists.[8] Porter believed that the Communists had no interest in achieving justice for the two men, but had all along looked forward to their martyrdom—a stunning betrayal exposing the frightening extremes of authoritarian politics.

After her time in Berlin, Porter's antiauthoritarianism only became more central to her creative imagination and to the ironic narrative perspective that became the signature of her writing in the 1930s and 1940s. Her first version of "Hacienda," which she apparently wrote during her time in Berlin and which drew from her experiences observing Sergei Eisenstein direct *Que Viva Mexico!* in Tetlapayac in 1932, exposed the failures of the Mexican Revolution, focusing on the irony that the motion picture, portraying a peasant uprising that sweeps away an oppressive feudal system, was filmed at a hacienda still operating according to that very feudal system.[9] At one point in the sketch, a visitor to the hacienda who has returned after a sixty-year absence looks about and comments, "How beautiful. Nothing has changed at all."[10] Spoken without irony, the visitor's comment nonetheless echoes ironically throughout the sketch and voices its central point: despite the revolution in Mexico, the old ways continue. The Mexico of "Hacienda" is a world of false hopes, with people basking in the rhetoric of revolution while masters still rule and peasants still suffer. Indeed, all that is left of the revolution is the rhetoric, the "slogans invented by bright young men in the Universities to drape upon the figure-head of Zapata, who is safely dead and can no longer embarrass them by acting upon their theories" (566). The peasants, meanwhile, remain besotted with a literal opiate of the people—pulque, the powerful drink described by the narrator as a "corpse-white liquor" that brings "forgetfulness by the riverful" (565). Even the Russian film-makers care only about their film, oblivious to both the overall plight of the peasants and the specific problems of those who are working for them. When one of the actors is accidentally killed and another carted off to jail, the Russians' only concern is the production schedule.

In her revision of "Hacienda," which she worked on in 1932 and 1933, after her time in Berlin had deepened her frustrations with Communist politics, Porter kept the basic story line but expanded the ironic commentary. To underscore the illusory nature of the revolution's gains, Porter describes the swarm of government agents who follow the Russian film crew, making sure that everything they film reflects on the glory of Mexico and the revolution. "Dozens of helpful observers, art experts, photographers, literary talents, and travel guides swarmed about them to lead them aright," Porter writes, "and to show them all the most beautiful, significant, and characteristic things in the national life and soul: if by chance anything not beautiful got in the way of the camera, there was a very instructed and sharp-eyed committee of censors whose duty it was to see that the scandal went no further than the cutting room" (*CSP* 146). Porter likewise expanded the commentary on the damage wrought by pulque, adding a passage describing a chain of greed, deceit, and profit that leads straight to the government: "The white flood of pulque flowed without pause; all over Mexico the Indians would drink the corpse-white liquor, swallow forgetfulness and ease by the riverful, and the money would flow silver-white into the government treasury; don Genaro and his fellow-hacendados would fret and curse, the Agrarians would raid, and ambitious politicians in the capital would be stealing right and left enough to buy such haciendas for themselves. It was all arranged" (*CSP* 168). But the most damning addition comes in a description of the revolutionist Velarde, whose career underscores the fact that the revolution has changed nothing but the names of the bosses:

> He was the most powerful and successful revolutionist in Mexico. He owned two pulque haciendas which had fallen to his share when the great repartition of land had taken place. He operated also the largest dairy farm in the country, furnishing milk and butter and cheese to every charitable institution, orphans' home, insane asylum, reform school and workhouse in the country, and getting just twice the prices for them than any other dairy farm would have asked. He also owned a great aguacate hacienda; he controlled the army; he controlled a powerful bank; the president of the Republic made no appointments to any office without his advice. He fought counter-revolution and political corruption, daily upon the front pages of twenty newspapers he had bought for that very purpose. He employed thousands of peons. (156)

Very little happens in "Hacienda," a fact some critics have complained about, but that is Porter's point: revolutions and counterrevolutions come and go, but the oppressive structures stay the same.

Almost all of Porter's work written while she was in Europe interrogates authoritarian power and oppression, though not always on the scale of "Hacienda." Significantly, it was during this time that Porter became enthusiastically interested in her family's genealogy and history. This new interest, combined with her concern about authoritarianism, led to a significant reinterpretation of her southern origins, and of southern culture more generally, from a perspective derived largely from her experiences in Europe. Evidence that Porter was aligning her memories of childhood with her German experiences surface first in her daybooks. In one entry from 1931 she contextualizes her anxiety in Berlin by discussing her anxieties as a child:

> Berlin 1931—I really suffer from a feeling of personal danger, I have no faith in tomorrow in this place, and surely this [is] communicated to me from the awful climate of painful insecurity—nobody around me is in the least happy, or hopeful, the young seem reckless and cynical, the elders disheartened.
>
> It is true that I am used to anxiety, to insecurity, but it was my own, I believed, not communicated and not shared by those around

me. . . . As a child I lived in an anxious house where there was very little love, and this seemed the natural explanation for my incurable disturbance of the mind and desolation of my heart. But in this place the oppressive constant threat of disaster comes from without. I seemingly absorb it and cannot reject it again, it is an insidious gas settling in the air.[11]

A year later, in some comments on Faulkner, Porter explicitly describes the forbidding and oppressive southern atmosphere at which she had previously only hinted. She writes that characterizing Faulkner's South is "an overtone, something ominous, terrible in the very air, something dreadful and subhuman that scares you to the heart, and yet you do not quite know where it comes from. I don't know if any but a southerner would feel this. Something deathly in the air that has been breathed off from the long and painful relations between the black and white, a dreadful memory between them that poisons the very daylight."[12] Echoing her observations about Berlin's "insidious gas," Porter describes a toxic southern atmosphere circulating with unnameable fears and dread, clearly her view not only of Faulkner's South but of her own.

Although she rarely attempted the type of gothic horror found in much of Faulkner's fiction, her increasing concern about southern authoritarianism spurred Porter sometime in 1933 or 1934 to begin work on a lynching story that, even in its fragmented state (the story was never finished), suggests something of the violent extremes marking Faulkner's fiction.[13] The story focuses on the aftermath of a black man's lynching, and particularly on the guilt-laden responses by the white family whose black servant is the victim's grandmother. One of the family's daughters reaches a particularly terrifying realization: the people she loves and respects are also murderers; behind the mask of southern chivalry stand cold-hearted killers. "It was all too mixed up," the girl concludes, "too cr[u]el and unreasonable and nobody should be asked to live in such a place and under such conditions."[14] As Jan Gretlund observes, the story indicts the entire community and more generally the southern way of life, a point emphasized in the description of the lynched man: "He hangs there, dark among the branches, a reproach and a witness, not only against the murderers, but to the shame of those who believed they were his friends."[15] While she does not say so explicitly, Porter suggests that the image of the hanged black man, rather than traditional images of southern gentility (the plantation house, the southern belle, etc.), best represents the core of southern culture. Significantly, Porter considered entitling the story "The Never-Ending Wrong," the same title she later used for her memoir on the Sacco and Vanzetti protests, which describes the two men crushed between dueling authoritarian powers, the government and the Communists.[16]

Porter's deep-seated response to the authoritarianism she found in Germany in the early 1930s also shaped the novel that she began in Berlin, originally entitled "Many Redeemers" and then later "Legend and Memory." As her second title suggests, Porter intended the novel to unite her interest in southern repression (as codified in cultural legends, the narratives that spread the net of southern ideology) with her interest in her own family and her upbringing (as captured in her memories, shaped and understood now at a time of looming world crisis). Undated notes for the novel, which remained unfinished, indicate that she envisioned a sweeping work following several generations of a family that included the character Miranda, who became the protagonist of many of Porter's southern stories.[17] The novel was to have three parts: book 1, tentatively entitled "Introduction to Death," following the family up to World War I; book 2, "Midway of This Mortal Life," tracing the disruption of the family, including Miranda's sojourn in Mexico; and book 3, "Beginning Again: The End," portraying the family members dispersing into "the present scene, the rich and crumbling society with some of the cures offered by diverse Saviours."[18] Porter's outline suggests several ideas that later became central in her Miranda stories: that the legends of the South and the family cannot withstand the social disruptions arising from the world's disorder (as unleashed by World War I); that with modern society tottering over the abyss, "Saviours" (certainly meant to be those espousing new political orders) offer various solutions for remaking the world; and that in the end all efforts at improvement come to naught, with characters, together with the family, flying apart rather than coming together. The title of book 3 evokes the novel's dark subtext: besides the simple idea that the characters' efforts to begin again close the novel, the title also suggests that reconstructing the self and the culture from the ruins is *the end*; that is, the effort is futile.

Porter's letters from Paris during the time she was working on her lynching story and her novel indicate her growing concern about the possibility of war and point to the grim undercurrents that were becoming central to her imaginative vision and fiction, summed up in a letter to her father dated 21 January 1933: "The whole situation here is very bad" (*LP* 90). In another letter to her father (2 March 1933) she described the grave situation in Germany and her earlier meeting with Göring: "The country is in a panic and people are running away. Did I tell you I met Goering, Hitler's right hand man, at a dinner party in Berlin last year, and he talked with me a whole evening about what Hitler was going to do, and I was skeptical, and thought, it is just politician's boasting. But it is all coming true, frightfully" (*LP* 93). Porter's only trip to Germany after the Nazis assumed power occurred in August 1934, when she attended the Salzburg Opera Festival and took day trips into Munich. The trip stoked her fears of Nazi aggression. In a letter to Barbara Harrison (29 July 1934) several days before she left for Austria (and several days after the failed Nazi putsch that had left the Austrian chancellor, Englebert Dollfuss, dead) Porter wrote that "the news from Austria is not very pretty" (*LP* 107). Her conversations with a Russian refugee had deepened her concerns. "It can't be very cheering-up to have to run for your life because you aren't an Aryan," Porter wrote, referring to the Russian's plight. "It may have been merely that he *hoped* all Germany and all Austria would blow up. They damn near have, judging by what I can gather from the newspapers, no two of which print the same lies, so its [*sic*] a little confusing" (*LP* 108). After returning from her trip (she was in Germany immediately before the national plebiscite to confirm Hitler's assumption of full power as chancellor and *Führer*), Porter wrote to Glenway Wescott and Monroe Wheeler (22 August 1934) commenting on the strangeness of being a sightseer "in a city with Hitler flags waving from every window—by order—a nasty picture of Hitler glaring at us from every taxi and shop and hotel window, and a confusion of loud speakers, set up even in the churches, working up the mass enthusiasm for the plebescite [*sic*], which took place not too gloriously the next day." "Munich is probably not so pleasant as it was," she concluded. "People go about in restaurants and in the street swinging their arms up in each others' faces and saying Heil Hitler!" (*LP* 115). She also noted that her program from *Figaro*, full of quotes from Mozart, identified the composer as German—an observation that looked eerily forward to the German annexation of Austria and suggested how easily dictatorial governments rewrote history.

While the lynching story and the southern novel remained unfinished, Porter completed three of her stories about Miranda while in Europe, "The Grave," "The Circus," and "The Journey." By this time Porter was developing her ideas on memory as central to her fiction and her artistic process. She saw memory not as the passive recall of events but as the active reworking of a person's thoughts about those events, an act of creative imagination that stood opposed to the ironclad, "official" versions of history sanctioned by the authoritarian state.[19] "This constant exercise of memory seems to be the chief occupation of my mind, and all my experience seems to be simply memory, with continuity, marginal notes, constant revision and comparison of one thing with another," Porter wrote in some 1936 notes from Paris. "Now and again thousand of memories converge, harmonize, arrange themselves around a central idea in a coherent form, and I write a story."[20] "The Grave," "The Circus," and "The Journey" all point to the conclusion that in the mid-1930s Porter looked back to her southern upbringing for subject matter for her fiction, with her memories arranged as commentaries on southern authoritarianism. This reconfiguration of childhood memories by the knowledge and fear of authoritarianism became the trademark of Porter's Miranda stories.

With its focus on Sophia Jane, Miranda's grandmother and the family's controlling force, "The Journey" laid the groundwork for Porter's presentation of southern culture's suffocating traditionalism. Sounding like Lillian Smith later would in *Killers of the Dream*, but without the emphasis on segregation, Porter showed that resistance to time and change undergirded southern traditionalism, the entire structure maintained by a strict obedience to roles and duties. As head of the family, Sophia Jane gives herself over entirely to her position of authority, suppressing whatever doubts and questions she has so as to maintain both order and the Order. She performs her duties without hesitation: "The Grandmother's rôle was authority, she knew that; it was her duty to portion out activities, to urge or restrain where necessary, to teach morals, manners, and religion, to punish and reward her household according to a fixed code. Her own doubts and hesitations she concealed, also, she reminded herself, as a matter of duty" (*CSP* 328). Perhaps her most important task, which she performs with her longtime black helper, Nannie, involves instructing the children in their roles and duties. For Sophia Jane and Nannie, "childhood was a long state of instruction and probation for adult life, which was in turn a long, severe, undeviating devotion to duty, the largest part of which consisted in bringing up children" (*CSP* 329). The children under Sophia Jane's rule simultaneously enjoy the security and chafe at the restrictions. Most problematic for the children, even if they do not understand the situation as well as the narrator, is Sophia Jane and Nannie's tireless focus on the past, a focus that configures people's lives, not as lines moving into the future, but as circles endlessly repeating previous events and patterns. "They talked about the past, really—always about the past," the narrator says of Sophia Jane and Nannie. "Even the future seemed like something gone and done with when they spoke of it. It did not seem an extension of their past, but a repetition of it" (*CSP* 327). Miranda's eventual frustration with the restraints of southern traditionalism, as seen in later stories, derives in large part from her growing sense that she has no choice in charting her future; she eventually realizes that unless she actively rebels, she is destined to retrace the circle the family has plotted for her.

The two Miranda stories from 1935, "The Circus" and "The Grave," both reveal weak points in southern traditionalism's construction of meaning and order, bringing the young Miranda face to face with aspects of the world for which her upbringing has left her unprepared. Brought up in a household of restraint and propriety, Miranda in "The Circus" is panic stricken when she confronts what appear to be terrifying manifestations of human savagery and evil. At the circus for the first time, having had no schooling in the conventions of the big top, Miranda confronts the barrage of startling stimuli—the loud music and bright lights, the bold costumes and exaggerated makeup, the roaring crowds, the death-defying acts—as if they were not scripted, as if the performers' looks of fright and terror were sincere. To Miranda's untrained eyes, a clown walking a tightrope appears as "a creature in a blousy white overall with ruffles at the neck and ankles, with bone-white skull and chalk-white face, with tufted eyebrows far apart in the middle of his forehead, the lids in a black sharp angle, a long scarlet mouth stretching back into sunken cheeks, turned up at the corners in a perpetual bitter grimace of pain" (*CSP* 344). The roars from the delighted crowd are to her ears yells of "savage delight, shrieks of dreadful laughter like devils in delicious torment" (*CSP* 345). Already emotionally undone, Miranda on her way out faces her most malicious tormentor, a dwarf who "made a horrid grimace at her, imitating her own face." After she strikes out at him, the dwarf gives "a look of haughty, remote displeasure, a true grown-up look. She knew it well. It chilled her with a new kind of fear: she had not believed he was really human" (*CSP* 345).

Miranda's later recognition that the circus is really scripted entertainment only deepens her despair and fear. She recognizes that people at home might be playing a similar game and that southern gentility might be masking people's "circus" selves. Furthermore, she realizes that unless she follows her scripted role, wearing her designated mask, she will be derided and scorned, a point Dicey underscores when she drags her home, mumbling under her breath, "little ole meany . . . little ole scare-cat . . . gret big baby . . . never go nowhere . . . never see nothin . . . come on here now, hurry up—always ruinin everything for othah folks" (*CSP* 345–46). For the young Miranda, the circus is not, as it is for the others, a temporary escape from southern traditionalism, but a frightening manifestation of southern traditionalism's system of power and control.

In "The Grave," Miranda comes to another disturbing recognition when, now nine years old, she witnesses the dissection of a pregnant rabbit, which makes her piercingly aware of the mysteries of sexuality and her body. Structuring the story is the tension between two models of womanhood: the proper and sexually pure southern lady (represented by the ring Paul finds in one of the dug-up family graves); and Miranda's sexualized body, with its own desires and demands (represented in the rabbit Paul shoots and dissects). After the tomboyish Miranda slips the ring Paul finds onto her finger, suggesting her marriage to tradition and a "circular" life, she imagines herself in the role of a southern woman. She wants to go back home to "take a good cold bath, dust herself with plenty of Maria's violet talcum powder—provided that Maria was not present to object, of course—put on the thinnest, most becoming dress she owned, with a big sash, and sit in a wicker chair under the trees. . . . She had vague stirrings of desire for luxury and a grand way of living which could not take precise form in her imagination but were founded on family legend of past wealth and leisure" (*CSP* 365). Quite different "stirrings of desire" arise after she witnesses the womb of the cut-open rabbit, with its "bundle of tiny rabbits, each wrapped in a thin scarlet veil" (*CSP* 366). After touching one of the unborn rabbits, Miranda trembles with recognition of her budding sexuality, understanding "a little of the secret, formless intuitions of her own mind and body, which had been clearing up, taking form, so gradually and so steadily she had not realized that she was learning what she had to know" (*CSP* 366–67). Recognition quickly gives way to fright and confusion, as Miranda has no way to integrate the two different worlds of womanhood. Returning home, she buries her memories of that day, locking away what she knows by her family's standards is forbidden knowledge.

"The Grave" ends twenty years later in a brief coda, with Miranda's memories of her fateful day with Paul exploding unexpectedly into her consciousness as she walks through a market in Mexico. It is a dreadful vision, called forth by the sight of a tray of candy shaped as small animals and the smell of "mingled sweet and corruption" (*CSP* 367). But almost instantly Miranda recovers, repressing her fearful vision of her body's complex sexuality and its eventual aging and decay with a vision of twelve-year-old Paul, happy and aglow, repeatedly turning over and over in his hands the casket ornament, a silver dove, which Miranda had found that day. Her vision of Paul with the ornament underscores that Miranda remains enmeshed in the ideology of her upbringing: like the dove, she is caught in an endless repetition, a repetition that in Miranda's case represents an idealized past that glosses over the more complicated and messy present.

All three of these stories illustrate Porter's deep concern about the controlling power of southern authoritarianism and furthermore point to her larger concern about political authoritarianism in general. As the European situation worsened in the late 1930s and early 1940s, Porter closely followed political developments abroad and grew increasingly alarmed at the domestic threat Fascism posed to American democracy. Porter feared subversive actions not only from Fascist agents and sympathizers in the United States but from the U.S. government itself; she worried that America might be headed for its own version of Fascism. When war broke out in Europe, she was incensed that Hitler's power had not been countered earlier, believing that the United States, France, and England, through cowardly and greedy foreign policies, had worked to ensure Germany's emergence as a military power. A few days after the fall of Paris, Porter wrote to Cinina and Robert Penn Warren (20 June 1940) that Hitler and the Nazis were "a majestic sort of Nemesis overtaking a cowardly and divided world," and she described a chain of events that had made that nemesis possible: "If England had not backed Mussolini, in its fear of Russia, M[ussolini] . . . could never have kept his power. Having his power, if he had not supported Hitler at the crisis, Hitler could have been nipped. England, France, and America combined in a race for trade in re-arming Germany, those three put the weapons in Germany's hand to destroy themselves. We are now selling to Japan all she needs to arm against us. . . . I think we need not be surprised when the Furies come, having been so often and persistently invited" (*LP* 182). In a letter to Donald Elder (9 April 1941) Porter even went so far as to say that should America go to war, she would feel better if she "could find out which side we are fighting on . . . that this war exists at all is due to one thing, or another: subhuman stupidity on the part of the of the English and American and French governments, or subhuman malignity: either way I don't feel reassured" (*LP* 200).

On the domestic front, too, Porter felt that the government was not doing enough to curb Fascist sympathizers. In the same letter to the Warrens, Porter cited a comment by Göring that the Nazis would defeat the United States from within, and she argued for swift action against Fascist sympathizers. To drive her point home, she described her dismay at witnessing a Fascist parade in Boston not long after her return from Europe.[21] Recalling watching the marchers go by, with their banners saluting Mussolini and Italy, Porter wrote that she had thought the parade should never have been permitted and that in its efforts to protect freedom of expression "Democracy was bending backward, and would get a broken spine at that rate" (*LP* 182). She asked the Warrens whether they could imagine a prodemocracy parade taking place in a Fascist country, with "waving banners saying Up Roosevelt, American Democracy Shall Conquer the World, etc," and then she answered herself: "Neither can I. They would never even have been permitted to gather, and rightly too" (*LP* 182). Porter's solution to the problem of Fascists in the United States was simple: get rid of them. "In the last war I was all for tolerance," Porter wrote. "Now I should like to see boatloads of them simply deposited in the midst of those governments they are so loyal to. That is where they belong. I hope to see them there very soon. I am quite willing to help with the project" (*LP* 182–83).

At the same time that she was railing against the dangers of Fascist authoritarianism, Porter jettisoned whatever lingering sympathies she had for Communism and espoused instead a bare-bones libertarian belief in individual rights, particularly regarding the protection of privacy. (She apparently did not acknowledge the contradictions between her radical individualism and her calls for deporting disloyal individuals.) Her celebration of the individual no doubt was tied to her belief in the integrity of the artist, particularly in the artist's freedom to work without political constraint. In her essay on Thomas Hardy, written in 1940, she discusses that relationship by focusing on Hardy's unyielding individualism and his refusal to bow down to religious authority. Porter observes that rather than resting easy in religious doctrine, Hardy's courageous, questioning mind "led him out of the tradition of orthodoxy into another tradition of equal antiquity, equal importance, equal seriousness, a body of opinion running parallel throughout history to the body of law in church and state: the great tradition of dissent. He went, perhaps not so much by choice as by compulsion of *belief*, with the Inquirers rather than the Believers."[22] In the remainder of the essay she enumerates the forces lined up against the heroic loner, forming one of Porter's fullest depictions of the power of the authoritarian state. She zeroes in on religious orthodoxy and its service to the ruling elite:

> Grant that the idea of God is the most splendid single act of the creative human imagination, and that all his multiple faces and attributes correspond to some need and satisfy some deep desire in mankind; still, for the Inquirers, it is impossible not to conclude that this mystical concept has been harnessed rudely to machinery of the most mundane sort, and has been made to serve the ends of an organization which, ruling under divine guidance, has ruled very little better, and in some respects, worse, than certain rather mediocre but frankly manmade systems of government. And it has often lent its support to the worst evils in secular government, fighting consistently on the side of the heavy artillery. And it has seemed at times not to know the difference between Good and Evil, but to get them hopelessly confused with legalistic right and wrong; justifying the most cynical expedients of worldly government by a high morality; and committing the most savage crimes against human life for the love of God. (8)

In Porter's view, it was precisely the injustices of the authoritarian state, "the kind committed by entrenched authority and power upon the helpless" (8), that Hardy railed against. With one eye on the deteriorating situation in contemporary Europe, Porter writes that Hardy stood up against "the military police of orthodoxy" (7) and that he understood the dirty politics that lead inevitably to war. He demanded, furthermore, "that those who made wars would admit the real motives; aside from the waste and destruction, which he viewed with purely humane feelings, he objected to the immoralities of statecraft and religion in the matter" (9). Once the United States entered the World War II, Porter took a stance very similar to the one she ascribed to Hardy.

Porter's three great works from the mid- to late 1930s—"Noon Wine," "Old Mortality," and "Pale Horse, Pale Rider"—collected as *Pale Horse, Pale Rider: Three Short Novels* (1939), all explore conflicts between individuals and authoritarian forces, clustered around issues generated by Porter's responses to the rise of Fascism, particularly the menace to individual integrity. That menace Porter perhaps best expressed a few years later in a letter to her nephew Paul (16 December 1941): "The individual is all that matters, and the evil of war, as of Fascism, is precisely this destruction of identity, this notion of herd life and mass death" (*LP* 215). The earliest of the three stories, "Noon Wine," much of which Porter wrote while in Europe in the early 1930s, stands apart from the other two in that it concerns neither Miranda and her family nor the suffocating stranglehold of southern traditionalism. Nonetheless, in the figure of bounty hunter Homer T. Hatch, Porter portrays a type of figure, derived from her concern with authoritarian governments, that increasingly came to haunt her imagination: the government agent who invades the lives of everyday people, pressuring them to follow the system's mandates—a manifestation of the incipient Fascism that Porter believed was beginning to infect America.[23] Almost as soon as he sets foot on the Thompson farm, Hatch invokes his authority, saying to Thompson, "Yes, sir, Homer T. Hatch is my name and America is my nation" (*CSP* 244). Without signaling his purpose, Hatch delicately guides the conversation, extracting bits of information and confusing Thompson into saying things that he has no intention of saying. As the narrator puts it, "He had a way of taking the words out of Mr. Thompson's mouth, turning them around and mixing them up until Mr. Thompson didn't know himself what he had said" (*CSP* 248). Hatch eventually reveals his intentions (and reveals that he has sweet-talked Helton's mother into bankrolling his trip—he told her he would visit her son and get all the news about him), threatening the reluctant Thompson with both the law and public embarrassment. "Now a course, if you won't help, I'll have to look around for help somewheres else," he says to Thompson. "It won't look very good to your neighbors that you was harbring an escaped loonatic who killed his own brother, and then you refused to give him up. It will look mighty funny" (*CSP* 255). Before long, Hatch's intrusive actions end in complete destruction: Hatch and Helton are killed, Thompson is dead by suicide, and the Thompson family and its farm are in ruins.

With "Old Mortality" and "Pale Horse, Pale Rider" Porter returned to Miranda and her family, exploring, as she had done in the earlier Miranda stories, the authoritarian power of southern traditionalism, particularly its rigid belief system buttressed by cultural legend. In "Old Mortality" Miranda and her sister Maria struggle to exert their individuality while dogged and pressured by family history, particularly that of Aunt Amy. Part 1 shows the two girls learning that the family demands unthinking acceptance of its legends, even in the face of contradictory facts. They are astonished, for instance, to hear their father claim that there were never any fat women in the family, when they know full well the size of their great-aunt Keziah, "who quite squeezed herself through doors, and who, when seated, was one solid pyramidal monument from floor to neck" (*CSP* 174). The two girls see that "something seemed to happen to their father's memory" (*CSP* 174) when he talks about the family; they soon realize that the family legends dictate "truth" no matter what contradicts them. It is analogous to Porter's witnessing the Germans claiming Mozart as German—the legend has become fact.

If Maria and Miranda at first find the family stories intriguing and mysterious, they eventually understand the extent to which the stories restrict their lives. Rather than infusing the world with mystery, the legends sap mystery from it; with the past forever towering above the present, the present becomes merely a pale shadow of what has come before, diminished, used up, insignificant. To their dismay, since they have most of their lives in front of them, Maria and Miranda realize that no matter what they do, no matter what exciting things they experience, "there was always a voice recalling other and greater occasions" (*CSP* 179). Eventually, in a mad dash for freedom, Miranda runs away from school and gets married.

Miranda still has much to learn about the warping power and tenacious grip of southern traditionalism, and her education continues when she later meets another of the family's rebels, Cousin Eva. Ostracized and cruelly treated as a child because of her unglamorous looks, Eva has torn herself from the family to become a fiery suffragist. Soon after meeting Miranda, she launches into a blistering tirade about the family's fictitious histories and the sordid reality they mask, concluding that the institution of the family is "the root of all human wrongs" and "should be wiped from the face of the earth" (*CSP* 217). Miranda realizes that Eva demonizes the past as much as the family romanticizes it and that she has created a legend as distorted and restrictive as the family's (an irony of which Eva remains unaware; like those in the family, she is chained to the past, only hers is a different past). Miranda vows that she will be different; she says that in moving forward into the future she will free herself from fictions and discover her own truths:

> Ah, but there is my own life to come yet, she thought, my own life now and beyond. I don't want any promises, I won't have false hopes. I won't be romantic about myself. I can't live in their world any longer, she told herself, listening to the voices back of her. Let them tell their stories to each other. Let them go on explaining how things happened. I don't care. At least I can know the truth about what happens

to me, she assured herself silently, making a promise to herself, in her hopefulness, her ignorance. (221)

That final word, *ignorance,* undercuts all that Miranda has planned, suggesting that her quest for independence and individualism is doomed to failure and that she will never be able to escape completely from the suffocating grip of southern traditionalism.

"Pale Horse, Pale Rider" picks up Miranda's story six years later, near the end of World War I, showing her still struggling for independence. Following the trail of so many before her, she has fled west to start anew and is now a newspaper reporter in Denver. But the story's opening, a dream filled with images from her childhood, indicates that she is still gripped by the past, with "the tough filaments of memory and hope pulling taut backwards and forwards holding her upright between them" (*CSP* 304). Moreover, her freedom is thwarted by forces from her present life, including two government agents (reincarnations of Homer T. Hatch) who pressure Miranda to buy war bonds. Their very looks connect them to an intrusive, authoritarian government: one wears "a square little mustache," a clear reference to Hitler, while the other stares at Miranda with a look described as "really stony, really viciously cold, the kind of thing you might expect to meet behind a pistol on a deserted corner" (*CSP* 272). Badgering her and questioning her loyalty, the agents press her to buy a Liberty bond, using threats that make it clear she has no liberty. "You can't lose by it," one of the agents says, speaking of the purchase program, "and you can lose a lot if you don't" (*CSP* 273).

More general social pressures also cut into Miranda's freedom, demanding that she, together with other young women, volunteer for war-related programs. At one point Miranda bitterly imagines their duties: "So rows of young girls, the intact cradles of the future, with their pure serious faces framed becomingly in Red Cross wimples, roll cock-eyed bandages that will never reach a base hospital, and knit sweaters that will never warm a manly chest, their minds dwelling lovingly on all the blood and mud and the next dance at the Acanthus Club for the officers of the flying corps. Keeping still and quiet will win the war" (*CSP* 290). Keeping quiet, she also knows, is important for staying out of trouble. "The Lusk committee will get you if you don't watch out," she thinks to herself at one point (*CSP* 291).[24] And while Miranda fears the reach of the government, she fears even more the numbing conformity demanded by society. "There must be a great many of them here who think as I do," she thinks despairingly, "and we dare not say a word to each other of our desperation, we are speechless animals letting ourselves be destroyed, and why? Does anybody here believe the things we say to each other?" (*CSP* 291).

Later, after nearly dying in the influenza epidemic, Miranda gives up her dreams of freedom. Protest, she believes, is futile, since she now perceives that the nation is in the grips of a vast conspiracy that deceives everyone into believing that they are happy and fulfilled. To cope, she will pretend that she is like everyone else. "For it will not do to betray the conspiracy and tamper with the courage of the living," she decides; "there is nothing better than to be alive, everyone has agreed on that; it is past argument, and who attempts to deny it is justly outlawed" (*CSP* 315). Miranda now accepts a world of drab sameness and totalitarian conformity. The story ends with Miranda about to leave the hospital to go back to the "noiseless houses with the shades drawn, empty streets, the dead cold light of tomorrow" (*CSP* 317). "Now there would be time for everything" (*CSP* 317), Miranda tells herself, even as she recognizes that in this nightmarish world of authoritarian control everything has become nothing.

Not long after the publication of *Pale Horse, Pale Rider,* Porter wrote her only story set in Germany, "The Leaning Tower," drawn loosely from her stay in Berlin in 1931–32. The Berlin of the story is strikingly similar to the world to which Miranda awakens at the end of "Pale Horse, Pale Rider": grim, gray, and locked down in tight conformity and strict regimentation. In the words of the story's protagonist, Charles Upton, Berliners live in "complete hopelessness and utter endurance" (*CSP* 442). Upton early on notices that people in the street seem to have lost their individuality. At one point Upton sees a small crowd of men and women standing before a shop window full of everything pig—toys, candy, and meat—and he observes that the people "were all strangely of a kind, and strangely the most prevalent type. The streets were full of them—enormous waddling women with short legs and ill-humored faces, and round-headed men with great rolls of fat across the backs of their necks, who seemed to support their swollen bellies with an effort that drew their shoulders forward" (*CSP* 442). Upton adds that the crowds seem transfixed "in a trance of pig worship" and that "they resembled the most unkind caricatures of themselves, but they were the very kind of people that Holbein and Dürer and Urs Graf had drawn, too: not vaguely, but positively like, their late-medieval faces full of hallucinated malice and a kind of sluggish but intense cruelty that worked its way up from their depths slowly through the layers of helpless gluttonous fat" (*CSP* 443). Upton gets his own lesson in German conformity when a barber insists upon giving him a Hitler cut, long on top and clipped to the skin at the back and sides. That is the only acceptable style, the barber tells him, and indeed, as the narrator observes, "the streets were full of such heads" (*CSP* 451).

More threatening than the faceless crowds is the militarism voiced by Upton's fellow boarders. Most vocal is Hans von Gehring (a name close in sound to *Göring*, as Thomas Carl Austenfeld points out),[25] who repeatedly defends the glory of the Germanic people at the expense of other Europeans. He dismisses all talk of social and cultural influence between nations as "oblique, feminine, worthless," adding: "Power, pure power is what counts to a nation or a race. You must be able to tell other peoples what to do, and above all what they may not do, you must be able to enforce every order you give against no matter what the opposition, and when you demand anything at all, it must be given you without question. That is the only power, and power is the only thing of value or importance in this world" (*CSP* 486). From this he derives a very simple foreign policy: attack before your enemies do. Identified at one point as "the youthful oracle" (*CSP* 485), Hans looks hopefully forward to the next war, when, he says, Germany will not stumble as it had in World War I. "We Germans were beaten in the last war," he says to Upton, "thanks partly to your great country, but we shall win the next" (*CSP* 486); and a bit later, he adds: "You'll see. The next time, there will be no mistakes on our side" (*CSP* 487).

Near the end of the story, Upton ponders the significance of Hans's words, together with the meaning of his landlady's plaster tower, which he earlier accidentally broke and which now seems somehow extremely significant. But he cannot get very far because of his dizzy hangover: "There was an answer if he could think what it was, but this was not the time. But just the same, there was something terribly urgent at work, in him or around him, he could not tell which. There was something perishable but threatening, uneasy, hanging over his head or stirring angrily, dangerously, at his back" (*CSP* 495). Of course, this uneasy, dangerous "something" is the German menace; and at the end it is that menace that Upton fails to recognize, falling on his bed and covering himself up, as a child might, hoping that when he emerges the threat will be gone. Upton's denial in the early 1930s would soon be Europe's and America's as the decade progressed. "The Leaning Tower" ponders the disastrous results of these denials, ultimately suggesting that the fractured plaster tower represents, not Nazi Germany, but Western civilization at the brink of destruction.

While she certainly understood the threat posed by the Nazis, Porter was slow in coming around to supporting America's entry into the war, primarily because she feared that the nation had a tough enough battle on its hands against big business and domestic Fascists. Porter explained her position in a letter to Donald Elder (9 April 1941), which she began by citing approvingly a letter she had clipped and enclosed from a recent *Nation*. That letter, which she did not identify, was Digby B. Whitman's response to Henry R. Luce's call to war in his *Life* editorial "The American Century."[26] Luce argued, as we saw in the chapter on the Nashville Agrarians, that America's entry into the war would be a major step in creating what he called "the first great American century,"[27] with America's way of life and ideals spreading to all corners of the world. In responding to Luce, Whitman wrote that he supported war, not to disseminate American ideals, but to counter Hitler's threat to America's tradition of freedom. He added that American freedom was also under domestic attack by big business, spearheaded by the likes of Luce and radio commentator W. J. Cameron, who had recently made a call to war similar to Luce's on his program *The Ford Sunday Evening Hour Talks*. Whitman called for a two-pronged attack to defeat both Hitler and "Luce-Cameronism in this country."[28] After praising Whitman's comments to Elder, Porter added: "Won't it be a jolly war, with Mister Luce cheering on the valiant cohorts, Mister Ford managing the Commissary (though his sumpter mules seem to have balked) and Miss Clare Booth as Head Vivandière of the whores de combat" (*LP* 200–201).

Even after America entered the war, Porter continued her assaults on corporate power's threat to American democracy, following Whitman's argument that there were two wars to be fought, one abroad and one at home. The most succinct statement of her position came in a letter to her nephew Paul (16 December 1941) in which she savagely attacked the power politics that had led the world into war. "I believe in our form of government," she wrote, "I think it is the best ever devised in human affairs, in spite of the abuses, in spite of the perversions that have deformed it in practice. This war will decide whether we are going to have another chance for a real democracy here or will this country be turned over again to the Morgans, the Fords and the Standard Oil Company. First we have this war with the foreign enemy, and then there is a second war to be fought here afterward with the internal enemy" (*LP* 215). In her only published piece specifically on the war,

"Act of Faith: 4 July 1942," Porter muted her argument somewhat, mentioning the need to fight internal enemies but without identifying them, though she made their identity clear enough when she wrote that American democracy's hardest and bitterest fight has been "to create an economy in which all the people were to be allowed access to the means and materials of life, and to share fairly in the abundance of the earth."[29]

Committed as she was to individual freedom, Porter by the early 1940s viewed Fascism and Communism as essentially similar totalitarian tyrannies that reduced individuals to unthinking automatons, and she railed against supporters of both systems. In a letter to Freda Kirchwey (5 February 1942) Porter denounced American Communists as traitors: "The people I hate and find detestable in their political morals, political tactics, and general life point of view are the American Communists of either wing [Stalinism or Trostkyism]; I think their acts are treasonable at this time, and even if they are anti-Fascist, they are also anti-American; the sole reason that they are not as dangerous as the Fascists who find so easy entrance into this country is, they are not so numerous and they are more easily watched" (*LP* 221–22). If Porter believed that domestic Fascists were more difficult to spot and combat, she did not seem to have any trouble spotting them; in fact, she found them just about everywhere—in the State Department, the Roman Catholic Church, the FBI, the Republican Party, to name merely a few of the organizations she believed were infiltrated, if not controlled, by Fascists.

Finding Fascist culprits was so easy for Porter largely because she used the term *Fascist* to label any person or organization (not already identified as Communist) that she believed in some way limited individual liberties. She leveled much of her harshest criticism at the FBI, which she often designated as America's Gestapo.[30] In a letter to Donald Elder (28 February 1942), who was thinking about looking for defense work, Porter advised him not to be intimidated by the FBI's background check, a vetting she believed was being used to keep loyal Americans from key jobs. "Please don't let the gestapo discourage you too much from getting some kind of job in defense work," she wrote. "Don't let the Nazis get everything. As you know it is part of their strategy to get office[s] or jobs in key places, and it wouldn't surprise me if FBI didn't do a good deal to help them. For this reason FBI would naturally put as many stumbling blocks in the way of such as you as they can devise. . . . Get over or around them someway, Don. Make it your business to get over them" (*LP* 229–30). She added that she herself was ready to go to battle: "I am in such a cold and grim fighting mood I'd just enjoy a good fight with the FBI or almost anybody on the other side" (*LP* 230).

Porter soon had the opportunity to do such battle. Several months after her letter to Elder, an FBI special agent contacted her regarding a background investigation of Josephine Herbst, a longtime friend and fellow writer who recently had begun work in information services in the Office of Facts and Figures. Whatever battle Porter waged during the confidential interview, however, appears to have been only with herself, for she provided the agent with damning information on Herbst, much of it apparently made up.[31] While Porter's motives for betraying Herbst remain unknown— she never admitted her act and later even wrote Herbst that she was horrified to learn about her friend's being dismissed from her job[32]—she probably persuaded herself that abetting the FBI was perfectly justifiable, since Herbst indeed had worked previously with Communist front organizations. Whatever her motives, Porter's comment two years later in a letter to her nephew Paul (27 March 1944) in all likelihood stands as her explanatory (but unacknowledged) confession: "The very thing about people that makes the human race interesting is also the thing that makes it so hard to get anything done without the most horrible confusions: no two people think exactly the same way about anything, and very few people are capable of faithfulness to a love or an idea, and everybody in the long run loves himself the best of all. And there is a natural Judas sleeps in the heart of too many" (*LP* 283–84).

During the war, Porter worked on several stories about Miranda and her family that continued her portrayal of southern traditionalism's authoritarianism: "The Source," "The Witness," and "The Last Leaf." As its title suggests, "The Source" portrays the family's central figure of control, Miranda's grandmother, as "a tireless, just and efficient slavedriver" (*CSP* 324) who oversees all aspects of the family's life. "The Witness" and "The Last Leaf" portray the cruelty and coercive restrictions underlying southern traditionalism's mask of civility and contentment. In "The Witness" Uncle Jimbilly's stories about the horrors of slavery give the children an alternative history to the family's legend of slavery's benevolence. Having once believed slavery to be so distant from their lives as to be the stuff of fairy tales, the children realize, after listening to Uncle Jimbilly, that it is the family legend, rather than the reality of slavery, that belongs in the realm of make-believe. In "The Last Leaf" the children likewise see that the blacks at the family farm are tied to the family less by affection than by bondage; they are stunned into this recognition when Aunt Nannie, supposedly utterly devoted to the family, moves out of the family house into her own cabin, transforming herself from "the faithful old servant Nannie, a freed slave" into "an aged Bantu woman of independent means, sitting on the steps, breathing the free air" (*CSP* 349).

At about the time that she was completing these three stories, Porter began a thoroughgoing reconfiguration of her public and artistic persona. Once the critic of southern traditionalism, Porter soon became its champion, as she came to see, in a stunning reversal of thinking, that southern traditionalism, for all its constraints, in the end nurtured strong-willed individuals who stood against the modern corporate state. Porter now portrayed herself, entirely fictitiously, as a distinguished southern lady from the aristocratic South, modeling herself on the grandmother in the Miranda stories. And it was from the position of the independent, aristocratic southerner that Porter now critiqued modern authoritarianism and its diminishment of the individual.[33]

Porter announced her new critical position in "Portrait: Old South," a 1944 essay affirming her binding connection with her ancestors, particularly her grandmother. Porter opens the essay with a forthright declaration: "I am the grandchild of a lost War, and I have blood-knowledge of what life can be in a defeated country on the bare bones of privation."[34] After describing her ancestors' fortitude during the Civil War and Reconstruction, Porter locates her strength of character squarely in those members of her family who held fast to their beliefs and codes of conduct through cataclysmic upheavals: "My elders all remained nobly unreconstructed to their last moments, and my feet rest firmly on this rock of their strength to this day" (161). Perhaps Porter's highest praise goes to her grandmother: "She was an individual being if I ever knew one" (164). In all this, southern traditionalism becomes the bedrock of virtue on which Porter takes her stand.

Maintaining individual vision in the face of world disorder became the touchstone for almost all of Porter's literary criticism from the late 1940s and early 1950s. She presents her strongly traditionalist view of the artist in "The Future Is Now," an essay praising a craftsman-artist for his careful construction of a table, undistracted by the noisy life outside his window. "He was full of the deep, right, instinctive, human belief that he and the table were going to be around together for a long time," Porter writes. "Even if he is off to the army next week, it will be there when he gets back. At the very least, he is doing something he feels is worth doing now, and that is no small thing."[35] Generalizing from the artisan's work, Porter characterizes artistic creation as the bringing of a "little handful of chaos . . . to coherency within a frame" (200).

In essays on other writers, Porter repeatedly invoked the ideal of remaining true to one's vision. In "Reflections on Willa Cather" Porter praises Willa Cather for holding "firmly for what she had found for herself" in an age "in which very literally everything in the world was being pulled apart, torn up, turned wrong side out and upside down; almost no frontiers left unattacked, governments and currencies falling; even the very sexes seemed to be changing back and forth and multiplying weird, unclassifiable genders. And every day, in the arts, as in schemes of government and organized crime, there was, there had to be, something New."[36] She similarly lauds E. M. Forster ("Indeed, Mr. Forster is an artist who lives in that constant state of grace which comes of knowing who he is, where he lives, what he feels and thinks about his world"),[37] Virginia Woolf ("The world of the arts was her native territory; she ranged freely under her own sky, speaking her mother tongue fearlessly"),[38] and even Ezra Pound, whom Porter admired for his ferocious artistic integrity, despite his Fascist politics. Porter comments that Pound understood that "greatness in art is like any other greatness: in religious experience, in love, it is great because it is beyond the reach of the ordinary, and cannot be judged by the ordinary, nor be accountable to it. The instant it is diluted, popularized, and misunderstood by the fashionable mind, it is no longer greatness, but window dressing, interior decorating, another way of cutting a sleeve."[39]

In her social commentary, Porter used her unreconstructed traditionalism as the vantage point from which to diagnose American society and to expose what she saw as polluting elements of Fascism and Communism. She was never shy in delivering her findings, as the opening paragraph in a letter to the editor of the *Nation* shows:

> It is quite true that strategic positions are occupied methodically by Communists, not only in departments of government here and abroad, but in our schools and universities, the press, the publishing business, industry, the motion pictures. You find them everywhere; they mean business and they are dangerous. But judging by the present drive against the Communists, I should say there are even more fascists in public office, or at least more powerfully placed: the Rankins of this country are as bitter enemies of democratic govern-

ment as any Communist, and the legislation proposed by them seeks the suppression of all liberty of speech or opinion; if they are not stopped here and now, we shall find ourselves with a "subversive-thoughts" law on our books.[40]

One can only wonder what J. F. Powers, a Roman Catholic who had gone to prison during World War II as a conscientious objector, thought when Porter wrote to him (5 November 1947) that she feared Fascism more than Communism because "it has the Pope at its head, and is Protean in its forms, and I hear people talking about Fascism and acting it out without knowing what name to call it by" (*LP* 350).

Such extreme thinking, coupled with a virulent racism that was now surfacing (a dark underside of her unreconstructed southernness), weighed heavily on Porter's artistic imagination, pushing her ultimately toward the cruel satiric vision and contrived allegorical structure of *Ship of Fools*, which she had begun in the early 1940s but which she did not finish until 1962. *Ship of Fools* illustrates the extremes to which Porter's antitotalitarianism eventually took her, tipping her into an unrelenting cynicism that often evolved into paranoia; her fear of Fascist infiltration of the government became in the novel her fear that deep down all humanity was Fascist, that behind masks of goodness and gentility human beings were vicious, bestial, and hateful, psychological if not always political monsters. Several years before she finished *Ship of Fools*, Porter wrote to her agent, Cyrilly Abels (20 February 1958), describing the novel as an exposé of human calumny: "It is a long exposition of the disastrous things people do to each other out of ignorance, prejudice, presumptuousness, self-love and self-hate, with religion, or politics, or race, or social distinctions, or even just nationality or a difference in customs . . . and—this is the other side of the question, out of inertia, moral apathy, timidity, indifference, and even a subconscious criminal collusion, people allow others to do every kind of wrong, and even, if the wrongdoers are successful, finally rather approve of them, perhaps envy them a little" (*LP* 546–47). Given the sweeping, universal vision of *Ship of Fools*, it is not surprising that Porter would turn to caricature and allegory, drawing inspiration (and title) from Sebastian Brant's 1494 *Das Narrensnshiff*. But for all its ambitions and scope, *Ship of Fools* in the end is a sad conclusion to Porter's career, evidence that Porter finally could not control what had become her cruel and damning vision, the origins of which stretch back to her trip to Germany in 1931.

8

DISPATCHES FROM THE HOME FRONT

CARSON MCCULLERS

In her essay "The Russian Realists and Southern Literature" Carson McCullers explored the connections between the Russian realists—particularly Chekhov, Tolstoi, Dostoievsky, and Gogol—and modern southern writers. McCullers was in large part responding, as she made clear from the very beginning, to charges that recent southern writing, and particularly that of William Faulkner, routinely exploited violence for pornographic effect. As we have already seen, leftist critics during the 1930s frequently denounced southern writing, largely because of its violent extremes, as being dangerously close to Fascist irrationalism. While not specifically discussing that allegation, McCullers argued that southern writing's explosive quality derived not from irrationalism but from its "bold and outwardly callous juxtaposition of the tragic with the humorous, the immense with the trivial, the sacred with the bawdy, the whole soul of man with a materialistic detail" (*MH* 252–53).[1] In defending southern literature, McCullers was clearly defending her own work, which in the early 1940s had come under the same type of attacks as Faulkner's had.[2]

Any suggestion linking her work to Fascist irrationalism no doubt rankled McCullers, for she not only repeatedly voiced anti-Fascist political views but also deliberately used her fiction to explore what she saw as both Fascism's dangerous psychology and its frightening manifestations in southern society. Indeed, of all the fiction writers treated in this study, McCullers was the most ambitious in juxtaposing foreign and domestic concerns and in depicting the operation of Fascist principles within southern culture. During the period of her finest achievement, roughly from 1939 to 1946, McCullers fashioned a South that was, in the words of her biographer Virginia Spencer Carr, "an inverted, nightmarish world—a World War II world,"[3] and in some ways, in terms of the psychological damage to her characters, this world was as fragmented and chaotic as the battlefield itself. But even more importantly, McCullers's South was a version of the Fascist systems that America was fighting against, a powerful cultural system that brutally enforced its demands for conformity and allegiance.

—* * * *—

McCullers's alienation from southern culture derived in part from the isolation and loneliness she felt during her childhood and adolescence in Columbus, Georgia. Her own sense of personal impoverishment (she felt freakishly unattractive) drew her eyes to the more general impoverishment of the town's mill workers and the blacks, with whom she identified. In high school she began establishing a more sophisticated understanding of her own alienation and of the town's oppressiveness through her reading of fiction and history. That education took a decidedly leftist turn when in 1934, as a high-school senior, she befriended Edwin Peacock. A few years older than McCullers and outspokenly political, Peacock introduced McCullers to the work of Karl Marx and an array of social-protest authors, including Erskine Caldwell, John Dos Passos, John Steinbeck, and James T. Farrell.[4] McCullers's political sophistication sharpened further after Peacock introduced her to her future husband, Reeves McCullers. The three often joined up to hash out current events, politics, and literature. In a letter to Virginia Spencer Carr, Peacock recalled their talks during the summer of 1935: "When we were all together, our evenings were filled with talk, talk, talk—the Civil War in Spain [actually, that war did not begin until 1936], *The Nation* and *The New Republic*, Hemingway, Faulkner, Eliot, and the other 'in writers' of the period."[5] About this time, McCullers looked into starting a political magazine, writing to a friend, Gin Tucker, that political commitment demanded more than talk.[6]

While the idea of the magazine went awry, McCullers began writing fiction that reflected her interest in politics and specifically the deteriorating situation in Europe. Most of these early stories explore issues that later became central in McCullers's vigorous anti-Fascism, particularly the numbing alienation and isolation of modern life, which she believed had led many Europeans to turn to Fascism for meaning and order. "Court in the West Eighties," one of her earliest stories (probably written in 1935, when McCullers was a student in New York), examines such alienation in a student living in New York City, following her thoughts and observations as she watches people in apartments whose windows look onto hers. "Our eyes would meet and then one of us would look away," the student observes and then goes on to note the irony that the window-sharers share a community of sorts yet remain steadfastly separate. "You see all of us in the court saw each other sleep and dress and live out our hours away from work, but none of us ever spoke" (*MH* 26). At another point the protagonist muses about the increasing political tensions in Europe, writing in her journal that *"fascism and war cannot exist for long because they are death and death is the only evil in the world"* (*MH* 23). Her comment here, together with her enigmatic and compelling attraction to a red-haired man she observes from her window, suggests the connection between the protagonist's alienation and that of Europeans who have turned to spellbinding dictators to break out of their despair. "No matter how peculiar it sounds I still have this feeling that there is something in him that could change a lot of situations and straighten them out," the protagonist muses at the end of the story. "And there is one point in a thing like this—as long as I feel this way, in a sense it is true" (*MH* 29).

"The Aliens," possibly written as early as 1935, is even more striking in its indication of McCullers's developing political vision.[7] The story follows a Jewish refugee, Felix Kerr, on a bus trip from New York to a town in the South where he will start a new life. Two years earlier, in 1933, the year Hitler took power, Kerr and his family had fled Munich to escape Nazi persecution. Most of the story focuses on Kerr's psychological burdens and sufferings as a refugee. "This was no ordinary traveller," McCullers writes. "He was no denizen of the great city he had left behind him. The time of his journey would not be measured by hours, but by years—not by hundreds of miles, but by thousands. And even such measurements as these would be in only one sense accurate. The journey of this fugitive—for the Jew had fled from his home in Munich two years before—more nearly resembled a state of mind than a period of travelling computable by maps and timetables. Behind him was an abyss of anxious wandering, suspense, of terror and of hope" (*MH* 91). McCullers's striking description of Kerr's grief for his elder daughter, who apparently did not make it out of Germany and whose fate remains unknown, points to her sympathetic identification with those who had fled the Nazis. More significantly, her equating the sufferings of Kerr under the Nazis with those of the deformed black woman who boards the bus (the other alien of the title) suggests that McCullers was already using what she knew about the Nazis' persecution of the Jews to deepen her understanding of southern racial practices.

In another early story, designated only as "Untitled Piece" when it was published posthumously, McCullers explored, as she had less explicitly in "Court in the West Eighties," the potentially dangerous prospect of alienated moderns giving themselves over to the calls of mesmerizing leaders and to dreams of power. Andrew Leander, who fled to New York because he felt out of place in his hometown in Georgia, is now returning, three years later, still confused and directionless. Thinking about his childhood despair, he recalls a time when, haunted by "a peculiar quiver of fear," he said to a quiet Jewish boy: "There ought to be a time when you see everything like you're looking through a periscope. A kind of a—colossal periscope where nothing is left out and everything in the world fits in with every other thing. And no matter what happens after that it won't—won't stick out like a sore thumb and make you lose your balance" (*MH* 114). Still haunted by a desire for order, Andrew later recalls that as a youth he once climbed to the rooftop of an unfinished house and imagined himself as a great leader unifying people with his visionary words: "He would be a great man, a kind of God, and what he called out would make things that bothered him and all other people plain and simple. His voice would be great and like music and men and women would come out of their houses and listen to him and because they knew that what he said was true they would all be like one person and would understand everything in the world" (*MH* 110). Andrew's memory of his rooftop reveries points not only to his own wish for an ordered, unalienated life but also, in terms of the world in the late 1930s, to the mesmerizing appeal of Fascist dictators who forge the alienated masses into a unified nation-state of loyal and unquestioning citizens. Of course, while Andrew never rallies anybody nor creates any order, Fascist dictators in real-world Europe by the time of the story had done just that; and McCullers hints that she had Hitler in mind in describing Andrew's rooftop fantasy when the flustered boy, unable to find the right words for his speech, feels driven to sing the music of Wagner, the composer adored by Hitler and often associated with Nazi nationalism.[8]

During the mid- to late 1930s, when McCullers was writing these and other stories, the ominous developments in Europe were becoming increasingly significant to her. By 1938, married to Reeves and living first in Charlotte and then in Fayetteville, North Carolina, she was stridently anti-Fascist and interventionist, fearing that America's isolationist policy would leave

Europe vulnerable to Hitler. Summarizing McCullers's activism during the critical years of 1938 and 1939, Virginia Spencer Carr writes that she "had become passionate about the European situation, zealous in her attack on fascism and nazism, and indignant at racism and what she considered the gross mistreatment of blacks in Fayetteville and in her own hometown."[9] Carr also notes that Reeves and McCullers were now considering adopting a refugee child, primarily to assert their solidarity with victims of Fascist oppression. While Carr does not point to McCullers's anti-Fascism as influencing her strong condemnation of southern racism and her desire to leave the South (which she and Reeves did in 1940), certainly her commitment to anti-Fascist politics was doing just that, a fact further suggested by *The Heart Is a Lonely Hunter* (1940), wherein issues foregrounded by the European conflict permeate the text.

The Heart Is a Lonely Hunter explores the loneliness and confusion warping the lives of several characters in a small southern town, examining in depth issues of modern alienation and dictatorship that McCullers had begun to explore in her early short stories. At first glance, the small-town world of the novel seems far from the social and political problems of Europe, but as soon becomes clear, forces of worldwide change have penetrated into the deepest recesses of town life and are transforming the town's fundamental structures and dynamics. Ihab Hassan rightly observes that the events of the novel call forth "the economic distress of the thirties and reverberate with the distant echoes of Nazi tyranny" and that the novel's "spirit shudders with the 'strangled South.'"[10] As Hassan suggests, not only are large-scale economic forces, labor strife, and civil rights activism altering the town's social and economic fabric but so, too, is the news from Europe, which repeatedly surfaces in the characters' discussions, dreams, and ideals. Most of these characters eventually come to see the European turmoil as emblematic of their own confusions and despair in a fast-changing world and end up, not unlike people living under Fascist dictatorships, looking to a leader whom they can worship as a savior.

The character most concerned with the rise of Fascism and Nazism is Harry Minowitz, Mick's Jewish friend. Minowitz's monstrous, all-consuming obsession with Fascism dominates his life. His standard of judgment—of people, ideas, politics, just about everything—boils down to one question: Fascist or anti-Fascist? Early in the novel, when Mick says she is humming a Mozart song, Harry immediately becomes suspicious because of the German-sounding name. "I say is that Mozart a Fascist or a Nazi?" he asks her (*HLH* 112). On other occasions Minowitz rarely misses an opportunity to lecture Mick on world politics and to foretell the coming war, when all people will have to choose between democracy and Fascism. "You see, there's just two things nowadays," he tells Mick. "It's the truth, there's just two things ahead nowadays.... Militant Democracy or Fascism.... Either one or the other. And although I don't believe in war I'm ready to fight for what I believe is right" (*HLH* 242). So consuming is Harry's obsession that he abandons his previous dream of being a prominent doctor, lawyer, or engineer. "All I can think about is what happens in the world now," he tells Mick. "About Fascism and the terrible things in Europe—and on the other hand Democracy. I mean I can't think and work on what I mean to be in life because I think too much about this other. I dream about killing Hitler every night" (*HLH* 246).

No other character shares Minowitz's passionate obsession with Fascism, but almost everyone ponders in one way or another its growing threat. While Minowitz makes no connection between oppressive conditions in Nazi Germany and those in the South—his focus remains on the Nazis' treatment of Jews—several other characters do. Blount's militantly anti-Fascist politics, for instance, fundamentally structure his analysis of what he calls "the strangled South. The wasted South. The slavish South" (*HLH* 294). At one point in a conversation with Dr. Copeland, Blount, spinning a globe in his hands, says that "three fourths of this globe is in a state of war or oppression" (*HLH* 294) and that the most uncivilized area in the world is the American South. Blount argues further that the corporate state's undermining of the founding principles of the nation—"the freedom, equality, and rights of each individual" (*HLH* 295)—is most evident in the South. "And here in these thirteen states the exploitation of human beings is so that— that it's a thing you got to take in with your own eyes," he says. "In my life I seen things that would make a man go crazy. At least one third of all Southerners live and die no better off than the lowest peasant in any European Fascist state" (*HLH* 295). Blount argues that the corporate system exploits the language of democracy to deceive the workers into thinking that despite the impoverishment from which they can never escape, they live in a nation guided by freedom and equality. "And the funny thing is that this has been drilled into the heads of sharecroppers and lintheads and all the rest so hard that they really believe it," he says (*HLH* 297). He implies, further, that what he terms the "capitalistic democracy" (*HLH* 297) of the United States differs little from Fascism, an idea underscored in one of the manifestos lying in his room, "The Affinity Between Our Democracy and Fascism." Like Minowitz, Blount sees the world facing a stark choice: "There remain only two roads ahead. One: Fascism. Two: reform of the most revolutionary and permanent kind" (*HLH* 297).

Dr. Copeland shares many of Blount's views on the oppressive South, but he focuses on racial politics and goes even further than Blount in explicitly connecting European totalitarianism and southern society. "Do not forget the Negro," he tells Blount. "So far as I and my people are concerned the South is Fascist now and always has been" (*HLH* 297). Linking the racial oppression of the Nazis with that of the South deepens his knowledge of both: "The Nazis rob the Jews of their legal, economic, and cultural life. Here the Negro has always been deprived of these. And if wholesale and dramatic robbery of money and goods has not taken place here as in Germany, it is simply because the Negro has never been allowed to accrue wealth in the first place." "The Jew and the Negro," Copeland continues. "The history of my people will be commensurate with the interminable history of the Jew— only bloodier and more violent" (*HLH* 297). Like the other two political activists in the novel, Minowitz and Blount, Dr. Copeland embraces a rigid, all-or-nothing stand against Fascism, which for him means making a complete commitment to working for the rights of blacks in the Fascist South. "You must give of your whole self without stint, without hope of personal return, without rest or hope of rest," he explains to Blount. "In the South and here in this very county. And it must be either all or nothing. Either yes or no" (*HLH* 301).[11]

Other characters in the novel, while not making such explicit connections between Nazi Germany and the South, nonetheless repeatedly find the European crisis surfacing in and shaping their thoughts. Early in the novel, and before her talks with Minowitz, Mick writes graffiti on a wall, printing the names "EDISON," "MUSSOLINI," and "DICK TRACY" before signing her initials, "M.K.," and adding, as she says, "a very bad word—PUSSY" (*HLH* 37). Mick's graffiti, erupting from her subconscious, encapsulates the Fascist dynamics manifested in the novel (even if she remains unaware of the significance of her words): Mussolini, like Thomas Edison and Dick Tracy, is a man of action and a popular hero, and he gives his followers purpose, identity, and sexual fantasy. And when Mick signs her initials to the graffiti, she mimics those who "sign up" and fall into line behind the leader.

Mick's drawings also point to the lurking presence of matters generated by Fascism and the world crisis; almost all of her pictures depict horrifying scenes of disaster awash with people scrambling to save themselves, both far away on the oceans and close by in her hometown. Her pictures include an airplane crashing, with people leaping into the sea; an ocean liner sinking, with everyone struggling to get into one small lifeboat; a huge fire on a street in her hometown, with some people lying dead and others fleeing; a factory torn apart by a boiler explosion, with men jumping out the windows and running from the scene. What she judges her best picture depicts a full-scale street battle in her town, although Mick is utterly mystified by it: she does not know why she painted it or why the people are fighting, and she has no idea what she should call it, though she is convinced that the right title is lurking somewhere in the back of her mind. Even if she cannot recognize it, the picture clearly expresses her fear that the world's growing tensions might lead to disastrous conflict at home.

The accelerating world crisis also deeply concerns Biff, who is struggling to understand the spiraling complexities of international, national, and local events. Since the close of World War I, Biff has been systematically filing newspaper articles to bring some kind of order to his thinking: "Three sets of outlines—one international beginning with the Armistice and leading through the Munich aftermath, the second national, the third all the local dope from the time Mayor Lester shot his wife at the country club up to the Hudson Mill fire. Everything for the past twenty years docketed and outlined and complete" (*HLH* 132). He hopes his filing system will help him overcome the general confusion of his life.[12] "Why?" the narrator reports Biff thinking at one point. "The question flowed through Biff always, unnoticed, like the blood in his veins. He thought of people and of objects and of ideas and the question was in him. Midnight, the dark morning, noon. Hitler and the rumors of war. The price of loin of pork and the tax on beer. Especially he meditated on the puzzle of the mute" (*HLH* 221). And a bit later a concatenation of Biff's thoughts, echoing Mick's graffiti, suggests not only that the European crisis has penetrated his consciousness but that in all likelihood is the disruptive force that leaves his shattered thoughts in "broken pictures [lying] like a scattered jigsaw puzzle in his head": "Alice soaping in the bathtub. Mussolini's mug. Mick pulling the baby in a wagon. A roast turkey on display. Blount's mouth. The face of Singer" (*HLH* 235). Amidst the "broken pictures" of Biff's thoughts two faces stand out: those of Mussolini and Singer, the "leaders" to whom people faraway and nearby have turned.

Underscoring the presence of the world's political crisis in the town, the war surfaces in almost all of Biff's musings on his own and the town's life.

Early in the novel, Biff conjoins the near and the faraway when he reads two stories from the newspaper, one on the money needed for local traffic signals and one on the war in the Orient. He senses that together they epitomize his disordered world: "Biff read them both with equal attention. As his eyes followed the print the rest of his senses were on the alert to the various commotions that went on around him. When he had finished the articles he still stared down at the newspaper with his eyes half-closed. He felt nervous" (*HLH* 17). Near the end of the novel, with the world moving quickly toward war, Biff specifically connects the world's dark future with his own. On the night of 21 August 1939 (the day German troops moved into Danzig, before the full-scale invasion of Poland) Biff listens uneasily to a radio broadcast discussing Hitler's intentions with regard to Poland: "He could not decide for certain whether the voice was German, French, or Spanish. But it sounded like doom. It gave him the jitters to listen to it" (*HLH* 354). Sensing the world crisis to be a version writ large of his own instability, Biff feels as if he now hangs suspended "between radiance and darkness," "between bitter irony and faith." He sees before him "a future of blackness, error, and ruin" (*HLH* 356). At the end of the novel, Biff still has not grasped how he will face this looming threat, his ambivalent and cautious stance resembling that of many Americans who in 1939 were unsure how their country should respond to the Nazi danger. "But, motherogod, was he a sensible man or not?" the narrator reports him thinking as he struggles to face up to the perilous days ahead. "And how could this terror throttle him like this when he didn't even know what caused it? And would he just stand here like a jittery ninny or would he pull himself together and be reasonable? For after all *was* he a sensible man or not?" (*HLH* 356).

Biff's questions at the end evoke the issues he has been struggling with all along, not only when he thinks about the crisis in Europe but also when, along with other characters, he feels compellingly drawn to Singer. Once again, the local mirrors the international, the attraction to Singer reflecting on a small scale the alienated masses' identification with Fascist leaders.[13] In this regard, Biff senses that Singer holds the key to his puzzlement and fragmentation and can show him the way out of his confusion. Besides his own pull to Singer, Biff observes that others feel likewise drawn toward him, including Blount and Mick, who to Biff's eyes go so far as to construct him into "a sort of home-made God" (*HLH* 230). He is both troubled and fascinated by the spectacle of these others making Singer into something they need for structuring their lives: "Owing to the fact he was a mute they were able to give him all the qualities they wanted him to have. Yes. But how could such a strange thing come about? And why?" (*HLH* 230–31). Only Singer's suicide reveals the false promise of their efforts at overcoming alienation; at the center of their imagined community is precisely the loneliness and alienation from which the characters had hoped to escape.

Besides Biff's struggles, Minowitz's admission that he was once drawn to the Fascist enterprise explicitly connects the psychological needs of the characters in McCullers's small-town South with those of Europeans lured to Fascism. "You know all the pictures of the people our age in Europe marching and singing songs and keeping step together," he explains to Mick. "I used to think that was wonderful. All of them pledged to each other and with one leader. All of them with the same ideals and marching in step together. I didn't worry much about what was happening to the Jewish minorities because I didn't want to think about it. And because at the time I didn't want to think like I was Jewish. You see, I didn't know. I just looked at the pictures and read what it said underneath and didn't understand. I never knew what an awful thing it was. I thought I was a Fascist. Of course later on I found out different" (*HLH* 245). As Minowitz suggests, the dream of social connection often blinds people to the pathologies structuring the causes they embrace.

Singer's bizarre dream picturing Antonapoulis kneeling naked atop a flight of stone steps also points to the terrifying ends to which aspirations of connection can carry people. A parable of blind submission enacted by those worshiping an all-powerful leader, Singer's dream at the same time is a frightening evocation of the tribal lore that typically characterized Nazi hero worship. In the dream, Singer and others kneel below Antonapoulis, transfixed by their apparent leader and the object he holds over his head:

> Out of the blackness of sleep a dream formed. There were dull yellow lanterns lighting up a dark flight of stone steps. Antonapoulis knelt at the top of these steps. He was naked and he fumbled with something that he held above his head and gazed at it as though in prayer. He himself knelt halfway down the steps. He was naked and cold and he could not take his eyes from Antonapoulis and the thing he held above him. Behind him on the ground he felt the one with the mustache and the girl and the black man and the last one. They knelt naked and he felt their eyes on him. And behind them there were uncounted crowds of kneeling people in the darkness. His own hands

were huge windmills and he stared fascinated at the unknown thing that Antonapoulis held. The yellow lanterns swayed to and fro in the darkness and all else was motionless. Then suddenly there was a ferment. In the upheaval the steps collapsed and he felt himself falling downward. He awoke with a jerk. (*HLH* 215)

Other haunting echoes of Nazi Germany appear throughout the novel. At one point, Jake tells Blount that he looks like "a Jew in Germany" (*HLH* 224), and at another, Mick, taunting Harry, raises her arm in the characteristic Nazi salute. More significant is the racial violence inflicted upon blacks. Willie's brutal torture in prison, resulting in his loss of his feet to gangrene, calls to mind the gruesome conditions of the Nazi concentration camps and more generally the iron-fisted power of totalitarian regimes. That power is also suggested when Copeland, seeking to register a complaint about Willie's mistreatment, is manhandled by the police. "That's the trouble with this country," the sheriff says after striking Copeland in the face for speaking back to him. "These damn biggity niggers like him" (*HLH* 259).

Thus, *The Heart Is a Lonely Hunter* recasts the rise of Fascism in Europe in a small southern town fractured by fast-changing times and beset with numbing alienation. The novel both explores the dangerous appeal that Fascism offers to the lost and lonely and exposes the authoritarian power of southern society. Not too long after the novel appeared, McCullers said that she viewed it as an "ironic parable of fascism," concerned with "the spiritual rather than the political side of the phenomenon."[14] As Oliver Evans put it, the novel is, finally, an "absurdly grim game of follow-the-leader" in which "the ultimate leader, the power beyond the power, is a lunatic"[15]—words that could also apply to Germany and Italy at the time.

Although much less explicit in its evocation of the Fascist menace, McCullers's second novel, *Reflections in a Golden Eye*, which she wrote in 1939, can also be read as an ironic parable of Fascism and the psychology of the Fascist mind, particularly in its exploration of the explosive forces of the irrational.[16] The novel focuses on the sexual and marital dynamics of two couples living on a southern military base, with all four characters suffering from a loneliness and alienation similar to that plaguing the characters of *The Heart Is a Lonely Hunter*. If her first novel explores characters in search of purpose and order, *Reflections* portrays characters destroying themselves by failing to channel in healthy ways what McCullers elsewhere describes as "man's revolt against his own inner isolation and his urge to express himself as fully as is possible."[17] Without this channeling, the mind's irrational forces explode in destructive fury, severing the fragile bonds that establish and hold together relationships. In portraying this explosion in the lives of four characters, McCullers illustrates, on a small canvas, the dangerous forces she saw being unleashed and mobilized by Fascism.[18]

Reflections furthermore depicts America, and specifically its military, as lacking what commentators of the day were calling "a fighting faith," that is, a central belief that citizens could enthusiastically support and rally behind in time of war. Indeed, everyone in the novel is entirely self-absorbed. Even those in the army—an organization whose purpose, creed, and hierarchy offer isolated individuals membership in a community—live without camaraderie and commitment, a stark contrast (though unstated in the novel) to the discipline and order structuring the Fascist state. At least one reviewer, Edward Weeks, bemoaned McCullers's depiction of the nation's military forces, writing that if McCullers's novel "is a fair sample of army life, and if the country is soon to pour itself into the army, then God save the Union!"[19]

Weeks made his comments in April 1941, when the European situation was much graver than when McCullers completed the manuscript, in mid-1939. Even so, as we have already seen, by 1939 McCullers was deeply concerned about the growing power of Fascism, and while it might seem strange that in a novel about military life she fails to mention the European crisis, its absence is arguably McCullers's point—that rather than recognizing the dangers of Fascism, the nation remains fixed in an inward-turning isolationism as pathological as the psychic disorders plaguing the characters of the novel. As the characters drift without purpose and duty, so too does the nation, both failing to confront the irrational forces mounting against them.

McCullers was soon making explicit calls for national unity and for intervention. Her anti-Fascism hardened dramatically after she and Reeves moved to New York City in June 1940, not only because war had broken out on the Continent but because she had befriended, and was now profoundly influenced by, a number of European refugees. Not long after moving to New York, she met Klaus and Erika Mann, children of Thomas Mann, both of whom had long been active in anti-Nazi resistance, and through them she met Annemarie Clarac-Schwarzenbach, a striking Swiss writer who was then involved in refugee relief. McCullers began to spend time with Erika and Annemarie, including attending meetings of the Emergency Rescue

Committee, where she met many other European exiles. Underscoring the significance of these two women to McCullers's personal and political development, Virginia Spencer Carr describes McCullers's devotion as a sacred discipleship, one in which she "spent long hours at their feet, enthralled by their tales of adventure and woe."[20] In large part because of her new circle of friends, McCullers began to see herself in them—as an exile from a repressive homeland, in her case the American South. This identification deepened her political commitment, pushing her both to write openly patriotic nonfiction about the conflict in Europe and to continue to explore the authoritarian structures of the South in her fiction.

McCullers's surging patriotism can be seen in a series of three political commentaries on America and the war, all of which exhorted Americans to rally around the ideals of democracy in facing the Fascist challenge.[21] In "Look Homeward, Americans," the first of her three commentaries, which appeared near the end of 1940, McCullers calls for a rejuvenation of democratic spirit. She begins by observing that because of the spreading war, Americans, who are fundamentally lonely and restless, can no longer easily travel abroad to reinvigorate themselves amidst the foreign and strange. She therefore urges Americans to rediscover and recommit themselves to their homeland, saying that they must convert the yearning for the foreign into the yearning for a strong and great nation. "We must make a new declaration of independence, a spiritual rather than a political one this time," McCullers writes, adding that "we must now be homesick for our own familiar land, this land that is worthy of our nostalgia."[22]

McCullers's other two wartime commentaries, "Night Watch over Freedom" and "We Carried Our Banners—We Were Pacifists, Too," are strongly interventionist. The need to support Britain underlies "Night Watch over Freedom," a short piece characterizing Big Ben as a worldwide symbol of freedom, its tolling at the new year described as "the heartbeat of warring Britain—somber, resonant, and deeply sure."[23] More explicitly interventionist is "We Carried Our Banners," which describes McCullers helping a friend, Mac, get ready to report for military duty.[24] A longtime leftist and pacifist, Mac has come to realize the necessity of going to war to stop Hitler, a decision he now sees he should have made long ago. "But why did it take me so long? Huh?" he asks. "Glued to the radio, talking, talking. Doing nothing. Why? Answer me that one!"[25] Mac remembers his days of pacifism, when "war was evil, Fascism was evil—they were the same. We never knew then that we would ever have to choose between them" (224). Seconding Mac's observations, McCullers comments on the general failure of Americans to grasp the severity of the European crisis and notes that those who are gearing up to "to fight for the betterment of Democracy, and to fight with Democratic means" (224) have reoriented their vision and purpose:

> We never knew that the full force of our barrage would have to be turned outward in order to escape complete annihilation. We have been demoralized. It has taken us long, too long, to come to terms with our inward selves, to adjust our traditions to necessity, to reach the state of conviction that impels action. We have had to re-examine our ideals, and to leave much behind. We have had to face a moral crisis for which we were scantily equipped. But at last we have reached our conclusions and are ready to act. We have come through.
>
> Democracy—intellectual and moral freedom, the liberty to work and live in the way most productive for us, the right to establish our individual spiritual values—that is the breath of the American ideal. And we Americans will fight to preserve it. We have clenched our giant fist; it will not open until we are victorious. (224)

McCullers's comment on Mac expresses her own resolve and commitment: "He knows what it will cost his generation in personal self-denial and in suffering. But he is done with questioning, finished with doubt" (226).

Once America entered the war, McCullers followed developments obsessively, particularly after Reeves reenlisted in 1942 and was sent to England in November 1943, participating in the Normandy invasion and further action on the Continent.[26] Apparently she even explored the possibility of becoming a war correspondent, though nothing came of her efforts. At the request of *Mademoiselle*, she wrote "Love's Not Time's Fool," a war wife's open letter to her departing husband, in which she declared her commitment to both her spouse and the war effort. "For you and me, and for all of us, there is an urgent necessity to believe in something larger than ourselves and our individual destinies," McCullers writes. "We know a deep necessity to affirm life, to believe in a future of creation rather than destruction, to have faith in ourselves and in the future of mankind. Because never have the forces of destruction and hate been so intricately organized. Never has there been more need in the world for love."[27]

McCullers's wartime fiction drew from both her haunting sense of exile from the South and her deep concerns about the war and the spread of

Fascism. In 1940 she apparently started work on a novel, never completed, about a Jewish refugee from Germany.[28] She told Klaus Mann, as he reported in his diary, that the novel was to be "about the Negro and the refugee," and in his notes Mann added that McCullers seemed well suited for the project: "Uncannily versed in the secrets of all freaks and pariahs, she should be able to compose a revealing tale of exile."[29] McCullers also wrote several of her best-known stories early in the war, together with her novella *The Ballad of the Sad Café*. Though none of these works made explicit reference to the war, they focused on the broader issues of isolation and loneliness, which she found at the heart of modern life and which she believed had in part precipitated the European crisis.

The Ballad of the Sad Café is particularly significant in its portrayal of a small southern town suffering under a crushing, totalitarian-like authoritarianism—precisely the South from which McCullers felt she was exiled. "The town itself is dreary," the short novel begins, and this dreariness, as soon becomes clear, has less to do with material culture than with human culture, which has been all but smothered, making life "lonesome, sad, and like a place that is far off and estranged from all other places in the world" (*BSC* 1). The narrator remembers an earlier time, when Miss Amelia ran her café with Cousin Lymon and life in the town was freer and more congenial. At the café, which quickly became the center of town life, the townsfolk gathered for pleasure and relaxation, with all manner of folk enjoying an amiable intimacy. Miss Amelia's café was a refuge from the controlling order, a place of "fellowship, the satisfactions of the belly, and a certain gaiety and grace of behavior" (*BSC* 16).[30]

That refuge was eventually destroyed by Marvin Macy, Miss Amelia's long-lost and vengeful husband, who represents the overwhelming power of southern patriarchy. With Amelia defeated and her café ransacked, the oppressive order is restored. After the fight Miss Amelia becomes a recluse, a madwoman if not quite in the attic, then almost; she lives alone on the second floor, occasionally peering out through the window. Her visage resembles "the terrible dim faces known in dreams—sexless and white, with two gray crossed eyes which are turned inward so sharply that they seem to be exchanging with each other one long and secret gaze of grief" (*BSC* 1). Actually there is not that much for her to see, for the townspeople have submissively returned to their rigidly controlled lives. Immediately after the fight, the people quietly disperse, each going his own way. "This was not a fight to hash over and talk about afterward," the narrator writes; "people went home and pulled the covers up over their heads" (*BSC* 51). Before long, the town is once again a place where "nothing moves" and "there is absolutely nothing to do" (*BSC* 53). "Walk around the millpond, stand kicking at a rotten stump, figure out what you can do with the old wagon wheel by the side of the road near the church," the narrator observes. "The soul rots with boredom. You might as well go down to the Fork Falls highway and listen to the chain gang" (*BSC* 53).

The Ballad of the Sad Café's brief coda, entitled "The Twelve Mortal Men," follows the narrator's suggestion to visit the chain gang at the Fork Falls highway. At first glance seemingly tangential to the rest of the short novel, the coda, with its description of the chain gang, actually comments directly on both the confining life in the town and the liberation that momentarily existed at Amelia's café. The coda suggests that with the destruction of the café, the only place of fellowship in McCullers's South is the chain gang. There blacks and whites, joined together, create a rich, soulful music, "intricately blended, both somber and joyful. . . . It is music that causes the heart to broaden and the listener to grow cold with ecstasy and fright" (*BSC* 54). "And what kind of gang is this that can make such music?" the narrator asks. "Just twelve mortal men, seven of them black and five of them white boys from this county. Just twelve mortal men who are together" (*BSC* 54). McCullers here suggests that those on the chain gang are freer than the people in town, their chains less confining than the invisible ones shackling the townspeople. The joyful creation of the convicts is not possible in the town itself, where rigid rules separate blacks and whites and where any attempt at creating a communal space of freedom and openness, such as Amelia's café, is crushed by the ruling forces. *The Ballad of the Sad Café* thus ends up suggesting that in McCullers's South everyone is a prisoner, everyone is working on one chain gang or another, literal or otherwise.[31] And although the short novel makes no explicit mention of the totalitarian politics of Fascist states, its depiction of the South's crushing conformity suggests that the traditional South operated by something close to those politics, a conclusion that W. J. Cash and Lillian Smith had also reached by this time. Indeed, if *The Heart Is a Lonely Hunter* is McCullers's "ironic parable of fascism," then *The Ballad of the Sad Café* is her ironic parable of totalitarianism.[32]

However speculative the connection between southern traditionalism and European totalitarianism in *The Ballad of the Sad Café*, McCullers explicitly connected them in *The Member of the Wedding*. Written almost entirely during World War II, the novel takes place in a small southern town during a time of ferocious change, both for its protagonist Frankie, who is struggling to understand the complexities of adolescent sexuality, and for the town itself, which is undergoing difficult transformations wrought by wartime mobilization and social unrest. The war in Europe, as it had in *The Heart Is a Lonely Hunter*, manifests itself just about everywhere in the town's daily life—in people's dreams and conversations; on the radio and in the newspaper; in the streets filled with soldiers. No one is affected more than Frankie, whose struggles with identity are in many ways shaped and defined by her understanding of and fears about the European crisis.

Frankie characterizes the time of the novel as "the summer of fear" (*MW* 21), a period when nothing in her own life or in the world at large seems stable and clearly defined. While her own instability derives largely from her troublesome body, which keeps growing and changing, she finds the world at large just as freakish and out of control. "It was the year when Frankie thought about the world," the narrator writes. "And she did not see it as a round school globe, with the countries neat and different-colored. She thought of the world as huge and cracked and loose and turning a thousand miles an hour. The geography book at school was out of date; the countries of the world had changed" (*MW* 19).

What is changing geography, as Frankie knows, is the world war, which she has learned about through reports in the newspaper and on the radio. She has trouble making sense of it all. Reading about the war only deepens her disorientation, as she cannot connect the barrage of events and places that fill the news. Likewise, when she tries to imagine the world at war, she finds herself lost in a jumble of images:

> She thought of the world, and it was fast and loose and turning, faster and looser and bigger than ever it had been before. The pictures of the War sprang out and clashed together in her mind. She saw bright flowered islands and a land by a northern sea with the gray waves on the shore. Bombed eyes and the shuffle of soldiers' feet. Tanks and a plane, wing broken, burning and downward-falling in a desert sky. The world was cracked by the loud battles and turning a thousand miles a minute. The names of places spun in Frankie's mind: China,

Peachville, New Zealand, Paris, Cincinnati, Rome. She thought of the huge and turning world until her legs began to tremble and there was sweat on the palms of her hands. (*MW* 31)

"I feel just exactly like somebody has peeled all the skin off me" (*MW* 31), Frankie says when she pulls herself free from this dizzying onslaught, conflating her confusion about the global disorder with her personal anxieties. "The war and the world were too fast and big and strange," the narrator comments at another point. "To think about the world for very long made her afraid" (*MW* 20). Adding to her confusion and fears are the radio broadcasts discussing the war that she hears at home (the radio stays on all day during her summer of discontent). Because of the poor reception, the news is scrambled with broadcasts from other stations, creating a bizarre mixture of the local and the global (mirroring her own disorientation) that the narrator describes as "a war voice crossed with the gabble of an advertiser, and underneath there was the sleazy music of a sweet band.... Music and voices came and went and crossed and twisted with each other" (*MW* 9).[33]

Despite her fears, Frankie actually does do a good bit of thinking about the world, usually in the kitchen with Berenice and John Henry. As Patricia Yaeger points out, the kitchen in the novel is a disruptive and subversive space, free from cultural constraint, where blacks and whites can congregate in an otherwise segregated society (clearly resembling Amelia's café in *The Ballad of the Sad Café*).[34] There Berenice speaks openly and freely, telling Frankie and John Henry stories about herself and other blacks in the community that they would not have heard otherwise. She also tells stories suggesting the dark underside of the town and of southern society more generally. "I have heard of many a queer thing," Berenice tells Frankie and John Henry as they eat together (itself a significant transgression of southern codes). "I have knew mens to fall in love with girls so ugly that you wonder if their eyes is straight. I have seen some of the most peculiar weddings anybody could conjecture.... I have knew womens to love veritable Satans and thank Jesus when they put their split hooves over the threshold. I have knew boys to take it into their heads to fall in love with other boys" (*MW* 66).

The kitchen is also a space where Frankie and John Henry can talk freely. With Berenice, they often mull over the rules that control their lives. Anguished about the identity into which her name has seemed to lock her, Frankie at one point envisions a world where people change their names whenever they wish, and she challenges Berenice to explain why the real world prohibits such freedom. "Now what kind of confusion do you think that would cause?" Berenice responds, pointing to the chaos that would ensue if Frankie suddenly named herself Joe Louis and John Henry took the name Henry Ford. "Nobody would ever know who anybody was talking about," she says, her examples suggesting that names anchor identity and gird boundaries of race, gender, and class. "The whole world would go crazy," she adds (*MW* 93), and of course she is right.

John Henry's drawings, which cover the kitchen's walls and give the room "a crazy look, like that of the room in the crazy-house" (*MW* 5), manifest the strange new patterns and configurations found in the stories told in the kitchen. Like the scrambled radio broadcasts, the drawings intertwine images of the everyday with the those of the war, creating a strange mélange of "Christmas trees, airplanes, freak soldiers, flowers" (*MW* 8), one more suggestion of the war's disruptive penetration of town, home, and consciousness. Already shaken by the world's confusion, Frankie finds the drawings deeply troubling, their distortions defamiliarizing her everyday feelings and perspectives, adding to her disorientation and instability.[35] Aware that the drawings somehow express her own inner disorder, Frankie attempts imaginatively to configure her face, unsuccessfully it turns out, as a John Henry drawing. "She would have liked for her expression to be split into two parts, so that one eye stared at Berenice in an accusing way, and the other eye thanked her with a grateful look," the narrator comments. "But the human face does not divide like this, and the two expressions cancelled out each other" (*MW* 91).

If John Henry's drawings defamiliarize the everyday world, so too does the game of imagining new worlds that Berenice and the two children often play in the kitchen. Berenice imagines a world without racial difference, what she calls "the world of the Holy Lord God Berenice Sadie Brown," where "all human beings would be light brown color with blue eyes and black hair. There would be no colored people and no white people to make the colored people feel cheap and sorry all through their lives. No colored people, but all human men and ladies and children as one loving family on the earth" (*MW* 79). Berenice's world would also be free of war and the violence that she says plagues both Europe and the South. Linking the oppression of European Jews with that of southern blacks (as Dr. Copeland does in *The Heart Is a Lonely Hunter*), Berenice says that there would be "no stiff corpses hanging from the Europe trees and no Jews murdered anywhere.... No killed Jews and no hurt colored people" (*MW* 79–80). Frankie's imagined world would have, among other things, a summer-free calendar and a War Island where people could go to fight if they felt like it. And most importantly, "people could instantly change back and forth from boys to girls, whichever way they felt like and wanted" (*MW* 80). John Henry imagines a world that "was a mixture of delicious and freak" (*MW* 73), with candy flowers, chocolate dirt, and lemonade rain, together with people having an arm that can stretch to California and an extra eye that can see almost as far.

Between them, Berenice and Frankie imagine worlds that question the formidable barriers of place, race, and gender that cement southern identity and culture. Both seek to do away with otherness, creating a world without exclusion and separateness where everyone is a member of the group. Although certainly benignly conceived, their imagined worlds nonetheless point disturbingly to the seductive appeal of overcoming alienation and loneliness by submerging the self entirely in the group, a process erasing difference and individuality that, as we have seen, McCullers saw as a cornerstone of Fascism. In this regard, Berenice's listing of common physical characteristics, including blue eyes, echoes the Nazi dream of Aryan superiority, although of course she herself makes no such connection and actually wants to do away with the notion of superiority. But the totalitarian echoes resonate anyway, as they do in Frankie's imagined world, as well as in her efforts to escape her isolation by joining a group. She wants to immerse herself in "the we of me" (*MW* 35). Further underscoring the troubling link between membership and militant nationalism are Frankie's attraction to the soldier and her fear of being left out of the war. "She was not afraid of the Germans or bombs or Japanese," the narrator tells us. "She was afraid because in the war they would not include her, and because the world seemed somehow separate from herself" (*MW* 20).

Near the end of the novel, in her final act of rebellion, Frankie tries to run away, only to be nabbed by a local policeman, who as a representative of cultural control is identified simply as "the Law" (*MW* 128). At this point, Frankie shelves her various dreams and decides to settle down as a member of her hometown society. Her decision brings her the security of acceptance but the loss of her creative and inquisitive individuality, as the rules of southern womanhood demand that Frankie repress her rebelliousness. From a young upstart with an adventurous imagination, Frankie turns into a giddy adolescent, consumed with the typical concerns of girls her age. Once looking to run away, Frankie now happily looks forward to going to school and moving to the suburbs; once imagining a new world order, she now dreams about traveling the world with her new girlfriend; once haunted by the chaos of the European war, she now pictures Europe merely as a continent of countries with pretty-sounding names, a wonderful tourist destination. "She did not see the earth as in the old days, cracked and loose and turning a thousand miles an hour," the narrator comments, adding, in a statement clearly indicating Frankie's fall from knowledge, that "the earth [to her] was enormous and still and flat" (*MW* 128).

Appropriate to her new identity, Frankie turns away from Berenice to her newfound friend Mary Littlejohn (and her mother) for comfort and guidance;[36] she cares little about Berenice's pending departure (Berenice will not work for Frankie's family once they move to the suburbs) and no longer listens to Berenice's stories. The barriers of segregation have been reestablished, even in the kitchen, where newly whitewashed walls cover over John Henry's drawings. Furthermore, Frankie has apparently "forgotten" all that Bernice ever told her about the controlling power of social convention, including her warning that "we all of us somehow caught. . . . And maybe we wants to widen and bust free. But no matter what we do we still caught" (*MW* 98). In distancing herself from Berenice (and her insights) and happily accepting her designated place in the cultural order, Frankie mindlessly follows the rituals enforced by southern tradition, what Lillian Smith characterized as "the dance that cripples the human spirit" (*KD* 96).

After World War II, McCullers's fiction thinned out, with the European political crisis no longer serving as an imaginative catalyst. Clearly the threat of Communism and developments in the cold war did not touch her imaginatively in the ways that the issues of World War II had. Her stage adaptation of *The Member of a Wedding* (which she began in 1946 but did not finish until 1949) offers some insight. Except for the last act, the play is set in August 1945, soon after the bombing of Hiroshima. While still haunted by the events of World War II, Frankie and Berenice now focus their concern on the unfathomable destruction of the atomic bomb. "The figures these days have got too high for me," Berenice says when she tries to imagine the destruction of Hiroshima. "Read in the paper about ten million peoples killed. I can't crowd that many peoples in my mind's eye."[37] With the entire world on the brink of similar nuclear catastrophe throughout the 1950s and 1960s, McCullers's creative imagination was perhaps as stymied as Berenice's, at least in terms of her being able to configure the South in the international context that marks her most significant fiction. Only in the 1930s and 1940s was McCullers able to see, and to write, with the vision that Biff in *The Heart Is a Lonely Hunter* struggles to forge, one bringing the local, the regional, and the international into simultaneous focus.

9

PRAGMATISM, IDEALISM, RESPONSIBILITY

ROBERT PENN WARREN

Throughout his career, Robert Penn Warren was deeply concerned with issues of American democracy and democratic theory, particularly the considerable problems facing the nation after it moved from a primarily agrarian order to a twentieth-century corporate state.[1] While as an Agrarian Warren was of course interested in the ramifications of this transformation for the South, his imagination was almost always drawn beyond specifically regional matters. At a reunion of the Fugitive poets at Vanderbilt University in 1956, Warren downplayed the regional character of the Agrarian cause, saying that in his view the movement had been "trying to find—in so far as we were being political—a rational basis for a democracy.... We were trying to find a notion of democracy which would make it possible for people to be people and not to be bosses, or exploiters, or anything else of other people, but to have a community of people, rather than a community of something else."[2]

Warren's words here point to an idea central to almost all of his work: that the modern industrial state was destroying the autonomy of the individual self, an autonomy that was crucial if democracy was to flourish. In the same talk at Vanderbilt, Warren commented that the efficiency of the modern state demanded ruthless dehumanization, a grinding conformity established to "disintegrate individuals, so you have no individual sense of responsibility and no awareness that the individual has a past and a place."[3] In a later interview, citing the work of Jacques Ellul, Warren said that the modern self was so hopelessly fragmented that it threatened to become merely a series of disconnected signifiers. As Warren put it, "If you go to a dentist, you're a tooth; if you work in a factory, you are number so-and-so; and in all your relations you are taken out of human context and put into a mechanical one."[4] In a discussion of Theodore Dreiser's *An American Tragedy* Warren commented that the "responsible self has been absorbed by the great machine of modern industrial secularized society, and reduced to a cog, a cipher, an abstraction."[5]

Warren feared that a citizenship reduced to mechanisms, cogs, and ciphers opened the way to authoritarian political rule. In *Democracy and Poetry* he foresaw the possibility of democracies peacefully evolving into totalitarian states, with individuals fading "into abstraction, into various successive, shadowy roles, with the highest abstraction, as Jung describes the matter, being the 'idea of the State as the principle of political reality'" (65). Continuing to draw from Jung, Warren described the individual self being subsumed into the state, so that "the moral responsibility of the individual, a mark of his selfhood, is 'inevitably replaced by the policy of the State,' and the 'moral and mental differentiations of the individual' replaced by 'public welfare and the raising of the living standard.' The self is absorbed, ultimately into *le raison d'état*—a situation which we have seen totally realized in some regimes of our century, and of which we have lately been able to detect a few symptoms in our own land" (65). Warren's comments here, written in 1971, look back to the central issues that structure almost all his work, particularly that of the 1930s and 1940s.

Although he began exploring issues of the self and democratic society in the 1920s, long before he was paying serious attention to the rise of Fascism in Europe, it was not until the late 1930s that Warren, profoundly shaken by Europe's political turmoil, began exploring and expressing these issues in the depth and complexity that mark his greatest art. Warren's comment from a later interview, though not referring specifically to his own work during this time, nevertheless speaks to his artistic response to the European crisis: "A period of cultural and moral shock, short of the final cataclysm, does breed art. . . . Deep conflicts of values can release tremendous amounts of energy. When the pieties are shaken, you are forced to reexamine the whole basis of life. A new present has to be brought in line with the past, and the other way around."[6] The cultural and moral shock of the European cataclysm forced Warren, as an artist, into just this sort of reexamination, compelling him not only to explore in his fiction and poetry political issues highlighted by the conflict but also to develop an aesthetics derived primarily from these same political issues.[7]

PRAGMATISM, IDEALISM, RESPONSIBILITY: ROBERT PENN WARREN

—x—x—x—x—

Warren's interest in the threats to and shortcomings of American democracy surfaced in his first book, *John Brown: The Making of a Martyr* (1929), which focuses on the dangerous extremes to which Brown took his uncompromising pursuit of the higher good. Warren portrays Brown's fanaticism, anchored in the certainty that his will coincided with God's, as a dangerous threat to the democratic social and political order; Brown seemed untroubled by trampling on the laws of the state, including committing murder, when those laws conflicted with his own higher law. Warren underscores the dangers of Brown's thinking by surveying the wild-eyed views of those who lionized him, particularly the New England Transcendentalists. He notes that Theodore Parker praised Brown by quoting Cromwell's declaration that "there is one general grievance, and that is the law!"[8] and that Bronson Alcott characterized Brown's abolitionist enterprise as "superior to any legal traditions" (318). But it was Emerson who perhaps most adored Brown, anointing him "the rarest of heroes, a pure idealist, with no by-ends of his own" and declaring that rather than the nation's violating one word of Brown's ideals it would be "better that a whole generation of men, women, and children should pass away by a violent death" (245). "That is a big value to place on a 'word,'" Warren comments wryly, taking quite seriously the frightening possibilities should such demagogic rhetoric ever be realized in fact. Warren adds that Emerson, like Brown, "lived in words, big words, and not facts" (245) and was unconcerned about "the barbarous and pitiful consequences" (318) of Brown's or his own rhetoric. "When he tried to deal with matters of fact," Warren says of Emerson, "words made him a common demagogue" (246).

Years later Warren commented in *Who Speaks for the Negro?* (1965) that writing *John Brown* "was my real introduction into some awareness of the dark and tangled problem of motives and values."[9] It was also the first of his many examinations of the dangers of absolutist thinking.[10] Strongly influenced by William James, Warren characteristically critiqued absolutist thinking from a tough-minded pragmatism that demanded accountability and responsibility, particularly to one's society. Warren's pragmatism lies behind his observation in his biography of Brown that however noble Brown's ideals, when those ideals led to murder and armed rebellion, "John Brown was as responsible for his actions as are the general run of criminals who have suffered similar penalties" (421).

Warren's pragmatism in part explains his lukewarm efforts on behalf of the Agrarians. Not only did he early on chafe at what he considered the group's undemocratic decision making, even going so far as to suggest that the organization was in the hands of a dictatorship,[11] but he resisted the group's southern chauvinism. Although sympathetic to Agrarian ideals, Warren nonetheless hesitated to support the group's strategy of challenging the American political system by appealing to a "higher" law based on southern idealism; in other words, he did not want the group to take a stand similar to John Brown's. Warren's contribution to *I'll Take My Stand*, "The Briar Patch," which very much upset some of the Agrarians (particularly Davidson), illustrates his pragmatic perspective.[12] Assigned the task of defining the role of blacks in the South's segregated society, Warren examined the policy of separate but equal, arguing that for southern society to achieve a restoration of balance and security, the letter of the law must be upheld; that is, blacks must be given equal opportunity and equal rights. Embracing what he called "a democratic ideal of equal opportunity" (*ITMS* 249), Warren endorsed segregation while advocating improvements for both blacks and whites in education, vocational opportunity, and labor relations, with a particular emphasis on eliminating strife between blacks and poor whites. "What the white workman must learn, and his education may be as long and laborious as the negro's," Warren wrote, underscoring the need for black and white workers to work together, "is that he may respect himself as a white man, but, if he fails to concede the negro equal protection, he does not properly respect himself as a man" (*ITMS* 260). In looking forward to an improved South, Warren drew upon the example of the ultrapragmatic Booker T. Washington rather than a hard-line white segregationist (of which there were plenty in the Agrarians), quoting Washington on the possibility that segregation could both maintain separation of the races and encourage a common effort toward social improvement: "We can be as separate as the fingers, yet one as the hand in all things essential to mutual progress" (*ITMS* 254).

With his own enthusiasm for the Agrarian cause waning and with the movement in disarray, by the mid-1930s Warren was beginning to shift his primary focus from cultural criticism to literary criticism.[13] Warren quickly became one of the key proponents of the New Criticism, which favored complex, ironic literature over literature of direct statement. In his early criticism Warren characteristically contrasted the complexity of artistic knowledge with what he saw as the simplicity of scientific analysis. Warren believed that the artist interrogated the multiplicity of experience, whereas the scientist attempted to reduce all knowledge and values to neatly organized systems of verifiable facts. Soon, however, in response to the worsening situation in Europe in the late 1930s and to America's gearing up for war, Warren reconfigured the opposition between the artist and the scientist as that between the artist and the patriot. With the nation in the midst of a patriotic revival, Warren came to see writers facing increasing pressures, both from the government and from the public, to write literature openly supporting democracy's stand against Fascism; at his most fearful, he likened such pressures to totalitarian oppression. Once believing that only writers who lived under authoritarian regimes felt compelled to support national ideals, by the early 1940s Warren was suggesting that American writers faced similar demands, even if they were not as rigidly enforced as in Nazi Germany or Fascist Italy.

In reconfiguring his critical focus, Warren was in part specifically responding to Archibald MacLeish's and Van Wyck Brooks's stinging attacks on what they saw as the widespread political irresponsibility of modern artists. As we saw in chapter 1, MacLeish in his essay "The Irresponsibles" attacked both artists and scholars for failing to defend Western culture from the anticivilizational forces threatening to destroy it, forces MacLeish characterized as "a revolution of negatives, a revolution of the defeated, a revolution of the dispossessed, a revolution of despair."[14] Rather than facing this crisis, MacLeish wrote, modern scholars and writers were retreating from political commitment, turning away from the world and their responsibilities as citizens to seek purity and transcendence in their scholarship and art. MacLeish described thusly their "purity of devotion":

> To the scholar impartiality, objectivity, detachment were ideal qualities he taught himself laboriously and painfully to acquire. To the writer objectivity and detachment were his writer's pride. Both subjected themselves to inconceivable restraints, endless disciplines to reach these ends. And both succeeded. Both writers and scholars freed themselves of the subjective passions, the emotional preconceptions which color conviction and judgment. Both writers and scholars freed themselves of the personal responsibility associated with personal choice. They emerged free, pure and single into the antiseptic air of objectivity. And by that sublimation of the mind they prepared the mind's disaster. (34)

Similarly, Van Wyck Brooks argued in *Opinions of Oliver Allston* (1941) that modern writers stood fundamentally opposed to everything that made great literature, which he referred to as "primary literature," great. Primary literature, he wrote, expressed faith in human progress and humanity, affirming life over death, its themes being "those by virtue of which the race has risen, courage, justice, mercy, honour, love."[15] "Coterie literature," in contrast, which Brooks said was that written by most modern writers, was mired in gloom and disillusionment, its fundamental theme being "life was ugly and men were base, and there was next to nothing to be done about it." Brooks added that modern writers, whose heroes "were gunmen or moral cripples, human jelly-fish or hobbledehoys," "had turned literature into a sort of wailing wall from which nothing rose but the sound of lamentations and curses" (196). Like MacLeish, Brooks argued that the negativism of modern writers had sapped the moral fortitude of their readers, leaving society helpless against the Fascist threat, and he pointed to the fall of France as evidence. Closer to home, Brooks faulted the New Critics, particularly John Crowe Ransom and Cleanth Brooks, for disregarding world affairs in their criticism; he declared that the New Criticism was not even criticism, because it entirely evaded what was justly the matter of criticism—"the whole world of values" (243).

Warren's response to what had quickly become known as the "Brooks-MacLeish Thesis" was swift and stinging. In a review of *Opinions of Oliver Allston* Warren likened Brooks to Cato the Elder, the pedantic censor who, among other things, strived to keep Roman culture free of foreign influence; and in his essay "Pure and Impure Poetry" he refuted Brooks and MacLeish's theory of pure poetry by arguing that the very structure of poetry involved resistance and tension between its elements (including language, rhythm, ideas, structure, metaphor, etc.).[16] Warren also declared that Brooks's and MacLeish's calls for political didacticism came close to mirroring the censorship and conformity enforced by totalitarian states.[17] He added that he could envision "certain, probably preliminary, attempts to legislate literature into becoming a simple, unqualified 'pure' statement of faith and ideal" (254) and that he feared that soon those writers who did not fall into line would be seen as treasonous. In defending the independence of modern writers, Warren wrote:

> We have seen the writers of the 1920's called the "irresponsibles." We have seen writers such as Proust, Eliot, Dreiser, and Faulkner called

writers of the "death drive." Why are these writers condemned? Because they have tried, within the limits of their gifts, to remain faithful to the complexities of the problems with which they are dealing, because they refused to take the easy statement as solution, because they tried to define the context in which, and the terms by which, faith and ideals could be earned. But this method will scarcely satisfy the mind which is hot for certainties; to that mind it will seem merely an index to lukewarmness, indecision, disunity, treason. The new theory of purity would purge out all complexities and all ironies and all self-criticism. And this theory will forget that the hand-me-down faith, the hand-me-down ideals, no matter what the professed content, is in the end not only meaningless but vicious. It is vicious because, as parody, it is the enemy of all faith. (254)

As suggested here and in essays soon to follow, Warren championed writers of "impure" poetry, that is, poetry that resisted the dogmatic nationalism that he feared was undermining American democracy and pushing the nation toward the purity of totalitarianism, which spoke in one voice and repressed all others.

Opposed to the purity of totalitarianism was the impurity of democracy, a system of government that Warren likened to the impure poem, with its political elements of dissent, dialogue, and compromise resisting single-minded, extremist belief and action. In *The Legacy of the Civil War* (which appeared in 1961 but expressed ideas that Warren had long held) Warren characterized the impurity of the democratic system as "illogical," meaning that political parties rarely took beliefs to their logical extremes. Impure and illogical, democracy was also inefficient, but even so it protected the nation from single-minded and single-voiced tyranny, a lesson that Americans had learned well from the election of 1860:

> The election in which social, sectional, moral, and philosophical forces found logical projection into the party setup was that of 1860; and when the votes were counted, business was not resumed as usual. Somewhere in their bones most Americans learned their lesson from this election. They learned that logical parties may lead logically to logical shooting, and they had had enough of that. The American feels that logicality, when not curbed and channeled by common sense, is a step toward fanaticism; it tends to sharpen controversy to some exclusive and vindictive point. Chesterton said that logic is

all that is left to the insane; the American is almost prepared to go him one better and say that logic is the mark of the insane, at least of the politically insane. Illogicality, like apathy (which, according to David Reisman, has "its positive side as a safeguard against the over-politicization of the country"), makes life possible; it guarantees continuity. From the Civil War the American emerged confirmed in his tendency to trust some undefined sense of a social compact which undergirds and overarches mere political activity. (43–44)

In the late 1930s, as Warren witnessed nations giving themselves over to Fascist purity, the dangers of fanaticism became a central issue in his works of fiction, poetry, and drama.[18] His work from this period, while often set in the past, draws heavily upon political issues highlighted by the European crisis, exploring ways these issues took shape in the American experience, often through the portrayal of an idealist who is eventually destroyed—and who often destroys others—by his radical idealism. Warren later said that in writing fiction set in the past (he did not like the designation "historical novel"), he chose events that he believed commented upon current concerns, and he looked for "something that has the distance of the past but has the image of an issue." "It must be an image, a sort of simplified and distant framed image," he continued, "of an immediate and contemporary issue, a sort of interplay between the image and the contemporary world."[19]

Warren's first novel, *Night Rider* (1939), illustrates his choice of a historical event that resonated with current events, particularly the rise of Fascism in Europe and the problems plaguing contemporary American democracy.[20] Written with one eye on Kentucky and one eye on European dictatorships, the novel draws on events from the tobacco wars in Kentucky and Tennessee (now known collectively as the Black Patch War) and focuses on the increasingly violent involvement of a young lawyer, Percy Munn, in a nightriding terrorist organization, the Association of Growers of Dark Fired Tobacco. Munn is one of modernity's "little," or "hollow," men, adrift, isolated, and purposeless and thus well suited for recruitment into ideological politics. Eager to give himself over to something outside himself—a cause, a group, an ideal—in order to gain a fuller sense of identity, Munn becomes easy prey for the association's manipulative leaders. Early on, Munn relishes the purity of the association's political vision, which gives him a "general confidence and excitement" that makes "everything seem so easy, every difficulty so superficial, the future so clear."[21] Eventually, however, Munn comes to see that his pure ideals have degraded him, driving him, as a nightrider, to commit murder and destroy property and, as a human being, to betray friends, abuse his wife, and wallow in vanity and lust.

By the end of the novel, having himself been used and betrayed by the association, Munn is once again without purpose and grounding, a man who "could not, no matter how hard he tried, think beyond the moment. He did not have the seed of the future in himself, the live germ. It had shriveled up and died, like a sprouting grain of corn that has been washed out of the hill to lie exposed to the sun's heat. . . . and because the future was dead and rotten in his breast, the past, too, which once had seemed to him to have its meanings and its patterns, began to fall apart, act by act, incident by incident, thought by thought, each item into brutish separateness" (390). Munn's turnaround mirrors the novel's, as the apparently hopeful tale of social revolution, with the growers taking a stand against corporate power, ends up underscoring the dangers of revolution and of "pure" political idealism.

That *Night Rider* spoke compellingly about the contemporary political crisis was not lost on Warren's readers. In an early review, Christopher Isherwood characterized Munn as "the noble liberal gone astray in a world of power politics,"[22] and a few years later Irene Hendry deemed Munn "the new man, heir of all the ages, in whom there is no longer even the virtue of conflict, who functions completely and mechanically in terms of his environment, epitomized in the soldier of a modern mechanized army or the citizen of the totalitarian state."[23] Hendry underscored that while Munn's absorption into the association provided him with a sense of revolutionary purpose, ironically it entailed at the same time a loss of individuality, a further diminishment of his already diminished self. Kenneth Burke drew specific connections between Warren's novel and Fascist politics and psychology, using insights from G. A. Borgese's 1938 study of Italian Fascism, *Goliath: The March of Fascism*. In that work Borgese characterizes Fascism as "the Great Involution," arguing that despite its revolutionary pretensions, Fascism involved a myopic turning inward, with the state folding in upon itself to create a rigid system bolstered by tribal mysticism and hero worship.[24] Burke perceived a similar motion in Munn's path toward self-destruction, deeming it "the end of the line mode." He described it "as the peeling away of the successive layers of an onion, which would perfectly suggest such development by introversion, by inturning towards a non-existent core." Burke concluded: "It is the fascist involution which Warren has embodied and ritualistically slain."[25]

During the time that he was finishing up *Night Rider,* Warren made two trips to Italy, seeing the Fascist state firsthand. The first trip, in the summer of 1938, seems to have been fairly uneventful, with Warren, accompanied by his first wife, Cinina (who had family in the country), mainly vacationing and getting writing done, though during a brief visit to Rome he witnessed Mussolini delivering an emotion-charged speech to a crowd in the Piazza Vienza. The second trip, in the following year, was more threatening and ominous. Warren had won a Guggenheim Fellowship, and in July he and Cinina departed for what they hoped would be a year's stay. The situation in Europe was deteriorating quickly: Germany had moved into Austria and Czechoslovakia, and England was threatening to declare war if Germany invaded Poland. Warren noted a change in people's feelings even before he set foot in Italy. He wrote to Frank Owsley (14 August 1939) that the "people on the boat are pretty grim and pessimistic; a vast difference from last year" (*SLW* 219). Not long after the Warrens' arrival, Germany invaded Poland and war broke out, although Italy at this point maintained its neutrality. Warren and Cinina considered returning home immediately, but they decided to stay, keeping close watch on the political situation and ready to leave at a moment's notice. Describing these fraught days, Warren wrote Owsley (11 November 1939) that "everybody was running like rabbits to Switzerland . . . or back to England, or was sleeping on deck to get back to New York. Well, we just sat quietly, and listened to the radio broadcasts, and occasionally had a moral collapse" (*SLW* 226).

In the coming months, Warren and Cinina struggled to balance their desire for a comfortable routine and their fears for their safety. Their moods and feelings fluctuated wildly. Warren's letters home during this time suggest the unreality of the situation: everyday life in Italy remained casual and relaxed, and yet the war raged on. Warren paid close attention to developments, listening to radio broadcasts and reading newspapers; he was particularly struck by the Soviet Union's invasion of Finland and Finland's surprisingly fierce resistance. "A lot of our time and energy now, especially since the Finland business started, is taken up with reading the papers," Warren wrote Owsley (7 December 1939). "War is ruining, not only the civilized world, but my morning's work rather often, for I feel that I can't get settled to work until I've run to the corner to get the paper and find out about the latest horror; and then after I get the paper I have a hard time settling down anyway. I don't suppose that you can find many Stalinists at home now, and when they appear in society or in print they don't feel themselves, I imagine, exactly among friends" (*SLW* 240). Although hoping to stay until early summer, Warren and Cinina left Italy on 18 May 1940, after being warned by a friend that Italy would soon join the war.

Despite all the distractions, Warren did get a good deal of work done while in Italy, almost all of which shows him responding imaginatively to Fascism and the war, a fact he suggested in a letter to Paul M. Hebert, president of Louisiana State University (7 March 1940): "This is not exactly the year I would have chosen to be here, but in some respects the special circumstances are proving a good deal more instructive than those of more normal and happy times" (*SLW* 269). The most obvious influences appear in his verse play, *Proud Flesh*, which deals with a dictatorial southern governor, based loosely on Huey Long (the play later became the basis for his novel *All the King's Men* [1946] and for three other dramatic versions).[26] Even though he was awarded his Guggenheim Fellowship to write a second novel, once in Italy Warren immediately turned to his *Proud Flesh*; he wrote to Kenneth Burke (13 November 1939) that the play "seemed pretty ripe to me then and ready to pluck."[27] In the introduction to an Italian translation of a later version of the play, Warren noted that when he was finishing *Proud Flesh*, in the winter of 1939–40, he was listening "to the music of military bootheels on the cobbles" and that as a result "the shadow of a European as well as a home-grown dictatorship lies over the composition."[28] He mentioned that long shadow again in a later interview: "I was in Italy when I was writing the play—I finished it in Italy in the first year of the war—so I couldn't help but relate these things, being right in the middle of it. I was cut off from my own world and I suppose this made my senses more acute. I was bound to wonder what makes these events, what blankness had made it possible."[29]

Dictatorship and the abuse of absolute power lie at the heart of *Proud Flesh*, with Warren conflating his dictator, Willie Strong (in some of the drafts, Willie Talos), with both Huey Long and Mussolini. That Warren imaginatively united Long and Mussolini was far from unusual, as many political commentators, both before and after Long's death, invoked Fascist dictatorships in Europe in discussing and interpreting his political activities and aspirations.[30] In Warren's hands, the Long/Mussolini/Strong story explores the damage to democracy—and to individuals—wrought by a leader driven by political idealism. As an all-powerful governor, Strong is obsessed with his visionary desire to build the very best hospital to serve the impoverished people of his state, and he is willing to use any means to get the funding and legislative approval, including bringing the democratic system to its knees through bribery and graft. Many aspects of the play call to mind Mussolini and the Fascist state. The play opens, for instance, with a suggestion of Fascist storm troopers, as a chorus of highway patrolmen, immaculately uniformed and organized, praise Willie's power and achievements. The stage directions describe the men as "dressed in blue uniforms and black leather boots, and caps," and "standing in military formation, in postures of wooden rigidity."[31] Their remarkable opening statement describes the Willie's godlike power:

> What hand flings the white road before us?
> What hand over hills and the damplands,
> Over the highlands and swamplands,
> Gully and bayou? And flings us
> Fast as the slug from the gun-mouth,
> Hard as the word from his own mouth—
> Us nameless, and yet he has named us,
> And aimless, and yet he has aimed us
> And flung us, and flings us, a handful
> Of knives hurled, edged errand—O errand
> Blind with the glittering blindness of light!
> (23)

The final line points both to the patrolmen's blind loyalty to their leader and to the governor's blindingly clear orders: Willie rules with a purity of vision unhampered by doubt, questions, or scruples. The patrolmen proceed to sing the praises of their motorcycles and their pistols, both symbolizing not only the power they now wield (celebrated in phallic adoration) but also Willie's vision of the new order. Echoing the Fascist glorification of the airplane, Willie's men embrace the motorcycle, which they describe in a moment of poetic synecdoche as the wheel, always blazing forward with no "crossed aims, distractions, / Confusion or sick heart" (24). Speaking "retardedly as in a ritual," the patrolmen praise the motorcycle's power to crush everything that stands before it in its drive into the future:

> Road-roarer
> Way-wailer
> Light-dazzler
> Space-eater
> Time-cheater
> Distance-betrayer.
> (24)

If the motorcycle is the image of the new state, the pistol represents the state's power to enforce its mandates, and the patrolmen celebrate the pistol's power to kill both bodies and minds:

> Far-speaker
> Fire-darter
> Light-quencher
> Slug-hurler
> Flesh-plugger
> Brain-darkener.
> (24–25)

Besides the chorus's unmistakable evocation of the Fascist police state built on technologies of force and speed, other images throughout the play point to the Fascist character of Strong's empire. At the football game in the second act, the offstage cheering for the state university calls to mind Fascism's rabid nationalism:

> OFFSTAGE CHEERING. Rah, rah, rah! Rah for State!
> Our Alma Mater, she is great!
> We will fight and die for State!
> Rah, rah, rah! Die for State!
> (58)
>
> OFFSTAGE VOICES. For good old State we'll give our all!
> For good old State we'll fight and fall!
> Give our all,
> Fight and Fall!
> For good old State!
> (65)

Even more suggestive is the crooner's song at the end of the first scene of the third act. The following lyrics are directed to be sung variously as recitation (first seven lines), as madly hysterical (middle five lines), and as recitation again (final three lines), this time "with heavily marked accents" (75), suggestive of a foreign tongue:

> What if worlds and cultures fall today, Baby?
> If democracy is in decay, Baby,
> Crumbling now,
> Tumbling now?
> Yet though you find
> Values shot,
>
> You have got
> Love, love, love, love, love, love, loving!
> Though the maggots now are in the cheese, Baby,
> And constellations drift like falling leaves,
> Glimmering, and by short-wave, when the weather's good,
>
> We hear the inspired idiot's harangue, the shout,
> The frantic burst of applause like hail on a tin roof.
> But sometimes we can only get the local stations.
> (74–75)

Here is a world spiraling toward destruction, propelled along by a host of disasters: the clash of war; the decay of democracy; the loss of moral values and the accompanying sentimental worship of love; the rotting of culture from within; the subversion of spiritual faith by science; and the rise of Fascism.

At the end of the play, Willie is shot dead by Keith Amos, who hopes his act will restore a moral order that he believes Willie's actions have destroyed. Ironically, the two antagonists, Willie and Amos, mirror each other in that both are willing to go to any extreme to achieve their idealistic visions. Finally, the democratic system lies in ruins. Amos's murder of Willie does not clear the way for law and order; it only furthers the state's plunge into misrule, with Tiny Harper, one of Willie's henchman, standing in the wings to take charge at the end.

The shadow of Fascism also looms large in *Eleven Poems on the Same Theme* (1942).[32] Unlike the poems from Warren's previous collection, *Thirty Six Poems* (1935), those from *Eleven Poems* look dramatically outward to the social and political disruption of the era, showing individuals struggling with private matters that mirror the larger fears and terrors manifested in the contemporary social turmoil.³³ "Individual personalities become mirrors of their times, or the times become a mirror of the personalities," Warren said in a much later interview, discussing an idea that had become central to his thinking by the mid-1930s. "Social tensions have a parallel in the personal world. The individual is an embodiment of external circumstances, so that a personal story is a social story."³⁴ References to the world's disorder begin vaguely in the opening poems and become increasingly specific and significant as the poems proceed, so that the sequence's overall movement can be understood as the progressive merging of the personal with the social. In the final poem, "Terror," the individual and the social come together in the Fascist enterprise—a concluding vision that, in casting its shadow back on the previous poems, establishes the threatening context of the entire sequence.

In an uncharacteristically full commentary on "Terror," written just over a decade after the poem's completion, Warren identified the paradox that anchors the poem: that the human impulse toward understanding moves in two directions, one following "the yearning for mere survival as meaning" and the other the yearning for "the appetite for death as meaning" (543). "Yearning for mere survival" means for Warren the compulsion to find contentment in everyday life in order to suppress the unsettling awareness of the darker regions of the heart and the world; yearning for "the appetite for death" means the effort to locate all meaning in primal violence and savagery in order to erase the complications of the world and individual consciousness. To those lacking what the poet calls an "adequate definition of terror" (*CPW* 77), which Warren in his commentary glosses as "that proper sense of the human lot, the sense of limitation and the sense of the necessity for responsible action within that limitation" (543), neither impulse is finally fulfilling or meaningful. The first stanza of "Terror" addresses the inadequacy of mere adjustment to the world:

> Not picnics or pageants or the improbable
> Powers of air whose tongues exclaim dominion
> And gull the great man to follow his terrible
> Star, suffice; not the window-box, or the bird on
> The ledge, which mean so much to the invalid,
> Nor the joy you leaned after, as by the tracks the grass
> In the emptiness after the lighted Pullmans fled,
> Suffices; nor faces, which, like distraction, pass

> Under the street-lamps, teasing to faith or pleasure,
> Suffice you, born to no adequate definition of terror.
> (*CPW* 77)

The fourth stanza describes the inadequacy of living by violence, using the example of American volunteers who, driven less by ideals than by blood lust, first fought alongside the Russians in the Spanish Civil War and then fought against them in Finland:

> So some, whose passionate emptiness and tidal
> Lust swayed toward the debris of Madrid,
> And left New York to loll in their fierce idyll
> Among the olives, where the snipers hid;
> And now the North, to seek that visioned face
> And polarize their iron of despair,
> Who praise no beauty like the boreal grace
> Which greens the dead eye under the rocket's flare.
> They fight old friends, for their obsession knows
> Only the immaculate itch, not human friends or foes.
> (*CPW* 78)

In the startling fifth stanza the poet describes both impulses at their deadliest extremes. The first four lines suggest that spilling blood means nothing to those driven to violence; violent acts bring no awareness of terror, evil, or anything outside of the violence itself. The last two lines, describing efforts of the physician Alexis Carrel to keep a chicken heart alive in the laboratory, suggest the ultimate dream of those attempting through science to create a perfectly adapted life and environment.[35] In his commentary, Warren wrote that after reading a newspaper report that Carrel's laboratory heart had "died," he came to see that "the business about the chicken heart seemed to summarize a view current in our time—that science (as popularly conceived) will solve the problem of evil by reducing it merely to a matter of 'adjustment' in the physical, social, economic, and political spheres" (542). Between these descriptions of the extremes of humanity's misguided impulses comes a frightening evocation of the powerful appeal and power of Fascism and Nazism:

> You know, by radio, how hotly the world repeats,
> When the brute crowd roars or the blunt boot-heels resound

> In the Piazza or the Wilhelmplatz,
> The crime of Onan, spilled upon the ground.
>   (*CPW* 78)

As Anthony Szczesiul notes, the reference to Onan suggests both the collective masturbation of Fascist rallies and the effort by Fascists to create a new society based on the scientific manipulation of the natural order.[36] Fascism's terrifying appeal, as Warren said of these lines in his commentary, comes from its dangerous conflation of modernity's impulses toward violence and adaptation: "Nazism, Fascism, embody both of the elements of the paradox mentioned above—the glorification of violence and death, the offer of salvation through practical success, adjustment, etc., the 'rational' state. But the boot-heels beating the stones in the Piazza or Wilhelmplatz set up echoes of the same impulses and desires across the Atlantic—all part of the same world, the same modernity, on one level" (543).

"Terror" ends quietly, with the "you" of the poem wandering without guilt or concern in hotel lobbies and gardens, unaffected by the world's horror. Contrasting this state with Macbeth's haunting awareness of the nature of evil, Warren describes "you" cracking nuts "while the conscience-stricken stare / Kisses the terror; for you see an empty chair" (*CPW* 78). Lines from a stanza that Warren deleted from the poem's final version make it clear that the blindness and apathy of "you" characterize the blindness and apathy of modern society:

> So Civilization, blabbing, emulates
> The drivelled Roman in his bloody bath
> Who quoted Greek and puddled out his abstract wrath.[37]

In the end, "Terror" conflates the psychopathologies of modern individuals, of Fascism, and of Western civilization itself.

In closing the eleven-poem sequence, "Terror" drastically reconfigures the context of the other poems. The reader of "Terror" now knows, in returning to the other poems, that the intrusive darkness of the earlier poems is more threatening than perhaps originally read and, furthermore, that attempting to escape that darkness, rather than confronting it straightforwardly, has led, as the very sequence of poems shows, to the world of "Terror"—the world of Fascism. How much more disturbing, in hindsight, are the following lines from "Monologue at Midnight":

> And always at the side, like guilt,
> Our shadows over the grasses moved,
>
> Or moved across the moonlit snow;
> And move across the grass or snow.
> Or was it guilt? Philosophers
> Loll in their disputatious ease.
> (*CPW* 65)

Or these from "Bearded Oaks":

> Ages to our construction went,
> Dim architecture, hour by hour:
> And violence, forgot now, lent
> The present stillness all its power.
> (*CPW* 66)

Or, finally, these from "Love's Parable," which in echoing *Proud Flesh*'s depiction of an American Fascism suggests the timeliness of *Eleven Poems*'s commentary on modernity:

> But we have seen the fungus eyes
> Of misery spore in the night
> And marked, of friends, the malices
> That stain, like smoke, the day's fond light,
> And marked how ripe injustice flows,
> How ulcerous, how acid, then
> How proud flesh on the sounder grows
> Til rot engross the estate of men.
> (*CPW* 76)

Besides *Eleven Poems on the Same Theme,* Warren's experiences in Italy in 1939–40 profoundly shaped his second novel, *At Heaven's Gate* (1943), which he began during his Italian trip. That influence can be seen both in its depiction of the ruthlessness of corporatism and finance capitalism, which was clearly shaped by Warren's conceptions of the Fascist state, and in its use of Dante to contextualize modernity's ills. As he noted later in an interview, Warren drew particularly from the *Inferno*'s seventh circle, the underworld home of the violators against nature, in the novel's depiction of a world in which "nature is being violated one way or another, and all the characters are somehow *denying* nature."[38] Warren's words here recall his commentary on *Eleven Poems on the Same Theme* concerning the destructive impulses at play when modernity lacks an "adequate definition of terror"; that is, not unlike Alexis Carrel experimenting to create artificial life, corporate officers manipulate society to create "artificial" economies and social orders based entirely on financial exchange. Like *Eleven Poems*, *At Heaven's Gate* in the end suggests that the modern world is grinding its way toward Fascism and the totalitarian state.

At Heaven's Gate uses many of the fundamental ideas undergirding the Agrarians' second manifesto, *Who Owns America?* which argued that finance capitalism's system of abstract wealth (stock certificates, bonds, etc.), as opposed to traditional society's system of property ownership (land, homes, etc.), reduced everything, including individuals, to units of abstract value and inevitably evolved into economic and political tyranny. The corporate empire, as Warren wrote elsewhere, represents "the desiccating abstraction of power,"[39] a point underscored by Duckfoot Blake's comment on the novel's chief powerbroker, Bogan Murdock: "Bogan Murdock is just a dream Bogan Murdock had, a great big wonderful dream."[40] Blake here suggests not only the insubstantiality of Murdock's financial empire (which is substanceless, merely the stuff of ink on paper) but also the illusory nature of his power: he is a dream into which people pour their own dreams. Murdock, indeed, is another of Warren's powerful leaders (similar to John Brown and Willie Strong) who owe much of their strength to the emptiness of their followers; or as Warren put it in an interview, "power—the man of power—flows into a vacuum: a vacuum in society, government, or individuals" and "fulfills the weaknesses of others."[41]

Indeed, almost all of the characters swirling around Murdock live primarily by self-deception, rewriting their pasts and reconfiguring their self-images as if they were managing financial accounts, using whatever accounting method they need to give them the total they want. The most accomplished of them adapt easily to changing circumstances, taking paths of least resistance and least responsibility and looking outside themselves, to groups and leaders, for meaning and purpose. "He swims in a lie, and he is in the lie and the lie is in him and if you could hook him and pull him out he'd hang there with his gills puffing and his eyes popping and not know what to make of it," Sweetwater says of Sarrett (393). These words apply to almost everyone in the book, including Sweetwater himself, all of whom care more about adapting themselves to beneficial situations than about living by principle and with responsibility.

At Heaven's Gate shows democracy in ruins, corrupted by the corporate state and its radical dehumanization of people; responsible citizens, necessary for democracy's success, have devolved into the irresponsible mob, easily controlled by powerful leaders. Duckfoot Blake's comment when he hears a lynch mob breaking the jail's windows points to how far democracy has fallen in the novel: "The classic instrument of the sovereign people," Duckfoot announced, "the half brick, the alley apple, the seed of democracy, the fruit of the popular will" (370–71). In destroying democracy with its tyrannical plutocracy, the corporate state of *At Heaven's Gate* implicitly looks forward to an even more terrifying political tyranny, with which America was then at war: the Fascist state.

After completing *At Heaven's Gate*, Warren in the spring of 1943 began revising *Proud Flesh*, deciding almost immediately to rewrite the play as a novel, which became *All the King's Men*.[42] "The idea wasn't entirely new," he wrote in the introduction to a later edition of the novel. "Now and then I had entertained the possibility of making a novel of the story. But now, all at once, a novel seemed the natural and demanding form for it, and for me."[43] Certainly the most significant change that Warren made in moving from drama to fiction was to narrate the novel through Jack Burden, a newspaperman who joins Willie Stark's organization (Willie Strong/Willie Talos becomes in the novel Willie Stark). Warren uses Jack to explore not only the dynamics of Willie's power but also the psychology of one of his followers. "The idea of an all-knowing author felt all wrong," Warren said in an interview; "no principle for dramatizing development, no internal dramatization of the 'vacuum.' . . . So I got my vacuum fellow, or, as it were, my partial vacuum fellow, into the story. But the real center of gravity in the novel is the dynamics of power. The newspaperman helps illustrate it."[44]

These dynamics of power center on the irony Warren exposed in *Proud Flesh:* that political ideals are often destroyed by the means by which they are instituted. Warren's visionaries, blinded by their idealism into acting without thought of wider consequences, in a sense remain perpetually "innocent," lacking, to return to Warren's gloss on "Terror," "that proper sense of the human lot, the sense of limitation and the sense of the necessity for responsible action within that limitation." In the novel, Jack navigates between two such visionaries, Adam Stanton and Willie Stark, who represent, he later comes to see, two poles of the fractured modern consciousness. "As a student of history," the narrator notes, "Jack Burden could see that Adam Stanton, whom he came to call the man of idea, and Willie Stark, whom he came to call the man of fact, were doomed to destroy each other, just as each was doomed to try to use the other and to yearn toward and try to become the other, because each was incomplete with the terrible division of their age" (*AKM* 436).

The man of idea, Stanton is a romantic idealist who believes in a perfect world of goodness and order from which modernity has fallen—and which everyone should now devote themselves to reconstructing. Adam's vision of things, as Jack notes, is so reductive that "when Adam the romantic makes a picture of the world in his head, it is just like the picture of the world Adam the scientist works with. All tidy. All neat. The molecule of good always behaves the same way. The molecule of bad always behaves the same way" (*AKM* 248). Moreover, Adam's reductiveness leads to intolerance if not violent cleansing; when the world does not conform to Stanton's system, Jack adds, "he wants to throw the world away. Even if that means throwing out the baby with the bath. Which . . . it always does mean" (*AKM* 247).

In contrast to Stanton, Willie, the man of fact, is a radical pragmatist. "Process as process is neither morally good nor morally bad," Jack characterizes Willie's central credo, which he uses to justify whatever means are necessary to achieve his ends. "We may judge results but not process. The morally bad agent may perform the deed which is good. The morally good agent may perform the deed which is bad" (*AKM* 393–94). Underlying Willie's thinking, Jack also points out, is a "theory of historical costs" (*AKM* 393) that abstracts the workings of social change into the double columns of an accountant's ledger: since all social change comes with costs, one merely writes the costs off against the gains.

The dangers to democracy of both extremes are clear: Adam takes the law into his own hands, attempting to cleanse the world of those staining it; and Willie manipulates the law to fulfill his dreams, his efforts so brazen that he in effect dismantles the legal system.[45] Read in the larger context of totalitarian politics, Willie and Stanton represent two apparently contradictory impulses that Fascism combines to cement its overwhelming appeal: the worship of an idealized past (and the excluding, if not the exterminating, of everyone who does not measure up) and the ruthless pragmatism that creates a thoroughly modern state, with the costs in terms of human life debited in the death camp's ledger.[46] Warren himself suggests this larger context in the two names that he gave Willie while working on the novel. In the original manuscript, Warren named his dictatorial governor Willie Talos, a reference to the mechanical man in book 5 of Spenser's

Faerie Queene, who does the violent bidding of the Knight of Justice—ideals of justice, in other words, delivered through death and destruction.[47] "I was thinking that people like Hitler or Huey Long are machines, executing the will of Justice," Warren later explained.[48] At his editor's suggestion, Warren dropped the name Talos and chose the German word for "strong," *Stark*, which was Willie's name in some of the working versions of *Proud Flesh*. "What better name for a dictator, in 1946, than a German one?" Noel Polk comments.[49]

Willie's stunning rise to power itself of course suggests the larger context of European Fascism and its threats to democracy, particularly in the contrast between what was popularly conceived as the efficiency of Fascism and the inefficiency of democracy and parliamentarianism.[50] Willie rules with a two-fisted approach that makes for efficient governance, a point that no one in the novel questions. Indeed, Jack stands behind Willie in part because he recognizes his effectiveness, particularly in light of all the ineffectiveness that has gone before. "Doesn't it all boil down to this?" he says at one point. "If the government of this state for quite a long time back had been doing anything for the folks in it, would Stark have been able to get out there with his bare hands and bust the boys? And would he be having to make up so many short cuts to get something done to make up for the time lost all these years in not getting something done?" (*AKM* 125). Even Judge Irwin, though fearful of Willie's extremism and opposed to it, recognizes his power to get things done: "I can respect a man, and he's a man. I was almost for him at one time. He was breaking the windowpanes out and letting in a little fresh air. But . . . I began to worry about him knocking down the house, too" (*AKM* 343).

If Jack recognizes Willie's effectiveness, he also knows firsthand Willie's merciless wielding of power. At the same time, despite doing Willie's bidding, he believes that he himself bears no responsibility for any of Willie's misdeeds or those of his regime. Indeed, Jack repeatedly distances himself from Willie's policies and practices, claiming that he has no influence with Willie and is merely an underling in the organization. "I'm not a politician, I'm a hired hand," Jack says at one point to his mother's husband, the Young Executive(*AKM* 113); and to Miss Dumonde he likewise denies that he works in politics, adding: "I've just got a job. . . . I'm an office boy" (*AKM* 123). To his mother he says that he makes it his business not to know anything about what Willie's henchmen do, adding that he is "very careful not to ever know what anybody anywhere does any time" (*AKM* 126). Even to

Willie, Jack characterizes himself as an insignificant cog in the machine, one who merely follows directives rather than making decisions. When Willie later asks Jack's advice on handling a political crisis, Jack responds, "Thinking is not my line" (*AKM* 138), but then goes on to advise Willie all the same. Even more significantly, Jack denies responsibility for anything he does while working for Willie, using a line of thinking—that he was merely following orders—that many of the Nazi defendants would soon use during the Nuremberg trials (and that soon became popularly known as the "Nuremberg Defense").[51]

That defense is only one of the many Jack uses in his more general attempt to shirk responsibility for his actions, at work or elsewhere. One of these defenses is what he calls "the Great Sleep" (*AKM* 189), in which he escapes besetting problems by plunging into monstrous periods of sleeping and staying in bed; another is his conception of "the Great Twitch" (*AKM* 314), a view of life that reduces all human activity to the workings of microbiology, characterized by Jack as "the dream that all life is but the dark heave of blood and the twitch of the nerve" (*AKM* 311). Both defenses strongly suggest issues relating to Nazi Germany. The Great Sleep calls to mind the image used by Churchill in *While England Slept* (1938) to describe the West's refusal to acknowledge the dangers of Nazi Germany, an image, attesting to its powerful resonance, that John F. Kennedy used slightly later in *Why England Slept* (1940). The Great Twitch, even more significantly, suggests the thinking used by Nazis to dehumanize Jews and others deemed misfits and enemies and finally to justify their extermination. Jack's configuring human beings as "unique agglomeration[s] of atomic energy" (*AKM* 331) with names—and names, he points out, "meant nothing," since in the world of the Great Twitch "all the words we speak meant nothing, and there was only the pulse in the blood and the twitch of the nerve, like a dead frog's leg in the experiment when the electric current goes through" (*AKM* 310)—ultimately leads to a clinical detachment in which all human activity, including suffering and killing, becomes merely a matter of scientific data. In hanging a man, Jack says, "you just change the length of his neck and give him a quizzical expression," adding that "in an electrocution you just cook some bouncing meat in a wholesale lot" (*AKM* 317). During his self-liberating trip to California, Jack at one point lies down and closes his eyes, seeing a vision of the world, as configured by the Great Twitch, that calls to mind the Nazi death camps: "I saw in the inward darkness as in mire the vast heave and contortion of numberless bodies, and limbs detached from bodies, sweating and perhaps bleeding from inexhaustible wounds" (*AKM* 310). Jack's response underscores the depths to which he has fallen: "But finally this spectacle, which I could summon up by the mere act of closing my eyes, seemed merely funny to me. So I laughed out loud" (*AKM* 310).

By novel's end Jack has come to see the error of his ways, accepting responsibility for his actions and shelving his shielding tactics. He has also, in relation to politics and democracy, come to understand that the liberating power of pragmatism must somehow be tempered by morality and responsibility. In his final stage of political development, Jack represents the mean between the two extremes of Adam and Willie, drawing something from both, not welding their positions together into the iron fist of Fascism, but balancing them in complicated, messy, and democratic interplay. It is this lesson of responsibility that lies at the heart of the Cass Mastern story, manifested most clearly in the famous passage describing Cass's knowledge "that the world is all of one piece. He learned that the world is like an enormous spider web and if you touch it, however lightly, at any point, the vibration ripples to the remotest perimeter" (*AKM* 188). Once seeing Cass's story as a stinging reproach to his own irresponsible life, Jack by the end of the novel turns to it as a guiding principle for his responsible pragmatism, seen so clearly when he lies to his mother about the circumstances of Judge Irwin's death—a lie not to protect him, but to protect her, made in a spirit of love for the mother he had once so vehemently condemned. Jack's decision to reconnect with Hugh Miller, furthermore, signals his moral reorientation, as Miller stands for the same type of pragmatism now endorsed by Jack, summed up in his response to Willie's methods: "History is blind, but man is not" (*AKM* 436).

All the King's Men concludes in the summer of 1939, with Jack and Anne about to leave Burden's Landing and the world about to erupt in war. Before departing, Jack warns his mother about traveling overseas: "You better stay out of Europe. . . . All hell is going to break loose over there and not long either" (*AKM* 430). Jack's warning points to his knowledge that a similar conflict has just been avoided in his home state and that his story is relevant to the events taking place in Europe. Indeed, that relevance is a fundamental point of the novel, a point James Justus underscores in his comment that the "confused moral principles working themselves out in a southern state in the 1930s, especially as they are registered on a tortured sensibility, have their louder political resonance in the ideological debates in Europe."[52] Justus notes further that behind the abstractions of Jack's famous declaration at the novel's close—to step "into the convulsions of the world, out of history into history and the awful responsibility of Time" (*AKM* 438)—"are those specific public convulsions that give resonance to and that perhaps are the literal referents of these abstractions: Spain, Poland, Czechoslovakia, France; the Channel War, Dresden, Belsen, Stalingrad. These public eruptions, varied as they were militarily, demonstrate a common fact, the inescapable entanglement of the moral and the political—which is also the inescapable lesson that Jack Burden learns. History is neutral, but man is not" (206). In no other work would Warren probe so deeply into the political and cultural confusion wrought by the threat of dictatorship; in no other work would the convulsions of Europe, though virtually absent from the text, be so profoundly present.

In his next novel, *World Enough and Time* (1950), much of which was written on a visit to Italy in 1948, Warren continued to explore a legal question called forth by Willie Stark's dictatorship when he manipulated the law to get the results he needed: how flexible should the law be when its principles seem inadequate to face the needs of society?[53] As he had in *Night Rider*, Warren used events from American history, specifically the financial panic of 1819, which plunged the country into a large-scale depression, to shed light on contemporary matters, most importantly the function of law under democracy. Issues surrounding World War II and the European political crisis permeate the novel, particularly those concerning the strengths and weaknesses of an embattled democracy. Emphasizing the interplay between past and present, the novel is told by a modern-day historian/editor who presents the autobiographical manuscript of Jeremiah Beaumont, a man deeply involved in the legal turmoil of 1820s Kentucky, and discusses the manuscript's relevance to contemporary affairs, including the conflict in Europe.

As revealed in his autobiography, Beaumont is caught in a turmoil similar to Jack Burden's, pulled between romantic idea and radical fact. Expressed in legal terms, these poles—designated as the Old Court and the New Court—underlie the fiercely contested political debates in which Beaumont, together with his Kentucky society, is embroiled:

> The Old Court said: The law exists, The Constitution exists. They exist by the sanction of Nature and Society. They are not Justice, for Justice is a spirit never seen, but only through them can Justice speak. Untune them and all is a jangle.

> The New Court said: The Law exists. The Constitution exists. But they exist only by the decision of man and what man can make he can unmake. As for Justice, that is the name for the needs of man. Justice is man's Goddess but is also his slave. Let man seize her naked and make her speak. (*WET* 313)

On a personal level, Jeremiah struggles with a similar conflict: should he follow an established moral authority, or should he continually make and unmake ideals according to changing circumstances? Jeremiah swings wildly between the two positions, eventually murdering a man in the name of justice, an act that ironically betrays, rather than validates, that ideal. The world to which he flees—the swampland empire of La Grand' Bosse, a Hobbesian world of filth, decay, and violence—underscores both the depths to which he has fallen and the depths to which society plunges when driven by radical pragmatism.[54] Eventually Jeremiah, like Jack Burden, accepts responsibility for his acts, deciding to return to face trial; he hopes to redeem himself by facing judgment, a decision that he sees balancing the two poles of existence that have torn his life apart. Jeremiah never reaches that redemption, however, for he is killed on his return journey, and his autobiography ends with his unresolved questions: "And in my crime and vainglory of self is there no worth lost? Oh, was I worth nothing, and my agony? Was all for naught?" (*WET* 512).

The narrator closes the novel by repeating Jeremiah's final words, "Was all for naught?" (*WET* 512), pointing not only to the narrator's own ambivalence regarding Jeremiah's story (he too swings in his commentary between positions of judgment) but also to the nation's ambivalence regarding the law, as seen in the disjunction between ideals and fact. Near the end of the novel, the narrator comments that despite America's firmly established legal system and its universal ideals of justice, justice has not been fully established in American society. In Kentucky, the narrator says, "*the Negro is emancipated and can vote and if he is smart he can even get paid for voting (just like white folks), and anyway he is free and can die of tuberculosis in a Louisville slum if he wants to and nobody will stop him (for it is his legal right and is damned near the only right the white folks will let him have)*" (*WET* 510), and he adds that "*in this fair land there is little enough justice yet, heart-justice or belly-justice*" (*WET* 511). The narrator's discussion here underscores that defining and enacting justice, however easy in theory, remains deeply problematic in practice, and he goes on to point out that while modern Americans easily pass judgment on the irrationalism of early Kentucky folkways, they do not recognize a similar irrationalism in their own world. Thinking about dueling in early Kentucky and the recent end of World War II, the narrator comments that "we may be like the dunces [who participate in duels]. We do not stand up at dawn, but we lie in a scooped-out hole in a tropical jungle and rot in the rain and wait for the steel pellet whipping through the fronds. We go down in the deep sea in a steel casket full of mechanisms like a watch, and wait for the shudder of the depth charge. At five thousand feet in the air we ride a snarling motor into the veil of flak. For Hecuba may be something to us, after all" (*WET* 128).

The narrator's observation brings us back to World War II, back to the European nightmare, back to the rise of totalitarianism, all of which haunt his imagination as he ponders the relevance of Jeremiah Beaumont's story to contemporary America. The political extremism that led to World War II, the narrator suggests, lies ultimately in the terrifying compulsions of the vengeful human heart, fittingly understood as versions writ large of Hecuba's exacting revenge for her youngest son's murder and of Jeremiah Beaumont's murderous life. Living entirely by idea or entirely by fact, entirely by idealism or entirely by pragmatism, blinds one to the human condition and ultimately leads to a dictatorial world in which all acts, even the most unjust and inhumane, can be easily justified.

World Enough and Time, and indeed almost all of Warren's work from the 1930s and 1940s, implicitly works from a political position that society should be structured like the well-made poem, not in a single voice but in many contending voices that ultimately affirm the complicated, multivalent nature of knowledge and existence. Such affirmation comes, as Warren wrote in an essay published a few years after *World Enough and Time*, when "out of a progressive understanding of this interpenetration, this texture of relations, man creates new perspectives, discovers new values—that is, a new self—and so the identity is continually emerging, an unfolding, a self-affirming and, we hope, a self-corrective creation."[55] That is how the self grows, and that is also how its mirror image, society, grows. Warren's description here echoes his many descriptions of the complexity of poetic experience, an echo that becomes even louder when he affirms, later in the essay, that poetry is knowledge and that knowledge of poetry is knowledge of form. This knowledge, however, as Warren immediately points out, is "the furthest thing possible from any doctrine that might go as sheer formalism" (191) and instead comes in an understanding of all the relations in a poem.

One gains this knowledge both by acting upon and by submitting to the poem, a fit description of the citizen's role in a democratic society. Warren goes on:

> When we ourselves must combat the force of some absurd or dangerous image of man—the image of man, say, that stood behind Nazism—we run the risk of assimilating the horror in the very act of wrestling with it. We run that risk because such an image, horrible though it may be, could not exist at all, or compel the imagination of millions, if it did not spring from, and satisfy, certain human needs, and give scope for certain human virtues. By our own similar needs and similar virtues we are vulnerable to the temptation of that image. As Coleridge says, all beliefs are true; at least, the fact of their existence proves that there is a kind of truth in them. To say this is not to condone a horror, but to realize its fullness in the fact that its energies of evil are a perversion of energies [sic] potential for good, that the will for destruction is but the will for creation swayed from its proper end. (188–89)

In Warren's mirrored understanding of poetry, self, and society the enemy of one becomes the enemy of the others, and to diminish one diminishes all three. For Warren, humanity must always be vigilant, ready not merely to take a stand against forces seeking this diminishment but also to come to terms with these forces, understanding their appeal and their threat:

> The form is a vision of experience, but of experience fulfilled and redeemed in knowledge, the ugly with the beautiful, the slayer with the slain, what was known as shape now known as time, what was known in time now known as shape, a new knowledge. It is not a thing detached from the world but a thing springing from the deep engagement of spirit with the world. This engagement may involve not only love for the world, but also fear and disgust, but the conquest, in form, of fear and disgust means such a sublimation that the world which once provoked the fear and disgust may now be totally loved in the fullness of contemplation. The form is the flowering of that deep engagement of spirit, the discovery of its rhythm. And the form is known, by creator or appreciator, only by experiencing it, by submitting to its characteristic rhythm. (191–92)

As Warren indicates here, Fascism, and more generally totalitarianism, is never far from his thinking about poetry, self, and society. Warren found in Fascism humanity's darkest enemy, the darkest inner reaches of the human heart made real. Almost all of Warren's writing from the mid-1930s to 1950 show him wrestling in one way or another with this dark enemy, though not with the patriotic clarity that many critics demanded. Straightforwardly instructive literature for Warren was not a defense against totalitarianism but the voice of totalitarianism, and the best way to silence that voice was to write contested, complex, and ironic literature whose very form embodied and affirmed intellectual freedom and democracy.

10

RAVAGERS OF THE EARTH

LILLIAN HELLMAN

During the 1930s and 1940s Lillian Hellman devoted herself to political work, vigorously supporting a host of left-wing causes. A 1939 article in the *New York World-Telegram* marveled at Hellman's activism, commenting that "instead of loafing in the country, she's been rushing to Washington to help the Union for Concerted Peace Action. She's been helping raise money for the Friends of the Lincoln Brigade and other groups aiding Loyalist refugees from Spain. She's been doing her job as vice president of the League of Women Shoppers, as a leader of The Screen Writers' Guild, as a member of the League of American Writers and a whole raft of other liberal groups."[1] Hellman was almost as stridently activist as an artist, with all of her work from the 1930s and 1940s, even that not obviously dealing with contemporary politics, driven and shaped by her fierce political vision, which by the late 1930s was militantly anti-Fascist. All of this work, moreover, interrogated an idea that was central to her anti-Fascism: the reluctance of soft-hearted liberals to take a stand against thieving, Machiavellian powerbrokers. Counterpoised against the Fascist enterprise, which she broadly characterized as an extension of capitalism and the corporate state, was the Communism of Soviet Russia, which in most ways stood as Hellman's guiding star, representing to her and many other intellectuals of the period a way of life that valued social equality and justice rather than profits. The contrasting ideals that she found in Fascism and Communism structure almost all of her drama and screenplays, both establishing their melodramatic character and underscoring their political urgency and significance.

RAVAGERS OF THE EARTH: LILLIAN HELLMAN

—x—x—x—x—

For someone so deeply involved in politics, Lillian Hellman never saw herself as a die-hard revolutionary. She was, as she herself acknowledged, too much the rebel, by which she meant that she was too independent to give herself over completely to one cause or one way of thinking. "It saddens me now to admit that my political convictions were never very radical, in the true, best, serious sense," she wrote in *An Unfinished Woman*. "Rebels seldom make good revolutionaries, perhaps because organized action, even union with other people, is not possible for them" (*UW* 118). Hellman's rebelliousness also compelled her to question not merely authority but just about everything else—a trait that led her father, in his irritation, to declare that she "lived within a question mark" (*UW* 119). No doubt the fact that most of her upbringing was split between New Orleans and New York City added to her sense of social awareness, the two very different milieus—and her identity within each—continually at play against each other. Her rebelliousness also apparently drew her to the kitchen, where she could talk with the black women who worked for her family, soaking up a perspective on her family's life quite different from what she heard otherwise.[2] "You got a hard road to go," Lillian recalled one of these women telling her. "Part what you born from is good, part a mess of shit" (*P* 85).

By age fourteen, according to Hellman, she was well on the way to fully recognizing the social injustice underlying the discrepancies between the rich and the poor, a recognition that further alienated her from her mother's family, the rich and powerful Newhouses of Louisiana. As Hellman herself put it, her adolescent anger was "a damaging combination" of repulsion from and attraction toward those with money. "I rebelled against my mother's family," she wrote, "and thus all people who were rich, but I was frightened and impressed by them; and the more frightened and impressed I grew the more aimless became my anger, which sometimes expressed itself in talk about the rights of Negroes and on two Sundays took the form of deliberately breaking plates at my grandmother's table. By fourteen my heart was with the poor except on the days when it was with those who ground them under" (*P* 63–64). As she grew older, she added, "I understood that I lived under an economic system of increasing impurity and injustice for which I, and all those like me, pay with ridiculous wounds to the spirit" (*P* 64).

By her own recollection, Hellman first became aware of the dangers of Fascism in 1929, during a trip to Germany that she took for respite from her foundering marriage to Arthur Kober. Not long after her arrival, she decided to stay for a year of study at the University of Bonn. While waiting for the term to begin, Hellman lived at a student boardinghouse, where she befriended a group of German students who were members of a youth group committed to a new German Socialism. Thinking that the students were voicing a leftist Socialism, Hellman found herself drawn to the group and its ideas.[3] It was only when she was asked to join the group, which entailed declaring that she was not a Jew, that Hellman understood her mistake. Scalded with shame and now painfully aware through her own experience of Nazism's seductive appeal, she immediately left Germany, henceforth a committed anti-Fascist. "Then for the first time in my life I thought about being a Jew," she later wrote. "But I was not only listening to anti-Semitism. I was hearing from people my own age the boasts of hopeful conquerors, the sounds of war" (*ST* 41–42). Hellman further noted that her time in Germany marked a decisive turn in her political education, with the aimless rebel discovering that her "rebelliousness was putting down a few young political roots" (*ST* 42).

Those roots took deeper hold after she became involved with Dashiell Hammett, whom she met in Hollywood in 1930. Forming an instantaneous bond, the two would remain deeply committed to each other, despite many very acrimonious times, until Hammett's death in 1961. By the time that they met, Hammett was already a wildly successful author, having published *Red Harvest* (1929), *The Dain Curse* (1929), and *The Maltese Falcon* (1930), and Hellman, an aspiring writer, quickly came under his sway. Almost immediately, Hammett began challenging Hellman to focus her thinking, as he was doing, on political developments in the world, particularly in Europe.[4] Hammett's maxim for political engagement, which he wrote to his daughter Mary (11 September 1936) and no doubt also told Hellman, entailed following one simple rule: "Be in favor of what's good for the workers and against what isn't. Follow that, and you may not be the most brilliant person in the world, but you'll at least be able to hold your head up when you look at yourself in the mirror."[5] In the late 1930s Hellman accompanied Hammett to meetings of a newly formed Communist Party USA cell in Hollywood, and she later became involved with a number of issues and causes backed by the party; she also became a strong supporter of Stalin and the Soviet Union.[6] Beginning in 1936 and extending into the 1940s, Hammett in his letters to

Hellman often lovingly and teasingly addressed her variously as "Lilushka," "Darlink," and most often "Lilishka."

Hellman's first play, *The Children's Hour* (1934), exhibited little of the leftist politics to which she had by this time gravitated, but it did focus on a concern that would become increasingly important to her in both her politics and her art: the moral cowardice of those who stand by and allow forces of evil to reign unchecked. Based loosely on a nineteenth-century trial in Edinburgh involving two teachers accused of lesbianism (Hellman read about the case, at Hammett's suggestion, in William Roughead's *Bad Companions*), *The Children's Hour* portrays the havoc wrought in a contemporary Massachusetts town by a rebellious girl's lie that two teachers at her girls' school were lovers. While most criticism of the play discusses the apparent gratuitous malice of Mary Tilford, the teachers' accuser, the play actually focuses more tellingly on the weak-kneed and easily duped characters who enable Mary to wield her power.[7] Mary, indeed, is less devil than misguided rebel, a point that Hellman herself made in the introduction to the 1942 edition of her collected plays, where she recalled drawing from her own childhood stratagems in creating Mary. Hellman's comments suggest a begrudging admiration of Mary's grit and spunk in manipulating the system, despite her vindictive motives. Carl Rollyson points out that in working notes for the play Hellman wrote approvingly of Mary's stand "against the completely accepting minds of the rest."[8]

It is at these accepting minds, most notably Mrs. Tilford and Dr. Cardin but also the accused teachers themselves, Karen Wright and Martha Dobie, that Hellman most takes aim. By refusing to act by their principles in the face of Mary's accusations and instead buckling under to the pressures of the status quo, these characters enable Mary to control events; and in this they resemble the wishy-washy liberals who in Hellman's later, more openly political plays empower manipulative politicians and powerbrokers, including Fascists. As Philip Armato observes, Karen and Martha's overriding concern that the school run smoothly opens the way for their own destruction, as they act less by principles of fairness, compassion, and loyalty than by narrow self-interest, seen most disturbingly in their rash punishment of Mary and their banishment of Martha's aunt, Lily Mortar.[9] Other characters act equally irresponsibly. Driven by concern for propriety, Mary's grandmother, Mrs. Tilford, immediately judges Karen and Martha guilty, without hearing them out and without looking beyond Mary's accusations. Even Dr. Cardin, the teachers' most ardent defender, admits in the final scene that he is not completely sure about their innocence; unable to put his faith completely in Karen, he remains doomed, as Carl Rollyson points out, "to half-believing in the lie" that he has publicly done everything to refute.[10] Finally, there is Martha herself, who reveals her true feelings for Karen only after it is too late; even then she cannot live by those feelings and chooses suicide to escape the judgment of Karen and, by extension, of the larger world. By the end of the play the Machiavellian Mary has revealed through her lie that those who profess principles rarely live by them and thus are themselves "liars"—and, furthermore, that people uncommitted to principles, along with the society of which they are a part, remain vulnerable to manipulation by those savvy enough to recognize their shortcomings.

Taking a stand on principle in the face of public and professional pressures (and often blackmail and deceit) would henceforth be central to Hellman both personally and artistically.[11] After the successful staging of *The Children's Hour* and her return to Hollywood in 1935, Hellman became involved in her first activist campaigns. Hired as a screenwriter by Samuel Goldwyn, she almost immediately began campaigning for passage of the Wagner Act, which guaranteed workers the right to organize and to participate in collective bargaining without retaliation; and she quickly became one of the most vocal supporters of the Screen Writers Guild in its bitter labor disputes with the studios. By early 1936, with two screenplays behind her, including an adaptation of *The Children's Hour* released as *These Three*, she began work on her second play, *Days to Come*, which centered on labor strife in a small Ohio town.

Days to Come reverses the situation in *The Children's Hour*. The play focuses on people, on both sides of the labor divide, who try to act with dignity and principle in a world that no longer operates by these values. Blind to the social and economic realities of the industrial economy, with its focus on the bottom line and nothing else, these characters become pawns to the powerful magnates who, from behind closed doors, ruthlessly operate the system. On one side of the divide is Andrew Rodman, a factory owner who, facing a strike after cutting wages, follows the advice of his pragmatic lawyer, Henry Ellicott, to hire a group of strikebreakers to keep his factory running. Remaining mired in a nostalgic illusion of workers and bosses living and working together as friends, Rodman has no idea that bringing in strikebreakers may lead to violent upheaval, and he is sure that once the workers return to their jobs his kind-hearted paternalism will restore harmony. Only after the strike's violent end do Rodman's eyes clear, although by then the damage has been done and there is nothing he can do to rectify the situation.

Equally blind, from the other side of the economic divide, is Tom Firth, a factory worker and longtime friend of Rodman's. Firth has joined the strike only because of duty to the union, and he has stood up for Rodman during the hard times and trusts his friend to resolve the labor issue fairly. When Leo Whalen, the hard-nosed union organizer, tells him to wise up, Firth fires back: "You and nobody is going to make me act blind. You and nobody is going to make me hate a man who's been my friend" (*SP* 92). But of course it is Firth who is blind; loyalty and friendship keep him from seeing that economic pressures and bottom-line concerns, rather than longtime personal commitments, are now behind Rodman's decisions (as formulated by Ellicott), as well as those of Rodman's creditors.

Firth recognizes the truth of Whalen's comments only after the strike's violent conclusion, which leaves Firth's daughter dead. Near the end of the play, with the strike broken, he voices both his resignation at the outcome and his recognition that the factory—and the town—are now operating by a new set of rules. "We'll go on back, make the best of it," he says, speaking of the factory workers. "And if the time comes again, we'll be different. We'll know.... We won't forget" (*SP* 136). When Firth adds that he blames Rodman for his child's death, Whalen gives him his final bit of advice, telling him that in the end Rodman had very little to do with anything that happened, since he was acting less as an individual than as a man enmeshed in the capitalist system, ultimately responsible to the market and creditors. "He's got to go his way, and you've got to go yours," Whalen tells Firth. "And they're not the same way.... You're on one side. He's on the other" (*SP* 136–37).

Whalen's commentary throughout *Days to Come* points to Hellman's own hard-nosed critique of people who did not face up to the new realities of the fast-changing world, a position that soon became central in her strident anti-Fascism. Hellman believed that comforting political illusions blinded people to the realities of the new world order, in which the twin goals of making money and maintaining power stood behind all relations, from those of the home to those of the marketplace—and beyond, to the realm of national and international politics. Not to recognize this was to fall victim to manipulation by the pragmatic and power hungry and, even more significantly, to open the door for any number of dangerous forces, including European Fascism, to rush in and take control.

While Hellman was writing *Days to Come*, the Spanish Civil War broke out, and for the next several years she devoted herself to political work supporting the Loyalists. In January 1937, along with Archibald MacLeish and Dorothy Parker, Hellman formed a foundation, Contemporary Historians, to raise money for Joris Ivens's documentary on the war, *The Spanish Earth*; shortly thereafter she began collaborating with MacLeish on the script and planning a trip to Spain with Ivens and the film crew. Before making that excursion, however, Hellman fell ill with pneumonia and pulled out of the project, but later that year she traveled to Europe on her own, first stopping in Paris and then traveling on to Moscow. At a time when the Moscow purge trials, which had been under way for more than a year, were shaking the faith of many Communist supporters outside Russia, Hellman remained steadfast in her support of Stalin, believing that attacks on the trials were mainly trumped-up anti-Soviet propaganda.[12] Cementing her loyalty to the Soviet government was its support of the Spanish Republicans, a position that stood in stark contrast to America's declaration of neutrality, which included a barring of arm sales, through an unusual interpretation of the Neutrality Act, to both the Republicans and the Nationalists.[13]

After Moscow, Hellman traveled to Spain, at the urging of Otto Simon, the director of Agence Espagne, the news service of the Republican government. She had met Simon during her stay in Paris, before she left for Moscow, and he had persuaded her to visit the country to see the war's devastation firsthand. "It didn't take much persuasion," Hellman later wrote: "I had strong convictions about the Spanish war, about Fascism-Nazism, strong enough to push just below the surface my fear of the danger of war" (*UW* 82). As indicated by her diary entries and her reportage, which focused primarily on the suffering of the civilians and the courage of the foreign volunteers supporting the Republicans, Hellman was deeply struck by her experiences.[14] She described such suffering in one of her sketches from her essay "Day in Spain," recalling waiting out a night of shelling in Madrid and discovering the destruction the next morning: shells had hit two hotels, a grocery store, the press office, and several houses in the poorest section of the city; eighty people were dead, including a blind woman who had received soup every night from a kitchen near Hellman's hotel.[15] "Not much sense to this kind of killing," Hellman reports an Englishman saying, his comments both a bitter indictment of the Fascists' shelling strategy and a grim foretelling of a larger war soon to come. "They don't even try for military objectives any more, or for men. When I was on the Franco side, a few months ago, I heard the German technicians call this 'the little war.' They're practising. They're testing, testing the guns. They're finding the accuracy of the guns, they're finding the range" (298). Hellman closes the sketch with her own scathing words on the Fascist enterprise: "Finding the range on a blind woman eating a bowl of soup is a fine job for a man" (298).

In another sketch from "Day in Spain," describing her trip to a base hospital at Benicasim, Hellman focuses on the bravery of those fighting the Fascists. At the hospital, she marvels at the courage and camaraderie of the foreign volunteers, at the same time feeling shame and guilt for her lack of bravery and resolve, being merely an observer to the war. Despite her distrust of inflated language, she is moved to describe the volunteers as heroic:

> Later that night, lying on a straw bed next to the wife of a Czech army officer, I thought that these foreigners from everywhere were noble people. I had never used the word noble before, and it came hard, even to say it to myself. They had come a long way to Spain, most of them making the cruel sixteen-hour walk across the Pyrenees. When it was over, if they came out alive, or with enough arms and legs to seem alive, there would be no glory and no reward. They had come because they thought that if a man believed in democracy he ought to do something about it. That's all they would go home with—wherever home was. Lying there, I prayed, for the first time in many years, that they would get what they wanted. (298)

Hellman's two other accounts of her experiences at Benicasim, a slightly revised version of the original sketch published in 1942 and her much later and fuller account in *An Unfinished Woman*, both comment upon her developing political commitment. In the 1942 version, Hellman suggests that her experiences at Benicasim, which she said made her feel "like being a child again," marked a rebirth, bringing her a new life with a new direction.[16] In the version in *An Unfinished Woman*, Hellman elaborates on the shame she suffers when, as someone not giving herself entirely to the war against Fascism, she hears the wife of the Czech army officer lash out at her countrymen who have resigned themselves to the Nazi takeover: "Liberal pigs," the officer's wife calls them, adding: "They will kill all the rest of us with their nothing-to-be-done-about-it stuff. They will save themselves when the time comes, the dirty pigs" (*UW* 91).

Fresh from her experiences at Benicasim, on her voyage back to the

United States Hellman began planning *The Little Foxes*, a play that signaled both her adoption of a more aggressively political stance (clearly spurred by her experiences in Spain) and her effort to reinterpret the world of her southern upbringing (the play is drawn loosely from Hellman's memories of her mother's family) in light of what she had learned in Spain. Although set in 1900, *The Little Foxes* bristles with cultural tensions similar to those Hellman found manifested in the Spanish Civil War and the advent of Fascism, particularly those arising from modern society's transformation into the industrial state. Although never fully visible, this transformation shadows the play, as in Addie's famous comment, "Well, there are people who eat the earth and eat all the people on it like in the Bible with the locusts. Then there are people who stand around and watch them eat it. Sometimes I think it ain't right to stand around and watch them do it" (*SP* 205). Placing the machinations of the Hubbard family in this broader context, Addie's comment suggests that the Hubbards' lust for power and wealth will soon be replayed on a grander scale by nations and rulers. For audiences in 1939, when the play opened, that grander scale—nations eating other nations while other nations idly look on—no doubt called to mind the contemporary turmoil in Europe.[17]

Addie's comment is prompted by the Hubbards' headlong pursuit of wealth, power, and dictatorial control of their community. As becomes clear early in the play, the Hubbards have made and consolidated their wealth by adapting speedily to changing economic times, all the while keeping their eyes on profit, the only value they value. In the social and economic chaos of the post–Civil War South the Hubbards thrived, while the once-wealthy plantation owners, who remained loyal to their agricultural traditions, were plunged into ruin, unable to cope in the new social and economic landscape. Now, at the turn of the century, the Hubbards are hoping to increase their fortune and bring more people under their financial control by building a cotton mill and creating a factory town. With their move into industry, as Ben says to Regina, the Hubbards will be participating in a process of historical change that will eventually lead them and others like them to control America. "The century's turning, the world is open," he says. "Open for people like you and me. Ready for us, waiting for us. After all, this is just the beginning. There are hundreds of Hubbards sitting in rooms like this throughout the country. All their names aren't Hubbard, but they are all Hubbards and they will own this country some day" (*SP* 222–23).

The Hubbards wield their power so effectively in part because they face so little resistance. As Addie reveals in a talk with Horace, Ben has already laid the groundwork for the town's transformation by an effective campaign of misinformation, telling people that the mill will bring wealth to everyone. When Horace expresses surprise that the townsfolk believe Ben's story, Addie makes it clear that Ben does not ask people to believe, he orders them to. "Believe it?" she says to Horace. "They use to believing what Mr. Ben orders. There ain't been so much talk around here since Sherman's army didn't come near" (*SP* 202). The only person with the means to mount any effective resistance is Horace, whose corporate bonds the family needs to finance the factory deal, but he is no match for the combined forces of the Hubbards. Before he dies, however, Horace delivers several stinging commentaries on the family's power plays. At one point, in response to Ben's glee that poor whites and blacks will willingly work for remarkably low wages, Horace bitterly comments that they will end up accepting even less when Ben gets around "to playing them off against each other. You can save a little money that way, Ben. And make them hate each other just a little more than they do now" (*SP* 192). And at another point, Horace angrily asks Regina why he should give his money to the family. "To pound the bones of this town to make dividends for you to spend?" he says. "You wreck the town, you and your brother, *you* wreck the town and live on it" (*SP* 199).

Horace's attacks in the end pose little threat to the Hubbards' empire; in fact, the serious conflicts facing the Hubbards in their drive for power involve not those opposing them but themselves, as each jockeys for greater control of the family enterprise. Put another way, the play's conflicts boil down to, in William Wright's words, "evil versus evil, and evil triumphs, with the decent characters merely impotent onlookers."[18] Evil may stand triumphant, but in the end one person does stand forthrightly against the Hubbards—Alexandra, who vows to fight to cleanse the world of people like them. Clearly a manifestation of Hellman's rejuvenated political self after her experiences in Spain, Alexandra understands the threat the Hubbards pose, an understanding she has reached largely through guidance by Addie, Horace, and Birdie. Horace has helped her by deliberately not shielding her from the family's deliberations and internal fights, wanting her to see the family in all its ugliness. At one point he tells Addie, who is sorry that Alexandra has heard some disturbing things about the family, that it was better that she was listening:

> So you didn't want Zan to hear? It would be nice to let her stay innocent, like Birdie at her age. Let her listen now. Let her see everything. How else is she going to know that she's got to get away? I'm trying to show her that. I'm trying, but I've only got a little time left. She can even hate me when I'm dead, if she'll only learn to hate and fear this. (*SP* 207)

Birdie's influence is more direct: near the end of the play she warns Alexandra that if she does not escape from the family, she will be ground down psychologically just as Birdie herself has been, so that "in twenty years you'll just be like me. They'll do all the same things to you. . . . And you'll trail after them, just like me, hoping they won't be so mean that day or say something to make you feel so bad" (*SP* 206). Listening to Birdie, Alexandra sees that that process has already begun. "I guess we were all trying to make a happy day," she says. "You know, we sit around and try to pretend nothing's happened. We try to pretend we are not here. We make believe we are just by ourselves, some place else, and it doesn't seem to work" (*SP* 206).

Alexandra's words here echo Hellman's belief, which her time in Spain had only confirmed, that contemporary liberals ignored the Fascist threat, pretending that it did not exist. Likewise, Alexandra's declaration at the end of the play, that she will leave and fight to prevent the type of world the family represents, echoes both the commitment Hellman found in the international volunteers in Spain and her own resolve to live by a similar commitment. When Regina says that she is not going to make Alexandra stay with the family, Alexandra responds:

> You couldn't, Mama, because I want to leave here. As I've never wanted anything in my life before. Because now I understand what Papa was trying to tell me. All in one day: Addie said there were people who ate the earth and other people who stood around and watched them do it. And just now Uncle Ben said the same thing. Really, he said the same thing. Well, tell him for me, Mama, I'm not going to stand around and watch you do it. Tell him I'll be fighting as hard as he'll be fighting some place where people don't just stand around and watch. (*SP* 225)

Alexandra vows to rid the earth of the "little foxes," the predators despoiling the land, the financiers and magnates ravaging the world.[19]

At the same time that *The Little Foxes* was making its successful run,

Hellman was deeply involved in supporting the Spanish Republicans and various anti-Fascist organizations. She remained a staunch supporter of Stalin and the Soviet Union even after Stalin and Hitler agreed to their non-aggression pact in August 1939 and the Soviet Union invaded Finland that November. The invasion of Finland generated a particularly nasty controversy for Hellman. Not long after the invasion, several of the cast members from *The Little Foxes*, including Talullah Bankhead (who was playing Regina), suggested a benefit performance to support Finland, only to have their request denied by Hellman and the play's director, Herman Shumlin. Bankhead was furious at the rejection, and Hellman was furious at the request, and the two fought bitterly and publicly. Maintaining her solidarity with Stalin, Hellman claimed that the Soviet invasion was justified and suggested that Finland was pro-Nazi. In one of her comments, she said that in a visit to Helsinki in 1937 (a visit she almost certainly never made) she had been stunned by the country's pro-Nazi sentiments: "I don't believe in that fine, lovable little Republic of Finland that everyone gets so weepy about. I've been there and it looks like a pro-Nazi little Republic to me."[20] She also suggested that supporting Finland would inflame warmongering; she told the *New York Times* that "theatrical benefits for Finnish relief would give a dangerous impetus to war spirit in this country."[21]

Despite publicly supporting the Stalin-Hitler nonaggression pact, Hellman maintained her passionate anti-Fascist beliefs. As William Wright observes, however much Hellman was enthralled with Soviet Communism, she hated German Fascism even more, a point underscored by the fact that in 1940 she began work on her anti-Fascist play *Watch on the Rhine* and publicly voiced fears of domestic Fascism.[22] In a January address to the American Booksellers Association she said that the increasingly stultifying climate of censorship and propaganda suggested that a homegrown Fascism might be emerging. "Unless we are very careful and very smart and very protective of our liberties," she said, "a writer will be taking his chances if he tells the truth, for as the lights dim over Europe, they seem to flicker a little here too."[23] With an obvious nod to the Nazis' persecution of the Jews, she commented on her own fears of similar persecution:

> I am a writer and I am also a Jew. I want to be quite sure that I can continue to be a writer and that if I want to say that greed is bad or persecution is worse, I can do so without being branded by the malice of people who make a living by that malice. I also want to be able

to go on saying that I am a Jew without being afraid of being called names or end[ing up] in a prison camp or be[ing] forbidden to walk down the street at night.[24]

Later in the year, in an article for *PM* covering the Republican National Convention in Philadelphia, Hellman similarly suggested that domestic Fascism might be brewing, as she saw an increasingly repressive political system stomping upon Americans' civil liberties. She wrote that in the convention hall political stooges were cutting deals among themselves, while outside the working people toiled, silenced not only in the political process but in simply expressing their beliefs, since people were now fearful that talking too much might get them in trouble. She concluded that "uptown the party of Abraham Lincoln is making deals in a city in which at least three white men and two black men are too suspicious and too tired and too frightened to exercise their primary right of free and easy speech. And I thought that Lincoln might not like that."[25]

During the time that she was commenting on America's drift toward authoritarianism, Hellman was working on *Watch on the Rhine*, which focused on the easygoing isolationism of liberal Americans who believed that Fascism was merely a European problem, not to be worried over and certainly not something to go to war over. In an interview at the play's opening, Hellman identified the central tension of the play as the contrast between "two ways of life—ours with its unawakened innocence and Europe's with its tragic necessities."[26] Into the innocent world of the Farrellys, a well-to-do family who live just outside the nation's capitol, come two Europeans, one a Fascist and one an anti-Fascist. Their squabbles and conflicts bring the Farrellys face to face with the conflict in Europe, making them finally see that it is necessary for Americans, if they really do believe in freedom, to commit themselves to the war against Fascism. "The political challenge does not ring with strident battle alarums, drums, uniforms, and party salutes, yet the terrifying face of Fascism hangs like a gargoyle over the Farrelly household," Richard Moody observes. "No longer can the Atlantic and Potomac shield us from the Nazi menace."[27]

The face of Fascism, or at least the face of a man who wants to be a Fascist, is Count Teck De Brancovis. Teck is a refugee from Romania (a country beset with a particularly virulent form of anti-Semitic Fascism)[28] who apparently years before had gotten into serious financial trouble after misjudging the political position of the German steel magnate Fritz Thyssen, who early on provided Hitler with crucial financial backing and whose company eventually became the backbone of the Nazi war machine. While never identifying himself as a Fascist, Teck nonetheless represents the type of person who Hellman believed embodied Fascism: a wiley, self-interested person who was willing to do anything, including betraying others, to advance himself and his power. Teck, in other words, is an up-to-date version of the Hubbards from *The Little Foxes*, and like them, he is constantly concerned with striking deals, making money, and collecting information for bribery and blackmail.[29] "What is my business?" Teck says at one point, responding to his wife's discomfort with his incessant probing into the past of the anti-Fascist Kurt Müller. "Anything might be my business now" (*SP* 256). That business, once he has collected the information he needs, is blackmail. He threatens to reveal Kurt's identity to the Nazis unless Kurt pays him ten thousand dollars from the money Kurt has raised to help buy the freedom of imprisoned anti-Fascists. "Now," he says to Kurt, as he lays out his terms. "Let us do business" (*SP* 288). Teck's offer does not surprise Kurt, who knows full well how Fascists operate, and in the end Kurt murders Teck, not because he would not stoop to paying off a Fascist if it were politically expedient, but because he knows that Teck almost certainly will betray him to the Nazis even if he is paid off.

In contrast to Teck, Kurt cares nothing about money, except for its use in the fight against Fascism. As we learn early in the play, Kurt has given up a successful career as an engineer to work in the resistance, a job, he notes at one point, with some irony, "that does not pay well" (*SP* 251). His work entails both danger and hardship, not only for himself but also for his family (Kurt is married to the Farrellys' daughter, Sarah), but as he makes clear, he had no choice but to give himself to the cause, and he has no regrets. He says that when he saw the Nazis kill twenty-seven people in a street riot in 1931, he knew that he, like Martin Luther, had to take his stand: "I cannot stay by now and watch. My time has come to move. I say with Luther, 'Here I stand. I can do nothing else. God help me. Amen'" (*SP* 253). Kurt's stand against the Nazis has nothing to do with personal gain and everything to do with making the world a better place. Near the end of the play, after killing Teck, Kurt explains to his children that he and others like him must at times do bad things in order to help make things better. Those working against the evils of Fascism, he tells them, "want what I want: a childhood for every child. For my children, and I for theirs. Think of that. It will make you happy. In every town and every village and every mud hut in the world, there is always a man who loves children and who will fight to make a good world for them" (*SP* 299).

The conflict between Teck and Kurt shakes the Farrellys out of their liberal complacency. They now see, as Bosley Crowther observed in a 1943 review of the film version of the play, "that the fundamental clash in civilization is between those bent on self-aggrandizement and those who are not and that 'it doesn't pay in money to fight for that in which we believe.'"[30] Kurt's repeated deflations of the stature of the Nazis, describing them as little men, help guide the Farrellys toward this understanding. "What a magnificent work Fascists have done in convincing the world that they are men from legends," Kurt says at one point, adding that it is only because the Nazis "came in on the shoulders of the most powerful men of the world," industrialists such as Fritz Thyssen, that they seem to be "men from the planets" (*SP* 282). However, the Nazis are not superheroes, Kurt assures the Farrellys, but merely everyday people who became Fascists for the everyday reasons of self-interest and greed. Thus, Fascist society merely replicates the capitalist society from which it sprang:

> There are those who give the orders, those who carry out the orders, those who watch the orders being carried out. Then there are those who are half in, half hoping to come in. They are made to do the dishes and clean the boots. Frequently they come in high places and wish now only to survive. They come late: some because they did not jump in time, some because they were stupid, some because they were shocked at the crudity of the *German* evil, and preferred their own evils, and some because they were fastidious men. For those last, we may well some day have pity. They are lost men, their spoils are small, their day is gone. (*SP* 288)

Kurt adds that German successes on the battlefield have come, not because Nazi soldiers possess superhuman power, but because an efficient industrial system, with corporate magnates working hand in hand with Hitler, undergirds the Nazi war machine.

"We are all Anti-Fascists," Fanny says early in the play, after hearing Kurt talk about leaving his engineering job to join the anti-Fascist resistance. "Yes," Sarah replies. "But Kurt works at it" (*SP* 251). What Sarah knows is what Fanny and her son David only much later come to understand: that it is not enough, in terms of fighting Fascism, merely to declare oneself an anti-Fascist while living in comfort and security; to be an anti-Fascist means actively fighting against Fascism, often with terrible sacrifice. By not immediately calling the police after Teck's murder, giving Kurt the two days he needs to make his escape, Sarah and David make that commitment, becoming complicit in Kurt's act. Both now see that the stand against Fascism is a stand for human dignity. As she affirms her choice to help Kurt, Fanny mentions something her husband told her not long before his death, that "the Renaissance American is dying" (SP 297). She recalls her husband's words:

> "A Renaissance man," he said, "is a man who wants to know. He wants to know how fast a bird will fly, how thick is the crust of the earth, what made Iago evil, how to plow a field. He knows there is no dignity to a mountain, if there is no dignity to man. You can't put that in a man, but when it's *really* there, and he will fight for it, put your trust in him." (SP 297)

Fanny now sees, as does David, that Kurt is precisely this Renaissance man, one to be both trusted and emulated. Fanny and David see, furthermore, that Fascism is life-destroying and anticivilizational, representing the death of all that the Renaissance man affirms. The Fascist is the man who, like Teck, is committed to nothing but his own advancement, little more than a man on the make. Teck, Fanny observes in disgust, summarizing Hellman's own view of the Fascist, is "the picture of a man selling the lives of other men" (SP 289).

Once America entered the war, Hellman became involved in a number of home-front activities, including efforts to drum up popular support for the Soviet Union's efforts in the Allied cause.[31] In 1942, apparently in response to a suggestion from the Roosevelt administration to Samuel Goldwyn, she and the director William Wyler began exploring the possibilities of making a documentary film on the war in Russia.[32] Although she and Wyler gained the support of the Soviet government after making their case for the project at the embassy in Washington, the plans fell through after Wyler enlisted in the armed forces and Hellman decided she did not want to go forward with a different director. She did agree, however, to write the screenplay for a feature film, *The North Star,* about Soviet peasants warring with the Nazis, to be directed by Lewis Milestone. In all likelihood, Hellman found Milestone acceptable not only because he was a seasoned director of war films (best known for his direction of *All Quiet on the Western Front*) but also because the film Milestone was then completing, *Edge of Darkness*, centered on the Nazi occupation of a Norwegian village and thus dovetailed nicely with her plans for *The North Star*, which focused on the Nazi occupation of a Soviet farming collective.

Hellman's collaboration with Milestone, however, was short-lived. After reading Hellman's script and making wholesale revisions, Milestone sent her a fifty-page document suggesting further changes. Hellman was floored, and after her unsuccessful appeal to Goldwyn she angrily quit the project. It is not hard to understand Hellman's frustration. Although Milestone stuck with Hellman's broad plot outline and the script's harsh depiction of the Nazis, he thoroughly redid her realistic presentation of the farming collective, turning much of the first part of the film into a musical, with villagers repeatedly breaking into highly choreographed song and dance (with music by Aaron Copland and lyrics by Ira Gershwin). Hellman called this part of the film an "extended opera bouffe peopled not by peasants, real and alive, but by musical comedy characters without a thought or care in the world."[33] Years later, Richard Moody wrote that the film's villagers (whose cast included, among others, Anne Baxter, Dana Andrews, Ann Harding, Dean Jagger, Walter Brennan, and Farley Granger) pranced about "as if they were strays from *Oklahoma*."[34] No doubt to distance herself from the film, Hellman published the master script she had originally submitted to Milestone (she had paid $30,000 to buy herself out of the contract with Goldwyn and to retain rights for her work), and it appeared the same month as the film's premiere, November 1943.

Aside from the brutality of the invasion itself, Hellman's script focuses its attacks on the Nazis on events at the Nazis' field hospital. Most damning is the Nazi doctors' bleeding children to death to increase the army's blood supply. Early in the script, before the Nazi invasion of Russia has begun, a Soviet radio newscast announces this medical practice, reporting that in Warsaw 112 children have died from forced transfusions. When, later in the play, the invading Germans overrun the farming collective, they immediately establish a base hospital and round up children to begin taking blood. In depicting the Nazis as vampirish child-killers, Hellman makes graphically real what in *Watch on the Rhine* she had only metaphorically suggested in Kurt's declaration that anti-Fascism was the guardian of posterity. In another echo to *Watch on the Rhine*, the forced transfusions make real the song Kurt recalls German anti-Fascists singing during the Spanish Civil War:

> This time we fight for people.
> This time the bastards will keep their hands away.
> Those who sell the blood of other men, this time,
> They keep their hands away.
> (*SP* 269)

The Nazis in *The North Star*, in fact, go one step further than the bastards of the song: they do not sell blood, they steal it.

Hellman's script centers on the two doctors who perform the bloodletting. One doctor, Richter, is a die-hard Nazi totally given to the cause, repeatedly voicing the Nazi party line in all situations. The other, Von Harden, is entirely cynical about the Nazis and their dreams of conquest, repeatedly mocking Richter's loyalties while at the same time performing Nazi dirty work. Von Harden is another of Hellman's dastardly liberals, aware of social injustice but doing nothing to oppose it. Worse, he has himself become an agent of Fascism, even as he mocks the Nazi enterprise. All this is clear to the Soviet doctor Kurin, who before murdering both German doctors denounces Von Harden as the more foul and dangerous. Speaking first of Richter and then of Von Harden, Kurin says:

> That, that kind, is nothing. They will go when their bosses go. But men like you who have contempt for men like him, to me *you* are the real filth. Men who do the work of the Fascists and pretend to themselves they are better than those for whom they work. Men who do murder while they laugh at those who order them to do it. It is men like you who sold your people to men like him.[35]

In his willingness to trade the life of others for his own self-preservation, Von Harden closely resembles Teck from *Watch on the Rhine*, though with a difference: Teck blackmails others, but Von Harden blackmails himself.

Hellman's attacks on Fascism, together with the liberals whose weakness she believed helped make it possible, continued with her most straightforwardly political play, *The Searching Wind*, which premiered in 1944. Using flashbacks to highlight crucial moments in the histories both of the characters and of Fascism, the play suggests that the personal and the political are all of the same piece, with choices made (or not made) in love and life mirroring those made in affairs of state. While all of Hellman's works in varying ways suggest this connection, *The Searching Wind* explicitly draws parallels between an American diplomat's relationships with his former lover and his wife and the Fascist takeover of Europe. Carl Rollyson astutely observes that *The Searching Wind* "reflects Hellman's restless quest to chart history, to put it on a human scale, to make it amenable to judgment, to *personalize* it."[36] But actually *The Searching Wind* goes even further, showing that history is always personalized, always driven forward by the choices and actions of individuals, even when large historical forces seem to be holding sway. One of *The Searching Wind*'s original cast members, Eugene Earl (Earl Fleischman), commented on the historical perspective underlying the play:

> [Hellman] is relentless and unmerciful in driving home her point that individuals "messy" in their private lives, when multiplied by millions, make a "messy" world—a world so weakened by moral slack, so undermined by blind selfishness and careless disregard for consequences, that it is easy prey to the Hitlers, Mussolinis, and Tojos. To Miss Hellman there is a fundamental bond between the moral verities which hold between individuals in their personal lives and those which govern the relations between nations.[37]

Like much of Hellman's work, *The Searching Wind* focuses less on acts performed than on acts *not* performed, with characters refusing to affirm their beliefs in situations demanding that affirmation. As we see through the flashbacks, Alex Hazen repeatedly downplays both the rising tide of Fascism and the complicated conflicts involved in his ongoing relationship with his ex-lover Cassie. He is skilled in diplomacy, as a lover and as a politician, avoiding confrontation by compromising his beliefs and by always seeking out appeasement. Sounding a good bit like Dr. Von Harden in *The North Star*, Alex complains about positions he must defend but defends them anyway; in the flashback to Rome in 1922, as Mussolini is marching to power, Alex tells his future father-in-law, Moses Taney, that the United States must remain impartial so as not to endanger relations with Italy. "I don't like this, and I don't like your thinking I do," he tells Moses. "But another few months of the kind of misery and starvation they've had, and there would have been a revolution. If Mussolini can put it down that doesn't make me like him, or the money behind him, or the people. But somebody had to do it, and you don't pick gentlemen to do the job" (*SW* 41). Alex similarly protects American interests rather than his American ideals in 1923 Berlin. He opposes Nazi Party street violence, not because (as Cassie argues) the uprising against Jewish shop owners is shameful and frightening, but because Americans in Berlin might get caught in the fighting. Later, in Paris in 1938 (on the eve of the Munich Agreement, which ceded the Sudetenland to the Nazis), Alex meets with a German diplomat, Count Von Stammer, who diligently presents the Nazi demands and then reveals that he is another liberal appeaser, a Nazi counterpart to Alex. "I speak this afternoon as if I thought it is wise to be on the side of my country," Von Stammer tells Alex. "But I do not always think that. And I do not much care. In two months I buy a house in Switzerland" (*SW* 75). Not long after Von Stammer leaves, Alex writes his analysis of the imminent Munich summit, criticizing those who view it as a capitulation to Hitler even though he believes that Hitler will soon be making more demands and that Germany will soon be at war with Russia. When Moses secretly reads his report, his damning judgment no doubt voices Hellman's: "Difficult world, eh Alex? So many men doing so many strange things. All we can do is compromise. Compromise and compromise. There's nothing like a good compromise to cost a few million men their lives" (*SW* 86).

All the while that he embraces appeasement in foreign policy, Alex works desperately to appease his wife and his lover. Through finagling and deception Alex keeps both women in his life, committing himself fully to neither. Ironically, both Emily and Cassie recognize Alex's machinations; it is only because both have also compromised themselves, choosing to remain in an unfulfilling relationship with him rather than demanding that he choose between them, that domestic balance is preserved. Both women, furthermore, in spite (or perhaps because) of their own self-compromises, criticize Alex for his: Cassie repeatedly chides him for failing to be a more forceful and upright diplomat, and Emily rebukes him for blithely living on her family's wealth while deliberately remaining ignorant of its origins, including investments in banks doing business with Axis countries. At one point Emily confronts him:

> I don't mean to influence you with my money. I have it, I'm glad I have it, and it's never meant much to me. But I'm not willing to lie to myself about money, or where and how I was born, or the world I've lived in. But sometimes I think you pretend to yourself that you have no world that influences you—that you have no connections and no prejudices. Why don't you try to see that they all have something to do with you? Maybe it isn't all on the basis of honor. (*SW* 81)

Neither Cassie's nor Emily's jabbings bring Alex out from his comfortable psychological cocoon; as his family name suggests, he would rather be hazy and live in haze. Haziness also marks his writing, a point Moses drives home when he helps Sam, Alex and Emily's son, cut through the smokescreen of his father's prose by summarizing one of his reports: "In three thousand words of diplomatic double talk it says that sometimes democracies have to deal with people they don't approve and sometimes, in order to save something or other, you have to do something else or other" (*SW* 8).

To the end, Alex sticks to self-deception and noncommitment, though he may be taking a small step toward clarity after the stinging rebuke from Sam that closes the play. Wounded in Italy and now home to recuperate, Sam tells his parents that while at the front he read a newspaper column about a dinner party attended by his mother and a number of Europe's rich and famous. At first proud and hopeful, thinking that the people at the party were Europe's finest and would rebuild the Continent once the war was over, he received a political awakening from his friend Leck:

> "Sam, that banker the piece talked about, he used to deal with the Germans before it got too hot. He's a no good guy. And the rest of those people, they're all old tripe who just live in our country now and pretend they are on the right side. When the trouble came in their countries they sold out their people and beat it quick, and now they make believe they're all for everything good. My God, Sam," he said, "if you come from that you better get away from it fast, because they helped to get us where we are." (*SW* 95)

Leck's comments haunted and shamed Sam, but not until later, when he listens to his parents talk, does he fully understands his feelings. He now sees that Leck was right: his parents are indeed like those with whom they associate, and whatever their patriotic rhetoric, they have failed to stand up for the nation's ideals and thus are part of the wide-scale appeasement that has brought the world to war. After asserting his love for America, Sam says to his parents: "And I don't want any more fancy fooling around with it. I don't want any more of Father's mistakes, for any reason, good or bad, or yours, Mother, for I think they do it harm. . . . I am ashamed of both of you, and that's the truth. I don't want to be ashamed that way again" (*SW* 96). While it is not clear how Alex and Emily will ultimately respond to Sam's challenge, it is clear that Sam is showing them the way to emerge from their rationalizations and deceptions. "It takes a searching wind to find the tree you sit in," one of the black women who worked for Hellman once said (*UW* 232), and indeed that is the point Hellman drives home here: it takes a searching challenge to one's beliefs to discover what one really believes.

Several months after *The Searching Wind* opened in April 1944, Hellman departed for Moscow, apparently with the approval of the Roosevelt administration, which at the time was supporting goodwill "cultural missions" to the Soviet Union.[38] Her arduous fourteen-day trip across the country (she entered Russia from Alaska and then suffered through a grueling series of flights in an unheated C-47, falling ill with pneumonia along the way), together with the grim conditions in Moscow, did little to dampen her enthusiastic support for the Soviets and Stalin.[39] Upon returning to the United States in early 1945, Hellman immediately held a press conference highlighting her trip[40] and jumped right back into the political fray. In the coming months, Hellman lashed out at the evils of Fascism and excoriated critics of the Soviet Union. As she looked forward to the postwar world, she feared that growing anti-Soviet sentiment in the United States would undermine international peace. Her fears increased when, after Roosevelt's death on 12 April 1945, Truman's hard-line stance against Communism became clear. The call announcing the First Conference on American-Soviet Cultural Cooperation in November 1945, a conference in which she participated, summed up her postwar views regarding foreign policy: "The future of all of us depends to a very large extent upon whether or not there can be successful cooperation and understanding between the United States and the Soviet Union."[41]

Ever the supporter of what she saw as the Soviet Union's moral and humanitarian aims, Hellman probably agreed with the postwar assessment of John Melby, an American diplomat whom she had met in Moscow in 1944 and with whom she was deeply involved romantically for a number of years. A week after the German surrender, Melby wrote Hellman (14 May 1945) about what he saw as the loss of American vision following Roosevelt's death and the growing anti-Soviet sentiments within government high circles:

> Very badly the moral genius and personality of Roosevelt are missed. And for lack of them in the direction, the feeling of a cause, the crusading spirit which has always been so completely American are [*sic*] not to be found and the little men push special interests and quibble over words. Coincidentally the moral leadership is drifting by default into Russian hands. It is precisely what has happened in so many

countries in Europe. We have gone in, destroyed the existing forms, and offered nothing in their place claiming to leave that to the local populace. Inevitably the Russians are sucked into the resultant vacuum. Of course we are hurt and bewildered and see the wily hand of the devil at work. The conspiratorial theory becomes an obsession. And it never occurs to anyone to look at our own hands and ask the obvious question. So, here we are merrily betraying almost every ideal we are supposed to believe in. It is a strange, depressing, frightening spectacle.[42]

Two months earlier, Melby had written Hellman (15 March 1945) suggesting what she too already feared: that there were powerful forces of Fascism at work in the United States. For Melby, as for Hellman, Fascism was integrally bound up with the fundamental values of capitalist enterprise, which elevated property over individuals:

It is possible to get awfully fed-up with endless hoopla in the Russian press about the need to cleanse this and that of fascism. It is of course fashionable to say that it is the cover plan for ulterior and dastardly plans. The fact of course is that the Russians understand the nature, the sources, the methods, and the objectives of fascism infinitely better than we do. Nor does a Marxist make the mistake of identifying it solely with German Nazis. He can see it potentially in any individual, group of individuals, or society, and I think correctly, which has as its primary objective the sanctity of property or the glorification of the physical State (which is after all just another form of property). Property, rather than labor or human life, is the criterion used. And this becomes all entangled and covered up with the hoary shibboleths of free enterprise etc. etc. . . . The weakness in our system—which did not become particularly pertinent until we reached the limit of our physical expansive power—was and IS that the vested interests in property, whether it be great wealth or merely a supposed security in a clerical job, in [their] insecurity comes to place property above the values of personality. This influence is opposed to and at least unconsciously tends to undermine and eventually to destroy the true sources of our strength. . . . Fascism, then, I would define as the corruption of things. And the problem: Can an individual once corrupted by things be made honest again?[43]

Melby's concluding question points precisely to Hellman's portrayal of the Hubbards in *The Little Foxes*, a powerful family whose loyalties and values are pegged entirely to their pursuit of wealth; the Hubbards trample on anyone who gets in their way, including family members. They may not be Fascists (yet), but their transformation of values represents the weakening of American democracy and the potential for American Fascism.

Given her perspective on the postwar world, it is not surprising that Hellman returned to the Hubbards in her next play, *Another Part of the Forest* (1946), a prequel to *The Little Foxes* set in 1880 and portraying the sordid origins of the Hubbard family's wealth and power. While at first glance *Another Part of the Forest* seems to have little to do with post–World War II politics, Carl Rollyson points out that both the play and Hellman's contemporary political concerns focus broadly on the same issue: the shifting balance of power in a postwar world in which social, economic, and political paradigms have been disrupted.[44] More specific commentary on the contemporary political situation emerges, furthermore, when one reads the Hubbards as representative American capitalists, their drive for power and wealth a version writ small of the forces driving contemporary American enterprise and commerce—and foreign policy.

Although *Another Part of the Forest* everywhere portrays the Hubbards acting corruptly, Marcus's trading with the enemy during the Civil War most typifies—and condemns—their business practices. Rather than fighting in the war (which of course would entail loyalty outside of individual gain), Marcus profits from it, running the Yankee blockade to procure much-needed salt for reselling to his community. Altruism has nothing to do with Marcus's venture; it is all business, and a lucrative one: he charges his neighbors exorbitant prices, which they have no alternative but to pay. But as becomes clear, they do not forget his dealings, even after many years have passed. Lavinia at one point comments that early in the war, before she knew any better, she thought Marcus's actions were heroic, even though he was dealing with the enemy. "People were dying for salt and I thought it was good to bring it to them," she says, adding that once she finally understood what Marcus was up to, she was shocked. "Imagine taking money for other people's misery" (*SP* 369). Even Laurette, dismissed by Ben as a whore, looks down on the Hubbards. "I'm not better than anybody, but I'm as good as piney wood crooks" (*SP* 344), she says, speaking of the Hubbards; and another time, she drives her point home to Marcus, telling him that "everybody in this country knows how you got rich, bringing in salt and making poor, dying people give up everything for it. Right in the middle of the war, men dying for you, and you making their kinfolk give you all their goods and money" (*SP* 356). When early on Oscar coaches her to pretend she is as good as the Hubbards, Laurette spits back: "*Pretend?* Pretend I'm as good as anybody called Hubbard? Why, my Pa died at Vicksburg. He didn't stay home bleeding the whole state of Alabama with money tricks, and suspected of worse" (*SP* 344). Bleeding people—the same image Hellman uses in her explicitly anti-Fascist plays to characterize the dynamics of Fascism.

The suspicions swirling around Marcus to which Laurette alludes involve a massacre during the war in which twenty-seven Confederate recruits were killed. While the community believed that Marcus had led the Yankees to the training camp, his guilt was never proved. Marcus, we discover, is indeed guilty, and in the end his treachery leads to his own betrayal by his son Ben, who blackmails him to relinquish his assets, one more in a chain of betrayals by Hubbard family members as they struggle among themselves for dominance.[45] Looking happily forward to a future when the family's jockeying for power will be replaced by large-scale power plays by corporations and industrial giants, Ben croons, "Big goings on all over the country. Railroads going across, oil, coal" (*SP* 391). Also opening up, although unmentioned here, is a political void left by the demise of American democracy, bled dry by the likes of Ben and those coming after him. In 1880 Ben is looking many years ahead to an uncharted future; in 1946 Hellman is looking many years back, to the origins of the political crisis that she now feared America was facing, a political vacuum that might be filled by some form of Fascism.

That fear took visible shape for Hellman in work of the House Un-American Activities Committee (HUAC), which by 1947 was ratcheting up its investigations of Communist subversion within American society. In that year the committee turned its eyes to Hollywood, looking for evidence that Communists controlled the film industry. A number of witnesses were called to the hearings; some gave damning information, some did not, and some refused to testify altogether. During the investigation, the executive producers stepped in, declaring that they would sweep the industry clean of subversives, firing all Communists and members of groups that called for the overthrow of the government; moreover, they would blacklist everyone who refused to sign a loyalty oath and everyone who refused to appear before HUAC. Hellman was appalled at what she saw as hysterical witch hunts, believing that the committee and its "friendly" witnesses were engaging in the type of blackmail that she had from the beginning portrayed in her drama, except that this blackmail carried the weight and authority of Congress.

In her article "The Judas Goats" Hellman savaged the HUAC hearings, calling them "sickening, sickening, immoral and degraded."[46] "It was a week of turning the head in shame," Hellman begins her article; "of the horror of seeing politicians make the honorable institution of Congress into a honky tonk show; of listening to craven men lie and tattle, pushing each other in their efforts to lick the boots of their vilifiers; publicly trying to wreck the lives, not of strangers, mind you, but of men with whom they have worked and eaten and played, and made millions" (7). In answer to the question of why the hearings were taking place, Hellman suggests that it was a stratagem for those wishing war, noting parallels to the machinations used by influence brokers to bring Hitler to power. "Remember that when it was needed, in Europe, they had to find the house painter and gangster to make fear work and terror acceptable to the ignorant," Hellman writes of these men's efforts, and then she looks forward to the possibility of a terrifying future, with HUAC's frightened witnesses, "the Judas goats," starting a widespread stampede toward an American Fascism: "Judas goats; they'll lead the others, maybe, to the slaughter for you. The others will be the radio, the press, the publishers, the trade unions, the colleges, the scientists, the churches—all of us. All of us who believe in this lovely land and its freedom and rights, and who wish to keep it good and make it better" (7). She ends the article with a call to fight the true enemies of American democracy, HUAC and weak-willed witnesses (versions of the liberal appeasers of her plays) who give the committee all that it wants to proceed with its witch hunts.

Hellman's next dramatic work, an adaptation of Emmanuel Roblès's *Montserrat*, set during the revolution in Venezuela led by Simon Bolívar, centers on what was for her a crucial issue then facing America: the necessity of taking a stand against state-sponsored blackmail.[47] *Montserrat* portrays the trials of a Spanish officer who betrays his country by secretly helping Bolívar escape from his Spanish pursuers. After Montserrat is apprehended, along with six innocent people, his superior, Izquierdo, delivers an ultimatum: the six hostages will be executed, one at a time, unless Montserrat reveals Bolívar's location. Faced with this terrifying blackmail, Montserrat struggles to maintain his revolutionary faith as the hostages plead for their lives and Izquierdo proceeds with the executions. In the end,

Montserrat holds firm, but only after one of the hostages, before she is led away to death, urges him to reveal nothing.

Clearly Hellman saw Montserrat's crushing dilemma as an extreme manifestation of the pressures facing Americans called before HUAC; and just as clearly, she offered Montserrat as an example of the courage required to maintain one's dignity and ideals in the face of government strong-arming. Izquierdo, moreover, represents Hellman's characterization of those leading the anti-Communist witch hunt; despite his apparent political zealotry, he is actually another of Hellman's unprincipled men, liberal in the sense of being not truly committed to any faith outside of himself. Izquierdo is driven by two entirely personal motives: to enact revenge on the revolutionaries for his earlier suffering as a prisoner and to secure his position in the power structure. "Understand me, I have no moral objection to what they do," Izquierdo tells Montserrat, commenting on the revolutionary forces' treatment of prisoners. "I have no such judgments. I leave them to you. I care only what was done to me. *After* that, I serve a King. But I am not fool enough to believe in him. If he dies tomorrow, no hopes of mine go with him. There will be another, and it will make no difference."[48]

Montserrat premiered in 1949, the same year that Hellman (as reported in her FBI file) attended a rally denouncing HUAC and contributed $250.00 to help support those called before the committee.[49] That same year, she also helped organize the Cultural and Scientific Conference for World Peace, which took place in New York City in March and drew representatives from around the world, including the Soviet Union and Soviet bloc nations. The conference, not surprisingly, generated a great deal of controversy and protest. The State Department denounced the proceedings, claiming that Communists controlled the conference and that the conference agenda, focusing on issues of world peace, was merely a smokescreen for the Soviet Union's plans for world conquest.[50] A bitter article covering the conference in *Life* included a two-page sidebar with head shots of fifty prominent Americans who had attended, including one of Hellman. "Dupes and Fellow Travelers Dress Up Communist Fronts" read the sidebar's title, and the article called these fifty and others like them "weapons" of the Communists, "prominent people who, wittingly or not, associate themselves with a Communist-front organization and thereby lend it glamor, prestige or the respectability of American liberalism," thus accomplishing "quite as much for the Kremlin in their glamorous way as a card holder in his drab toil."[51]

In three years Hellman herself would be called to testify before HUAC for her political activities, but in the interim she finished another play, *The Autumn Garden*, which premiered in 1951. Given the turmoil in the world and in Hellman's life, *The Autumn Garden* is surprisingly quiet and restrained, focusing on the everyday problems of its characters and making few references to national or international matters.[52] Even so, in uncovering the complicated motives underlying the betrayal of friends and beliefs, the play delivers a stinging commentary on the repressive political climate in America, presenting in a domestic setting the type of self-examinations and self-recriminations that were occurring at the time when Americans were being called to testify against themselves and others.[53] By the end of the play, most characters have come to see that their self-constructed flattering self-images mask the fact that they live entirely by expediency, holding no fundamental beliefs or ideals that would give their lives meaning and purpose. "I feel so lost, Ned," Constance says, having come to see that without belief she is without definition. "As if I distrusted myself, didn't have anything to stand on. I mean, right now, if you asked me, I just wouldn't know what I thought or believed, or ever had. . . . Well, what *have* I built my life on?" (*SP* 391). Griggs reaches a similar conclusion, telling Crossman that he suffers from the "worst disease of all," explaining, "I'm all gone. I've just looked and there's no Benjamin Griggs." Griggs continues, in the play's most famous passage:

> So at any given moment you're only the sum of your life up to then. There are no big moments you can reach unless you've a pile of smaller moments to stand on. That big hour of decision, the turning point in your life, the someday you've counted on when you'd suddenly wipe out your past mistakes, do the work you'd never done, think the way you'd never thought, have what you'd never had—it just doesn't come suddenly. You've trained yourself for it while you've waited—or you've let it all run past you and frittered yourself away. I've frittered myself away, Crossman. (*SP* 491)[54]

Constance and Griggs are versions of the political liberals Hellman had all along been castigating in her work, those who follow any ideology or leader to protect their own comfort and security. In her previous work, Hellman typically highlighted liberalism's catastrophic effects on society, showing how a society of the faithless opened the door to rapacious powerbrokers and ultimately Fascism. Here she focuses on liberalism's catastrophic effects on the individual, showing how those living without faith and commitment waste away in spirit and identity, suffering, as Griggs observes, the "worst disease of all." *The Autumn Garden,* together with her earlier work from the 1930s and 1940s, shows Hellman as a master diagnostician, one who knows that the ills of the individual eventually manifest themselves in the ills of society, the worst disease of the individual opening the way for the worst disease of society—Fascism. In both her art and her activism Hellman did what she could to expose and, she hoped, to eradicate those diseases.

Coda

THE LONG SHADOW

The twelve writers examined in this book clearly demonstrate that political developments in Europe, particularly the rise of Fascism, profoundly influenced the ways white southern writers understood themselves and the South. As the shape of this study suggests, with its chapters on individual writers, no particular school of white southern writing collected around the issue of Fascism (unless one counts a brief solidarity among the Nashville Agrarians during their crisis years); rather, individual writers, through their own traveling, reading, and thinking, came up against a question that would haunt their identity as southerners and their imaginative vision: what does the authoritarianism and the racial politics of European Fascism, and most particularly that of Nazi Germany, have to do with southern culture?

As varied as the writers' answers were, parallels and connections do emerge, at least in broad terms. Writers who cast their allegiance with southern traditionalism, asserting that southern culture stood fundamentally opposed to Fascism and political authoritarianism, typically emphasized the ongoing lines of hardy individualism and premodern allegiances that they saw defining the white southern experience, with Donald Davidson's tall men of Tennessee the most compelling example. In this traditionalist configuration the tall men of the South stand opposed to the small men of modernity, the faceless masses created by the modern industrial state, which in its final evolution was the Fascist state. This line of thinking was broadly followed by the Nashville Agrarians and William Alexander Percy, though in *Lanterns on the Levee* Percy suggested that the sweeping flood of modernity had already destroyed the traditional South, leaving the few remaining tall men isolated and forlorn, holding fast to their individual honor and private stoicism. In contrast, writers who found disturbing parallels between Fascism and southern culture emphasized, not the premodern nature of southern traditionalism, but its modernity, manifested in its authoritarian control of its citizens. The most obvious examples here are W. J. Cash and Lillian Smith, both of whom attempted to unmask the mystifying power of southern tradition and its totalitarian structures.

Writers of fiction and drama also typically worked with one of these two models. Carson McCullers's savaging of southern authoritarianism in *The Heart Is a Lonely Hunter* and *The Member of the Wedding* is the clearest example of the portrayal of the South as something close to a Fascist state. Katherine Anne Porter worked from both positions during her career: in her work up until roughly the mid-1940s she portrayed southern culture as so controlling as to be totalitarian; and then, when she changed stances to champion southern traditionalism and its tall men and women who stood against the modern state, she presented herself as one of those tall women, complete with a thoroughly fictitious genealogy to prove it. Lillian Hellman radically revised the traditionalist model of cultural continuity, finding that unbroken line in the ongoing pursuit of capital, a pursuit that eventually led straight to the Fascist state. Signaling his new artistic vision developed during World War II, Faulkner likewise reconfigured the traditionalist model (after initially invoking it in his three home-front stories), positing instead an ongoing line of tall-man heroism, but one originating with the figure of Abraham Lincoln. Faulkner had become a nationalist. In a broad sense, so too were Thomas Wolfe and Robert Penn Warren eventually to become nationalists in their exploration of Fascism and the South, both struggling with fundamental issues concerning the nature of democracy and fanaticism.

Fascism compelled all the writers in this study to look far beyond the borders of Dixie to comprehend themselves and their homeland, pushing them toward an understanding of what today is called in southern studies "the global South." All, in a sense, strove to attain the type of unified vision, endorsed by Lillian Smith and Paula Snelling, that superimposed the local, the national, and the international. "Unless we keep the world map open before us we shall slip back into the old, bad habit of looking down at our own feet, and if we do we shall find ourselves at the same place where we first began," Smith and Snelling wrote. "We must learn to read our maps simultaneously: regional map, national map, world map."[1] One reason for concluding my study at (roughly) 1950 is that with the end of World War II and the defeat of Nazi Germany and Fascist Italy, southern writers faced a new international map and context, one shaped largely by the cold war and by the end of empire, which brought independent nationhood to former colonies of African and Asian. Closer to home, in addition, was the quickly burgeoning civil rights movement, which of course was itself integrally bound up with global affairs. The local, the national, and the global thus all looked profoundly different in the 1950s, as did the relevance of Fascism—and, more generally, of totalitarianism. Coping with these new contexts, those white southern writers of this study who were still alive in 1950 (all but W. J. Cash and William Alexander Percy) necessarily reformulated their conceptions of the South, though typically recurring to the same fundamental issues of southern traditionalism and authoritarianism.

One can see this intellectual reconfiguring clearly in the work of Lillian Smith, particularly in her revised edition of *Killers of the Dream*, published in 1961 with several new chapters specifically addressing southern segregation in the context of the cold war.[2] In her foreword to the revised edition, Smith noted that examination of segregation's destructive work in 1949 was piercingly relevant in 1961 to the world's future, particularly as African and Asian nations stepped free from their colonial bondage. "What was based on intuition, on a kind of prophetic guess," Smith wrote, speaking of her observations in the 1949 edition, "is now boldly acting itself out on a world-size stage. I had felt the curve of approaching events but I could only warn, I could not prove. And now here it is: the new African nations, the hatred of colonialism, and the Communists' shrewd exploitation of this word so fatefully tied to 'the white man' and to Western democracy—and to everyone's future."[3] Foreign aid was not enough to bring developing nations under American influence, wrote Smith; to court these nations, America must first renounce the ideology of white supremacy and then rid the nation of its most visible manifestation, southern segregation. "The President may try, the State Department, the USIA and Peace Corps may try, but no matter what they do or say, the offer of help and friendship will be without psychic and moral substance as long as we practice segregation here at home," Smith wrote. "And at the critical moment, many of these nations, too, will turn to communism, rejecting what they call 'white democracy'" (17). The urgency of the 1961 edition of *Killers of the Dream* lies right here: the fate of the world, torn in conflict between Communism and democracy, hangs in the balance, as developing nations cast their lot with one side or the other. In her new concluding chapter, Smith reiterated this argument, thus in effect grounding her entire analysis of southern segregation in her anti-Communist foreign policy.

Other writers in this study undertook similar if not always as obvious reappraisals of the South and totalitarianism during the cold war. And it seems certain that many younger, emerging white southern writers were having to come to terms with the relevance—or, if they so decided, the irrelevance—of cold-war politics to their understanding and representation of southern society.[4] But that is another story, long and complicated, outside the boundaries of this study, a story that is still to be told.

Amidst all the changes that the region, the nation, and the world have undergone since 1950, however, the specter of Fascism and its relevance to understanding the South never entirely dissipated. In this connection I would like to close with a quick look forward to two novels from the late 1970s, Walker Percy's *Lancelot* (1977) and William Styron's *Sophie's Choice* (1979), both of which, from very different perspectives, point to the continuing and troubling presence of Nazi Germany in the white southern literary imagination, a presence that challenges the virtues generally associated with traditional southern culture. For Percy, the specter of Nazi Germany provided, in the tumultuous 1970s, a means to interrogate the extremes to which southern antimodernism might extend, while for Styron, the horrors of the Holocaust gave him the context in which to explore the legacy of southern slavery.

Percy's *Lancelot* follows a conversation over several days between Lancelot Lamar, who has been confined to a psychiatric hospital after committing deadly acts of vengeance, and his boyhood friend and now priest, Percival. One of the things Lance talks to Percival about is the new society he wants to start once he is freed, what he calls at one point "the new Reformation" (*L* 177). As becomes clear through his descriptions, Lance envisions his new order as standing upon the chivalric ideals of the Old South, particularly its rigid code of personal honor. But as also becomes clear, Lance envisions a new world that takes Old South ideology to its logical extremes—a new world that resembles Nazi Germany. Indeed, Lance's hospital/prison commentary analyzing the chaos of the modern world and offering his alternative to it shares a good bit with Hitler's prison statement, *Mein Kampf,* which describes his rejection of bourgeois society and his program for a new society. Lance directs much of his anger, as did Hitler, against the breakdown of order and tradition that characterized modernity, a breakdown that he believes shattered ideals and propelled society into a morass of humanitarian bilge. Lance rages at Percival for what he sees as the Roman Catholic Church's complicity in this breakdown, saying that the church's once rigid articles of faith and conduct have eroded into feel-good-about-yourself love feasts led by the likes of the Singing Nun. Lance's new order, what he comes to characterize, in another echo of Nazi Germany, as "the Third Revolution," will, he says, reestablish, with a vengeful sword, the fallen structures of belief. "We are going to set it out for you, what is good and what is bad, and no Jew-Christian waffling bullshit about it," he tells Percival. "What we are is the last of the West. What we are is the best of you, Percival, and the best of me, Lancelot, and of Lee and Richard and Saladin and Leonidas and Hector and Agamemnon and Richthofen and Charlemagne and Clovis and Martel" (*L* 177–78).

Lance's comment that those of the Third Revolution will be "the last of the West" recalls the Nashville Agrarians' characterization of traditional southern society as the last remnant of Western civilization, a further suggestion that Lance's conception of his new order carries the ideals of the traditional South to their logical extremes. Most of these ideals, at least in Lance's configuration, derive from the stern stoicism that upholds personal honor, chivalry, and the purity of women. It is all or nothing for Lance. There is no middle ground, no compromising. A man is either a gentleman or a thief; a woman is either a lady or a whore—and everyone in Lance's world of clearly marked boundaries will be able to distinguish a person's identity:

> We know who we are and where we stand. There will be leaders and there will be followers. There are now, only neither knows which is which. There will be men who are strong and pure of heart, not for Christ's sake but for their own sake. There will be virtuous women who are proud of their virtue and there will be women of the street who are there to be fucked and everyone will know which is which. You will do right, not because of Jew-Christian commandments but because we say it is right. There will be honorable men and there will be thieves, just as now, but the difference is one will know which is which and there will be no confusion, no nice thieves, no honorable Mafia. There are not many of us but since we are ready to die and no one else is, we shall prevail. (*L* 177–78)

Appropriately, Lance plans to start his new order in the South's heartland, Virginia, specifically the Shenandoah Valley. At one point he imagines a scene (recalling the poetry of hard-line Agrarian Donald Davidson) representing the life he sees coming: a young man with a rifle keeps watch over a mountain pass, his eyes turned toward the dying cities of the Northeast.

Whatever the appeal of such romantic, postapocalyptic thinking, Lance's repeated screeds against modernity, in particular the promiscuity of modern women, underscore the forbidding extremes of his Third Revolution. The women's liberation movement and its championing of female desire, Lance says, has unmanned the American male and led to what he characterizes as "the great whorehouse and fagdom of America" (*L* 176). "Christ what a country!" he says to Percival at one point. "A nation of 100 million voracious cunts" (*L* 177). "Which is a better world," he asks him at another, "this cocksucking cuntlapping assholelicking fornicating Happyland U.S.A. or a Roman legion under Marcus Aurelius Antonius? Which is worse, to die with T. J. Jackson at Chancellorsville or live with Johnny Carson in Burbank?" (*L* 158). No doubt anticipating Percival's objections, Lance tells him not to confuse his plans with those of the Nazis, adding that "the new order will not be based on Catholicism or Communism or fascism or liberalism or capitalism or any ism at all, but simply on that stern rectitude valued by the new breed and marked by the violence which will attend its breach" (*L* 158). Lance reassures Percival that "killings will not be necessary" to usher in the Third Revolution; once people hear his message they will willingly follow. And then he adds ominously: "Millions agree with me and know that this age is not tolerable, but no one will act except the crazies and they are part of the age. The mad Mansons are nothing more than the ultimate spasm-orgasm of a dying world. We are only here to give it the *coup de grâce*. We shall not wait for it to fester and rot any longer. We will kill it" (*L* 159–60).

Despite his denials, Lance's thinking shares much with Nazi ideology, particularly his attacks on modernity and his celebration of a mythic rebirth of a national culture based on discipline, faith, and honor. Echoes of the Nazis abound in his commentary, although they are not always specifically identified as such. Lance's attacks on engulfing women, for instance, recall the profoundly misogynist fears that underlay the thinking of the German Freikorps, as illustrated so clearly in the work of Klaus Theweleit.[5] Moreover, Lance's analysis of the mass appeal of his new order—that modern people, alienated and isolated, crave to be told what to do and believe—echoes Eric Fromm's analysis of the psychological appeal of Fascism and totalitarianism.[6] That Percy had the frighteningly powerful appeal of Nazism in mind when writing *Lancelot* is furthermore suggested by the fact, as mentioned above in chapter 3, that on a trip to Nazi Germany in 1934

Percy apparently felt drawn to the mystique and purposefulness of the Hitler Jugend.[7]

In his last novel, *The Thanatos Syndrome* (1987), Percy rewrote his 1934 experiences in Nazi Germany into those of his character Father Smith. Father Smith recalls that during a visit to Germany in the mid-1930s he befriended a Hitler Jugend enthusiast, Helmut, and quickly came under his and his group's spell. He remembers that he saw in Helmut what he had never before seen in a person: complete and absolute dedication to a group and a belief. "He was ready to die," Father Smith comments. "I had never met anyone ready to die for a belief. . . . I can only think—and this may seem strange—of the young Jesuits of the seventeenth century who were also soldiers knowing they were probably going to die in some place like India, England, Japan, Canada. Or perhaps a young English Crusader signing up with Richard to rescue the holy places from the infidel."[8] Father Smith then confesses what has long haunted him: that had he been German, he would have eagerly followed Helmut into the Hitler Jugend.

Father Smith, of course, did not become a Nazi, but he did become a Catholic priest, a set of alternatives similar to those laid out by Lance at the end of the earlier novel, even if he does not specifically identify his Third Revolution as Nazism. "Very well," he says to Percival. "But you know this! One of us is wrong. It will be your way or it will be my way" (*L* 257). With Lance's declaration, Percy was almost certainly reworking in fictional extremes a similar choice that he himself had faced earlier in his career— to embrace either southern stoicism, as taught to him by William Alexander Percy, or the Roman Catholic faith. Percy of course chose the latter, but he certainly did not leave all his feelings toward Uncle Will's stoicism entirely behind him, particularly his admiration for its stern, dignified nobility in the face of the world's overwhelming disorder. Yet, as Percy makes clear in *Lancelot*, and as he had already made clear in several of his essays and in his earlier novels, particularly *The Last Gentleman* (1966), southern stoicism, for all its virtues, was finally a dead end—literally because its uncompromising intolerance and radical individualism no longer worked in the modern society and figuratively because stoicism's grim pessimism, its schadenfreude, celebrated nothing more so than death. "The South's virtues were the broadsword virtues of the clan," Percy wrote in "Stoicism in the South" (1956), "as were her vices, too—the hubris of *noblesse* gone arrogant."[9] "*Noblesse* gone arrogant" underlies Lancelot's plans for the Third Revolution—and, as has already been suggested, Lance carries that vice to its logical extremes, ending with a vision that Percy characterized in an interview as Lance's "own peculiar brand of fascism."[10]

Percy's comments on stoicism in "The Failure and the Hope" shed further light on Lance's "peculiar brand of fascism." In that essay, Percy wrote that stoicism "had little relevance in the political and social order," because stoics tended to "wash [their] hands of prevailing social evils."[11] In *Lancelot*, however, Percy portrays Lancelot as an old-school stoic who rather than washing his hands of social evils takes them head-on; in doing so, Lance uses stoicism's "broadsword virtues," which were intended for self-control, in order to enforce social control. The results are disastrous, with the old-school stoic transformed into the new-school Fascist. We are left at the end of *Lancelot* with a dangerous man and his dangerous political ideology, one that emphasizes anger, intolerance, arrogance, and violence.

If Percy in *Lancelot* connects the extremes of southern traditionalism with Nazi ideology, exploring his own rejection of traditionalism and his turn to Catholicism, Styron in *Sophie's Choice* explores the legacy of white guilt over the horrors of slavery by connecting that legacy to that of the Nazi extermination camps. *Sophie's Choice* follows in the long line of southern novels, most of them written between the early 1920s and the mid-1940s, that portray characters agonizing over their southern heritage, and particularly that of slavery and racial violence. Styron's narrator, Stingo, describes his early life as a young writer in New York, torn between his southern and his modern loyalties. It soon becomes clear that for the young Stingo to mature as an individual and an artist, he must somehow integrate these two loyalties, finding a way to accept his heritage without being bound by it, thus remaining responsible to his southern past (and identity) while pursuing his thoroughly modern aspirations. Styron complicates Stingo's psychological turmoil by connecting, at least through suggestion, the horrors of chattel slavery with those of the Holocaust. That connection comes in a narrative move positing that the logical end of southern slavery in the nineteenth century is the Nazi extermination camp in the twentieth. As a result, the burden of southern history for Stingo becomes in a sense the burden of German history; Stingo must come to terms not only with the transgressions of southern slavemasters but also with those of the Nazis.

Initially, however, Stingo's only burdens as a young man in New York are of the mundane sort—he is short of money, without a job, and he needs a place to live. That begins to change when he receives a letter from his father containing his share of a family inheritance that accumulated originally from the sale of a family slave, Artiste, who had been accused, falsely it turns out, of improper conduct with a white woman. The great-grandfather who sold Artiste, Stingo learns from his father, had been wracked by guilt after the discovery of Artiste's innocence. "Not only had he committed one of the truly unpardonable acts of a slave-owner—breaking up a family—but he had sold off an innocent boy of 16 into the grinding hell of the Georgia turpentine forests," Stingo's father comments, adding that the great-grandfather had later searched desperately, without success, to find Artiste in order to buy him back (*SC* 32). In large part because he already knew that his ancestors were slaveholders, Stingo initially has few misgivings about the origins of the inheritance; he feels more fortunate than guilty for receiving the money. Over the course of his friendship with Nathan and Sophie, however, he grows more uncomfortable with the inheritance, particularly as he learns from Sophie about the Germans' use of slave labor at Auschwitz.

If he does not initially connect southern and Nazi slavery, Stingo nevertheless certainly better understands the dark heritage of southern slavery after hearing of Sophie's sufferings. The inheritance he originally deemed a "phenomenal stroke of luck" (*SC* 27), he thereafter deems "blood money" (*SC* 420); and when he is later robbed of what is left of the inheritance, he admits he is relieved. No longer holding the blood money, Stingo feels freed from direct connection to his family's slave-owning heritage. But he quickly realizes how naive he is to think that a simple theft could exorcize his haunting guilt of slavery:

> Yet how could I *ever* be rid of slavery? A lump rose in my gorge, I whispered the word aloud, "Slavery!" There was dwelling somewhere in the inward part of my mind a compulsion to write about slavery, to make slavery give up its most deeply buried and tormented secrets, which was every bit as necessary as the compulsion that drove me to write, as I had been writing today, about the inheritors of that institution who now in the 1940s floundered amid the insane apartheid of Tidewater Virginia—my beloved and bedeviled bourgeois New South family whose every move and gesture, I had begun to realize were played out in the presence of a vast, brooding company of black witnesses, all sprung from the loins of bondage. And were not all of us, white and Negro, still enslaved? I knew that in the fever of my mind and in the most unquiet regions of my heart I would be shackled by slavery as long as I remained a writer. (*SC* 420–21)

Stingo now sees, in other words, that his fate as an artist is integrally bound up with the fate of Artiste.

It is not only Sophie who prods Stingo toward confronting the darker aspects of his southern identity and heritage. Indeed, the more visible and vocal challenge to Stingo's complacency comes from Nathan, who repeatedly both belittles the South and its history of racial violence and accuses Stingo of shirking his responsibility, as a privileged white southerner, for the South's shameful treatment of black people. When he is really worked up, Nathan goes even further, claiming that racial violence is the bedrock of southern culture, the work not of a demented few but of the entire society, in which racism has been institutionalized. Southern racial violence, Nathan concludes, mirrors that of Nazi Germany, lynchings being as barbaric as the death camps.[12] Early in the novel, Nathan zeroes in on a recent, gruesome lynching of a black man, Bobby Weed, asking Stingo if he agrees that Weed's emasculation and death "at the hands of white southern Americans is as bottomlessly barbaric as any act performed by the Nazis during the rule of Adolph Hitler!" (*SC* 70). Stunned, shocked, but most of all offended as a southerner, Stingo lashes back at Nathan's characterization of southern barbarity, voicing allegiances that he typically rarely acknowledges out loud or maybe even to himself. "I'm *Southern* and I'm *proud* of it, but I'm not one of those pigs—those *troglodytes* who did what they did to Bobby Weed! I was born in Tidewater Virginia, and if you'll pardon the expression, I regard myself as a gentleman!" (*SC* 70). Nathan then continues his attack:

> Aren't you able to perceive the simple truth? Aren't you able to discern the truth in its awful outlines? And that is that your refusal to accept responsibility in the death of Bobby Weed is the same as that of those Germans who disavowed the Nazi party even as they watched blandly and unprotestingly as the thugs vandalized the synagogues and perpetrated the *Kristallnacht*. Can't you see the truth about yourself? About the South? (*SC* 71)

Although convinced of what he sees as Nathan's irrational error, Stingo is so shaken by Nathan's accusations, challenging his once unquestioned identity as it has never been challenged before, that he is reduced, not merely to silence, but to gibberish, responding to Nathan with only "an odd chirping sound in the back of my throat" (*SC* 71).

Later, Stingo is likewise stymied by Nathan in a conversation about the Mississippi senator Theodore Bilbo. While waiting for a meeting with

Nathan, Stingo reads an article about Bilbo's declining health, thinking to himself how appropriate it is that the man whose mouth has spilled forth so much vileness is now suffering from cancer of the mouth and, furthermore, how glad he is that Bilbo, who had become an embarrassment to many in the South, would in all likelihood soon be dead and gone. Among other things, Stingo notes that Bilbo publicly railed against blacks and Jews, deeming blacks "niggers," "coons," and "jigaboos" and Jews "dagos" and "kikes," even when addressing the likes of New York City's Mayor LaGuardia. Despite his feelings about Bilbo, Stingo later refuses to join in Nathan's toast to Bilbo's pending death, saying he would never toast anyone's suffering and demise. Enraged, Nathan asks him if he would toast the death of Hitler, a question that ignites Stingo's southern partisanship. "*Of course* I would toast the death of Hitler," Stingo responds. "But that's a fucking different matter! Bilbo's not Hitler!" (*SC* 205). Stingo then launches into a fierce attack on what he sees as Nathan's uncalled-for attacks on the South and his willful blindness about the region. He concludes with a rousing defense of Bilbo's achievements as a populist governor of Mississippi, achievements that include, Stingo points out, the creation of a highway commission, the implementation of a tuberculosis program, and the institution of a tick-eradication program to fight Texas fever in cattle. Nathan's fierce interruption stops Stingo dead in his tracks: "You fool, you silly klutz. Texas fever! You *clown!* You want me to point out that the glory of the Third Reich was a highway system unsurpassed in the world and that Mussolini made the trains run on time?" (*SC* 207). As before, Stingo collapses in the face of Nathan's charges, crumbling, as he says, in "the shambles of my defeat" (*SC* 207). Nathan's seemingly irrational tirade linking the South with Nazi Germany once again not only flushes out Stingo's cherished southern allegiances but exposes *their* fundamental irrationality, which is why Stingo is speechless when he tries to reason with Nathan and why he later says that he defended Bilbo in the heat of fury, after "semi-hysteric energy" propelled him "into regions of deep asininity" (*SC* 206).

This last judgment comes from Stingo as the narrator of the novel, some thirty years after his conversation with Nathan. The young Stingo would never have suggested that his southern loyalties resided in "regions of deep asininity," and indeed he characteristically rebounds quickly when Nathan is no longer present, reasserting his southernness and deflecting Nathan's charges as merely the ravings of a self-righteous, arrogant Yankee Jew. That Stingo's deep-seated southern attitudes remain fundamentally unchanged (even while he is more self-consciously aware of them) by his experiences with Sophie and Nathan becomes absolutely clear when, near the end of the novel, he and Sophie head South toward the family farm where Stingo envisions he and Sophie settling. Awash with the agrarian dream of the traditional South, Stingo imagines an idyllic life of self-sufficient farming, with Sophie his happy wife overseeing their home and children. While a part of him recognizes that he is wallowing in rose-colored escapism, he refuses to accept that his plans could go astray—until, that is, during one of his conversations with Sophie about the happy life he foresees for them, she pulls away, shaken and distraught. "Oh, Stingo, I need a drink so bad," she says, responding to Stingo's agrarian vision (*SC* 493). Sophie's words burst Stingo's bubble, his southern pastoralism overwhelmed by her sufferings during the Holocaust. So crushing is the moment that Stingo feels as if he is one of the European refugees, torn from home and dead to the world. Once Sophie's suitor and savior, he now sees himself *as* Sophie, psychologically mangled by Auschwitz. "I had identified so completely with Sophie that I felt Polish," Stingo comments, remembering the experience, "with Europe's putrid blood rushing through my arteries and veins. Auschwitz still stalked my soul as well as hers. Was there no end to this? No end?" (*SC* 493).

Actually there is an end to Stingo's despair, and it comes at the conclusion of the novel, when, in an emotional outburst, he gives himself over to his deep grief, shedding tears not only for the deaths of Sophie and Nathan but also for the other victimized people he has known, or known of (including Artiste and Bobby Weed), people he describes as "a few of the beaten and butchered and betrayed and martyred children of the earth" (*SC* 515). It marks the beginning of his maturity, the novel ending with a rebirth as Stingo awakes from a night of sleeping on the beach, having been staggered the evening before by his grief. But with the new day he is ready to start anew, wiser and more responsible, and he recites to himself words that announce his emergence from the dark depths of his recent life: "'Neath cold sand I dreamed of death / but woke at dawn to see / in glory, the bright, the morning star" (*SC* 515).

It is significant that during his emotional breakdown the previous night, Stingo shed tears for those he held dear but not for those lost in the Holocaust, "the six million Jews or the two million Poles or the one million Serbs or the five million Russians." He was, he explained, "unprepared to weep for all humanity" (*SC* 515). Thirty years later, as narrator of the novel, the elder Stingo is much better prepared to weep for the Holocaust victims and indeed for all humanity. He is not merely older and wiser; he is much more informed about the Holocaust and its significance to both the history of the American South and the history of Western culture. Comments throughout the novel indicate that since the startling events of 1947, Stingo has pondered and read deeply about the Holocaust; writers he comments upon include, among others, Hannah Arendt, Bruno Bettleheim, Richard Rubenstein, George Steiner, and Elie Wiesel. By the time that he writes about his experiences with Sophie, Stingo is a successful novelist, a writer on both the contemporary South and Old South slavery. His narrative of the events of 1947 is his attempt to understand himself and his southern vision, we now see, in the larger scope of Western culture and the Holocaust. Early in the novel, Nathan tells Stingo that southern writing is a "worn-out tradition" and that "another genre is going to have to take its place" (*SC* 115). Stingo may not have believed Nathan in 1947, but the novel he writes much later indicates that he has finally come around to something close to Nathan's perspective.

As the narrator of the novel and a commentator on the Holocaust, Stingo is clearly a stand-in for Styron himself (a connection that Styron all but announces by patterning Stingo's literary career so closely on his own),[13] and certainly Stingo's musings on southern and Nazi oppression voice Styron's own probings of what he called elsewhere "the most compelling theme in history, including the history of our own time—that of the catastrophic propensity on the part of human beings to attempt to dominate one another."[14] These words come from Styron's 1978 essay-review of Richard Rubenstein's *The Cunning of History: The Holocaust and the American Future,* and specifically from a discussion comparing Rubenstein's work on the Holocaust to Stanley Elkins's on slavery in the South. Both Elkins and Rubenstein stand as guiding lights for Styron in the making of *Sophie's Choice,* for it was largely through their work that he came to see a historical continuum linking southern slave plantations with Nazi concentration camps, a continuum in the novel that Stingo the narrator in the 1970s understands but that Stingo the aspiring novelist of 1947 does not.

What Styron found so intriguing in the work of Elkins and Rubenstein, and what linked the two writers, was their positing that the Nazi concentration camp was best understood less as a death factory than as, in the words of Elkins, "a special and highly perverted instance of human slavery," a form of human mastery anticipated by the slave system of the American South. In *Slavery: A Problem in American Institutional and Intellectual Life* Elkins uses studies of the crushing psychological trauma undergone by inmates of concentration camps to explore what he believes was similar trauma experienced by southern slaves as they adjusted to and, in some cases, resisted a system of absolute power. "The only mass experience that Western people have had within recorded history comparable in any way with Negro slavery was undergone in the nether world of Nazism," Elkins writes. "The concentration camp was not only a perverted slave system; it was also—what is less obvious but even more to the point—a perverted patriarchy."[15] Elkins elaborates on the connections between the slave plantation and the concentration camp:

> Both were closed systems from which all standards based on prior connections had been effectively detached. A working adjustment to either system required a childlike conformity, a limited choice of "significant others." Cruelty per se cannot be considered the primary key to this; of far greater importance was the simple "closedness" of the system, in which all lines of authority descended from the master and in which alternative social bases that might have supported alternative standards were systematically suppressed. The individual, consequently, for his very psychic security, had to picture his master in some way as the "good father," even when, as in the concentration camp, it made no sense at all. But why should it not have made sense for many a simple plantation Negro whose master did exhibit, in all the ways that could be expected, the features of the good father who was really "good"? If the concentration camp could produce in two or three years the results that it did, one wonders how much more pervasive must have been those attitudes, expectations, and values which had, certainly, their benevolent side and which were accepted and transmitted over generations. (128–30)

Styron, who first read Elkins when he was beginning work on *The Confessions of Nat Turner,* found in his essay-review that *Slavery: A Problem in American Institutional and Intellectual Life* boldly shed "fresh light on American Negro slavery" (95). Elkins's book, he wrote, struck "violently through the obfuscations and preconceptions that had dictated, often self-righteously, the views of the apologists for slavery on the one hand and those of its adversaries on the other, and, in effect, demanded that the institution be examined from any number of new and different angles objectively, in all of its difficult complexity" (97).

Styron felt that Rubenstein's work on the Nazi concentration camp, which focused on Auschwitz and drew upon Elkins's ideas, similarly opened up the debate on the complexities of the Holocaust, avoiding the thoroughly understandable emotional extremes that characteristically shaped interpretations of the Nazi camps. A paragraph from Styron's essay-review neatly expresses the towering significance he found in what he saw as Rubenstein's groundbreaking (and ground-clearing) work:

> I am saying that, like Elkins, Rubenstein is forcing us to re-interpret Auschwitz—especially, although not exclusively, from the standpoint of its existence as part of a continuum of slavery which has been engrafted for centuries onto the very body of Western civilization. Therefore, in the process of destroying the myth and the preconception, he is making us see that the encampment of death and suffering may have been more horrible than we had ever imagined. It was slavery in its ultimate embodiment. He is making us understand that the etiology of Auschwitz—to some, a diabolical, perhaps freakish excrescence which vanished from the face of the earth with the destruction of the crematoriums in 1945—is actually embedded deeply in a cultural tradition which stretches back to the Middle Passage from the coast of Africa, and beyond, to the enforced servitude in ancient Greece and Rome. Rubenstein is saying that we ignore this linkage, and the existence of the sleeping virus in the bloodstream of civilization, at the risk of our future. (97–98)

As Styron notes, Rubenstein's basic thesis asserts that with Auschwitz the Nazis created a society of total domination, one that took to their limits the cultural forces of secularization and rationality that had long been propelling the evolution of Western society toward ever more complicated manifestations of the modern industrial state and its intricate bureaucracy. In terms of the future of Western culture, Rubenstein thus finds Auschwitz, with its slave-labor system, more threatening than the camps that were solely extermination centers. "An execution center can only manufacture corpses," Rubenstein writes; "a society of total domination creates a world of the living dead that can serve as a prototype of a future social order, especially in a world confronted by catastrophic crises and ever-increasing, massive population redundancy."[16]

In his essay-review of *The Cunning of History*, Styron tipped his hat to both Elkins and Rubenstein, writing that "if slavery was the great historical nightmare of the eighteenth and nineteenth centuries in the Western world, slavery's continuation in the horror we have come to call Auschwitz is the nightmare of our own century" (95). Besides suggesting that *Sophie's Choice* might be read as a continuation of *The Confessions of Nat Turner*, at least in terms of the exploration of slavery's psychological impact on the enslaved, Styron's comment goes far in explaining why he would write a novel about Auschwitz in the first place—it is the nightmare for all people of the twentieth century. It is that nightmare, of course, that Stingo in 1947 discovers in his relationship with Sophie, and it is that nightmare that goes on to haunt him as he matures as a person and a writer. But as Styron makes clear in the novel, attempting to grasp the significance of Auschwitz is only half of Stingo's challenge; the other half is understanding what the significance of Auschwitz has to do with his identity as a white southerner and his responsibility to the South's benighted history.

And this brings us back to Theodore Bilbo. As we have already seen, Stingo justifies Bilbo's political career by pointing to his achievements as a populist governor while glossing over his disgraceful late years as a U.S. senator and suggesting that Bilbo's racist ranting and shenanigans are merely what his constituency demands of him.[17] From Stingo's perspective, which he developed in a college term paper on southern demagogues, Bilbo is less a villain than a victim of the South's racist system. Nathan's retort, pressing the comparison between Nazi Germany and the South, is that no matter what the social and political pressure to conform, people have to take responsibility for their acts, including their complicity, either active or passive, with the ruling regime.

Whatever Nathan's madness and paranoia, Stingo must come to understand his fundamental point about accepting responsibility, an understanding that he appears to be moving toward at the end of the novel when he weeps for, among others, Nat Turner and other black victims of the South's racist system. As Stingo's comments as narrator thirty years later make clear, his insight into Nathan's retort deepened over the years as he continued his study of the Holocaust, aided by the work of both Elkins and Rubenstein. So too did his understanding of Bilbo and the specific issue of the individual's responsibility within an oppressive and unjust system, aided by his reading of Hannah Arendt's *Eichmann in Jerusalem*, which Stingo the narrator mentions favorably in his comments (and which Styron read closely when researching *Sophie's Choice*).

The youthful Stingo needs to see—but cannot yet see—that Eichmann had a choice and so did Bilbo. And so does he. In fact, in 1947 Bilbo himself issued a challenge to Stingo and other Americans to make a choice regarding America's future: either segregate blacks completely or witness America's destruction "by the slow but certain process of sin, degradation, and mongrelization."[18] Bilbo's manifesto for black repatriation to Liberia, *Take Your Choice: Separation or Mongrelization*, indeed eerily echoes the Nazis' initial plans for sending German Jews to Madagascar and their later decision to send them instead to a divided Poland. And while Bilbo's plan of course differed crucially from the Nazis' in that American blacks would not be forced to move (after enough blacks moved of their own volition, Bilbo predicted, those remaining in America "will get lonesome and be more than glad to go" [290]), and while he nowhere advocated that blacks be sent to extermination camps, Bilbo's rhetoric is so apocalyptic that it does not take much imagination to foresee Bilbo, had he lived, later offering a Nazi-like solution if blacks resisted repatriation. Certainly, Bilbo lays the groundwork in *Take Your Choice* for such a solution, announcing right off that "the writer of this book would rather see his race and his civilization blotted out with the atomic bomb than to see it slowly but surely destroyed in the maelstrom of miscegenation, interbreeding, intermarriage, and mongrelization" (np).

"Bilbo is not Hitler," the youthful Stingo says in the novel. Stingo is right—Bilbo was not a mass murderer—but what Stingo has yet to see, but will see eventually, is that ultimately he must judge Bilbo not only in the context of populist governors but also in the context of the violent racism—and slavery—of the South and Nazi Germany, a realization that will lead him to accept a further and more important insight with which Nathan challenged him: that as a privileged white Southerner, a Virginian gentleman, Stingo shares responsibility for the South's racial violence and that in the end he must judge himself not only alongside other white Southerners who did little to stop racial violence but also alongside the German populace who stood passively by while the Nazis led their nation from the street violence of *Kristallnacht* to the slave camp of Auschwitz.

Percy's and Styron's work in the 1970s points to the continuing presence of European Fascism, and more generally totalitarianism, in the white Southern imagination, a haunting that, as we have seen, began in earnest during the 1930s. Their work furthermore suggests that, not unlike Katherine Anne Porter's Miranda, who at the end of "Old Mortality" vowed to discover her own truths and create her own legends, white Southern writers in the post–World War II South have discovered that it is all but impossible to step entirely free from the past. Remaining haunted by long memories of anguish and guilt, they have learned that the fears and obsessions of their ancestors are in many ways their own, however much history separates them, however much Southern society has changed for the better. And finally, and perhaps most significantly, the work of Percy and Styron suggests that the long shadow of Nazi Germany continues to shade white Southerners' perceptions of their homeland and to serve as a touchstone for understanding the South's benighted history, stretching from the days of slavery to the days in which we now live.

NOTES

INTRODUCTION

1. It is not known whether Smith accurately reported the camper's words or fabricated them for a powerful effect.

2. While I am well aware of the many conflicting theories of the origins and manifestations of Fascism, together with the different structures and ideologies of Nazi Germany and Fascist Italy, throughout the book I use the term *Fascism* in the same way that most of the writers in this study used it during the 1930s and 1940s: to suggest broadly the totalitarian systems of both Fascist Italy and Nazi Germany. While southern writers of this period typically did not distinguish between the two when they spoke of Fascism, they generally had Nazi Germany foremost in mind, both because of Nazi racial ideology and practice, which cast a disturbing light on the South's system of segregation, and because of the grave military threat posed by Nazi Germany and Hitler. For various interpretations of Fascism, see esp. Hannah Arendt, *The Origins of Totalitarianism*, new ed. (New York: Harcourt Brace Jovanovich, 1973); Roger Eatwell, *Fascism: A History* (New York: Penguin, 1997); Renzo De Felice, *Interpretations of Fascism*, trans. Brenda Huff Everett (Cambridge, MA: Harvard University Press, 1977); Roger Griffin, ed., *International Fascism: Theories, Causes, and the New Consensus* (New York: Oxford University Press, 1998); Walter Laqueur, *Fascism: Past, Present, Future* (New York: Oxford University Press, 1996); George L. Mosse, *The Fascist Revolution: Toward a General Theory of Fascism* (New York: Howard Fertig, 1999); and Stanley G. Payne, *A History of Fascism, 1914–1945* (Madison: University of Wisconsin Press, 1995).

3. Examining the South in a global context is one of the foundations of what many critics are now calling "the new southern studies." As Kathryn McKee and Annette Trefzer write in their preface to a recent symposium on southern studies in *American Literature*, the new southern studies focuses on the "global South," giving rise to series of questions extending far beyond regional and national borders and frameworks: "What happens when we unmoor the South from its national harbor, when it becomes a floating signifier in a sea of globalism? How does the South participate in the global networks of culture and economy? How have the South's culture and history always already been global? What are the global gestures in liter-

ary texts that we were formerly interpreting as regional or national issues?" "Preface: Global Contexts, Local Literatures; The New Southern Studies," *American Literature* 78 (December 2006): 678. Not surprisingly, much of the work done on the global South has focused on the South's relationship to the Caribbean and to Central and South America. For further discussion of the issue of the new southern studies and for some examples of scholarship on the global South, see esp. Houston A. Baker, Jr., and Dana D. Nelson, "Preface: Violence, the Body and 'The South,'" ibid. 73 (June 2001): 231–43; Michael Kreyling, "Toward 'A New Southern Studies,'" *South Central Review* 22 (Spring 2005): 4–18; John Lowe, "'Calypso Magnolia': The Caribbean Side of the South," ibid., 54–80; Kathryn McKee and Annette Trefzer, eds., "The U.S. South in Global Contexts: A Collection of Position Statements," *American Literature* 78 (December 2006): 691–739; Deborah N. Cohn, *History and Memory in the Two Souths: Recent Southern and Spanish American Fiction* (Nashville, TN: Vanderbilt University Press, 1999); Douglas Sullivan-Gonzales and Charles Reagan Wilson, eds., *The South and the Caribbean* (Jackson: University Press of Mississippi, 2001); Suzanne W. Jones and Sharon Monteith, eds., *South to a New Place: Region, Literature, Culture* (Baton Rouge: Louisiana State University Press, 2002); Jon Smith and Deborah N. Cohn, eds., *Look Away! The U.S. in New World Studies* (Durham, NC: Duke University Press, 2004); and James L. Peacock, Harry L. Watson, and Carrie R. Mathews, eds., *The American South in a Global World* (Chapel Hill: University of North Carolina Press, 2005).

4. Franklin D. Roosevelt, *The Continuing Struggle for Liberalism: 1938; The Public Papers and Addresses of Franklin D. Roosevelt* (New York: Macmillan, 1941), 167–68.

5. Jennifer Rae Greeson, "The Figure of the South and the Nationalizing Imperatives of Early United States Literature," *Yale Journal of Criticism* 12 (Fall 1999): 209.

6. C. Vann Woodward, *The Burden of Southern History*, rev. ed. (Baton Rouge: Louisiana State University Press, 1968); see esp. his chapters "The Irony of Southern History" and "A Second Look at the Theme of Irony."

7. In a recent study exploring the complex interplay between the South and the rest of America in the first half of the twentieth century, Leigh Anne Duck brilliantly explores how the trope of the backward South crucially shaped the nation's political self-definition as it modernized and then faced the crises of the Great Depression and World War II. Duck explores the various ways southern writers from the period negotiated the regional-national dynamic, focusing most tellingly on the issue of time, often expressed in the tension between the nation's progressive line into the future and the South's stubbornly embraced stasis. See Leigh Anne Duck, *The Nation's Region: Southern Modernism, Segregation, and U.S. Nationalism* (Athens: University of Georgia Press, 2006).

8. Jean Toomer, *Cane* (1923; New York: Liveright, 1975), 27.

9. Richard Wright, "The Ethics of Living Jim Crow," in *Uncle Tom's Children* (1940; New York: HarperPerennial, 1993), 13.

10. Carl Carmer, *Stars Fell on Alabama* (New York: Blue Ribbon Books, 1934), xiii (hereafter cited in text).

11. In this description of a policelike state, Carmer was challenging the position characteristically taken by southern newspapers in refuting the charge that southern persecution of blacks, and particularly lynching, mirrored the Nazis' persecution of the Jews. As Johnpeter Horst Grill and Robert L. Jenkins point out, in defending southern racial practices southern editorials typically argued that "lynchings were against the law, while anti-Jewish actions in Germany were supported by the state." "The Nazis and the American South in the 1930s: A Mirror Image?"

Journal of Southern History 58 (November 1992): 686. See also John T. Kneebone, *Southern Liberal Journalists and the Issue of Race, 1920–1944* (Chapel Hill: University of North Carolina Press, 1985).

12. Hermann Rauschning, *The Revolution of Nihilism: Warning to the West*, trans. E. W. Dickes (New York: Alliance Book Corporation, 1939).

13. Ibid., xii.

14. Wilhelm Reich, *The Mass Psychology of Fascism*, trans. Vincent R. Carfagno (New York: Farrar, Straus and Giroux, 1970).

15. Virginius Dabney, "If the South Had Won the War," *American Mercury* 39 (October 1936): 200 (hereafter cited in text).

16. Regarding the reference to the Sands Point washroom, in September 1933, Long had attended a charity party at the Sands Point Bath Club on Long Island, New York. When visiting the rest room, the inebriated Long apparently had urinated on a man's leg after he would not move away from the urinal for him; the man had smashed Long in the face, bloodying him. The incident had been a great embarrassment for Long, and his detractors often referred to the incident when mocking him.

17. I am grateful to the work of Morton Sosna for insights on the democratic revival and the South, specifically "Democratic Discourse: Implications for the South" (paper presented at the annual meeting of the Southern Historical Association Meeting, 1987). See also Philip Gleason, "Americans All: World War II and the Shaping of American Identity," *Review of Politics* 43 (October 1981): 483–518; Edward A. Purcell, Jr., *The Crisis of Democratic Theory: Scientific Naturalism and the Problem of Value* (Lexington: University Press of Kentucky, 1973); and Benjamin L. Alpers, *Dictators, Democracy, and American Public Culture: Envisioning the Totalitarian Enemy, 1920s–1950s* (Chapel Hill: University of North Carolina Press, 2003).

18. While Mead does not mention the South explicitly here, her call for the "segregation" of those societies infected with nondemocratic irrationalism suggests a turning of the tables on the white South.

19. Robert L. Dorman, *Revolt of the Provinces: The Regionalist Movement in America, 1920–1945* (Chapel Hill: University of North Carolina Press, 1993).

20. Melvin Rader, *No Compromise: The Conflict between Two Worlds* (New York: Macmillan, 1939).

21. Ibid., 337.

22. Excellent discussions of the political controversies surrounding regionalist painting include James M. Dennis, *Renegade Regionalists: The Modern Independence of Grant Wood, Thomas Hart Benton, and John Steuart Curry* (Madison: University of Wisconsin Press, 1998); Erika Doss, *Benton, Pollock, and the Politics of Modernism: From Regionalism to Abstract Modernism* (Chicago: University of Chicago Press, 1991); and Cécile Whiting, *Antifascism in American Art* (New Haven, CT: Yale University Press, 1989).

23. Stuart Davis, "Davis Rejoinder," *Art Digest* 9 (1 April 1935): 13 (hereafter cited in text).

24. Peyton Boswell, "The Grant Wood Controversy," ibid. 17 (1 December 1942): 3.

25. H. W. Janson, "Benton and Wood, Champions of Regionalism," *Magazine of Art* 39 (May 1946): 184 (hereafter cited in text).

26. Doxey A. Wilkerson, "Freedom—Through Victory in War and Peace," in *What the Negro Wants*, ed. Rayford W. Logan (Chapel Hill: University of North Carolina Press, 1944), 196.

27. Walter White, *A Rising Wind* (Garden City, NY: Doubleday, Doran, 1945), 154 (hereafter cited in text).

28. Zora Neale Hurston, "Seeing the World as It Is," in appendix to *Dust Tracks on a Road* (1942; New York: HarperPerennial, 1991), 250–51 (hereafter cited in text).

29. Mark Christian Thompson, in *Black Fascisms: African American Literature and Culture Between the Wars* (Charlottesville: University of Virginia Press, 2007), which came out after my manuscript was completed, argues that Zora Neale Hurston and Richard Wright, along with several other prominent African American writers, embraced "a uniquely black form of generic fascism" (2) in their critiques of American democracy and European totalitarianism. Particularly significant in terms of this study is that in analyzing "fascistic fantasies" (13) in African American writing, Thompson locates Hurston and Wright in a national rather than a regional context, downplaying their southernness and linking their work instead to that of Marcus Garvey, George Schuyler, and Claude McKay. Although not explicitly, Thompson thus supports my point that Hurston's and Wright's feelings about Fascism (whether or not one agrees with Thompson's controversial interpretation of those feelings) primarily shaped their attitudes concerning America's, rather than the South's, failings.

30. In their wartime focus on the national and international scope of racial discrimination, black southern writers were largely in line with the prevailing view among black American intellectuals. This view is everywhere evident, for instance, in Rayford W. Logan's influential collection of essays *What the Negro Wants*, published in 1944. Logan selected contributors from a wide political spectrum—he says in the preface that he assembled four conservatives, five liberals, and five radicals—and while they differed in political perspective and strategy, they all underscored that what the Negro wanted was full democratic rights and status, not just in the South but everywhere in America. Logan established the overarching theme of the collection in his opening essay, which he entitled "The Negro Wants First-Class Citizenship" and which begins, "The Negro problem in the United States is today a national problem" (1). The international scope of racial discrimination was emphasized by several of the contributors, including George S. Schuyler, who in his essay, "The Caucasian Problem," bluntly concluded that "the basic philosophy of the white rulers here is the same as that elsewhere [throughout the world]. It is not a national problem but a world problem" (294). Other contributors included Mary McLeod Bethune, Sterling A. Brown, W. E. B. Du Bois, Gordon B. Hancock, Leslie Pinckney Hill, Langston Hughes, Frederick D. Patterson, A. Philip Randolph, Willard S. Townsend, Charles H. Wesley, Doxey A. Wilkerson, and Roy Wilkins.

31. Richard Wright, "How 'Bigger' Was Born," in *Richard Wright: Early Works* (New York: Library of America, 1991), 864 (hereafter cited in text).

32. Richard Wright, *Native Son*, in ibid., 829 (hereafter cited in text).

33. The quotations from Canfield Fisher's letter to Wright are from Jeff Karem, "'I Could Never Really Leave the South': Regionalism and the Transformation of Richard Wright's *American Hunger*," *American Literary History* 13 (Winter 2001): 702.

34. Richard Wright, *Black Boy: A Record of Childhood and Youth*, restored text of *American Hunger* (New York: HarperPerennial, 1993), 312.

35. Richard Wright, *Black Boy: A Record of Childhood and Youth* (New York: Harper and Brothers, 1945), 228.

36. Dorothy Canfield [Fisher], "*Black Boy* by Richard Wright," *Book-of-the-Month Club News*, February 1945, 2 (hereafter cited in text).

37. Inside front jacket, *Black Boy*, 1945 ed. Further underscoring the patriotic thrust of the reconstructed *Black Boy*, the inside back jacket issues a call to buy war bonds, targeting black workers and purportedly written by Wright (his signature follows the appeal). Under the title

"Don't Wear Your 'Sunday Best' Every Day," the jacket copy reads: "Down South where I was born we called our good clothes our 'Sunday Best,' and we wore them only on Sundays. Today we are all making big war money, but there aren't enough goods to buy. So I'd say let's put our money away in WAR BONDS until peace (Sunday) comes. Don't be a dude: All dressed up and nowhere to go. Dudes usually get into trouble. And you'll get into trouble—INFLATION—if you spend war dollars unnecessarily. The war is far from over; millions of boys overseas want to come back home. So pull off your 'Sunday Best'—shed your dollars—and buy WAR BONDS. That's the sensible way to do it!"

38. The trend to look outside the South to understand the South no doubt will have a large impact on new interpretations of southern literature. For a brilliant reading of southern literature from the 1930s and 1940s, showing the interplay between the South and the rest of the nation, see Duck, *Nation's Region*, discussed briefly in n. 7 above.

39. See, e.g., Thomas Carl Austenfeld, *American Women Writers and the Nazis: Ethics and Politics in Boyle, Porter, Stafford, and Hellman* (Charlottesville: University Press of Virginia, 2001); Anne Goodwyn Jones, "Every Woman Loves a Fascist: Writing World War II on the Southern Home Front," in *Remaking Dixie: The Impact of World War II on the American South*, ed. Neil R. McMillan (Jackson: University Press of Mississippi, 1997), 111–30; Barbara Ladd, "'Writing against Death': Totalitarianism and the Nonfiction of Eudora Welty at Midcentury," in *Eudora Welty and Politics: Did the Writer Crusade?* ed. Harriet Pollack and Suzanne Marrs (Baton Rouge: Louisiana State University Press, 2001), 155–78; and Ted Atkinson's chapter on Faulkner and Fascism, "Power by Design: Faulkner and the Specter of Fascism," in his *Faulkner and the Great Depression: Aesthetics, Ideology, and Cultural Politics* (Athens: University of Georgia Press, 2006), 115–72.

40. There are other white writers who struggled with these issues who are not included in this study, including Clarence Cason, Richard Weaver, Stetson Kennedy, James Agee, and Erskine Caldwell. At some point, in a long study such as this one, comprehensiveness had to give way to selection.

CHAPTER I

1. A fourth Agrarian, Robert Penn Warren, is treated in a later chapter. Warren stands apart from Ransom, Tate, and Davidson in that he was not one of the group's leaders and was not actively involved in the group's political efforts.

2. Tate was heavily influenced by the British historian Christopher Hollis, who in *The American Heresy* (1927) argued that the Civil War had been the watershed event for the creation of the all-powerful plutocracy ruling over twentieth-century America. Hollis wrote that with the destruction of the South, the only region in America that lived by the ideals of Jeffersonian republicanism (liberty and equality depended on the widespread distribution of property as found in agricultural societies), forces of rapacious industrialism had ruled unchecked and eventually taken control of the American political system. Tate acknowledged his debt to Hollis in a bibliographical note to *Jefferson Davis*, writing that "in so far as the general point of view of this volume is not the author's—in so far as it is indebted to influences too minute or too remote to be acknowledged—it is that of a book called *The American Heresy*, by Christopher Hollis. The book is incomplete and inaccurately documented, but it is the first effort to comprehend the supposedly mixed forces of American history under a single idea." Allen Tate,

Jefferson Davis: His Rise and Fall; A Biographical Narrative (New York: Minton, Balch, 1929), 303. For discussions of Hollis's influence on Tate, see esp. Paul H. Buck, "American Heresies," *Hound and Horn* 6 (January–March 1933): 357–67; and Alexander Karanikas, *Tillers of a Myth: Southern Agrarians as Social and Literary Critics* (Madison: University of Wisconsin Press, 1966), 28–30.

3. Tate, *Jefferson Davis*, 301–2.

4. Robert H. Brinkmeyer, Jr., *Remapping Southern Literature: Contemporary Southern Writers and the West* (Athens: University of Georgia Press, 2000), 4; the first chapter talks extensively about the contrast of East and West in twentieth-century southern literature.

5. Sarah Newman Shouse, *Hillbilly Realist: Herman Clarence Nixon of Possum Trot* (University: University of Alabama Press, 1986), 57.

6. Robert Penn Warren, *The Selected Letters of Robert Penn Warren*, vol. 1, *The Apprenticeship Years, 1924–1934*, ed. William Bedford Clark (Baton Rouge: Louisiana State University Press, 2000), 185.

7. Ibid., 187.

8. In a few years, as the threat of Fascism grew, the Agrarians revised their thinking, seeing the centralization brought about through finance capitalism as evolving into either Fascism or Communism.

9. To signal the unanimity of the group, Ransom's introduction went unsigned.

10. Donald Davidson, "Social Science Discovers Regionalism," in *The Attack on Leviathan: Regionalism and Nationalism in the United States* (Chapel Hill: University of North Carolina Press, 1938), 64.

11. It is not difficult to see Tate's attraction to the right-wing politics of L'Action Française, which, among other things, called for the restoration of the monarchy in France and the establishment of Roman Catholicism as the state religion. By the time of Tate's letter, L'Action Française was strongly endorsing the authoritarian rule of Benito Mussolini, and it would later support that of Francisco Franco.

12. In his survey of these reviews, Paul Conkin notes that it hardly mattered from what perspective reviewers approached the symposium; in the end "almost no one endorsed or unqualifiedly praised the book." Paul K. Conkin, *The Southern Agrarians* (Knoxville: University of Tennessee Press, 1988), 87.

13. Gerald W. Johnson, "No More Excuses: A Southerner to Southerners," *Harper's*, February 1931, 333.

14. Gerald W. Johnson, "The South Faces Itself," *Virginia Quarterly Review* 7 (January 1931): 157.

15. Johnson, "No More Excuses," 337.

16. Of the three other traditionalist groups with which Collins brought the Agrarians into contact, the British Distributists had the most influence on their ideas and strategies, particularly Tate's. The Distributists were vocal antimodernists, deeply admired by Collins, who called for an end to finance capitalism and the industrial state and supported the widespread distribution of land and the creation of a guild economy, taking their inspiration from Catholic societies of the Middle Ages. Tate was bowled over when he read the Distributists; he shared more with them than did the other Agrarians, particularly in his admiration for the authority of the Catholic Church and in his belief that the Agrarian movement needed a well-defined religious center. If the other Agrarians did not quite share Tate's enthusiasm for the Distributists, most of them nonetheless eventually realized that the Distributist agenda, particularly its call

for redistributing land to resist political and economic collectivism and to protect individual freedom, gave them a structure for their own practical proposals. Before long, the Agrarians' rhetoric was sounding very much like the Distributists'. Collins fully outlined his reasons for bringing together the four antimodernist groups in the first issue of the *American Review*. See Seward Collins, "Editorial Notes," *American Review* 1 (April 1933): 122–27. For further discussion of Collins and the *American Review*, see esp. Albert E. Stone, Jr., "Seward Collins and the *American Review*: Experiment in Pro-Fascism, 1933–37," *American Quarterly* 12 (Spring 1960): 4–19.

17. Collins's meeting with the Agrarians is discussed in Conkin, *Southern Agrarians*, 107–9. The Agrarian plan to manipulate Collins is discussed in Thomas A. Underwood, *Allen Tate: Orphan of the South* (Princeton, NJ: Princeton University Press, 2000), 203–4.

18. For further discussion of Tate's dispute with Collins, see esp. Underwood, *Allen Tate*, 202–3.

19. Quoted in ibid., 204.

20. There is evidence that Tate was reading the journal closely. Tate declared in a letter to Collins (14 April 1933) that it was "the only magazine I've ever read every word of which I was able to agree with." Quoted in ibid., 206.

21. Harold Goad, "The Corporate State," *American Review* 1 (April 1933): 93.

22. Collins, "Editorial Notes," 127.

23. Seward Collins, "Editorial Notes: The Revival of Monarchy," *American Review* 1 (May 1933): 245, 252 (hereafter cited in text).

24. In an essay shortly thereafter, Collins made his most ambitious attempt to explain his understanding of Fascism: "Fascism betokens the revival of monarchy, property, the guilds, the security of the family and the peasantry, and the ancient ways of European life." Seward Collins, "Editorial Notes: *The American Review*'s First Year," *American Review* 3 (April 1934): 124. Although he did not put it exactly in these words, Collins clearly saw Fascism as combining the best of the journal's four antimodernist perspectives—Distributism, Neo-Humanism, Neo-Scholasticism, and Agrarianism. Put another way, as the essence of traditionalism, Fascism was the center holding together the antimodernist alliance.

25. See, e.g., the following essays by Ransom: "Land! An Answer to the Unemployment Problem," *Harper's*, July 1932, 216–24; "What Does the South Want?" *Virginia Quarterly Review* 12 (April 1936): 180–94; and "The South Is a Bulwark," *Scribner's Magazine* 99 (May 1936): 299–303.

26. John Crowe Ransom, "A Capital for the New Deal," *American Review* 1 (December 1933): 129–42.

27. See William Yandell Elliott, *The Need for Constitutional Reform: A Program for National Security* (New York: McGraw-Hill, 1935); Frank Owsley, "The Pillars of Agrarianism," *American Review* 4 (March 1935): 529–47; and Donald Davidson, "Where Regionalism and Sectionalism Meet," *Social Forces* 13 (October 1934–May 1935): 23–31.

28. Allen Tate, "The Problem of the Unemployed: A Modest Proposal," *American Review* 1 (May 1933): 146 (hereafter cited in text).

29. After the Italian invasion of Ethiopia in 1935 and then G. K. Chesterton's death in 1936, the more moderate Distributists fell away from the movement, leaving Distributism mainly in the hands of Hillaire Belloc and other hard-liners, including A. J. Penty and Douglas Jerrold, all of whom were admirers of Mussolini. The most prolific Distributist contributors to the *American Review*, these were the ones most associated with the Agrarian alliance.

30. Grace Lumpkin, "I Want a King," *Fight against War and Fascism* 3 (February 1936): 3 (hereafter cited in text).

31. Quoted in Underwood, *Allen Tate*, 229.

32. The editors of the *New Republic* entitled the exchange between Tate and Lumpkin "Fascism and the Southern Agrarians," and they introduced the letters with a short commentary that included excerpts from Lumpkin's interview of Collins. See "Fascism and the Southern Agrarians," *New Republic*, 27 May 1936, 75–76.

33. Allen Tate, open letter to Grace Lumpkin, in "Fascism and the Southern Agrarians," 75 (hereafter cited in text).

34. Tate's essay was published in *I'll Take My Stand*. Rather than a literal call to arms, Tate's lines speak about the psychological violence that modern southerners had to perform in order to embrace Old South traditionalism: they had somehow to wrench themselves free from their modern rationality and then will themselves, with deliberate calculation, into an emotional connection with their heritage. But, as Tate explained, the very condition of self-consciousness, of having to *choose* traditionalism rather than living it unthinkingly, finally voided the traditional. "Indeed," writes Tate, "the act of loyalty, or the fact of loyalty, must be spontaneous to count at all; tradition must, in other words, be automatically operative before it can be called tradition" (*ITMS* 162).

35. Grace Lumpkin, open letter to Allen Tate, in "Fascism and the Southern Agrarians," 76 (hereafter cited in text).

36. Fletcher's essay appeared in *ITMS*, 92–121.

37. Albert E. Stone, Jr., conjectures, probably correctly, that Malcolm Cowley was responsible for the title. Stone, "Seward Collins and the *American Review*," 17.

38. Seward Collins, letter to the editor, in "The Sunny Side of Fascism," *New Republic*, 10 June 1936, 131 (hereafter cited in text).

39. Grace Lumpkin, letter to the editor, in ibid., 132.

40. Virginia Rock observes that Malcolm Cowley probably wrote the commentary. Virginia Rock, "The Making and Meaning of *I'll Take My Stand*: A Study in Utopian Conservatism, 1925–1929" (PhD diss., University of Minnesota, 1961), 405.

41. Editors' note to "The Sunny Side of Fascism," 132.

42. For discussions of the trial and its significance as a flashpoint for discussion of southern racial practices, see esp. Dan T. Carter, *Scottsboro: A Tragedy of the American South* (Baton Rouge: Louisiana State University Press, 1979); and James Goodman, *Stories of Scottsboro: The Rape Case That Shook 1930's America and Revived the Struggle for Equality* (New York: Pantheon, 1994).

43. The fullest discussion of the Scottsboro case by an Agrarian is Frank Owsley, "Scottsboro, the Third Crusade: The Sequel to Abolition and Reconstruction," *American Review* 1 (June 1933): 257–85. Tate talked about the case in a letter to John Brooks Wheelwright (25 February 1932), warning that a vicious backlash against blacks loomed because of the agitators' attempts to use the case as an attack on segregation. In that same letter he also commented on the power dynamics structuring southern segregation: "You have no idea what it is to live—and not merely sympathize from Boston or New York—with another race; and for that and all the complicating reasons I see the negro question in terms of power. When there are two unassimilable races one of them must rule; and being white I prefer white rule, and I will not give up the slightest instrument of white rule that seems necessary. It's too bad that the negro has

no interested protector—for example, an owner—and is at the mercy of the mob. I see no solution." Quoted in Underwood, *Allen Tate*, 293.

44. John Gould Fletcher, "Is This the Voice of the South?" letter to the editor, *Nation*, 27 December 1933, 735 (hereafter cited in text).

45. Frank Owsley, "The Foundations of Democracy," in *Who Owns America? A New Declaration of Independence*, ed. Herbert Agar and Allen Tate (1936; Wilmington, DE: ISI Books, 1999), 92.

46. Lyle H. Lanier, "Big Business in the Property State," in ibid., 30–31.

47. Herbert Agar, "But Can It Be Done?" in ibid., 144.

48. Allen Tate, "Notes on Liberty and Property," in ibid., 123, 122.

49. Owsley, "Foundations of Democracy," 82–83.

50. Donald Davidson, "That This Nation May Endure," in *Who Owns America?* 162, 163.

51. Robert Penn Warren, "Literature as a Symptom," in ibid., 353 (hereafter cited in text).

52. Dwight McDonald, review of Agar and Tate, *Who Owns America? Common Sense* 5 (August 1936): 27.

53. V. F. Calverton, "The Bankruptcy of Southern Culture," *Scribner's*, May 1936, 298.

54. John Chamberlain, "Agrarianism, American Style," review of Agar and Tate, *Who Owns America? Saturday Review of Literature*, 25 July 1936, 17.

55. Corliss Lamont, *You Might Like Socialism: A Way of Life for Modern Man* (New York: Modern Age Books, 1939), 52, 53.

56. Quoted in Thomas Daniel Young, *Gentleman in a Dustcoat: A Biography of John Crowe Ransom* (Baton Rouge: Louisiana State University Press, 1976), 262.

57. Quoted in Underwood, *Allen Tate*, 251.

58. Donald Davidson, "American Heroes," in Davidson, *Attack on Leviathan*, 217.

59. Donald Davidson, "Mr. Cash and the Proto-Dorian South," *Southern Review* 7 (Summer 1941): 1–20; idem, "Preface to Decision," *Sewanee Review* 53 (July–September 1945): 394–412 (hereafter both essays cited in text).

60. Davidson was not the only southern traditionalist to attack Cash's connecting Nazi Germany with southern culture. Richard Weaver, who was much influenced by John Crowe Ransom and the Agrarians in general, opened his dissertation (most of which was written in 1941–42, though it was not published until years later, in 1968, as *The Southern Tradition at Bay*) with a clear reference to Cash: "The mind of the South, which has been conspicuous for its resistance to the spiritual disintegration of the modern world, is traditional in the sense that it exhibits important connections with European civilization. The habit of contemporary publicity has been to treat it in terms of superficial contrasts and to ignore the fact that it rests upon conceptions more fundamental in human nature than those envisaged by certain modern philosophies." *The Southern Tradition at Bay: A History of Postbellum Thought*, ed. George Core and M. E. Bradford (1968; Washington, DC: Regnery Gateway, 1989), 31. Weaver went further than most traditionalists in noting similarities between Fascism and southern traditionalism, linking them as revolts against modernity. But he argued that Fascism, despite its antimodernist impulse, ultimately transformed itself into modernity's worst nightmare—the authoritarian state. Weaver thus concluded that apparent similarities between the traditional South and the Fascist state were insignificant, as the two systems were finally fundamentally opposed to each other. In an essay written near the end of the war that discussed this issue further Weaver wrote: "In the ideological conflict between the South and Fascist Europe the world before the French

Revolution looks at the world after the French Revolution and finds it hateful." "The South and the Revolution of Nihilism," in *The Southern Essays of Richard M. Weaver*, ed. George M. Curtis III and James J. Thompson, Jr. (Indianapolis, IN: Liberty Press, 1987), 184.

61. Donald Davidson, *The Tennessee*, vol. 1, *The Old River: Frontier to Secession* (1946; Nashville, TN: J. S. Sanders, 1991), 17–18.

62. Donald Davidson, *The Tennessee*, vol. 2, *The New River: Civil War to TVA* (1948; Nashville, TN: J. S. Sanders, 1992), 251.

63. John Crowe Ransom, "Criticism as Pure Speculation," in *The Intent of the Critic*, ed. Donald Stauffer (Princeton, NJ: Princeton University Press, 1941), 108 (hereafter cited in text).

64. John Crowe Ransom, "Muses and Amazons," *Kenyon Review* 3 (Spring 1941): 240 (hereafter cited in text).

65. John Crowe Ransom, "We Resume," ibid. 4 (Autumn 1942): 405 (hereafter cited in text).

66. John Crowe Ransom, "Artists, Soldiers, Positivists," ibid. 6 (Spring 1944): 276 (hereafter cited in text).

67. John Crowe Ransom, "Art and the Human Economy," ibid. 7 (Autumn 1945): 686 (hereafter cited in text).

68. Allen Tate, "The Present Function of Criticism," *Southern Review* 6 (Autumn 1940): 238 (hereafter cited in text).

69. Allen Tate, preface to *Reactionary Essays on Poetry and Ideas* (New York: Charles Scribner's Sons, 1936), xii (hereafter cited in text).

70. MacLeish first delivered "The Irresponsibles" as a lecture to the American Philosophical Society on 19 April 1940. It was published in the *Nation* on 18 May 1940 (618–23), and later in the year it was published as a small book, *The Irresponsibles: A Declaration*, by Duell, Sloan and Pierce of New York.

71. Allen Tate, preface to *Reason in Madness: Critical Essays* (New York: G. P. Putnam's Sons, 1941), x (hereafter cited in text).

72. For further discussion of the creation of the Office of the Coordinator of Information, see Anthony Cave Brown, *The Last Hero: Wild Bill Donovan* (New York: Random House, 1982), 165–71.

73. Cleanth Brooks and Allen Tate, *Cleanth Brooks and Allen Tate: Collected Letters, 1933–1976*, ed. Alphonse Vinh (Columbia: University of Missouri Press, 1998), 83 (hereafter cited in text).

74. As it turned out, the *Southern Review* ceased publication in 1942, not because of government suppression but because of financial problems facing Louisiana State University resulting from the war.

75. Allen Tate, "Anti-Axis Poetry," letter to the editor, *New Republic*, 16 November 1942, 643.

76. Davidman's response to Tate's letter, published several weeks later in the *New Republic*, chastised him as an irresponsible defeatist and a "snob-poet of the culture-hounds," a man completely out touch with reality, in contrast to the genuine poet, who was "a passionate participant in the life of the men around him." While not flat-out calling Tate unpatriotic, she wrote that Tate's poetic objectives embodied "the worst sort of passive defeatism" and were expressed in "the kind of escapist poetry which tries to pretend the war isn't there at all." "This way lies madness," she commented; "this way lie irresponsibility and disintegration. Mr. Tate is opposing my 'mere call to action' with a mere call to inaction, which is not only the less courageous but the less poetic of the two." Joy Davidman, "A Reply to Mr. Tate," letter to the editor, *New Re-*

public, 21 December 1942, 829. Davidman's dismissal of Tate's poetics and her questioning of his national loyalties represented to Tate precisely the type of authoritarian demands that he believed American writers were then facing.

77. Allen Tate, "The State of Letters," *Sewanee Review* 52 (October–December 1944): 610 (hereafter cited in text).

78. Allen Tate, *The Fathers* (New York: G. P. Putnam's Sons, 1938), 5 (hereafter cited in text).

79. Quoted in Underwood, *Allen Tate*, 267.

80. Tate's interest in salvaging humane values in a world spiraling toward barbarism can also be seen in his reconfiguration of his understanding of the Agrarian movement. In a decided turn from his earlier views, Tate declared early in the war that, at least to him, the Agrarian movement had been primarily an affirmation of the values of Western civilization rather than an effort at practical politics. No doubt Tate surprised Davidson when he wrote his friend (4 December 1942) that "you evidently believe that agrarianism was a failure; I think it was and *is* a very great success; but then I never expected it to have any political influence. It is a reaffirmation of the humane tradition, and to reaffirm that is an end in itself" (*LCDT* 328). This would be Tate's take on Agrarianism for the rest of his career; at the reunion of the Fugitive poets at Vanderbilt in 1956 he declared that Agrarianism was simply religious humanism. See *Fugitives' Reunion: Conversations at Vanderbilt, May 3–5, 1956*, ed. Rob Roy Purdy (Nashville, TN: Vanderbilt University Press, 1959).

81. John Peale Bishop and Allen Tate, *The Republic of Letters in America: The Correspondence of John Peale Bishop and Allen Tate*, ed. Thomas Daniel Young and John J. Hindle (Lexington: University Press of Kentucky, 1981), 197.

82. Radcliffe Squires, *Allen Tate: A Literary Biography* (New York: Pegasus, 1971), 159.

83. For a very fine discussion of this poem and Tate's use of Drayton, see M. E. Bradford, "Angels at Forty Thousand Feet: 'Ode to Our Young Pro-Consuls of the Air' and the Practice of Poetic Responsibility," in *Generations of the Faithful Heart: On the Literature of the South* (La Salle, IL: Sherwood Sugden, 1983), 183–99.

84. Henry R. Luce, "The American Century," *Life*, 17 February 1941, 63 (hereafter cited in text).

85. Bradford, "Angels at Forty Thousand Feet," 197. Cabell made his comments in *Let Me Lie: Being in the Main an Ethnological Account of the Remarkable Commonwealth of Virginia and the Making of Its History* (New York: Farrar, Straus, 1947), 15.

86. Tate had considered becoming a Catholic as early as 1929, a possibility that had shocked his Agrarian friends, particularly Davidson, who had written to Tate (29 July 1929) advising him against making this religious step, adding that "your services are badly needed in a big fight which I foresee in the immediate future" (*LCDT* 227). That battle, of course, was the Agrarian assault on finance capitalism, which Davidson proposed should begin with political, and not religious, commitment.

87. Norman Cousins and Harrison Smith, "Ezra Pound and the Bollingen Award," *Saturday Review of Literature*, 11 June 1949, 21 (hereafter cited in text).

88. Hillyer's two essays were "Treason's Strange Fruit," ibid., 11 June 1949, 9–11, 28, and "Poetry's New Priesthood," ibid., 18 June 1949, 7–9, 38; the quotation is from the second essay, 38 (hereafter cited in text).

89. Robert Gorham Davis, "The New Criticism and the Democratic Tradition," *American Scholar* 19 (Winter 1949–50): 11 (hereafter cited in text).

CHAPTER 2

1. W. J. Cash, "Problem in Definition: Now, What Is a Liberal?" *Charlotte News*, 6 November 1938. Cash's journalism from the *Charlotte News* is most readily available from a Cash Web site and online resource, "W. J. Cash: Quandaries of the Mind," available at www.wjcash.org (hereafter citations to Cash's journalism are from this resource and are identified in the text with the date of publication).

2. For a fine discussion of locating Cash's ideas on authoritarianism and totalitarianism, particularly in contrast with the those of the Agrarians and, even more significantly, Richard Weaver, see Richard King, "Cash and the Crisis of Political Modernity," in *W. J. Cash and the Minds of the South*, ed. Paul D. Escott (Baton Rouge: Louisiana State University Press, 1992), 67–87.

3. Quoted in Joseph L. Morrison, *W. J. Cash: Southern Prophet; A Biography and Reader* (New York: Alfred A. Knopf, 1967), 52.

4. W. J. Cash, "The Mind of the South," *American Mercury* 18 (October 1929): 185 (hereafter cited in text).

5. Cash claimed that he had written sixty thousand words in his application for a Guggenheim Fellowship submitted in October 1932. See Morrison, *W. J. Cash*, 59.

6. Quoted in ibid. Cash's comments are from his 1936 fellowship application to the Guggenheim Foundation.

7. The exception is Cash's 1933 essay "Buck Duke's University," *American Mercury* 30 (September 1933): 102–10. Cash concludes this essay by observing that liberal forces at Duke will eventually overcome the conservative stranglehold put in place by James Buchanan Duke: "In time, it seems certain, this university founded as a Babbitt mill will go over, lock, stock, barrel, hoof and horn, to Theory, and take up its place beside its neighbor, that University of North Carolina which old Buck distrusted, as a militant champion of civilization and a dangerous critic of the *status quo*" (110). But Fred Hobson observes that Cash's original ending suggests that the conservative forces at Duke would prevail. Fred C. Hobson, Jr., *Serpent in Eden: H. L. Mencken and the South* (Chapel Hill: University of North Carolina Press, 1974), 115. Mencken objected to Cash's downbeat conclusion and advised him to change it, which he did.

8. W. J. Cash, "The War in the South," *American Mercury* 19 (February 1930): 169.

9. W. J. Cash, "Close View of a Calvinist Lhasa," ibid. 28 (April 1933): 449 (hereafter cited in text).

10. W. J. Cash, "Holy Men Muff a Chance," ibid. 31 (January 1934): 113 (hereafter cited in text).

11. W. J. Cash, "Genesis of the Southern Cracker," ibid. 35 (May 1935): 106 (hereafter cited in text).

12. Bruce Clayton, *W. J. Cash: A Life* (Baton Rouge: Louisiana State University Press, 1991), 156.

13. The abridged English translation approved by the Nazi government cut some of Hitler's most extreme anti-Semitic and bellicose comments. The full, unexpurgated text was not commercially available in English until 1939. Before that, in the United States, Allen Cranston, then a journalist, distributed copies of a translation of the complete version until he was forced to stop when the court ruled in favor of the Nazi government in its suit to stop distribution.

14. Cash particularly admired the work of Dorothy Thompson, who was expelled from Germany in 1934 for publishing an unflattering interview with Hitler and whose syndicated columns on the European turmoil repeatedly commented on the Nazi danger. Cash fervently praised *Let the Record Speak* (1939), a collection of Thompson's commentary. See Cash's review,

"Dorothy Thompson Hits the Nail on the Head on Foreign Affairs: Uncanny Accuracy in Her Predictions," *Charlotte News*, 27 August 1939.

15. In the face of the European crisis, Cash in the mid-1930s also cut his ties with his former mentor, H. L. Mencken, whose elitist and antidemocratic positions were at odds with Cash's emergent liberalism. Cash bitterly attacked Mencken and his call for sterilization of America's poor in his editorial "Biological Suggestion: Henry Is Loose Again; Mr. Mencken's Idea," *Charlotte News*, 1 August 1937. While sympathetic with some of Mencken's concerns, such as the need to reduce the large number of the poor and to raise their standard of living, Cash found that his sterilization proposal would not only violate fundamental American civil liberties (following through on Mencken's proposal, Cash wrote, would "set a great many teeth to rattling for the safety of the Flag and the Republic") but also be inhumane, if not barbaric. While making no direct reference to Nazi eugenic theory and practice, Cash almost certainly had that in mind when he quoted Mencken's observation that without mass sterilization Americans faced the "wholesale degeneration of the American stock."

16. Scott was best known for her critiques of southern culture's demeaning and confining models of womanhood. Born Elsie Dunn, Scott and her lover Frederick Creighton Wellman changed their names (he became Cyril Kay Scott) to protect their identities after they secretly ran away to Brazil in 1913. Her autobiography, *Escapade* (1923), describes her escape from the South, and several of her novels, including *The Narrow House* (1921), *Narcissus* (1922), and *The Golden Door* (1925), portray the sufferings of women locked in conventional marriages.

17. Cash's speech can be found in print and audio versions (Cash was recorded reading the speech) online at "W. J. Cash: Quandaries of the Mind."

18. The immediate reference is to Anne Morrow Lindbergh's book *The Wave of the Future: A Confession of Faith* (New York: Harcourt, Brace, 1940), which Cash saw as a traitorous capitulation to Nazism. During the spring of 1941 Cash repeatedly attacked both Anne Morrow Lindbergh and, even more aggressively, her husband Charles A. Lindbergh for their ties to Nazi Germany and their calls for appeasement. Charles A. Lindbergh, as Cash noted, was very close to Alexis Carrel, a Nobel Prize–winning physician who was a strong supporter of eugenics and who in the mid-1930s voiced support for the Nazi enforced eugenics campaign, which included mass sterilization and euthanasia.

19. The reference is to R. H. Markham's rebuttal of Anne Morrow Lindbergh's argument, *The Wave of the Past* (Chapel Hill: University of North Carolina Press, 1941). Cash favorably reviewed Markham's answer to Anne Morrow Lindbergh in a review in the *Charlotte News* on 3 April 1941.

20. Certainly Cash's fear of the South's possible fall into barbarism helped push him toward the madness that led to his suicide only months after *The Mind of the South*'s publication. In spite of all his efforts to free the South from its ancient pattern, with his suicide Cash became another of that pattern's victims.

21. Anne Goodwyn Jones, "The Cash Nexus," in *The Mind of the South: Fifty Years Later*, ed. Charles W. Eagles (Jackson: University Press of Mississippi, 1992), 43.

CHAPTER 3

1. For biographical information on Percy, see esp. Lewis Baker, *The Percys of Mississippi: Politics and Literature in the New South* (Baton Rouge: Louisiana State University Press, 1983)

(hereafter cited both parenthetically in text and in notes); and Bertram Wyatt-Brown, *The House of Percy: Honor, Melancholy, and Imagination in a Southern Family* (New York: Oxford University Press, 1994).

2. The extent to which Percy's sexuality affected his aesthetic and rhetorical decisions, and particularly those necessary to reconcile his homosexuality and his admiration for a society in which it had no place, has yet to be fully explored. Much of the material in Percy's archive is severely restricted. For further discussion of Percy's sexuality, see esp. William Armstrong Percy III, "William Alexander Percy (1885–1942): His Homosexuality and Why It Matters," in *Carryin' On in the Lesbian and Gay South*, ed. John Howard (New York: New York University Press, 1997), 75–92.

3. Jay Tolson, *Pilgrim in the Ruins: A Life of Walker Percy* (New York: Simon and Schuster, 1992), 72.

4. For a fuller discussion of Walker Percy's request to travel to Germany, see ibid., 114–15.

5. Walker Percy's trip to Germany and its impact on his fiction is discussed in more depth in the coda.

6. Quoted in Phil McCombs, "Century of Thanatos: Walker Percy and His Subversive Message," *Southern Review*, n.s., 24 (Autumn 1988): 809.

7. Certainly Percy's retreat in verse to classical times was spurred in part by the displacement he suffered, but could not otherwise acknowledge, as a homosexual living in the traditional South.

8. Quoted in Fred C. Hobson, Jr., *Tell about the South: The Southern Rage to Explain* (Baton Rouge: Louisiana State University Press, 1983), 276.

9. Quoted in ibid.

10. For a good discussion of these issues, see Baker, *Percys of Mississippi*, 123–27; and Michael Kreyling, *Figures of the Hero in Southern Narrative* (Baton Rouge: Louisiana State University Press, 1987), 157–59.

11. In his reading of Frederick II, Lawson draws from Eric Voegelin's *The New Science of Politics*, Norman Cohn's *The Pursuit of the Millennium*, and Marjorie Reeves's *The Influence of Prophecy in the Later Middle Ages*. Lewis A. Lawson, "William Alexander Percy, Walker Percy, and the Apocalypse," *Modern Age* 24 (Fall 1980): 396–406 (hereafter cited in text).

12. Once the European war broke out, Percy worked hard locally to publicize the dangers of Nazi tyranny, including arranging lectures advocating American intervention. See David L. Cohn, "Eighteenth-Century Chevalier," *Virginia Quarterly Review* 31 (Autumn 1955): 574.

13. Quoted in Billups P. Spalding, "William Alexander Percy: His Philosophy of Life as Reflected in His Poetry" (MA thesis, University of Georgia, 1957), 57.

14. Quoted in ibid., 59.

15. At about this time, another white conservative much concerned with defending southern traditionalism, Richard Weaver, was also using the issue of hybridity in defending southern culture. In his dissertation, "The Confederate South, 1865–1910: A Study in the Survival of a Mind and a Culture," most of which was written in 1941 and 1942 (and which was published much later as *The Southern Tradition at Bay: A History of Postbellum Thought*, ed. George Core and M. E. Bradford [1968; Washington, DC: Regnery Gateway, 1989]), Weaver characterized southern traditionalism as a revolt against the sweeping forces of modernity unleashed by the French Revolution. Intriguingly, he also saw Fascism as a similar revolt, and in a remarkable passage he discussed the similarities of the Fascist and southern revolts:

> It is undeniable that there are numerous resemblances between the Southern agrarian mind and the mind of modern fascism, and I would affirm that fascism too in its ultimate character is a protest against materialist theories of history and society. This is certain despite the fact that fascism immersed itself in materialist techniques for its conquests, and thereby failed. This other society too believes in holiness and heroism; but it is humane, enlightened, and it insists on regard for personality more than do modern forms of statism under liberal and social-democratic banners. Above all, in meeting the problem of motivation it does what social democracy has never been able to do. Now that truth can once more be told, let us admit that fascism had secret sympathizers in every corner of the world and from every social level. It attracted by its call to achievement, by its poetry, by its offer of a dramatic life. It attracted even by its call to men to be hard on themselves. Social democracy will never be able to compete with this by promising to each a vine-covered cottage by the road and cradle-to-grave security. People who are yet vital want a challenge in life; they want opportunity to win distinction, and even those societies which permit distinction solely through the accumulation of wealth and its ostentatious display, such as ours has been, are better than those that permit none. From the bleakness of a socialist bureaucracy men will sooner or later turn to something stirring; they will decide again to live strenuously, or romantically. (379–80)

Ultimately, however, Weaver concluded that Fascism and southern traditionalism were violently opposed to each other, since Fascism, he argued, was traditionalism gone wrong. For Weaver, Fascism was a revolt against modernity that in the end embraced modernity in its assertion of values, becoming a hybrid monster.

16. Scott Romine's brilliant reading of *Lanterns on the Levee* explores this problem, persuasively arguing that Percy's aesthetic code represents his attempt to preserve his idealized community before the onslaught of history, an attempt that ends in failure and narrative exhaustion. My reading of Percy is similar to Romine's, though our emphases are different: Romine's analysis focuses on Percy's concealing of a coercive and self-interested aristocratic culture behind the image of communal assent and harmony; my analysis focuses on Percy's masking of the modernity of southern culture, including its possible connections to Nazi ideology, behind the image of traditional culture. See Scott Romine, "The Aesthetics of Community: William Alexander Percy's *Lanterns on the Levee*," in *The Narrative Forms of Southern Community* (Baton Rouge: Louisiana State University Press, 1999), 112–48.

17. Quoted in Baker, *Percys of Mississippi*, 170.

18. As Johnpeter Horst Grill and Robert L. Jenkins point out, equating the activities of the Ku Klux Klan with those of the Nazis was standard practice in southern newspapers during the 1930s. That position, of course, deflected criticism of southern racism away from mainstream southern culture. "The Nazis and the American South in the 1930s: A Mirror Image?" *Journal of Southern History* 58 (November 1992): 666–94.

19. For further discussion of the new Ku Klux Klan's middle-class origins, see esp. Nancy MacLean, *Behind the Mask of Chivalry: The Making of the Second Ku Klux Klan* (New York: Oxford University Press, 1995). Ironically, the very title of MacLean's book, suggesting the Klan's strategy of masking itself with chivalric ideals, also suggests Percy's narrative strategy in masking the aristocracy in *Lanterns on the Levee*.

20. LeRoy Percy, "The Modern Ku Klux Klan," *Atlantic Monthly*, July 1922, 124.

21. John M. Barry describes LeRoy Percy's attempts to import labor, including a scheme that went astray to recruit Italians to the Delta. See John M. Barry, *Rising Tide: The Great Mississippi Flood of 1927 and How It Changed America* (New York: Simon and Schuster, 1997), 108–13.

22. Besides LeRoy Percy, Barry identifies the powerbrokers as banker Joe Weinberg, planter Alfred Stone, and attorney Billy Wynn. See ibid., 143–44.

23. For a full discussion of General Ferguson and his embezzlement of levee funds, see William F. Holmes, "William Alexander Percy and the Bourbon Era in the Yazoo-Mississippi Delta," *Mississippi Quarterly* 26 (Winter 1972–73): 71–99.

24. Percy describes discovering much later that his father had been behind the flood committee's decision not to evacuate the blacks. There was nothing of noblesse oblige in that decision, as even Percy admits: it was a matter "of the dispersal of our labor" (*LL* 258); that is, the planters feared that evacuated blacks would not return, exacerbating an already existing labor shortage.

25. For conditions at the Greenville relief camp, see esp. Barry, *Rising Tide*, 310–17.

26. Percy at one point does connect relief efforts in Belgium to those during the flood, but only in terms of logistics. He asks himself whether the blacks, if they are not evacuated, should be fed "from centralized kitchens as the Belgians had been fed?" (*LL* 256). Percy makes no connection between the German treatment of the Belgians and the planters' treatment of Greenville's blacks.

27. Although Percy presents Fode suggesting these personal failings, he does not go so far as to have Fode comment on Percy's homosexuality (Fode was apparently one of Percy's lovers). Percy's essentialist taxonomy, allowing members of the aristocracy to be honorable no matter how they act, in all likelihood was in part rooted in his own alienation and self-loathing as a homosexual in Greenville; that is, his taxonomy allows him to remain pure as an aristocrat despite his "impure" sexual orientation. It is clear that Percy felt cowed before the figures of his father and grandfather, both of whom he casts as large, heroic figures, precisely what Percy saw himself as not being. The subtitle of *Lanterns on the Levee*, "Recollections of a Planter's Son," underscores his own sense of diminishment as a Percy, as does his admission in the text that, in contrast to his hard-living forebears, "I was blessed with no endearing vices: drunkenness made me sick, gambling bored me, rutting per se, unadorned, I considered overrated and degrading. In charitable mood one might call me an idealist, but, more normally, a sissy" (*LL* 125–26). One can read *Lanterns on the Levee* as Percy's defense of himself before his father's judgmental eyes. Near the end of the text, Percy looks back on his life and counts his failures—"at law undistinguished, at teaching unprepared, at soldiering average, at citizenship unimportant, at love second-best, at poetry forgotten before remembered" (*LL* 348). Even so, as an aristocrat and a "nice" person, he demands recognition from his father; and *Lanterns* ends with Percy fantasizing about a pilgrim (clearly Percy himself) passing before the High God (clearly Percy's father). To the God's question, "Who are you?" the text ends with these words: "The pilgrim I know should be able to straighten his shoulders, to stand his tallest, and to answer defiantly: 'I am your son'" (*LL* 348).

28. Quoted in Baker, *Percys of Mississippi*, 169. Percy made his comment in 1940. Three years later, Albert Jay Nock, another conservative (although not a southerner), echoed Percy's comment in *Memoirs of a Superfluous Man* (New York: Harper and Row, 1943). Robert M. Crunden, in the introduction to *The Superfluous Men: Conservative Critics of American Culture, 1900–1945* (Austin: University of Texas Press, 1977), argues that many conservative think-

ers from the period felt out of place in American society and withdrew from public involvement, cultivating instead their inner lives. Crunden does not discuss William Alexander Percy, but certainly Percy's life illustrates Crunden's thesis.

29. Whereas invisibility was a powerful tool for the poor whites in infiltrating the Delta, invisibility for the aristocracy was the last step before extinction, an emptying of presence in the present.

30. Besides seeing poor whites as threats to the gentry's purity, Percy identifies them as the cause of the South's destruction, in a sense designating them as "Jew figures," scapegoats for all of the failings of the white South. Percy also draws upon Jewish stereotypes when he links poor whites with forces of modernity.

31. In stark contrast to Percy's ideas on hybridization are those of another southern commentator, Stetson Kennedy, particularly in his blistering polemic *Southern Exposure* (Garden City, NY: Doubleday, 1946), which attacked both what he called "Southern-styled fascism" and the Fascist thinking he saw driving finance capitalism. Regarding racial hybridization, Kennedy answered southerners who decried the destruction of the white race through "mongrelization" (as did "their Nazi prototypes") by arguing that "the white-Negro combination results in a sound ethnic type with physical and mental characteristics equal and often superior to their parents" (334) and that such intermixing, quoting the observations of M. F. Ashley Montagu (author of *Man's Most Dangerous Myth: The Fallacy of Race*), leads humanity genetically forward not backward: "Hybridization is one of the most fundamental processes of evolution. In man it is an age-old process which was unquestionably operative among his proto-human ancestors. The genes combine to produce new types which are always novel and often recognizably superior in some traits to their parental stocks" (334).

32. Which is precisely Cash's point in *The Mind of the South*. See the discussion of Cash's interpretation of Reconstruction in chapter 2.

33. C. Vann Woodward, *Thinking Back: The Perils of Writing History* (Baton Rouge: Louisiana State University Press, 1986), 74.

34. See Leo Marx, *The Machine in the Garden: Technology and the Pastoral Ideal in America* (New York: Oxford University Press, 1964).

35. James C. Cobb, *The Most Southern Place on Earth: The Mississippi Delta and the Roots of Regional Identity* (New York: Oxford University Press, 1992), 141.

36. While Percy never mentions the popular racialist historians Lothrop Stoddard and Madison Grant, his configuring of Delta history as primarily racial shares similarities with their thinking. Both Percy and Stoddard, for instance, use the image of the dike (or levee) in advocating protection against the flood of alien races threatening the superior white race and civilization. Stoddard entitles one section of *The Rising Tide of Color against White World-Supremacy* (New York: Charles Scribner's Sons, 1921) "The Deluge on the Dikes," and he includes chapters titled "The Outer Dikes" (on regions of the world under white political control but with little white settlement) and "The Inner Dikes" (on regions of white settlement). Stoddard and Grant are discussed in greater depth in chapter 5.

CHAPTER 4

1. Lillian Smith, Dope with Lime, *North Georgia Review* 6 (Winter 1941): 5–6, 6 (hereafter cited in text).

2. Most other leftist critics of the South, unlike Smith, were liberal gradualists who spoke out against racial violence but not segregation. Smith characteristically attacked these southern liberals even more fiercely than she did avowed racists, in large part because she believed that liberals lacked the courage to live their beliefs and thus denied the South its needed leadership. The significant exception was Stetson Kennedy, a radical prolabor commentator who located Fascism in both southern racism and the workings of monopoly capitalism, commenting that "it is safe to say that anyone who is given to racism, religious bigotry, anti-unionism, or plutocracy is potentially if not actually a fascist" (*Southern Exposure* [Garden City, NY: Doubleday, 1946], 190). Viewing the South alongside Nazi Germany, Kennedy concluded that native-born Fascism in the South mirrored in many respects that of the Nazis:

> In the matters of peonage, feudalism, exploitation, and denial of suffrage to her own citizens, the South is 100 per cent as fascistic as was Nazi Germany. The overlords of the South are at least as adept as the Nazis in the techniques of divide-and-rule. Southern sectionalism, often bordering upon nationalism, serves essentially the same reactionary purposes as Nazi nationalism. In many respects the South's racial discriminations are more gross than the peacetime discriminations of the Nazis. The segregation and confinement in black ghettos of the South's ten million Negro citizens is at least as rigorous as the Nazis' peacetime segregation of the Jews. In the South the Kloran of the KKK has been substituted for the Constitution of the U.S.A. in much the same manner as the Nazis subverted the German Constitution. There are in the South an uncounted number of would-be fuehrers, and an untold number of organizations every bit as fascistic as the Nazi party. And, finally, the storm troopers of Southern fascism—the Klan, police, state guardsmen—are preparing for *Der Tag* when they can demonstrate that they can be just as terroristic as the Nazis. (191)

Unlike Smith, Kennedy looked to the Soviet Union as a model society, repeatedly praising it as "anti-fascist, anti-aggression, anti-imperialist, and anti-exploitation" (189). Arguing that there were two kinds of totalitarianism, "majority and minority; democratic and fascistic; good and evil" (189), Kennedy said that the Soviet Union's totalitarian system was fundamentally benevolent.

3. Quoted in Anne C. Loveland, *Lillian Smith: A Southerner Confronting the South* (Baton Rouge: Louisiana State University Press, 1986), 40.

4. Quoted in ibid.

5. Quoted in ibid.

6. For insightful commentary on Smith's unpublished fiction, see Margaret Rose Gladney, "Becoming a Writer," introduction to *How Am I to Be Heard? Letters of Lillian Smith,* ed. Gladney (Chapel Hill: University of North Carolina Press, 1993), 9–11; and Loveland, *Lillian Smith,* 17–18.

7. Lillian Smith and Paula Snelling, editorial statement, *Pseudopodia* 1 (Spring 1936), 6.

8. Ibid.

9. Louise Blackwell and Francis Clay, *Lillian Smith* (New York: Twayne, 1971), 27.

10. Lillian Smith, "Dope with Lime," *Pseudopodia* 1 (Spring 1936), 7.

11. While certainly Allen and Smith shared a fundamental perspective on the Agrarians, it is not clear whether in 1936 Smith would have gone as far as Allen in finding them fundamentally Fascist. To Allen's comment that the Agrarians would prefer Fascism over Communism, for instance, Smith and Snelling attached this footnote: "'I am so deeply opposed to fascism

that I would choose communism if it were the alternative,' Mr. Tate replied in New Republic, May 27, to Mrs. Grace Lumpkin who interprets his writings as Mr. Allen and many others do" (2). Quoted in John D. Allen, "Southern Agrarianism: Revised Version," ibid. 1 (Summer 1936): 2. For a full discussion of the Grace Lumpkin–Allen Tate controversy, see chapter 1.

12. Ibid., 14 (hereafter cited in text).

13. Lillian Smith and Paula Snelling, "From Lack of Understanding," ibid. 1 (Fall 1936): 9.

14. Lillian Smith, Dope with Lime, *North Georgia Review* 2 (Winter 1937–38): 2.

15. Lillian Smith, "He That Is Without Sin . . . ," ibid., 31–32 (hereafter cited both parenthetically in text and in notes).

16. Smith makes it clear earlier in the essay that the slogan "making the world safe for democracy" is a smokescreen for making the world safe for capitalistic enterprise. She notes that America had entered World War I "because munitions must be made, loans must be protected, cotton must be sold, faces saved." Ibid., 32.

17. Smith argues in a 1938 Dope with Lime column that America should measure its defense capabilities in terms of the nation's internal health and not its military might. "Our country's defense against external enemies is only so impregnable as its internal strength," Smith writes, adding that the nation's internal strength is measured "in terms of health, economic security, conservation of natural resources and the emotional stability of its citizens." Lillian Smith, Dope with Lime, ibid. 3 (Spring 1938): 2.

18. Lillian Smith, Dope with Lime, ibid. 5 (Spring 1940): 4 (hereafter cited in text). "Martian panic" refers to the public scare following the radio broadcast of Orson Welles's adaptation of H. G. Wells's "War of the Worlds" on 30 October 1938.

19. Lillian Smith, Dope with Lime, ibid. 6 (Winter 1940–41): 5 (hereafter cited in text).

20. Lilliam Smith, "Mr. Lafayette, Heah We Is—," ibid. 4 (Spring 1939): 14 (hereafter cited in text).

21. Lillian Smith and Paula Snelling, "As We Go to War," ibid. 6 (Winter 1941): 25 (hereafter cited in text).

22. Lillian Smith and Paula Snelling, "Winning the World with Democracy: A Symposium of Questions and Answers concerning Aims and Strategies, Ends and Means," *South Today* 7 (Spring 1942): 8 (hereafter cited in text).

23. The respondents included Louis Adamic, Sherwood Eddy, Channing H. Tobias, Gerald W. Johnson, Guy B. Johnson, Jessie Daniel Ames, Edward R. Embree, Tarleton Collier, James A. Dombrowski, Ira De A. Reid, Roger Baldwin, Phillips Russell, and Howard Kester.

24. The magazine's printers refused to print this issue because they feared that the monologue (originally titled "There Are Some Things White Folks Can't Say") might incite racial trouble. For Smith's description of the incident, see her letter to Walter White (2 June 1942), in *LLS,* 59.

25. Lillian Smith, "Portrait of the Deep South Speaking to Negroes on Morale," *South Today* 7 (Spring 1942): 35 (hereafter cited in text).

26. Smith commented on "Portrait of the Deep South Speaking to Negroes on Morale" in a letter to Walter White (2 June 1942), in *LLS,* 59.

27. Lillian Smith and Paula Snelling, "Buying a New World with Old Confederate Bills," *South Today* 7 (Autumn–Winter 1942–43): 11 (hereafter cited in text).

28. Morton Sosna, *In Search of the Silent South: Southern Liberals and the Race Issue* (New York: Columbia University Press, 1977), 105–20.

29. Ibid., 111.

30. Quoted in ibid., 106.

31. Quoted in John Egerton, *Speak Now against the Day: The Generation before the Civil Rights Movement* (Chapel Hill: University of North Carolina Press, 1994), 216. Ethridge's words were widely publicized in defenses of segregation during the 1940s. Theodore Bilbo used them to buttress his argument for racial separation in his tirade *Take Your Choice: Separation or Mongrelization* (Poplarville, MS: Dream House, 1947), 49.

32. David L. Cohn, "How the South Feels," *Atlantic Monthly*, January 1944, 50.

33. Virginius Dabney, "Nearer and Nearer the Precipice," ibid., January 1943, 94.

34. Smith described the encounter with Harris in a letter to Walter White (17 January 1943), in *LLS*, 64.

35. Journalists were not alone in attacking Smith. Harassment by public officials included an effort to deny *South Today* a mailing permit, a threatened investigation by the Georgia legislature, and surveillance and investigation by the FBI (in the first memo in her case file, an unnamed source described Smith as "a social uplifter in favor of the negroes"). Will Brantley obtained Smith's FBI file through a Freedom of Information/Privacy Act request, and he discusses its contents in his essay "The Surveillance of Georgia Writer and Civil Rights Activist Lillian Smith: Another Story from the Federal Bureau of Investigation," *Georgia Historical Quarterly* 85 (Spring 2001): 59–82; the quotation above from Smith's file is on p. 65.

36. Besides the novel's being banned in Boston, the U.S. Postal Service declared it obscene and prohibited the book's transport through the mails; postal officials also advised publications not to advertise the book. President Roosevelt quickly lifted the ban, at the urging of his wife, Eleanor.

37. Tracy first experiences this new way of seeing things while serving in Europe during World War I; far from home, with no one to tell him how or what to think, Tracy sees Nonnie in all her beauty and in all his love. In this liberating wartime experience in Europe, Tracy appears to share much with William Alexander Percy, who, as described in *Lanterns on the Levee*, experienced a similar liberation while serving in Europe. Once back in the South, both Tracy and Percy eviscerate themselves emotionally in order to take their "rightful" place in society.

38. Lillian Smith, *Strange Fruit* (1944; Athens: University of Georgia Press, 1986), 356.

39. Lillian Smith, "Addressed to Intelligent White Southerners," *South Today* 7 (Autumn–Winter 1942–43): 39 (hereafter cited in text).

40. Smith continued to see child development as crucial for the creation of democracy for the rest of her career. On 31 May 1954, not long after the *Brown v. Board of Education* decision, Smith wrote a letter to the *Atlanta Constitution* stressing the broad implications of the decision, particularly for the rights of children. "It is every child's Magna Carta," she wrote. "All are protected by the magnificent statement that no artificial barriers, such as laws, can be set up in our land against a child's right to learn and to mature as a human being." See *LLS*, 146.

41. Lillian Smith, "Humans in Bondage," in *The Winner Names the Age: A Collection of Writings by Lillian Smith*, ed. Michelle Cliff (New York: W. W. Norton, 1978), 32–33 (hereafter cited in text).

42. For further discussion of Americans' interpretations of Nazi Germany and the Soviet Union as totalitarian societies, see Les K. Adler and Thomas G. Patterson, "Red Fascism: The Merger of Nazi Germany and Soviet Russia in the American Image of Totalitarianism, 1930's–1950's," *American Historical Review* 75 (April 1970): 1046–64.

43. Jay Watson, "Uncovering the Body, Discovering Ideology: Segregation and Sexual

Anxiety in Lillian Smith's *Killers of the Dream,*" *American Quarterly* 49 (September 1997): 470–503.

44. Regarding my reference to George Orwell's *1984*, there are a number of striking similarities between Orwell's novel and *Killers of the Dream*, both of which appeared in 1949. Perhaps most striking is the congruence between Orwell's "doublethink" and Smith's segregated mind. This is Orwell: "To know and not to know, to be conscious of complete truthfulness while telling carefully constructed lies, to hold simultaneously two opinions which cancelled out, knowing them to be contradictory and believing in both of them, to use logic against logic, to repudiate morality while laying claim to it, to believe that democracy was impossible and that the Party was the guardian of democracy, to forget whatever it was necessary to forget, then to draw it back into memory again at the moment when it was needed, and then promptly to forget it again, and above all, to apply the same process to the process itself—that was the ultimate subtlety: consciously to induce unconsciousness, and then, once again, to become unconscious of the act of hypnosis you had just performed." George Orwell, *1984* (New York: Harcourt Brace Jovanovich, 1949), 36. While Smith obviously had not read *1984* when she was working on *Killers of the Dream*, at least the 1949 edition, it is possible that she had read *Animal Farm* (1946), though I have found no evidence of this. If Smith did read *Animal Farm*, she perhaps drew from Orwell's example in using elements of fable to make political points. One final parallel: Orwell's famous words "ALL ANIMALS ARE EQUAL BUT SOME ANIMALS ARE MORE EQUAL THAN OTHERS" fittingly describe the political logic of the segregated South Smith describes. George Orwell, *Animal Farm* (1946; New York: Harcourt, Brace and World, 1954), 148.

45. Smith echoed her comment from "Addressed to White Southerners" later in *Killers of the Dream*. Responding to a camper who objected to Smith's attempts to reeducate her campers, Smith fired back: "In other words, you would make little Nazis out of them" (*KD* 47).

CHAPTER 5

1. Not only his love for travel drew Wolfe to Europe: he looked to the Continent for literary models and was early on attracted to modernist aesthetics and particularly to James Joyce; his first novel, *Look Homeward Angel*, owes much to Joyce's *Ulysses.*

2. As Hugh Holman points out, from 1924 on Wolfe spent about one-quarter of his life in Europe. C. Hugh Holman, *The Loneliness at the Core: Studies in Thomas Wolfe* (Baton Rouge: Louisiana State University Press, 1975), 139.

3. Thomas Wolfe, "The Story of a Novel," in *The Autobiography of an American Novelist*, ed. Leslie Field (Cambridge, MA: Harvard University Press, 1983), 27.

4. Hemingway, in return, characterized Wolfe as "a glandular giant with the brains and guts of three mice" and "the over-bloated Lil Abner of literature." Quoted in David Herbert Donald, *Look Homeward: A Life of Thomas Wolfe* (Boston: Little, Brown, 1987), 278.

5. Quoted in ibid., 244. Donald gives a good overview of Wolfe's response to the 1930 elections.

6. H. M. Ledig-Rowohlt, "Thomas Wolfe in Berlin," *American Scholar* 22 (Spring 1953): 187, 191.

7. Donald, *Look Homeward*, 324.

8. Wolfe, "Story of a Novel," 29.

9. Stoddard's and Grant's popularity in the 1920s and 1930s was widespread. As already noted, William Alexander Percy may have drawn from Stoddard's *Rising Tide of Color against White World-Supremacy* in his construction of racial taxonomy in *Lanterns on the Levee*. See chapter 3, n. 36.

10. Henry Fairfield Osborn, preface to *The Passing of the Great Race; or The Racial Basis of European History*, by Madison Grant, rev. ed. (New York: Charles Scribner's Sons, 1918), viii.

11. Lothrop Stoddard, *The Rising Tide of Color against White World-Supremacy* (New York: Charles Scribner's Sons, 1920), 300 (hereafter cited in text).

12. Grant, *Passing of the Great Race*, 161 (hereafter cited in text).

13. Madison Grant, introduction to Stoddard, *Rising Tide of Color*, xxix.

14. Wolfe's essay "The London Tower" was originally published in the *Asheville Citizen*, 19 July 1925.

15. Thomas Wolfe, *The Letters of Thomas Wolfe to His Mother*, ed. C. Hugh Holman and Sue Fields Ross (Chapel Hill: University of North Carolina Press, 1968), 49 (hereafter cited in text).

16. Thomas Wolfe, *Of Time and the River* (New York: Charles Scribner's Sons, 1935), 413 (hereafter cited in text).

17. See the discussion of Wolfe's story "The Child by Tiger," below.

18. Thomas Wolfe to Aline Bernstein, 1 December 1926, quoted in Donald, *Look Homeward*, 155.

19. Thomas Wolfe, *The Web and the Rock* (New York: Harper and Brothers, 1939), 547 (hereafter cited in text).

20. For a discussion of this phenomenon in the work of British modernists, see Andrea Freud Lowenstein, *Loathsome Jews and Engulfing Women: Metaphors of Projection in the Works of Wyndham Lewis, Charles Williams, and Graham Greene* (New York: New York University Press, 1993).

21. Adolf Hitler, *Mein Kampf*, trans. Ralph Manheim (Boston: Houghton Mifflin, 1943), 61, 58.

22. Thomas Wolfe, quoted in Ledig-Rowohlt, "Thomas Wolfe in Berlin," 194–95.

23. Ledig-Rowohlt, "Thomas Wolfe in Berlin," 196–97.

24. Thomas Wolfe, *You Can't Go Home Again* (New York: Harper and Brothers, 1940), 625–26 (hereafter cited in text).

25. Thomas Wolfe, "Writing and Living," in *Autobiography of an American Novelist*, 142–43, 143.

26. For a discussion of this encounter, see Donald, *Look Homeward*, 389–90. "I Have a Thing to Tell You" was originally serialized in the *New Republic*, 10 March 1937, 132–26; 17 March 1937, 159–64; and 24 March 1937, 202–7.

27. The new title, "I Have a Thing to Tell You," refers to the expression Wolfe's German friend H. M. Ledig-Rowohlt often used when he spoke to Wolfe about Nazi oppression.

28. Richard S. Kennedy, *The Window of Memory: The Literary Career of Thomas Wolfe* (Chapel Hill: University of North Carolina Press, 1962), 332.

29. Bella Kussy, "The Vitalist Trend and Thomas Wolfe," *Sewanee Review* 50 (July–September 1942): 322 (hereafter cited in text).

30. During the early 1930s, Wolfe was also spending time with a number of leftist writers and critics, and he contributed without fee several stories for *Modern Monthly*. For a discussion of Wolfe's politics during this period, see Donald, *Look Homeward*, 303–4.

31. Thomas Wolfe, *Look Homeward, Angel: A Story of the Buried Life* (New York: Charles Scribner's Sons, 1929), 471.

32. Wolfe, *Of Time and the River,* 895. Although Wolfe is not entirely despairing about America's future in this novel—American spirit, despite all, remains unquenchable—nonetheless his descriptions highlight the wretchedness of much of American life. The novel primarily looks back to a better America now lost rather than forward to coming better times.

33. Wolfe, "Writing and Living," 145.

34. Wolfe, notes from 1938, quoted in Donald, *Look Homeward,* 436.

35. Wolfe, "Story of a Novel," 88, 89.

36. According to David Donald, Wolfe had been nagged by the rumor that his father's mother was a Jew at least since 1933. See Donald, *Look Homeward,* 430.

37. Whether Wolfe's letter to Anderson was ever mailed is not certain, as only a carbon copy exists.

38. Donald, *Look Homeward,* 443–44.

39. Underscoring the racial roots of Prosser's violence, Wolfe originally entitled the story "Congo." His portrayal of the poor whites' degeneracy likewise suggests that their acts derive from befouled genetics.

40. Wolfe, *Web and the Rock,* 154. Originally published in the *Saturday Evening Post,* 11 September 1937, 10–11, 92–102, "The Child by Tiger" was later incorporated into *The Web and the Rock.*

CHAPTER 6

1. Joseph Blotner, *Faulkner: A Biography* (New York: Random House, 1974), 1597.

2. Alan Reynolds Thompson, "The Cult of Cruelty," *Bookman* 74 (January–February 1932): 481.

3. Harry Hartwick, *The Foreground of American Fiction* (New York: American Book Company, 1934), 166.

4. Granville Hicks, *The Great Tradition: An Interpretation of American Literature since the Civil War* (New York: Macmillan, 1933), 266.

5. Phillip Rahv, review of *Absalom, Absalom!* in *William Faulkner: The Critical Heritage,* ed. John Bassett (London: Routledge and Kegan Paul, 1975), 208–10.

6. Robert Penn Warren, "Cowley's Faulkner," in Bassett, *William Faulkner,* 328.

7. Maxwell Geismar, *Writers in Crisis: The American Novel between Two Wars* (Boston: Houghton Mifflin, 1942), 164 (hereafter cited in text).

8. Malcolm Cowley, ed., *The Faulkner-Cowley File: Letters and Memories, 1944–1962* (New York: Viking, 1966), 10.

9. Malcolm Cowley, "Sanctuary," review of *The Wild Palms,* by William Faulkner, *New Republic,* 25 January 1939, 349.

10. Blotner, *Faulkner,* 1030.

11. Ibid.

12. Faulkner frequently left apostrophes out of contractions.

13. William Faulkner, "Snow," in *The Uncollected Stories of William Faulkner,* ed. Joseph Blotner (New York: Random House, 1979), 665, 677. Because of the story's similarities to "Mistral" and "Evangeline," some critics have suggested that Faulkner in all likelihood wrote the

main part of "Snow" in the late 1920s or early 1930s, returning to it in 1942 merely to tack on the beginning and ending frame to give the story contemporary reference.

14. William Faulkner, "Knight's Gambit," carbon typescript, in *William Faulkner Manuscripts 18, Knight's Gambit: Typescripts and Miscellaneous Typescript Pages*, ed. Thomas L. McHaney (New York: Garland, 1987), 326.

15. William Faulkner, "Delta Autumn," in *Uncollected Stories*, 269.

16. Faulkner may have had in mind Donald Davidson's poem "The Tall Men." There, when a man from the North inquires why there are so many tall men in Tennessee, the poet responds: "Why, since you ask, / Tallness is not in what you eat or drink / But in the seed of man." See Donald Davidson, "The Tall Men," in *Poems, 1922–1961* (Minneapolis: University of Minnesota Press, 1966), 119.

17. As Joe Karaganis points out, "Shall Not Perish" shares with the Gettysburg Address "not only a vocabulary and, to a considerable degree, a tone, but also the larger purpose of transforming mourning into an act of rededication to the national cause." "Negotiating the National Voice in Faulkner's Late Work," in *A Gathering of Evidence: Essays on William Faulkner's "Intruder in the Dust,"* ed. Michel Gresset and Patrick Samway, SJ (Philadelphia: St. Joseph's University Press, 2004), 103.

18. Besides being a call to arms in the present war, Pete's vision looks forward to the rhetoric of American foreign policy during the early years of the Cold War. One of the architects of that policy, Arthur M. Schlesinger, Jr., several years later echoed Faulkner in *The Vital Center: The Politics of Freedom* (Boston: Houghton Mifflin, 1949), calling for a renewal of democratic *élan* manifested as a "fighting faith" (245) that would be the vital center in America's ideological battle against totalitarianism. Quoting Whitman, although he could just as easily have quoted Faulkner, Schlesinger calls for a "large resolute breed of men" (251) for that defense.

19. As I have argued elsewhere, Ike attempts to stop the decline of his family and the South through an act of radical asceticism, emulating the Desert Fathers by withdrawing from his community. Ike hopes to empower himself as a spiritual leader, a strategy that Faulkner himself commented on years later, in a classroom discussion at the University of Virginia, saying that Ike was the type of person who, rather than actively engaging problems, would instead "go off into a cave or climb a pillar to sit on." *Faulkner in the University: Class Conferences at the University of Virginia, 1957–1958*, ed. Frederick L. Gwynn and Joseph L. Blotner (Charlottesville: University of Virginia Press, 1959), 246. In his study of early Christian ascetics, "The Rise and Function of the Holy Man in Late Antiquity," *Journal of Roman Studies* 61 (1971): 80–101, Peter Brown discusses the type of strategy to which Ike turns, noting that ascetics who withdrew from their societies did so to gain power and influence within those societies. By deliberately striving to attain Christ-like purity through isolation and self-mortification, the early ascetics came to be seen as semidivine, angelic beings mediating between God and humanity. Their actions symbolized God's presence and power in the world, and their words carried divine force and objectivity. For this reason, village leaders in the late Roman Empire actively consulted the ascetics for advice, healing, and arbitration. "Above all, the holy man is a man of power," Brown writes, commenting on the ascetics' far-reaching influence in providing early societies with identity and guidance (87). Ike, however, fails to achieve this authority. While he does teach the ways of the hunt to many of the area's boys—becoming in this regard "uncle to half a county and father to no one" (*GDM* 3)—Ike's lasting influence appears negligible, as suggested by the hunters in "Delta Autumn," who have cast aside the rituals that Ike taught them and that he himself embodies. Roth's question to Ike in the same story—"where have

you been all the time you were dead"? (*GDM* 329)—suggests that in his eyes, and most likely in those of others in the community, Ike's ascetic striving to become dead to the world means exactly that and nothing more. Most people in the community apparently see Ike as an anachronism, a person to humor but not to emulate or consult; they see his renunciation as an act of weakness rather than strength, a shirking rather than an assumption of responsibility. See: Robert H. Brinkmeyer, Jr., "*Go Down, Moses* and the Ascetic Imperative," in *Faulkner and the Short Story,* ed. Evans Harrington and Ann J. Abadie (Jackson: University Press of Mississippi, l992), 206–28.

20. The exchange between Roth and Ike, suggesting that the European war stands as a distant backdrop in the novel, points to the possibility that not only the Desert Fathers but also Hitler shadows Ike's attempts to gain power and stature. Although Ike and Hitler are of course entirely different in their fundamental humanity and the visions for which they desire leadership, they share a great deal in terms of their visions to lead their societies by reversing the process of history's depletion. Ike and Hitler both see destabilizing forces of modernity undermining their cultures, with Ike's complaints about the greed and self-interest tearing apart southern culture dovetailing with Hitler's views, as expressed in *Mein Kampf,* trans. Ralph Manheim (Boston: Houghton Mifflin, 1943), that German society was floundering in "humanitarian bilge" (226), "the pettiest utilitarianism" (266), and "the hollowness of comfortable life" (21), so that Aryan men of strength and heroism—versions of Ike's "tall men"— were fast disappearing. As leaders, furthermore, both Ike and Hitler choose models fundamentally ascetic. Ike chooses the way of the eremite, withdrawal from society for purifying the individual; Hitler chooses the way of the cenobite, creation of a tightly controlled community, based on the monastic model, whose goal is to purify its members. Hitler's ghostly presence in *Go Down, Moses* ultimately points to Ike's failure as a leader. While Faulkner no doubt found Ike's idealism admirable, he also found it ineffectual; unlike Hitler, who rallied Germany into a powerful society, Ike fails miserably at centering and unifying his community in traditional values. See: Brinkmeyer, "*Go Down, Moses* and the Ascetic Imperative."

21. From Hollywood Faulkner continued to look into obtaining a pilot's commission. Apparently, just being in Los Angeles, a potential bombing target and a city churning with wartime activity, made Faulkner feel closer to the conflict. Meta Carpenter later remembered Faulkner's fixation on the war while in California, writing that "the tensions and turbulence of wartime Los Angeles stretched Faulkner like a fine wire." Meta Carpenter Wilde and Orin Borsten, "Faulkner: Hollywood: 1943," in William Faulkner, *Faulkner: A Comprehensive Guide to the Brodsky Collection,* ed. Louis Daniel Brodsky and Robert W. Hamblin, vol. 4, *"Battle Cry": A Screenplay by William Faulkner* (Jackson: University Press of Mississippi, 1985), xii (hereafter cited as *"Battle Cry"*). Evidence of war was everywhere, she added, and it was central to Faulkner's life. "Servicemen, WAVES, uniformed nurses, and British, Canadian and Free French soldiers and sailors enlivened the passing parade downtown and on Hollywood and Sunset Boulevards," Carpenter wrote describing wartime Los Angeles. "Endless convoys with lights glowing in the daylight passed along main arteries between military installations, and in transit between San Diego and San Francisco, then onward to Portland and Tacoma and Seattle. Newspaper headlines screamed of death and disaster. Faulkner, hunched forward in his chair, listened intently to the terse broadcasts about war by Edward R. Murrow and William L. Shirer. He would pause in his writing to turn on the radio at the Highland (Avenue) Hotel to hear Lowell Thomas, Gabriel Heatter, and Raymond Gram Swing" (xi–xii).

Faulkner best expressed his feelings about participating in the war in a letter to his nephew

Malcolm (5 December 1942), who had recently joined the service. Saying that no sane man really wanted to go to war, Faulkner added that "it is the biggest thing that will happen in your lifetime. All your contemporaries will be in it before it is over, and if you are not one of them, you will always regret it." Faulkner wrote that the compulsion for war was primal, "something in the meat and bone and blood from the old cave-time," and that "it's a strange thing how a man, no matter how intelligent, will cling to the public proof of his masculinity: his courage and endurance, his willingness to sacrifice himself for the land which shaped his ancestors." He concluded by making it clear that he was describing his own situation, saying that while he did not really want to go to war, "when I can, I am going too, maybe only to prove to myself that I can do (within my physical limitations of age, of course) as much as anyone else can to make secure the manner of living I prefer and that suits my kin and kind" (*SLF* 166).

22. In their introduction to the screenplay, Louis Daniel Brodsky and Robert W. Hamblin point out that the vision underlying the work "increasingly came to characterize the work of Faulkner's late years." Introduction to William Faulkner, *Faulkner: A Comprehensive Guide to the Brodsky Collection*, ed. Brodsky and Hamblin, vol. 3, *"The De Gaulle Story" by William Faulkner* (Jackson: University Press of Mississippi, 1984), xxxiii (hereafter cited as *"De Gaulle Story"*).

23. William Faulkner, "Free France: Story Treatment," in ibid., 50; hereafter citations to this and other working versions of this screenplay are from this edition and appear in the text.

24. For a full discussion of the origins and sources of "Battle Cry," see Daniel Brodsky and Robert W. Hamblin's excellent introduction to *"Battle Cry."*

25. What Faulkner was calling the "Lincoln Cantata" was actually "The Lonesome Train," a cantata written by Millard Lampell, with music by Earl Robinson. "The Lonesome Train" aired on Norman Corwin's CBS radio show *Columbia Presents Corwin* on 21 March 1944. Faulkner's directions for "Battle Cry" indicate that he wanted Paul Robeson to sing the cantata in the film.

26. William Faulkner, "'Battle Cry': Second Temporary Screenplay," in *"Battle Cry,"* 190; hereafter citations to this and other working versions of this screenplay are from this edition and appear in the text.

27. Brodsky and Hamblin, introduction to *"Battle Cry,"* xxi. In "The Lonesome Train" Lincoln upbraids a woman who says to him, "Well I say: America for Americans! / What happens on the other side of the ocean shouldn't be any skin off our backs. / Isn't that right Mr. Lincoln?" Lincoln responds: "Well I'll tell you, Ma'am: / It seems to me the strongest bond of human sympathy, outside your family, of course, / should be the one uniting all working people of all nations, tongues, and kindred!" See Millard Lampell and Earl Robinson, "The Lonesome Train," http://showcase.netins.net/web/creative/lincoln/education/lonesome.htm.

28. David Minter, *William Faulkner: His Life and Work* (Baltimore: Johns Hopkins University Press, 1980), 200.

29. Further evidence of Faulkner's suspicions about the origins of his work include his comment, in a letter to Malcolm Cowley (20 September 1945), that in looking back at *Light in August* he now saw that Percy Grimm "was the Fascist galahad who saved the white race by murdering Christmas. I invented him in 1931. I didn't realize until after Hitler got into the newspapers that I had created a Nazi before he did" (*SLF* 202).

30. One of the most astute readers of Faulkner's postwar work, Joseph R. Urgo, argues that in his late fiction Faulkner deliberately presented an alternative world-view to what Urgo calls the "mythic" interpretation of the South that Malcolm Cowley and other critics found in

Faulkner's earlier Yoknapatawpha fiction. Urgo sees Faulkner's late vision as deeply political, focused on a critique of state power and an endorsement of the individual's resistance to that power, writing that this vision "stands as a political and ideological alternative to what Faulkner considered to be the totalitarianism of modern society." Joseph R. Urgo, *Faulkner's Apocrypha: "A Fable," "Snopes," and the Spirit of Human Rebellion* (Jackson: University Press of Mississippi, 1989), 4. In opposing the "mythic," this late vision is, according to Urgo, "apocryphal." While largely agreeing with Urgo's interpretation of Faulkner's postwar political vision, I think that Faulkner instead came to see his prewar work as, to use Urgo's term, "apocryphal," believing that his later works were his most authentic and important and thus finally stood as his canonical works.

31. Faulkner, *Faulkner in the University*, 6.

32. William Faulkner, "Appendix Compson: 1699–1945," in *The Sound and the Fury*, corrected text with appendix (New York: Modern Library, 1992), 339 (hereafter cited in text).

33. Although Caddy's motives for riding with the Nazi general remain unknown, it is perhaps significant that several of Faulkner's wartime works portray women befriending Nazis in order to destroy them. In *"De Gaulle Story,"* for instance, women in the French resistance manipulate their Nazi acquaintances; and in "Snow" a woman avenges the death of her husband by killing her Nazi companion.

34. Faulkner's fears concerning the diminishment of American individualism and individual rights are fully expressed in his 1955 essay "On Privacy (The American Dream: What Happened to It?)," published in *Essays, Speeches and Public Letters by William Faulkner*, ed. James B. Meriwether (New York: Random House, 1965). There Faulkner declares that the once free and independent individual has become "one more identityless integer in that identityless anonymous unprivacied mass which seems to be our goal" (71). On the loss of national purpose, Faulkner writes that individuals who once spoke together "in mutual unification of one mutual hope and will" now speak "a cacophony of terror and conciliation and compromise babbling only the mouthsounds; the loud and empty words which we have emasculated of all meaning whatever—freedom, democracy, patriotism—with which, awakened at last, we try in desperation to hide from ourselves that loss" (65–66).

35. William Faulkner, *Intruder in the Dust* (1948; New York: Vintage International, 1991), 211.

36. In conflating the issues of black equality and individual rights, Stevens's gradualism often gets messy and complicated, losing clear focus and leading to contradiction and misunderstanding—problems Faulkner himself faced when he publicly voiced similar views in the 1950s.

37. In Lucas and Chick's relationship Faulkner rewrites a relationship in "The De Gaulle Story" between a French woman and a Nazi soldier. The woman, despite her hatred of the Nazis, one day reaches out to the soldier in an instinctive act of kindness. Her act sets off a chain of events in which the soldier ends up helping the French resistance, never quite knowing how he is being manipulated but knowing that he must repay the debt to the woman. Chick likewise must repay his original debt to Lucas; and in the process, Lucas manipulates Chick for his own advantage, eventually using him to solve the murder with which he has been charged. This giving and returning of personal debts represents for Faulkner the process of change that undoes oppression. In a passage already cited, but which bears relevance here, Faulkner wrote of the Nazi soldier in "The De Gaulle Story": "Through him we can show how Naziism is inherent in its own downfall to the extent that Nazis are at bottom human beings, too, when this quality can be reached." Faulkner, "Free France: Story Treatment," 48.

38. At the same time that Faulkner was reevaluating his political views in light of the Soviet Union, Faulkner's reputation was being reevaluated in that same context. As Lawrence Schwartz has shown, once seen as proto-Fascist, Faulkner after World War II became representative of the modern artist in America, free to explore whatever he wanted in whatever way he wanted, in contrast to the Soviet artist, who was straightjacketed by the strong arm of totalitarian dictatorship and censorship. Lawrence H. Schwartz, *Creating Faulkner's Reputation: The Politics of Modern Literary Criticism* (Knoxville: University of Tennessee Press, 1988).

39. William Faulkner, "Interviews in Japan," in *Lion in the Garden: Interviews with William Faulkner, 1926–1962*, ed. James B. Meriwether and Michael Millgate (New York: Random House, 1968), 162–63.

40. Urgo, *Faulkner's Apocrypha*, 105, 107.

41. William Faulkner, *A Fable* (1954; New York: Random House, 1978), 232.

CHAPTER 7

1. Katherine Anne Porter, "Remarks on the Agenda," in *The Collected Essays and Occasional Prose of Katherine Anne Porter* (New York: Delacorte, 1970), 220, 223.

2. Porter's leftist sympathies date from both her upbringing in an area of Texas awash with radical ferment and her time spent in revolutionary Mexico during the 1920s. For a discussion of the politics of Porter's home country during her childhood, see Janis P. Stout, *Katherine Anne Porter: A Sense of the Times* (Charlottesville: University Press of Virginia, 1995), 41–46. Much good work has been done on Porter's time in Mexico and its impact upon her career, both aesthetically and politically. Besides my own book, *Katherine Anne Porter's Artistic Development: Primitivism, Traditionalism, and Totalitarianism* (Baton Rouge: Louisiana State University Press, 1993), and Stout's, see esp. Thomas F. Walsh, *Katherine Anne Porter and Mexico: The Illusion of Eden* (Austin: University of Texas Press, 1992); Darlene Unrue, *Truth and Vision in Katherine Anne Porter's Fiction* (Athens: University of Georgia Press, 1985); Joan Givner, *Katherine Anne Porter: A Life*, rev. ed. (Athens: University of Georgia Press, 1991); William L. Nance, "Katherine Anne Porter and Mexico," *Southwest Review* 55 (Spring 1970): 143–53; and Colin Partridge, "My Familiar Country: An Image of Mexico in the Work of Katherine Anne Porter," *Studies in Short Fiction* 7 (Fall 1970): 597–614.

3. Thomas Carl Austenfeld, *American Women Writers and the Nazis: Ethics and Politics in Boyle, Porter, Stafford, and Hellman* (Charlottesville: University Press of Virginia, 2001), 33–34. Concerning the Germany in which Porter found herself, Austenfeld notes that it was in political chaos, with extremists and paramilitary groups battling in the streets and with the nation fearing civil war. Joan Givner notes that 1931 was Germany's "*annus terribilis,* a time of desperate hardship when over five million workers were unemployed and when shortages of food and fuel were so severe that Chancellor Brüning was known as the 'hunger dictator.'" Givner, *Katherine Anne Porter,* 252.

4. Apparently Porter had worked for a short while with ROSTA, the forerunner of TASS, in New York in the late 1920s, a fact that no doubt helped her make connections with the Soviet news agency in Berlin. See Stout, *Katherine Anne Porter,* 63.

5. Givner, *Katherine Anne Porter,* 259.

6. Ibid., 261–62.

7. Ibid., 261.

8. Porter's feelings about the Sacco and Vanzetti executions clearly affected her depiction of the Salem witch trials in her unfinished biography of Mather. She describes Mather manipulating the proceedings in order to consolidate his power rather than to seek justice. See Katherine Anne Porter, "A Goat for Azazel (A.D. 1688)," in *Collected Essays and Occasional Prose*, 331–42. Porter wrote much later about the Sacco and Vanzetti case and her involvement in the protests in *The Never-Ending Wrong* (Boston: Atlantic–Little, Brown, 1977).

9. As Darlene Unrue suggests, in portraying the failure of the Mexican Revolution, "Hacienda" complements well "Flowering Judas," a story written two years earlier portraying a character in the process of pulling back from revolutionary commitment, the hopes and dreams of the revolution almost but not entirely gone. Unrue, *Truth and Vision*, 83–84.

10. Katherine Anne Porter, "Hacienda," *Virginia Quarterly Review* 8 (October 1932): 567 (hereafter this first version cited in text).

11. Quoted in Walsh, *Katherine Anne Porter and Mexico*, 167.

12. Ibid. I am indebted to Walsh for quoting these two daybook entries and for his insightful discussion of the material; however, my reading of the entries differs somewhat from his. While noting that Porter used her childhood anxieties to understand her depression in Berlin, Walsh concludes that Porter's understanding of the deathly air of the South derived from her linking the South with Mexico, not Germany, as I argue. See ibid., 167–68.

13. Givner describes Porter working on the manuscript in Paris at this time. Givner, *Katherine Anne Porter*, 298. See also Jan Nordby Gretlund, "'The Man in the Tree': Katherine Anne Porter's Unfinished Lynching Story," *Southern Quarterly* 31 (Spring 1993): 8. The manuscript of the unfinished story is not much more than a string of fragmentary passages, with alternative titles, passages, names, and story lines. For piecings together of "The Man in the Tree," see Givner, *Katherine Anne Porter*, 298–99; Gretlund, "The Man in the Tree"; and Stout, *Katherine Anne Porter*, 136–37.

14. Quoted in Stout, *Katherine Anne Porter*, 136.

15. Quoted in Gretlund, "The Man in the Tree," 9.

16. Other titles that Porter considered for the story included "The Man in the Tree," "All the Evidence?" and "The Southern Story," all of which suggest the broad cultural significance of the lynching.

17. Porter later incorporated parts of the unfinished novel into short stories.

18. Quoted in Walsh, *Katherine Anne Porter and Mexico*, 172–73.

19. For a fuller discussion of this idea, see esp. Brinkmeyer, *Katherine Anne Porter's Artistic Development*, chap. 1.

20. Katherine Anne Porter, "Notes on Writing," in *Collected Essays and Occasional Prose*, 449.

21. It is not clear that Porter ever went to a parade of Fascist supporters in Boston or, indeed, that such a parade ever took place.

22. Katherine Anne Porter, "On a Criticism of Thomas Hardy," in *Collected Essays and Occasional Prose*, 6 (hereafter cited in text).

23. Porter's description of Hatch's eyes as "wicked and pig-like" (*CSP* 252) connects him to Germany and the Gestapo (Porter characteristically described Germans as porcine) and to the domestic Fascist threat that Porter increasingly feared after the United States entered the war. By 1942 she was railing against the power of the FBI and what she saw as its infiltration by the Gestapo. The following year, she wrote to her nephew Paul (20 July 1943) that "my fear is that the very thing we are fighting in Europe is seeping up here among us like a kind of miasma out of the very earth under our feet.... There never was such a concerted assault on human liberty

as we see now, since the first idea of human liberty was ever fought for. And our worst enemies are here at home, most dangerous because you can't walk over them with an army" (*LP* 271). Porter's words here look back to the end of "Noon Wine," where the order of Thompson's world has been destroyed by Hatch's machinations. For further evidence of Porter fears of domestic Fascism, see esp. her letter to Donald Elder of 28 February 1942, in *LP*, 228–30.

24. Porter's mention here of the Lusk Committee is anachronistic, as the committee was not formed until 1919, a year after the events of the story. She makes her point, nonetheless.

25. Austenfeld, *American Women Writers and the Nazis*, 42.

26. Digby B. Whitman, "Against Luce Thinking," *Nation*, 5 April 1941, 419; Henry R. Luce, "The American Century," *Life*, 17 February 1941, 61–65.

27. Luce, "American Century," 65.

28. Whitman, "Against Luce Thinking," 419.

29. Katherine Anne Porter, "Act of Faith: 4 July 1942," in *Collected Essays and Occasional Prose*, 195.

30. Porter was particularly fearful of Nazi infiltration of the FBI after reading a profile of Harry Bridges in the *New Yorker*, in which the labor leader talked about outsmarting federal agents who had him under surveillance. See St. Clair McKelway, "A Reporter at Large: Some Fun with the F.B.I.," *New Yorker*, 11 October 1941, 53–57.

31. For the fullest discussion of Porter's betrayal of Herbst, see Elinor Langer, *Josephine Herbst* (Boston: Little, Brown, 1984), 249–56.

32. Katherine Anne Porter to Josephine Herbst, 28 December 1943, quoted in ibid., 256.

33. Despite her long-term friendships with a number of southern writers, particularly Allen Tate and Robert Penn Warren, before the mid-1940s Porter had rarely taken the enterprise of celebrating southern identity and culture very seriously. She had enjoyed hanging out with Tate and Caroline Gordon, for instance, and could easily be drawn into conversations laden with southern nostalgia, but that was about as far as it went. Her interest in the South had been almost entirely literary, having to do with the subject matter of her fiction, which, as we have seen, unmasked rather than idealized southern traditionalism.

34. Katherine Anne Porter, "Portrait: Old South," in *Collected Essays and Occasional Prose*, 160 (hereafter cited in text).

35. Katherine Anne Porter, "The Future Is Now," in ibid., 199 (hereafter cited in text).

36. Katherine Anne Porter, "Reflections on Willa Cather," in ibid., 38, 33–34.

37. Katherine Anne Porter, "E. M. Forster," in ibid., 74.

38. Katherine Anne Porter, "Virginia Woolf," in ibid., 71.

39. Katherine Anne Porter, "It Is Hard to Stand in the Middle," in ibid., 46. A few years earlier, Porter had not been so generous with regard to Pound's work for the Italian Fascists. In a letter to Kay and James Powers (14 December 1947) Porter wrote about the declaration of Pound's insanity: "So much to say there. I know this though: if ever I committed treason, or any other crime, personal or political, it would infuriate me to be considered insane. I insist on being held absolutely responsible for my words and deeds. I know the meaning of both, and would loathe being waved away as a nit-wit. To be an artist does not mean that one is outside the manifold predicaments of human beings. They should have hanged Ezra—(and he wouldn't have been the first poet put to death for political beliefs) or they should have set him free" (*LP* 354).

40. Katherine Anne Porter, "A Letter to the Editor of *The Nation*," in *Collected Essays and Occasional Prose*, 203.

CHAPTER 8

1. The essay was originally published in *Decision* 2 (July 1941): 15–19.

2. The early reviews of *Reflections in a Golden Eye* were decidedly negative. In the *New York Herald Tribune*, 16 February 1941, Rose Feld wrote that McCullers was too talented to be writing fiction that depended "upon the grotesque and the morbid for effect"; she added that with *Reflections*, McCullers seemed "almost deliberately to be seeking something that could match [Faulkner] at his morbid" (8). Clifton Fadiman, in the Books section of *New Yorker*, 15 February 1941, went further in the Faulkner comparison, saying that "Mrs. McCullers' characters make Mr. Faulkner's seem like the folks next door" (78). Basil Davenport, in the *Saturday Review of Literature*, 22 February 1941, wrote that the novel "is a vipers'-knot of neurasthenic relationships among characters whom the author seems hardly to comprehend, and of whose perversions she can create nothing" (12). While none of these reviewers suggested that McCullers's sordidness somehow equated with the Fascist enterprise, they nonetheless found her work disturbing all in the wrong ways; indeed, Feld wrote that Alison Langdon's self-mutilation in the novel was "as physically unnerving to the reader as anything that has appeared in print."

3. Virginia Spencer Carr, *The Lonely Hunter: A Biography of Carson McCullers* (New York: Doubleday, 1975), 194.

4. For discussions of Peacock's early influence on McCullers, see ibid., 36–39; and Oliver Evans, *The Ballad of Carson McCullers: A Biography* (New York: Coward-McCann, 1965), 27–28.

5. Quoted in Carr, *Lonely Hunter*, 57.

6. Ibid.

7. "The Aliens" may have been written later, as in 1940 McCullers described plans for a novel whose plot dovetails with that of the story. Carr suggests that the story was written in 1935. Ibid., 56.

8. In a much later essay, "The Flowering Dream: Notes on Writing," which appeared in 1959 and is reprinted in *The Mortgaged Heart*, McCullers commented on Hitler's (mis)appropriation of Nietzsche and Wagner. One passage reads: "It is paradoxical that a great philosopher like Nietzsche and a great musician like Richard Wagner could have contributed so much to the world's suffering in this century. Partial understanding for an ignorant person is a warped and subjective understanding, and it was with this type of understanding that the philosophy of Nietzsche and the creations of Richard Wagner were the mainstay of Hitler's emotional appeal to the German people. He was able to juggle great ideas into the despair of his time, which we must remember was a real despair" (*MH* 278).

9. Carr, *Lonely Hunter*, 84.

10. Ihab H. Hassan, "Carson McCullers: The Alchemy of Love and Aesthetics of Pain," *Modern Fiction Studies* 5 (Winter 1959–60): 315.

11. Copeland's abstract, theory-ridden approach to life, underscored by his affection for Spinoza, isolates him, his strict logic overriding human concerns and empathy; his inflexibility and fervor broadly and ironically mirror that of the Fascist enemy he rails against. Copeland strives for dictatorial control and power over both his family and the town's blacks, repeatedly delivering pronouncements declaring how everyone should live and act. Time and again he stresses the need for self-sacrifice for the black race and its future; not insignificantly, he campaigns most fervently for birth control and eugenic practices, entitling his project "Eugenic Parenthood for the Negro Race" (*HLH* 73).

12. Biff is trying to see with the type of vision advocated by Lillian Smith and Paula Snelling, who, as we have seen, argued that southerners needed a vision that brought the local, national, and international simultaneously into focus. They used the image of maps in one of their editorials: "Unless we keep the world map open before us we shall slip back into the old, bad habit of looking down at our own feet, and if we do we shall find ourselves at the same place where we first began. We must learn to read our maps simultaneously: regional map, national map, world map." "Buying a New World with Old Confederate Bills," *South Today* 7 (Autumn–Winter 1942–43): 7–30.

13. Almost from the very beginning, as we have seen, this was a central idea in McCullers's fiction and thinking. She felt that Americans were particularly susceptible to this psychological compulsion, as she declared forthrightly in "Loneliness . . . An American Malady." "No motive among the complex ricochets of our desires and rejections seems stronger or more enduring than the will of the individual to claim his identity and belong," McCullers wrote, adding later that "after the first establishment of identity there comes the imperative to need to lose this new-found sense of separateness and to belong to something larger and more powerful than the weak, lonely self. The sense of moral isolation is intolerable to us" (*MH* 259–60).

14. Quoted in Isabel Paterson, "Turns with a Bookworm," *New York Herald Tribune Books*, 23 June 1940, 11. While McCullers no doubt was making connections between violent manifestations of southern racism and Fascist racism, Chester Eisinger probably overstates the case when he argues that McCullers's comment "makes sense only if we assume that the economics of capitalism and the racial practices of the South suggest to her the barbarism of fascism." Chester E. Eisinger, *Fiction of the Forties* (Chicago: University of Chicago Press, 1963), 251.

15. Evans, *Ballad of Carson McCullers*, 43.

16. That McCullers had the context of Fascism in mind in constructing *Reflections* is suggested by the source for much of the novel, D. H. Lawrence's story "The Prussian Officer," which is concerned with, among other things, militarism, authoritarianism, and sadomasochism. At the time when McCullers was working on *Reflections*, leftist critics were proleptically linking Lawrence's fiction to Fascist ideology, particularly in its celebration of the martial spirit, irrationalism, and primitivism. (The attacks on Lawrence resemble those being leveled at Faulkner and other writers tagged as students of "the school of cruelty.") For example, in a 1936 review of *Phoenix: The Posthumous Papers of D. H. Lawrence* published in the *New Republic* Granville Hicks concluded that Lawrence's thought "gives encouragement to the fascist mind," an assertion Newton Arvin defended a few weeks later in the same magazine. Granville Hicks, "D. H. Lawrence as Messiah," review of *Phoenix: The Posthumous Papers of D. H. Lawrence*, ed. Edward D. McDonald, *New Republic*, 28 October 1936, 359; Newton Arvin, "D. H. Lawrence and Fascism," ibid., 16 December 1936, 219. More elaborate discussions were appearing by the late 1930s, including Christopher Caudwell's *Studies in a Dying Culture* (London: John Lane, 1938) and William York Tindall's *D. H. Lawrence and Susan His Cow* (New York: Columbia University Press, 1939). Bitterly denouncing Lawrence, Caudwell wrote that in spurning bourgeois culture Lawrence embraced ideas "ultimately Fascist," turning backward "to old primitive values, to mythology, to racialism, nationalism, hero-worship, and *participation mystique*. This Fascist art is like the regression of the neurotic to a previous level of adaptation" (56). Tindall concluded, in a chapter entitled "Lawrence among the Fascists," that Lawrence was best read as "a theocratic fascist" (179).

17. Carson McCullers, "Author's Outline of *The Mute*" (later published as *The Heart Is a Lonely Hunter*), in *MH*, 124.

18. McCullers's understanding of Fascism seems close to that of Wilhelm Reich, who characterized it as "the expression of the irrational structure of mass man." Wilhelm Reich, *The Mass Psychology of Fascism*, trans. Vincent R. Carfagno (New York: Farrar, Straus and Giroux, 1971), xx.

19. Edward Weeks, "First Person Singular," *Atlantic Monthly*, April 1941, xx. Weeks's book column reviewing *Reflections in a Golden Eye*, it might be noted, was sandwiched between reviews of two books depicting the dangers of Nazi Germany: Hermann Rauschning's *The Redemption of Democracy: The Coming Atlantic Empire*, trans. Barrows Mussey (New York: Alliance Book Corporation, 1941), and William E. Dodd's *Ambassador Dodd's Diary, 1933–38*, ed. William E. Dodd, Jr., and Martha Dodd (New York: Harcourt, Brace, 1940). Rauschning's book, criticizing isolationism and appeasement in the face of the Nazi threat, calls for the type of democratic fighting faith that one finds absent in McCullers's novel. Dodd's diary chronicles his years as ambassador to Germany. In his introduction to the Dodd book, Charles A. Beard uses Rauschning's phrase "the revolution of nihilism" to characterize Nazism (vii).

20. Carr, *Lonely Hunter*, 101.

21. In this, McCullers was voicing ideas similar to those being voiced by other literary figures, such as Van Wyck Brooks and Archibald MacLeish, who advocated the political responsibility of the artist. The critical positions of Brooks and MacLeish are discussed further in chapters 1 and 9.

22. Carson McCullers, "Look Homeward, Americans," *MH*, 212, 213.

23. Carson McCullers, "Night Watch over Freedom," ibid., 215.

24. While it is possible that she was describing a real event, in all likelihood McCullers created Mac (as his very name suggests) as a mouthpiece for her own views.

25. Carson McCullers, "We Carried Our Banners—We Were Pacifists, Too," *MH*, 222 (hereafter cited in text).

26. Reeves and Carson divorced in 1942, but during his military training before leaving for England they were reconciled, though they decided, at this point, against remarriage. Once Reeves shipped out, the distance apart brought them closer together, and the two exchanged numerous letters, with Reeves sending back graphic descriptions of the fighting and suffering and Carson voicing her passionate concern for his safety and for Allied victory. Their wartime letters have been collected in *Illumination and Night Glare: The Unfinished Autobiography of Carson McCullers*, ed. Carlos L. Dews (Madison: University of Wisconsin Press, 1999).

27. Carson McCullers, "Love's Not Time's Fool," *Mademoiselle*, April 1943, 95. McCullers signed the letter "A War Wife."

28. See above, n. 7. This may have been a new work or an expansion of her story "The Aliens."

29. Klaus Mann, quoted in Carr, *Lonely Hunter*, 100.

30. Miss Amelia's café created the type of free and open space, nurturing fellowship and community, that McCullers found in Brooklyn, as described in her essay "Brooklyn Is My Neighbourhood," which she wrote in 1941. The atmosphere in Miss Amelia's café (which doubled as a bar—Miss Amelia sold moonshine from her still) closely resembles the atmosphere in McCullers's descriptions of the bars along Brooklyn's Sand Street, where life was "as vivacious as a country fair" (*MH* 218). At one bar, McCullers notes, in a detail looking forward to *The Ballad of the Sad Café*, "there is a little hunchback who struts in proudly every evening, and is petted by everyone, given free drinks, and treated as a sort of mascot by the proprietor" (*MH* 219).

31. The conformity demanded by the traditional South stands in direct opposition to the life McCullers found in Brooklyn, a community awash with diverse and quirky people who share a common identity in their allegiance to the neighborhood. This shared identity, as McCullers drives home in the final lines of "Brooklyn Is My Neighbourhood," embraced rather than restricted difference, nurtured rather than oppressed: "That is one of the things I love best about Brooklyn. Everyone is not expected to be exactly like everyone else" (*MH* 220).

32. Taken one step further, *The Ballad of the Sad Café* might also be read as a parable of Nazi Germany's destruction of Weimar culture, which was popularly associated with the nightclubs and cabarets.

33. When Jarvis comes home to visit before the wedding, he turns off the radio. During the time when Frankie has transformed herself into F. Jasmine and feels secure in the world, the radio remains off and Frankie makes sure that it stays off. At one point, after Bernice suggests they turn on the radio, Frankie responds: "No. . . . I can't explain why. But I don't want to have that radio turned on again" (*MH* 75).

34. Patricia Yaeger, *Dirt and Desire: Reconstructing Southern Women's Writing, 1930–1990* (Chicago: University of Chicago Press, 2000), 159.

35. Yaeger suggests that John Henry's drawings resemble surrealistic art in their distortion of conventional images and patterns. See ibid., 161–62.

36. At the end of the novel, for instance, following Mrs. Littlejohn's advice, Frankie avoids going to the freak show at the fair.

37. Carson McCullers, *The Member of the Wedding: A Play* (New York: New Directions, 1951), 90.

CHAPTER 9

1. Warren believed that the Civil War set in motion developments that plagued modern democratic society, culminating in World War II. In *The Legacy of the Civil War* he argued that the war had transformed the social order by stimulating economic and technological enterprise, "catapult[ing] America from what had been in considerable part an agrarian, handicraft society into the society of Big Technology and Big Business," with "the old sprawling, loosely knit country disappeared into the nation of Big Organization." *The Legacy of the Civil War: Meditations on the Centennial* (New York: Random House, 1961), 8, 9 (hereafter cited both parenthetically in text and in notes). The aftermath of the war, Warren believed, unleashed plutocratic tyranny, unbridled consumerism, and environmental destruction. Warren frequently turned to Herman Melville, and particularly his collection of verse *Battle-Pieces* (1866), to characterize the forbidding underside of post–Civil War America. With *Battle-Pieces*, Warren wrote, Melville became "the first American writer to sniff the dead rat behind the baseboard [of American politics]." *Democracy and Poetry* (Cambridge, MA: Harvard University Press, 1975), 8 (hereafter cited in text).

2. Quoted in *Fugitives' Reunion: Conversations at Vanderbilt, May 3–5, 1956*, ed. Rob Roy Purdy (Nashville, TN: Vanderbilt University Press, 1959), 213–14.

3. Ibid., 209.

4. Quoted in "Interview with Eleanor Clark and Robert Penn Warren," in *Robert Penn Warren Talking*, 263.

5. Robert Penn Warren, *Homage to Theodore Dreiser on the Centennial of His Birth* (New York: Random House, 1971), 129 (hereafter cited both parenthetically in text and in notes).

6. Quoted in "A Conversation with Robert Penn Warren," by Frank Gado, in *Robert Penn Warren Talking*, 85–86.

7. In *The Legacy of the Civil War*, in another context, Warren posed some of the same questions that he repeatedly examined in his own work: "Is it possible for the individual, in the great modern industrial state, to retain some sense of responsibility? Is it possible for him to remain an individual? Is it possible, in the midst of all the forces making for standardization and anonymity, for society to avoid cultural starvation—to retain, and even develop, cultural pluralism and individual variety, and foster both social and individual integrity? Can we avoid, in its deep and more destructive manifestations, the tyranny of the majority, and at the same time keep a fruitful respect for the common will?" (48–49).

8. Robert Penn Warren, *John Brown: The Making of a Martyr* (1929; Nashville: J. S. Sanders, 1993), 318 (hereafter cited in text).

9. Robert Penn Warren, *Who Speaks for the Negro?* (New York: Random House, 1965), 320 (hereafter cited both parenthetically in text and in notes).

10. Warren noted in the same passage from *Who Speaks for the Negro?* that a French critic had rightfully observed that "the mythic Brown figure recurs again and again in my fiction, in various disguises, the man who at any cost, would strike for absolute solutions" (320).

11. Warren and Allen Tate made this complaint in a letter to Donald Davidson and John Crowe Ransom (6 September 1930), with particular reference to the decision to entitle the Agrarian symposium *I'll Take My Stand* rather than *Tracts Against Communism*. See Robert Penn Warren, *Selected Letters of Robert Penn Warren*, vol. 1, *The Apprenticeship Years, 1924–1934*, ed. William Bedford Clark (Baton Rouge: Louisiana State University Press, 2000), 188–91.

12. After reading Warren's essay in manuscript, Davidson fired off a letter to Tate (21 July 1930) expressing his shock and dismay. "It hardly seems worthy of Red, or worthy of the subject," Davidson wrote. "And it certainly is not very closely related to the main theme of our book. It goes off at a tangent to discuss the negro problem in general (which, I take it, is not our main concern in the book), and it makes only two or three points that bear on our principles at all." Even worse, Davidson continued, "the ideas advanced about the negro don't seem to chime with our ideas as I understand them. Behind the essay, too, are implications which I am sure we don't accept—they are 'progressive' implications, with a pretty strong smack of latter-day sociology." Angry at and befuddled by Warren, Davidson finally threw up his hands, declaring that the essay veered so far away from the Warren he knew that he was almost inclined "to doubt whether RED ACTUALLY WROTE THIS ESSAY!" (*LCDT* 251). While Davidson did not speak for the entire group, his words nonetheless point to the fact that Warren was often out of sync with the rest of the Agrarians.

13. Hastening Warren's withdrawal from the Agrarians were the attacks by leftist critics asserting that regionalism—and agrarianism—shared ideological ties with Fascism. Warren noted these attacks on regional writing in his 1936 essay "Literature as a Symptom," which appeared in *Who Owns America? A New Declaration of Independence*, ed. Herbert Agar and Allen Tate (1936; Wilmington, DE: ISI Books, 1999). As discussed in chapter 1, Warren commented that because of their emphasis on localism (rather than on internationalism, as endorsed by

leftist writers), regional writers were often characterized as mindless proponents "of antiquated religion, patriotism, or even fascism" (353). Warren was also aware of Seward Collins's interview by Grace Lumpkin, which appeared that same year in *Fight against War and Fascism*; in that interview, as we have already seen, Lumpkin asserted that the Agrarians shared many of Collins's Fascist ideas, even if they themselves did not see the connections. Grace Lumpkin, "I Want a King," *Fight against War and Fascism* 3 (February 1936): 3, 14. A month after Lumpkin's interview appeared, Warren and Cleanth Brooks sent Allen Tate a copy of a newspaper article reporting that Lumpkin was attacking the Agrarians in public talks. The article quotes her as saying at a meeting of the Young Women's Christian Association in New Orleans that a rising tide of Fascism was threatening America and that "already there are 'highbrow Fascists' who are paving the way for such a government in America today." Lumpkin pointed a finger at Tate and writers connected with the *Southern Review* (Brooks and Warren were its editors), who she said were promoting Fascist thinking. Tate, she said, believed that "people must be pushed back to medieval times, that there shall be lords and kings and a few masters to rule an abject and hopeless mass of workers," and she noted that one of the key backers of Agrarians, Seward Collins, admired Hitler and Mussolini and "wanted a government with a few people chosen to run the whole system, with the rest in virtual slavery." "Sharecroppers in Distress, Novelist Says," *New Orleans Morning Tribune*, 17 March 1936, 2. In their letter to Tate, Brooks and Warren, wondered whether a lawsuit against Lumpkin was in order.

14. Archibald MacLeish, *The Irresponsibles: A Declaration* (New York: Duell, Sloan and Pierce, 1940), 16 (hereafter cited in text).

15. Van Wyck Brooks, *Opinions of Oliver Allston* (New York: E. P. Dutton, 1941), 211 (hereafter cited in text).

16. Robert Penn Warren, "Homage to Oliver Allston," review of *Opinions of Oliver Allston*, by Van Wyck Brooks, *Kenyon Review* 4 (Spring 1942): 259–63; idem, "Pure and Impure Poetry," ibid. 5 (Spring 1943): 228–54 (hereafter cited in text). In his essay Warren followed the lead of Allen Tate and John Crowe Ransom, both of whom had already responded to the Brooks-MacLeish Thesis in a *Partisan Review* symposium on the topic. See "On the 'Brooks-MacLeish Thesis,'" *Partisan Review* 9 (January–February 1942): 38–47. Also participating in the symposium were William Carlos Williams, Henry Miller, Louise Bogan, James T. Farrell, and Lionel Trilling.

17. In the same *Partisan Review* symposium on Brooks and MacLeish's ideas, Allen Tate reached a similar conclusion, pointing out that Brooks in particular extended his moralistic and didactic view of literature into the realm of nationalism and patriotism. In Brooks's call for artistic conformity along nationalist lines Tate heard the call for censorship and repression, and he noted how close to the Nazis Brooks sounded: "Nobody who follows the drift of opinion in this country can fail to see the parallel between the Brooks-MacLeish school and Dr. Goebbels' Hitler-inspired attack on 'modern' art. It is wholly irrelevant whether a nationalist-patriotic censorship of the imagination is set up in the interest of democracy or of totalitarianism; the results may turn out to be the same. The best defense of democracy, or of any other political order, in terms of the creative imagination, is no defense at all; and the worst defense of democracy, or of any other political order, in terms of the imagination, is the effort to prove that the arts prefer any one political system." Allen Tate, in "On the 'Brooks-MacLeish Thesis,'" *Partisan Review* 9 (January–February 1942): 38.

18. While Warren's concern about political fanaticism was not new, in the late 1930s that concern became central to his imaginative vision, anchoring just about all of his work.

19. Quoted in "An Interview in New Haven with Robert Penn Warren," by Richard B. Sale, in *Robert Penn Warren Talking*, 128–29.

20. Warren French goes so far as to suggest that *Night Rider* was constructed entirely as a commentary on contemporary politics, with Warren deliberately manipulating historical events and chronology in order to "make the reader uncomfortably aware of the parallel between the events that destroyed the society of this remote and isolated region and those that threatened, when Warren wrote, the whole Western world." Warren French, *The Social Novel at the End of an Era* (Carbondale: Southern Illinois University Press, 1966), 185.

21. Robert Penn Warren, *Night Rider* (1939; Nashville, TN: J. S. Sanders, 1992), 43 (hereafter cited in text).

22. Christopher Isherwood, "Tragic Liberal," review of *Night Rider*, by Robert Penn Warren, *New Republic*, 31 May 1939, 108.

23. Irene Hendry, "The Regional Novel," *Sewanee Review* 53 (January–March 1945): 101.

24. See G. A. Borgese, *Goliath: The March of Fascism* (New York: Viking, 1938).

25. Kenneth Burke, *The Philosophy of Literary Form: Studies in Symbolic Action* (Baton Rouge: Louisiana State University Press, 1941), 84, 88.

26. The best discussion of Warren's different versions of the play and of the textual difficulties in the existing multiple versions, see *Robert Penn Warren's "All the King's Men": Three Stage Versions*, ed. James. A. Grimshaw, Jr., and James A. Perkins (Athens: University of Georgia Press, 2000).

27. Quoted in Joseph Blotner, *Robert Penn Warren: A Biography* (New York: Random House, 1997), 175.

28. Warren's introductory statement appeared originally in the Italian magazine *Sipario* and is reprinted in its entirety in the introduction to *Robert Penn Warren's "All the King's Men,"* 9–10.

29. Quoted in "Conversation with Robert Penn Warren," 78.

30. Perhaps the most well known example is Harnett Kane's *Louisiana Hayride: The American Rehearsal for Dictatorship, 1928–1940* (1941; Gretna, LA: Pelican, 1990), in which Kane frequently compares Long to Hitler and Mussolini, seeing all three pursuing absolute power and dictatorship. Kane writes that Long created "a thing that most Americans thought impossible: a systematic totalitarianism on North American soil, functioning under the Constitution, under the flag, to the tune of *The Star-Spangled Banner* (with some minor notes of *Dixie*). The most complete despotism in the nation's history used the institutions of democracy to crush democracy" (4). Kane also argues that Long's rise to power was not necessarily an isolated event; he declares that a similar takeover could happen in any state and that the federal government was also at risk.

31. Robert Penn Warren, *Proud Flesh*, in *Robert Penn Warren's "All the King's Men,"* 23 (hereafter cited in text).

32. Warren worked on several of the poems from the collection, including "Love's Parable" and "Terror" (and probably "Crime"), while in Italy in 1939–40. In his biography, Joseph Blotner says that Warren also wrote "Pursuit" while in Italy, though comments from Warren suggest otherwise. In his author's note in the anthology *Modern Poetry* Warren said that he had begun "Pursuit" in August 1940, while in Gambier, Ohio, and completed it that October, while in Baton Rouge. See Robert Penn Warren, "Author's Note to 'Terror,'" in *Modern Poetry: British and American*, ed. Kimon Friar and John Malcolm Brinnin (New York: Appleton-Century-Crofts, 1951), 542–43 (hereafter cited in text).

33. While most of the poems in *Thirty-Six Poems* make no reference to large social and political issues, two poems that Warren wrote in 1935, "Letter from a Coward to a Hero" and "Ransom," do invoke the turmoil facing modernity, clearly looking forward to Warren's poems of the early 1940s. Particularly striking in this regard are lines from "Letter from a Coward to a Hero" in which the sound of autumn guns signals both the hunting in the woods and fighting on the battlefield: "Guns blaze in autumn and / The quail falls and / Empires collide with a bang / That shakes the pictures where they hang / And democracy shows signs of dry rot / And Dives has and Lazarus not / And the time is out joint" (*CPW* 47).

34. Quoted in "Conversation with Robert Penn Warren," 71–72.

35. As noted above, in n. 18 to chapter 2, Carrel was a Nobel Prize–winning physician who strongly supported eugenics, including the Nazis' program of enforced sterilization and euthanasia.

36. Anthony Szczesiul, *Racial Politics and Robert Penn Warren's Poetry* (Gainesville: University Press of Florida, 2002), 54.

37. Quoted in John Burt's "Textual Notes to 'Terror,'" in *CPW*, 655.

38. Quoted in "Robert Penn Warren: An Interview," by Marshall Walker, in *Robert Penn Warren Talking*, 182.

39. Robert Penn Warren, introduction to *All the King's Men* (1946; New York: Modern Library, 1953), iii.

40. Robert Penn Warren, *At Heaven's Gate* (New York: New Directions, 1943), 373 (hereafter cited in text).

41. Quoted in "An Interview with Robert Penn Warren," by Peter Stitt, in *Robert Penn Warren Talking*, 233.

42. For my comments on *All the King's Men*, I use the 1946 text as originally published by Harcourt, Brace. Where appropriate, I comment upon differences between this text and Noel Polk's new "restored edition," which reproduces Warren's original typescript, free from the deletions and changes demanded by his editors. For discussion of the changes Warren made to his original manuscript, see Noel Polk, afterword to *All the King's Men*, restored ed., ed. Noel Polk (New York: Random House, 2001).

43. Warren, introduction to *All the King's Men*, vii.

44. Quoted in "Conversation with Robert Penn Warren," 76, 77–78.

45. Willie's position represents an extreme form of legal realism, an interpretation of the law, largely influenced by Justice Oliver Wendell Holmes, that asserted that rather than by precedent (the position of legal formalism), laws should be determined by social needs. Warren was extremely interested in Holmes and his legal reasoning. In his later discussion of Holmes in *Homage to Theodore Dreiser*, Warren characterized him in terms that echo his depiction of Willie, arguing that Holmes's championing of the common people was far overshadowed by his grim view of human worth and his belief that power politics were necessary for instituting change. Warren cited Holmes's well-known letter to Sir Sidney Pollack in which Holmes wrote that "the sacredness of human life is a purely municipal ideal of no validity outside the jurisdiction. I believe that force, mitigated so far as may be by good manners, is the *ultima ratio*, and between two groups that want to make inconsistent kinds of worlds I see no remedy except force. I may add what I no doubt have said often enough, that it seems to me that every society rests on the death of men" (60–61). Willie shares a similar disdain for humanity (as expressed in one of his favorite observations, "Man is conceived in sin and born in corruption and he passeth from the stink of the didie to the stench of the shroud" [*AKM* 49]) and a simi-

lar belief in power. At one point, Willie describes the law as "always too short and too tight for growing humankind. The best you can do is do something and then make up some law to fit and by the time that law gets on the books you would have done something different. Do you think half the things I've done were clear, distinct, and simple in the constitution of this state?" (*AKM* 136). And when Hugh Miller counters that the state supreme court has always upheld Willie, he responds that "they ruled because I put 'em there to rule it, and they saw what had to be done. Half the things *weren't* in the constitution but they are now, by God. And how did they get there? Simply because somebody did 'em" (*AKM* 136). Here is Warren's vision of where he feared radical legal realism might end: a world of radical relativism governed by iron-fisted dictatorship.

46. In his discussion of Warren's exploration of pragmatism, particularly the ideas of William James, in *All the King's Men*, Cushing Strout points out that it was the perceived pragmatism of Mussolini, carrying Italy forward into the future with a vision unchecked by liberal conscience, that in part explained his appeal outside Italy. In 1926 Mussolini himself expressed his debt to James, saying that "James taught me that an action should be judged rather by its results than by its doctrinary basis. I learnt of James that faith in action, that ardent will to live and fight, to which Fascism owes a great part of its success." See Cushing Strout, "All the King's Men and the Shadow of William James," *Southern Review*, n.s., 6 (October 1970): 920–34; the quotation from Mussolini is on 921.

47. Significant, too, is that in book 5 of the *Faerie Queene* Artegall, the Knight of Justice, defeats the giant, who represents early ideas on democracy.

48. Quoted in Stitt, "Interview with Robert Penn Warren," 233.

49. Polk, afterword to *All the King's Men*, 636.

50. As noted earlier in this study, commentators in the American press often emphasized the efficiency of Fascism. Even those who deeply believed in democracy often suggested that representative government might be too cumbersome and inefficient to handle the increasingly complex problems of modernity. "If Mussolini Had Ruled Detroit," an editorial from the 11 December 1929 *Christian Century*, commented that while "the fascist scheme of government is all wrong," nonetheless "it sometimes succeeds by its autocratic methods in accomplishing something that is of more social significance than making the trains run on schedule." The editorial noted approvingly that Mussolini had stepped in to protect factory workers when an Italian automobile manufacturer announced layoffs. "We wonder what Mussolini would have done when Mr. Ford laid off his factory force while maturing plans for 'Model A,' if Detroit had been in Italy," the editorial quipped. "We are glad that Detroit is not in Italy, and that Mussolini was not at the head of a band of black-shirts governing Detroit. Nevertheless, the hope of democracy will revive when it learns how to do the things that need to be done as efficiently as autocracy does them" (1534). Praise of efficiency also lies behind the *Wall Street Journal*'s ditty on Mussolini: "On formula and etiquette / He seems a trifle shy; / But when it comes to 'go and get,' / He's some two-fisted guy." Quoted in Edward A. Purcell, Jr., *The Crisis of Democratic Theory: Scientific Naturalism and the Problem of Value* (Lexington: University Press of Kentucky, 1973), 122. See also Benjamin L. Alpers, *Dictators, Democracy, and American Public Culture: Envisioning the Totalitarian Enemy, 1920s–1950s* (Chapel Hill: University of North Carolina Press, 2003).

51. Preparations for trying the Nazi leadership as war criminals began long before the Nuremberg trials opened in November 1945. Several important steps in those preparations took place in 1943, the year that Warren began work on the novel. On 30 October Winston Churchill, Franklin Roosevelt, and Joseph Stalin signed the Moscow Declaration, which in-

cluded a section citing evidence of Nazi war atrocities and the necessity for bringing Nazi war criminals to trial at war's end. At their meeting in Tehran later that year (28 November–1 December), the three leaders further discussed the future prosecution of war criminals. During the summer of 1945, when Warren was revising the manuscript of the novel, the United States, France, the United Kingdom, and the Soviet Union signed the Charter of the International Military Tribunal, establishing the tribunal and the procedures for prosecuting the major Axis war criminals. Two of the charter's articles specifically addressed the matter of a person's responsibility for crimes committed while serving in an official government capacity:

> Article 7: The official position of defendants, whether as Heads of State or responsible officials in Government departments, shall not be considered as freeing them from responsibility or mitigating punishment.
> Article 8: The fact that the defendant acted pursuant to order of his Government or of a superior shall not free him from responsibility, but may be considered in mitigation of punishment if the Tribunal determine that justice so requires. (53)

See Michael R. Marrus, ed., *The Nuremberg War Crimes Trial, 1945–46: A Documentary History* (Boston: Bedford Books, 1997).

52. James H. Justus, *The Achievement of Robert Penn Warren* (Baton Rouge: Louisiana State University Press, 1981), 205 (hereafter cited in text).

53. As Warren reveals in his letters from his trip to Italy, he was deeply interested in observing post-Mussolini politics, and he closely followed the election campaigns and other political developments. He was particularly taken with Sicily, which reminded him of the American South. In a letter to his friend Brainard Cheney (5 August 1948), Warren observed that Sicily was "a damned strange country, with people I like very much, and in a peculiar way it is a useful look at Mississippi or Louisiana, for in more than geography Sicily is the South of Italy." Robert Penn Warren, *Selected Letters of Robert Penn Warren*, vol. 3, *Triumph and Transition, 1943–1952*, ed. Randy Hendricks and James A. Perkins (Baton Rouge: Louisiana State University Press, 2006), 313.

54. As James Justus characterizes him, La Grand' Bosse is a "bestial dictator," a frightening echo to Willie Stark. His fiefdom, located, appropriately, in a swamp, points to the misrule to which Willie was taking his state. See Justus, *Achievement of Robert Penn Warren*, 220.

55. Robert Penn Warren, "Knowledge and the Image of Man," *Sewanee Review* 63 (April–June 1955): 186–87 (hereafter cited in text).

CHAPTER 10

1. Quoted in Katherine Lederer, "The Critical Reaction to the Dramatic Works of Lillian Hellman" (PhD diss., University of Arkansas, 1967), 27–28.

2. A refuge that recalls the kitchen in McCullers's *The Member of the Wedding*.

3. Hellman discussed her stay in Bonn in both *Unfinished Woman* and *Scoundrel Time*. See *UW*, 54; and *ST*, 41–42.

4. A former Pinkerton agent and strikebreaker, Hammett by this time had reversed himself to become a committed Marxist and champion of the working class. Later, the outbreak of the Spanish Civil War apparently was a watershed event for Hammett, pushing him into active politics.

5. Dashiell Hammett, *Selected Letters of Dashiell Hammett, 1921–1960*, ed. Richard Layman with Julie M. Rivett (Washington, DC: Counterpoint, 2001), 109–10.

6. Hammett joined the Communist Party USA in 1937. It is not clear whether Hellman made the same step, though she probably did not. Given her rebellious nature, she probably found that party membership demanded artistic and intellectual submission that was impossible to tolerate.

7. Representative of criticism focusing on Mary Tilford's evil is Barrett Clark's conclusion that *The Children's Hour* is not about good and evil, but about "evil alone," and that evil, manifested in Mary's actions, "is a kind of unattached and almost meaningless power. It is like a phenomenon of nature, which cannot be eradicated, hardly perhaps even dealt with." Barrett H. Clark, "Lillian Hellman," *College English* 6 (December 1944): 128.

8. Quoted in Carl Rollyson, *Lillian Hellman: Her Legend and Her Legacy* (New York: St. Martin's, 1988), 66.

9. Philip M. Armato, "'Good and Evil' in Lillian Hellman's *The Children's Hour*," in *Critical Essays on Lillian Hellman*, ed. Mark W. Estrin (Boston: G. K. Hall, 1989), 74–75.

10. Rollyson, *Lillian Hellman*, 70.

11. For a discussion of the theme of blackmail in Hellman's plays, see Jacob H. Adler, "The Dramaturgy of Blackmail in the Ibsenite Hellman," in Estrin, *Critical Essays on Lillian Hellman*, 31–42.

12. For a fuller discussion of Hellman's response to the trials, see esp. William Wright, *Lillian Hellman: The Image, The Woman* (New York: Simon and Schuster, 1986), 138–40. Hellman later claimed, in *An Unfinished Woman*, that when she arrived in Moscow she was unaware that the Soviet Union was "in the middle of the ugliest purge period"; discussion of the trials by American diplomats was so mixed with blind hatred for Soviet Russia, she added, that "one couldn't pick the true charges from the wild hatred" (*UW* 81).

13. Even though the Neutrality Act did not specifically bar arms sales to warring sides in civil wars, it was invoked with regard to the Spanish Civil War.

14. Although the factual accuracy of Hellman's diary entries has been called into serious question, the entries nonetheless reveal, in terms of Hellman's personal perspective, that her experiences in Spain had a tremendous impact on her political thinking and commitment. For a withering attack on the factual errors in Hellman's writings on Spain, see Martha Gellhorn, "On Apocryphism," *Paris Review* 23 (Spring 1981): 280–301.

15. "Day in Spain" was originally commissioned by Walter Winchell for inclusion in one of his syndicated columns. Upon reading her article, however, William Randolph Hearst, the owner of the syndicating company that distributed Winchell's columns, ordered that the column with Hellman's commentary not be distributed to subscribing newspapers. Hellman subsequently published "Day in Spain" in the *New Republic* 94 (13 April 1938): 297–98 (hereafter cited in text).

16. Lillian Hellman, "The Little War," in *This Is My Best*, ed. Whit Burnett (New York: Dial, 1942), 990.

17. Addie's observation, furthermore, directly echoes Hellman's praise for the international volunteers in "Days in Spain"; they are heroes in battling against, rather resigning themselves to, Fascist aggression.

18. Wright, *Lillian Hellman*, 153.

19. It seems clear that "little foxes" was for Hellman an apt label for those engaged in the Fascist enterprise, little men out to increase their power. Hellman's entitling her play "The Little

Foxes," with its epigraph from *Song of Solomon* 2:15, "Take us the foxes, the little foxes, that spoil the vines; for our vines have tender grapes," may have derived from an incident she describes in one of her sketches in "Day in Spain." In this sketch, Hellman describes herself eating grapes with two soldiers in Madrid during an attack by Italian bombers that killed sixty-three people in another part of the city. Read in this light, the Fascist enterprise represents the end to which the Hubbards are heading and perhaps the enemy against which Hellman imagined Alexandra someday fighting.

20. Quoted in Wright, *Lillian Hellman*, 161. Much later, in *Pentimento*, Hellman again claimed that she had been to Finland in 1937. Of her supposed experiences there she wrote: "I had been in Helsinki for two weeks and had turned my head each day from the giant posters of Hitler pasted to the wall of my hotel. One night a member of our Olympic team, a man of Finnish descent, had taken me to a large rally of Hitler sympathizers and translated for me their admiring speeches. I needed no translator for the raised arms, the cheers, the Wessel song" (*P* 183).

21. Quoted in Rollyson, *Lillian Hellman*, 151.
22. Wright, *Lillian Hellman*, 182.
23. Quoted in ibid., 168.
24. Ibid.
25. Lillian Hellman, "The Little Men in Philadelphia," *PM*, 25 June 1940, 6.
26. Quoted in Lederer, "Critical Reaction," 53.
27. Richard Moody, *Lillian Hellman: Playwright* (New York: Pegasus, 1972).
28. Hannah Arendt, in *Eichmann in Jerusalem*, concludes that "it is hardly an exaggeration to say that Rumania was the most anti-Semitic country in prewar Europe." She notes that so savage were the attacks on Jews by Romanians during the war that "even the S.S. were taken aback, and occasionally frightened, by the horrors of old-fashioned, spontaneous pogroms on a gigantic scale; they often intervened to save Jews from sheer butchery, so that the killing could be done in what, according to them, was a civilized way." Hannah Arendt, *Eichmann in Jerusalem: A Report on the Banality of Evil* (1963; New York: Penguin, 1994), 190.
29. In perhaps a nod to *The Little Foxes*, Fanny recalls her mother saying of the Chandlers, hard-driving business people who trade in bootleg munitions, that "they never should have learned to walk on two feet. They would have been more comfortable on four" (*SP* 268). When Fanny asks Teck if he minds that Sam Chandler is a bootleg arms dealer, he responds, "Mind? I have not thought about it" (*SP* 268).
30. Bosley Crowther, "The Cream of the 1943 Crop," *New York Times*, 28 August 1943, sec. 2, p. 3.
31. Early in the war, working with Paul Robeson and others, she also devoted a good bit of energy to ending segregation in the armed forces and the federal government. In addition, she wrote a screenplay for a short propaganda film, *The Negro Soldier*, which, while acknowledging the often violent racism blacks faced at home, nonetheless urged them to join in the war effort, since, as one character says, "if you're going to make the lot of the black man better, you got to fight for the white man, too." The film was produced, but Hellman's script was completely rewritten, and she was not listed in the film's credits. The quotation is from Hellman's screenplay, as cited in Rollyson, *Lillian Hellman*, 193. Rollyson provides a good discussion and overview of *The Negro Soldier*, as well as further information on Hellman's wartime work against racial discrimination.

32. For a fuller discussions of the planned film, see esp. Moody, *Lillian Hellman*, 139–40; and Rollyson, *Lillian Hellman*, 199–200.

33. Theodore Straus, "On Lillian Hellman, a Lady of Principle: The Author of *Watch on the Rhine* and *North Star* Stands by Her Guns," *New York Times*, 29 August 1943, sec. 2, p. 3.

34. Moody, *Lillian Hellman*, 140.

35. Lillian Hellman, *"The North Star": A Motion Picture about Some Russian People* (New York: Viking, 1943), 113.

36. Rollyson, *Lillian Hellman*, 207.

37. Earl E. Fleischman (Eugene Earl), "*The Searching Wind* in the Making," *Quarterly Journal of Speech* 31 (February 1945): 25.

38. Hellman apparently was invited by group of Russian artists to see productions of *The Little Foxes* and *Watch on the Rhine*, which were then in rehearsals in Moscow. For the fullest discussion of Hellman's trip to the Soviet Union in 1944, see Robert P. Newman, *The Cold War Romance of Lillian Hellman and John Melby* (Chapel Hill: University of North Carolina Press, 1989). Of Roosevelt's strategy of sending cultural ambassadors to the Soviet Union, Newman writes: "Roosevelt sought every possible stratagem to mollify Stalin. One of his tactics was sending a series of goodwill emissaries to the Soviet Union, sometimes with personal messages to Stalin, sometimes not. Wendell Willkie, Joseph E. Davies, Eric Johnston, Patrick Hurley, and Henry Wallace were among those whom Roosevelt dispatched largely for goodwill reasons. Lillian Hellman's trip was part of this effort" (16).

39. Near the end of her trip, Hellman traveled to the Polish front and may have visited Majdanek, the recently liberated concentration camp on the outskirts of Lublin. In her article "I Meet the Front-Line Russians," in *Collier's*, 31 March 1945, Hellman praised the camaraderie and bravado of the Russian soldiers, observing that her conversations with them cemented her belief that "one of the most remarkable of Russian qualities is their ability to speak about war, death, love and hate without self-consciousness and without fake toughness; they speak simply, like healthy people who have never, fortunately, learned to be ashamed of emotion" (71). In other words, there was no wishy-washy, hazy liberalism about the Russians. Hellman made no mention of visiting Majdanek in the *Collier's* article, but in *An Unfinished Woman* she described her horror at visiting the camp (*UW* 153–54).

40. "Russia Acclaimed by Miss Hellman: Home, She Says, Soviet Will Deal with Fascism—Hopes We Do the Same," *New York Times*, 2 March 1945, 5. As Robert Newman notes, the *Times* printed two versions of this story, with a fuller version appearing in the paper's early edition. That edition is no longer readily available, as the paper's late edition, carrying an abbreviated version of the article, is the one that was microfilmed and archived. Newman read the original article in the FBI files on Hellman that he obtained through the Freedom of Information Act. See Newman, *Cold War Romance*, 54.

41. Quoted in Newman, *Cold War Romance*, 94.

42. Quoted in ibid., 66.

43. Quoted in ibid., 47–48.

44. Rollyson, *Lillian Hellman*, 242–43.

45. The massacre of the twenty-seven Confederate recruits recalls the Nazi street massacre witnessed by Kurt in *The Watch on the Rhine*, which also left twenty-seven dead. The different responses to the massacres underscore the difference between Kurt and Ben: Kurt gives up his financial security and becomes an anti-Fascist after witnessing the Nazi terror; Ben, after he be-

comes aware of the truth about the massacre, blackmails Marcus and takes his place as head of the family, thereby enmeshing himself in, rather than stepping free from, the massacre's chain of responsibility.

46. Lillian Hellman, "The Judas Goats," *Screenwriter*, December 1947, 7 (hereafter cited in text).

47. Hellman saw Roblès's play in Paris in 1948, during a trip that also took her to Prague and then to Belgrade, where she attended the opening of *The Little Foxes* and interviewed Tito.

48. Lillian Hellman, *Montserrat*, adapted from the play by Emmanuel Roblès (New York: Dramatists Play Service, 1949), 71–72.

49. Rollyson, *Lillian Hellman*, 278.

50. For fuller accounts of the conference, see esp. ibid., 276–78; and Wright, *Lillian Hellman*, 225–29.

51. "Red Visitors Cause Rumpus," *Life*, 4 April 1949, 42, 43.

52. With *The Autumn Garden* Hellman turned from the melodramatic problem play, inspired by Ibsen, to the more subtle and impressionist drama of Chekhov. Unlike her earlier plays, in which a central problem controlled the action, *The Autumn Garden* involves the self-revelations that emerge in the interactions between the characters.

53. For a fine discussion of *The Autumn Garden* in the context of the cold war, see Rollyson, *Lillian Hellman*, 295–96.

54. In their final form, Griggs's comments on frittering his life away were actually written by Dashiell Hammett, although the thoughts are Hellman's. Hammett rewrote two of Hellman's drafts before coming up with the final version.

CODA

1. Lillian Smith and Paula Snelling, "Buying a New World with Old Confederate Bills," *South Today* 7 (Autumn–Winter 1942–43): 12.

2. Besides adding three chapters, Smith made extensive changes to her original text that illustrate her revised perspective, clearly shaped by the cold war. Rather than exhaustively analyzing these changes, however, I limit my brief discussion to two of the new chapters, since they are the most clear and obvious expressions of her new position.

3. Lillian Smith, *Killers of the Dream*, rev. ed. (New York: W. W. Norton, 1961), 15 (hereafter cited in text).

4. See, e.g., Jon Lance Bacon's intriguing reading of Flannery O'Connor, *Flannery O'Connor and Cold War Culture* (New York: Cambridge University Press, 1993).

5. Klaus Theweleit, *Male Fantasies*, trans. Stephen Conway, 2 vols. (Minneapolis: University of Minnesota Press, 1987).

6. See esp. Eric Fromm, *Escape from Freedom* (1941; New York: Holt, Rinehart and Winston, 1976).

7. For a discussion of Percy's trip to Germany, see Jay Tolson, *Pilgrim in the Ruins: A Life of Walker Percy* (New York: Simon and Schuster, 1992), 114–19.

8. Walker Percy, *The Thanatos Syndrome* (New York: Farrar, Straus and Giroux, 1987), 247–48.

9. Walker Percy, "Stoicism in the South," in *Signposts in a Strange Land*, ed. Patrick Samway (New York: Farrar, Straus and Giroux, 1991), 84.

10. Walker Percy, "An Interview with Zoltán Abádi-Nagy," by Zoltán Abádi-Nagy, in *Signposts in a Strange Land*, 383.

11. Walker Percy, "The Failure and the Hope," in ibid., 333.

12. Nathan's extreme views, connecting lynching with the death camps, here echo the views of Lillian Smith.

13. For autobiographical elements in the novel, see esp. James L. W. West III, *William Styron, A Life* (New York: Random House, 1998), 411–27.

14. William Styron, "Hell Reconsidered," in *"This Quiet Dust" and Other Writings* (New York: Random House, 1982), 95 (hereafter cited in text).

15. Stanley M. Elkins, *Slavery: A Problem in American Institutional and Intellectual Life* (Chicago: University of Chicago Press, 1959), 104 (hereafter cited in text).

16. Richard L. Rubenstein, *The Cunning of History: Mass Death and the American Future* (New York: Harper and Row, 1975), 79.

17. It should be noted, in terms of Stingo's glossing of Bilbo's career, that only a few months before the time of the novel the U.S. Senate had refused to seat Bilbo, citing allegations of voter intimidation in his 1946 election campaign and of accepting bribes from defense contractors. "The way to keep the nigger from the polls is to see him the night before," Bilbo was reported to have said during his campaign. Bilbo is quoted in Chester M. Morgan, *Redneck Liberal: Theodore Bilbo and the New Deal* (Baton Rouge: Louisiana State University Press, 1985), 250.

18. Theodore Bilbo, preface to *Take Your Choice: Separation or Mongrelization* (Poplarville, MS: Dream House, 1947), np (hereafter cited in text).

BIBLIOGRAPHY

Adler, Jacob H. "The Dramaturgy of Blackmail in the Ibsenite Hellman." In Estrin, *Critical Essays on Lillian Hellman*.
Adler, Les K., and Thomas G. Patterson. "Red Fascism: The Merger of Nazi Germany and Soviet Russia in the American Image of Totalitarianism, 1930's–1950's." *American Historical Review* 75 (April 1970): 1046–64.
Agar, Herbert. "But Can It Be Done?" in Agar and Tate, *Who Owns America?*
———. *Land of the Free*. Boston: Houghton Mifflin, 1935.
Agar, Herbert, and Allen Tate, eds. *Who Owns America? A New Declaration of Independence*. 1936. Wilmington, DE: ISI Books, 1999.
Allen, John D. "Southern Agrarianism: Revised Version." *Pseudopodia* 1 (Summer 1936): 1–3, 14.
Alpers, Benjamin L. *Dictators, Democracy, and American Public Culture: Envisioning the Totalitarian Enemy, 1920s–1950s*. Chapel Hill: University of North Carolina Press, 2003.
Anderson, Sherwood. *Sherwood Anderson's Memoirs*. New York: Harcourt Brace, 1942.
Andrews, William L. "In Search of a Common Identity: The Self and the South in Four Mississippi Autobiographies." *Southern Review*, n.s, 24 (Winter 1988): 47–64.
Arendt, Hannah. *Eichmann in Jerusalem: A Report on the Banality of Evil*. 1963. New York: Penguin, 1994.
———. *The Origins of Totalitarianism*. New ed. New York: Harcourt Brace Jovanovich, 1973.
Armato, Philip M. "'Good and Evil' in Lillian Hellman's *The Children's Hour*." In Estrin, *Critical Essays on Lillian Hellman*.

Arvin, Newton. "D. H. Lawrence and Fascism." *New Republic*, 16 December 1936, 219.
Atkinson, Ted. *Faulkner and the Great Depression: Aesthetics, Ideology, and Cultural Politics*. Athens: University of Georgia Press, 2006.
Austenfeld, Thomas Carl. *American Women Writers and the Nazis: Ethics and Politics in Boyle, Porter, Stafford, and Hellman*. Charlottesville: University Press of Virginia, 2001.
Bacon, Jon Lance. *Flannery O'Connor and Cold War Culture*. New York: Cambridge University Press, 1993.
Baker Houston A., Jr., and Dana D. Nelson. "Preface: Violence, the Body and 'The South.'" *American Literature* 73 (June 2001): 231–43.
Baker, Lewis. *The Percys of Mississippi: Politics and Literature in the New South*. Baton Rouge: Louisiana State University Press, 1983.
Barr, Stringfellow. "American Dreams." Review of *Who Owns America? A New Declaration of Independence*, ed. Herbert Agar and Allen Tate, and *The Coming American Fascism*, by Lawrence Dennis. *Virginia Quarterly Review* 12 (July 1936): 476–80.
Barry, John M. *Rising Tide: The Great Mississippi Flood of 1927 and How It Changed America*. New York: Simon and Schuster, 1997.
Bassett, John, ed. *William Faulkner: The Critical Heritage*. London: Routledge and Kegan Paul, 1975.
Beard, Charles A. Introduction to Dodd, *Ambassador Dodd's Diary*.
Benton, Thomas Hart. "American Regionalism: A Personal History of the Movement." *University of Kansas City Review* 18 (Autumn 1951): 41–75.
Bevilacqua, Winifred Farrant. *Josephine Herbst*. Boston: Twayne, 1985.
Bilbo, Theodore. *Take Your Choice: Separation or Mongrelization*. Poplarville, MS: Dream House, 1947.
Bingham, Emily S., and Thomas A. Underwood. *The Southern Agrarians and the New Deal: Essays after "I'll Take My Stand."* Charlottesville: University Press of Virginia, 2001.
Bishop, Ferman. *Allen Tate*. New York: Twayne, 1967.
Bishop, John Peale, and Allen Tate. *The Republic of Letters in America: The Correspondence of John Peale Bishop and Allen Tate*. Ed. Thomas Daniel Young and John J. Hindle. Lexington: University Press of Kentucky, 1981.
Blackwell, Louise, and Francis Clay. *Lillian Smith*. New York: Twayne, 1971.
Blotner, Joseph. *Faulkner: A Biography*. New York: Random House, 1974.
———. *Robert Penn Warren: A Biography*. New York: Random House, 1997.
Blum, John Morton. *V Was for Victory: Politics and American Culture during World War II*. New York: Harcourt Brace Jovanovich, 1976.
Booker, Margaret. *Lillian Hellman and August Wilson: Dramatizing a New American Identity*. New York: Peter Lang, 2003.
Borgese, G. A. *Goliath: The March of Fascism*. New York: Viking, 1938.

Boris, Eileen. "'Arm and Arm': Racialized Bodies and Colored Lines." *Journal of American Studies* 35 (April 2001): 1–20.
Boswell, Peyton. "The Grant Wood Controversy." *Art Digest* 17 (1 December 1942): 3.
Boyd, Valerie. *Wrapped in Rainbows: The Life of Zora Neale Hurston*. New York: Scribner, 2003.
Bradford, M. E. "Angels at Forty Thousand Feet: 'Ode to Our Young Pro-Consuls of the Air' and the Practice of Poetic Responsibility." In Bradford, *Generations of the Faithful Heart*, 183–99.
———. *Generations of the Faithful Heart: On the Literature of the South*. La Salle, IL: Sherwood Sugden, 1983.
Brantley, Will. *Feminine Sense in Southern Memoir: Smith, Glasgow, Welty, Hellman, Porter, and Hurston*. Jackson: University Press of Mississippi, 1993.
———. "The Surveillance of Georgia Writer and Civil Rights Activist Lillian Smith: Another Story from the Federal Bureau of Investigation." *Georgia Historical Quarterly* 85 (Spring 2001): 59–82.
Brinkmeyer, Robert H., Jr. "*Go Down, Moses* and the Ascetic Imperative." In *Faulkner and the Short Story*, ed. Evans Harrington and Ann J. Abadie, 206–28. Jackson: University Press of Mississippi, 1992.
———. *Katherine Anne Porter's Artistic Development: Primitivism, Traditionalism, and Totalitarianism*. Baton Rouge: Louisiana State University Press, 1993.
———. *Remapping Southern Literature: Contemporary Southern Writers and the West*. Athens: University of Georgia Press, 2000.
Brooks, Cleanth. "Edna Millay's Maturity." *Southwest Review* 20 (July 1935), Book Supplement, 3.
Brooks, Cleanth, and Allen Tate. *Cleanth Brooks and Allen Tate: Collected Letters, 1933–1976*. Ed. Alphonse Vinh. Columbia: University of Missouri Press, 1998.
Brooks, Cleanth, and Robert Penn Warren. *Cleanth Brooks and Robert Penn Warren: A Literary Correspondence*. Ed. James A. Grimshaw, Jr. Columbia: University of Missouri Press, 1998.
Brooks, Van Wyck. *Opinions of Oliver Allston*. New York: E. P. Dutton, 1941.
Brown, Anthony Cave. *The Last Hero: Wild Bill Donovan*. New York: Random House, 1982.
Brown, Peter. "The Rise and Function of the Holy Man in Late Antiquity." *Journal of Roman Studies* 61 (1971): 80–101.
Buck, Paul H. "American Heresies." *Hound and Horn* 6 (January–March 1933): 357–67.
Burke, Kenneth. *The Philosophy of Literary Form: Studies in Symbolic Action*. Baton Rouge: Louisiana State University Press, 1941.
Busby, Mark, and Dick Heaberlin, eds. *From Texas to the World and Back: Essays on the Journeys of Katherine Anne Porter*. Fort Worth: Texas Christian University Press, 2001.

Cabell, James Branch. *Let Me Lie: Being in the Main an Ethnological Account of the Remarkable Commonwealth of Virginia and the Making of Its History.* New York: Farrar, Straus, 1947.

Calverton, V. F. "The Bankruptcy of Southern Culture." *Scribner's,* May 1936, 294–98.

Canfield [Fisher], Dorothy. "*Black Boy* by Richard Wright." *Book-of-the-Month Club News,* February 1945, 2.

Carlson, John Roy. *Under Cover: My Four Years in the Nazi Underworld of America—The Amazing Revelation of How Axis Agents and Our Enemies Within Are Now Plotting to Destroy the United States.* Philadelphia: E. P. Dutton, 1943.

Carmer, Carl. *Stars Fell on Alabama.* New York: Blue Ribbon Books, 1934.

Carr, Virginia Spencer. *The Lonely Hunter: A Biography of Carson McCullers.* New York: Doubleday, 1975.

———. *Understanding Carson McCullers.* Columbia: University of South Carolina Press, 1990.

Carter, Dan T. *Scottsboro: A Tragedy of the American South.* Baton Rouge: Louisiana State University Press, 1979.

Cash, W. J. "Buck Duke's University." *American Mercury* 30 (September 1933): 102–10.

———. "Close View of a Calvinist Lhasa." *American Mercury* 28 (April 1933): 443–51.

———. "Genesis of the Southern Cracker." *American Mercury* 35 (May 1935): 105–8.

———. "Holy Men Muff a Chance." *American Mercury* 31 (January 1934): 112–18.

———. "Jehovah of the Tar Heels." *American Mercury* 17 (July 1929): 310–18.

———. "Literature and the South." *Saturday Review of Literature,* 28 December 1940, 3–4, 18–19.

———. "The Mind of the South." *American Mercury* 18 (October 1929): 185–92.

———. *The Mind of the South.* 1941. New York: Vintage, 1991.

———. "Paladin of the Drys." *American Mercury* 24 (October 1931): 139–47.

———. "The War in the South." *American Mercury* 19 (February 1930): 163–69.

———. "W. J. Cash: Quandaries of the Mind." http://www.wjcash.org.

Casper, Leonard. *Robert Penn Warren: The Dark and Bloody Ground.* Seattle: University of Washington Press, 1960.

Caudwell, Christopher. *Studies in a Dying Culture.* London: John Lane, 1938.

Chamberlain, John. "Agrarianism, American Style." Review of *Who Owns America? A Declaration of Independence,* ed. Herbert Agar and Allen Tate. *Saturday Review of Literature,* 25 July 1936, 17.

Churchill, Winston S. *While England Slept: A Survey of World Affairs, 1932–1938.* Ed. Randolph S. Churchill. New York: G. P. Putnam's Sons, 1938.

Clark, Barrett H. "Lillian Hellman." *College English* 6 (December 1944): 127–33.

Clark, Eleanor, and Robert Penn Warren. "Interview with Eleanor Clark and Robert Penn Warren." In *Robert Penn Warren Talking,* 318–35.

Clark, William Bedford, ed. *Critical Essays on Robert Penn Warren.* Boston: G. K. Hall, 1981.

Clayton, Bruce. *W. J. Cash: A Life*. Baton Rouge: Louisiana State University Press, 1991.
Clurman, Harold. "Roblès, Hellman, Blitzstein." *New Republic*, 5 December 1949, 21–22.
Cobb, James C. *The Most Southern Place on Earth: The Mississippi Delta and the Roots of Regional Identity*. New York: Oxford University Press, 1992.
Cohn, David L. "Eighteenth-Century Chevalier." *Virginia Quarterly Review* 31 (Autumn 1955): 561–75.
———. "How the South Feels." *Atlantic Monthly*, January 1944, 47–51.
Cohn, Deborah N. *History and Memory in the Two Souths: Recent Southern and Spanish American Fiction*. Nashville, TN: Vanderbilt University Press, 1999.
Coley, Lem. "Memories and Opinions of Allen Tate." *Southern Review*, n.s., 28 (October 1992): 944–64.
Collins, Seward. "Editorial Notes." *American Review* 1 (April 1933): 122–27.
———. "Editorial Notes: *American Review*'s First Year." *American Review* 3 (April 1934): 118–28.
———. "Editorial Notes: The Revival of Monarchy." *American Review* 1 (May 1933): 243–56.
———. Letter to the editor. In "The Sunny Side of Fascism." *New Republic*, 10 June 1936, 131–32.
Conkin, Paul K. *The Southern Agrarians*. Knoxville: University of Tennessee Press, 1988.
Corrin, Jay P. *Catholic Intellectuals and the Challenges of Democracy*. Notre Dame, IN: University of Notre Dame Press, 2002.
———. *G. K. Chesterton and Hillaire Belloc: The Battle against Modernity*. Athens: Ohio University Press, 1981.
Couch, W. T. "The Agrarian Romance." *South Atlantic Quarterly* 36 (October 1937): 419–30.
Cousins, Norman, and Harrison Smith. "Ezra Pound and the Bollingen Award." *Saturday Review of Literature*, 11 June 1949, 20–21.
Cowley, Malcolm. "A Game of Chess." Review of *Reactionary Essays on Poetry and Ideas*, by Allen Tate. *New Republic*, 29 April 1936, 348–49.
———. "Sanctuary." Review of *The Wild Palms*, by William Faulkner. *New Republic*, 25 January 1939, 349.
———, ed. *The Faulkner-Cowley File: Letters and Memories, 1944–1962*. New York: Viking, 1966.
Cox, James M. "Trial for a Southern Life." *Sewanee Review* 97 (Spring 1989): 238–52.
Crowther, Bosley. "The Cream of the 1943 Crop." *New York Times*, 28 August 1943, sec. 2, p. 3.
Crunden, Robert M, ed. *The Superfluous Men: Conservative Critics of American Culture, 1900–1945*. Austin: University of Texas Press, 1977.

Dabney, Virginius. "If the South Had Won the War." *American Mercury* 39 (October 1936): 199–205.

———. "Nearer and Nearer the Precipice." *Atlantic Monthly,* January 1943, 94–100.

Daniel, Pete. *Deep'n as It Come: The 1927 Mississippi River Flood.* 1977. Fayetteville: University of Arkansas Press, 1996.

Dardis, Tom. *Some Time in the Sun: The Hollywood Years of Fitzgerald, Faulkner, Nathaniel West, Aldous Huxley, and James Agee.* New York: Charles Scribner's Sons, 1976.

Davenport, Basil. "McCullers . . ." Review of *Reflections in a Golden Eye,* by Carson McCullers. *Saturday Review of Literature,* 22 February 1941, 12.

Davidman, Joy. "A Reply to Mr. Tate." Letter to the editor. *New Republic,* 21 December 1942, 828–29.

Davidson, Donald. "Agrarianism and Politics." *Review of Politics* 1 (April 1939): 114–25.

———. *The Attack on Leviathan: Regionalism and Nationalism in the United States.* Chapel Hill: University of North Carolina Press, 1938.

———. *Lee in the Mountains and Other Poems.* Boston: Houghton Mifflin, 1938.

———. "Mr. Cash and the Proto-Dorian South." *Southern Review* 7 (Summer 1941): 1–20.

———. "The Nervous Man." *Virginia Quarterly Review* 26 (Spring 1950): 214–15.

———. *Poems, 1922–1961.* Minneapolis: University of Minnesota Press, 1966.

———. "Political Regionalism and Administrative Regionalism." *Annals of the American Academy of Political and Social Science* 207 (January 1940): 138–43.

———. "Preface to Decision." *Sewanee Review* 53 (July–September 1945): 394–412.

———. *The Tennessee.* Vol. 1, *The Old River: Frontier to Secession.* 1946. Nashville, TN: J. S. Sanders, 1991.

———. *The Tennessee.* Vol. 2, *The New River: Civil War to TVA.* 1948. Nashville, TN: J. S. Sanders, 1992.

———. "That This Nation May Endure." In Agar and Tate, *Who Owns America?*

———. "Where Regionalism and Sectionalism Meet." *Social Forces* 13 (October 1934–May 1935): 23–31.

Davidson, Donald, and Allen Tate. *The Literary Correspondence of Donald Davidson and Allen Tate.* Ed. John Tyree Fain and Thomas Daniel Young. Athens: University of Georgia Press, 1974.

Davis, Robert Gorham. "The New Criticism and the Democratic Tradition." *American Scholar* 19 (Winter 1949–50): 9–19.

Davis, Stuart. "Davis Rejoinder." *Art Digest* 9 (1 April 1935): 12–13, 26–27.

Davis, Thaddious M. *Games of Property: Law, Race, Gender, and Faulkner's "Go Down, Moses."* Durham, NC: Duke University Press, 2003.

De Felice, Renzo. *Interpretations of Fascism.* Trans. Brenda Huff Everett. Cambridge, MA: Harvard University Press, 1977.

Dennis, James M. *Renegade Regionalists: The Modern Independence of Grant Wood, Thomas Hart Benton, and John Steuart Curry.* Madison: University of Wisconsin Press, 1998.

DeVoto, Bernard. The Easy Chair. *Harper's,* May 1944, 525–28.

———. The Easy Chair. *Harper's,* November 1944, 554–57.

Dick, Bernard F. *Hellman in Hollywood.* Rutherford, NJ: Fairleigh Dickinson University Press, 1982.

Diggins, John P. "Flirtation with Fascism: American Pragmatic Liberals and Mussolini's Italy." *American Historical Review* 71 (January 1966): 487–506.

———. *Mussolini and Fascism: The View from America.* Princeton, NJ: Princeton University Press, 1972.

Dodd, William E. *Ambassador Dodd's Diary, 1933–38.* Ed. William E. Dodd, Jr., and Martha Dodd. New York: Harcourt, Brace, 1940.

Donald, David Herbert. *Look Homeward: A Life of Thomas Wolfe.* Boston: Little, Brown, 1987.

Dorman, Robert L. *Revolt of the Provinces: The Regionalist Movement in America, 1920–1945.* Chapel Hill: University of North Carolina Press, 1993.

Doss, Erika. *Benton, Pollock, and the Politics of Modernism: From Regionalism to Abstract Modernism.* Chicago: University of Chicago Press, 1991.

Duck, Leigh Anne. *The Nation's Region: Southern Modernism, Segregation, and U.S. Nationalism.* Athens: University of Georgia Press, 2006.

Duffy, Bernard K., and Martin Jacobi. *The Politics of Rhetoric: Richard M. Weaver and the Conservative Tradition.* Westport, CT: Greenwood, 1993.

Dunbar, Leslie W. "A Southerner Confronting the South." *Virginia Quarterly Review* 64 (Spring 1988): 202–14.

Dupuy, Edward J. "The Dispossessed Garden of William Alexander Percy." *Southern Quarterly* 29 (Winter 1991): 31–41.

Eagles, Charles W., ed. *The Mind of the South: Fifty Years Later.* Jackson: University Press of Mississippi, 1992.

Eatwell, Roger. *Fascism: A History.* New York: Penguin, 1997.

Editors' note to "Fascism and the Southern Agrarians." *New Republic,* 27 May 1936, 75.

Editors' note to "The Sunny Side of Fascism." *New Republic,* 10 June 1936, 132.

Egerton, John. *Speak Now against the Day: The Generation before the Civil Rights Movement.* Chapel Hill: University of North Carolina Press, 1994.

Eisinger, Chester E. *Fiction of the Forties.* Chicago: University of Chicago Press, 1963.

Elkins, Stanley M. *Slavery: A Problem in American Institutional and Intellectual Life.* Chicago: University of Chicago Press, 1959.

Elliott, William Yandell. *The Need for Constitutional Reform: A Program for National Security.* New York: McGraw-Hill, 1935.

Erenberg, Lewis A., and Susan E. Hirsch, eds. *The War in American Culture: Society and Consciousness during World War II*. Chicago: University of Chicago Press, 1996.

Escott, Paul D., ed. *W. J. Cash and the Minds of the South*. Baton Rouge: Louisiana State University Press, 1992.

Estrin, Mark W., ed. *Critical Essays on Lillian Hellman*. Boston: G. K. Hall, 1989.

Evans, Oliver. *The Ballad of Carson McCullers: A Biography*. New York: Coward-McCann, 1965.

Fadiman, Clifton. Books. *New Yorker*, 15 February 1941, 78–81.

Falk, Doris V. *Lillian Hellman*. New York: Frederick Ungar, 1978.

Fant, Joseph L., III, and Robert Ashley, eds. *Faulkner at West Point*. Jackson: University Press of Mississippi, 2002.

Faulkner, William. *The Collected Stories of William Faulkner*. New York: Random House, 1950.

———. *Essays, Speeches and Public Letters by William Faulkner*. Ed. James B. Meriwether. New York: Random House, 1965.

———. *A Fable*. 1954. New York: Vintage, 1978.

———. *Faulkner: A Comprehensive Guide to the Brodsky Collection*. Ed. Louis Daniel Brodsky and Robert W. Hamblin. Vol. 3, *"The De Gaulle Story" by William Faulkner*. Jackson: University Press of Mississippi, 1984.

———. *Faulkner: A Comprehensive Guide to the Brodsky Collection*. Ed. Louis Daniel Brodsky and Robert W. Hamblin. Vol. 4, *"Battle Cry": A Screenplay by William Faulkner*. Jackson: University Press of Mississippi, 1985.

———. *Faulkner in the University: Class Conferences at the University of Virginia, 1957–1958*. Ed. Frederick L. Gwynn and Joseph L. Blotner. Charlottesville: University of Virginia Press, 1959.

———. *Go Down, Moses*. 1942. New York: Vintage International, 1990.

———. *Intruder in the Dust*. 1948. New York: Vintage International, 1991.

———. *Lion in the Garden: Interviews with William Faulkner, 1926–1962*. Ed. James B. Meriwether and Michael Millgate. New York: Random House, 1968.

———. *Selected Letters of William Faulkner*. Ed. Joseph Blotner. New York: Random House, 1977.

———. *The Sound and the Fury*. Corrected text with appendix. New York: Modern Library, 1992.

———. *The Uncollected Stories of William Faulkner*. Ed. Joseph Blotner. New York: Random House, 1979.

———. *William Faulkner Manuscripts 18, Knight's Gambit: Typescripts and Miscellaneous Typescript Pages*. Ed. Thomas L. McHaney. New York: Garland, 1987.

Feld, Rose. Review of *Reflections in a Golden Eye*, by Carson McCullers. *New York Herald Tribune Books*, 16 February 1941, 8.

Fleischman, Earl E. (Eugene Earl). "*The Searching Wind* in the Making." *Quarterly Journal of Speech* 31 (February 1945): 22–28.

Fletcher, John Gould. "Is This the Voice of the South?" Letter to the editor. *Nation*, 27 December 1933, 734–35.

———. *The Two Frontiers: A Study in Historical Psychology*. New York: Coward-McCann, 1930.

French, Warren. *The Social Novel at the End of an Era*. Carbondale: Southern Illinois University Press, 1966.

Friar, Kimon, and John Malcolm Brinnin, eds. *Modern Poetry: British and American*. New York: Appleton-Century-Crofts, 1951.

Fromm, Erich. *Escape from Freedom*. 1941. New York: Holt, Rinehart and Winston, 1976.

Fussell, Paul. *The Great War and Modern Memory*. New York: Oxford University Press, 1975.

Geismar, Maxwell. *Writers in Crisis: The American Novel between Two Wars*. Boston: Houghton Mifflin, 1942.

Gellhorn, Martha. "On Apocryphism." *Paris Review* 23 (Spring 1981): 280–301.

Genovese, Eugene D. *The Southern Front: History and Politics in the Cultural War*. Columbia: University of Missouri Press, 1995.

Givner, Joan. *Katherine Anne Porter: A Life*. Rev. ed. Athens: University of Georgia Press, 1991.

Gladney, Margaret Rose. "Becoming a Writer." Introduction to Lillian Smith, *How Am I to Be Heard?*

Gleason, Philip. "Americans All: World War II and the Shaping of American Identity." *Review of Politics* 43 (October 1981): 483–518.

Goad, Harold. "The Corporate State." *American Review* 1 (April 1933), 80–93.

Godden, Richard. *Fictions of Labor: William Faulkner and the South's Long Revolution*. Cambridge: Cambridge University Press, 1997.

Goodman, James. *Stories of Scottsboro: The Rape Case That Shook 1930's America and Revived the Struggle for Equality*. New York: Pantheon, 1994.

Grant, Madison. Introduction to Stoddard, *Rising Tide of Color*.

———. *The Passing of the Great Race; or The Racial Basis of European History*. Rev. ed. New York: Charles Scribner's Sons, 1918.

Graves, John Temple. *The Fighting South*. New York: G. P. Putnam's Sons, 1943.

Gray, Richard. *The Life of William Faulkner: A Critical Biography*. Oxford: Blackwell, 1994.

———. *Southern Aberrations: Writers of the American South and the Problems of Regionalism*. Baton Rouge: Louisiana State University Press, 2000.

———. *Writing the South: Ideas of an American Region*. Cambridge: Cambridge University Press, 1986

Greenbaum, Leonard. *The Hound and Horn: The History of a Literary Quarterly.* The Hague: Mouton, 1966.

Greeson, Jennifer Rae. "Expropriating *The Great South* and Exporting 'Local Color': Global and Hemispheric Imaginaries of the First Reconstruction." *American Literary History* 18 (Fall 2006): 496–520.

———. "The Figure of the South and the Nationalizing Imperatives of Early United States Literature." *Yale Journal of Criticism* 12 (Fall 1999): 209–48.

Gresset, Michel, and Patrick Samway, SJ, eds. *A Gathering of Evidence: Essays on William Faulkner's "Intruder in the Dust."* Philadelphia: St. Joseph's University Press, 2004.

Gretlund, Jan Nordby. "'The Man in the Tree': Katherine Anne Porter's Unfinished Lynching Story." *Southern Quarterly* 31 (Spring 1993): 7–16.

Griffin, Roger, ed. *International Fascism: Theories, Causes, and the New Consensus.* New York: Oxford University Press, 1998.

Grill, Johnpeter Horst, and Robert L. Jenkins. "The Nazis and the American South in the 1930s: A Mirror Image?" *Journal of Southern History* 58 (November 1992): 666–94.

Grimshaw, James A., Jr. *Robert Penn Warren's "Brother to Dragons": A Discussion.* Baton Rouge: Louisiana State University Press, 1983.

Grimwood, Michael. *Heart in Conflict: Faulkner's Struggles with Vocation.* Athens: University of Georgia Press, 1987.

Gulledge, Jo, ed. "William Alexander Percy and the Fugitives: A Literary Correspondence, 1921–1923." *Southern Review,* n.s., 21 (April 1985): 415–27.

Guttenberg, Barnett. *Web of Being: The Novels of Robert Penn Warren.* Nashville, TN: Vanderbilt University Press, 1975.

Hammett, Dashiell. *Selected Letters of Dashiell Hammett, 1921–1960.* Ed. Richard Layman with Julie M. Rivett. Washington, DC: Counterpoint, 2001.

Hamovitch, Mitzi Berger, ed. *The Hound and Horn Letters.* Athens: University of Georgia Press, 1982.

Hannon, Charles. "'The Ballad of the Sad Café' and Other Stories of Women's Wartime Labor." In *Bodies of Writing, Bodies in Performance,* ed. Thomas Foster, Carol Siegal, and Ellen E. Berry. New York: New York University Press, 1996.

Harpham, Geoffrey Galt. *The Ascetic Imperative in Culture and Criticism.* Chicago: University of Chicago Press, 1987.

Hartwick, Harry. *The Foreground of American Fiction.* New York: American Book Company, 1934.

Hassan, Ihab H. "Carson McCullers: The Alchemy of Love and Aesthetics of Pain." *Modern Fiction Studies* 5 (Winter 1959–60): 311–26.

Havard, William C., and Walter Sullivan, eds. *A Band of Prophets: The Vanderbilt Agrarians after Fifty Years.* Baton Rouge: Louisiana State University Press, 1982.

Hellman, Lillian. *Conversations with Lillian Hellman.* Ed. Jackson R. Bryer. Jackson: University Press of Mississippi, 1986.
——. "Day in Spain." *New Republic,* 13 April 1938, 297–98.
——. "I Meet the Front-Line Russians." *Collier's,* 31 March 1945, 11, 68, 71.
——. Introduction to *Four Plays by Lillian Hellman.* New York: Modern Library, 1942.
——. Introduction to *The Selected Letters of Anton Chekhov,* ed. Lillian Hellman, trans. Sidonie Lederer. New York: Farrar, Straus, 1955.
——. "The Judas Goats." *Screenwriter,* December 1947, 7.
——. "The Little Men in Philadelphia." *PM,* 25 June 1940, 6.
——. "The Little War." In *This Is My Best,* ed. Whit Burnett. New York: Dial, 1942.
——. *Maybe.* New York: Little, Brown, 1980.
——. *Montserrat.* Adapted from the play by Emmanuel Roblès. New York: Dramatists Play Service, 1949.
——. *"The North Star": A Motion Picture about Some Russian People.* New York: Viking, 1943.
——. *Pentimento: A Book of Portraits.* Boston: Little, Brown, 1973.
——. *Scoundrel Time.* New York: Little, Brown, 1976.
——. *"The Searching Wind": A Play in Two Acts.* New York: Viking, 1944.
——. *Six Plays.* New York: Modern Library, 1960.
——. *An Unfinished Woman: A Memoir.* Boston: Little, Brown, 1969.
Hendrick, Willene, and George Hendrick. *Katherine Anne Porter.* Rev. ed. Boston: Twayne, 1988.
Hendricks, Randy. *Lonelier Than God: Robert Penn Warren and the Southern Exile.* Athens: University of Georgia Press, 2000.
Hendry, Irene. "The Regional Novel." *Sewanee Review* 53 (January–March 1945): 84–102.
Herbst, Josephine. "Miss Porter and Miss Stein." *Partisan Review* 15 (May 1948): 568–72.
Hicks, Granville. "D. H. Lawrence as Messiah." Review of *Phoenix: The Posthumous Papers of D. H. Lawrence,* ed. Edward D. McDonald. *New Republic,* 28 October 1936, 358–59.
——. *The Great Tradition: An Interpretation of American Literature since the Civil War.* New York: Macmillan, 1933.
Hillyer, Robert. "Poetry's New Priesthood." *Saturday Review of Literature,* 18 June 1949, 7–9, 38.
——. "Treason's Strange Fruit." *Saturday Review of Literature,* 11 June 1949, 9–11, 28.
Hitler, Adolf. *Mein Kampf.* Trans. Ralph Manheim. Boston: Houghton Mifflin, 1943.
Hobson, Fred. C., Jr. *But Now I See: The White Southern Racial Conversion Narrative.* Baton Rouge: Louisiana State University Press, 1999.

———. *Serpent in Eden: H. L. Mencken and the South*. Chapel Hill: University of North Carolina Press, 1974.

———. *Tell about the South: The Southern Rage to Explain*. Baton Rouge: Louisiana State University Press, 1983.

Hodgson, Godfrey. *The World Turned Right Side Up: A History of Conservative Ascendancy in America*. Boston: Houghton Mifflin, 1996.

Holdsworth, Carolyn. "The Gorgon's Head and the Mirror: Fact versus Metaphor in *Lanterns on the Levee*." *Southern Literary Journal* 14 (Fall 1981): 36–45.

Holman, C. Hugh. *The Loneliness at the Core: Studies in Thomas Wolfe*. Baton Rouge: Louisiana State University Press, 1975.

Holmes, William F. "William Alexander Percy and the Bourbon Era in the Yazoo-Mississippi Delta." *Mississippi Quarterly* 26 (Winter 1972–73): 71–99.

Horkheimer, Max, and Theodore W. Adorno. *Dialectic of Enlightenment: Philosophical Fragments*. 1944. Ed. Gunzelin Schmid Noerr. Trans. Edmund Jephcott. Stanford, CA: Stanford University Press, 2002.

Hurston, Zora Neale. *Dust Tracks on a Road*. 1942. New York: HarperPerennial, 1991.

"If Mussolini Had Ruled Detroit." *Christian Century*, 11 December 1929, 1534.

Isherwood, Christopher. "Tragic Liberal." Review of *Night Rider*, by Robert Penn Warren. *New Republic*, 31 May 1939, 108.

James, Judith Giblin. "Carson McCullers, Lillian Smith, and the Politics of Broadway." In *Southern Women Playwrights: New Essays in Literary History and Criticism*, ed. Robert L. McDonald and Linda Rohrer Paige, 42–60. Tuscaloosa: University of Alabama Press, 2002.

Jancovich, Mark. *The Cultural Politics of the New Criticism*. Cambridge: Cambridge University Press, 1993.

Janson, H. W. "Benton and Wood, Champions of Regionalism." *Magazine of Art* 39 (May 1946): 184–86, 198–200.

———. "The International Aspects of Regionalism." *College Art Journal* 2 (May 1943): 110–15.

Jenkins, McKay. "Metaphors of Race and Psychological Damage in the 1940s American South: The Writings of Lillian Smith." In *Racing and (E)Racing Language: Living with the Color of Our Words*, ed. Ellen J. Goldner and Safiya Henderson-Holmes, 99–123. Syracuse, NY: Syracuse University Press, 2001.

Johnson, Diane. *Dashiell Hammett: A Life*. New York: Random House, 1983.

Johnson, Gerald W. "No More Excuses: A Southerner to Southerners." *Harper's*, February 1931, 331–37.

———. "The South Faces Itself." *Virginia Quarterly Review* 7 (January 1931): 152–57.

———. "When to Build a Barricade." *Virginia Quarterly Review* 14 (Spring 1938): 161–76.

Jones, Anne Goodwyn. "The Cash Nexus." In Eagles, *The Mind of the South: Fifty Years Later.*
——. "Every Woman Loves a Fascist: Writing World War II on the Southern Home Front." In *Remaking Dixie: The Impact of World War II on the American South*, ed. Neill R. McMillan, 111–30. Jackson: University Press of Mississippi, 1997.
Jones, Suzanne W., and Sharon Monteith, eds. *South to a New Place: Region, Literature, Culture.* Baton Rouge: Louisiana State University Press, 2002.
Justus, James H. *The Achievement of Robert Penn Warren.* Baton Rouge: Louisiana State University Press, 1981.
Kane, Harnett T. *Louisiana Hayride: The American Rehearsal of Dictatorship, 1928–1940.* 1941. Gretna, LA: Pelican, 1990.
Karaganis, Joe. "Negotiating the National Voice in Faulkner's Late Work." In Gresset and Samway, *Gathering of Evidence,* 97–130.
Karanikas, Alexander. *Tillers of a Myth: Southern Agrarians as Social and Literary Critics.* Madison: University of Wisconsin Press, 1966.
Karem, Jeff. "'I Could Never Really Leave the South': Regionalism and the Transformation of Richard Wright's *American Hunger.*" *American Literary History* 13 (Winter 2001): 694–715.
Kennedy, John F. *Why England Slept.* New York: Wilfred Funk, 1940.
Kennedy, Richard S. *The Window of Memory: The Literary Career of Thomas Wolfe.* Chapel Hill: University of North Carolina Press, 1962.
Kennedy, Stetson. *Southern Exposure.* Garden City, NY: Doubleday, 1946.
King, Richard H. "Anti-Modernists All!" *Mississippi Quarterly* 64 (Spring 1991): 193–201.
——. "Cash and the Crisis of Political Modernity." In Escott, *W. J. Cash and the Minds of the South,* 67–87.
——. "Politics and Literature: The Southern Case." *Virginia Quarterly Review* 64 (Spring 1988): 189–201.
——. *A Southern Renaissance: The Cultural Awakening of the American South, 1930–1955.* New York: Oxford University Press, 1980.
Kneebone, John T. *Southern Liberal Journalists and the Issue of Race, 1920–1944.* Chapel Hill: University of North Carolina Press, 1985.
Kreyling, Michael. *Figures of the Hero in Southern Narrative.* Baton Rouge: Louisiana State University Press, 1987.
——. *Inventing Southern Literature.* Jackson: University Press of Mississippi, 1998.
——. "Toward 'A New Southern Studies.'" *South Central Review* 22 (Spring 2005): 4–18.
Krutch, Joseph Wood. "An Open Letter on Critics and Criticism." *Nation,* 1 August 1942, 95–96.

Kussy, Bella. "The Vitalist Trend and Thomas Wolfe." *Sewanee Review* 50 (July–September 1942): 306–24.

Ladd, Barbara. "'Writing against Death': Totalitarianism and the Nonfiction of Eudora Welty at Midcentury." In *Eudora Welty and Politics: Did the Writer Crusade?* ed. Harriet Pollack and Suzanne Marrs, 155–78. Baton Rouge: Louisiana State University Press, 2001.

Lamont, Corliss. *You Might Like Socialism: A Way of Life for Modern Man.* New York: Modern Age Books, 1939.

Lampell, Millard, and Earl Robinson. "The Lonesome Train." http://showcase.netins.net/web/creative/lincoln/education/lonesome.htm.

Langer, Elinor. *Josephine Herbst.* Boston: Little, Brown, 1984.

Lanier, Lyle H. "Big Business in the Property State." In Agar and Tate, *Who Owns America?*

Laqueur, Walter. *Fascism: Past, Present, Future.* New York: Oxford University Press, 1996.

Lawson, Lewis A. "William Alexander Percy, Walker Percy, and the Apocalypse." *Modern Age* 24 (Fall 1980): 396–406.

Lederer, Katherine. "The Critical Reaction to the Dramatic Works of Lillian Hellman." PhD diss., University of Arkansas, 1967.

———. *Lillian Hellman.* Boston: Twayne, 1979.

Ledig-Rowohlt, H. M. "Thomas Wolfe in Berlin." *American Scholar* 22 (Spring 1953): 185–201.

Leverette, William E., Jr., and David E. Shi. "Agrarianism for Commuters." *South Atlantic Quarterly* 79 (Spring 1980): 204–18.

Lilienthal, David. *TVA: Democracy on the March.* New York: Harper and Brothers, 1944.

Lindbergh, Anne Morrow. *The Wave of the Future: A Confession of Faith.* New York: Harcourt, Brace, 1940.

Logan, Rayford W. "The Negro Wants First-Class Citizenship." In Logan, *What the Negro Wants.*

———, ed. *What the Negro Wants.* Chapel Hill: University of North Carolina Press, 1944.

Loveland, Anne C. *Lillian Smith: A Southerner Confronting the South.* Baton Rouge: Louisiana State University Press, 1986.

Lowe, John. "'Calypso Magnolia': The Caribbean Side of the South." *South Central Review* 22 (Spring 2005): 54–80.

Lowenstein, Andrea Freud. *Loathsome Jews and Engulfing Women: Metaphors of Projection in the Works of Wyndham Lewis, Charles Williams, and Graham Greene.* New York: New York University Press, 1993.

Lubick, George M. "Restoring the American Dream: The Agrarian-Decentralist Movement, 1930–1946." *South Atlantic Quarterly* 84 (Winter 1985): 63–80.

Luce, Henry R. "The American Century." *Life,* 17 February 1941, 61–65.
Lumpkin, Grace. "I Want a King." *Fight against War and Fascism* 3 (February 1936): 3, 14.
———. Letter to the editor. In "The Sunny Side of Fascism." *New Republic,* 10 June 1936, 132.
———. Open letter to Allen Tate. In "Fascism and the Southern Agrarians." *New Republic,* 27 May 1936, 76.
Lytle, Andrew, and Allen Tate. *The Lytle-Tate Letters: The Correspondence of Andrew Lytle and Allen Tate.* Ed. Thomas Daniel Young and Elizabeth Sarcone. Jackson: University Press of Mississippi, 1987.
MacLean, Nancy. *Behind the Mask of Chivalry: The Making of the Second Ku Klux Klan.* New York: Oxford University Press, 1995.
MacLeish, Archibald. *The Irresponsibles: A Declaration.* New York: Duell, Sloan and Pierce, 1940. Originally published in *Nation,* 18 May 1940, 618–23.
Malvasi, Mark G. *The Unregenerate South: The Agrarian Thought of John Crowe Ransom, Allen Tate, and Donald Davidson.* Baton Rouge: Louisiana State University Press, 1997.
Marling, William. *Dashiell Hammett.* Boston: Twayne, 1983.
Markham, R. H. *The Wave of the Past.* Chapel Hill: University of North Carolina Press, 1941.
Marrus, Michael R., ed. *The Nuremberg War Crimes Trial, 1945–46: A Documentary History.* Boston: Bedford Books, 1997.
Marx, Leo. *The Machine in the Garden: Technology and the Pastoral Ideal in America.* New York: Oxford University Press, 1964.
Mathews, John T. "Recalling the West Indies: From Yoknapatawpha to Haiti and Back." *American Literary History* 16 (Summer 2004): 238–62.
McCombs, Phil. "Century of Thanatos: Walker Percy and His Subversive Message." *Southern Review,* n.s., 24 (Autumn 1988): 808–24.
McCullers, Carson. *"The Ballad of the Sad Café" and Collected Short Stories.* Boston: Houghton Mifflin, 1955.
———. *The Heart Is a Lonely Hunter.* Boston: Houghton Mifflin, 1940.
———. *Illumination and Night Glare: The Unfinished Autobiography of Carson McCullers.* Ed. Carlos L. Dews. Madison: University of Wisconsin Press, 1999.
———. "Love's Not Time's Fool." *Mademoiselle,* April 1943, 95, 166–68.
———. *The Member of the Wedding.* Boston: Houghton Mifflin, 1946.
———. *The Member of the Wedding: A Play.* New York: New Directions, 1951.
———. *The Mortgaged Heart: Selected Writings.* Ed. Margarita G. Smith. Boston: Houghton Mifflin, 1971.
McDonald, Dwight. Review of *Who Owns America? A New Declaration of Independence,* ed. Herbert Agar and Allen Tate. *Common Sense* 5 (August 1936): 26–27.
McDonald, Robert L., and Linda Rohrer Paige, eds. *Southern Women Playwrights:*

New Essays in Literary History and Criticism. Tuscaloosa: University of Alabama Press, 2002.

McDowell, Margaret B. *Carson McCullers.* Boston: Twayne, 1980.

McKee, Kathryn, and Annette Trefzer. "Preface: Global Contexts, Local Literatures; The New Southern Studies." *American Literature* 78 (December 2006): 677–90.

———, eds. "The U.S. South in Global Contexts: A Collection of Position Statements." *American Literature* 78 (December 2006): 691–739.

McKelway, St. Clair. "A Reporter at Large: Some Fun with the F.B.I." *New Yorker,* 11 October 1941, 53–57.

Mead, Margaret. *And Keep Your Powder Dry: An Anthropologist Looks at America.* New York: William Morrow, 1942.

Meiners, R. K. *The Last Alternatives: A Study of the Works of Allen Tate.* Denver: Alan Swallow, 1963.

Mellen, Joan. *Hellman and Hammett: The Legendary Passion of Lillian Hellman and Dashiell Hammett.* New York: HarperCollins, 1996.

Menninger, Karl A. *Man against Himself.* New York: Harcourt, Brace, 1938.

Mensch, Barbara. *D. H. Lawrence and the Authoritarian Personality.* New York: St. Martin's, 1991.

Milkman, Paul. *PM: A New Deal in Journalism, 1940–1948.* New Brunswick: Rutgers University Press, 1977.

Minter, David. *William Faulkner: His Life and Work.* Baltimore: Johns Hopkins University Press, 1980.

Moody, Richard. *Lillian Hellman: Playwright.* New York: Pegasus, 1972.

Morgan, Chester M. *Redneck Liberal: Theodore Bilbo and the New Deal.* Baton Rouge: Louisiana State University Press, 1985.

Morrison, Joseph L. *W. J. Cash: Southern Prophet; A Biography and Reader.* New York: Alfred A. Knopf, 1967.

Mosse, George L. *The Fascist Revolution: Toward a General Theory of Fascism.* New York: Howard Fertig, 1999.

Murphy, Paul V. *The Rebuke of History: The Southern Agrarians and American Conservative Thought.* Chapel Hill: University of North Carolina Press, 2001.

———. "The Sacrament of Remembrance: Southern Agrarian Poet Donald Davidson and His Past." *Southern Cultures* 2 (Fall 1995): 83–102.

Nance, William L. "Katherine Anne Porter and Mexico." *Southwest Review* 55 (Spring 1970): 143–53.

"National Defense: A Progressive Policy." *New Republic,* 30 March 1938, suppl., 233–58.

Newman, Robert P. *The Cold War Romance of Lillian Hellman and John Melby.* Chapel Hill: University of North Carolina Press, 1989.

Nixon, Herman Clarence. *Forty Acres and Steel Mules.* Chapel Hill: University of North Carolina Press, 1938.

Nock, Albert Jay. *Memoirs of a Superfluous Man*. New York: Harper and Row, 1943.
O'Brien, Michael. *Conjectures of Order: Intellectual Life in the American South, 1810–1860*. 2 vols. Chapel Hill: University of North Carolina Press, 2004.
"On the 'Brooks-MacLeish Thesis.'" *Partisan Review* 9 (January–February 1942): 38–47.
Orwell, George. *Animal Farm*. 1946. New York: Harcourt, Brace and World, 1954.
———. *1984*. New York: Harcourt Brace Jovanovich, 1949.
Osborn, Henry Fairfield. Preface to Grant, *Passing of the Great Race*.
Owsley, Frank. "The Foundations of Democracy." In Agar and Tate, *Who Owns America?*
———. "The Pillars of Agrarianism." *American Review* 4 (March 1935): 529–47.
———. "Scottsboro, the Third Crusade: The Sequel to Abolition and Reconstruction." *American Review* 1 (June 1933): 257–85.
Partridge, Colin. "My Familiar Country: An Image of Mexico in the Work of Katherine Anne Porter." *Studies in Short Fiction* 7 (Fall 1970): 597–614.
Paterson, Isabel. "Turns with a Bookworm." *New York Herald Tribune Books*, 23 June 1940, 11.
Payne, Stanley G. *A History of Fascism, 1914–1945*. Madison: University of Wisconsin Press, 1995.
Peacock, James L., Harry L. Watson, and Carrie R. Mathews, eds. *The American South in a Global World*. Chapel Hill: University of North Carolina Press, 2005.
Pells, Richard H. *Radical Visions and American Dreams: Culture and Social Thought in the Depression Years*. New York: Harper and Row, 1973.
Percy, LeRoy. "The Modern Ku Klux Klan." *Atlantic Monthly*, July 1922, 122–28.
Percy, Walker. "The Failure and the Hope." In Walker Percy, *Signposts in a Strange Land*, 326–39. Originally published in *Katallagete* 1 (December 1965): 16–21.
———. "An Interview with Zoltán Abádi-Nagy." By Zoltán Abádi-Nagy. In Walker Percy, *Signposts in a Strange Land*, 373–96.
———. *Lancelot*. New York: Farrar, Straus and Giroux, 1977.
———. *Signposts in a Strange Land*. Ed. Patrick Samway. New York: Farrar, Straus and Giroux, 1991.
———. "Stoicism in the South." In Walker Percy, *Signposts in a Strange Land*, 83–88. Originally published in *Commonweal* 64 (6 July 1956): 342–44.
———. *The Thanatos Syndrome*. New York: Farrar, Straus and Giroux, 1987.
Percy, William Alexander. *The Collected Poems of William Alexander Percy*. New York: Alfred A. Knopf, 1943.
———. *Lanterns on the Levee: Recollections of a Planter's Son*. 1941. Baton Rouge: Louisiana State University Press, 1973.
Percy, William Armstrong, III. "William Alexander Percy (1885–1942): His Homosexuality and Why It Matters." In *Carryin' On in the Lesbian and Gay South*, ed. John Howard, 75–92. New York: New York University Press, 1997.

Perry, Keith. *The Kingfish in Fiction: Huey P. Long and the Modern American Novel.* Baton Rouge: Louisiana State University Press, 2004.

Polk, Noel. Afterword to *All the King's Men,* by Robert Penn Warren. Restored ed. Ed. Noel Polk. New York: Random House, 2001.

Porter, Katherine Anne. *The Collected Essays and Occasional Writings of Katherine Anne Porter.* New York: Delacorte, 1970.

———. *The Collected Stories of Katherine Anne Porter.* New York: Harcourt, Brace and World, 1965.

———. "Hacienda." *Virginia Quarterly Review* 8 (October 1932): 556–69.

———. *Katherine Anne Porter: Conversations.* Ed. Joan Givner. Jackson: University Press of Mississippi, 1987.

———. *The Letters of Katherine Anne Porter.* Ed. Isabel Bayley. New York: Atlantic Monthly Press, 1990.

———. *The Never-Ending Wrong.* Boston: Atlantic–Little, Brown, 1977.

———. *Ship of Fools.* Boston: Atlantic–Little, Brown, 1962.

Purcell, Edward A., Jr. *The Crisis of Democratic Theory: Scientific Naturalism and the Problem of Value.* Lexington: University Press of Kentucky, 1973.

Purdy, Rob Roy, ed. *Fugitives' Reunion: Conversations at Vanderbilt, May 3–5, 1956.* Nashville, TN: Vanderbilt University Press, 1959.

Quinlan, Kieran. *John Crowe Ransom's Secular Faith.* Baton Rouge: Louisiana State University Press, 1989.

Rader, Melvin. *No Compromise: The Conflict between Two Worlds.* New York: Macmillan, 1939.

Rahv, Phillip. Review of *Absalom, Absalom!* by William Faulkner. In Bassett, *William Faulkner,* 208–10. Originally published in *New Masses* 20 (24 November 1936): 20–21.

Rainey, Glenn W. "A Brief for Freedom." *North Georgia Review* 2 (Summer 1937): 5–6, 22–23.

Ransom, John Crowe. "Art and the Human Economy." *Kenyon Review* 7 (Autumn 1945): 683–88.

———. "Artists, Soldiers, Positivists." *Kenyon Review* 6 (Spring 1944): 276–81.

———. "A Capital for the New Deal." *American Review* 1 (December 1933): 129–42.

———. "Criticism as Pure Speculation." In Stauffer, *Intent of the Critic.*

———. *God without Thunder: An Unorthodox Defense of Orthodoxy.* 1930. Hamden, CT: Archon Books, 1965.

———. "Happy Farmers." *American Review* 1 (October 1933): 513–35.

———. "Land! An Answer to the Unemployment Problem." *Harper's,* July 1932, 216–24.

———. "Moholy-Nagy's New Arts." *Kenyon Review* 3 (Summer 1941): 372–74.

———. "Muses and Amazons." *Kenyon Review* 3 (Spring 1941): 240–42.

———. *Selected Essays of John Crowe Ransom.* Ed. Thomas Daniel Young and John Hindle. Baton Rouge: Louisiana State University Press, 1984.

———. *Selected Letters of John Crowe Ransom.* Ed. Thomas Daniel Young and George Core. Baton Rouge: Louisiana State University Press, 1985.
———. "The South Is a Bulwark." *Scribner's*, May 1936, 299–303.
———. "War and Publication." *Kenyon Review* 4 (Spring 1942): 217–18.
———. "We Resume." *Kenyon Review* 4 (Autumn 1942): 405–6.
———. "What Does the South Want?" *Virginia Quarterly Review* 12 (April 1936): 180–94.
Rauschning, Hermann. *Men of Chaos.* New York: G. P. Putnam's Sons, 1942.
———. *The Redemption of Democracy: The Coming Atlantic Empire.* Trans. Barrows Mussey. New York: Alliance Book Corporation, 1941.
———. *The Revolution of Nihilism: Warning to the West.* Trans. E. W. Dickes. New York: Alliance Book Corporation, 1939.
———. *Time of Delirium.* Trans. Richard Winston and Clara Winston. New York: D. Appleton-Century, 1946.
"Red Visitors Cause Rumpus." *Life*, 4 April 1949, 39–43.
Reeves, Paschal. *Thomas Wolfe's Albatross: Race and Nationality in America.* Athens: University of Georgia Press, 1968.
Reich, Wilhelm. *The Mass Psychology of Fascism.* Trans. Vincent R. Carfagno. New York: Farrar, Straus and Giroux, 1970.
Riordan, Mary Marguerite. *Lillian Hellman: A Bibliography, 1926–1978.* Metuchen, NJ: Scarecrow, 1980.
Robbins, Rossell Hope. *The T. S. Eliot Myth.* New York: Henry Schuman, 1951.
Rock, Virginia. "The Making and Meaning of *I'll Take My Stand*: A Study in Utopian Conservatism, 1925–1929." PhD diss., University of Minnesota, 1961.
———. "They Took Their Stand: The Emergence of the Southern Agrarians." *Prospects* 1 (1975): 205–95.
Rocks, James E. "The Art of *Lanterns on the Levee*." *Southern Review*, n.s., 12 (October 1976): 814–23.
Rollyson, Carl. *Lillian Hellman: Her Legend and Her Legacy.* New York: St. Martin's, 1988.
Romine, Scott. *The Narrative Forms of Southern Community.* Baton Rouge: Louisiana State University Press, 1999.
Roosevelt, Franklin D. *The Continuing Struggle for Liberalism: 1938; The Public Papers and Addresses of Franklin D. Roosevelt.* New York: Macmillan, 1941.
Rowley, Hazel. *Richard Wright: The Life and Times.* New York: Henry Holt, 2001.
Rubenstein, Richard L. *The Cunning of History: Mass Death and the American Future.* New York: Harper and Row, 1975.
Rubin, Louis D., Jr. *The Wary Fugitives: Four Poets and the South.* Baton Rouge: Louisiana State University Press, 1978.
"Russia Acclaimed by Miss Hellman: Home, She Says, Soviet Will Deal with Fascism—Hopes We Do the Same." *New York Times*, 2 March 1945, 5.

Sancton, Thomas. "Trouble in Dixie: The Bloody Shirt Once More." *New Republic*, 11 January 1943, 50–51.

———. "Trouble in Dixie: Race Fear Sweeps the South." *New Republic*, 18 January 1943, 81–83.

———. "Trouble in Dixie: The Returning Tragic Era." *New Republic*, 4 January 1943, 11–14.

Schaub, Thomas Hill. *American Fiction in the Cold War.* Madison: University of Wisconsin Press, 1991.

Schlesinger, Arthur M., Jr. *The Politics of Upheaval.* Boston: Houghton Mifflin, 1960.

———. *The Vital Center: The Politics of Freedom.* Boston: Houghton Mifflin, 1949.

Schuyler, George S. "The Caucasian Problem." In Logan, *What the Negro Wants.*

Schwartz, Lawrence H. *Creating Faulkner's Reputation: The Politics of Modern Literary Criticism.* Knoxville: University of Tennessee Press, 1988.

Scotchie, Joseph. *Barbarians in the Saddle: An Intellectual Biography of Richard Weaver.* New Brunswick, NJ: Transaction, 1997.

———, ed. *The Vision of Richard Weaver.* New Brunswick, NJ: Transaction, 1995.

Shapiro, Edward S. "American Conservative Intellectuals, the 1930's, and the Crisis of Ideology." *Modern Age* 23 (Fall 1979): 370–80.

———. "The Southern Agrarians and the Tennessee Valley Authority." *American Quarterly* 22 (Winter 1970): 791–806.

"Sharecroppers in Distress, Novelist Says." *New Orleans Morning Tribune*, 17 March 1936, 2.

Shi, David E. *The Simple Life: Plain Living and High Thinking in American Culture.* New York: Oxford University Press, 1985.

Shouse, Sarah Newman. *Hillbilly Realist: Herman Clarence Nixon of Possum Trot.* Tuscaloosa: University of Alabama Press, 1986.

Singal, Daniel Joseph. *The War Within: From Victorian to Modernist Thought in the South, 1919–1945.* Chapel Hill: University of North Carolina Press, 1982.

Smith, Henry Nash. "Realism vs. Revelation." Review of *A Southern Vanguard*, ed. Allen Tate. *Saturday Review of Literature*, 11 October 1947, 19–20.

Smith, Jon, and Deborah N. Cohn, eds. *Look Away! The U.S. in New World Studies.* Durham, NC: Duke University Press, 2004.

Smith, Lillian. "Addressed to Intelligent White Southerners." *South Today* 7 (Autumn–Winter 1942–43): 34–43.

———. Dope with Lime. *Pseudopodia* 1 (Spring 1936): 7, 12.

———. Dope with Lime. *North Georgia Review* 2 (Winter 1937–38): 2, 32.

———. Dope with Lime. *North Georgia Review* 3 (Spring 1938): 2, 31–32.

———. Dope with Lime. *North Georgia Review* 5 (Spring 1940): 4–6.

———. Dope with Lime. *North Georgia Review* 5 (Winter 1940–41): 4–8.

———. Dope with Lime. *North Georgia Review* 6 (Winter 1941): 4–6.

———. "He That Is without Sin . . ." *North Georgia Review* 2 (Winter 1937–38): 16–19, 31–32.

———. *How Am I to Be Heard? Letters of Lillian Smith*. Ed. Margaret Rose Gladney. Chapel Hill: University of North Carolina Press, 1993.

———. "Humans in Bondage." In Lillian Smith, *Winner Names the Age*, 32–55. Originally published in *Social Action* 10 (15 February 1944): 1–32.

———. *Killers of the Dream*. New York: W. W. Norton, 1949.

———. *Killers of the Dream*. Rev. ed. New York: W. W. Norton, 1961.

———. "Mr. Lafayette, Heah We Is—." *North Georgia Review* 4 (Spring 1939): 14–17.

———. "Portrait of the Deep South Speaking to Negroes on Morale." *South Today* 7 (Spring 1942): 34–37.

———. *Strange Fruit*. 1944. Athens: University of Georgia Press, 1986.

———. *The Winner Names the Age: A Collection of Writings by Lillian Smith*. Ed. Michelle Cliff. New York: W. W. Norton, 1978.

Smith, Lillian, and Paula Snelling. "As We Go to War." *North Georgia Review* 6 (Winter 1941): 25–26.

———. "Buying a New World with Old Confederate Bills." *South Today* 7 (Autumn–Winter 1942–43): 7–30.

———. Editorial statement. *Pseudopodia* 1 (Spring 1936): 6.

———. "From Lack of Understanding." *Pseudopodia* 1 (Fall 1936): 8–9.

———. "Winning the World with Democracy: A Symposium of Questions and Answers concerning Aims and Strategies, Ends and Means." *South Today* 7 (Spring 1942): 7–24.

Smith, Ted J., III, ed. *Steps toward Restoration: The Consequences of Richard Weaver's Ideas*. Wilmington, DE: ISI Books, 1998.

Sosna, Morton. "Democratic Discourse: Implications for the South." Paper presented at the annual meeting of the Southern Historical Association, Charlotte, NC, 1987.

———. *In Search of the Silent South: Southern Liberals and the Race Issue*. New York: Columbia University Press, 1977.

Spalding, Billups P. "William Alexander Percy: His Philosophy of Life as Reflected in His Poetry." MA thesis, University of Georgia, 1957.

Spalding, Phinizy. "A Stoic Trend in William Alexander Percy's Thought." *Georgia Review* 12 (Fall 1958): 241–51.

Squires, Radcliffe. *Allen Tate: A Literary Biography*. New York: Pegasus, 1971.

Stauffer, Donald, ed. *The Intent of the Critic*. Princeton, NJ: Princeton University Press, 1941.

Stoddard, Lothrop. *The Rising Tide of Color against White World-Supremacy*. New York: Charles Scribner's Sons, 1920.

Stone, Albert E., Jr. "Seward Collins and the *American Review*: Experiment in Pro-Fascism, 1933–37." *American Quarterly* 12 (Spring 1960): 4–19.

Stout, Janis P. *Katherine Anne Porter: A Sense of the Times.* Charlottesville: University Press of Virginia, 1995.

Straus, Theodore. "On Lillian Hellman, a Lady of Principle: The Author of *Watch on the Rhine* and *North Star* Stands by Her Guns." *New York Times,* 29 August 1943, sec. 2, p. 3.

Strout, Cushing. "*All the King's Men* and the Shadow of William James." *Southern Review,* n.s., 6 (October 1970): 920–34.

Styron, William. "Hell Reconsidered." In *"This Quiet Dust" and Other Writings,* 95–106. Originally published in *New York Review of Books,* 29 June 1978, 10–14.

———. *Sophie's Choice.* New York: Random House, 1979.

———. *"This Quiet Dust" and Other Writings.* New York: Random House, 1982.

Sullivan-González, Douglas, and Charles Reagan Wilson, eds. *The South and the Caribbean.* Jackson: University Press of Mississippi, 2001.

Symons, Julian. *Dashiell Hammett.* New York: Harcourt Brace Jovanovich, 1985.

Szczesiul, Anthony. *Racial Politics and Robert Penn Warren's Poetry.* Gainesville: University Press of Florida, 2002.

Tate, Allen. "Anti-Axis Poetry." Letter to the editor. *New Republic,* 16 November 1942, 643.

———. *Collected Poems, 1919–1976.* New York: Farrar, Straus and Giroux, 1977.

———. *Essays of Four Decades.* New York: Swallow, 1968.

———. *The Fathers.* New York: G. P. Putnam's Sons, 1938.

———. *Jefferson Davis: His Rise and Fall; A Biographical Narrative.* New York: Minton, Balch, 1929.

———. "Literature as Knowledge: Comment and Comparison." *Southern Review* 6 (Spring 1941): 629–57.

———. "Mr. Davidson and the Race Problem." *Sewanee Review* 53 (October–December 1945): 659–60.

———. "Notes on Liberty and Property." In Agar and Tate, *Who Owns America?*

———. Open letter to Grace Lumpkin. In "Fascism and the Southern Agrarians." *New Republic,* 27 May 1936, 75.

———. Preface to *Reactionary Essays on Poetry and Ideas.* New York: Charles Scribner's Sons, 1936.

———. Preface to *Reason in Madness: Critical Essays.* New York: G. P. Putnam's Sons, 1941.

———. "The Present Function of Criticism." *Southern Review* 6 (Autumn 1940): 236–46.

———. "The Problem of the Unemployed: A Modest Proposal." *American Review* 1 (May 1933): 129–49.

———. "The State of Letters." *Sewanee Review* 52 (October–December 1944): 608–14.

———. "A Traditionalist Looks at Liberalism." *Southern Review* 1 (Spring 1936): 731–44.

———. "Where Are the People?" Review of *The People's Choice*, by Herbert Agar. *American Review* 2 (December 1933): 231–37.
Theweleit, Klaus. *Male Fantasies*. Trans. Stephen Conway. 2 vols. Minneapolis: University of Minnesota Press, 1987.
Thompson, Alan Reynolds. "The Cult of Cruelty." *Bookman* 74 (January–February 1932): 477–87.
Thompson, Mark Christian. *Black Fascisms: African American Literature and Culture between the Wars*. Charlottesville: University of Virginia Press, 2007.
Tindall, William York. *D. H. Lawrence and Susan His Cow*. New York: Columbia University Press, 1939.
Tolson, Jay. *Pilgrim in the Ruins: A Life of Walker Percy*. New York: Simon and Schuster, 1992.
Toomer, Jean. *Cane*. 1923. New York: Liveright, 1975.
Twelve Southerners. *I'll Take My Stand: The South and the Agrarian Tradition*. 1930. Baton Rouge: Louisiana State University Press, 1977.
Underwood, Thomas A. *Allen Tate: Orphan of the South*. Princeton, NJ: Princeton University Press, 2000.
Unrue, Darlene Harbour, ed. *Critical Essays on Katherine Anne Porter*. New York: G. K. Hall, 1997.
———. *Truth and Vision in Katherine Anne Porter's Fiction*. Athens: University of Georgia Press, 1985.
———. *Understanding Katherine Anne Porter*. Columbia: University of South Carolina Press, 1988.
Urgo, Joseph R. *Faulkner's Apocrypha: "A Fable," "Snopes," and the Spirit of Human Rebellion*. Jackson: University Press of Mississippi, 1989.
Voegelin, Eric. *The New Science of Politics: An Introduction*. Chicago: University of Chicago Press, 1952.
Wade, John Donald, and Donald Davidson. *Agrarian Letters: The Correspondence of John Donald Wade and Donald Davidson*. Ed. Gerald J. Smith. Macon, GA: Mercer University Press, 2003.
Waite, Robert G. L. *The Psychopathic God: Adolf Hitler*. New York: Basic Books, 1977.
Walker, Marshall. *Robert Penn Warren: A Vision Earned*. New York: Harper and Row, 1979.
Walsh, Thomas F. *Katherine Anne Porter and Mexico: The Illusion of Eden*. Austin: University of Texas Press, 1992.
Warren, Robert Penn. *All the King's Men*. 1946. New York: Harcourt Brace Jovanovich, 1982.
———. *All the King's Men*. Restored ed. Ed. Noel Polk. New York: Random House, 2001.
———. *At Heaven's Gate*. New York: New Directions, 1943.

———. "Author's Note to 'Terror.'" In *Modern Poetry: British and American*, ed. Kimon Friar and John Malcolm Brinnin, 542–43. New York: Appleton-Century-Crofts, 1951.
———. "The Blind Poet: Sidney Lanier." *American Review* 2 (November 1933): 27–45.
———. *Brother to Dragons: A Tale in Verse and Voices*. New York: Random House, 1953.
———. *The Collected Poems of Robert Penn Warren*. Ed. John Burt. Baton Rouge: Louisiana State University Press, 1998.
———. "A Conversation with Robert Penn Warren." By Frank Gado. In *Robert Penn Warren Talking*.
———. "Cowley's Faulkner." In Bassett, *William Faulkner*.
———. *Democracy and Poetry*. Cambridge, MA: Harvard University Press, 1975.
———. "Homage to Oliver Allston." Review of *Opinions of Oliver Allston*, by Van Wyck Brooks. *Kenyon Review* 4 (Spring 1942): 259–63.
———. *Homage to Theodore Dreiser on the Centennial of His Birth*. New York: Random House, 1971.
———. "An Interview in New Haven with Robert Penn Warren." By Richard B. Sale. In *Robert Penn Warren Talking*.
———. "An Interview with Robert Penn Warren." By Peter Stitt. In *Robert Penn Warren Talking*.
———. Introduction to *All the King's Men*. 1946. New York: Modern Library, 1953.
———. *John Brown: The Making of a Martyr*. 1929. Nashville, TN: J. S. Sanders, 1993.
———. "Knowledge and the Image of Man." *Sewanee Review* 63 (April–June 1955): 182–92.
———. *The Legacy of the Civil War: Meditations on the Centennial*. New York: Random House, 1961.
———. "Literature as a Symptom." In Agar and Tate, *Who Owns America?* 343–64.
———. *Night Rider*. 1939. Nashville, TN: J. S. Sanders, 1992.
———. "A Note on the Hamlet of Thomas Wolfe." *American Review* 5 (May 1935): 191–208.
———. *Proud Flesh*. In *Robert Penn Warren's "All the King's Men."*
———. "Pure and Impure Poetry." *Kenyon Review* 5 (Spring 1943): 228–54.
———. "Robert Penn Warren: An Interview." By Marshall Walker. In *Robert Penn Warren Talking*.
———. *Robert Penn Warren's "All the King's Men": Three Stage Versions*. Ed. James A. Grimshaw, Jr., and James A. Perkins. Athens: University of Georgia Press, 2000.
———. *Robert Penn Warren Talking: Interviews, 1950–1978*. Ed. Floyd C. Watkins and John T. Hiers. New York: Random House, 1980.
———. *The Selected Letters of Robert Penn Warren*. Vol. 1, *The Apprenticeship Years*,

1924–1934. Ed. William Bedford Clark. Baton Rouge: Louisiana State University Press, 2000.

———. *Selected Letters of Robert Penn Warren.* Vol. 2, *The "Southern Review" Years, 1935–1942.* Ed. William Bedford Clark. Baton Rouge: Louisiana State University Press, 2001.

———. *Selected Letters of Robert Penn Warren.* Vol. 3, *Triumph and Transition, 1943–1952.* Ed. Randy Hendricks and James A. Perkins. Baton Rouge: Louisiana State University Press, 2006.

———. "Some Don'ts for Literary Regionalists." *American Review* 8 (December 1936): 142–50.

———. "T. S. Stribling: A Paragraph in the History of Critical Realism." *American Review* 2 (February 1934): 463–86.

———. "Twelve Poets." *American Review* 3 (May 1934): 212–27.

———. "Uncorrupted Consciousness: The Stories of Katherine Anne Porter." *Yale Review* 55 (December 1965): 280–90.

———. *Who Speaks for the Negro?* New York: Random House, 1965.

———. *World Enough and Time: A Romantic Novel.* New York: Random House, 1950.

Warren, Robert Penn, and Cleanth Brooks, Jr. "Dixie Looks at Mrs. Gerould." *American Review* 6 (March 1936): 585–95.

———. "The Reading of Modern Poetry." *American Review* 8 (February 1937): 435–49.

Watson, Charles S. *The History of Southern Drama.* Lexington: University Press of Kentucky, 1997.

Watson, Jay. "Uncovering the Body, Discovering Ideology: Segregation and Sexual Anxiety in Lillian Smith's *Killers of the Dream.*" *American Quarterly* 49 (September 1997): 470–503.

Weaver, Richard M. *Ideas Have Consequences.* 1948. Chicago: University of Chicago Press, 1984.

———. *In Defense of Tradition: Collected Shorter Writings of Richard Weaver, 1929–1963.* Ed. Ted J. Smith III. Indianapolis, IN: Liberty Fund, 2000.

———. *The Southern Essays of Richard Weaver.* Ed. George M. Curtis III and James J. Thompson, Jr. Indianapolis, IN: Liberty Press, 1987.

———. *The Southern Tradition at Bay: A History of Postbellum Thought.* Ed. George Core and M. E. Bradford. 1968. Washington, DC: Regnery Gateway, 1989.

———. *Visions of Order: The Cultural Crisis of Our Time.* 1964. Wilmington, DE: ISI Books, 1995.

Weeks, Edward. "First Person Singular." *Atlantic Monthly,* April 1941, xx.

West, James L. W., III. *William Styron: A Life.* New York: Random House, 1998.

White, Walter. *A Rising Wind.* Garden City, NY: Doubleday, Doran, 1945.

Whiting, Cécile. "American Heroes and Invading Barbarians: The Regionalist Response to Fascism." In *Prospects: An Annual of American Cultural Studies*, vol. 13, ed. Jack Salzman. New York: Cambridge University Press, 1988.

———. *Antifascism in American Art.* New Haven, CT: Yale University Press, 1989.

Whitman, Digby B. "Against Luce Thinking." *Nation,* 5 April 1941, 419.

Wilde, Meta Carpenter, and Orin Borsten. "Faulkner: Hollywood: 1943." In Faulkner, *Faulkner: A Comprehensive Guide to the Brodsky Collection,* vol. 4.

Wilkerson, Doxey A. "Freedom—Through Victory in War and Peace." In Logan, *What the Negro Wants.*

Wilson, Edmund. "Tennessee Agrarians." *New Republic,* 29 July 1931, 279–81.

Winchell, Mark Royden. *Where No Flag Flies: Donald Davidson and the Southern Resistance.* Columbia: University of Missouri Press, 2000.

Wolfe, Thomas. *The Autobiography of an American Novelist.* Ed. Leslie Field. Cambridge, MA: Harvard University Press, 1983.

———. *The Letters of Thomas Wolfe.* Ed. Elizabeth Nowell. New York: Charles Scribner's Sons, 1956.

———. *The Letters of Thomas Wolfe to His Mother.* Ed. C. Hugh Holman and Sue Fields Ross. Chapel Hill: University of North Carolina Press, 1968.

———. *Look Homeward Angel: A Story of the Buried Life.* New York: Charles Scribner's Sons, 1929.

———. *The Notebooks of Thomas Wolfe.* Ed. Richard S. Kennedy and Paschal Reeves. 2 vols. Chapel Hill: University of North Carolina Press, 1970.

———. *O Lost: A Story of the Buried Life; The Original Version of "Look Homeward Angel."* Ed. Arlyn Bruccoli and Mathew J. Bruccoli. Columbia: University of South Carolina Press, 2000.

———. *Of Time and the River.* New York: Charles Scribner's Sons, 1935.

———. "The Story of a Novel." In Wolfe, *Autobiography of an American Novelist.*

———. *The Web and the Rock.* New York: Harper and Brothers, 1939.

———. "Writing and Living." In Wolfe, *Autobiography of an American Novelist.*

———. *You Can't Go Home Again.* New York: Harper and Brothers, 1940.

Wolfe, Thomas, and Aline Bernstein. *My Other Loneliness: The Letters of Thomas Wolfe and Aline Bernstein.* Ed. Suzanne Stutman. Chapel Hill: University of North Carolina Press, 1983.

Woodward, C. Vann. *The Burden of Southern History.* Rev. ed. Baton Rouge: Louisiana State University Press, 1968.

———. *Thinking Back: The Perils of Writing History.* Baton Rouge: Louisiana State University Press, 1986.

Wright, Richard. *Black Boy: A Record of Childhood and Youth.* New York: Harper and Brothers, 1945.

———. *Black Boy: A Record of Childhood and Youth.* Restored text of *American Hunger.* New York: HarperPerennial, 1993.

———. "The Ethics of Living Jim Crow." In Wright, *Uncle Tom's Children.*

———. "How 'Bigger' Was Born." In Wright, *Richard Wright*.
———. *Native Son*. In Wright, *Richard Wright*.
———. *Richard Wright: Early Works*. New York: Library of America, 1991.
———. *Uncle Tom's Children*. 1940. New York: HarperPerennial, 1993.
Wright, William. *Lillian Hellman: The Image, The Woman*. New York: Simon and Schuster, 1986.
Writers at Work: The Paris Review Interviews. 3rd ser. New York: Viking Press, 1967.
Wyatt-Brown, Bertram. *The House of Percy: Honor, Melancholy, and Imagination in a Southern Family*. New York: Oxford University Press, 1994.
Yaeger, Patricia. *Dirt and Desire: Reconstructing Southern Women's Writing, 1930–1990*. Chicago: University of Chicago Press, 2000.
Young, Fred Douglas. *Richard M. Weaver, 1910–1963: A Life of the Mind*. Columbia: University of Missouri Press, 1995.
Young, Thomas Daniel. *Gentleman in a Dustcoat: A Biography of John Crowe Ransom*. Baton Rouge: Louisiana State University Press, 1976.
Young, Thomas Daniel, and M. Thomas Inge. *Donald Davidson*. New York: Twayne, 1971.

INDEX

Absalom, Absalom! (Faulkner), 177, 179
acculturation, 136, 155, 157
Adams, Leonie, 68
aesthetics, 14, 54–56, 68; and politics, 48, 52, 252; and traditionalism, 70, 341n16
African Americans, 44, 126, 136, 190, 330n29; and protest, 15; and women, 261, 301; as writers, 5, 16–20, 197, 330n29, 330–31n37. *See also* civil rights movement; miscegenation; National Association for the Advancement of Colored People (NAACP); race; racism
Agar, Herbert, 40, 45, 47–48
Agee, James, 331n40
Agrarians. *See* Nashville Agrarians
Aiken, Conrad, 68
Alcott, Bronson, 253
Alexander, T. H., 28
alienation, 48, 134, 230–31, 233, 238–39, 248, 342n27
All the King's Men (Warren), 261, 270–75, 364n42, 365n46
Allen, John D., 122
American dream, 62, 122, 181–82, 190
American Mercury, 8, 72, 74–75
American Review, 33, 34, 35, 37, 38, 39, 40, 42
And Keep Your Powder Dry (Mead), 9–11
Anderson, Sherwood, 172

Andrews, Dana, 296
Another Part of the Forest (Hellman), 303–4
antiauthoritarianism, 68, 206
antimodernism, 35, 332–33n16; and fascism, 43, 312, 333n24, 335–36n60; regionalism of, 24, 87
anti-Semitism, 151, 157–60, 166, 282, 292, 338n13, 368n28
appeasement, 298–99, 300, 339n18, 359n19
Arendt, Hannah, 321, 324, 368n28
aristocracy, 30, 81, 108, 116, 226, 341n16, 342n27
Armato, Philip, 283
Aryanism, 80, 86, 109, 211, 248, 351n20
At Heaven's Gate (Warren), 268–70
Atlantic Monthly, 110, 132
Attack on Leviathan (Davidson), 49
Auden, W. H., 61, 68
Auschwitz, 317, 320, 323–25
Austenfeld, Thomas, 205, 222, 354n3
authoritarianism, 30, 201–2, 292; and the Agrarians, 34, 51–52, 56, 58, 60, 62, 68–70, 335–36n60; in America, 14, 69, 83–84, 134; and Cash, 72–77, 82, 86–88, 90–95, 120, 338n2; and McCullers, 239, 241, 243; in Nazi Germany, 23, 81, 99–100, 108–10, 166, 309; and Porter, 204, 206, 208–10, 212, 215–21, 225–26; and Smith, 134, 136–

INDEX

authoritarianism *(continued)*
  38, 144–45; in the South, 134, 198–99, 310–11; and Warren, 252, 255
Autumn Garden, The (Hellman), 307–8

Babbitt, Irving, 34
Baker, Lewis, 100–101
Ballad of a Sad Cafe, The (McCullers), 243–45
Bankhead, Talullah, 291
Barr, Stringfellow, 32
Baxter, Anne, 296
Bedichek, Roy, 11
Belgium, 16, 98, 114, 342n26
Belloc, Hillaire, 34, 38, 333n29
Benton, Thomas Hart, 11, 13, 14, 43
Berlin, 149, 203–11, 221, 298–99
Bernstein, Aline, 147, 157, 173, 175
Bettleheim, Bruno, 321
Bilbo, Theodore, 318–19, 324–25, 346n31, 371n17
Bishop, John Peale, 62–63
Black Boy (Wright), 20–21, 197, 330–31n37
Blackwell, Louise, 122
Blease, Cole, 8
Blotner, Joseph, 179, 363n32
Boas, Franz, 80–81
Bogan, Louise, 68
Borgese, G. A., 259
Boswell, Peyton, 14
bourgeois society, 42, 57, 122, 312, 317, 358n16
Bradford, M. E., 67
Brennan, Walter, 296
Brodsky, Daniel, 191, 352n22
Brooks, Cleanth, 59, 256, 361–62n13
Brooks, Van Wyck, 58–61, 66, 255–56, 359n21, 362n17. See also *Opinions of Oliver Allston* (Brooks)
Buchenwald, 140
Burke, Kenneth, 259–60, 261

Cabell, James Branch, 67
Caldwell, Erskine, 5, 77, 230, 331n40
call to arms, 69, 136, 171, 188, 334n34, 350n18
Calverton, V. F., 47
Cameron, W. J., 223

Cane (Toomer), 5, 113
capitalism, 36, 56, 314, 332n16, 337n86; alternatives to, 12, 41, 167; and communism, 26, 45, 332n8; and fascism, 23, 268–69, 280, 332n8, 343n31, 344n2, 358n14; vis-à-vis regionalism, 12, 88
Carmer, Carl, 5–7, 328n11
Carter, Hodding, 132
Cash, W. J., 71–72, 338–39n14, 339n15, 339n18; and frontierism, 73, 84; later essays of, 75–78; *Mind of the South*, 49–51, 74, 82–83, 93–95, 96–97, 119–120, 131; and Nazism, 79–80; and race relations, 85, 88–89, 110; and totalitarianism of the South, 23, 81, 86–87, 90–92, 109, 199, 244, 310–11, 335–36n60
Carr, Virginia Spencer, 230, 233, 241
Carrel, Alexis, 266, 269, 339n18
Cason, Clarence, 331n40
Cather, Willa, 227
Central Intelligence Agency (CIA), 58–59
centralization, 13, 31–32, 51, 332n8
Cerf, Bennett, 196, 197
Chamberlain, John, 47–48
Chamberlain, Neville, 50
Chapin, Katherine Garrison, 68
Charlotte News, 71, 77, 120, 338n1
Chekhov, Anton, 229
Cheney, Brainerd, 366n53
Chesterton, G. K., 34, 38, 257, 333n29
Chicago Defender, 103, 113–14
Children's Hour, The (Hellman), 283–84, 367n7
China, 120–21, 133, 136; and imperialism, 15, 125; and relationship with Japan, 18, 78, 123–24
Christianity, 139, 159, 313, 350–51n19; and colonialism, 121; in Tate's poetry, 63; and totalitarianism, 137. See also religion
Churchill, Winston, 50, 273, 365–66n51
CIA. See Central Intelligence Agency (CIA)
citizenship, 57, 193, 195, 199–201, 252
civil liberties, 45, 71–72, 161, 292, 339n15
civil rights movement, 19, 70, 127, 143, 233, 311
Civil War, 4, 62, 64, 156, 226, 331n2; and

402

psychology of defeat, 8, 30, 44, 49; and Southern primitivism, 84, 86; vis-a-vis Europe, 25, 190–93, 360n1
Clarac-Schwarzenbach, Annemarie, 240
class: and alleged inferiority, 106, 167, 199; and alleged superiority, 85, 87, 110–11, 119, 122; and middle level, 13, 110–11, 341n9; and planters, 105, 118
Clay, Frances, 122
Cobb, James, 118
Cohn, David, 101, 132
cold war, 70, 138, 202, 249, 311–12, 350n18, 370n2
Coleridge, Samuel, 278
Collins, Seward, 33–43, 45, 47–48, 332–33n16, 333n24, 361–62n13
colonialism, 15, 121, 125–26, 311
Communism, 142–43, 205, 225, 227–28, 249, 314; Agrarian attitudes toward, 28–29, 36, 40–47, 49, 332n8, 344–45n11; Smith's attitudes toward, 124, 311–12; in Soviet Russia, 280, 291, 306; and totalitarianism, 3, 137–38, 142, 144, 201–2, 206, 216, 224. *See also* Communist Party USA
Communist Party USA, 282
concentration camps, 2, 38, 47–48, 140, 142, 239, 273, 316, 321–23, 325, 369n39. *See also* Auschwitz; Buchenwald; Dachau
Confessions of Nat Turner, The (Styron), 322, 324
conformity, 75, 86, 251, 256; enforcement of in the South, 49–51, 90, 131, 230, 244, 322, 360n31; in literature, 61, 199, 220–22, 362n17; and politics, 53–54
Conrad, Joseph, 68, 79
contagion, 10, 162
Contemporary Historians, 286
Copland, Aaron, 296
corporate state, 226, 234, 251, 270, 280
Cousins, Norman, 68–69
Cowley, Malcolm, 54, 178–79, 197
Crowther, Bosley, 294
Cult of Cruelty, 177
Cultural and Scientific Conference for World Peace, 306
Curry, John Steuart, 11, 13, 14, 43

D'Arcy, Father, 34
Dabney, Virginius, 8, 132–33
Dachau, 140, 142
Dain Curse (Hammett), 282
Daniels, Jonathan, 104, 167
Dante, 63, 99, 268
Davidman, Joy, 59–60, 336–37n76
Davidson, Donald, 25, 50, 56, 99, 313, 337n80, 338n86; *I'll Take My Stand* title dispute, 28–34, 361n12; perspectives on Fascism, 40, 46, 309, 335–36n60; and race relations, 51; and regionalism, 37, 48–49, 52
Davis, Jeff, 8
Davis, Robert Gorham, 69–70
Davis, Stuart, 13
Dawson, Christopher, 34
Days to Come (Hellman), 284–86
De Voto, Bernard, 60–61
Decline of the West (Spengler), 75–76
defeat, 336–37n76; as foundational myth of the South, 4, 30, 49, 64, 103, 226; as World War II goal, 59, 142, 168–69, 216, 223, 319
degeneracy, 153; as class marker, 76, 106–7, 339n15; and modernism, 13; and race, 173, 175, 349n39
dehumanization, 17, 41, 76, 251, 270, 273
demagoguery, 71, 119, 253; as aspect of Southern culture, 4, 8, 33, 137–38, 324; and Fascism, 43
democracy, 35, 58, 64–65, 234–35, 340–41n15, 362n17, 365n50; and aesthetics, 14, 47, 50–53, 70; celebrations of, 194–95; criticisms of, 20, 56, 107–8, 119, 154, 167–69, 330n29, 345n16, 347n44; defense of, 82, 85, 124–29, 132, 136, 145, 171–73, 176; and nationalism, 61; potential destruction of, 264, 270–72; in the South, 138–39, 142–43, 186–92, 199–202, 310–11; theories of, 251–53, 255, 257–58; threats to, 2–3, 8–9, 12, 25, 43–45, 197, 215–16, 223–24, 303–5
Democracy and Poetry (Warren), 252
Democratic Party, 16, 75, 91
depression (psychological), 101, 179, 204, 355n12
disruption (societal), 210, 246–47, 264; as function of class, 100, 106–8, 115; as prod-

disruption (societal) *(continued)*
   uct of capitalism, 62, 71; as product of war, 67, 303
Distributists, 40–42, 45, 46, 48, 332–33n16
Dobie, J. Frank, 11
Dobie, Martha, 283
Dollfuss, Englebert, 211
Donald, David Herbert, 149, 347n5
Donovan, William "Wild Bill," 59
Dorman, Robert, 11
Dos Passos, John, 230
Dostoievsky, Fyodor, 229
Drayton, Michael, 65–66
Dreiser, Theodore, 252, 256, 364–65n45
Duck, Leigh Anne, 328n7, 331n38
Duke, Jams Buchanan, 73, 338n7
Dust Tracks on a Road (Hurston), 16, 20

education, 203–4, 230; and Agrarianism, 38; deficit of, 4, 156; in the South, 73, 92, 132, 254
Eisenstein, Sergei, 206
Elder, Donald, 215, 223–25
Eleven Poems on the Same Theme (Warren), 264–69
Eliot, T. S., 68–69, 230, 256
Elkins, Stanley, 321–24
Elliott, William Yandell, 37
Ellul, Jacques, 251
Emerson, Ralph Waldo, 253
equalitarianism, 24, 70, 107, 153
Ethridge, Mark, 132, 346n31
eugenics, 151, 339n18, 364n35
Evans, Oliver, 239

Fable, A (Faulkner), 196, 201
Fadiman, Clifton, 49–50, 357n2
fanaticism, 33, 78, 253, 257–58, 310, 362n18
farming, 33, 37, 104–6, 182, 296, 320
Farrell, James T., 230
Fascism, 2–3, 16, 22, 36, 340n15, 365n50; in America, 43, 45, 169, 215, 268, 303, 305; and association with Agrarians, 25, 38–43, 46–49, 61, 69, 122, 332n8, 335–36n60; Cash's obsession with, 72, 77–78, 83, 91; cultural roots of, 197, 252, 309; defined as, 7–15, 43, 327n2, 333n24, 359n18; Faulkner's perspectives on, 176, 178–79, 181, 188, 192–93; Hellman's perspectives on, 280, 282, 285–88, 291–98, 301–5, 307–8; McCullers's perspectives on, 229–31, 233–35, 238–41, 243–44, 248, 358n16; perceived horrors of, 60, 278, 312, 368n28, 369n39; and Walker Percy's perspectives on, 314, 316, 325; William Alexander Percy's perspectives on, 96, 98, 343n31; Porter's perspectives on, 217–18, 224, 227–28; and racism, 17, 22, 81, 344n2; Smith's perspectives on, 122–24, 126–27, 143, 344n2, 344–45n11; Southern writers' responses to, 2–3, 22, 309–10, 330n29; and totalitarianism, 22–23, 202, 311; Warren's perspectives on, 255, 258–59, 261, 263–64, 266–69, 271–72, 274, 279, 361–62n13; Wolfe's perspectives on, 162–63, 169–170, 172; and World War II, 16, 195, 203
Fathers, The (Tate), 62
Faulkner, Malcolm, 188, 195, 351–52n21
Faulkner, William, 77, 99, 118, 350n18, 351–52n21, 352–53n30, 353n34; *Absalom, Absalom!* 177, 179; and Fascism, 15, 23, 352n29, 354n38; *Go Down, Moses*, 179, 181, 187–89, 197, 350–51n19, 351n20; *Intruder in the Dust*, 199, 201; *Knight's Gambit*, 179, 181; and modernism, 310; *Sound and the Fury, The*, 197–99; *Wild Palms, The*, 179
FBI (Federal Bureau of Investigation), 224–25, 306, 346n35, 355–56n23, 356n30
federal government, 49, 113; and segregation, 132, 368n31; and states' rights, 37, 46, 51, 200
Feldman, Charles, 190
Ferguson, Samuel Wragg, 112–13
feudalism, 3, 9, 26, 30, 344n2
Fight against War and Fascism, 38, 39
Finland, 260, 266, 291, 368n20
First Conference on American-Soviet Cultural Cooperation, 301
Fisher, Dorothy Canfield, 20, 21, 22
Fitzgerald, F. Scott, 146
Fletcher, John Gould, 41, 44, 45
folk culture, 6, 13, 31, 43, 277

Foreground of American Fiction, The (Hartwick), 177
Forster, E. M., 227
France, 16, 332n11; and Agrarians, 35; and World War II, 78, 98, 189, 198, 215, 256, 365–66n51
Franco, Francisco, 179, 286, 332n11
Frank, Waldo, 12
Frederick II, 99–100
Freud, Sigmund, 7
Friends of the Lincoln Brigade, 280
Fromm, Eric, 314
frontier, 62, 73, 84, 86, 88–89, 93, 154

Geismar, Maxwell, 178–79
gender, 227, 247, 248. *See also* sexuality; women
German Communist Party, 205
Germany, 56; Cash's perspective on, 72, 78, 81, 87, 90, 94, 97; compared to the South, 3, 16, 41, 90, 234–35, 309, 311–14, 324–26, 335–36n60; Faulkner's perspective on, 192, 199, 351n20; Hellman's perspective on, 282, 299; and Hitler, 36, 47, 50, 80, 128, 327n2; and Jews, 36, 80, 137, 235, 239, 243, 328–29n11; McCullers's perspective on, 231, 234, 239, 243; Walker Percy's perspective on, 315; William Alexander Percy's perspective on, 98, 108, 114; Porter's perspective on, 203–5, 210–11, 215, 223, 228, 354n3, 355–56n23; Smith's perspective on, 122, 124, 140, 344n2; Styron's perspective on, 318–19; as totalitarian state, 2, 200; Warren's perspective on, 255, 260, 273; Wolfe's perspective on, 146–51, 153, 160–67, 171, 175; Wright's perspective on, 17–19
Gershwin, Ira, 296
Gettysburg Address, 184, 190, 350n17
global South, 2, 310, 327–28n3
globalism, 327–28n3
Go Down, Moses (Faulkner), 179, 181, 187–89, 197, 350–51nn19–20
Goad, Harold, 35
Gogol, Nikolai, 229
Goldwyn, Samuel, 284, 295–96

Gordon, Caroline, 28, 204–5, 356n33
Göring, Hermann, 205, 211, 216
gradualism, 193, 200, 344n2, 353n36
Granger, Farley, 296
Grant, Madison, 151–56, 343n36, 348n9
Great Depression, 12, 75, 156, 167, 171, 175, 187, 328n7
Great Tradition, The (Hicks), 177
Green, Paul, 68
Greeson, Jennifer Rae, 4
Gretlund, Jan Nordby, 209
Grill, Johnpeter Horst, 328–29n11, 341n18
Griswold, Francis, 120
grotesque, 102, 105, 177, 357n2
Guggenheim Foundation, 33, 79, 203, 260–61

Haas, Robert, 179–80, 196–97
Hamblin, Robert, 191, 352n22
Hammett, Dashiell, 282–83, 366n4, 367n6, 370n54
Hammett, Mary, 282
Harding, Ann, 296
Hardy, Thomas, 75, 216–17
Harris, Joel Chandler, 33
Harris, Julian, 133
Hartwick, Harry, 177
Hassan, Ihab, 233
Hawks, Howard, 190
Heart Is a Lonely Hunter, The (McCullers), 233–39, 250
Hebert, Paul M., 261
Heflin, Tom, 8
Hellman, Lillian, 367n6, 367nn14–15, 368n31; *Autumn Garden, The*, 307–8, 370n52; *Children's Hour, The*, 283–84, 367n7; *Days to Come*, 284–86; and Fascism, 23, 368n20, 369n40; *Little Foxes, The*, 288–93, 303, 367–68n19; *Searching Wind, The*, 297–301; *These Three*, 284; and totalitarianism, 310; *Unfinished Woman, An*, 281, 286–87, 301, 367n12, 369n39; *Watch on the Rhine*, 291–97, 369–70n45
Helper, Hinton, 85
Hemingway, Ernest, 146, 178, 230
Hendry, Irene, 259
Herbst, Josephine, 204–6, 225

INDEX

Hicks, Granville, 177, 358n16
Hillyer, Robert, 69–70
Hitler, Adolph, 15, 41, 47, 50, 128, 293–94, 299; and admiration of by Americans, 18, 38–39, 42–43, 141; and criticism of by Southern writers, 81, 98–99, 109, 124, 149, 161, 190, 192, 197, 215, 241, 312, 315; rise to power of, 36, 44, 77, 160, 205, 231, 305, 351n20; and treatment of Jews, 13, 80, 126, 160, 173, 319, 325, 338n13
Holland, 16
Hollywood, 188, 282, 284, 304, 351n21
Holocaust, 312, 316, 320–21, 323–24. *See also* concentration camps
homogeneity, 13, 154
homosexuality, 98, 340n2, 340n7, 342n27
Hopper, Edward, 13
horror (in literature), 202, 209
House Un-American Activities Committee (HUAC), 304–7
HUAC. *See* House Un-American Activities Committee (HUAC)
Hurston, Zora Neale, 16, 20, 330n29

I'll Take My Stand, 28, 35, 37, 41; as antimodernist text, 26–27, 29, 32–33, 62; as defense of Southern culture, 26–27, 334n34; and Ransom, 24, 26–27, 361n11; and Tate, 334n34, 361n11; and Warren, 254, 361n11
immigration, 153, 155–56, 206
imperialism, 15, 16, 67, 101, 121, 125
individualism, 70, 201, 216, 220; and connections to Fascism, 309; as contrary to community, 27, 166, 181–82; as distinctively Southern, 84, 86, 92, 315, 353n34
industrialism, 104, 178, 331–32n2; Agrarian critiques of, 28–29, 32, 37–38, 44, 122; as force of modernity, 24; in the South, 26–27, 73, 76, 88
instability (psychological), 237, 245, 247
Institute of International Education, 203
intellectual freedom, 52, 279
internationalism, 2, 14, 361–62n13
interventionism, 101, 123, 200, 232–33, 241
intolerance, 92, 271, 315n16

Intruder in the Dust (Faulkner), 199, 201
irrationalism, 8, 25, 197, 229, 277, 329n18, 358n16
Isherwood, Christopher, 259
isolationism, 100–101, 135, 138, 232–33, 240, 292, 359n19
Italy, 2, 23, 41, 78, 122, 327n2; American sympathies for, 35, 45; Cash's perspective on, 49, 72, 91; compared to the South, 3, 49, 72, 91, 311; Hellman's perspective on, 298; McCullers's perspective on, 239; Porter's perspective on, 216; Warren's perspective on, 260–61, 268, 275, 365n46
Ivens, Joris, 286

Jackson, Stonewall, 182
Jagger, Dean, 296
James, William, 253, 365n46
Janson, H. W., 14
Japan, 10, 18, 72, 78, 123, 124, 201, 215, 315
Jeffers, Robinson, 177
Jefferson Davis: His Rise and Fall (Tate), 25–26
Jenkins, Robert L., 328–29n11, 341n18
Jerrold, Douglas, 45, 333n29
Jervey, Huger, 101
Jews, 247, 173, 368n28; Germany's treatment of, 36, 39, 44, 80, 88, 140, 159, 291–92, 325, 328–29n11; identity politics of, 157; and McCullers's work, 231–32, 234–35; and Porter's work, 205; in Smith's work, 126–27; in the South, 106; in Styron's work, 319–20; in Wolfe's work, 158–59, 161, 163, 172, 173; in Wright's work, 13, 19
Jim Crow, 5, 128, 139, 142
jingoism, 13, 14, 43, 65, 127, 184
John Brown: The Making of a Martyr (Warren), 253–54
Johnson, Charles S., 51
Johnson, Gerald, 33
Johnson, Guy B., 134–35
Jones, Anne Goodwyn, 94
Journey Down, The (Bernstein), 173
Joyce, James, 148, 347n1
Jung, Karl, 7, 86, 252
justice, 256; for African Americans, 44–45,

92; in Faulkner's work, 177; in Hellman's work, 280–81; in William Alexander Percy's work, 113, 117; in Porter's work, 206, 217, 297; in Smith's work, 132, 135–36, 145; in Warren's work, 272, 275–76; in Wolfe's work, 167; in Wright's work, 18, 20–21;
Justus, James, 274, 366n54

Kennedy, John F., 273
Kennedy, Richard, 166
Kennedy, Stetson, 331n40, 343n31, 344n2 (chap. 4)
Kenyon Review, 48, 53–54
Killers of the Dream (Smith), 1, 120, 138, 144, 212, 249, 311, 347n44, 347n45
Kirchwey, Freda, 224
Kirk, David, 202
Knight's Gambit (Faulkner), 179, 181
Knopf, Blanche, 72–73
Kober, Arthur, 282
Ku Klux Klan, 6, 133, 142, 341n18, 344n2; in Cash's work, 81, 89–90; in William Alexander Percy's work, 108–10, 341n19; in Wright's work, 17
Kussy, Bella, 166–167

L'Action Française, 32, 35, 332n11
labor, 48, 74, 302; in Germany, 98, 317, 323; organization of, 108, 144, 185; in the South, 104, 110, 254, 342n21, 342n24; and unrest, 233, 284–85
LaGuardia, Fiorello, 319
Lamont, Corliss, 48
Lancelot (Percy), 312–16
Lanier, Lyle, 45
Lanterns on the Levee (Percy), 96–103, 110–11, 115, 118–19, 309, 341n16, 342n27
Last Gentleman, The (Percy), 315
Lawson, Lewis, 100
League of American Writers, 179, 280
League of Nations, 80, 99
League of Women Shoppers, 280
Ledig-Rowohlt, H. M., 149, 161, 348n27
Lee, Robert E., 26, 190, 200
leftists, 3, 176, 179, 241; and criticisms of art, 13, 177, 197, 229, 358n16; Southerners as, 120, 167, 204, 205, 230, 282–83, 254n2; and tensions with the South, 44, 344n2, 361–62n13
Legacy of the Civil War, The (Warren), 257–58
liberalism, 70, 75, 122, 138, 306, 307, 314, 339n15
Life, 223, 306
Lincoln, Abraham, 39, 49, 184, 190–92, 195, 280, 292, 310
Lindbergh, Anne Morrow, 83, 339n18
Lindbergh, Charles, 339n18
Linscott, Robert, 199
Linton, Ralph, 80
Little Foxes, The (Hellman), 288–93, 303, 367–68n19
localism, 14, 25, 43, 45–46, 361–62n13
Logan, Rayford W., 51, 330n30
Look Homeward Angel (Wolfe), 166
Long, Huey, 8, 13, 261–62, 272, 329n16, 363n30
Lost Cause, 86, 97
Lost Generation, 147
Louis, Joe, 192, 247
Louisiana, 8, 281
Louisville Courier-Journal, 40, 132
Lowell, Robert, 68
Luce, Clare Booth, 223
Luce, Henry R., 66–67, 223
Lumpkin, Grace, 38–43, 361–62n13
lynching, 4, 33, 107, 133, 132; in fiction, 17, 173, 209–11, 270, 318, 371n12; and racial code enforcement, 5, 44, 50–51, 88, 140, 328n11
Lytle, Andrew, 27–30, 32, 35, 38

MacLeish, Archibald, 58–59, 66, 255–56, 286, 359n21, 362n17
Maltese Falcon (Hammett), 282
Mann, Erika, 240
Mann, Klaus, 240–41, 243
Mann, Thomas, 240
mapping, 5, 8, 142
Markham, R. H., 83, 339n19
Marshall, Margaret, 54

INDEX

Marx, Karl, 230
Marx, Leo, 118
masturbation, 19, 141, 267
materialism, 158, 194, 229, 340–41n16
Mather, Cotton, 206, 355n8
McCullers, Carson, 23, 358n13, 359n21, 360n31; "Aliens, The" 231–32; and attacks on authoritarianism, 310, 357n8, 357n14, 359n18; *Ballad of a Sad Cafe, The*, 243–45; *Heart Is a Lonely Hunter, The*, 233–39, 250; *Member of the Wedding, The*, 245–49; *Reflections in a Golden Eye*, 239–40, 357n2, 357n16; "Untitled Piece," 232
McCullers, Reeves, 230, 232–33, 240, 242, 359n26
McDonald, Dwight, 47
McDonald, James G., 80
McGill, Ralph, 133
McKee, Kathryn, 327–28n3
Mead, Margaret, 9–11, 329n18
Mediterranean and Other Poems, The (Tate), 48
Mein Kampf (Hitler), 79, 160, 312, 351n20
Melby, John, 301–3
Member of the Wedding, The (McCullers), 245–49
memoir: by Carmer, 5; by Smith, 1; by William Alexander Percy, 116, 118; by Porter, 210
memory, 151, 170; as changing process, 203, 347n14; as fodder for art, 197, 200, 209, 211–12, 219–20, 232; and the Lost Cause, 86, 97
Mencken, H. L., 72–73, 338n7, 339n15
Mexican Revolution, 205–6
Milestone, Lewis, 295–96
Miller, Perry, 94
Mind of the South (Cash), 72, 96–97; criticisms of, 49; as critique of the South, 81–83, 90–91, 93–95, 119–20, 131, 339n20; writing process of, 74, 76–77. *See also* Cash, W. J.
Minter, David, 196
miscegenation, 117, 133, 325
misogyny, 158, 159, 198, 314. *See also* women
modernism, 13, 22, 99, 159, 347n1

modernity, 116, 118, 365n50; criticisms of, 62, 87, 90, 96–97, 106–9, 178, 267, 341n16; in Southern literature, 22, 178, 188, 258, 268–69, 314, 364n33; and threats to traditional culture, 12, 24, 98–99, 100–104, 113, 116, 309–10, 312, 335–36n60, 340–41n15, 351n20
Montserrat, 305–6
Moody, Richard, 292, 296
More, Paul Elmore, 34
Morrison, Cameron, 75
Mumford, Lewis, 11
Mussolini, Benito, 15, 41–44, 81, 363n30; admiration of, 18, 38, 332n11, 333n29, 361–62n13, 365n50; and European turmoil, 77–78, 215–16; in fiction, 235–36, 260–62, 298, 365n46

NAACP. *See* National Association for the Advancement of Colored People (NAACP)
Nashville Agrarians, 44–45, 207, 223, 332–33n16; and alleged connections to Fascism, 23, 35–36, 38–43, 170, 309, 332n8, 335–36n60, 344–45n11; Cash's perspectives on, 72, 90–91, 97; and Davidson, 28–29, 33–34, 48–52; as defenders of regionalism, 11, 14, 24–25, 87, 90, 313; and industrialism, 29, 37; William Alexander Percy's perspectives on, 96, 97, 108, 309; and Ransom, 27, 29, 33–34, 37, 48, 53–56; Smith's perspectives on, 122; and Tate, 26, 28–33, 37, 40–43, 56–68, 337n80, 337n86; and Warren, 46–47, 254, 269, 361–62n13
Nashville Tennessean, 28
Nation, 44, 52, 171, 223, 227, 230
National Academy of Arts and Letters, 170
National Association for the Advancement of Colored People (NAACP), 15, 132
National Guard, 114, 180
National Socialism, 14, 57
nationalism, 123, 171, 248, 358n16; and the Agrarians, 25, 49, 61, 257, 263, 361–62n17; and effects on regionalism, 2; and Nazism, 13, 43, 86, 160, 232, 344n2
Native Son (Wright), 17, 19–20
nativism, 151, 154, 157, 160, 172, 173, 175

INDEX

Nazism, 322, 359n19; Cash's perspectives on, 77–80, 339n18; Faulkner's perspectives on, 193, 201; Hellman's perspectives on, 282, 286; McCullers's perspectives on, 233; Walker Percy's perspectives on, 313, 315; William Alexander Percy's perspectives on, 98–99, 109; Smith's perspectives on, 129, 136–37; and Southern traditionalism, 72; Warren's perspectives on, 266–67, 278; Wolfe's perspectives on, 149, 151, 166, 170–71
Neutrality Act, 286, 367n13
New Criticism, 52, 68–69, 254, 256
New Deal, 51, 92, 182
New Republic, 40, 42–43, 54, 59, 166, 230, 334n32
New South, 73, 76, 88, 118, 317
New York Sun, 170
New York Times, 137, 139, 142, 144, 155, 170, 291
New York Times Sunday Book Review, 170
New York World-Telegram, 280
Night Rider (Warren), 258–60
nihilism, 7, 79
Nixon, Clarence, 28
noblesse oblige, 104–5, 110, 114–15, 315, 342n24
North Georgia Review, 120, 122
North Star, The, 295–98
Nowell, Elizabeth, 166
Nuremberg trials, 273, 365–66n51

Ober, Harold, 196
obscenity, 177, 346n36
occupation (military), 22, 51, 78, 123, 148, 189, 296
Odum, Howard, 73, 122–23
Of Time and the River (Wolfe), 154, 166, 168, 349n32
Office of the Coordinator of Information. See Central Intelligence Agency (CIA)
Old South, 24, 26, 118, 226; and authoritarianism, 83–87; failures of, 30–31, 34, 68, 334n34; and paternalism, 88, 191, 321; and sentimentality, 28, 73, 84, 89, 102, 121, 312
Opinions of Oliver Allston (Brooks), 256

oppression, 124, 192, 208, 353n37; of African Americans, 19, 20, 199, 235, 247; in Nazi Germany, 20, 80, 149, 175, 189, 233, 235, 247, 255, 321; in the South, 17, 20, 33, 76, 234–35, 247
ownership, 36, 46, 105, 269
Owsley, Frank, 37, 45–46, 260, 334–35n43

Page, Thomas Nelson, 33, 178
Pale Horse, Pale Rider (Porter), 217–21
Parker, Dorothy, 286
Parker, Theodore, 253
pastoralism, 12, 55–56, 98, 101, 104–6, 118, 320
paternalism, 88, 115, 284
patriotism, 58, 66, 81–82, 241; and American identity, 9, 25, 127, 190, 195, 255; and art, 48, 52, 54, 60, 181, 187–89, 279, 353n34; and Fascism, 46, 168, 362n17; in the South, 88–89
Patterns of Negro Segregation (Johnson), 51
Peacock, Edwin, 230
Pearl Harbor, 59, 127, 180–81, 183, 192
peasantry, 104, 206–7, 234, 295–96
Percy, LeRoy, 99–100, 102, 110, 118, 342n21
Percy, Walker, 98–99, 312–16
Percy, William Alexander, 107–8, 340n2, 341n16; and fascist-southern connection, 23, 96; and the Ku Klux Klan, 108–10; *Lanterns on the Levee*, 100–103, 111, 119; and the Lost Cause, 97; as Nazism critic, 98–99, 309; and race, 111–12, 114–15, 117, 348n9; and sentimentality, 102, 104–6, 114–15, 118, 175; and sexuality, 340n2; 342n27; and Walker Percy, 315
Perkins, Maxwell, 148–49, 150
plantation system, 76, 86, 88, 104
Poland, 79, 237, 260, 275, 325
poor whites, 100, 103, 106, 109, 116, 343n30; political power of, 8, 107–8, 343n29; and relations with African Americans, 5, 106, 110–11, 112, 173–75, 254, 289; victimizations of, 76–77, 84, 85
Porter, Katherine Anne, 23, 68, 209–11, 356n30; and "Hacienda," 206–8, 355n9; leftist politics of, 204, 354n2; *Ship of*

Porter, Katherine Anne *(continued)*
 Fools, 228; short stories of, 207–8, 212–15, 218–22, 225–26, 355–56n23; as witness to European Fascism, 203–6, 211, 354n3
Pound, Ezra, 68–69, 227, 356n39
poverty, 33, 86, 106, 121, 123, 137, 149; as by-product of industrialism, 76; as foundational myth of South, 4, 102, 134
Powers, J. F., 228, 356n39
pragmatism, 253–54, 271, 274, 277, 365n46
Pressly, Eugene, 204–5
primitivism, 156, 358n16
prisons, 239, 306, 312; as central to Southern culture, 4, 20, 73, 75, 244; in World War II, 228, 292
propaganda, 150, 170, 188, 291; for democracy, 59, 125, 368n31; and the Nazis, 109; and the Soviets, 286
Proud Flesh (Warren), 261–62, 268, 270, 272
Proust, Marcel, 256
provincialism, 24, 27, 43, 47
Pseudopodia, 120–21
psychoanalysis, 7, 144

race, 80, 85; and alleged taxonomies, 112, 151–52, 155, 173, 175, 348n9; and Germans, 11; and identity, 106, 111–12, 155; and mixed-race couplings, 1. *See also* African Americans; Aryanism; whites
racism, 117; and attitudes of superiority, 116, 152, 154; codes of, 5, 134; and conciliation, 110; ideologies of, 44, 80–81, 85, 97, 327n2; and politics, 193, 235, 309; and violence, 5, 109, 175, 239, 316, 318, 325, 344n2, 368n31. *See also* segregation
Rader, Melvin, 12
Rahv, Philip, 177
Rainey, Glenn, 124
Ransom, John Crowe, 48, 68, 70; and aesthetics, 52–56, 256; and commentary on Southern culture, 24–25, 27–29, 335–36n60; *I'll Take My Stand*, 32–33; and industrialism, 37
Rauschning, Hermann, 7, 79, 359n19
Reconstruction, 86, 90, 108, 113, 118, 133; and effects on Southern culture, 30, 44, 84, 87–88; Southern attitudes toward, 8, 51, 226
Red Harvest (Hammett), 282
Reeves, Pascal, 153–55, 172
Reflections in a Golden Eye (McCullers), 239–40
regionalism, 37, 49, 59; and authoritarianism, 12–13, 14, 43, 45–46, 361–62n13; and democracy, 11; and modernism, 12, 52
Reich, Wilhelm, 7
Reisman, David, 258
religion, 61, 68, 217; and the Agrarians, 34, 41, 46, 56, 361–362n13; Cash's perspectives on, 49, 76; Porter's perspectives on, 212, 228; and Protestantism, 30; and Roman Catholicism, 30, 68, 224, 228, 313–16, 332n11, 332–33n16, 337n86; Smith's perspectives on, 141, 143
repression, 14, 49, 57, 149, 164–65, 210, 362n17
Republican Party, 143, 224, 292
resistance, 60, 157, 189, 190, 256, 260; to industrialism, 32; to modernism, 13, 22, 52, 87, 212, 335–36n60; to Nazism, 21, 149, 198, 240, 293–94, 353n33, 353n37
Richmond Times-Dispatch, 8
Roberts, Margaret, 167, 170
Robeson, Paul, 352n25, 368n31
Robles, Emmanuel, 305
Rollyson, Carl, 283–84, 298, 303
romanticism, 84, 86, 166, 271, 275, 314
Roosevelt, Franklin D., 16, 50, 58, 71, 169, 301; and relationship with the South, 3–4, 9, 92, 105; and World War II, 124–25, 216, 365–66n51
Roughead, William, 283
Rubenstein, Richard, 321–24

Sacco, Ferdinando Nicola, 206, 210, 355n8
Samuel, Maurice, 178
Sandoz, Maria, 11
Sands Point, 8, 329n16
Saturday Review of Literature, 47, 69, 120, 170

schizophrenia, 134, 143
Schuyler, George S., 330nn29–30
Scott, Evelyn, 81, 339n16
Scottsboro trials, 44, 334–35n43
Screen Writers' Guild, 280, 284
Sea Island Lady (Griswold), 120
Searching Wind, The (Hellman), 297–301
secularization, 252, 323
segregation, 22, 88; African American protest against, 15; Agrarian support of, 43, 49, 51, 334–35n43; comparisons to Nazism, 16, 80, 130, 137, 140, 327n2; Faulkner's perspective on, 176, 193, 199–200, 202; historical effects of, 1–4, 10, 120–21, 134–35, 160; McCullers's perspectives on, 249; Porter's perspectives on, 212; Smith's perspectives on, 125, 129, 130–33, 138–39, 141, 145, 311–12, 344n2; Warren's perspectives on, 254
Sewanee Review, 60–61
sexuality, 235, 239; between races, 117, 141–42; emergence of, 245; and women, 151, 159, 214–15. *See also* homosexuality; masturbation; miscegenation
shame, 19, 21, 62, 103, 166, 174; as part of American psyche, 169, 287, 299, 305; as part of Southern psyche, 4, 136, 318; and race, 121, 209, 318
sharecropping, 4, 104, 105, 106, 114, 126, 128, 234
Ship of Fools (Porter), 228
Shumlin, Herman, 291
Simmons, William Joseph, 108
Simon, Otto, 286
slavery, 6, 85, 88, 105, 139, 170; and comparisons to concentration camps, 312, 316–17, 322–26; in the Old South, 132, 155, 190–93, 225, 321, 325–26
Smith, Harrison, 68–69
Smith, Lillian: and communism, 124, 311–12; and Fascism, 122–24, 126–27, 143, 344n2, 344–45n11; and Germany, 122, 124, 140, 344n2; *Killers of the Dream*, 1, 120, 138, 144, 212, 249, 311, 347nn44–45; and the Soviet Union, 291, 295–96, 301, 344n2;

Strange Fruit, 133; and views on authoritarianism, 134, 136–38, 144–45
Snelling, Paula, 120–23, 127–28, 130–32, 310, 344–45n11, 358n12
social realism, 13
social responsibility, 55, 92, 175
socialism, 12, 14, 45, 57, 122, 167, 282
Solid South, 138, 144
Sophie's Choice (Styron), 312, 316–21
Sosna, Morton, 132, 329n17
Sound and the Fury, The (Faulkner), 197–99
South Today, 120, 136, 346n35
Southern Regions of the United States (Odum), 122
Southern Review, 39, 54, 59, 336n74
Soviet Union, 201, 260, 282, 291, 295–96, 301, 344n2; and communism, 280; and industrialism, 29; and the savage ideal, 49, 91; as totalitarian state, 2, 108, 137–38, 200–202
Spanish Civil War, 230, 266, 286, 288, 296–97, 366n4
Spengler, Oswald, 75–76, 78
Squires, Radcliffe, 64
Stalin, Joseph, 50, 365–66n51, 369n38; Hellman's support for, 282, 286, 291, 301; and totalitarianism, 138–39, 142
Stars Fell on Alabama (Carmer), 5–7
Steinbeck, John, 230
Steiner, George, 321
Stoddard, Lothrop, 151–56, 343n36, 348n9
stoicism, 116, 310, 313, 315–16
Strange Fruit (Smith), 133
Straus, Harold, 101
Strout, Cushing, 365n46
Styron, William, 312, 316, 321–26
subversion, 7, 94, 215, 228, 246, 264, 304
Szczesiul, Anthony, 267

taboos, 49, 85, 117, 141
TASS, 205, 354n4
Tate, Allen, 35, 332n11, 334–35n43, 337n80, 344–45n11; and aesthetics, 52, 70, 336–37n76, 362n17; and the Agrarians, 26, 28–33, 37, 40–43, 56–68, 337n80, 337n86;

Tate, Allen *(continued)*
  Fathers, The, 62; *I'll Take My Stand*, 24, 334n34, 361n11; and industrialism, 38, 332–33n16; *Jefferson Davis: His Rise and Fall*, 25–26, 331–32n2; poetry of, 48, 63
Tennessee Valley Authority (TVA), 51–52
Tennessee, The (Davidson), 51–52
terror, 81, 113, 264, 266–67, 269–70, 353n34; and communism, 144; and Nazism, 80–81, 94, 165, 199, 231, 237, 265, 344n2, 369–70n45; and segregation, 16, 140, 258, 344n2
textile industry, 74–75, 88, 118, 124, 288
Thanatos Syndrome, The (Percy), 315
These Three (Hellman), 284
Theweleit, Klaus, 314
Thompson, Alan Reynolds, 177
Thorp, Willard, 68
Thyssen, Fritz, 292–93, 294
Tillman, Benjamin R., 8
Tolson, Jay, 98
Tolstoi, Leo, 229
Toomer, Jean, 5
totalitarianism, 45–47, 57–58, 71–72, 82–83, 105, 327n2; and American culture, 16, 20, 56, 64–65, 197, 330n29, 363n30; and Christianity, 137; and communism, 3, 137–38, 142, 144, 201–2, 206, 216, 224; and Fascism, 22–23, 164, 202, 239, 244–45, 255, 269, 279, 311; in the South, 23, 49, 51–53, 81, 85–87, 90–92, 109, 120, 131, 140, 191, 199, 244, 310–11, 325, 335–36n60; in the Soviet Union, 2, 108, 137–38, 200–202, 344n2; and Stalin, 138–39, 142
Tracts Against Communism. See *I'll Take My Stand*
traditionalism, 70, 309–10, 335–36n60, 340–41n15; and the Agrarians, 49, 334n34; Cash's views on, 75, 87, 91, 199; William Alexander Percy's commitment to, 96–97, 100–104, 106–10, 113, 115–16; Porter's critique of, 212–14, 218–20, 225–27, 356n33; and Nazism, 72, 244–45, 316, 333n24; and race, 44; Smith's critique of, 119, 136, 199; versus industrialism, 27–28, 44
transcendentalists, 253
Trefzer, Annette, 327–28n3

tribalism, 72, 154
Truman, Harry S., 301
Tucker, Gin, 230
Turner, Frederick Jackson, 49
TVA. *See* Tennessee Valley Authority (TVA)

U. S. Congress, 16, 305. *See also* House Un-American Activities Committee (HUAC)
U. S. State Department, 224, 304, 311
U. S. Supreme Court, 8
Unfinished Woman, An (Hellman), 281, 286–87, 301, 367n12, 369n39
uniformity, 34, 49, 51–52, 72
Union for Concerted Peace Action, 280
Unrue, Darlene, 355n9
urbanism, 26, 43
Urgo, Joseph P., 201–2, 352–53n30

Vanzetti, Bartolomeo, 206, 210, 355n8
Vardaman, James K., 102
Velarde, Ramón López, 208
violence, 29, 77, 127, 229, 265–68; and alleged connections to industrialism, 41, 334n34; Cash's perspectives on, 92; and labor, 73–74; and Nazi Germany, 15, 247, 298, 325; and race, 5, 17, 44–45, 88, 90, 109, 134, 175, 239, 316–18, 325, 344n2
Virginia Quarterly Review, 32, 170
voting rights, 4, 13

Wagner Act, 284
Warner Brothers, 188, 189
Warren, Cinina, 215, 260–61
Warren, Robert Penn: *All the King's Men*, 261, 270–75, 364n42, 365n46; *At Heaven's Gate*, 268–70; and authoritarianism, 252, 255; critique of Fascism, 255, 258–59, 261, 263–64, 266–69, 271–72, 274, 279, 361–62n13; *Democracy and Poetry*, 252; *Eleven Poems on the Same Theme*, 264–69; *I'll Take My Stand*, 254, 361n11; *John Brown: The Making of a Martyr*, 253–54; *Legacy of the Civil War, The*, 257–58; *Night Rider*, 258–60; *Proud Flesh*, 261–62, 268, 270, 272; *Who Speaks for the Negro?* 253; *World Enough and Time*, 275–77

Washington, Booker T., 254
Watch on the Rhine (Hellman), 291–97, 369–70n45
Watson, Jay, 141
Watson, Tom, 8
Weaver, Richard, 331n40, 335–36n60, 340–41n15
Web and the Rock, The (Wolfe), 159, 173
Web, Walter Prescott, 11
Wecter, Dixon, 166
Weeks, Edward, 240
Wescott, Glenway, 211
Wheeler, Monroe, 211
While England Slept (Churchill), 273
White, Walter, 15, 132
whites: as southerners, 2, 3, 14–16, 22–23, 51, 142, 151, 309, 311–12, 318, 325; as supremacists, 75, 113, 137–140, 145, 311; and whiteness, 106, 121
Whitman, Digby B., 223
Who Owns America? 38, 40, 45–47, 122, 269
Who Speaks for the Negro? (Warren), 253
Why England Slept (Kennedy), 273
Wild Palms, The (Faulkner), 179
Wiesel, Elie, 321
Wilkerson, Doxey A., 15
Wilson, Woodrow, 99
Wolfe, Fred, 148
Wolfe, Thomas, 23, 310, 348n30, 349n32, 349n36, 349n39; and Jews, 158–59, 161, 163, 172, 173; *Look Homeward Angels*, 166; and Nazism, 149, 151, 166, 170–71; *Of Time and the River*, 154, 166, 168, 349n32; perspectives on Fascism, 162–63, 169–70, 172; *Web and the Rock, The*, 159, 173; *You Can't Go Home Again*, 163–64, 166, 168, 171

women, 6, 19, 199; and class, 174–75; and race, 44, 94, 117, 178, 280–81, 301; and sexuality, 151, 158–59, 313–14. *See also* misogyny
Wood, Grant, 11, 13, 14, 43
Woodward, C. Vann, 4, 118
World Enough and Time (Warren), 275–77
World War I, 114, 152, 222, 345n16; and effect on the South, 84, 89; William Alexander Percy's perspectives on, 98, 100–101
World War II, 7, 22, 79, 142, 176, 328n7; and connection to Civil War, 185, 190–93; and erosion of localism, 14–16; and industrialism, 65–66, 325–26, 360n1
Woolf, Virginia, 227
Wright, Richard, 17–20, 197, 330n29, 330–31n37
Wright, William, 289, 291
Writers in Crisis (Geismar), 178–79
Wyler, William, 295

Yaeger, Patricia, 246, 360n35
You Can't Go Home Again (Wolfe), 163–64, 166, 168, 171

Zapata, Emiliano, 207

www.ingramcontent.com/pod-product-compliance
Lightning Source LLC
Chambersburg PA
CBHW051241300426
44114CB00011B/843